THE OXFORD BIBLE C

THE OXFORD BIBLE COMMENTARY

THE PAULINE
EPISTLES

EDITED BY
JOHN MUDDIMAN
AND
JOHN BARTON

ASSOCIATE EDITORS
Dr Loveday Alexander
Dom Henry Wansborough, *OSB*

OXFORD
UNIVERSITY PRESS

OXFORD
UNIVERSITY PRESS

Great Clarendon Street, Oxford OX2 6DP

Oxford University Press is a department of the University of Oxford.
It furthers the University's objective of excellence in research, scholarship,
and education by publishing worldwide in

Oxford New York

Auckland Cape Town Dar es Salaam Hong Kong Karachi
Kuala Lumpur Madrid Melbourne Mexico City Nairobi
New Delhi Shanghai Taipei Toronto

With offices in

Argentina Austria Brazil Chile Czech Republic France Greece
Guatemala Hungary Italy Japan Poland Portugal Singapore
South Korea Switzerland Thailand Turkey Ukraine Vietnam

Oxford is a registered trade mark of Oxford University Press
in the UK and in certain other countries

Published in the United States
by Oxford University Press Inc., New York

British Library Cataloguing in Publication Data
Data available

Library of Congress Cataloging in Publication Data
Data available

Typeset by SPI Publisher Services, Pondicherry, India
Printed in Great Britain
on acid-free paper by
Clays Ltd., St Ives plc

ISBN 978-0-19-958026-2

1 3 5 7 9 10 8 6 4 2

LIST OF CONTENTS

List of Contributors		vi
Abbreviations		vii
1.	General Introduction	1
2.	Introduction to the New Testament	7
3.	Introduction to the Pauline Corpus	27
4.	Romans	57
5.	1 Corinthians	91
6.	2 Corinthians	126
7.	Galatians	151
8.	Ephesians	170
9.	Philippians	189
10.	Colossians	204
11.	1 Thessalonians	216
12.	2 Thessalonians	235
13.	The Pastoral Epistles	244
14.	Philemon	263
	Bibliographical Guide	268
	Index	273

LIST OF CONTRIBUTORS

Leslie Houlden, *formerly Professor of Theology, King's College, London*

Terence L. Donaldson, *Professor of New Testament Studies, Wycliffe College, Toronto* ·

Craig C. Hill, *Professor of New Testament, Wesley Theological Seminary, Washington DC*

John Barclay, *Professor, Department of Religion and Theology, University of Durham*

Margaret MacDonald, *Professor, Department of Religious Studies, Francis Xavier University, Nova Scotia*

G. N. Stanton, *formerly Lady Margaret's Professor of Divinity and Fellow of Fitzwilliam College, University of Cambridge*

J. D. G. Dunn, *Emeritus Lightfoot Professor of Divinity, University of Durham*

Robert Murray, *SJ, formerly University of London*

Jerome Murphy-O'Connor, *Professor of New Testament, École Biblique et Archéologique Française, Jerusalem*

Philip F. Esler, *Professor of Biblical Criticism, University of St Andrews*

Clare Drury, *formerly University of Cambridge*

Craig S. Wansink, *Associate professor of Religious Studies, Virginia Wesleyan College, Norfolk, Virginia*

ABBREVIATIONS

GENERAL

AB	Anchor Bible
ABD	D. N. Freedman (ed.), *Anchor Bible Dictionary* (6 vols.; New York: Doubleday, 1992)
AnBib	Analecta biblica
ANRW	*Aufstieg und Niedergang der römischen Welt*
b.	Babylonian Talmud
BAGD	W. Bauer, W. F. Arndt, F. W. Gingrich, and F. W. Danker, *Greek–English Lexicon of the NT and other Early Christian Literature* (Chicago: Univ of Chicago Press, 1979 rev. edn.)
BBB	Bonner biblische Beiträge
BBR	*Bulletin for Biblical Research*
BCE	Before Common Era
BDF	F. Blass, A. Debrunner, and R. W. Funk, *A Greek Grammar of the New Testament* (Chicago: Univ of Chicago Press, 1961)
BETL	Bibliotheca ephemeridum theologicarum lovaniensium
Bib.	*Biblica*
BJRL	*Bulletin of the John Rylands Library*
BNTC	Black's New Testament Commentaries
BR	*Biblical Research*
BZNW	Beihefte zur ZNW
CBC	Cambridge Bible Commentary
CBQ	*Catholic Biblical Quarterly*
CD	Cairo Geniza, Damascus Document
CE	Common Era
CGTC	Cambridge Greek Testament Commentaries
Ebib	Études bibliques
EDNT	H. Balz and G. Schneider (eds.), *Exegetical Dictionary of the New Testament* (3 vols.: Grand Rapids: Eerdmans, 1990)
EKKNT	Evangelisch-katholischer Kommentar zum Neuen Testament
ET	English Translation
ETL	*Ephemerides theologicae lovanienses*
FBBS	Facet Books, Biblical Series
FRLANT	Forschungen zur Religion und Literatur des Alten und Neuen Testaments

Gk.	Greek
GNB	Good News Bible
GNS	Good News Series
HB	Hebrew Bible
HBC	J. L. Mays *et al.* (eds.), *Harper's Bible Commentary* (San Francisco: Harper & Row, 1988)
Heb.	Hebrew
HTR	*Harvard Theological Review*
ICC	International Critical Commentary
JBL	*Journal of Biblical Literature*
JSNT	*Journal for the Study of the New Testament*
JSNTSup	Journal for the Study of the New Testament—Supplement Series
JSOT	*Journal for the Study of the Old Testament*
JTS	*Journal of Theological Studies*
LCL	Loeb Classical Library
LXX	Septuagint
MeyerK	H. A. W. Meyer, Kritisch-exegetischer Kommentar über das Neue Testament
MLB	Modern Language Bible
MNTC	Moffatt New Testament Commentary
MS	Monograph Series; manuscript
Mt.	Mount
NCB	New Century Bible
NIBC	New International Bible Commentary
NICNT	New International Commentary on the New Testament
NIGTC	New International Greek Testament Commentary
NIV	New International Version
NJB	H. Wansbrough (ed.), *New Jerusalem Bible*
NJBC	R. E. Brown, J. A. Fitzmyer, and R. E. Murphy (eds.), *The New Jerome Biblical Commentary* (London: Geoffrey Chapman, 1989)
NovT	*Novum Testamentum*
NovTSup	Novum Testamentum, Supplements
NTS	*New Testament Studies*
OCB	*Oxford Companion to the Bible*
PG	J. Migne, *Patrologia graeca*
QD	Quaestiones disputatae

RAC	*Reallexikon für Antike und Christentum*
RB	*Revue biblique*
RTR	*Reformed Theological Review*
SBL	Society of Biblical Literature
SBLDS	SBL Dissertation Series
SBLSBS	SBL Sources for Biblical Study
SBT	Studies in Biblical Theology
SCM	Student Christian Movement
SJLA	Studies in Judaism in Late Antiquity
SNTSMS	Society for New Testament Study Monograph Series
SNTW	Studies of the New Testament and its World
SP	Sacra Pagina
SPCK	Society for Promoting Christian Knowledge
ST	*Studia theologica*
SUNT	Studien zur Umwelt des Neuen Testaments
S.V.	Sub vide
t.	Tosefta
TDNT	G. W. Bromiley (ed. and trans.), *Theological Dictionary of the New Testament* (10 vols.; Grand Rapids: Eerdmans, 1964–78)
TU	Texte und Untersuchungen
v.	versus
WBC	Word Biblical Commentary
WUNT	Wissenschaftliche Untersuchungen zum Neuen Testament
ZNW	*Zeitschrift für die neutestamentliche Wissenschaft*

CLASSICAL

Ap.	Apuleius
Met.	*Metamorphoses*
Apoc. Abr.	*Apocalypse of Abraham*
Did.	*Didache*
Ep. Arist.	*Epistle of Aristeas*
Ign.	Ignatius
Eph.	*Ephesians*
Magn.	*Letter to the Magnesians*
Trall.	*Letter to the Trallians*

Jos.	Josephus
Ag. Ap.	*Against Apion*
Ant.	*Antiquities of the Jews*
J.W.	*Jewish War*
Jub.	*Jubilees*
Mart. Pol.	*Martyrdom of Polycarp*
Pal. Tg.	*Palestinian Targum*
Phil.	Polycarp, *Letter to the Philippians*
Philo	Philo Judaeus
Conf. Ling.	*De confusione linguarum*
Flacc.	*In Flaccum*
Pliny	
Ep.	*Epistulae*
Nat. Hist.	*Natural History*
Plut.	Plutarch
Mor.	*Moralia*
Polycarp	
Phil.	*Letter to the Philippians*
1QpHab	Qumran Cave 1, *Pesher on Habakkuk*
1QS	Qumran Cave 1, *Serek hayyahad (Rule of the Community, Manual of Discipline)* [2h dot]
4QpNah	Qumran Cave 4, *Pesher on Nahum*
11QTemple	Qumran Cave 11, *Temple Scroll*
Šabb.	*Šabbat*
Sanh.	*Sanhedrin*
Strabo	
Geog.	*Geographical Sketches*
Tac.	Tacitus
Ann.	*Annales*
Hist.	*Historia*
Tert.	Tertullian
Adv. Marc.	*Adversus Marcionem*
Apol.	*Apologeticus*
T. Judah	*Testament of Judah*
T. Naph.	*Testament of Naphtali*
tr(s).	translation(s), translated (by)
v.	versus

1. General Introduction

A. Studying the Bible. 1. People's reasons for studying the Bible—and therefore for using a biblical commentary—are many and various. The great majority of Bible readers have a religious motivation. They believe that the Bible contains the 'words of life', and that to study it is a means of deepening their understanding of the ways of God. They turn to the Bible to inform them about how God desires human beings to live, and about what God has done for the human race. They expect to be both challenged and helped by what they read, and to gain clearer guidance for living as religious believers. Such people will use a commentary to help them understand the small print of what has been disclosed about the nature and purposes of God. The editors' hope is that those who turn to the Bible for such religious reasons will find that the biblical text is here explained in ways that make it easier to understand its content and meaning. We envisage that the Commentary will be used by pastors preparing sermons, by groups of people reading the Bible together in study or discussion groups, and by anyone who seeks a clearer perspective on a text that they hold in reverence as religiously inspiring. Jews, Catholics, Protestants, and Orthodox Christians have different expectations of the Bible, but we hope that all will find the Commentary useful in elucidating the text.

2. A somewhat smaller group of readers studies the Bible as a monument to important movements of religious thought in the past, whether or not they themselves have any personal commitment to the religious systems it represents. One of the most striking developments of recent decades has been the growth of interest in the Bible by those who have no religious commitment to it, but for whom it is a highly significant document from the ancient world. Students who take university or college courses in theology or religious or biblical studies will often wish to understand the origins and meaning of the biblical text so as to gain a clearer insight into the beginnings of two major world religions, Judaism and Christianity, and into the classic texts that these religions regard as central to their life. We hope that such people will find here the kinds of information they need in order to understand this complex and many-faceted work. The one-volume format makes it possible to obtain an overview of the whole Bible before going on to use more advanced individual commentaries on particular biblical books.

3. Finally, there are many Bible readers who are committed neither to a religious quest of their own nor to the study of religion, but who are drawn by the literary quality of much of the Bible to want to know more about it. For them it is a major classic of Western—indeed, of world—literature, whose influence on other literature, ancient and modern, requires that it should be taken seriously and studied in depth. A generation ago 'the Bible as literature' was regarded by many students of the Bible, especially those with a religious commitment to it, as a somewhat dilettante interest, insufficiently alert to the Bible's spiritual challenge. Nowadays, however, a great deal of serious scholarly work is being done on literary aspects of the Bible, and many commentaries are written with the needs of a literary, rather than a religious, readership in mind. We think that those who approach the Bible in such a way will find much in this Commentary to stimulate their interest further.

B. Biblical Criticism. 1. The individual authors of commentaries have been free to treat the biblical books as they see fit, and there has been no imposition of a common editorial perspective. They are, however, united by an approach that we have called 'chastened historical criticism'. This is what is traditionally known as a *critical* commentary, but the authors are aware of recent challenges to what is generally called biblical criticism and have sought (to a greater or lesser extent) to take account of these in their work. Some explanation of these terms is necessary if the reader is to understand what this book seeks to offer.

2. Biblical criticism, sometimes known as historical criticism of the Bible or as the historical-critical method, is the attempt to understand the Bible by setting it in the context of its time of writing, and by asking how it came into existence and what were the purposes of its authors. The term 'historical' is not used because such criticism is necessarily interested in reconstructing history, though sometimes it may be, but because biblical books are being studied as anchored in their own time, not as freely floating texts which we can read as though they were contemporary with us. It starts with the acknowledgement that the Bible is an ancient text. However much the questions with which it deals may be of perennial interest to human beings (and perhaps no one would study it so seriously if they were not), they arose within a particular historical (and geographical) setting. Biblical criticism uses all available means of access to information about the text and its context, in order to discover what it may have meant when it or its component parts were written.

3. One precondition for a critical understanding of any text is a knowledge of the language in which it is written, and accordingly of what individual words and expressions were capable of meaning at the time of the text's composition. The critical reader is always on guard against the danger of anachronism, of reading later meanings of words into their use in an earlier period. Frequently, therefore, commentators draw attention to problems in understanding particular words and phrases, and cite evidence for how such words are used elsewhere in contemporary texts. A second prerequisite is that the text itself shall be an accurate version of what the author actually wrote. In the case of any ancient text this is an extremely difficult thing to ensure, because of the vagaries of the transmission of manuscripts down the centuries. Copying by hand always introduces errors into texts, even though biblical texts were often copied with special care because of their perceived sacred status. In all the individual commentaries here there are discussions of how accurately the original text is available to us, and what contribution is made to our knowledge of this by various manuscripts or ancient translations. The art of textual criticism seeks to explain the evolution of texts, to understand how they become corrupted (through miscopying), and how their original form can be rediscovered.

4. In reading any piece of text, ancient or modern, one needs to be aware of the possibility that it may not be a unity. Some documents in our own day come into existence through the work of several different authors, which someone else then edits into a reasonably unified whole: such is the case, for example, with documents produced by committees. In the ancient world it was not uncommon for books to be produced by joining together, and sometimes even interweaving, several already existing shorter texts, which are then referred to as the 'sources' of the resulting single document. In the case of some books in the Bible it is suspected by scholars that such a process of production has resulted in the texts as we now have them. Such hypotheses have been particularly prevalent in the case of the Pentateuch (Genesis–Deuteronomy) and of the Synoptic Gospels (Matthew, Mark, and Luke). The attempt to discover the underlying sources is nowadays usually called 'source criticism', though older books sometimes call it 'literary criticism' (from German *Literarkritik*, but confusing in that 'literary criticism' usually means something else in modern English), or 'higher criticism'—by contrast with 'lower', that is, textual criticism. It is important to see that biblical critics are not committed to believing that this or that biblical book is in fact the result of the interweaving of sources (R. N. Whybray's commentary on Genesis in this volume argues against such a hypothesis), but only to being open to the possibility.

5. A further hypothesis that has had a long and fruitful history in the study of both Testaments is that our present written texts may rest on materials that were originally transmitted orally. Before the biblical books were written, the stories or other units of which they are composed may have had an independent life, circulating orally and being handed on from parent to child, or in circles where stories were told and retold, such as a 'camp-fire' or a liturgical context. The attempt to isolate and study such underlying oral units is known as form criticism, and it has been much practised in the case of the gospels, the stories in the Pentateuch and in the early historical books of the Old Testament, and the prophetic books. Again, by no means all critics think that these books do in fact rest on oral tradition, but all regard the question whether or not they do so as important because it is relevant to understanding their original context.

6. Where texts are composite, that is, the result of weaving together earlier written or oral sources, it makes sense to investigate the techniques and intentions of those who carried out the weaving. We should now call such people 'editors', but in biblical studies the technical term 'redactor' tends to be preferred, and this branch of biblical criticism is thus known as 'redaction criticism'. Once we know what were a biblical redactor's raw materials—which source and form criticism may be able to disclose to us—we can go on to ask about the aims the redactor must have had. Thus we can enquire into the intentions (and hence the thought or the 'theology') of Matthew or Luke, or of the editor of the book of Isaiah. Redaction criticism has been a particular interest in modern German-speaking biblical study, but it is also still widely practised in the English-speaking world. It is always open to the critic to argue that a given book is not composite in any case and therefore never had a redactor, only an author. Most scholars probably think this is true of some of the shorter tales of the Old Testament, such as Jonah or Ruth, or of many of Paul's epistles. Here too what makes study critical is not a commitment to a particular outcome, but a willingness to engage in the investigation. It is always possible that there is simply not enough evidence to resolve the matter, as R. Coggins argues in the case of Isaiah. This conclusion does not make such a commentary 'non-critical', but is arrived at by carefully sifting the various critical hypotheses that have been presented by previous scholars. An uncritical commentary would be one that was unaware of such issues, or unwilling to engage with them.

7. Form and redaction criticism inevitably lead to questions about the social setting of the underlying units that make up biblical books and of the redactors who put them into their finished form. In recent years historical criticism has expanded to include a considerable interest in the contribution the social sciences can make to understanding the Bible's provenance. The backgrounds of the gospels and of Paul's letters have been studied with a view to discovering more about the social context of early Christianity: see, for example, the commentary here on 1 Thessalonians by Philip Esler. In the study of the Old Testament also much attention has been directed to questions of social context, and this interest can be seen especially in D. L. Smith-Christopher's commentary on Ezra–Nehemiah.

C. Post-Critical Movements. 1. In the last few decades biblical studies has developed in many and varied directions, and has thrown up a number of movements that regard themselves as 'post-critical'. Some take critical study of the Bible as a given, but then seek to move on to ask further questions not part of the traditional historical-critical enterprise. Others are frankly hostile to historical criticism, regarding it as misguided or as outdated. Though the general tone of this commentary continues to be critical, most of its contributors believe that these newer movements have raised important issues,

and have contributed materially to the work of biblical study. Hence our adoption of a critical stance is 'chastened' by an awareness that new questions are in the air, and that biblical criticism itself is now subject to critical questioning.

2. One important style of newer approaches to the Bible challenges the assumption that critical work should (or can) proceed from a position of neutrality. Those who write from feminist and liberationist perspectives often argue that the older critical style of study presented itself as studiedly uncommitted to any particular programme: it was simply concerned, so its practitioners held, to understand the biblical text in its original setting. In fact (so it is now argued) there was often a deeply conservative agenda at work in biblical criticism. By distancing the text as the product of an ancient culture, critics managed to evade its challenges to themselves, and they signally failed to see how subversive of established attitudes much of the Bible really was. What is needed, it is said, is a more engaged style of biblical study in which the agenda is set by the need for human liberation from oppressive political forces, whether these constrain the poor or some other particular group such as women. The text must be read not only in its reconstructed 'original' context but also as relevant to modern concerns: only then will justice be done to the fact that it exercises an existential claim upon its readers, and it will cease to be seen as the preserve of the scholar in his (sic) study.

3. Such a critique of traditional biblical criticism calls attention to some of the unspoken assumptions with which scholars have sometimes worked, and can have the effect of deconstructing conventional commentaries by uncovering their unconscious bias. Many of the commentators in this volume are aware of such dangers in biblical criticism, and seek to redress the balance by asking about the contribution of the books on which they comment to contemporary concerns. They are also more willing than critics have often been to 'criticize' the text in the ordinary sense of that word, that is, to question its assumptions and commitments. This can be seen, for example, in J. Galambush's commentary on Ezekiel, where misogynist tendencies are identified in the text.

4. A second recent development has been an interest in literary aspects of the biblical texts. Where much biblical criticism has been concerned with underlying strata and their combination to make the finished books we now have,

some students of the Bible have come to think that such 'excavative' work (to use a phrase of Robert Alter's) is at best only preparatory to a reading of the texts as finished wholes, at worst a distraction from a proper appreciation of them as great literature just as they stand. The narrative books in particular (the Pentateuch and 'historical' books of the Old Testament, the gospels and Acts in the New) have come to be interpreted by means of a 'narrative criticism', akin to much close reading of modern novels and other narrative texts, which is alert to complex literary structure and to such elements as plot, characterization, and closure. It is argued that at the very least readers of the Bible ought to be aware of such issues as well as those of the genesis and formation of the text, and many would contend, indeed, that they are actually of considerably *more* importance for a fruitful appropriation of biblical texts than is the classic agenda of critical study. Many of the commentaries in this volume (such as those on Matthew and Philippians) show an awareness of such aesthetic issues in reading the Bible, and claim that the books they study are literary texts to be read alongside other great works of world literature. This interest in things literary is related to the growing interest in the Bible by people who do not go to it for religious illumination so much as for its character as classic literature, and it is a trend that seems likely to continue.

5. Thirdly, there is now a large body of work in biblical studies arguing that traditional biblical criticism paid insufficient attention not only to literary but also to theological features of the text. Here the interest in establishing the text's original context and meaning is felt to be essentially an antiquarian interest, which gives a position of privilege to 'what the text meant' over 'what the text means'. One important representative of this point of view is the 'canonical approach', sometimes also known as 'canonical criticism', in which biblical interpreters ask not about the origins of biblical books but about their integration into Scripture taken as a finished whole. This is part of an attempt to reclaim the Bible for religious believers, on the hypothesis that traditional historical criticism has alienated it from them and located it in the study rather than in the pulpit or in the devotional context of individual Bible-reading. While this volume assumes the continuing validity of historical-critical study, many contributors are alive to this issue, and are anxious not to make imperialistic claims for historical

criticism. Such criticism began, after all, in a conviction that the Bible was open to investigation by everyone, and was not the preserve of ecclesiastical authorities: it appealed to evidence in the text rather than to external sources of validation. It is important that this insight is not lost by starting to treat the Bible as the possession of a different set of authorities, namely historical-critical scholars! Canonical approaches emphasize that religious believers are entitled to put their own questions to the text, and this must be correct, though it would be a disaster if such a conviction were to result in the outlawing of historical-critical method in its turn. Contributors to this volume, however, are certainly not interested only in the genesis of the biblical books but are also concerned to delineate their overall religious content, and to show how one book relates to others within the canon of Scripture.

6. Thus the historical-critical approach may be chastened by an awareness that its sphere of operations, though vital, is not exhaustive, and that other questions too may reasonably be on the agenda of students of the Bible. In particular, a concern for the finished form of biblical books, however that came into existence, unites both literary and canonical approaches. Few scholars nowadays believe that they have finished their work when they have given an account of how a given book came into being: the total effect (literary and theological) made by the final form is also an important question. The contributors to this volume seek to engage with it.

D. The Biblical Canon. 1. Among the various religious groups that recognize the Bible as authoritative there are some differences of opinion about precisely which books it should contain. In the case of the New Testament all Christians share a common list, though in the centuries of the Christian era a few other books were sometimes included (notably The Shepherd of Hermas, which appears in some major New Testament manuscripts), and some of those now in the canon were at times regarded as of doubtful status (e.g. Hebrews, Revelation, 2 and 3 John, 2 Peter, and Jude). The extent of the Old Testament varies much more seriously. Protestants and Jews alike accept only the books now extant in Hebrew as fully authoritative, but Catholics and Orthodox Christians recognize a longer canon: on this, see the Introduction to the Old Testament. The Ethiopic and Coptic churches accept also *Enoch* and

Jubilees, as well as having minor variations in the other books of the Old Testament.

2. In this Commentary we have included all the books that appear in the NRSV—that is, all the books recognized as canonical in any of the Western churches (both Catholic and Protestant) and in the Greek and Russian Orthodox churches and those in communion with them. We have not included the books found only in the Ethiopic or Coptic canons, though some extracts appear in the article Essay with Commentary on Post-Biblical Jewish Literature.

3. It is important to see that it is only at the periphery that the biblical canon is blurred. There is a great core of central books whose status has never been seriously in doubt: the Pentateuch and Prophets in the Old Testament, the gospels and major Pauline epistles in the New. Few of the deutero-canonical books of the Old Testament have ever been of major importance to Christians—a possible exception is the Wisdom of Solomon, so well respected that it was occasionally regarded by early Christians as a New Testament book. There is nowadays comparatively little discussion among different kinds of Christian about the correct extent of the biblical canon (which at the Reformation was a major area of disagreement), and our intention has been to cover most of the books regarded as canonical in major churches without expressing any opinion about whether or not they should have canonical status.

E. How to Use this Commentary. 1. A commentary is an aid towards informed reading of a text, and not a substitute for it. The contributors to this volume have written on the assumption that the Bible is open before the reader all the while, whether in hard copy or electronic form. The NRSV is the normal or 'default' version. When other versions or the commentator's own renderings are preferred this is indicated; often this is because some nuance in the original has been lost in the NRSV (no translation can do full justice to all the possible meanings of a text in another language) or because some ambiguity (and these abound in the text of the Bible) has been resolved in a way that differs from the judgement of the commentator.

2. The NRSV is the latest in a long line of translations that go back to the version authorized by King James I of England in 1611. It is increasingly recognized as the most suitable for the purposes of serious study, because it is based on the best available critical editions of the original texts, because it has no particular confessional allegiance, and because it holds the balance between accuracy and intelligibility, avoiding paraphrase on the one hand and literalism on the other. But comparison between different English translations, particularly for the reader who does not know Hebrew or Greek, is often instructive and serves as a reminder that any translation is itself already an interpretation.

3. *The Oxford Annotated Bible*, based on the NRSV, is particularly useful for those who wish to gain a quick overview of the larger context before consulting this Commentary on a particular passage of special interest. It is useful in another way too: its introductions and notes represent a moderate consensus in contemporary biblical scholarship with which the often more innovative views of the contributors to this Commentary may be measured.

4. When a commentator wishes to draw attention to a passage or parallel in the Bible, the standard NRSV abbreviations apply. But when the reference is to a fuller discussion to be found in the Commentary itself, small capitals are used. Thus (cf. Gen 1:1) signifies the biblical text, while GEN 1:1 refers to the commentary on it. In the same way GEN A etc. refers to the introductory paragraphs of the article on Genesis. The conventions for transliteration of the biblical languages into the English alphabet are the same as those used by *The Oxford Companion to the Bible* (ed. B. M. Metzger and M. Coogan, Oxford: Oxford University Press, 1994).

5. The traditional kind of verse-by-verse commentary has in recent times come under attack as a 'disintegrating' approach that diverts the attention of the reader from the natural flow of the text. The paragraph or longer section, so it is argued, is the real unit of thought, not the verse. However, certain commentators commenting on certain texts would still defend the traditional approach, since they claim that readers chiefly need to be provided with background information necessary to the proper historical interpretation of the text, rather than a more discursive exposition which they could work out for themselves. Examples of both the older and newer methods are to be found in the commentaries below. But even when a particular commentator offers observations on individual verses, we would recommend readers to read the whole paragraph or section and not just the comment on the verse that interests them, so as to gain a more rounded picture. And to encourage this we have not peppered

the page with indications of new verses in capitals (V.1) or bold type (**v.1**), but mark the start of a new comment less obtrusively in lower case (v.1).

6. The one-volume Bible commentary, as this genre developed through the twentieth century, aimed to put into the hands of readers everything they needed for the study of the biblical text. Alongside commentaries on the individual books, it often included a host of general articles ranging from 'Biblical Weights and Measures' to 'The Doctrine of the Person of Christ'. In effect, it tried to be a Commentary, Bible Dictionary, Introduction (in the technical sense, i.e. an analysis of evidence for date, authorship, sources, etc.) and Biblical Theology all rolled into one. But it is no longer possible, given the sheer bulk and variety of modern scholarship, even to attempt this multipurpose approach: nor indeed is it desirable since it distracts attention from the proper task of a commentary which is the elucidation of the text itself. Readers who need more background information on a particular issue are recommended to consult *The Oxford Companion to the Bible* or the six volumes of *The Anchor Bible Dictionary* (ed. D. N. Freedman, New York: Doubleday, 1992), though older bible dictionaries may be used instead: the basic factual information they contain remains largely reliable and relatively stable over time.

7. Each article concludes with a bibliography of works cited. But in addition at the end of the volume there is an aggregated bibliography that points the reader towards the most important specialist works in English on the separate books of the Bible, and also major reference works, introductions, theologies, and so forth.

8. The contributors to *The Oxford Bible Commentary*—and this will probably apply to its users as well—belong to different faith traditions or none. They have brought to their task a variety of methods and perspectives, and this lends richness and depth to the work as a whole. But it also creates problems in coming to an agreed common terminology. As we have noted already, the definition of what is to be included in the Bible, the extent of the canon, is disputed. Further, should we refer to the Old and New Testaments, or to the scriptures of Israel and of early Christianity; to the Apocrypha or the deutero-canonical literature? How should dates be indicated, with BC and AD in the traditional manner or with BCE and CE in reference to the *Common Era*? The usages we have actually adopted should be understood as simple conventions, without prejudice to the serious issues that underlie these differences. A particular problem of a similar kind was whether or not to offer some assistance with a welter of texts, dating from the late biblical period up to 200 CE, which, while not biblical on any definition, are nevertheless relevant to the serious study of the Bible: these are the Dead Sea scrolls, the Old Testament pseudepigrapha, and the apocryphal New Testament. The compromise solution we have reached is to offer not exactly commentary, but two more summarizing articles on this literature (chs. 55 and 82) which, however, still focus on the texts themselves in a way consistent with the commentary format. Some readers may wish to distinguish sharply between the status of this material and that in the Bible; others will see it as merging into the latter.

9. In addition to the overall introductions to the three main subdivisions of the commentary, there are other articles that attempt to approach certain texts not individually but as sets. The Pentateuch or Five Books of Moses functions not only doctrinally but also in terms of its literary history as one five-part work. Similarly, the letters of Paul were once a distinct corpus of writings before they were expanded and added to the growing canon of the New Testament. The four gospels may properly be studied separately, but, both as historical and theological documents, may also be read profitably 'in synopsis'. No attempt has been made by the editors to make these additional articles that group certain texts together entirely consistent with the individual commentaries on them, for the differences are entirely legitimate. The index of subjects at the end of the volume relates only to this introductory material and not to the commentaries themselves. To locate discussions of biblical characters, places, ideas etc. the reader is recommended to consult a concordance first and then to look up the commentary on the passages where the key words occur.

The Bible is a vast treasury of prose and poetry, of history and folklore, of spirituality and ethics; it has inspired great art and architecture, literature and music down the centuries. It invites the reader into its own ancient and mysterious world, and yet at the same time can often surprise us by its contemporary relevance. It deserves and repays all the efforts of critical and attentive reading which the *Oxford Bible Commentary* is designed to assist.

2. Introduction to the New Testament

LESLIE HOULDEN

A. Introduction. 1. This article sets out to 'introduce' the New Testament. But in literature as in life, introductions may be of two kinds. At a formal lecture or public meeting, the speaker is usually introduced with a factual account of career and achievements. We receive in effect the speaker's credentials, flattering him or her and reassuring the audience as it settles to what lies ahead. Such introductions, with their battery of facts, generally bear no close relation to the substance of the ensuing utterance, except that they lead the listener to expect a display of some competence in, say, economics, but none in civil engineering.

2. Introductions at social gatherings are of a different character. When we are introduced to someone, we do not expect a monologue of information about our new acquaintance to flow from the introducer, still less from the person who faces us. No, introduction is a mere beginning. It offers the prospect of conversation where we shall range around for points of contact and explore possible features of character and opinion; so that gradually, but quite unsystematically, we may build up a picture of the one who has been introduced to us. If the introduction leads to sufficient interest, we shall hope that it leads to further meetings, so that our sketchy picture may become fuller and more exact. We shall take steps to ensure that the process continues from this propitious beginning. We shall certainly not expect that the first encounter provides more than a few unrelated bits of information and half-formed impressions. Loose ends will not worry us in the least.

3. This Introduction is of this second kind. At many points, the reader who is new to the subject will wish to question and clarify, and may even be frustrated by the incompleteness of what is provided. The aim, however, is to open subjects rather than to close them. Moreover, though a range of ideas on a particular subject will often be given, to indicate that it is not all plain sailing and where the rocks and shoals lie, this Introduction represents only one among the many possible perspectives on its subject. Further information on many topics comes in the detailed articles that follow, or else in other works of reference, such as Bible dictionaries or encyclopedias or in fuller commentaries on particular NT books. The aim here is to stimulate curiosity, even to incite to discontent, so that the New Testament may continue to fascinate as well as edify its readers.

B. The Idea of the New Testament. 1. It is natural to suppose that the NT is virtually as old as Christianity itself. It is equally natural to assume that the NT has always been part and parcel of Christianity, integral to its very being. It is refreshing to the mind to recognize that the truth is not so simple. We shall list some of the facts that cast doubt on those assumptions about the NT.

2. But first we should identify what we have in mind when we think of 'the NT'. Most people will visualize a slim volume containing twenty-seven writings from early Christianity, or else think of the second part of the Christian Bible, most of it occupied by the OT. These writings vary in type (though most are either gospels or letters) and in length (from the 28 chapters of Matthew's gospel and Acts to the few lines of the 2nd and 3rd Letters of John). Though there are connections between some of them, by way of authorship (e.g. the letters of Paul) or in a literary way (dependence among the first three gospels and common material in Colossians and Ephesians), each is in origin a separate work, composed in its own time and place for its own particular purpose.

3. These writings differ also in accessibility: we are likely to feel most at home with the gospels and Acts, with their strong story-line, much less at home with some of the letters and the Revelation of John; and when we survey the list, there may be some titles that we have scarcely heard of. It is interesting then how rapidly diversity among these writings forces itself on our attention, even though we are attending to the NT as a single entity. Clearly this is not a single entity at all in some senses of that term, either in itself or in our awareness of its contents.

4. The NT we think of is probably in the English language. But every bit of it began in the Greek language of the first century of our era (apart from a handful of words taken over from Hebrew, Aramaic, or Latin); so what we have is a translation, never a simple operation and always involving decisions that amount to interpretation. Until fairly recently, it would have been overwhelmingly likely that the NT in our hand or in our memory was the translation issued in England in 1611, usually known simply (and confidently) as 'The Authorised Version', or sometimes as the King James Version, after James I in whose reign and by whose authority the work was done.

5. In the last fifty years, however, a plethora of different translations has appeared, each attempting the task in a particular way or even looking at the NT from a particular doctrinal standpoint. Most aim to give a more modern English version than that of 1611: old words have changed sense or gone out of use, new ways of putting things have come in. Some recent versions do their modernizing in a way that stays close to the old version (e.g. the RS Version), others break right away from it (e.g. the NEB and the GNB). In a determination to make the NT speak today, they may go so far as to amend the strong masculine assumptions of former times, embodied in the Bible, by producing gender-neutral renderings simply absent from the original. Churches, using the NT in worship or for study by their members, take varying views about new versions, some favouring the resonance and familiarity of traditional language, others seeing it as an obstacle to the use of the NT by modern people.

6. It is not just a question of modernizing the English or not, though often the subject is discussed as if it were. There are also issues of accuracy. For one thing, because of the discovery since the seventeenth century of numerous very old manuscripts of the NT, some going back to within a hundred years or so of the original writing, we have a better idea of the NT authors' precise wording than was available to our ancestors (Metzger 1964; Birdsall 1970). (Never lose sight of it: until the invention of printing, every copy of the NT was made by hand, with all the inevitable slips and blunders, and even the alteration of the text to bring it into line with what the copyist believed the scriptural writer 'must' or 'should' have put.) Despite this opportunity for a better informed judgement about the text itself, however, there remain numerous places of disagreement; and translations differ as they reflect differences of judgement in what are often nicely balanced decisions. All this is in addition to unavoidable variations of style and emphasis as translators view the text before them. Again, the NT is far from the stable entity that it appears at first sight.

7. And there is more to come. Look at the NT historically. Only gradually did these writings come to be accepted in the Christian churches in such a way that they could begin to be seen as a single book with a name of its own. This is not the place to go into details of the process whereby this came about (von Campenhausen 1972; Metzger 1987). Suffice it to say that a collection of Paul's letters was probably made before the end of the first century; that the idea of Christians needing both a gospel (i.e. the story of Jesus) and Paul's letters caught on soon after; that the end of the second century saw the acceptance in a number of major Christian centres (e.g. Rome, Alexandria) of something close to the present collection (four gospels, Acts, Paul's and other letters; but that it was four centuries before most churches accepted more or less the set of writings that have remained to this day as those authorized for official use—it is a list that has survived (despite occasional marginal hesitations) all the great divisions of the church, the same for all. The negative corollary of this progressivist way of putting things is of course that the church, viewed as a whole, managed for four centuries or so without the NT as we know it.

8. Again it cannot be our concern here, but it is worth recognizing that there was no discernible inner drive towards the production of such a thing as the NT: that makes it sound much too purposive. Historically speaking, it was all more haphazard. It is more realistic to look at it this way: the Christian communities, widely scattered around the Mediterranean within a few decades of Jesus' lifetime, had certain needs that had to be met if their life and mission were to flourish and if they were to have any coherence as (despite their plurality) a single phenomenon—the Christian church, or even 'Christianity'. They needed first to communicate with each other and to profit from one another's experience and wisdom, not to speak of bringing one another into line. Hence the early importance of letters. Even if these originally addressed passing situations and had no eye on the long term, they might profitably be preserved against future crises or simply for encouragement and edification. Inevitably, they would be circulated and acquire authority, both forming and buttressing church leaders in their work.

9. The Christian communities also needed to have ways of recalling Jesus, both in his time on earth and in terms of present relationship with his heavenly reality. The content of the letters (e.g. of Paul) might often help with the second, as did the eucharistic worship and prayers of the church; the gospels were essential for the first. There is a question about how early this need came to be strongly felt; but soon the gospels were used as tools for teaching and, from at least the middle of the second century but probably earlier, as an element in the Christian gatherings for worship, where extracts were read to the community and were no doubt the subject of preaching. In this way, the parts of the NT were prior to the whole—that is, in the church's use of these writings. The more one looks at the matter from the point of view of use, the more the final production of a single entity, 'the NT', appears to be an afterthought, a tidying up.

10. That is was more than this is to do with the fact that an element of selection entered into the matter. The NT is far from containing the whole of early Christian literature (Schneemelcher (ed.) 1991, 1992; Staniforth and Louth (eds.) 1987). We know there were numerous other writings, from the second century if not from the first, because copies of them have survived, often in fragments and extracts. Some of them indeed are as old as at least the later of the writings included in the NT itself. It is apparent then that the authorized collection did not come together simply on the basis of antiquity—it was not just the early church's archives. It looks as if a number of factors played a part: simply, popularity and usefulness on a sufficiently wide scale; but also the attachment of an apostolic name, that is the name of one of the earliest Christian leaders, increasingly venerated as authorities, perhaps as martyrs, certainly as close to Jesus. These two factors were not wholly distinct: indeed it looks as if a bid could be made for the authoritativeness of a writing by attaching to it an apostle's name, whether Paul or Peter or John. It is not clear how far this was done in what we should regard as a deliberately fraudulent way and how far it was a matter of claiming the revered figure's patronage—this is what he would have written if he had been in our shoes. Both strategies can be paralleled in the relevant parts of the ancient world. It is not even wholly clear whether it is legitimate to draw a sharp distinction between them ('Pseudonymity', in *A B D* 5). However that may be (and modern literary ethics are surely inappropriate), there was a Christian literature far larger than the NT itself that failed to win general endorsement.

11. In any case, it is evident that the NT grew piecemeal, both in its parts and as a whole. Evident too that it is an instrument of the church, which for all the authority that, in whole and in parts, it came to have in the church, came into being within the already existing life and work of the Christian communities. In so far as the church had a Bible from the start, it consisted of the Jewish Scriptures, eventually designated by Christians 'the Old Testament', which it interpreted in the light of the career and person of Jesus, seen as its fulfilment. More will be said about this at the end of this section.

12. If the church managed without a fully formed and authorized NT for its first few centuries, it is equally true that, in a contrary movement, the NT has undergone a disintegrative process in the last three or four centuries. This has not occurred primarily (often scarcely at all) in the official life of the churches, but in the realm of scholarship, itself church sponsored (especially in mainstream Protestantism) if not church endorsed in many of its results (Houlden 1986; Carroll 1991). During that period, the NT writings have been subjected to all kinds of analytical procedures. Almost all of these have involved treating them as separate units, often indeed identifying possible sources behind them (notably in the case of the gospels) or possible earlier units that have gone to form them as composite wholes (some of the letters, e.g. 2 Cor). Mostly, it has been a matter of attempting to suggest the original form, setting, and intention of each of the writings by the use of informed historical imagination and literary observation. Nearly always the effect has been to break down in the reader's mind the sense of NT as a whole, which was so laboriously built up in the early centuries. The NT comes to be seen very much as a collection of independent, or semi-independent, works, each to be examined in its own right as well as in relevant wider contexts.

13. The upshot is that, in the strict sense, the heyday of the NT as a compact entity (the book within the covers) was in the middle millennium of the church's 2,000-year history; even then, its most characteristic use, the form in which it was mainly experienced, was in bits—sometimes as little as a few words, that would support a doctrinal or ethical point, more often a longer section recited in liturgy or, especially in the later part of the period, used in private meditative prayer. It is interesting to note that for much of that middle period, Christian imagination was filled not only with material derived from Scripture but with legendary stories that the church had specifically rejected from the authorized canon. In for example, the sequence of windows at Chartres

Cathedral, details of Jesus' family, birth, and childhood drawn from the Protevangelium of James (2 cent.) figure alongside those drawn from the gospels.

14. At the same time, in whole or in substantial parts, 'the NT' played a recognized part in Christian life. The NT as a volume came in medieval times to carry the sacred weight of an icon, as did the gospels, bound separately—to be reverenced, viewed with awe, even feared, as charged with numinous power. The ceremonial carrying of the book of the gospels in Eastern Orthodoxy and (much less often now) in the Western eucharistic liturgy retains this sense. So, at a more mundane level, still sometimes tinged with superstition, does the use of the NT in courts of law in some countries for the swearing of oaths. More grandly, the British coronation ritual includes the monarch's oath-taking on the fifth-century NT manuscript (actually far from complete), the Codex Bezae. In these residual uses, 'the NT' survives in a way that our medieval ancestors saw as wholly normal: and notice, this use of it did not necessitate its being opened or read at all. Of course, for the many Christians who remain immune to the analytical endeavours of scholarship, the NT, in whole and in parts, retains its verbal authority, speaking to the reader as God's very utterance, with Paul and his fellow-writers as no more than instruments. There are of course many intermediate stages between such literalism and the recognition of variety within the NT, understood in the light of the diverse settings of the various writings (Houlden (ed.) 1995).

15. This brings us to the final recognition that tends towards the breaking up of the NT as we may now read it. Once we attend to the likely origins of the various writings, we find that they do not all sing the same tune. Certainly, we must abandon any idea that they were the result of some kind of collaborative exercise—an impression that the single, tightly bound volume easily creates. It may be retorted that divine inspiration—the idea that, through the various human agents, the one divine 'pen' is at work—implies a transcending singleness of mind. But it is not wholly transparent that, even on such a strong view of inspiration, God necessarily favours singleness of statement at the expense of (for example) the emergence of truth by way of dialogue or controversy, even in early Christianity whose memorial the NT is. At all events, a candid historical view of the NT writings, while recognizing their overall unity of purpose and

interest, is bound to recognize that they represent different viewpoints in the early church, and even that some of them look as if they were written to correct and refute others. For instance, it is likely that the Gospels of Matthew and Luke were designed, not simply to amplify but rather to improve on the Gospel of Mark, eradicating what were seen as its inadequacies. The formal opening of Luke, the first four verses, seems to suggest as much. And the Pastoral Epistles (1 and 2 Tim, Titus) and perhaps Ephesians (as well as the latter half of Acts) were probably designed to put Paul in a different light from that in which his letters had come to place him: they smooth out the sense of him as a strident and pugnacious figure, ready to take on esteemed church leaders when in his view the gospel dictated it. The Letter of James seems to subvert one of the crucial emphases of Paul's teaching. The NT does not support the view that the early church enjoyed harmonious unanimity of opinion or homogeneity of teaching. Their disputes may often have related to issues long since dead, so that we tend to discount them, but the battles were real enough in their day, sometimes have modern counterparts, and in any case caution us against over-ready adoption of a particular idea or teaching as *the* NT view of the subject in question. On almost every topic of importance, there was diversity and conflict.

16. There is one more important point. Throughout this section we have had in mind the NT as a self-contained work, bound in its own covers, albeit a collection of twenty-seven distinct writings. But more often than not, we encounter the NT as the second (and much the smaller) part of the Bible: in sheer prominence, it can even look like a sort of adjunct to the OT. From the fourth century, Bibles have been produced by Christians consisting of these two parts, and both parts have been in constant use in Christian worship and Christian study. This combination of the NT with the OT compels us to consider the relation between the two. It is impossible here to detail the many different ways in which that relation has been seen. But, despite the comparative brevity of the NT, Christians have always seen it as the climax and goal of the Bible as a whole. Most commonly (as was hinted earlier), they have seen the NT as fulfilling the OT; or, more precisely, Jesus as fulfilling the old Scriptures and the NT as commenting on the manner of that fulfilment. In the NT's own terms, the fulfilment was expressed by way of OT images and themes which were taken up and applied to him (e.g. king of Israel, son of God, lamb), often with startling paradox and originality; also by way of statements in the OT which were read through fresh eyes and seen as relevant to some aspect or detail of Jesus' life or teaching. Most NT books, most obviously the Gospels of Matthew (e.g. 1–2) and John, contain many such applications of OT quotations to Jesus (Lindars 1961). The modern reader who looks up the original OT context will often see audacity (or even fraudulence) in many of these applications—a difficulty removed or at least alleviated once it is understood that the NT writers are using techniques of scriptural interpretation current in Judaism at the time, and applying them creatively to their own subject-matter. Again from a modern point of view, it is necessary to recognize that they were reading Scripture as sheer words, God-given, with only a minimal sense of historical context such as modern scholarship has so vigorously pursued. So words that originally related to the birth of a child in the royal house in Jerusalem in the late eighth century BCE (Isa 7:14) are applied to the birth of Jesus many centuries later and taken to illuminate its character (Mt 1:23; Brown 1993).

C. The Background of the New Testament. 1. So far we have considered the *idea* of the NT. In terms of introduction, this has been the stage of sizing up the new acquaintance. Another important aspect of introduction lies a little behind the scenes and is often slow to emerge. It concerns the world and the culture from which the new acquaintance comes. Only if we find out about that will the introduction progress and lead to understanding.

2. As we face this matter, we immediately encounter what can seem a puzzling fact. All the NT books were written in Greek (though just possibly Hebrew sources lie somewhere behind one or two of them), but their culture is chiefly Jewish. There are in these writings only occasional instances of Hebrew or Aramaic (the Semitic vernacular of the area), the words of Jesus from the cross in Mk 15:34 (Aramaic = Mt 27:46 Hebrew) being much the most extensive. In one way this creates an obstacle—when for example we hope to read the very words of Jesus. While (as we shall see) there is a chance that Jesus knew some Greek, the overwhelming probability is that the main vehicle of his teaching was Aramaic. Therefore, at best (i.e. even if no other factors are involved) we have in

the gospels renderings of Jesus' words into a foreign tongue—with the distortions that translation cannot but entail.

3. It is worth noting at this point that, apart from a few words and references to a few military or legal institutions, Latin culture has left little mark on the NT: these writings reflect life in the eastern half of the Mediterranean world, parts of the Roman empire with their own strong and often mixed cultures, with Greek as the dominant force in many areas of life. True, descendants of Roman army veterans with Latin names (e.g. Tertius, Rom 16:22) appear in the church at Corinth; Roman officials are not inconspicuous in Acts, Pilate is a key figure in the gospel story, and the empire sometimes broods over the scene, as in Revelation, or is an acknowledged presence, as in 1 Peter and Philippians; but even so, Roman cultural penetration is not deep in the circles from which the NT comes.

4. Yet the obstacle referred to above is modified once we realize that in the first century there was no impenetrable wall between Greek language and Jewishness, or indeed between Jewish and Greek cultures. It is only fair to say that some aspects of the first-century situation, even quite important ones, remain obscure and contentious. But two major facts are clear. First, Palestine, at least as far as the towns were concerned, had become deeply affected by Greek culture during the three centuries before the time of Jesus. It showed itself in public matters such as civic architecture (e.g. Herod's Temple in Jerusalem, built just before Jesus' time), leisure provision (amphitheatres, games), commerce and language (Greek inscriptions on buildings and burial urns); in matters of the mind, so that for example the old Jewish tradition of wisdom writing (classically represented in Proverbs) seems to have absorbed elements of Greek thought (e.g. in Job and Eccesiasticus). While politically the area that would later be called Syria Palestina was, in Jesus' day, part of the Roman empire, its Herodian rulers and many aspects of the Jewish life over which they presided were in practice deeply affected by Hellenistic culture especially in the upper reaches of Jewish society. It is much less clear how far the countryside was affected: throughout the Mediterranean world, old indigenous cultures tended to survive intact outside the limits of the towns and cities. The town of Sepphoris, only a few miles from Nazareth, was being rebuilt along Hellenistic lines in the years of Jesus' youth, but it is impossible to be sure how far such a place would radiate its influence and in exactly what respects. Certainly it is never referred to in the gospels. We shall discuss the setting of Jesus' own life later: suffice it to say here that the extent of his exposure to things Greek *may* have been minimal.

5. Secondly, in the Diaspora (i.e. among the Jews living in the cities of the Mediterranean world), Greek was the predominant medium— even the Scriptures had been translated (the Septuagint); and it is this more firmly Hellenized Judaism that forms the background for most, perhaps all, the NT writers and their books. That does not imply total cultural homogeneity: there were many styles and grades of the conditioning of Judaism by Hellenistic thought and Greek language, and the early Christians whose outlook is encountered through the books of the NT differ a good deal along these lines. None of them displays more than a perfunctory acquaintance with Greek literature (Acts 17:28; 1 Cor 15:33): overwhelmingly their literary formation comes from the Jewish Scriptures, mostly in their Greek form, and often with emphasis on some parts more than others—depending perhaps on the availability of expensive and cumbersome scrolls.

On the other hand, some of them show knowledge of Greek literary forms. Thus, there is a good case for saying that the gospels have affinities with Roman and Greek lives of celebrated figures (Burridge 1992). To judge from books of the period, Luke's preface (1:1–4) indicates that he saw himself as providing a kind of handbook about Jesus, whether for the Christian community or for a wider public (Alexander 1993). Mark shows signs of a degree of training in rhetoric as taught in the Greek schools of the period (Beavis 1989), and the same may be true of Paul (Betz 1979). These writers, for all the Jewishness of their thought and culture, were dependent also on the Greek culture of the setting in which they had been formed—and unselfconsciously so. In their very different ways—and the same variety is found among Jewish writers of the period—they drew upon Greek models. They were part and parcel of their habitat. Partly because of this close interweaving of Judaism and Hellenism by this time, it is not always easy to assign a given feature of a NT book to Jewish or Greek influence. It can still be discussed, for example, whether the prologue of the Gospel of John owes more to the Jewish tradition of 'wisdom' writing or to Greek philosophical discourse of a

Platonist kind; and though current opinion tends to the former opinion, the matter is immediately complicated by the understanding that the wisdom tradition itself had already been open to strands of Platonist thinking (Hengel 1974; Meyers and Strange 1981).

6. Attempts to produce more exotic sources for central early Christian ways of thinking or behaving have failed to earn a permanent place in our picture of the time. The suggestion is made that Paul's ideas on baptism, seeing it in terms of dying and rising with Christ (Rom 6:3–11), and perhaps John's on the eucharist, in terms of eating and drinking Christ's flesh and blood (6: 51–8), have links to supposed beliefs of mystery cults or other esoteric sects, but the chronological difficulties in making some of these connections (especially if gnostic links are introduced) can scarcely be removed and the match of mental worlds is a long way from being exact (Wagner 1967; Wedderburn 1987). At points like these, there must be space for real Christian originality. On any showing, Paul and John were figures of great creativity. Equally, whatever the roots and affinities of his teaching, the impact of Jesus and his followers in the years following his lifetime was so great and so novel that it is vain to hope that every aspect of thought about him, every item of Christian observance, can be shown to be derived easily and directly from phenomena already present in one circle or another in the vastly diverse religious scene of the first-century Mediterranean world. Jesus, the new, unique factor, produced new patterns, new ways of looking at the world. In the gospel's own words, it really was a case of new wine even when there might be old bottles to contain it.

7. Let us look a little more closely at some of the varieties of Hellenized Jewishness, now Christianized, that are visible to us in the NT. With the possible exception of the author of Luke–Acts (and even he was imbued with Jewish lore and culture), every one of the main NT writers was almost certainly Jewish in birth and upbringing. But they exhibit a variety of styles of Jewishness as currently found in various parts of the Jewish world. None of them matches the sophisticated Platonized mentality that Philo of Alexandria was bringing to bear on traditional Jewish themes and biblical texts at precisely the time of Christianity's birth. But Matthew's gospel, for example, with its many scriptural quotations, is the work of someone skilled in the contemporary scribal techniques of biblical interpretation, as abundant examples in the Dead Sea scrolls have demonstrated (Stendahl 1968; Goulder 1974). The kind of training to which they testify, in a work written in Greek, comes most naturally from a Syrian context, affected by the methods elaborated in nearby Palestine and by issues (of law observance) that were hotly debated in the sectarian life of the Jewish heartland in the period (Sanders 1992). Paul and John show similar expertise in the handling of scriptural texts, and the former tells of his background in Pharisaism (Phil 3:5), which operated in a thought-world of such interpretation. John's gospel can be seen as a thoroughgoing reworking of scriptural themes and symbols (light, life, bread, shepherd, lamb), applying them to the determinative figure of Jesus.

8. Luke's reliance on the traditional Scriptures comes out in an ability to write in a Septuagintal style where the context demands it. So, while the stories of the birth of John Baptist and Jesus (1–2) contain no biblical quotations, their language is biblical from end to end, and the characters they depict evoke familiar scriptural figures, most obviously Hannah (1 Sam 2) in the case of Mary, but also couples such as Abraham and Sarah and Manoah and his wife (Jdt 13), who serve to create an ethos of profound biblical piety and solid embeddedness in history for the life of Jesus which follows. Luke is deeply imbued with biblical language and the biblical story.

9. The latter comes out in passages such as Stephen's speech (Acts 7), with its survey of Jewish history presented in a manner reminiscent of numerous Jewish writings (most notably and extensively the contemporary historian Josephus), including its mixture of example and warning. In the NT, the same feature appears in Hebrews, most explicitly in ch. 11.

10. In the NT it is plain that we are reading the work of people soaked in the stories, images, themes and language of the Jewish Scriptures (chiefly in their Greek translation). This sense of thorough permeation comes across nowhere more strongly than in the Revelation of John, where there are no quotations yet almost everything is owed to a disciplined reflection on the books of Ezekiel, Zechariah, and Daniel in their own symbolic and linguistic terms. To call it pastiche would be to undervalue the degree of ingenuity and visionary creativity displayed in this reminting of old motifs in the light of Jesus and beliefs about his person and significance (Farrer 1949; Sweet 1979).

11. The Jewish background of the NT writings comes out as clearly and distinctively as anywhere in the cosmic framework within which their reflection on Jesus and his achievement is set. It is true that much Jewish religious energy went into the minutiae of the application of the Law to daily living, both in spheres that we should call secular and in matters of plain religious observance: Judaism drew no line between the two as far as the applicability of the Law was concerned. In other words, Judaism was (and is) a faith and a lifestyle that viewed the present with intense seriousness and subjected daily conduct to the closest scrutiny (Sanders 1985, 1992).

12. But alongside this concern with the details of present living, and to our eyes perhaps at variance with it, we find, sometimes (as at Qumran) in the same circles, an equally intense interest in the future destiny of the individual, of Israel, and indeed of the world as a whole. This concern with the future and with the cosmic dimension is part and parcel of the Jewish mentality which the first Christians inherited, and both in many of its characteristics and in its strength it differentiated Judaism from other speculative systems and 'end-expectations' of the time. This strength is generally thought to be closely related to the cohesiveness of the Jewish people (despite geographical dispersion) and to the many national catastrophes and disappointments they had endured. These pressures gave rise to extravagant and even desperate hopes of divine intervention and the restoration of Israel. But the power and grandeur of this understanding was enhanced by the strong underlying tradition of monotheism. It was the one God of the universe whose purpose would soon be fulfilled (Rowland 1982).

13. Christian expressions of this world-outlook, centring on the figure of Jesus as God's agent in the hoped-for intervention, are to be found in one form or another in most of the NT books, most notably in the Revelation, a work that is (apart from the letters in chs. 2–3) wholly couched in the idiom of apocalyptic, focused on the heavenly realities and the consummation about to be revealed.

14. But this perspective is by no means confined to Revelation. Jesus himself is depicted as imbued with it in all the gospels, but especially in the first three (Mk 13; Mt 24; Lk 17, 21; but also Jn 5:24–7). Not only does it therefore carry his authority, but its presence as an important constituent in these works lends to each of them as a whole an apocalyptic character: if the modern reader is inclined to skip over these passages, that is simply a symptom of the gap between then and now. Moreover, the actual expression of this feature goes well beyond the chapters that are formally labelled 'apocalyptic', extending, for example, to parables which look forward to cosmic judgement (eg Mt 13:36–43; 25:1–46; Lk 12:35–40). This placing of apocalyptic material cheek by jowl with narrative is already found in Jewish models such as Daniel and serves to place the story as a whole against a cosmic backcloth: we may seem to be reading about events in Galilean villages, but in fact the story is set in the context of the whole universe, heaven and earth and Hades. What is being described has a meaning far beyond that of earthly events and words, however impressive or profound. Further, while the Gospel of John has little explicit apocalyptic material in a formal sense, and its precise literary background is not easily defined, there is a good case for saying that in this work Jesus is seen in his entire career as a manifestation of the divine from heaven—with the consummation of God's purposes both embodied and so concretely anticipated in his life and death. It is a revelatory work *par excellence* (Meeks in Ashton (ed.) 1986; Ashton 1991).

15. Paul too clearly works within an eschatological framework that is apocalyptic or revelatory in character, that is, he sees history, under God's energetic providence, moving rapidly to a climax of judgement and of renewal for his people; and in expressing this conviction he uses the revelatory imagery familiar, in various forms and combinations, in Judaism. There will be judgement according to moral deserts (2 Cor 5:10; Rom 2:16); there will be a resurrection seen as the transformation of God's faithful ones into the form of spiritual bodies (1 Cor 15:35–56); there will even be what amounts to a new creation (2 Cor 5:17; Gal 6:15).

16. For both Paul and John, especially, this picture is linked strikingly to the coming of Jesus and in effect given a new shape as a result of the conviction that the fulfilment of God's purpose centres on him. This conviction necessitates an intensifying of the apocalyptic sense and a shift in its temporal framework. If Jesus is the decisive revelation of God and agent of his purpose, then the process of cosmic consummation is already under way and those who adhere to him embody the fulfilment of Israel's hope. Here is the essential (and radical) amendment to the Jewish picture of things that makes for Christian distinctiveness. It may have taken

some decades to be widely manifest and institutionally plain, but from our earliest source (the letters of Paul) the Christian movement was on its own new path. From a Jewish point of view, this was a fatal distortion of the heritage—especially when, already for Paul, it involved the free inclusion of Gentiles within the new people of God. From the Christian side, it is the goal to which all has tended. No wonder Christians immediately had to set about the appropriation of the old Scriptures—the agreed data—to their picture of things; no wonder the Scriptures were the battleground in the struggle to decide whose right it was to inherit the mantle of Israel's history and God-given privileges.

17. The attaching of a hitherto future hope to the career of Jesus, now past, and to the life of the church, the people that stemmed from him, was a decisive shift; all the more so when (as we shall see) that career was by no means the obvious match to the terms of that hope. In order to accomplish the shift, the apparatus or imagery of apocalyptic was the most readily available tool. So: Jesus was cast (and had perhaps cast himself) in the role of instigator of the fulfilment of God's purpose; the resurrection process began in his own rising on the third day; the Spirit of God, whose outpouring in a new God-given vitality was associated with the coming consummation, was already experienced in the Christian groups (1 Cor 12:1–13; Rom 8); judgement could be seen as linked to the act of adherence to Jesus or the refusal to make that act—to accept the shelter of his gift of overwhelming grace was to come safely to the far side of judgement and into a state of reconciliation with God (Rom 5:1–11; 2 Cor 5:17–21; Jn 5:24). It made a breathtaking offer and no wonder it was put in the most audacious terms.

18. Paul and John saw the implications of this reworking of old categories more clearly than others: it is certainly carried through in their work more thoroughly than in any other of the NT writings. For both of them, concentration on the decisiveness of Jesus is combined with a sense of driving on towards an assured end. The Jewish framework of the one God of the universe, the achieving of whose purpose of salvation will assuredly be realized, is preserved intact. What is new is, first, that it centres on Jesus and is seen as visibly guaranteed by his life, death, and resurrection (and that very attachment to an actual human career, capable inevitably of numerous assessments, opened the door immediately to controversy); and, second, that the fulfilment now has both an urgency and an institutional frame (the church). Only the Qumran sect could rival it in Judaism in this sense of urgency and expectancy, and that group lacked universality of vision and missionary drive, so that its failure to survive the Jewish rebellion of 66–73 CE is in no way surprising. By that time, the followers of Jesus, with their openness to all-comers, Jew and Gentile alike, were well established in the main towns and cities of the Mediterranean world.

19. Only in some of the later books of the NT (1 and 2 Tim, Titus, 2 Pet) do we begin to get a sense of the slackening of the kind of dynamism we have been noticing, a loss of the creative theological vision which had set the people of Jesus on their own distinctive path. The church is here just beginning to be the defender of a system, of both thought and organization, rather than the originator of a novel response to God's action in the world. Sociology teaches us to see such a development as inevitable (von Campenhausen 1969; Holmberg 1990). It is a remarkable fact about the Gospel of John that, in these same last years of the first century, it is able to produce a more thoroughly creative reworking of the traditional Jewish pattern of history, in the light of Jesus, than any other early Christian writing. Anyone inclined to think in terms of single-track, linear development should reflect that, with regard to the basic perspectives that we have been discussing, we find an essential community of mind between Paul, the first Christian writer of all, and John, writing towards the end of the period.

20. Anyone who knows about the ancient world will wish to raise questions about this account of the NT's cultural milieu. The pervasive Hellenizing of the life of the societies around the Mediterranean, especially in the East, must surely point to certain influences on which nothing has been said. Was this not a world in which the great philosophical achievements of Plato and Aristotle, not to speak of Stoics, Cynics, and Pythagoreans, were currents in the prevailing air? It has to be said that the great philosophies have left little trace in these writings. This is not wholly explained by their dominant Jewishness, for, as the case of Philo shows, Judaism was not in itself inimical to the Platonist idiom of thought. It is more a matter of the social strata from which the NT writers came. They were, by definition, not illiterate, but either their education was scriptural or scribal in content and manner or it stopped at a stage on the ladder below that where serious philosophical teaching would

have occurred. All we get then is perhaps a few scraps of Stoicism, possibly affecting Paul's teaching on 'nature' in Rom 1 and 2:14–15, and showing itself in the discussion of the divine in Acts 17:22–31, and in a few other features; and, a subject of much current discussion, Cynic moral wisdom as a factor behind some aspects of Jesus' teaching. It is a disputed question, not so much whether parallels can be identified, as whether, in the circumstances of Jesus' Galilee (or indeed of the evangelists), Cynic influence is at all probable. The day was not far distant, however, when philosophy (chiefly Platonist and Stoic) was to provide a framework of thought in which Christian thinkers sought to operate. Within a few years of the writing of the last books to find a place in the NT (120 CE?), such attempts were beginning to get into their stride.

D. The Church of the New Testament. 1. The Christian church is both depicted in most of the books of the NT and presupposed by all of them. Every one of them is the product of one setting or another in the early Christian communities. Sometimes the location of that setting is actually stated; in other cases it is not hard to see a good deal about its character. Though most of the books bear the name of a single author, there is good reason to think that, even if those ascriptions were in fact accurate (and most of them probably are not), we ought to see these writings partly as productions of the church. While they reflect the thought of some single mind—a genuine author—they were not written in isolation in some equivalent of a modern author's secluded retreat, but from the midst of a particular group of Christians with whom the author was in close interaction. Even the author of Revelation, shut away on Patmos, has his mind on the fellow-Christians from whom he is separated.

2. But, as we saw earlier, churches were not all of one kind or, in many matters, of a single mind. They differed in geographical location; in exposure to some of the cultural features that have been described; in their relation to Jewish observances and the local Jewish community; in attitudes to leading Christian figures such as Peter and Paul; in social composition (Jews, Gentiles, rich, poor); in the handling of moral problems, such as divorce and the scope of generosity. While the Christian churches were a far closer network than any other organization of the time that is at all comparable (and this is surely a major factor in their success, both now and later), held together by visits, letters, and a measure of supervisory responsibility felt by founders and leaders and by one church for another, they were nevertheless often strung out across great distances and surely were compelled to engage in much independent decision-making. As letters such as Galatians and 1 Corinthians show very well, the independence and the supervision could find themselves on a collision course. Many of the NT writings were indeed both an instrument of cohesion (as in due course they recommended themselves to a variety of communities) and a product of difference (in so far as they were designed to meet local and transient needs, or to counter or correct lines taken in other writings and places).

3. If our interest is in the churches within or for whom the NT books were produced, then the most obvious place to begin—and the place where we shall get the most direct results—is the corpus of genuine letters by the apostle Paul. Here is the most transparent (or at any rate the least opaque) window available to us as we seek to look at the life of early Christian communities. That immediately creates narrowness, for they cover only a limited range of churches—in Greece and Macedonia (1 and 2 Cor, 1 and 2 Thess, Phil), Asia Minor (Gal, Col, Philem), and Italy (Rom). (Other letters are of uncertain Pauline authorship or unclear geographical destination: Eph, 1 and 2 Tim, Titus.) Moreover, they vary a great deal in the degree to which they illuminate for us the lives of those to whom they are addressed—as distinct from the thought and interests of Paul who addresses them. Clearest of all is the church in Corinth, where we have the two NT letters (the first of them directly concerned with a welter of practical problems) and personal information from Rom 16, written at Corinth and including greetings from members of the Corinthian church. And Acts 18 gives an account of Paul's initial mission in the city. There is also archaeological and literary material shedding light on the Corinthian background (Theissen 1982; Meeks 1983; Murphy-O'Connor 1983).

4. What is perhaps most surprising about this community, established in the early 50s, is the small degree to which its manifold problems appear to reflect difficulties that are related to Christianity's Jewish origins. There were, it appears, some Jewish members, but what one might expect to be their concerns (Law observance, relations to Gentile members, and scriptural interpretation) scarcely figure. This was,

already, largely a Gentile community, and most of its problems sprang from overexuberant and élitist religiosity on the part of the most articulate and wealthy members. More clearly than any other NT writings, these letters give evidence of a church whose cohesion was made precarious by the dominance of these religious 'experts'. Precarious, that is, in the eyes of Paul, who insists that all-embracing dependence on Christ implies the transcending of social and racial divisions (1 Cor 1–4; 12:13) and the giving of full honour and consideration to the simpler and poorer members (11:17–34; 12:1–13). In Paul's perception, the Lord's supper was to be the outward manifestation of this basic equality of generous love, rather than the focus of social division that it had become in Corinthian practice. They were simply continuing to run their meetings along the hierarchical lines taken for granted in a place such as Corinth in households and in guilds and associations of various kinds.

5. Galatians gives evidence of a different situation. Here it is indeed the implications of Christ for the adherence of his followers to Jewish observance that is in question, in particular the traditional Jewish identity-markers of circumcision, sabbath, and food rules. This letter gives a vivid picture of the bitterness caused by this issue (1–2 especially). Whether or not Paul was the first to see adherence to Christ as transcending this observance, and so as eliminating it at least as far as Gentile Christians were concerned (and therefore in effect dethroning it for all Christians), he it was who gave a rationale, scripturally based at that, for resistance to the imposition of the old Jewish marks of valid membership of God's people (3–4; see also Rom 4).

6. Some writings point to there being groupings of churches, whether on a geographical basis, or in relation to a shared missionary-founder. There would often be a shared language—a particular idiom or set of ideas in which to express Christian belief. This is most easily seen in the case of the communities visible in the Johannine Epistles. Here we have evidence of a number of Christian groups (it is unclear how many), where there is a limited degree of common acquaintance (3 Jn) and so perhaps a fairly wide geographical spread, but all sharing some sort of organizational unity (2 Jn 1)—and having to struggle to maintain it (3 Jn). The basis of this unity, fragile as it was, was the form of Christian belief whose classic expression was in the Gospel of John, with its distinctive, finely tuned vocabulary of key words (light, life, truth, word), endlessly rewoven like elements in a complex fugue. But it is plain that there was no machinery for the exerting of rigid discipline among these Johannine Christians: the occasion for the first two letters is the emergence of division about the interpretation of their manner of belief concerning the person of Jesus. It is also plain that, even in the short time that must have elapsed between the writing of the gospel and the letters, some of the key words changed subtly in sense, in response to the quarrels. 'Love', for example, becomes a duty confined to the like-minded (Brown 1979).

7. The Revelation of John, with its letters to seven churches in Asia Minor (chs. 2–3), may again testify to some kind of group consciousness among a set of congregations, though it is unclear whether the admonitory role adopted by the seer is self-appointed or represents a formal acceptance by these churches of a special relationship. That such groupings might not be tight or exclusive is suggested by the fact that the church in the major centre of Ephesus appears in three different sets: the seven churches of Revelation, the largely different seven churches who received letters from Ignatius of Antioch (c.110 CE), and the Pauline foundations (Acts 19). The speed with which the main NT writings seem to have circulated itself suggests the effectiveness of at least informal ties among the churches, as does such a project as the collecting of Paul's letters, presumably from the churches which had initially received them, a process perhaps concluded by the end of the first century.

8. What has been said so far about the early Christian communities may seem to point to virtual simultaneity among the situations depicted; and it may seem that as, at the outside, the time-span of their composition was no more than seventy years (say, 50–120 CE), and as the period is so distant and obscure, there is little scope for attempts to refine that approach. But we are not entirely without the possibility of identifying developments even within that relatively short period, though certainty very often eludes us.

9. The first development was the shift in the character of the Christian movement from the period of Jesus' ministry to the subsequent mission and the living of the Christian life. Our written sources in the NT itself, the gospels and Acts, present it as the smoothest of transitions. At first there was, it seems, a brief time of

Galilean ministry by Jesus and a small group of adherents, supported from time to time by transient and anonymous crowds. It was marked by constant movement, and a few references to Jesus' home (Mk 2:1, 15) scarcely modify this picture of endless mobility. The fact that the dominant mode of Christian life soon came to be settled and static speaks for the accuracy of this picture: any temptation to redescribe Jesus' circumstances in the light of later times has been resisted.

10. This time was also marked by the rural character of its setting: the big urban centres of Galilee in Jesus' day, notably Sepphoris and Tiberias, are conspicuous by their absence, even though the former was only a few miles from Nazareth where Jesus was brought up. There are of course numerous references to 'cities'; in general and by name, but none of them is much more than a village or small town in modern terms. They were small settlements in an overwhelmingly peasant-dominated and agriculture-centred world. We have already seen that, in congruity with this mode of life, this was a setting where Aramaic was the dominant language and where literacy and a wider culture were almost certainly rare. While, like the wandering character of Jesus' ministry, the rural setting has amply survived any attempt the evangelists might have been expected to make to conform their account of Jesus' activities to the urban setting of the churches of their own experience, the Semitic speech has been almost totally obliterated (Mk 5:41; 7:34; 14:36—all dropped by Matthew and Luke in their parallel passages), and Jesus is depicted as possessing both scriptural knowledge and technical interpretative skill, including the ability to read (Lk 4:17), and even perhaps some acquaintance with current popular moral teaching with Cynic affinities. The question attributed to the people in the synagogue (Mk 6:2), 'Where did this man get all this?' has never been satisfactorily answered, except in the terms of supernatural endowment—which the evangelist is no doubt content for us to entertain. However, it has to be said that evidence about synagogues in Galilee in this precise period (as distinct from a little later) and about educational opportunities at village level is practically non-existent and intelligent guesses vary, some more optimistic than the tone adopted here (Freyne 1988).

11. Leaving these matters aside, we do not have to look for the reason behind the original organizational simplicity, even indifference, of the movement that centred on Jesus. It lay surely in the vivid sense of God's imminent fulfilment of his saving purpose—to which, as we have seen, the gospels (not to speak of Paul and most other early Christian writers) bear witness. True, in the Qumran sect we have a Jewish group that combined such a sense (despite their existence for two centuries without its realization) with the most meticulous rules and observance covering every aspect of the common life. But in the case of both John Baptist and Jesus, the policy is different: open not secluded, of mass appeal not separatist, personal not immediately communal in its effects. There is not much sign in the gospels (and again the resistance of inevitable pressure to conform the story to later situations is impressive) of any attempt by either of these charismatic figures to ensure the survival and stability of a movement, with the structural provision which that requires. What there is, for example the commission to Peter (Mt 16:17–19), has all the marks of coming from later times: in this example, the words are added by Matthew to Mark's narrative, reducing it to confusion when we read on to 'Get behind me, Satan', addressed now to one just assured of the most crucial role in the church. Even when such material is taken into account, it does not amount to a blueprint: in the later first century, when the gospels were written, the church had still not reached a Qumran-like point, where every detail of life should be provided for by rule. The strong eschatological impulse from Jesus had not exhausted itself, despite the great changes which had nevertheless occurred.

12. Those changes were indeed momentous. Almost all the features of Jesus' ministry that have been described were replaced by their contraries. Mesmerized by the smoothness of the transition as described by Luke, as we move from his gospel to the beginning of Acts, readers have been reluctant to grasp how incongruous are the 'before' and the 'after'. Much attention has long been given to the question of how and why the Christian movement survived the death of its founder and the seeming failure of all his hopes and promises; and in answering that question, attention has focused chiefly on the resurrection of Jesus as offering, somehow, the key to the problem's solution. But there is the at least equally fascinating institutional problem. Evidence to shed light on it is almost non-existent, and Luke has thrown us off any scent there might be, encouraging us to see the move as the most natural thing you could imagine: of course, Jesus' followers simply established themselves in Jerusalem, where they happened to be, and started preaching.

13. In fact it was remarkable that, in institutional terms, the Christian movement survived the crisis. It was done at the cost of severe changes to some of its central attributes and perspectives. Most obviously, there was a shift from rural to urban settings, probably first in Jerusalem, as Acts says, but soon in other major cities—Antioch (one of the largest cities of the ancient world) and then, in due course, in Asia Minor, Greece, and Rome, in the 40s and 50s. The world of Galilee was left behind. Indeed, with the exception of a single allusion in Acts 9:31, we have no clear evidence of Christian activity there after Jesus left for Jerusalem. For all we can tell, his work there was without trace—a passing whirlwind. (References to appearances of the risen Jesus there, in Mt 28 and Jn 21, are of uncertain value in this regard and nothing visible follows from them.)

14. There was a shift too (and necessarily, given the urban locations) from itinerant to settled life, with missions undertaken from permanent urban centres. The result of this shift was that tensions arose between the more mobile missioners and the members of Christian congregations who did not normally reckon to leave their city boundaries and whose Christian life soon expressed also a change from a movement of unorganized individual adherents, many of them perhaps transiently impressed by the preaching of Jesus (the 'crowds' of the gospels), to one of tightly knit congregations, many of their members belonging probably to a small number of households in a given place and living quite circumscribed lives, marked in all kinds of ways by their Christian allegiance. We have seen that the letters of Paul testify amply to some of the problems resulting from this new allegiance, working its way within the social framework of such cities of the Graeco-Roman world as Corinth and Thessalonica.

15. We said that the strong sense of an imminent manifestation of God's power, to judge and then to save his own, survived the lifetime of Jesus—it is the framework of Paul's faith—and the shift to a more organized mode of existence. But certain of its concomitants in the earlier phase are no longer prominent. It was not practicable in the circumstances of an urban institution to follow the pattern of abandonment of family and property which is so strong in the preaching of Jesus. No doubt, with the exception of Jesus' immediate circle of itinerant preachers, there was always a measure of metaphor in the interpretation of this theme: Peter was married when he 'forsook all and followed' Jesus (Mk 1:16–20, 29–31), and remained so (1 Cor 9:5), and indeed Mark studiously omits wives from the list of relations to be left behind (10:29–31; cf. the prohibition of divorce in 10:1–12)—though Luke (looking back through ascetic rose-tinted spectacles?) does not (18:29). The message might be interiorized into attitudes of single-mindedness and self-abnegation, or modified to spur Christians into generosity (forsaking not all wealth but certainly some), whether to the needy of the Christian group or to outsiders (Lk 10:25–37). There is astonishingly little on these themes in the ethical sections of the letters of Paul (Rom 12:13; 16:1–2 on giving; and 1 Cor 7:12–16 on marital problems in relation to conversion); though it is hard to believe that passages such as Mk 1:16–20 did not resonate with people whose Christian decision cost them dear in terms of family relationships and inheritance (cf. Jn 9).

16. Christian family life, with its development of injuction and advice for its regulation, was not long in becoming a primary concern in the urban congregations. It had soon become an institution in its own right, and it figures in one form or another in many of the NT letters (1 Cor 7; Col 3:18–4:1; Eph 5:21–6:9; 1 Pet 2:18–3:7), in terms much like those found in both Jewish and Greek compendia dealing with the same themes. The church had become domesticated. The note of abandonment, as a constant sound in the Christian ear, was muted, as emphasis shifted to the maintenance of church life.

17. It has become common to give more attention to a second transition in church life during the period in which the NT books were written, and sometimes it has been exaggerated or misleadingly described, perhaps in surrender to the impulse to contrast an early golden age with subsequent decline. This is the development in the later years of the first century and the earlier years of the second, of a greater concern to formalize and legitimate Christian institutions of many kinds. The first moves towards an authorized body of Christian writings probably belong to this time and are one mark of this trend. Others include the final replacement of itinerant missionaries (such as Paul and his associates) by the leaders of local churches, so that the churches now bear the weight of Christian organization and authority: there is no outside body to turn to, except other churches comparable to one's own. Despite the emergence of networks and groupings,

local leaders became more prominent, and in more and more places, a single 'supervisor' (*episkopos*, later acquiring the status of a Christian technical term, 'bishop') came into being as the chief officer of the Christian community. As a matter of history, he probably arose from among the natural leaders of household-churches in a given place, but some bishops at least soon came to see their role in much more lofty terms: as representatives of God the Father and vehicles of the Spirit's utterance. The letters of Ignatius of Antioch (*c.*110 CE; Staniforth and Louth 1987) show us a man whose high sense of his place in the Christian scheme of things makes Paul's idea of an apostle pale by comparison (Campbell 1994).

18. There is little surviving evidence, but it is likely that forms of worship came to be formulated in the same period. The Didache (not in the NT and unknown until a single manuscript came to light in 1873) contains forms of eucharistic prayer from Syria, probably from the late first century. There are signs too of an increasing concern with conformity to whatever in a particular place was seen as orthodoxy: both the Johannine and the Pastoral Epistles show this trait, and in the latter case, there is more interest in urging such conformity than in elaborating on the beliefs actually involved. These pseudonymously Pauline letters are also insistent on the need for respectable behaviour, acceptable to society at large, and on the sober qualities required in church leaders (1 Tim 2:1–4; 3:1–11). It is all a far cry from the exuberance and brave independence of mind that mark the mission of Paul half a century before.

19. All the same, it does not do to paint too sharp a contrast between the solid and perhaps unexciting interests visible in some of the late NT writings and the enthusiasm and innovation of earlier days. If Paul is aware of the inspirational force of the Spirit in himself and among his converts, Ignatius shows comparable assurance, speaking with the voice of God. He is no mere ecclesiastical official, basing his position on human legitimation and just, as it were, doing a job for the church. On the other hand, Paul himself is far from being uninterested in due order in his Christian communities. It may sometimes have been hard to achieve or, as in Corinth, power had come to be concentrated in persons he disapproved of—even if they were themselves, it appears, claiming charismatic inspiration. But the whole tone of his correspondence shows an acute concern for properly accredited leadership, as 1 Cor 16:15–17 tactfully indicates. He was no lover of spiritual anarchy (Holmberg 1978).

20. However the matter is analysed in detail—and there is room for difference of opinion—it is evident that the churches underwent considerable changes, even within the relatively brief period to which the NT testifies and even to the extent of producing contradictory opinions and policies (for example on ethical questions such as the continuing role of the Jewish Law in daily life, Houlden 1973).

21. It is to be noted that all this took place among a still obscure body of people—spreading rapidly across the Mediterranean map and growing in numbers right through the century, but, in the writings available to us, showing little awareness of the world of the history textbook. There are, however, some marks of that world: the author of Revelation has his eyes on the fate of the Roman Empire and is aware of the rise and fall of emperors; Luke knows about Roman governors and other officials in the territories he describes, as well as something of the system they operate (Sherwin-White 1963; Lentz 1993). Yet the events that might be expected to have made an impact on the late first-century writings of a religious group with Jewish antecedents—the Jewish rebellion in Judea, the destruction of the Jerusalem Temple at Roman hands, and the mass suicide at Masada—have left only oblique traces, such as elements in a parable (Mt 22:7) and symbol-laden prophecies on Jesus' lips (Lk 21:20–4). On the face of it, this is astonishing, so much so that some critics have been led (in the teeth of all other considerations) to date the NT books well before those happenings of 66–73 CE (Robinson 1976). It may be better to see this silence as evidence of the degree to which the Christian communities responsible for these books had by the time of writing abandoned their Palestinian and, in many cases, their Jewish roots, at least in social and institutional terms. These events impinged, on people whose loyalties and interests now lay elsewhere and who were removed from the immediate scene, less than seems to modern people to be credible.

22. Finally, part of the explanation lies also in the high concentration that marked the self-understanding of the Christian communities: they had strongly formed beliefs not just about God and Jesus, but also about the church itself. In other words, the detached and analytical terms in which the church has been discussed in this article would have been wholly alien to them. In Jesus' own preaching, there can

be little doubt that, even if he did not establish 'cells' of followers in the Galilean countryside and villages (and there is no sign of such groups), his preaching of the dawn of God's kingdom, his visible and effective sovereignty, involved communal assumptions. What was to emerge was a purified and rejuvenated 'people of God'—some sort of 'Israel'.

23. The urbanizing of Christianity, visible in Paul and elsewhere, brought no break in this 'Israel-consciousness'. Above all in Rom 9–11, Paul produced a complex and ingenious theory to demonstrate the continuity between the Israel of the Scriptures and the Christian community, made up of Jews and Gentiles on equal terms (at least in Paul's determined view). But Paul also saw the church in a quite different perspective, one that was in tension, if not contradiction, with the idea of continuity which his Jewish roots and his sense of the one God of history would not allow him to forgo. This other perspective, for which he also argued with great skill and passion, centred on Christ and the sheer novelty that had come on the scene with him. It was nothing less than a new creation (2 Cor 5:17), with Jesus as a new Adam, starting the human journey off all over again (Rom 5:12–21; 1 Cor 15:22). In him, the human race was created afresh. Paul's highly concentrated image of the church as Christ's body encapsulates this consciousness, in which the Jew–Gentile divide is not so much overcome as undermined and rendered irrelevant (1 Cor 12; Rom 12; Gal 3:28). By clever scriptural arguments, chiefly involving the figure of Abraham (Gal 3; Rom 4), Paul sought to reconcile these two perspectives. They did not convince Jews, and while Christians mostly maintained that they were the true heirs of the old Israel, it was the idea of their membership 'in Christ', expressed in baptism and eucharist, and worked out in following his teaching as found in the gospels, that chiefly occupied their practical consciousness. John's gospel systematically shows Jesus, and then those attached to him as branches to vine and as sheep to shepherd (15; 10), as embodying and absorbing all the great attributes and properties that had belonged to Judaism and the people of Israel. They belonged now to the people of Jesus.

E. Jesus and the New Testament. 1. It might be expected that an introduction to the NT would open with an account of Jesus rather than delay the subject to the end. After all, directly or obliquely, Jesus is the subject of

most of the NT books, and is the most significant factor in their ever having been written at
all. There are, however, good reasons for the
roundabout approach to the heart of the matter. For, despite all his prominence, Jesus is in
the NT a figure to be approached with caution.
For one thing, much depends on the reader's
interest: whether, for example, you are keen to
find out about the facts and circumstances of
Jesus' life, personality, and teaching, or about
the origins and terms of faith in him. There is a
well-grounded distinction between Jesus as a
figure of early first-century Jewish history and
Jesus as the object of devotion and faith, presupposed by all the NT writers; with the resurrection (that most difficult of phenomena to pin
down) as the hinge between the two.

2. It is a basic truth that, whatever the claims
and the appearances, Jesus is never encountered
'neat' in the NT. Apart from the fact that the
gospels are unlikely to be the work of steno-
graphers who hung on Jesus' every word and of
adherents who witnessed his every act, those
brief books have all the inevitable distortion
that goes with selectivity; moreover, it is apparent that the selectivity was not unprincipled or
merely random. It worked by way of filters,
some obvious, others more hypothetical, by
which material was affected on its way into
the gospels we read. We have already referred
to the frequently ignored filter of translation of
speech from Aramaic into Greek. It is accompanied by the equally frequently ignored filter
by which the material moves from an originally
uneducated Galilean and rural setting to more
sophisticated urban settings, in Syria, Asia
Minor, or elsewhere, where much vital original
colouring must have been invisible. Sometimes
the provision of new colouring is obvious
enough: the well-known example of the tile-
roofed Hellenistic town house described in
Luke's version of the healing of the paralytic
(5:19; contrast the Palestinian house in Mk 2:4).
For all we know, there are many details, large
and small, in the gospels that are both harder to
spot and more significant for the general picture than that.

3. Equally important as a distorting factor is
the effect of developing convictions and attitudes in the church in the years following
Jesus' lifetime. Some instances have proved devastating in their results, above all the way the
gospels (increasingly as one succeeds another)
place responsibility for Jesus' death on Jewish
heads (on *all* Jewish heads, Mt 27:25), with Pon-
tius Pilate as their pliable but scarcely guilty

accomplice (Mt 27:24; Lk 23:22). There is good
reason to suppose that this is unlikely to represent the truth of the matter and that it reflects
instead the increasing tension between Christians and (other) Jews, as the former were virtually compelled to define themselves over
against the latter. Historically, the probability
is that, at a time of governmental nervousness
in a Jerusalem crowded for Passover, the Roman
authorities combined with the Jewish priestly
aristocracy who administered the Temple to
remove one whom they perceived to be a possible occasion of civil disorder. His execution
was, after all, by the Roman method in such
cases, that is crucifixion (Rivkin 1984; Brown
1994).

4. But this is only the most spectacular instance of a pervasive principle, often hard to
identify with assurance. Take, for example, the
matter of Jesus' attitude to the Jewish Law. Did
he simply take it for granted as the air he
breathed, perhaps taking one side or another
on subjects of current dispute, but not stepping
outside the limits, as currently seen, of legitimate debate? His society did not, it seems, operate
under a rigid orthodoxy and there was much
diversity of interpretation about such matters as
sabbath observance and tithing of produce. Or
did he go beyond such bounds, offering a radical critique of the Law's very foundations? If so,
it is puzzling that none of the gospels offers this
as the reason for his final condemnation
(though he is attacked for it in the course of
the story, e.g. Mk 3:1–6). But the gospels differ in
their presentation of Jesus' teaching on this
subject in the course of his ministry.

5. In brief, Mark depicts him as radical,
marginalizing food taboos and the priority of
sabbath observance (7:19; 2:23–3:6) and down-
playing the sacrificial system in favour of an
ethic of active love (12:28–34); while John
shows him superseding the Law in his own
person as the medium of God's disclosure to
his people (1:17; 2:21; 7:37–8). Matthew, by contrast, has Jesus endorse and intensify the
requirements of the Law (5:17–20; 23:23), while
he takes a humane view on certain currently
disputed issues (12:1–14; 19:1–9; adapting Mark).
And Luke places his attitude somewhere between Mark and Matthew, rather in the spirit
of the compromise he shows the Jerusalem
church arriving at later in the light of substantial Gentile conversions to the church (Acts 15).
It is hard to avoid the conclusion that all these
presentations have been affected by the diverse
resolutions of this problem, both pressing and

practical in the first decades of the Christian movement, that were adopted in various different quarters of the church.

6. Moreover, all the evangelists were writing after the shock of Paul's strong stand on this very matter, releasing Gentile converts from the adoption of the key marks of Jewish identity—sabbath observance, food laws, and circumcision—and thereby implicitly placing allegiance to Christ as the sole identity marker for all Christians. It appears that the whole subject remained contentious for some time, with a variety of positions being taken (though it remains a puzzle that neither radical nor conservative presentations in the gospels refer to the matter of circumcision on whose irrelevance Paul was so insistent, as Galatians in particular demonstrates). The upshot of all this is that we really cannot tell with certainty exactly what Jesus himself taught or practised, and scholarly opinion remains divided. Careful analyses of crucial sayings, fitting them plausibly into the setting of his time and place, always remain open to alternative interpretations which see them as reflections of the particular evangelists' views (Harvey 1982; Sanders 1993).

7. Jesus is obscured too by the fact that, by the time the gospels were written, interest in the sheer preservation of his words and ideas was overshadowed by his being the object of faith—and by the consequent need to make a case for that faith, which saw him not simply as a figure of the past who had once revealed God and his saving purposes and whose death and resurrection had given new insight into those purposes or marked their realization; but as the present heavenly Lord who enjoyed supreme triumph as God's co-regent and would soon return in the public display of that reality.

8. The scriptural text that seemed best to epitomize that faith was 'The Lord said unto my Lord, Sit at my right hand, till I make your enemies your footstool' (Ps 110:1). This text is quoted more widely across the gamut of NT authors than any other—closely followed by 'Thou art my son, this day I have begotten thee' (Ps 2:7), less precise but not dissimilar in import. It is impossible to believe that this faith failed to colour the memory of Jesus' earthly life, even if there had been in the churches a strongly archival sense, or, more likely, a reverence for Jesus' words and the stories of his deeds, which could stand alongside that faith: argument ranges back and forth on the balance of effect of these various aspects of the situation (Gerhardsson 1961; Stanton 1974; Meier 1991).

9. The faith in Jesus which prevents the gospels being neutral records (whatever that might mean) was largely articulated by means of material drawn from Judaism, and especially from the old Scriptures. This was partly for purposes of Christian self-understanding (to what other medium could the first Christians practically turn?) and partly for purposes of self-definition in relation to (other) Jews who did not share their assessment of Jesus and adherence to him. But this appeal to Scripture, which pervades the gospels, makes yet another screen between us and the realities of Jesus' historical life. It is an interpretative tool that was certainly used, in one form or another, by all schools of thought in the early church, but, when it comes to the gospels, we are faced with the question of whether Jesus himself initiated the process- -as in the depiction that is before us. Did he not, inevitably, interpret his own mission and person in scriptural terms? If so, to which models did he appeal? And to what extent did the amplifying of this mode of thought in the church, as evidenced in the gospels and elsewhere, merely build upon his foundations and continue along lines he laid down, as distinct from moving along altogether more ambitious paths? For example, when the Gospel of John views Jesus under the image of God's pre-existent Word, his copartner in the work of creation itself (1:1–18), thus drawing on a symbol current in Judaism (e.g. Ps 33:6; Wis 9:1), there is nothing to suggest that Jesus himself made use of that category of thought. It is quite otherwise with Jewish terms such as Messiah, son of God, or son of man. These appear on his lips or are inseparable from the tradition about him. None of them is easy to interpret, and if Jesus used them, it is as likely that they received, by the very fact of their application to him if not from his explicit teaching, twists of sense, perhaps to the extent of sheer paradox, that were novel. Jesus was, after all, on any showing a most un-messianic Messiah, given the nationalistic associations of the term—if indeed he did make any such claim. And the same would be true even if in reality the claim derives from his followers after his lifetime rather than from himself.

10. None of this caution, this indirectness, is designed to say that the gospels merely obscure the figure of Jesus or tell us nothing of value about him. There are certain features of his life and teaching that not only come across loud and clear but were less than wholly welcome in the early church—and would not therefore have survived if the church, like a traumatized individual, simply eliminated that which it no longer approved of or no longer served its purposes. We have seen that the renunciatory teachings of Jesus the Galilean charismatic preacher were toned down or repackaged quite rapidly in the more settled life of the urban churches. Yet we see them prominently displayed in the first three gospels. Much has been made (Hengel 1981) of the saying in Mt 8:22 ('Follow me, and let the dead bury their own dead'), advocating, in the name of the extreme urgency of God's call and of his kingdom, a stance of provocative immorality by the standards of virtually any culture and soon abandoned in the family ethic of the church, as Eph 6:4 demonstrates. It is these harder, more uncomfortable elements in the story of Jesus which, however they may sometimes visibly, as one evangelist modifies another, have been modified by the church, speak most powerfully for the tenacity and authority of Jesus' vision, simply because it was his (Harvey 1990).

11. A promising line of enquiry begins by bypassing the gospels altogether. We know when and where Jesus lived: what then can we learn from a knowledge of the times derived from other sources, such as archaeology and histories of the period? We have already made reference to evidence of this kind: the Qumran sect and the Dead Sea scrolls left by them (Vermes 1977, 1995); the probabilities about the circumstances of Jesus' death; the mixed culture of Galilee with its peasant countryside and Hellenistic cities. But can this approach bring us nearer to a realistic view of Jesus himself, at any rate to a view of his role in the society of his time—what sort of part he played, how he may have fitted into its structure and been perceived (Finegan 1992; Stanton 1995)?

12. This more detached and wider-ranging approach does not yield unquestioned results, but many would agree that it places Jesus in a category of persons recognizable in the period (Vermes 1973). In traditional terms, such persons have affinities with the prophets of former centuries, men who stood out from the prevailing religious culture and social system, declaring the will of God and the imminence of his judgement. More sociologically, we can refer to them as charismatics, that is people whose message threatens to turn the world upside down, challenging conventional values—even those whose morality seems unimpeachable—and looking towards an order of things where life is lived at a new level of righteousness and God

is all in all. Such people rarely get much of a hearing: often their day is brief or they are snuffed out by authorities who feel endangered by them. First-century Galilee, somewhat removed from the centre of power in Jerusalem and probably unstable in its rural economy, spawned several such figures, most of them leaving practically no trace. John Baptist had more identifiable effects: he comes into the story of Jesus, and the late first-century Jewish historian Josephus (like Mark and Matthew but in somewhat different terms) tells of his execution for his righteous meddling in the affairs of the great ones in the land—a classic prophet's predicament. Moreover (and somewhat mysteriously), like Jesus, he gave rise to a group of followers who, according to Acts 18:24–19:6, had spread to Ephesus in the later years of the century—thereafter they fade from view.

13. Much of the broad picture of Jesus in the gospels coheres with this identification of his social role: the radical, shocking teaching about ties to family and property; the call to 'follow' that brooks no delay, no appeal to prudence; the ready challenge to established religious groups, even the most pious, for their routines and their self-satisfaction; the challenge to central authority—if that is how we are to construe the incident in the Temple (Mk 11:15–17) which probably precipitated the perception of Jesus as a breacher of the peace and his speedy elimination; above all, the sense of the imminent realization of God's rule.

14. However, other readings are possible and win some support, even within the method we have been describing. The picture of Jesus as charismatic leader or prophet, once put forward, seems obvious: it makes best sense of the most basic recognition of modern scholarship—that Jesus was a Jew of his time. It brings it into sharp focus and takes us behind some of the other characterizations of Jesus (for example, as the heavenly one come to earth) that soon came to dominate Christian accounts of him (Rom 1:3; Gal 4:4). But it does less than justice to certain other aspects of the gospel material: such as the teaching about there being no need for anxiety, no need for complexity of lifestyle (Mt 6:25–34); or the picture of Jesus and his followers as a band of brothers espousing freedom and simplicity of life under God's heaven, somewhat after the manner of modern opters-out from society. Jesus' common meals with his followers (specially emphasized in Luke) were then the central symbol of this lifestyle, focused on the present.

15. This is a distinctly non-apocalyptic picture of Jesus and, in terms of Jewish heritage, seems to owe more to some facets of Jewish 'wisdom' tradition, with its provision for moral life here and now. But its associations and provenance may lie more in the teaching of Cynic philosophers who adopted values of this kind and whose influence had perhaps penetrated into northern Palestine. The straightforward view is of course, that Jesus himself sensed a directness and simplicity of filial relationship with God—it was his stance in daily life ('father' e.g. Mt 6:7–14). Alternatively, this picture may represent one style among others of church reflection on Jesus, as the tradition about him was exposed to the variegated culture of the Graeco-Roman world (Crossan 1991; 1994).

16. This discussion started, somewhat negatively, under the injunction to approach the figure of Jesus with caution: the nature of our evidence, literary and circumstantial, dictates it. But (to repeat) it would be a mistake to let caution lead to the conclusion that Jesus is a mere enigma, lost in the mists of time or a welter of church obfuscation of whatever clarity there might otherwise have been. As we have seen, some features are unmistakable and their strength shines through. But the equally unmistakable effects of church interpretation of various kinds are there in the gospels, and they lead us to our final topic: Jesus as the object of faith.

17. If we had only the letters of Paul, we should think that all that really mattered about Jesus' career was his death and resurrection: that is, its importance centred almost wholly on a period of some forty-eight hours—and if more than that, then what followed it (his heavenly rule and presence in his adherents) was more notable than what preceded it. That is the earliest Christian perspective of which we have evidence.

18. How different it is from the picture we get from the gospels. There, though the death and resurrection are plainly the climax of the narrative and occupy a disproportionate place from a purely biographical point of view, these elements are nevertheless parts of a much greater whole. To put it more succinctly, they form the end of a story, where in Paul they acted much more as the inauguration of a continuing state of affairs. It is not wholly satisfying simply to point out that these are different genres of writing and so naturally differ in their perspective. After all, none of these writers was compelled to write as he did, and each wrote in a particular way because, presumably, it reflected the 'shape' of his convictions about Jesus.

19. The two perspectives meet, however, precisely in the death and resurrection, and the latter in particular may be seen as the junction between them (Evans 1970; Marxsen 1970). Luke's two-volume work (Gospel and Acts) comes nearest to meeting the need to unite Jesus' life before the resurrection and the life of the church after it—though even this narrative probably ends before the time of writing, and so, like the gospels, looks back from the Christian present to an (albeit longer) normative history. On the other hand, though the gospels do indeed describe a past that culminates in Jesus' death and resurrection, they are nevertheless imbued with a present faith in the living Christ who, in his heavenly rule, may still be said to inspire his people and even to dwell in and among them: perhaps especially in Mark and John, the backdrop is that of Jesus' past life but he addresses the present of the gospels' readers. So much is this the case that, as we have seen, we must be alert to the effects of this factor as we read the gospels with a view to discovering simply what happened and how things were in Jesus' lifetime.

20. To take a small example, but significant for that very reason (and capable of being paralleled almost limitlessly): Mk 9:40 ('Whoever is not against us is for us') suggests that Jesus urged on his followers an open, expansive attitude to possible supporters and deflects them from any narrowness or the erection of barriers and the application of tests. This is, in the words of the church poster, a case of 'All welcome'. But Mt 12:30 ('He who is not with me is against me') reflects the precise opposite. Jesus makes stringent demands on potential followers and there is no easy entry to their company: adhering is sharply distinguished from remaining outside. The boundary wall is high. Must we not see here the effects of two different outlooks in different parts of the early church, both equally comprehensible, but contrasting in their policies—and far-reaching in their twin visions of Christian life? It does not take much imagination to see that the two statements betoken two very different ways of believing in Jesus' significance and the scope of his work, as they also may be seen as the founts of two different traditions in Christian life down to our own day. The gospels, accounts of the pre-resurrection life of Jesus, then reflect the faith of the post-resurrection church, in small ways as in great. These considerations go some way to mitigate the contrast that we drew between the perspectives of Paul and the gospels.

21. From another point of view, we may indeed say that these writings—and indeed almost all the NT books (the Letter of James is a strange exception)—testify to a remarkably homogeneous faith in the centrality of Jesus as the agent of God's saving purpose. True, they differ in certain respects, in emphasis and terminology, but the unanimity is striking. To return to the obvious: it is this common conviction about Jesus as the one who 'makes all the difference' that holds together the early Christian movement, and so the NT as its literary deposit—whatever other factors loomed large in its life and whatever the problems to which it had to attend.

22. Yet we may observe interesting variations of resonance even in the use of certain terms to express this conviction about Jesus. For example, many early Christian writers speak of him as 'son of God'. But what associations did this expression have for them? It is not, after all, an expression that simply comes out of the blue: it has numerous antecedents in Judaism, and without recognizable resonances it could scarcely have been used at all in its new context. In Paul, the earliest writer to use it, it is not altogether clear what is in mind, for he gives it multiple applications. In Rom 9:4, it receives one of its traditional applications, to Israel as a people (cf. Ex 4:22; Hos 11:1); in Gal 3:26 and Rom 8:14, it denotes Christian believers—a usage paralleled in Jewish wisdom writing (Wis 2:18), where it is applied to righteous servants of God. Yet clearly, for Paul, this application to Christians is now closely related (but exactly how?) to its central use for Jesus himself; just as God's 'fatherhood' of Jesus is related to their right to claim that same fatherhood (Gal 4:4–6; Rom 8:14–17). Paul perhaps comes nearest to showing his mind in Rom 8:32, where he appeals to the giving by Abraham of his son Isaac to death (narrowly averted, Gen 22) as a parallel to God's giving of Jesus: 'God did not spare his only son' (cf. Gen 22:16). That model of sonship splendidly and appropriately illuminates the death of Jesus and is an important ingredient in the quest for scriptural texts that could put that otherwise catastrophic event, as far as the hopes of Jesus' followers were concerned, in a positive light. Here was a case where the giving of a son by a father was the seed of total good—the establishing of the people of Israel (Byrne 1979).

23. The same model may play a part in the Markan story of Jesus' baptism, where his sonship is announced by God himself: the word 'beloved' in 1:11 is the Septuagint's repeated adjective for Isaac in Gen 22. But here, in what is for Mark the crucial opening scene, establishing Jesus' identity, it is joined with the words of Ps 2:7, 'Thou art my son', probably seen as messianic in import in the Jewish background upon which Mark draws.

24. In Matthew and Luke, Jesus' sonship is for the first time linked to his conception and birth, but even here the focus is not on physiology but on scriptural texts and models which are seen to foreshadow Jesus and to authenticate his role. In Matthew, for example, Isa 7:14 plays a crucial role (cf. 1:23). In Luke, the whole narrative of chs. 1 and 2 is couched in language that echoes the old stories of providential births, such as those of Isaac, Samson or Samuel.

25. In John, the sonship of Jesus in relation to God is taken further still. Partly by way of its associations with other terms and models, it now describes a relationship that does not begin at Jesus' baptism or conception, but exists from all eternity. Jesus' relationship with God, as Father, is, for the Gospel of John, anchored at that most fundamental level. From the vantage point of this climax in the development of the model (soon to be taken up in a more philosophical idiom), we can see how Jesus' representation of God comes to be seen in more and more extensive terms, until it operates on the scale of the cosmos itself.

26. This example of development and of many-sidedness could be paralleled for other expressions and ideas in which the Christians of the NT period clothed their belief in Jesus. Typically, it is based on a variety of scriptural passages, each pointing to its own associations and concepts. Typically too, even within the narrow temporal confines of the NT period, it is neither static nor universal. It is symptomatic of the explosion of symbolic energy which so imaginatively produced the new devotion that saw in Jesus the key to everything.

REFERENCES

Alexander, L. (1993), *The Preface to Luke's Gospel: Literary Convention and Social Context in Luke 1:1–4 and Acts 1:1* (Cambridge: Cambridge University Press).

Ashton, J. (1991), *Understanding the Fourth Gospel* (Oxford: Clarendon).

Beavis, M. A. (1989), *Mark's Audience: The Literary and Social Setting of Mark 4:1–12* (Sheffield, JSOT).

Betz, H. D. (1979), *Galatians*, Hermeneia (Philadelphia: Fortress).

Birdsall, J. N. (1970), 'The New Testament Text', in P. R. Ackroyd and C. F. Evans (eds.), *Cambridge History of the Bible* (Cambridge: Cambridge University Press), i. 308–77.

Brown, R. E. (1979), *The Community of the Beloved Disciple: The Life, Loves and Hates of an Individual Church in New Testament Times* (London: Geoffrey Chapman).

—— (1993), *The Birth of the Messiah: A Commentary on the Infancy Narratives in the Gospels of Matthew and Luke* (London: Geoffrey Chapman).

—— (1994), *The Death of the Messiah: A Commentary on the Passion Narratives* (London: Geoffrey Chapman).

Burridge, R. A. (1992), *What Are the Gospels? A Comparison with Graeco-Roman Biography* (Cambridge: Cambridge University Press).

Byrne, B. (1979), *'Sons of God'—'Seed of Abraham': A Study of the Idea of the Sonship of God of All Christians in Paul against the Jewish Background* (Rome: Biblical Institute Press).

Campbell, R. A. (1994), *The Elders: Seniority within Earliest Christianity* (Edinburgh, T. & T. Clark), 1994.

Campenhausen, H. von (1969), *Ecclesiastical Authority and Spiritual Power in the Church of the First Three Centuries* (London: A. & C. Black).

—— (1972), *The Formation of the Christian Bible* (London: A. & C. Black).

Carroll, R. P. (1991), *Wolf in the Sheepfold: The Bible as a Problem for Christianity* (London: SPCK).

Crossan, J. D. (1991), *The Historical Jesus: The Life of a Mediterranean Jewish Peasant* (Edinburgh: T. & T. Clark).

—— (1994), *Jesus: A Revolutionary Biography* (London: HarperCollins).

Evans, C. F. (1970), *Resurrection and the New Testament* (London: SCM).

Farrer, A. M. (1949), *A Rebirth of Images: The Making of St. John's Apocalypse* (Westminster: Dacre).

Finegan, J. (1992), *The Archeology of the New Testament: The Life of Jesus and the Beginning of the Early Church* (Princeton, NJ: Princeton University Press).

Freyne, S. (1988), *Galilee, Jesus and the Gospels: Literary Approaches and Historical Investigations* (Dublin: Gill & Macmillan).

Gerhardsson, B. (1961), *Memory and Manuscript: Oral Tradition and Written Transmission in Rabbinic Judaism and Early Christianity* (Lund: Gleerup).

Goulder, M. D. (1974), *Midrash and Lection in Matthew* (London: SPCK).

Harvey, A. E. (1982), *Jesus and the Constraints of History* (London: Duckworth).

—— (1990), *Strenuous Commands: The Ethics of Jesus* (London: SCM).

Hengel, M. (1974), *Judaism and Hellenism* (London: SCM).

—— (1981), *The Charismatic Leader and his Followers* (Edinburgh: T. & T. Clark).

Holmberg, B. (1978), *Paul and Power: The Structure of Authority in the Primitive Church as Reflected in the Pauline Epistles* (Lund: Gleerup).

—— (1990), *Sociology and the New Testament: An Appraisal* (Minneapolis: Fortress).

Houlden, J. L. (1973), *Ethics and the New Testament* (Edinburgh: T. & T. Clark).

—— (1986), *Connections* (London: SCM).

—— (ed.) (1995), *The Interpretation of the Bible in the Church* (London: SCM).

Lentz, J. C. (1993), *Luke's Portrait of Paul* (Cambridge: Cambridge University Press).

Lindars, B. (1961), *New Testament Apologetic: The Doctrinal Significance of the Old Testament Quotations* (London: SCM).

Marxsen, W. (1970), *The Resurrection of Jesus of Nazareth* (London: SCM).

Meeks, W. A. (1983), *The First Urban Christians: The Social World of the Apostle Paul* (New Haven: Yale University Press).

—— (1986), 'The Man from Heaven in Johannine Sectarianism', in J. Ashton (ed.), *The Interpretation of John* (London: SPCK), 141–73.

Meier, J. P. (1991), *A Marginal Jew: Rethinking the Historical Jesus* (New York: Doubleday).

Metzger, B. M. (1964), *The Text of the New Testament: Its Transmission, Corruption, and Restoration* (Oxford: Clarendon).

—— (1987), *The Canon of the New Testament: Its Origin, Development, and Significance* (Oxford: Clarendon).

Meyers, E. M., and Strange, J. F. (1981), *Archaeology, the Rabbis and Early Christianity* (London: SCM).

Murphy-O'Connor, J. (1983), *St Paul's Corinth: Texts and Archaeology* (Wilmington, Del.: Michael Glazier).

Rivkin, E. (1984), *What Crucified Jesus* (London: SCM).

Robinson, J. A. T. (1976), *Redating the New Testament* (London: SCM).

Rowland, C. C. (1982), *The Open Heaven: A Study of Apocalyptic in Judaism and Early Christianity* (London: SPCK).

Sanders, E. P. (1985), *Jesus and Judaism* (London: SCM).

—— (1992), *Judaism, Practice and Belief, 63BCE–66CE* (London: SCM).

—— (1993), *The Historical Figure of Jesus* (London: Allen Lane, Penguin).

Schneemelcher, W. (ed.), (1991; 1992), *New Testament Apocrypha* (Cambridge: James Clarke), i and ii.

Sherwin-White, A. N. (1963), *Roman Society and Roman Law in the New Testament* (Oxford: Clarendon).

Staniforth, M., and Louth, A. (eds.) (1987), *Early Christian Writings* (Harmondsworth: Penguin).

Stanton, G. N. (1974), *Jesus of Nazareth in New Testament Preaching* (Cambridge: Cambridge University Press).

—— (1995), *Gospel Truth? New Light on Jesus and the Gospels* (London: HarperCollins).

Stendahl, K. (1968), *The School of St Matthew and its Use of the Old Testament* (Philadelphia: Fortress).

Sweet, J. P. M. (1979), *Revelation* (London: SCM).

Theissen, G. (1982), *The Social Context of Pauline Christianity* (Edinburgh: T. & T. Clark).

Vermes, G. (1973), *Jesus the Jew: A Historian's Reading of the Gospels* (London: Collins).

—— (1977), *The Dead Sea Scrolls: Qumran in Perspective* (London: Collins).

—— (1995), *The Dead Sea Scrolls in English*, 4th edn. (Harmondsworth: Penguin).

Wagner, G. (1967), *Pauline Baptism and the Pagan Mysteries* (Edinburgh: T. & T. Clark).

Wedderburn, A. J. M. (1987), *Baptism and Resurrection* (Tübingen: Mohr).

3. Introduction to the Pauline Corpus

TERENCE L. DONALDSON

A. Overview. 1. No less than thirteen of the twenty-seven writings of the New Testament are letters attributed to the Apostle Paul. They constitute fully one-quarter of the New Testament's bulk; if one adds to this the portion of the Acts of the Apostles where Paul is the main character, Paul's proportion of the New Testament climbs to almost a third. The proportion devoted to the life and ministry of Jesus (i.e. the four gospels) is higher, but not by much.

2. The significance of Paul's literary legacy, of course, is not simply a matter of its quantity. His letters (at least those that can be attributed to him with some certainty) represent the earliest extant writings of the Christian movement. Further, they are real letters, written to actual congregations whose life circumstances are reflected, albeit with some ambiguity, in the texts themselves. In addition, they are at times highly personal letters, at least in the sense that the desires, emotions, thinking processes, and very personality of their author are vividly portrayed. Moreover, their author was no marginal figure. While his place within the early Christian movement needs to be determined with care, it is clear on any reading of Christian origins that, by virtue of the groundbreaking nature of his missionary activity among the Gentiles and the intellectual vitality that he brought to bear on the defence and nurture of his young congregations, Paul was a major player in the first, formative generation of the movement. In sum, then, Paul's letters represent a window into nascent Christianity of inestimable value.

3. The significance of the Pauline corpus is not restricted to its value as source material for the reconstruction of Christian origins, however. The letters not only play a passive role, providing a window into the circumstances lying behind them; they have also been agents in their own right, affecting the lives of their readers—both the original readers and those who subsequently read, as it were, over their shoulders—and thereby helping to shape the history of Christianity and of Western culture as a whole. The Epistle to the Romans, for instance, has had a striking chain of influence—from the unknown early readers who, for whatever reason, preserved the letter in the first place; to Augustine's conversion, precipitated by the random reading in a moment of crisis of a particularly pertinent passage (13:13–14); to Martin Luther's rediscovery of Augustine and his own experience of spiritual release while wrestling with the phrase, 'the just shall live by faith' (1:17) as he prepared lectures on the epistle; to John Wesley's experience of a heart 'strangely warmed' while listening to a reading of the Preface to Luther's commentary; to Karl Barth and his own commentary on the epistle, which represented a dramatic break with the sunny liberalism in which he had been nurtured and a rediscovery and reworking of Reformation themes. This chain of influence, of course, represents a particular strand of Christianity, one in which Paul has been especially revered. But Paul's influence has by no means been limited to the Reformed segment of Christendom. Hymnody, homilies, iconography and other forms of aesthetic representation, across the Christian spectrum and down through the centuries; the nineteenth-century missionary movement; the 'introspective conscience of the west' (Stendahl 1976: 78–96); popular idiom ('all things to all people'; 'thorn in the flesh'; 'charisma'); contemporary Jewish–Christian dialogue; social-scientific models of conversion—the influence of Paul has been pervasive and far-reaching.

4. For these reasons and more, Paul's letters are significant and deserve the careful attention not only of Christian readers but also of all who aspire to an informed perspective on the Western cultural inheritance. But the very things that make for Paul's significance also bring with them various problems that feed into and affect the experience of reading him.

5. For one thing, the sheer bulk of Pauline material in the NT can easily lead readers to overestimate his place and significance in early Christianity. Evidence even from his own letters indicates that Paul was somewhat of a maverick, operating for the most part outside the main circle of earliest Christianity and relating only awkwardly to its original leaders. He may well have represented the wave of the future: since the middle of the second century those characteristic elements that it took all his formidable resources to establish and defend—full and equal membership for Gentile believers, no obligation to adhere to the law of Moses, and so on—have simply been taken for granted as basic elements of the Christian faith. But the very success of Gentile Christianity can serve to obscure the degree to which Paul's mission represented radical innovation in his own day, and this in turn can result in misperceptions of the nature of his thought and rhetoric.

6. In addition, and partly for this reason, Paul has not always fared well at the hands of his interpreters—admirers and champions included. To cite one particular example, the Reformation reading of Paul, in which the theme of justification by faith is identified as the heart of his gospel and the interpretative centre of his thought, is increasingly being seen as a misreading; to approach Paul with the assumption that his concerns and contentions were analogous to those of a Luther or a Calvin is to look at him through a distorting lens that skews some aspects of his theological discourse and leaves others in obscurity. Further, the interpretation of a normative text in a religious culture inevitably has social effects. Thus Paul's name has come to be associated with developments in Western society that many have found undesirable: for example, the treatment of Jews and Judaism as a people rejected by God; the institution of slavery in the eighteenth and nineteenth centuries; the colonialization of Africa and the Far East, to which the activity of Christian missionaries was a contributing factor; patriarchal structures and the exclusion of women from full participation in church and society; intolerant attitudes towards those of homosexual orientation. Also, Paul has sometimes been blamed for constructing a complex religion centred on sin, guilt, and death, far removed from the life-affirming message of Jesus (cf. Muggeridge and Vidler 1972: 11–16).

7. The very factors making for Paul's significance, then, also serve to condition our perception of his writings, interposing between the modern reader and the letters themselves a set of lenses and filters that shape the reading process. These interposed optical paraphernalia should not be seen simply as an obstruction; the history of the effects of Paul's letters in the centuries between their time of writing and our own day is an important part of the overall significance of the letters themselves. Still, the first step in coming to terms with the letters is to try to bridge the intervening distance and to read the letters directly and on their own terms; put differently, to bracket out the particularities of our own contemporary perspectives and attempt to read the letters as they would have been understood by their original intended readers.

8. This is a laudable goal, towards which a formidable array of Pauline scholars have bent their collective energies over the past two centuries of historical-critical investigation. But here we encounter a second set of problems, arising from the letters themselves: as the author of 2 Peter observed long ago, many aspects of Paul's letters are 'difficult to understand' (2 Pet 3:16). In part, the difficulties are due to the fact that we are dealing with letters *per se*; in part, they derive from the particular way in which Paul writes letters. But in each case, the nature of these writings means that in order to understand them we need to go beyond them, to interpret them in the framework of at least three hypothetical scholarly reconstructions.

9. First, there are the individual contexts presupposed by the letters themselves. As Roetzel (1998) has reminded us, Paul's letters are 'conversations in context'; more to the point, in reading these letters we are hearing only one side of the conversation, with no clear indication of the context. As in any conversation, the epistolary author as conversation partner can simply take for granted a whole set of details crucial to the meaning of the letter but so well known to the intended readers that they require no explicit mention. Who, to take one simple example, was the 'famous brother' (2 Cor 8:17) who accompanied Titus in the delivery of 2 Corinthians 8 and so could remain unnamed in the letter? Or with what strand of early Christianity can we identify those who were 'unsettling' the Galatians (Gal 5:12), and what were their motives? Later readers like ourselves, who are not privy to the whole conversation and its context, are forced to draw out from whatever slender clues the text affords a sense of these contextual taken-for-granteds, as an essential first step in the determination of meaning.

10. Such reconstruction of provenance and life setting forms part of the interpretative task for any individual letter from antiquity (and—*mutatis mutandis*—for any ancient text at all). But in the case of Paul we are dealing not simply with one individual letter, but with a whole series of letters that evidently had an integral role to play in an extended missionary agenda. A proper understanding of any one of them, then, will depend to a certain extent on a second scholarly reconstruction, namely, the larger sequential framework of Paul's own life and activity within which the individual letter finds its place. Here the reconstructive task is both aided and complicated by the existence of the Acts of the Apostles, with its connected narrative of Paul's missionary activity. Aided, in that Acts deliberately sets out to provide us with the kind of sequential account that is glimpsed only occasionally, and with difficulty, in the letters. Complicated, in that the Acts account, partly because of the author's own purposes and partly because of the limitations within which the author did his work, is not infrequently at variance with the picture emerging from the letters themselves. Perhaps this is the place to mention the additional fact that several of the letters bearing Paul's name also bear characteristics that make it difficult to understand them as written by Paul himself. In at least some of these cases it is best to understand them as the product of a Pauline school carrying on his legacy into a subsequent generation. Further, a tradition going back as far as the second century sees the epistle to the Hebrews as written by Paul as well. While there is no scholarly justification for the attribution, the reference to 'our brother Timothy' in Heb 13:23 serves to situate this epistle somewhere in the larger Pauline circle. In any case, the reconstruction of the nature, *modus operandi*, sequence, chronology, and aftermath of Paul's missionary enterprise is another requisite element of the interpretative task.

11. Thirdly, there is an inherently theological dimension to the rhetoric of these letters. To be sure, the letters are not to be read as if they were theological treatises; a recognition of the essentially occasional and situational nature of the letters was a decisive step forward in Pauline scholarship. Nevertheless, while the letters must be seen as responses to particular circumstances in the life of Paul and his communities, it is also evident that to deal with these various contingent situations Paul engaged in a style of theological argumentation that drew on already-existing vocabulary, structures, and patterns of thought. As Dunn (1998: 15) has observed with reference to the search for the theology of Paul, 'the letters themselves indicate the need to go behind the letters themselves'. Again, however, the interpreter is faced with a difficult task. Partly because of the sheer fecundity of Paul's agile mind, and partly because the letters use and allude to his 'theology' without ever laying it out in any systematic way, it has been notoriously difficult to discern the central element or essential structure of his theological thought.

12. A proper understanding of Paul's letters, then, necessarily involves us in substantial projects of contextual reconstruction. In turn, these projects depend for their success on a larger engineering project, that of bridging the social and cultural gap between the modern reader and the first-century Graeco-Roman world. To a modern reader, for example, Paul's language of 'bewitchment' in Gal 3:1 may seem quaintly metaphorical. But in a culture where the power of the evil eye was widely feared, the text would have had quite a different impact (Elliott 1990). Likewise, ancient and modern readers would bring distinctly different cultural assumptions to a reading of 2 Cor 8–9, in which Paul is encouraging the Corinthian Christians to contribute to his collection for the Jerusalem church. In contrast to modern readers in the Western world, who tend to see charitable giving as a universal obligation, Paul's Corinthian converts would have understood benefaction to be the domain of the wealthy, who themselves would assume the role of benefactor less out of a sense of moral obligation than in expectation of public honour. What we think we know is often a greater barrier to understanding than what we do not know, and this is as true of the cultural assumptions we bring to a reading of the NT as of any other area of life.

13. The foregoing is not meant to discourage the casual or novice reader from reading Paul, as if one has to acquire a massive body of background and contextual knowledge before being able to approach the letters themselves. The process is spiral: initial familiarization with the text raises questions of interpretation and meaning that can be answered only on the basis of further information about the text's original context; increasing awareness of contextual background precipitates further questions that can be answered only on the basis of a more careful and critical reading of the text; and so on. Further, the process is ongoing and open-ended. It is not as if the range of questions diminishes as knowledge increases. As will become apparent not only in this introductory essay but also in the commentaries on the individual letters to follow, there is a great deal of disagreement and debate among Pauline scholars at almost every point. One enters this interpretative spiral, then, not so much to arrive at a definitive interpretation as to become a participant in an ongoing process of discussion, debate, and new insight.

14. The process may be ongoing, but it is not without its key moments and fresh phases. Indeed, this is a particularly exciting time to be engaged in the discussion of Paul and his letters. The previous three decades have seen some significant developments: richer descriptions of Paul's cultural environment, both Jewish and Graeco-Roman; fundamental shifts in the way his thought is perceived and put together, especially with reference to his Jewish upbringing and 'conversion'; fruitful application of methods and insights drawn from the social sciences: increased appreciation of the rhetorical and epistolary conventions at work in the letters; and so on.

The purpose of this introductory essay is to lead readers into the interpretative spiral described above and to convey some sense of the current state of the discussion. To do this, the material will be organized as follows.

B. The Sources. 1. Our two main sources of biographical information concerning Paul are the Acts of the Apostles and the letters themselves. There are some additional snippets in later Christian writings—e.g., a stylized descriptive portrait in *Acts of Paul* 3.1; accounts of his martyrdom under Nero (1 *Clem.* 5.5–7; 6.1; Eusebius *Hist. Eccl.* 2.25). But even if we were to exploit them to the full (e.g. Riesner 1998), we would simply be adding minor embellishments to a portrait based primarily on our two main sources.

At first glance these two sources seem to complement each other neatly. Acts provides us with biographical information on Paul's life and ministry, and the circumstances in which the individual churches were founded; the letters provide us with direct information on his thought and his interaction with churches after he had moved on to new fields of mission. We might seem to be in the happy position of being able to combine two complementary sources to construct a full picture.

2. As has already been observed, however, the use of Acts as a source for Paul is not without problems. For one thing, despite the impression given by the author of Acts (let us for convenience call him Luke) that he is providing us with a full and continuous account of Paul's itinerary. Paul himself makes reference to details—for example, trips (the hasty and painful visit to Corinth in 2 Cor 2:1) and various incidents of hardship (2 Cor 11:23–7, especially the references to shipwrecks, synagogue discipline, and imprisonments)—about which Luke seems unable to tell us anything.

Further, at points where the two accounts do overlap, they are sometimes strikingly at odds. The parade example of this is the narration of Paul's first post-conversion visit to Jerusalem in Gal 1:18–24 and Acts 9:26–30. In Acts, it is a high-profile visit. Although the disciples were 'all afraid of him', after Barnabas had convinced 'the apostles' of the reality of his new-found faith, Paul 'went in and out among them in Jerusalem, speaking boldly in the name of the Lord', at least until opposition from the (non-Christian) Hellenists increased to the point that the 'brothers' felt it necessary to escort him to safety in Caesarea. In Galatians, by contrast, the visit is a much less public affair. Paul's purpose in going up to Jerusalem was 'to visit Cephas', which he did for fifteen days, not seeing 'any other apostle except James the Lord's brother'. Even after his departure, he was 'still unknown by sight to the churches of Judea that are in Christ', who simply had oral reports that their former persecutor was now 'proclaiming the faith he once tried to destroy'.

Even when one gives full weight to the diverging purposes of Luke (who wants to emphasize harmony in the early church and the smooth progression of the faith outwards from Jerusalem) and Paul (who wants to downplay his contacts with Jerusalem and to defend his independence as an apostle), the differences between the two accounts are substantial. Acts and the letters are not to be treated simply as equal and complementary sources. Paul's own testimony needs to be given primacy. The letters represent our primary source for his life and thought.

3. Nevertheless, Acts is not simply to be dismissed; Luke clearly has independent access to information about Paul's career. He displays no awareness of Paul as a letter-writer, which means that Acts cannot be seen merely as an embellished narrative presentation of details gleaned from the letters. Further, there are frequent points of contact, in details of itinerary, between Acts and the letters (see the list in Brown 1997: 424). Even the accounts in Gal 1 and Acts 9, as discussed above, despite their differences in detail and emphasis, contain a similar sequence: conversion near Damascus (Gal 1:15–17; Acts 9:1–19); subsequent trip to Jerusalem (Gal 1:18: Acts 9:26); time spent in Cilicia/Tarsus (Gal 1:21; Acts 9:30) and Syria/Antioch (Gal 1:21; Acts 11:25–6). Moving out from Galatians but still within the same sequence of events, the account of Paul's flight from Damascus in Acts 9:23–5 has its first-person counterpart in 2 Cor 11:32–3. Similar observations could be made about Paul's progression down the Greek peninsula (1 Thess 2–3; cf. Acts 16–18) or his final trip to Jerusalem with the collection money (1 Cor 16:1–4; 2 Cor 7–9; Rom 15:25–9; cf. Acts 19:21–21:19). Thus while Acts and the letters are not simply to be interlaced, critical and cautious use can be made of the Acts account to supplement the information on Paul's life and activity contained in the letters.

C. Paul's 'Conversion'. 1. Any biographical accounting of Paul needs to begin with what in popular parlance is called his 'conversion'. The appropriateness of the term is debated, and will be discussed a little later. Without foreclosing on the debate, we will refer to the event as Paul's Damascus transformation or Damascus experience. This experience—which Paul understands as an encounter with the risen Christ—is not only foundational for everything that follows, it is the perspective from which our sources present what they do about anything that precedes. Luke does not seem to tire of the story; after providing a full narrative in Acts 9, he repeats it (with some interesting variations in detail) on no less than two other occasions (22:3–21; 26:2–18). Modern readers might wish that he had used this space instead to fill in some of the gaps in his narrative—the activity of Peter, for example, or the origins of the church in Rome. Paul is somewhat more reticent, speaking of it on three occasions (Gal 1:15–16; 1 Cor 9:1; 1 Cor 15:8–10; perhaps also 2 Cor 4:6), but always in the context of some other issue. Still, the consequences of the experience—the conviction that God had raised Jesus, making him Christ and Lord; the conviction that God had commissioned Paul, making him apostle to the Gentiles—are everywhere present, as assumption or as theme.

2. To reconstruct Paul's biography, then, it is necessary to begin with his Damascus experience. To reconstruct it accurately, however, it is necessary to understand the nature of the experience. It was an event that divided Paul's life into a 'before'—'my earlier life in Judaism' (Gal 1:13)—and an 'after'—'an apostle' (Gal 1:1) 'entrusted with the gospel for the uncircumcised' (Gal 2:7); a proper understanding of Paul depends on how we correlate these three biographical points. More specifically, the characteristic features of Paul's apostolic self-understanding stand in such patent contrast to the typical 'life in Judaism' that one cannot really understand the later Paul without understanding how the transformation worked itself out. How was it that a self-proclaimed 'zealot for the traditions of [his] ancestors' (Gal 1:14) was transformed into a zealous advocate of a mission to Gentiles, offering them a righteous status before God not by adherence to the Torah but by faith in Christ?

3. It was mentioned above that there have been some significant shifts in Pauline scholarship in recent years; one such has to do with the understanding of Paul's Damascus transformation. Older scholarship tended to understand this transformation as involving a perception on Paul's part of some fundamental deficiency in Judaism and his consequent abandonment of Judaism for a different religion that was able to offer what Judaism lacked. In this family of interpretations the appropriateness of the term 'conversion' is assumed. There are several branches of the family. One, stemming from the Reformation, emphasizes Paul's polemical contrast between justification by works and justification by faith. It is assumed that this works/faith contrast represented Paul's fundamental critique of Judaism; he understood Judaism to be a legalistic religion, one in which a person's status with God was something earned through meritorious Torah observance (works) rather than something offered freely by God in divine grace, to be received in humble faith. The essence of Paul's conversion is understood, in this reading of it, to consist in the recognition that Judaism was a works-religion that did not work, and the correlative discovery that Christianity offered freely, on the basis of faith, the righteous status that Torah-religion was not able to provide. Sometimes such a recognition of the futility of Judaism is understood to be the essence of the Damascus experience itself; in encountering the risen Jesus Paul saw Judaism for the inferior and inadequate religion that it was. Often, however, the recognition is shifted further back, Paul's problem with Judaism seen as something emerging during his upbringing. It is argued, usually with appeal to Rom 7, that Paul's experience of Judaism was one of frustration and despair. He had tried hard to gain God's approval by keeping the law in a zealous fashion, but found that no matter how hard he tried he always fell short. In this reading, his conversion is seen as fundamentally the discovery that Christ provided the solution to an existential problem that he had already experienced in his Jewish upbringing.

4. This is not the only way in which Paul's Damascus transformation is perceived as essentially an abandonment of Judaism. Another interpretation takes its point of departure not from Paul's faith/works contrast but from his universal gospel. How is Paul's interest in Gentiles to be accounted for? The answer, it is suggested, is that Paul came to abandon a frame of reference in which the distinction between Jew and Gentile is central, for one in which that distinction is abolished, one in which 'there is no longer Jew or Greek' (Gal 3:28). Again, such an exchange of one type of religion (this time a particularistic one) for another (a universalistic one) is sometimes seen as the essence of the Damascus experience itself. Just as often, however, it is rooted in the idea that already in his upbringing Paul had experienced frustration with Jewish particularism and, in some interpretations, had struggled, valiantly but vainly, to suppress an attraction to the wider Hellenistic world.

5. Such interpretations, in which Paul's Damascus experience is seen as essentially an abandonment of a Jewish context for something different, have had a long and successful history, at least in part because they seem to provide a coherent explanation of central elements in Paul's post-Damascus frame of reference—especially his role as apostle to the Gentiles, and the gospel he preached to Gentiles, offering them a righteous status before God without demanding adherence to the Torah. But more recent study of Paul has tended to demonstrate that such coherence is purchased at a high price, specifically, an unacceptable level of incoherence with respect to the first of the three biographical points—Paul's earlier life in Judaism.

By the early part of the twentieth century Jewish scholars (e.g. C. Montefiore, S. Schechter, and later H.-J. Schoeps), along with Christians sympathetic to Judaism (e.g. G. F. Moore, J. Parkes), had already pointed out that Judaism was not the legalistic religion of meritorious achievement that it had often been made out to be. Jewish religion, they objected, started not with the Torah but with the covenant, a relationship between God and Israel established entirely on the basis of divine grace. The Torah was given as a means not of earning a relationship with God, but rather of responding in gratitude to God and of maintaining the relationship already established by God's gracious election of Israel. Further, Jewish religion did not require flawless performance of the law, as Paul's argument in Romans and Galatians seems to assume. The law itself recognized the inevitability of sin, making provision, in the sacrificial system, for repentance, atonement, and forgiveness—an aspect of Torah-religion that Paul studiously avoids in the pertinent passages. This more accurate depiction of Judaism has been most convincingly developed and demonstrated by E. P. Sanders (see Sanders 1977), who terms it a religion of 'covenantal nomism' rather than of legalism. Prior to Sanders's work, however, the conclusion often drawn from this argument about the true nature of Judaism has been that if the traditional reading of Paul is accurate, then Paul must have seriously misunderstood Judaism. If Paul really perceived Judaism as a religion of meritorious achievement requiring perfect performance, then his critique of Judaism is badly off-target from the outset.

6. One way of explaining this supposed misunderstanding of Judaism is to lay it at the door of Paul's diaspora upbringing; if Paul had been raised in Judea, closer to the source, he would have experienced a truer form of the faith and thus would have depicted it more accurately (Montefiore 1914: 14–101; Schoeps 1961:173). But this leads to a second way in which the traditional interpretations of Paul fail to integrate what we know about his earlier life in Judaism. Not only is it recognized that no sharp distinction can be drawn between Hellenistic and Palestinian Judaism, the idea that Paul fundamentally misunderstood Judaism does not square well with his own comments about his earlier life. For one thing, he locates himself within a traditional, covenant-centred form of the faith. He is a Hebrew of the Hebrews (Phil 3:5; cf. 2 Cor 11:22); a zealot for the traditions of his ancestors (Gal 1:14); a Pharisee, a group for which we have only Palestinian evidence (Phil 3:5; see Hengel and Schwemer 1997:36). Further, whenever he looks back on this period of his

life, he does so with a great deal of pride and satisfaction (Gal 1:13–14; Phil 3:4b–6: 2 Cor 11:22). Phil 3:6 is particularly instructive; as one of the grounds for which he might have confidence in the flesh, he points to the fact that 'as to right-eousness under the law, [he was] blameless'. The statement resonates with the pride of accomplishment (blameless!) rather than despair over the impossibility of the law's demands. With the recognition that the 'I' of Romans 7 is not autobiographical (Kümmel 1929), the way has been cleared to ask whether instead of Paul misunderstanding Judaism, Paul's interpreters have misunderstood him.

7. This question has been posed most force-fully by E. P. Sanders in his epoch-making book, *Paul and Palestinian Judaism* (1977). In the book Sanders demonstrates convincingly that Paul can be much better understood if we assume (1) that in his upbringing he had experienced Judaism as a religion of coven-antal nomism, but that (2) in his Damascus experience he had come to believe that God had provided Christ as a means of salvation for all on equal terms, and that (3) since entrance into the community of salvation was through Christ, Torah-observance could not be imposed as a condition of membership. Anticipating some discussion to follow, we need to observe that Sanders leaves a number of loose ends and logical disjunctions; in particular: why 'for all'? Why 'on equal terms'? Why are Christ and Torah mutually exclusive? But for present pur-poses, the significant point of Sanders's work is that it opens up the possibility of seeing Paul's Damascus experience as primarily the accept-ance of a new set of convictions about Jesus rather than the abandonment of an old set of convictions about Judaism. The way is open to see Paul not as a frustrated Jew, nor as one who fundamentally misunderstood the religion of his ancestors and contemporaries, but as a covenantal nomist who had an experience con-vincing him that the God of Israel had raised Jesus from death.

8. What emerges, then, is an understanding of Paul's Damascus experience in which it is seen not as the solution to an already-perceived prob-lem with Judaism, nor as the abandonment of one religion (Judaism) for another (Christianity). Instead, the outcome of the experience was in the first instance a new estimation of the person and significance of Jesus in the purposes of the God of Israel. This led to an unprecedented reconfiguration of the constituent elements of Judaism, for reasons that we will explore in a moment. But reconfiguration is quite a different thing from abandonment.

For this reason, 'conversion' has been seen as perhaps not the best term to use to describe Paul's experience. Both in popular parlance and in much social-scientific study, 'conversion' implies a transformation that is more radical, more discontinuous with the convert's past, and more driven by psychological imbalance, than was the case with Paul. At the same time, to describe the experience as a 'call', as Stendahl does (Stendahl 1976: 7–23), is not a fully satis-factory alternative either, even when one gives full value to Paul's use of prophetic call lan-guage in Gal 1:15 (cf. Isa 49:1; Jer 1:5). This term fails to do justice to the fact that Paul's experi-ence represented a much more decisive shift, a more sharply demarcated before and after (cf. Phil 3:4–11), than was ever the case with an Isaiah or a Jeremiah. While Paul continued to worship and serve the same God, his framework of service shifted decisively from one organiz-ing centre (Torah) to another (Christ). What term to use, then, for this decisive shift? One alternative is to return to 'conversion', redefin-ing it so that both continuity and discontinuity are preserved (Segal 1990). Such an approach can claim support from more recent social-scientific studies (e.g. Rambo 1993), which rec-ognize a much broader range of conversion types. Perhaps the safer approach, however, is to choose less loaded terms, such as transform-ation or reconfiguration.

9. But why was the reconfiguration so sharply polarized? Why were the two organizing centres—Torah and Christ—set over against each other in such an antithetical way? Or to pose the question with respect to the compara-tive biographies of Paul and James, who both became leaders in the church as the result of an experience understood to be an encounter with the risen Christ (for James, see 1 Cor 15:7): why did the experience lead in Paul's case to a Christ–Torah antithesis while in the case of James of Jerusalem, who seemed to be able to combine Christ-faith and Torah-religion in a much more harmonious way, it led rather to a Christ–Torah synthesis?

10. In contrast to Paul's conversion *per se*, the answer to this question does seem to lie in his pre-Damascus experience. Even prior to his own experience of Christ, Paul had already come to some conclusions about the incompat-ability of Christ-faith and Torah-religion. What is important here is not simply *that* Paul perse-cuted the church, but that he understood it as

an expression of *zeal* (Phil 3:6; cf. Gal 1:14). In the context of Torah-piety, zeal implies more than simply fervour. At least since the time of the Maccabees, zeal and zealotry referred to the willingness to use force to defend Torah-religion from some perceived threat (e.g. 1 Macc 2:24, 26, 27, 50; *Jub.* 30.18; Jdt 9:2–4; see Donaldson 1997: 285–6; Dunn 1998: 350–2). If Paul's persecution of the church was an act of zeal, then he must, even at this early stage, have seen Christ-religion and Torah-religion as mutually exclusive. Further, since even after his Damascus experience this in-compatability between Christ and Torah seems to have remained (even if transformed), the conflict between the two must have been of such a nature that it could not be resolved simply by changing his estimation of Jesus. The Christ–Torah antithesis must have been perceived as a more fundamental incompatibility.

11. What, then, was the nature of this incompatibility? Several possibilities have been explored in scholarly discussion (Donaldson 1997: 169–72). Some suggest that the idea of a suffering and dying Messiah was in itself an affront to Jewish expectation and thus incompatible with Torah-religion. Others focus on the specific means of Jesus' death—crucifixion—noting that the Torah itself sees as cursed 'anyone hung on a tree' (Deut 21:22–3), a text that by the first century was being interpreted with respect to crucifixion (4QpNah 1.7–8; 11QTemple 64.12; cf. Gal 3:13). Still others suggest that Paul's estimation of the Torah had been deeply affected by the fact that it was precisely his zeal for the law that had led him to persecute Christ's church. But none of these suggestions seem to produce a tension between Christ and Torah so intractable that a well-motivated Jewish believer could not have found a way to resolve it.

12. My suggestion moves in a different direction, and builds on two more fundamental aspects of Jewish and Jewish-Christian belief: (1) the relationship between Torah and Messiah in Jewish expectation; and (2) the unprecedented 'already/not yet' shape of early Christian belief. In Jewish patterns of thought (at least those that included the concept of a Messiah), the respective functions of Torah and Messiah were neatly differentiated by the distinction between this age and the age to come. In this age, the Torah functioned as a badge of membership or a boundary marker for the covenant people of God. To live a life of loyalty to the Torah was a mark of membership in the covenant community; to be a member in good standing was

to be righteous; it was the community of the righteous as demarcated by the Torah in this age that could expect to be vindicated by God in the age to come, when the Messiah appeared. There was thus no confusion of roles: the Torah served to determine the identity of the people whom the Messiah would come to deliver; put differently, the Messiah did not function as a boundary marker or badge of membership.

13. But the Christian message—that God had revealed the identity of the coming Messiah by raising Jesus from death—had the effect of blurring this neat distinction. The Christ who would come to redeem the righteous in the age to come had already appeared before this age was at an end. How, then, was the community of the righteous to be determined in the period between the resurrection and the end? Was it defined by adherence to Torah or to Christ? Would the community redeemed by Christ at the eschaton be one demarcated by Torah-observance or by Christ-adherence? The unprecedented two-stage appearance of the Messiah in Christian belief had the effect of putting Christ and Torah in tension with each other, as rival boundary markers for the people of God. The overlapping of the ages in Christian proclamation brought Christ and Torah into conflict.

14. My suggestion is that because of his perspective as an outsider, the pre-Christian Paul perceived this rivalry and conflict much more clearly than those inside. He was a faithful observer of the Torah, 'as to righteousness under the law, blameless' (Phil 3:6). But the Christian message as he heard it implied that this was not enough; to truly belong to the community of the righteous, he had to believe in Christ. He also observed that the church was prepared to admit as full members many who, 'as to righteousness under the law', were far from 'blameless'. Torah observance, it appeared, was also unnecessary. Undergirding his persecution of the church, then, was a fundamental perception that—whether the early Christians recognized it fully or not—the Christ they preached represented a categorical rival to the Torah in its community-defining role. Since this rivalry was rooted not simply in Paul's lack of belief in Christ but in the nature of the Christian message itself, it did not disappear with his new belief in Christ. The Christ–Torah antithesis remained, even though his perception of its implications shifted dramatically.

15. One final element of Paul's Damascus experience requires mention here, though we can deal with it only briefly. In the discussion carried out above concerning Paul's description of his experience as a 'call', we did not pay much attention to the focus of the call—'to proclaim [God's Son] among the Gentiles' (Gal 1:16). At least in retrospect, then, Paul sees his role as 'apostle to the Gentiles' (Rom 11:13) as the direct outcome and inner meaning of his Damascus experience. But how are we to understand his all-embracing concern for the salvation of the Gentiles?

This question, too, has been altered by the interpretative shift described above. In older patterns of interpretation, Paul's interest in the Gentiles has been understood as entailing, or as the result of, an abandonment of Judaism. In his conversion experience, it was argued, Paul left behind a world where the distinction between Jew and Gentile was fundamental, and entered a wider world where there was no differentiation. The ways in which this line of interpretation were worked out varied with the ways in which the process of abandonment was reconstructed (see above, and also Donaldson 1997: 18–27). But the heart of the matter in each case was that Paul's 'universalism' (i.e. his concern for Gentile salvation) was tied up with a rejection of Jewish particularism.

16. More recent study, however, has brought to the fore two things that suggest a different explanation. The first has to do with Paul himself, the second with Jewish attitudes towards Gentile salvation. First, it is clear that 'Jew' and 'Gentile' continue to be important categories for Paul. While he insists that there is no distinction with respect to sin ('all, both Jews and Greeks, are under ... sin', Rom 3:9) or salvation ('for there is no distinction between Jew and Greek', Rom 10:12), this does not mean that Jewishness has lost all theological significance for Paul. Indeed, by describing himself as apostle to the *Gentiles*, he indicates that he continues to inhabit a world where the distinction between Jew and Gentile is operative. Paul sees himself as a Jew (Rom 11:1), commissioned by the God of Israel to bring a message of salvation, not to an undifferentiated mass of generic humanity, but to Gentiles, that part of humanity that exists in distinction from Israel. Further, the ultimate goal of this mission is the final salvation of 'all Israel' (Rom 11:26). What is needed, then, is a much more Israel-centred understanding of Paul's interest in the Gentiles.

17. This brings us to the second point. While Jewish self-understanding is undeniably particularistic (the one God of all has chosen Israel from among the nations for a special covenanted relationship), Judaism also had its own forms of universalism. That is, by Paul's day Judaism had developed ways of finding a place for Gentiles within God's saving purposes for the world, ways that offered Gentiles a share in salvation without denying the special nature of Israel's own covenant relationship. One of these patterns of universalism, of course, was proselytism; the community of Israel was willing to accept as full members of the family of Abraham those Gentiles who embraced the Torah and its way of life (e.g. Jdt 14:10; Tacitus, *Hist.* 5.5.2). Another pattern, based on a quite different perception of things, was prepared to see the possibility of Gentiles being accounted righteous and having a share in the age to come *as Gentiles*, without having to accept those aspects of the Torah that differentiated Gentiles from Jews (e.g. Jos. *Ant.* 20.34–48; *t. Sanh.* 13.2). A third looked to the future, and expected that as one of the consequences of Israel's end-time redemption, many Gentiles would finally acknowledge the God of Israel and thus be granted a share in the blessings of the age to come (e.g. Isa 2:2–4; Tob 14:5–7).

18. This is not the place to survey the pertinent Jewish material in any detail (see Donaldson 2007). Nor is it possible here to explore Paul's conceptions concerning the Gentiles and their place 'in Christ' against this background (see Donaldson 1997). For present purposes it is sufficient to say that Paul's Gentile mission is best understood as a Christ-centred reinterpretation of one of these Israel-centred patterns of universalism. That is, Paul's concern for the Gentiles had its origin in attitudes already present in Judaism, even though with his Damascus experience they came to be oriented around a different centre. His call 'to proclaim [God's Son] among the Gentiles' results not from a rejection of Jewish particularism but from a reinterpretation, from his standpoint 'in Christ', of some aspect of Jewish universalism.

Later on in this introductory essay we will return to the matter of Paul's thought and its characteristic themes and structure. For the present, however, we need to discuss the temporal and geographical framework of his life.

D. Paul's Formative Years. 1. 'My earlier life in Judaism' (Gal 1:13): Paul does not tell us a great deal about his Jewish upbringing and pre-Christian activities. This is not due to reticence; when it serves his purposes, he can parade his credentials and accomplishments with great flourish

(esp. Gal 1:13–15; 1 Cor 15:9; Phil 3:4–6; 2 Cor 11:22; Rom 11:1). But his purposes are never purely biographical; what he tells us and how is determined by the rhetorical needs of the moment. In addition to the explicit information he does convey in passing, of course, the letters also contain a wealth of implicit evidence— familiarity with the Mediterranean world, facility in Greek, knowledge of the Septuagint and of Jewish interpretative tradition, and so on.

Still, the information conveyed to us by Paul himself is much less specific than that contained in the Acts account, where it appears both in the narration of his persecuting activity (7:58– 8:3; 9:1–3) and in the speeches of self-defence made after his final arrest (22:1–5, 19–20; 23:6; 26:4–12). But while its secondary status needs to be remembered, the information in Acts, with only two or three exceptions, is both consistent with Paul's own statements and not so patently in keeping with Luke's special purposes as to come under suspicion.

2. According to Luke, Paul was a diaspora Jew— specifically, a native of Tarsus, the prosperous chief city of the region of Cilicia (21:39; 22:3). The letters certainly confirm the general identification; even without Acts, Paul's facility in Greek and the ease with which he navigated the Hellenistic world identify him as a diaspora Jew. With respect to the more specific reference to Tarsus, the only evidence in the letters with a bearing on the matter is Paul's statement that after his first visit to Jerusalem he 'went into the regions of Syria and Cilicia' (Gal 1:21). Syria is understandable; someone who had spent time in Damascus (Gal 1:17) could readily gravitate to Antioch, an important centre of the Jewish diaspora. But Cilicia is less to be expected, unless, as Luke indicates. Paul had a special personal affinity for the area. This detail in Galatians, then, lends a definite plausibility to Luke's identification of Tarsus as Paul's home city.

Luke goes further, however, to identify Paul as a citizen both of Tarsus (21:39) and of Rome (16:37–9; 22:25–9; 23:27), the latter by birth. This is not outside the realm of possibility. Jews certainly could be Roman citizens without compromising their traditional observances (e.g. Jos. Ant. 14.228–37). Tarsus itself was lavishly rewarded for services rendered, both by Mark Antony after the death of Cassius and Brutus (Appian, Historia, 5.1.7), and by Octavian after the battle of Actium (Dio Chrysostom, Orationes, 34.8). One could readily imagine circumstances in which even a Jewish family would have been able to share in this largesse. At the same time,

however, full weight needs to be given to two additional items of information. First, Paul himself nowhere alludes to Roman citizenship, despite his readiness to boast about other items on his curriculum vitae when it served his purposes. Second, Paul's Roman citizenship could be seen as too neatly consistent with one of Luke's major themes—namely, that Roman officials repeatedly took the Christians' side, or at least demonstrated that they considered the movement to be no real threat to the order of the empire. But on the other hand, the sole premiss of Paul's final trip to Rome, as it is narrated in Acts, is his Roman citizenship, with the concomitant right of appeal to the imperial tribunal (Acts 25:10–12, 21; 26:32). Unless we are prepared to dismiss this whole account, despite the verisimilitude of its first-person narration (27:1–28:16), we need to give at least some credence to Luke's statements about Paul's citizenship.

3. As we have already observed, however, Paul's own self-description places more emphasis on his Jewish identity and credentials. To put this information into its proper perspective, we need to keep in mind the extent and significance of the Jewish diaspora. By the beginning of the first century, as was observed by the geographer and historian Strabo, 'this people [i.e. of Judea] has already made its way into every city, and it is not easy to find any place in the habitable world which has not received this nation and in which it has not made its power felt' (quoted by Jos. Ant. 14.114–18). Of interest in this statement is not only the geographical spread of Jewish communities (also Jos. J. W. 2.399; Ag. Ap. 2.38–9; Philo, Flacc. 7.45; Acts 2:5–11), but also what this translation calls their 'power', rendering a Greek verb that usually has the sense 'to gain the mastery of, to prevail over'. The word is not to be taken literally, as if Jews had become dominant in any of the cities where they had taken up residence. But it does describe the fact that in city after city Jews had been able to create and maintain Torah-centred islands in the midst of the larger Hellenistic sea. And perhaps this image distorts things somewhat, in that Jewish communities were by no means sealed off from the life and culture of the cities that sustained them. The example of Sardis, where the Jewish community was able to acquire space for their synagogue in the central civic edifice that also housed the bath and gymnasium, is perhaps a little late (3rd cent. CE) to be directly relevant. But any difference between this example and the

circumstances of diaspora Jews in the first century in Sardis and elsewhere is one of degree, not of kind. Diaspora realities can also be seen reflected in the long list, compiled by Josephus, of decrees issued by Julius Caesar and his successors which defined and protected the rights of the Jewish communities in various cities of Asia and elsewhere (Jos. *Ant.* 14.186–264). While not as much is known of the Jewish community in Tarsus as in some other cities, a Jewish presence in the first century is nevertheless 'well attested' (Murphy-O'Connor 1996: 33).

4. Paul's biographical statements, then, brief and tangential though they may be, come more vividly to life when placed in the context of this vibrant diaspora reality. It was in one of these Greek-speaking Jewish communities, integrated into the life of the larger city but without wholesale assimilation, that he was born (perhaps in the first decade of the century) and nurtured in the ancestral faith. There were inevitably different degrees of Hellenization within the diaspora, but Paul locates his origins at the more rigorously observant end of the spectrum. While most (male) Jews could presumably describe themselves, as Paul does in Phil 3:5, as 'circumcised on the eighth day', and 'a member of the people of Israel', not all would be able to name their tribe (Benjamin), or—since the term probably indicates facility in Hebrew or Aramaic—to categorize themselves as 'a Hebrew born of Hebrews' (cf. 2 Cor 11:22).

The next item in the Philippian catalogue—'as to the law, a Pharisee' (Phil 3:5)—is a little harder to envisage in a diaspora setting, however. While Jews everywhere were identified by their adherence to the law, the only evidence we have for Pharisees as a specific group stems from Judea. Here the information from Acts is relevant, for Luke identifies Jerusalem as the place of Paul's education. Speaking to the Jerusalem crowd after his arrest, Paul is depicted as saying: 'I am a Jew, born in Tarsus in Cilicia, but brought up in this city at the feet of Gamaliel, educated strictly according to our ancestral law' (Acts 22:3). This reading of the verse takes the latter two participial clauses (brought up, educated) as referring to the same process—study under Gamaliel. It is possible, however, to read the verse as referring to two stages—primary nurture (brought up in this city) and secondary training (educated strictly at the feet of Gamaliel according to our ancestral law). This latter reading, which suggests that Paul moved to Jerusalem as a child, is probably more consistent with the comment in Acts 23:6 that he was also the 'son of Pharisees'.

5. But is it consistent with Paul's own statements about Jerusalem? There is a significant body of scholarship that rejects wholesale Luke's identification of Jerusalem as the locale for both Paul's education and his persecuting activity (e.g. Knox 1950: 34–6; Haenchen 1971: 297, 625). This rejection is based partly on a consideration of Luke's purposes: it is in keeping with his interpretative programme (cf. Acts 1:8) to have the apostle responsible for taking the gospel 'to the ends of the earth' to be linked closely with Jerusalem. But further, it is based more fundamentally on Paul's own statement that even after his conversion and first visit to Jerusalem, he 'was still unknown by sight to the churches of Judea' (Gal 1:22). Surely, it is argued, the Jerusalem church would have known its chief persecutor.

6. In the context of Galatians, however, Paul is talking about his contacts with Jerusalem as a Christian: apart from Cephas and James, he declares, the church in Jerusalem and Judea had not seen the transformed Paul with their own eyes. With respect to the possibility of a period of residence in Jerusalem, then, Paul's statement that he was a Pharisee weighs in more heavily than does his comment about the churches in Judea (Murphy-O'Connor 1996: 52–4). This does not mean, however, that Luke's depiction is to be accepted *in toto*. Surely if Paul had had any meaningful association with Gamaliel it would have been included in one of his catalogues of Jewish credentials. The claim to be a 'son of Pharisees' probably belongs to a similar category.

7. In all probability, then, Paul journeyed to Jerusalem as a young man, where he joined the Pharisees, pursuing his 'zeal for the traditions of his ancestors', and 'advancing in Judaism beyond many of [his] people of the same age' (Gal 1:14). Probably we are to see him as attached to one of the Hellenistic synagogues in Jerusalem, perhaps even the 'Synagogue of the Freedmen' (Hengel 1991: 69), which included in its membership expatriates of Cilicia (Acts 6:9). It is also possible that during this period he took a special interest in Gentile proselytes. In Gal 5:11 he refers to a time when he 'was preaching circumcision'. In the context of Galatians, this statement means more than simply that he himself was once a Torah-observer; it means that he once was engaged in encouraging Gentiles to be circumcised and thus to become full adherents of Torah-religion (cf. Gal 5:3). When was this? It is unlikely that there was a period after his Damascus experience where he preached a kind of Judaizing gospel to Gentiles. The statement more likely refers to his pre-Damascus period, where we might envisage him as playing the same sort of role with Gentile synagogue-adherents as Eleazar did with King Izates of Adiabene (Jos. *Ant.* 20.43–5), namely, insisting that only by becoming full proselytes would they be pleasing to God.

8. It is also during this period that Paul's zeal 'for the traditions of [his] ancestors' (Gal 1:14) took particular expression in his persecution of the nascent Christian movement (Gal 1:14, 23; Phil 3:6; 1 Cor 15:9). As has been noted already, there is no need to set Gal 1:22 over against the Acts account, and to restrict Paul's persecuting activity to an area outside Judea (Damascus). We can accept the Acts account at least to this point, that it was in Jerusalem that Paul took offence at the activity of the early Christians, particularly the Greek-speaking 'Hellenists' (Acts 6) who formulated their message in a manner that was much more critical of the temple and much less acquiescent to the Jewish religious establishment (cf. Acts 7) than the 'Hebrews'. Perceiving the activity of the Hellenistic Jewish Christians as a threat to the well-being of the Torah-centred way of life, and also at a deeper level perceiving their basic message as setting Christ over against the Torah, he engaged in 'zealous' repression of the movement. When this resulted in the flight of Christians from Jerusalem to other Jewish centres, Paul became involved in attempts to repress the activity of the new movement in Damascus. That is, we can accept the basic itinerary of Acts 8 and 9, though some of the details (the ferocity of Saul's own activity, imprisonment rather than simple disciplinary action, official letters from the high priest) may well be the result of Lukan exaggeration.

9. 'When God was pleased to reveal his Son to (in) me' (Gal 1:15–16): Somewhere near Damascus (cf.'returned', Gal 1:17), Paul had an experience that led to a radical reassessment of the person of Jesus and a thoroughgoing reconfiguration of his foundational convictions. In the history of interpretation, various attempts have been made to account for this experience without remainder by appealing to psychological pre-conditioning or even physiological manifestations (e.g. an epileptic seizure). But to reduce the range of possible explanations in this way is to fail to recognize the reality of religious experience, on the phenomenological level at the very least. Religious phenomena certainly have their psychological and physiological dimensions, but it is unfair to religious communities in general to reduce religious experience to non-religious categories.

Paul, of course, understood this experience as an encounter with the risen Christ (Gal 1:15–16; 1 Cor 9:1; 15:8–9) and, moreover, as belonging to the same set of experiences as had brought the movement into being in the first place (1 Cor 15:5–8). But the reality of a religious experience is one thing, the interpretation placed on it by the subject quite another. Any attempt to assess the reality lying behind the statement, 'Christ appeared to me', belongs in a book whose purposes are quite different from those of a commentary such as this.

10. To understand Paul and his letters, however, it is necessary to recognize that he saw no gap or caesura between the experience and the interpretation. For him the subjective experience ('God...was pleased to reveal his Son *in* me', Gal 1:15–16, my lit. tr.) and the objective reality ('[Christ] appeared...*to* me'; 1 Cor 15:8) were a seamless unity.

Further, to understand Paul it is necessary to recognize two things that flowed from this experience. One was a reconfiguration of his basic, world-ordering convictions. Paul had already come to some conclusions about how the message of a crucified and risen Messiah related to the basic convictions of covenantal nomism. His previous perceptions of Christ 'according to the flesh' (2 Cor 5:16) produced the conviction that Christ and Torah were mutually exclusive; they were rival ways of marking the community of the righteous. Consequently his new conviction—that God had raised Jesus and that the claims made about him in Christian preaching were thus grounded in God's action—was not a simple, self-contained conviction; rather, it set in motion a thoroughgoing process of convictional restructuring. Not that his new convictions were simply the inversion of the old. He continued to believe in the God of Israel, in Israel's election, even in the divine origin of the Torah. But these native convictions were redrawn around a new centre, the foundational conviction that the crucified Jesus had been raised by God.

11. The second thing that flowed from Paul's Damascus experience was that it was also and at the same time a call to be an apostle. Despite the chronological gap between the first experiences recounted in 1 Cor 15:5–7 and Paul's own—a gap alluded to in v. 8 ('last of all, as to someone untimely born') but ultimately dismissed as inconsequential—Paul claims that it constituted him an apostle on an equal basis with the others (vv. 10–11; cf. Gal 1:1). One can readily imagine how this claim would have sounded to those 'who were already apostles before [him]' (Gal 1:17) and their Jerusalem followers, especially when this johnny-come-lately began to insist on a law-free mission to Gentiles with Paul himself as its divinely commissioned apostle. An uneasy relationship with the Jerusalem church marked Paul's ministry from the outset.

12. '*So that I might proclaim him among the Gentiles*' (Gal 1:16): Looking back, Paul locates the origin of his Gentile mission in the Damascus experience itself. Some interpreters have argued that this is just a matter of retrospect, Paul here collapsing a process that might have taken years, into the event that set the process in motion in the first place (e.g. Watson 1986: 28–38). But not only is there no evidence for such an intervening phase of any length, Paul's statements relating to his activity in Arabia suggest that from the very beginning he saw himself as commissioned to carry the gospel to Gentiles. Paul's sojourn in Arabia (Gal 1:17) is sometimes seen as a period of quiet reflection, where he contemplated the significance of his experience and worked out its theological implications. No doubt there was a period of time in which such reflection took place; certainly his new theological framework did not emerge instantaneously. But Paul's time in Arabia seems to have attracted the unfavourable attention of King Aretas himself (2 Cor 11:32). One does not usually arouse the ire of a ruling monarch by engaging in solitary theological reflection. Paul's Arabian experience suggests that he attempted to carry out an apostolic ministry among non-Jews at a very early date. If there was a period of reflection, we should think in terms of weeks, not years.

13. From a first-century Judean perspective, Arabia was the kingdom of the Nabataeans, with its capital in Petra (Jos. J.W.1.125: 'the capital of the Arabian kingdom, called Petra'). This means that Paul's sojourn in Arabia in Gal 1:17 needs to be co-ordinated with the account of his escape from the agents of King Aretas in Damascus (2 Cor 11:30–3). The reference here is to Aretas IV, king of the Nabataeans from about 9 BCE to 39 CE. Murphy-O'Connor (1996: 5–7) argues that Damascus came under Nabataean control in 37 CE, which would then have been when Paul's departure from Damascus took place, though certainty is not possible (cf. Riesner 1998: 84–9). Presumably Paul had created enough of a disturbance through his evangelizing activity in Arabia that he had to return to

Damascus (Gal 1:17), which in turn became too hot for him to remain once Aretas had gained control of the city. This evidence suggests, then, that Paul's statement in Gal 1:16 should be taken at its temporal face value: right from the beginning, he felt himself called as an apostle with a special commission for the Gentiles.

14. '*Up to Jerusalem . . . into the regions of Syria and Cilicia . . . Antioch*' (Gal 1:18, 21; 2:11): Of the other events in the period between his Damascus experience and the start of the missionary activity reflected in the letters, Paul tells us very little. 'After three years' he journeyed to Jerusalem, with the specific intention of 'getting to know' Cephas/Peter, or of 'making his acquaintance' (Gal 1:18; on this sense of the verb *historein*, see Jos. J. W. 6.81). Paul's larger purpose in Galatians 1 and 2 is to minimize his contacts with 'those who were already apostles before [him]' (Gal 1:17), in order to establish the point that he 'did not receive [his gospel] from a human source, nor was [he] taught it, but [he] received it through a revelation of Jesus Christ' (Gal 1:12). While this statement underlines the centrality of the Damascus experience for Paul's new commitment to Christ and the gospel, it should not be interpreted as implying that his early Christian experience was isolated and individual and that other Christians played no part in his formation. Presumably he did not baptize himself (Rom 6:3). Likewise, he was able to count on friends—Christians, in all probability—to help him over the city wall in Damascus (note the passive in 2 Cor 11:33: 'I was let down'). Even before his first visit to Jerusalem, then, he had been incorporated into a Christian community as a new convert, with all the socialization that would have entailed. Further, he describes such central Christian elements as the facts of the gospel itself (1 Cor 15:1–7) and the narrative of the last supper (1 Cor 11:23) as material that he had 'received' and then 'handed on', using the accepted, formal vocabulary for the transmission of tradition. It is probably not without significance that the two proper names mentioned in the summary of the gospel in 1 Cor 15:3–7 (Cephas, James) are precisely the two people that he met on his first Jerusalem visit (Gal 1:18–19). As C.H. Dodd is famously reported to have said, surely in two weeks Paul and Peter found more to talk about than simply the weather.

15. Of Paul's time in 'the regions of Syria and Cilicia' (Gal 1:21), very little can be said, unless we disregard the order in which these two geographical regions are listed and understand

'Syria' to refer to the kind of scenario recounted in Acts 11:25–6, where Paul was engaged as Barnabas's junior partner in a ministry of teaching and church leadership in Antioch. Be that as it may, other statements of Paul confirm the general picture arising from the Acts account: he was resident for a time in Antioch (both Cephas and James's delegation 'came' to Antioch, while Paul and Barnabas were already there; Gal 2:11–12); and he was associated with Barnabas in the earlier part of his known ministry but probably not later (the only evidence for direct association appears in Gal 2:1, 9, 13; cf. 1 Cor 9:6). Paul's arrival in Antioch brings his formative period to an end and sets the stage for the more public ministry narrated in Acts and reflected in his letters.

E. The Chronology and Sequence of Paul's Mission.
1. Any full chronological reconstruction of Paul's active ministry requires the co-ordination of three interdependent lines of investigation: (1) discerning the relative chronology of the different geographical stages of his mission; (2) identifying some fixed dates as anchor points for an absolute chronology; and (3) placing the letters at their appropriate points within this chronological framework. This is not the place, of course, to attempt any such reconstruction. Even if it were possible to do so in a reasonably concise way, it would be inappropriate here; the authors of each of the sections to follow must be allowed the freedom to interpret their assigned segment of the Pauline corpus within their own reconstruction of Paul's career. What is required at this point is a more general introduction to the problems inhering in the evidence, the points at which crucial decisions need to be made, and the resultant range of reconstructions.

2. As might well be expected, the role of Acts is once again a key factor in the discussion. In both Acts and the letters Paul's mission activity is punctuated by visits to Jerusalem, and the main reconstructions of Pauline chronology are differentiated by their approach to these visits. Acts recounts no less than five such visits:

Visit 1:	Post-conversion visit (9:26–30)
Intervening activity:	Time spent in Tarsus and Antioch (9:30; 11:25–6)
Visit 2:	Famine relief visit (11:27–9; 12:25)
Intervening activity:	Mission activity in Cyprus and southern Asia Minor (13:1–14:28)
Visit 3:	Jerusalem Council visit (15:1–30)
Intervening activity:	Mission activity in Macedonia and Achaia (16:1–18:17)
Visit 4:	Unspecified visit (18:18–23)
Intervening activity:	Mission activity in Ephesus and Asia (18:24–19:41)
Visit 5:	Collection visit (20:1–21:26)
Subsequent events:	Arrest, hearings, journey to Rome (21:27–28:31)

Two preliminary observations should be made about the final two visits. First, while Luke presents the fourth visit as a matter of some urgency to Paul (cf. 18:20–1), he provides no information at all about either the reason for the journey or its outcome. Second, while Luke is aware of the fact that the fifth visit was for the purpose of delivering collection money to Jerusalem (24:17), this aspect of the final journey is very much played down in Acts in comparison to the letters.

3. In the letters themselves, by contrast, there is evidence of only three visits:

Visit A.	Post-conversion visit (Gal 1:18)
Visit B.	Jerusalem consultation (Gal 2:1–10)
Visit C.	Collection visit (1 Cor 16:1–4; Rom 15:25; cf. 2 Cor 8–9).

Several preliminary observations should be made about this list as well. To start with, the first two visits are presented in conjunction with some additional chronological information: the first visit occurred three years after Paul's Damascus experience (Gal 1:18), and the second visit took place 'after fourteen years' (Gal 2:1)—though whether the fourteen-year period begins with the first visit or with the Damascus experience is not specified in the text and is a matter of some scholarly dispute. Further, since Paul's purpose in this section of Galatians is to make the point that his contacts with Jerusalem were minimal, the context requires that the list is complete. That is, the cogency of his argument would have been in jeopardy if he had failed to mention a visit; thus prior to the writing of Galatians, Paul had made two, and only two, visits to Jerusalem. Finally, the third visit, to deliver the 'collection for the saints' (1 Cor 16:1), appears only in prospect; in all the references it is still a journey that lies in the future.

Of these two sets of visits, the first and the last in each case obviously correspond with each other, despite differences in detail. It is more difficult, however, to make sense of what comes in between. There are evident similarities between the meetings recounted in Acts 15 and Gal 2:1–10: the same participants (Paul, Barnabas, Peter, James), dealing with the same issue (circumcision of Gentile converts), coming to the same general decision (legitimacy of the Gentile mission). The majority of interpreters take these two passages as variant accounts of the same event (i.e. B = 3), and develop a chronological framework on the basis of this and other evident points of contact between Acts and the letters (with varying estimations of the reliability of information found only in Acts).

4. In addition to this majority position, however, there are two other minority approaches to Paul's chronological framework that need to be mentioned. One of them originated with the work of William Ramsay (1907), who was particularly concerned to demonstrate the historical reliability of Acts. The majority viewpoint described above tends towards the conclusion that Luke was mistaken in recounting an intervening visit between the post-conversion visit and that of the Jerusalem Council (i.e. the famine relief visit), since Paul's argument in Galatians leaves no room for it. In the position developed by Ramsay and followed by a number of others (e.g. Bruce 1977), it is argued instead that the consultation described in Gal 2:1–10 took place during the famine relief visit (i.e. B = 2). They argue that the private nature of this consultation (Gal 2:2) is more in keeping with Acts 11 than with Acts 15, and that Paul's statement of his eagerness to remember the poor (Gal 2:10) can readily be correlated with the famine relief project. Essential to this approach are two assumptions about the letter to the Galatians: first, that Galatians was written prior to the Jerusalem Council of Acts 15—perhaps the same delegation from Jerusalem that was creating dissension in Antioch (Acts 15:1) was pressuring the Galatian churches as well; and second, that the 'churches of Galatia' were those founded by Paul and Barnabas in Pisidian Antioch, Iconium, Derbe, and Lystra during the so-called first missionary journey (Acts 13 and 14), cities that were located in the southern part of the Roman province of Galatia (though the region of the ethnic Galatians lay further to the north). While this approach is often dismissed as special pleading in defence of Acts, there is a case that could be made on the basis of Galatians itself, which contains details that might suggest an early date for the letter (e.g. the prominence of Barnabas

and absence of Timothy; the absence of any explicit mention of the collection project or injunctions to contribute; the restriction of his whereabouts between the first two visits to the regions of Syria and Cilicia).

5. The other minority viewpoint, pioneered by John Knox (1950), attempts to build a chronology almost entirely on the basis of information in the letters. In addition to the Jerusalem visits, there are three chronological sequences appearing explicitly in the letters: (1) from Damascus to the confrontation with Peter (Gal); (2) missionary activity in the Greek peninsula (1 Thess); (3) travels in connection with the collection (1 Cor, 2 Cor, Rom). Knox, followed by a number of others (e.g. Hurd 1965; Lüdemann 1984), have argued that according to Paul's own statements there could not have been any more than three visits to Jerusalem. The key to this reconstruction is the injunction in Gal 2:10 that Paul 'remember the poor', which is understood to mark the inception of the collection project. That is, at the Jerusalem Council, in return for the recognition of his Gentile mission, Paul undertook a project to raise money from his Gentile churches as a sign of good faith towards the Jerusalem church. Since this was the project that occupied much of his time during the final, Ephesus-based phase of his known missionary activity, the founding of churches in Galatia, Macedonia, and Achaia must have happened prior to the Jerusalem Council; that is, this missionary activity is located in the fourteen-year period mentioned in Gal 2:1. This reconstruction has the effect (though not the intent) of placing the Jerusalem Council at a point in the sequence corresponding to the unspecified visit of Acts 18:18–23.

6. To this point, the discussion has had to do with relative chronology. In order to develop an absolute chronology, it is necessary to determine some fixed dates. Paul himself is not all that helpful in this regard. The reference to King Aretas in 2 Cor 11:32 is the only instance where he names an otherwise identifiable secular figure. Still, one reference is better than none. As observed above, Murphy-O'Connor (1996: 5–7) has argued that Paul's departure from Damascus can be dated to about 37 CE; while this may represent more precision than the evidence allows, at least one can say that the event had to have taken place before Aretas's death in 39 or 40 (Riesner 1998: 84–9). The other possible anchor-point is provided by the reference to Paul's appearance before Gallio, the proconsul of Achaia (Acts 18:12). In 1905 an inscription

was discovered at Delphi containing the text of a letter from Claudius to the city, which also referred to Gallio as proconsul. Since the term of office for a proconsular governor of a province was normally one year, commencing on the first of July, it is possible to fix Paul's appearance before Gallio to some time in the latter part of 51 CE (Murphy-O'Connor 1996: 15–22; Riesner 202–11). This, of course, assumes that Luke's report is reliable; advocates of a letters-based chronology place Paul's time in Corinth much earlier, and thus are required to dismiss the Acts account entirely.

7. To illustrate how the different approaches to Paul's chronology work out in practice, it will be useful to compare three chronologies—that of Murphy-O'Connor (1996), representing an approach that makes significant, albeit critical, use of Acts; Bruce's framework based primarily on Acts (Bruce 1977); and Lüdemann's letters-based chronology (1984). Note the significant variations in the events lying in between the post-conversion visit and the Jerusalem Council.

Murphy-O'Connor:

Conversion	33
Post-conversion visit	37
Syria and Cilicia	37–?
Cyprus, S. Asia Minor	?–45
Antioch	45–6
Galatia, Macedonia, Corinth	46–51
Jerusalem Conference	51
Antioch	51–2
Ephesus and environs	52–6
Collection visit	56
Arrival in Rome	62

Bruce:

Conversion	33
Post-conversion visit	35
Syria and Cilicia	35–46
Famine relief visit	46
Cyprus, 'Galatia'	47–8
Jerusalem Council	49
Macedonia, Achaia	49–52
Unspecified visit	52
Ephesus and environs	52–7
Collection visit	57
Arrival in Rome	60

Lüdemann

Conversion	33
Post-conversion visit	36
Syria and Cilicia	
S. Asia Minor	
Macedonia (Galatia?)	
Arrival in Corinth	41
Jerusalem Council	50
Ephesus and environs	51–3
Collection visit	55

(Lüdemann also offers an alternative set of dates, not reproduced here, based on a date for the crucifixion of 27 CE rather than 30).

8. The final aspect of any chronological reconstruction is the placement of the letters within the larger chronological framework. Again we can leave these discussions for the commentaries on the individual letters that follow. Here only brief comments are necessary. There is little uncertainty about the relative position of 1 Thessalonians, the two Corinthian epistles, and Romans; in each case internal evidence provides reasonably clear indications of relative date (though the issue of the Corinthian correspondence is complicated by the probability that at least 2 Corinthians is a composite document). If 2 Thessalonians is authentic, then it is probably to be dated shortly after 1 Thessalonians, though some interpreters argue for an inverted sequence. Most commentators place Galatians prior to Romans and in the same general time-frame as the Corinthian correspondence, though as has already been observed there is a minority view that holds it to be the earliest of the letters. As for the 'prison epistles'—Philippians, Philemon, and Colossians (if authentic)—while traditionally they have been seen as written during Paul's Roman imprisonment, there is a growing body of opinion that would place some or all of them earlier, perhaps in an Ephesian imprisonment between 1 and 2 Corinthians (see 2 Cor 1:8; note the reference to many imprisonments in 2 Cor 11:23).

F. Paul's Apostolic *Modus Operandi*. 1. The number of churches addressed or referred to in the letters suggests that Paul was strikingly successful in gaining converts and founding new congregations. The letters provide us with very little direct information, however, on how he went about the process. Once again, the lack might seem to be supplied by the Acts account. Here Paul's activity in founding new churches tends to follow a recognizable pattern. He begins in the synagogue, where he takes advantage of opportunities to proclaim the gospel in a public forum (e.g. Acts 13:5, 14; 14:1; 16:13; 17:1–2, 10; 18:4). The preaching meets with a mixed response—a positive reception by some of the Jews and many of the Gentile proselytes and 'God-fearers' (13:43; 14:1; 17:4), but a hostile response by the larger proportion of the Jewish community (13:45; 14:2; 17:5–9, 13; 18:6). This opposition leads Paul to withdraw from the synagogue with his small group of converts, who become the nucleus of a separate community with a growing number of Gentile members (13:46–9; 14:3–4; 18:6–11), and an appointed body of leaders ('elders', 14:23; 20:17). Eventually local opposition or other considerations force Paul to depart and to move to a different city, where the process is invariably repeated.

2. Again, however, the Acts material should be used with caution; for when Paul describes his mission field, Jewish synagogues are nowhere in sight. While preaching to Jews is not categorically eliminated (1 Cor 9:20), Paul invariably characterizes his apostolic mission as directed towards Gentiles (1 Thess 2:16; Gal 2:2; Rom 1:5; 11:13; 15:16; Col 1:24–9); indeed, this was precisely the division of labour agreed to with Peter (Gal 2:7–9). Likewise, when he addresses his readers, he refers to them as Gentiles (1 Cor 12:2). In neither case is there any hint of a mixed group of Jews and Gentiles. Further, when he describes his Thessalonian converts as people who had 'turned to God from idols, to serve a living and true God' (1 Thess 1:9), he does not seem to leave room for the possibility that adherence to the synagogue had been for any of them a half-way house on the path from idolatry to their new faith, in contrast to Acts 17:4.

3. Still, the differences between Paul and Acts should not be exaggerated. For one thing, if some of his converts indeed had first been 'God-fearers' and synagogue adherents, Paul would have had his own reasons to play down this fact, not wanting his mission to be seen as dependent in any way on the synagogue; he is, after all, not a disinterested observer of his own mission. Further, the ease with which he can quote and allude to Scripture in his letters suggests a real familiarity with Jewish Scripture and tradition on the part of his Gentile readers, a fact not inconsistent with the idea that some of them had had a prior association with the synagogue. In addition, Paul's statement in 1 Cor 9:20 that 'to the Jews I became as a Jew, in order to win Jews', indicates that he did not consider Jews to be out of bounds for him. Indeed, given the evidence for Jewish communities in most of the cities where he worked, it would be difficult to imagine that he could have carried on a mission that did not impinge on the synagogue community in some way.

4. Nevertheless, Paul's letters represent our primary source, and we should not allow the more fully developed but nevertheless schematized picture in Acts to control or overshadow the information emerging from the letters themselves. Further, the task of setting the information from both Acts and the letters into a richer description of Paul's mission has been aided of late by more sociologically informed studies—both those that draw on models of how new religions grow and develop (on the Christian mission generally, see Stark 1996) and those that attempt detailed descriptions of Paul's social context (e.g. Meeks 1983). One emphasis arising from both types of study is the importance of various social networks in the spread of a new religious movement. While the role of public preaching and teaching should not be eliminated entirely, more emphasis should be placed on family networks (e.g. 1 Cor 7:13–16), on the extended household with its various networks of slaves, freedmen, tenants, clients, and so on (e.g. 1 Cor 1:16), and on the networks involved in the carrying out of a trade (Hock 1980). Indeed, the frequency of references to house-churches (1 Cor 16:19; Rom 16:3–5, 23; Philem 1; Col 4:15) suggests that households provided the primary social context in which Paul's churches were embedded (though other models such as voluntary associations may have helped shape the new communities as well; see Ascough 1997).

5. It is not easy to discern the shape of Paul's original preaching. The basic elements are clear enough; the summary in 1 Cor 15:3–8, with its focus on Christ's death and resurrection as a saving event, is reflected in other references sprinkled through the letters (e.g. 1 Cor 2:1–5; 1 Thess 1:9–10). But it is more difficult to discern how these basic elements were fleshed out. To take one sharply debated issue, how much biographical information about Jesus' life and teaching was included (Dunn 1998: 183–206)? Or, how central was Israel to Paul's preaching? Did he, for example, lead his converts to believe that they were full members of Abraham's family (Gal 3:29) or that they had been grafted into Israel's stock (Rom 11:17–24), or did these Israel-centred themes emerge only later and in response to external influences (see Donaldson 1994)?

6. In any case, after his initial preaching Paul spent a period of time consolidating his evangelistic gains and establishing a self-sufficient community. Most of his letters contain passing references back to this initial period of community-formation (e.g. 1 Cor 1:14–16; 2:1–5; 2 Cor 1:19; 12:12–13; Gal 4:13–15; Phil 4:9; 1 Thess

2:9–12; 2 Thess 3:7–10). During this period he did not request or accept financial support from the congregation, preferring to support himself through his own work (1 Cor 9:3–18; 1 Thess 2:9; 2 Thess 3:7–10) and contributions from already-founded congregations (2 Cor 11:7–11; Phil 4:15–16). With the exception of Phil 1:1, there seems to be little evidence of the kind of appointed 'elders' referred to in Acts (e.g. Acts 14:23). Indeed, a striking feature of the letters is that in dealing with local conflicts Paul does not bring local office-holders into the picture, either to instruct them or to encourage his readers to submit to them. He tended to operate more on the basis of a charismatic, gift-based leadership (Rom 12:4–7; 1 Cor 12: 1–31; cf. Eph 4: 11–16), though one should not underestimate the *de facto* leadership role played by the head of the household in which the church met.

7. After leaving the congregation and moving on to another city, Paul continued to feel 'daily pressure because of [his] anxiety for all the churches' (2 Cor 11:28). His anxiety took the positive form of an ongoing pastoral responsibility, exercised not only through his own follow-up visits (Phil 1:27; 2:24; 1 Cor 4:18–21), but also by means of appointed emissaries—for example, Timothy (1 Cor 4:16; 16:10–11; Phil 2:19–23) and Titus (2 Cor 7:6–16; 8:16–24)—and by means of the letters themselves. Through these agencies Paul extended his apostolic activity and authority; both emissaries (1 Cor 4:17) and letters (Gal 4:20) functioned as proxies—and sometimes as precursors—for his own apostolic presence (Funk 1967).

8. Paul founded self-sustaining congregations and then moved on. But where, and why? How did he decide which city he would move to next? More specifically, did Paul operate from some sense of a geographical plan or strategy? A number of pieces of evidence seem to suggest that he did. (1) Not only did he concentrate on cities, but the cities he chose to work in tended to be prominent ones, provincial capitals and the like. (2) He seems to have thought of these cities in terms of the provinces in which they were found, preferring to refer to his churches with provincial rather than city names; e.g. Achaia and Macedonia (Rom 15:26; 2 Cor 8:1; 9:2), Asia (Rom 16:5), Illyricum (Rom 15:19), Spain (Rom 15:24), and (probably) Galatia (Gal 1:2). (3) For years, he says, he had a desire to proclaim the gospel in Rome (Rom 1:10–13; 15:23), which he then wanted to use as a staging-post for a journey to Spain (Rom 15:24, 28). (4) The agreement between Peter and Paul recounted

in Gal 2:9—'that we should go to the Gentiles and they to the circumcised'—is at least open to a territorial (rather than solely ethnic) interpretation. (5) The geographical context in 2 Cor 10:12–18 suggests a territorial element in Paul's statement that 'we...will keep within the field that God has assigned to us' (v. 13). (6) Paul's statement in Rom 15:19, 24, to the effect that he is now free to travel to Rome because he has 'fully proclaimed the gospel of Christ' 'from Jerusalem and as far around as Illyricum', seems to suggest not only a notion of territoriality but also of a specific evangelizing agenda within that territory. Since there was still plenty of scope for preaching, not only in untouched cities but even in the cities where churches had been planted, his statement that his work was finished in this area must suggest that he was operating according to some more specific strategy than simply preaching to as many Gentiles as he could wherever he might find them. (7) Finally, the statement that the conversion of the 'full number of the Gentiles' would be the thing to trigger the coming of the End and the salvation of 'all Israel' (Rom 11:25–6), sets the whole mission within an eschatological framework: when the gospel was 'fully preached', not simply from Jerusalem to Illyricum but from Jerusalem to X (X being wherever he considered the end of the territory to be), then the parousia would take place.

9. While these pieces of evidence seem to add up to a geographical strategy of some kind, it is not any easy matter to discern what it might have been. The popular notion that Paul engaged in 'missionary journeys', with Jerusalem as his point of departure and return, owes more to Luke than to Paul—and actually owes more to the modern missionary movement than to Luke: as Townsend (1985) has observed, it was not until the onset of the missionary movement in the eighteenth century that anyone thought to describe Paul's apostolic activity in terms of 'three missionary journeys'. Another notion influenced by more modern Christian missionary strategy—namely, that Paul intended each of his churches to be centres of evangelism for the whole province of which it was a part (e.g. Dunn 1988: ii. 869)—founders on the fact that Paul nowhere urges his congregations to carry out the task of evangelism; strangely, his letters contain no injunctions to evangelize at all. Somehow he seems to consider his churches as representative of the provinces in which they are located, so that once a church was founded within a province, he could

say that the gospel had been 'fully preached' in that province.

10. But how did he determine which provinces in which to work? Knox has suggested that the word *kuklō* in Rom 15:19 ('from Jerusalem and *kuklō* as far as Illyricum') should be translated 'in a circular manner', arguing on this basis that Paul's plan was to work his way through a string of provinces circling the Mediterranean and ending up in Egypt (Knox 1964). Others have attempted to find a geographical template in Israel's Scriptures—either the sequence of nations listed in Isa 66:18–21 (Riesner 1998: 245–53) or the various 'tables of the nations' in Gen 10 and elsewhere (Scott 1995). Each proposal has its difficulties, however, not the least of which is the fact that there were many provinces between Jerusalem and Rome or Spain which Paul did not seem compelled to visit. The statement that he chose to work only where Christ had not 'already been named' (Rom 15:20) might suggest that he avoided other provinces because they had already been evangelized. But this would hardly have been true of Thrace, Moesia, or Gaul, to name only a few of the provinces in which he did no work. Moreover, Rom 15:20 cannot be pressed too hard, in that Paul was quite prepared to preach the gospel in Rome (Rom 1:13) and to consider it as part of his apostolic turf (Rom 1:5–6; 15:14–16) even though a church already existed there.

Perhaps the most that can be said is that Spain, considered by the ancients to be the 'end of the earth', represented for Paul the goal of his ever westerly-pressing mission. In this connection, it is worth noting that Paul seems to have conceived of his apostolic task in the light of the Servant passages of Isaiah (see the citations or allusions in Gal 1:15; 2 Cor 6:2; Rom 15:21) and that the Servant's task was to bring God's salvation 'to the end of the earth' (Isa 49:6; see further Donaldson 2006).

In all probability, however, Paul never made it to the 'end of the earth'. He journeyed to Rome not in apostolic freedom but as a prisoner. While it is possible that his Roman hearing resulted in release (Murphy-O'Connor 1996: 359–63), it is more likely that it resulted, eventually, in his execution.

G. The Letters. 1. Paul wrote neither theological treatises nor narratives but letters, and a proper understanding of his literary legacy requires that we take seriously its epistolary character. To do this, we must look not only at the letters themselves, but also at the letter-writing conventions that were present in the Graeco-Roman world. Fortunately, we are the beneficiaries of a century of careful comparative study, with the result that the shape and texture of Paul's letters are being brought ever more clearly into focus.

2. It is customary in discussions of the literary features of Paul's letters to begin with Adolf Deissmann and his work on the papyri that were coming to light in the latter part of the nineteenth century (Deissmann 1910). And with good reason. Deissmann was the first to realize the significance of these papyri for the study of Paul's letters, and his own observations have continued to shape the discussion. In contrast to the more literary epistles that had been preserved in the classical corpus, which were generally written for a wider reading public and with a view to preservation (e.g. those of Cicero or Seneca), the letters contained among the papyri findings were truly occasional writings. That is, they were addressed to the immediate situation that had prompted their writing, and they tended to be artless, spontaneous, and personal. On the basis of such a distinction between literary 'epistles' ('products of literary art') and real 'letters' ('documents of life'; ibid. 218), Deissmann argued that Paul's writings should be classed among the latter. That is, they are occasional writings, written 'not for the public and posterity, but for the persons to whom they are addressed' (ibid. 225), written not as the careful formulations of a systematic theologian but out of the pressing urgency of a pastoral situation.

3. As a first approximation, Deissmann's analysis is valid and perceptive, highlighting as it does the immediacy and situation-driven character of the letters. Even the Epistle to the Romans, containing the most sustained and systematic argumentation in the corpus and traditionally understood as a 'compendium of Christian Doctrine' (Melanchthon), should be understood instead as written out of specific circumstances (Paul's planned trip to Rome) and shaped in accordance with specific purposes (to win the acceptance of the Roman Christians by addressing their concerns about his Gentile mission). But Deissmann's categories are too crudely drawn and need to be significantly revised. For one thing, Paul's letters are not simply personal and private; he writes to whole congregations, even in such a 'personal' letter as Philemon (Philem 2), and addresses his readers from a self-conscious position of authority. Nor are they as brief, rough, and artless as many of the papyri letters on which Deissmann based his categories; while they may not display evidence of formal rhetorical training, they are nevertheless well-structured and carefully composed. In addition, further study of letters in antiquity has revealed a wide variety of different types of letter (Stowers 1986), from letters of rebuke (cf. Galatians) to letters of mediation (cf. Philemon), as well as a wider range of relationships between sender and recipient. With respect to the latter point, Aune has suggested a similarity between Paul's letters and 'official letters' sent from government officials to those under their authority (Aune 1987: 164–5).

4. Still, private letters provide the basic form on which all letters in Graeco-Roman antiquity were based, and a comparison between Paul and the epistolary papyri is very illuminating. Paul's letters are composed according to the conventional pattern of the day, although he adapted it in ways that made his letters particularly effective means of extending and reinforcing his apostolic activity.

Letters typically began with a prescript, consisting of the name of the sender, the name of the recipient, and a salutation. To use one of Deissmann's (1910: 167–72) examples, a second-century letter from a young Egyptian just arrived in Italy after having enlisted in the army begins this way: 'Apion to Epimachus his father and lord, many greetings.' The word 'greetings' (chairein) is a customary form of salutation in Hellenistic letters, though Jewish letters sometimes replace it with 'peace' (šālôm, eirēnē). Paul's letters follow the same format (A to B, greetings), but with several characteristic adaptations, some of them more or less the same from letter to letter, others particularly tailored to the needs of the situation. First, he usually adds a term descriptive of his own role and status, most frequently 'apostle' but also 'servant' or 'prisoner', completed in each case by 'of Christ Jesus'. Then he often names a co-sender (Romans being the only exception among the certainly authentic epistles), even though the letter itself is usually couched in the first person singular (e.g. Philemon). Then, where it suits his purposes, he will considerably expand either the sender or the recipient portion of the prescript. In Romans and Galatians, for example, where his own status as an apostle is in need of defence, he uses this portion of the letter to make an aggressive (Galatians) or subtle and extended (Romans; 6 verses) tdeclaration of his apostolic status and authority.

In 1 Corinthians, it is the recipients who are described more fully (1:2). Here the emphasis on their status as saints and on their membership in a wider community of Christians is an appropriate opening note to a letter addressed to a community marked by decidedly unsaintly behaviour (e.g. 5:1) and smug self-sufficiency (4:8; cf. 11:16). Finally, Paul ends the prescript with a salutation distinctively his own ('Grace to you and peace from God our Father and the Lord Jesus Christ'; minor variations in Colossians and 1 Thessalonians), yet adapted from current patterns. 'Grace' (charis), while part of Paul's characteristic Christian vocabulary, is close enough to chairein to be heard as an edifying wordplay; 'peace' is typical of Jewish letter-writing patterns.

5. The prescript in Graeco-Roman letters was frequently followed by a section in which the writer expressed wishes for the good health of the recipient, often couched in the form of a prayer, and/or offered thanksgiving to the gods for some benefit received. To illustrate, the letter cited above continues: 'First of all, I pray that you are in good health, and that you continue to prosper and fare well, with my sister and her daughter and my brother. I give thanks to the Lord Serapis that when I was in danger in the sea he saved me immediately.' Again this has its counterpart in Paul, though where in conventional letters it tended to be formulaic and perfunctory, in Paul each prayer/thanksgiving section is freshly composed for each letter, complimentary to the readers, and tailored in evident ways to the concerns of the letter. In 1 Corinthians, to take a particularly striking example, Paul gives thanks for characteristics in his readers that he will later scold them for not displaying: their richness (cf. 4:8) in speech (cf. ch. 14), in knowledge (cf. ch. 8), and in spiritual gifts (cf. chs. 12, 14). In Philemon, before pressing his request that Philemon receive Onesimus back with love (v. 16) and so refresh Paul's heart (v. 20), he gives thanks for Philemon's demonstrated 'love for all the saints' (v. 5) and for the way in which 'the hearts of the saints have been refreshed' already through Philemon. In less capable hands, this section would have been crudely manipulative. In Paul's more subtle and even elegant phrasing, however, this section functions as a kind of overture, introducing the themes to follow and predisposing the recipients to a receptive reading of the letter as a whole. The one exception is Galatians, where Paul moves straight from the prescript (concluded, unusually, with a doxology) to an

expression of astonishment at the culpable folly of the readers. Here the prayer/thanksgiving section is omitted for effect, or one could even argue that it has been replaced with a curse section (Gal 1:6–9).

6. At this point in both Graeco-Roman letters and in Paul we move into the body of the letter, where the sender sets out to accomplish the purpose for which the letter was being written. Here, the sheer variety of purposes and forms means that it is not as easy to identify epistolary patterns at work in letter bodies as a whole. Still, comparative work has by no means been fruitless (White 1972). For one thing, many of the formulae by which Paul introduces his subject-matter or takes up new themes are frequently found elsewhere: e.g. 'I am astonished that'; 'I want you to know that'; 'I beseech/appeal to you'; 'I rejoice that'; 'I am confident that'—all are frequent in Paul and richly documented in Graeco-Roman sources (Aune 1987: 188; Longenecker 1990: pp. cv–cviii). As observed already, letter bodies can be further categorized according to the particular function intended for the letter (Stowers 1986). Also, as will be picked up in more detail below, considerable new light has been shed on the letters, particularly on the letter bodies, by analysing them in terms of the conventions of ancient rhetoric. Finally, it is possible in at least some of the letters to identify a section of parenaesis at the end of the body proper (Rom 12:1–15:13; Gal 5:1–6:10; 1 Thess 4:1–5:22), i.e., a combination of instruction and encouragement, no doubt related to the particular circumstances prompting the letter, but in ways that are not always readily discerned.

7. Letter closings display less of a fixed form and have not been nearly as well studied, at least until recently (Weima 1994). Instead of essential elements, there appear to have been a number of conventions from which letter writers could make a selection according to preference or need: 'a farewell wish, a health wish, secondary greetings, an autograph, an illiteracy formula [i. e. indicating that the note had of necessity been written by a secretary], the date, and a postscript' (ibid. 55). Again Paul's usage both reflects current conventions and displays a Christian adaptation of them. His letters contain the following closing elements (ibid. 77–155): (1) a peace benediction, often a variation on the form 'may the God of peace be with you' (e.g. Rom 15:33; 2 Cor 13:11; Phil 4:9); (2) a final exhortation (e.g. 1 Cor 16:13–16; Phil 4:8–9); (3) greetings (first-, second-, and third-person),

together with an injunction to 'greet one another with a holy kiss' (Rom 16:16; also 1 Cor 16:20; 2 Cor 13:12, 1 Thess 5:26); (4) an autograph (explicit in 1 Cor 16:21; Gal 6:11; 2 Thess 3:17; Philem 19; Col 4:18); (5) a grace benediction, in the form 'the grace of the Lord Jesus be with you'. The one fixed element, found in all the letters, is the closing grace benediction, which taken in combination with the prescript means that each letter is framed with the wish for grace. In addition, each closing contains a selection of the other elements, with a tendency towards the order in which they were listed above.

8. In more recent years, epistolary analysis has been supplemented—or even rivalled—by a second type of analysis to which the letters have been subjected, that of rhetorical criticism. The pejorative overtones associated with the term 'rhetoric' in popular parlance (e.g. mere or empty rhetoric) is a measure of how far this once highly prized declamatory skill has fallen in esteem. In antiquity, however, rhetoric was one of the two possible capstones of an education (philosophy being the other) and the basic prerequisite for a public career. Shorn of its negative connotations, 'rhetoric' simply denotes the 'art of persuasion', and more recent study has recovered a sense of its place in antiquity and its potential for New Testament interpretation (Kennedy 1984).

9. Rhetorical criticism looks at argument in the NT from several angles (see Mack 1990), each of which can be fruitfully applied to the body of Paul's letters. One has to do with classification of argument types. Ancient rhetoricians divided argument into three categories—judicial (rendering verdicts on past actions), deliberative (making decisions about future courses of action), and epideictic (bestowing praise or blame)—and these have been brought to bear on Paul's letters. A second approach has to do with the classification of different elements within an argument. Aristotle distinguished between *ethos* (the establishment of the speaker's relationship with the audience and the basis of the speaker's authority), *logos* (the substance, structure and arrangement of the argument itself), and *pathos* (the ways in which the emotions of the audience are elicited and engaged in the service of the argument). These three categories can readily be applied to each of Paul's letters, with immediate and fruitful results. A third aspect of rhetorical criticism is concerned with the *logos* itself, especially with structures of ancient rhetoric as prescribed in the handbooks of Quintilian and others. In his work on Galatians, for example, Betz (1979) attempts to demonstrate that the argument in this epistle unfolds according to the prescribed sequence of the *exordium* (introductory section), the *narratio* (recitation of the facts of the case), the *propositio* (thesis to be demonstrated), the *probatio* (specific arguments or proofs), and the concluding *exhortatio*.

10. Occasionally one gets the sense in reading rhetorical criticism that text is being eclipsed by pattern; that is, that the text is being squeezed to fit a prescribed rhetorical pattern, or at least that demonstrating the pattern has taken precedence over revealing the text. Further, it is doubtful that Paul himself would have been exposed in an explicit way to the type of rhetorical training prescribed by the handbooks. Still, since rhetoric itself permeated the cultural air he breathed, he would have been deeply affected by rhetorical patterns and conventions at least in a secondary way. Moreover, any approach that encourages readers to attend carefully to the actual functioning of a text as it works its persuasive power on a reader is to be warmly welcomed.

11. Any discussion of the actual functioning of the individual letters themselves or of the ends to which their particular persuasive powers are turned is best left to the individual commentaries to follow. More generally, however, one can say that what Paul intends to accomplish by means of his letters is what he himself would do if he were there. As he says towards the end of his troubled correspondence with the Corinthians: 'So I write these things while I am away from you, so that when I come, I may not have to be severe in using the authority that the Lord has given me for building up and not for tearing down' (2 Cor 13:10). Or a little earlier in the same letter: 'Let such people understand that what we say by letter when absent, we do when present' (2 Cor 10:11). Further, the promise (threat?) of a visit in many of the letters (1 Cor 4:18–21; 16:5–9; 2 Cor 9:4; 13:1, 10; Phil 2:24; Philem 22) serves to reinforce the connection between action by letter and action in person (Funk 1967).

12. Of course the Corinthians themselves felt that, at least as far as the exercise of forceful discipline was concerned, Paul's letters were more effective than his presence! 'His letters are weighty and strong, but his bodily presence is weak and his speech contemptible' (2 Cor 10:10). But discipline was only one arrow in his epistolary quiver. What Paul was attempting to do in his letters—to continue the archery

metaphor by borrowing a phrase from Beker (1980)—was to direct a 'word on target' to the situation of his readers, to bring the 'coherent core' of his gospel to bear on the 'contingent circumstances' to which the letter was addressed. Paul's ultimate aim, in person or by letter, was to create and maintain for his converts a new world in which they might live and find meaning, a world grounded on the death and resurrection of Christ and the victory over the forces of evil and death that these had signalled.

13. This brings us close to the matter of Paul's 'theology', to which we will turn our attention in a moment. But first, two final items concerning the letters themselves. One of these has to do with two other agents with roles to play in the process of communication carried out by a letter. As was customary in a culture where the means of letter production were not readily available to all, Paul made use of a secretary to do the actual pen and papyrus work. This is implied by the autograph section in many of the letter closings, where Paul himself takes up the pen 'to write this greeting with [his] own hand' (1 Cor 16:21). It is stated explicitly in Rom 16:22 where, in the midst of a series of third-party greetings, the secretary breaks into the conversation to add his own word of greeting: 'I Tertius, the writer of this letter, greet you in the Lord.'

What was the role of the secretary in the production of Paul's letters? There is a range of possibilities, from simply producing a good copy from Paul's corrected first draft to actually composing the substance of the letter under Paul's general direction. The oral quality that comes through at many points, however, especially where sentences are broken off or new thoughts begun before old ones are fully completed (e.g. Rom 5:12; 8:3) or where verbs of speaking are used with respect to what is being said in the letter (Rom 11:13; 2 Cor 12:19), seems to suggest that Paul dictated his letters. This is also confirmed by a general evenness in style among the certainly authentic letters.

14. Perhaps more important for the process of communication was the role played by another agent—the person delivering the letter. In an era where there was organized postal service only for Roman imperial business, individual arrangements had to be made for the delivery of letters, preferably by someone known to the sender. Presumably the 'tearful letter' referred to in 2 Corinthians (2:3–4, 9; 7:8, 12) had the positive effect that it did (7:6–16) at least in part because Titus (who probably delivered the letter) had been present to interpret it, to ensure that it was being heard correctly, to mollify any who were upset by it, and perhaps even to negotiate a more positive response than if Paul had delivered his message in person. The role of the letter carrier also comes up in Col 4:7–9 where Paul (if Colossians is directly from Paul) commends Tychicus, again the probable letter carrier, who 'will tell you all the news about me'. Later readers, who have to piece together information about Paul's 'news' like a detective in a P. D. James novel, might wish that Paul had not left so much to the letter carrier, but had put more of the actual detail of his life and circumstances into the letters.

15. The reference in the previous paragraph to the disputed authenticity of Colossians brings us to the final item to be touched on in this section. Fully six of the thirteen letters that bear Paul's name display characteristics that have led many scholars to conclude that some or all of the six were not written directly by Paul. While the details need to be left for the individual commentaries to follow, the characteristics are a combination of elements: differences in vocabulary and style, differences in theological outlook, reflections of contextual circumstances that probably emerged only later, and so on. These characteristics are not uniformly present in the six letters: 2 Thessalonians, Colossians, and Ephesians are much more Pauline in their vocabulary, style, and theology than are the Pastorals (1 and 2 Timothy, Titus). There are also variations within these two groups. Ephesians, with its long sentences and its piling up of synonyms and genitive constructions (e.g. 'the working of the power of his strength', 1:19), sounds less Pauline than does Colossians or 2 Thessalonians. With respect to the Pastorals, some of the features that set these writings apart from the rest of the Pauline corpus (the concern for church order; the stiff and formal tone out of keeping with letters ostensibly written to close associates) are absent from 2 Timothy.

16. In each case scholars have entertained a range of possibilities. Some have defended authenticity by appealing to special circumstances that might account for the observed deviations from the norm. Others have pointed to the way in which Paul included others within his sphere of apostolic authority—those mentioned as co-senders of letters, for example—in order to argue that Paul may have given a secretary or co-worker greater latitude in the actual

composition of the letters in question. Still others—the majority in the case of Ephesians and the Pastoral epistles—believe that letters were written by former associates or later admirers of Paul some time after his death, written to bring the voice and authority of Paul to bear on pressing circumstances in the real author's own day.

17. Readers who encounter this discussion for the first time often interpret the latter suggestion as implying deliberate deception on the part of the real author. But even in our own day we are familiar with situations where it is considered quite appropriate for texts that have been written by one person to be attributed to another—political speeches, for example, or 'as told to' autobiographies, or unfinished manuscripts published posthumously after being edited and completed by a colleague or admirer of the deceased. Furthermore, the ancients tended to have different attitudes towards authorship than are standard in our own culture, with its notions of copyright and intellectual property. Take, for example, this statement by the late second-century Christian writer Tertullian: '[The Gospel] which was published by Mark may be maintained to be Peter's, whose interpreter Mark was, just as the narrative of Luke is generally ascribed to Paul. For it is allowable that that which disciples publish should be regarded as their master's work' (*Adv. Marc.* 6.5). Certainly cases of deception were known in antiquity, no less than in our own day. But there is a much broader range of options to be put into play in the discussion.

One of the factors in the discussion of authenticity, however, and one of the keys to Paul's enduring significance, is the presence in the certainly authentic letters of a distinctive set of theological themes and structures. To this we will now turn our attention.

H. The Thought within and beneath the Letters. 1. One cannot read through Paul's letters without being struck by the dazzling array of images, metaphors, terms, concepts, and typologies that he uses to describe the human situation and the work of Christ and its consequences. A classroom of even beginner-level students can quickly fill up a whole blackboard. In an order as random as a classroom brainstorming session: justification; sin; redemption; judgement; flesh; Spirit; spirit; body; law; works of the law; faith; grace; boasting; Christ; Lord; the first/last Adam; Son of God; sons of God; sons of Abraham; righteousness; reconciliation; adoption;

freedom; slavery; expiation; sanctification; enemy; wrath; love; for us; for our sins; blood; gospel; preaching; body of Christ; in Christ; putting on Christ; in the Spirit; crucified with Christ; dying with Christ; rising with Christ; walking; called; being one; bought and sold; first fruits; wisdom; glory; living sacrifice; faith, hope, and love; triumph; dying to the law; dying to sin; principalities and powers; elemental spirits; condemnation; fellowship—not to mention 'things that are not to be told, that no mortal is permitted to repeat' (2 Cor 12:4).

2. The list is a testimony to the vigour and vitality of Paul's mind. His was an active intellect, throwing off metaphors and ideas as a grindstone throws off sparks. Yet the very kaleidoscopic dazzle of his language makes it difficult to read him well, especially since his statements on some topics (the law, in particular) seem to be in considerable tension with each other. Is there a discernible pattern or an underlying structure that will help us make coherent sense of this welter of theological language? What, in other words, is the basic shape of Paul's theology?

3. The task is by no means easy. The puzzlement expressed by the author of 2 Peter, noted at the outset of this essay (2 Pet 3:16), is echoed by modern readers as well. In Franz Over-beck's delightfully paradoxical way of putting it: 'No one has ever understood Paul, except Marcion; and even he misunderstood him.' Or, in more expanded form: '[Paul's] greatness is shown in the very fact that he has found no congenial interpreter and probably never will. From Marcion to Karl Barth, from Augustine to Luther, Schweitzer or Bultmann, he has ever been misunderstood or partially understood, one aspect of his work being thrown into relief while others have been misunderstood and neglected' (Schoeps 1961: 13).

4. Some have decided that the very attempt to find a coherent pattern of thought in Paul is misdirected, either because Paul's significance is to be found instead in his spirituality or his exercise of pastoral care, or because his thinking contains an irreducible element of incoherence. Among those who think that the quest for coherence is worth pursuing, there have been several different ways of formulating the problem, or several different places in which the interpretative key has been sought. Some have looked to Paul's 'background', hoping to find in Paul's Jewish formation or Hellenistic environment (or a combination of the two) the grid-points around which his theological discourse can be plotted and patterned. Others have looked to his conversion (as has already been observed), hoping to find a biographical and experiential paradigm that might have generated— and thus might make sense of—his later argumentation. Still others have attempted to select from the larger set of terms and metaphors a primary image or a central theme around which the remainder can be arranged. 'Justification by faith not works' is probably the best-known example of such an attempt. These approaches have been supplemented from time to time by various developmental schemes, which try to discern a substantial progression of Paul's theology as he matured.

5. Perhaps the most promising approach, however, is one that sees Paul's 'theology' as a cumulative activity taking place between two other levels of cognition and perception. The foundational level, located in structures beneath the surface of the text, consists of Paul's set of basic convictions, things that he took to be axiomatic or self-evident. Some of these were native convictions, stemming from his primary formation in Judaism; others were secondary and reconstitutive, stemming from his Damascus experience. We have already discussed the way in which Paul's 'conversion' experience can be seen as a redrawing of his primary Jewish convictions around the new belief that God had raised Jesus from death and thus made him Saviour and Christ.

By contrast, the uppermost level, encountered at the rhetorical surface of the letters, is much more contingent, in that it is related to the specific situations that prompted Paul's epistolary response. This level is not to be simply identified with either the actual circumstances themselves or Paul's actual response, though both are involved. Rather, it is to be located in Paul's perception of the situation, as he views it through the lens of his basic gospel convictions.

6. What is commonly thought of as Paul's theology, then, can be seen as lying in between these two levels and produced by the dynamic interaction between them. New and unforeseen circumstances in his churches force Paul to develop the implications of his core convictions in order to be able to address them. Questions raised by opponents or sceptical hearers of his message raise to the surface tensions inherent in his new set of convictions, tensions that he needs to resolve if his message is to be heard. Especially prominent in this regard are those tensions arising from his new belief that Christ,

not Torah, is the true badge of membership in the family of Abraham. Paul's theology, then, is that developing body of thought that exists in between conviction and circumstance, driven in different ways by both and by the dynamic interaction between them.

7. This is obviously not the place to try to develop any full-scale description of this developing body of thought. The most recent (and highly successful) attempt to do this (Dunn 1998) ran to some 800 pages! But for present purposes, in addition to this suggestion of a multilevel approach to Paul's theology, it will be helpful to make a few further comments about the shift that is currently underway with respect to a central aspect of his thought, namely, the nature of the human plight and of the solution provided by God in Christ. An older pattern, shaped in large measure by the controversies of the Reformation era (though constructed from elements in existence ever since the church had become a distinctly Gentile institution), has been increasingly displaced by a new pattern owing much to a new appreciation of the Jewish context in which Paul carried out his apostolic mission. Of course, to reduce the complex field of Pauline interpretation to two 'patterns' is a considerable oversimplification; reality is much more complex than that. Still, it is often helpful to paint with broad strokes before working on the fine details, so there is value in a simplified sketch. In any case, both patterns deal with the central themes of sin and salvation, but in strikingly different ways.

8. The older approach assumes that for Paul the fundamental problem posed by sin was essentially that it left human beings guilty before a righteous God. God demands righteousness first and foremost, but humans are universally sinful and thus under divine condemnation. Christ's role, then, is conceived primarily as a way of removing this guilty verdict. His death makes it possible for God, though righteous, to forgive sin, and for humans, though sinful, to be considered righteous. In this 'objective' view of the atonement (the process by which Christ overcomes the problem posed by sin and effects a reconciliation between God and humankind), the problem posed by human sin is located ultimately with God; even though God might be willing to forgive, the standards of divine righteousness make this impossible. There are various ways in which this 'impossibility' has been understood. The most common, however, is that God's righteousness required that sin be punished. In his death—so runs this 'penal substitutionary' view of the atonement—Christ functioned as a substitute, experiencing death as the punishment for sin, even though he was not guilty of sin. With the penalty paid, God is then free to overlook sin, 'imputing' Christ's righteous status to those who believe.

9. If guilt and its consequence—condemnation—constitute the nub of the human plight, then the heart of salvation for Paul is to be found in its opposite, justification. Christ's fundamental accomplishment in this older view, then, was seen as opening up the possibility of justification, a new status attributed to the believer on the basis of faith. What gave Paul's doctrine of justification by faith its particular spin in the traditional line of interpretation was the way it was defined in contrast to 'works'. Faith and works were taken to be fundamental categories for Paul, representing two mutually exclusive personal stances or attitudes vis-à-vis God. 'Works' is understood as an attitude of self-confidence based on meritorious achievement, where one attempts to earn acceptance and standing before God on the basis of moral and religious accomplishment. While such standing might be theoretically possible, the pervasiveness of sin, it is argued, made it impossible in reality. Thus Paul's language of justification by faith is interpreted within the framework of two mutually exclusive religious frameworks—one operating on the basis of divine grace humbly accepted, the other on the basis of human achievement boastfully put forward.

In this reading of Paul, Judaism comes into the picture essentially as an example of a works religion—the one with which Paul was most familiar, but nevertheless just a particular example of a more general human tendency. Paul's interest in the Gentiles is taken for granted, in that it is assumed that he begins with a generically human problem—how can a sinful human being find acceptance before a righteous God?

10. In this way of construing Paul's thought, it can readily be seen how the distance between Luther and Paul has been collapsed, so that Paul's problem and solution are understood to replicate those of Luther himself. We have already seen one difficulty with this reading of Paul—the fact that its legalistic interpretation of Judaism represents a fundamental misunderstanding of how the law functioned with respect to the covenant. But there are other difficulties as well. One has to do with sin. It is hard to imagine how someone who read in his Scriptures that God was 'merciful and gracious, slow to anger and abounding in steadfast love' (Ps 103:8) could have believed that human guilt for sin was a fundamental obstacle to divine forgiveness. Another has to do with justification by faith. While juridical language (justification, etc.) looms large in Galatians and Romans, when one looks at the letters as a whole one is struck by the limited role it plays. Outside Galatians and Romans (and Phil 3) Paul never uses this doctrine as a fundamental first principle to be brought to bear on problems, in Corinth, say, or Thessalonica. Moreover, he quite happily issues all sorts of commands and injunctions to his congregations concerning 'works' they are to perform, without feeling any apparent compunction to warn them of the dangers of legalism. In fact, the only 'works' that Paul gets upset about are those that would turn Gentiles into Jews—circumcision, food laws, sabbath observance, and other Torah regulations. Since Romans and Galatians are written precisely for the purpose of defending the equal status of Gentile believers as Gentiles, against those who would in effect have them become Jews, it can be argued that instead of being his central theme, justification by faith is a particular line of argument developed for this purpose.

11. These observations could be developed at much greater length. But for present purposes this will suffice as an introduction to an alternative way of construing Paul's central story of plight and salvation, again sketched out in broad strokes. Rom 8:1–4 provides us with a convenient set of paints and brushes:

> There is therefore now no condemnation for those who are in Christ Jesus. For the law of the Spirit of life in Christ Jesus has set you free from the law of sin and of death. For God has done what the law, weakened by the flesh, could not do: by sending his own Son in the likeness of sinful flesh, and to deal with sin, he condemned sin in the flesh, so that the just requirement of the law might be fulfilled in us, who walk not according to the flesh but according to the Spirit.

At this point in Romans, Paul is bringing the argument of chs. 1–8 to a conclusion. He returns to the theme of justification: there is no condemnation—that is, there is justification—for those in Christ Jesus. Why? Not because Christ has endured a penalty that had to be meted out, but because Christ has performed an act of liberation: he has liberated you from the law of sin and death. For Paul, sin is conceived not simply as culpable wrongdoing, but more fundamentally as a power, a kind of force-field that 'has come into the world through one man' (Rom 5:12), bringing death in its train and holding the whole of humankind under its sway. Those in its power commit sins and incur guilt, of course, but precisely because of the power of sin already at work in them: 'If I do what I do not want, it is no longer I that do it but sin that dwells within me' (Rom 7:20). The problem posed by sin, then, is only secondarily one of guilt; more fundamentally, the problem is bondage. What is needed is not forgiveness *per se*; until the power of sin is nullified, forgiveness does not get at the root of the problem. What is needed, rather, is liberation.

12. Christ's accomplishment, then, is to be seen more fundamentally in terms of a confrontation with sin, breaking its power and opening up a new sphere in which life can be lived. What Christ has done in the flesh is to 'condemn sin' (v. 3). In context, this must mean more than simply to declare sin to be deserving of condemnation; the law was very good at doing this (ch. 7), but what Christ has done is something that the law 'could not do' (v. 3). Christ, for Paul, has not only pronounced the verdict but also carried out the sentence; he has won a victory over sin and emptied it of its power—at least for those who are 'in Christ' (v. 1) and who 'walk according to the Spirit' (v. 4).

13. While Christ's death makes possible a new objective status (of which justification is one metaphor), this is not the heart of salvation for Paul. Instead, salvation has to do with the real subjective experience of being liberated from sin's power and transferred to a sphere in which a different power is at work, the power of the Spirit. Those who are empowered by the Spirit—who 'walk according to the Spirit' (v. 4)—are thereby 'of Christ' (Rom 8:9) or 'in Christ' (v. 1) or have Christ in them (Rom 8:10). This language is part of a larger complex in Paul in which the Christian experience is described in participatory terms—i.e. as an experience of sharing with Christ in the process of dying to this age, an age in which sin and death are the regnant powers, and rising to the life of the age to come, where sin and death are finally defeated (Rom 6:1–11). While the process will not be complete until the End, believers even now experience the Spirit as a kind of first fruits (Rom 8:23) of the full harvest to come. Just as those under the power of sin were bound to transgress the law (Rom 7:14–20), so those who 'walk according to the Spirit' are enabled to 'fulfil' 'the just requirement of the law' (v. 4).

In contrast to the juridical language of justification by faith, this language of participation in Christ permeates the letters, functioning as the touchstone for ethics (e.g. Rom 6:1–11; Gal 5:16–26) and the fundamental first principle for dealing with community problems (e.g. 1 Cor 6:15–20; 10:14–22). If we begin here, we will be able to make much better sense of Paul than if we take justification by faith as the centre and starting-point. Faith is still fundamental, though what it does in the first instance is to open the door for the believer's incorporation into Christ.

14. In this portrayal of Paul's thought, Judaism comes into the picture not as an example of the wrong kind of religion: rather, in Paul's reinterpretation of Torah-religion, Israel becomes the place where the nature of the human plight was clarified and the decisive act of God's solution was carried out. Israel's role, as Paul understands it, was to be a kind of representative sample of the whole of humankind, in both plight and salvation. Within Israel, the Torah functioned to define and reveal sin (Rom 5:20; 7:7, 13), so that it could be clearly seen that all were under its power and subject to death; within Israel, Christ appeared to confront and defeat sin, so that all could be liberated from its power and share in the glory of the age to come. As a representative (Rom 11:1–6) of this representative sample, Paul felt himself called to announce this liberation to the nations out of which Israel had been called in the first place.

This is far from being even a sketch of Paul's theology; a rough outline of one section of a sketch would be more accurate. Still, if the letters cannot be understood without some sense of the convictional and theological levels operating beneath the surface, this sketch of a sketch might provide the reader with a bit of a glimpse of what might be going on beneath the surface and giving shape to what appears above.

I. The Collection and Enduring Significance of the Letters. 1. It was observed above that we have been able to arrive at a better understanding of Paul's letters by comparing them with ordinary letters of his own day, noting not only the similarities but also the differences. In addition to the differences already discussed, there is one further difference between Philemon, say, and Apion's letter to his father Epimachus (discussed above) that deserves reflection. The issue is that of preservation. That we are able to read the papyri

letters at all is purely due to happenstances of survival and discovery—the favourable Egyptian climate and the chancy circumstances of archaeological investigation. Paul's letters, by contrast, have been deliberately preserved by generations of reading communities that have continued to find them meaningful and have each taken great care to preserve them and hand them on to the next. Consequently the 'meaning' of these texts cannot be restricted to the limited confines of the original reading event. These texts have had a significant afterlife, continuing to speak in fresh ways to new situations, and this afterlife has added its own successive layers of meaning that hover like an aura around the texts as we read them today.

2. The actual process by which Paul's letters were collected in the first place can be only dimly discerned (Gamble 1975; 1985). That they have survived at all seems to indicate that they were preserved by their original recipients; the only other option—that Paul and his associates preserved a 'master file' of letters—is ruled out both by the absence of some letters (e.g. the one mentioned in 1 Cor 5:9) and by evidence that suggests the gradual emergence of a standard collection rather than the existence of a fixed corpus of letters from the outset (Gamble 1975). The reference in 2 Pet 3:16, along with the writings of Clement of Rome, Ignatius, and Polycarp, indicate that by the late first and early second centuries most of Paul's letters were known and were being cited as authoritative texts, though there is no indication of the shape or extent of the collection. The first extant list of Pauline writings is that of the 'heretic' Marcion in the mid-second century, a list containing all but the Pastorals. The Pastorals are included, however, in lists drawn up later in the century by Irenaeus, Tertullian, and Clement of Alexandria. These three authors also contributed significantly to the concept of a Christian canon of scripture, consisting of a set of 'apostolic' writings existing alongside the Scriptures originating with Israel; the terms 'Old' and 'New Testament' (the Latin equivalent of 'covenant') were contributed by the Latin writer Tertullian. By the end of the second century, then, the thirteen letters contained in our New Testament had been collected into a single Pauline corpus that formed part of a larger (though still somewhat fluid) collection of authoritative Christian Scripture.

3. This process of canonization represents a dramatic shift in the context within which these letters were read. At the outset, neither Paul nor his intended readers saw the letters as 'Scripture', even though Paul wrote both out of the conviction that God had 'spoken' in a new way in Christ (revelation being one component in the concept of 'Scripture'), and with a sense of divinely granted authority (a second component). No doubt these were factors in the initial preservation of the letters. But what happened next? In the absence of any hard data between the 50s and the 90s of the first century, there is room for a variety of possibilities. Some argue for a Pauline school—associates and later followers of Paul, who made collections of the letters in order to study the thought of the master, producing new letters to synthesize his thought (e.g. Ephesians) or to bring his voice to bear on new situations (the Pastorals). Others suggest that it was the publication of the Acts of the Apostles that produced a renewed interest in Paul and led churches to dig the letters out of the archives and copy them for circulation. Edgar Goodspeed and his followers (e.g. Knox 1959) link this with the imaginative idea that the one primarily responsible for the collection was none other than Onesimus, the slave for whose benefit the letter to Philemon was written. This theory rests on two (not completely implausible) suppositions: that the Onesimus of Philemon is the same person referred to by Ignatius (c.110CE) as bishop of Ephesus; and that the inclusion of the short, semi-personal letter to Philemon in the Pauline corpus requires some explanation. It is more probable, however, that the process of collection was both a more continuous and a more haphazard affair, with different collections emerging in different local settings through the latter part of the first century.

4. In any case, the basic fact is clear that the letters survived not because the early church was interested in preserving an archival record of its origins, but because those who first read the letters over the shoulders, as it were, of the original recipients felt that the letters transcended their original settings and had continuing meaning for readers and situations beyond the original context. While our understanding of the letters has been richly enhanced by careful scholarly reconstruction of their original contexts, it should not therefore be supposed (though a perusal of much scholarly literature suggests that it often has been supposed) that the question of the meaning of these texts is exhausted when a full recovery of this 'original meaning' is attained. At least three additional layers or dimensions of meaning need to be recognized.

5. The first is the canonical context. While the letters were first written as individual items of communication—part of an ongoing dialogue between Paul and the community in question, to be sure, but to be read independently of any other letter from Paul—they have been preserved in a canonical collection of which they are an integral part (Childs 1984). At least in the context of the church, then, one cannot read Galatians, say, with its polemical and extreme language about (some aspects of) Torah-centred religion, without reference to the more tempered and generous language of Romans. Likewise, the negative view of marriage in 1 Cor 7 has to be read alongside the more positive depiction in Eph 5; even if Ephesians is not by Paul himself, these texts have been preserved for us by a tradition that makes no distinction whatsoever between Pauline and Deutero-Pauline or post-Pauline literature.

6. To say this, of course, is to say nothing about how one goes about resolving tensions among the members of the collection; there are no rules to say that Romans trumps Galatians or that Eph 5 is to be preferred over 1 Cor 7 (or vice versa in either case). Tension and interpretative difficulty come with the canonical territory, even more so when the rest of the canon is brought into play (as indeed it should be). Of course, we can read the letters in isolation from each other if we choose to do so. But they have been preserved only as part of a collection where they are presented to us as 'the epistles of Saint Paul'. This process of canonization, then, is not simply the ecclesiastical equivalent of the dry sands of Egypt—a historical happenstance that has effected the preservation of these letters but that is extrinsic to their meaning. Intrinsic to the process of preservation is the development of a framework of meaning within which the letters have been handed on to subsequent generations.

7. This leads to a second 'value-added' stage in the process. Subsequent generations have not simply handed on the texts in their canonical framework of meaning. Each generation of Christian readers has engaged in the process of scriptural interpretation—of reading these letters within this framework in order both to enter more deeply into the text and to bring it to bear on the situations and circumstances of their own day. Scriptural interpretation is of necessity a collaborative and corporate exercise, but one that is impoverished when the voices of previous generations of interpreters are left out of the discussion. Recently there has been a revival of interest in the history of interpretation, evidenced for example by the series Ancient Christian Commentary on Scripture (Inter Varsity Press) and Pilgrim Classic Commentaries (Pilgrim Press), and this is helping to bring these voices back to the interpretative table.

8. But this is not the only way in which the transmission of Paul's letters through the years has generated levels of meaning that accompany them into the present. The Bible has existed not simply as an interpretative object; it has been a kind of subject or agent as well, impacting—indeed, shaping in fundamental ways—the culture in which it has been transmitted to us. One cannot come to a full understanding of Paul's letters without recognizing the social and cultural effects they have had. This type of study is still in its early stages (see, e.g., the series *Romans through History and Culture*, T & T Clark) but examples spring readily to mind. We have already observed at the outset of this essay the role played by the Epistle to the Romans in the conversions of Augustine, Martin Luther, and John Wesley. These conversions are significant not only for their own sake, but also for their farreaching social and historical consequences—Augustine and the 'introspective conscience of the West' (Stendahl 1976), Luther and the Reformation, Wesley and the evangelical revivals in Great Britain and the New World. It would take whole volumes of books to trace the historical consequences of Paul and his letters in these events alone.

9. To take another, quite different, example: during archaeological excavation of the city of Caesarea Maritima, a mosaic floor was discovered in a building dating from the Byzantine period (6th cent. CE) that originally served some public and bureaucratic function. The mosaic contained the text of Rom 13:3: 'Do you wish to have no reason to fear the authority? Then do what is good, and you will received its approval.' Here, probably not for the first time and certainly not the last, statements from Paul's letter to the church in Rome were used by ruling powers to encourage submission to the state. The role of this text in eliciting and reinforcing the church's acquiescence to the policies of the Nazi regime in Germany is a more extreme example of the same power of texts to shape social realities, for good or ill. The fact that the text was being misinterpreted in the process—what he said to the Roman Christians notwithstanding, Paul was quite prepared to engage in activity that the state considered disruptive enough to justify his arrest and imprisonment (2 Cor 11:23)—in no way diminishes the point.

10. The point could be elaborated at great length, and there is much interesting work waiting to be done on the epistles of Paul as factors in social history. But the most important thing to be said about the letters as subjects, as agents accomplishing effects, is that the potential for their functioning in this way is present every time they are read anew. In any fresh encounter with these texts they bring to the event the evocative power of their rhetorical voice, along with the reverberating echoes of the processes of meaning-production that have preserved them and brought them to us. We bring to the event our own personal subjectivities, along with whatever we have come to know about the texts themselves, the circumstances lying behind them, the structures of thought and conviction lying beneath them, and the history of preservation, interpretation, and effective agency opening up in front of them. What comes out of the encounter, happily, has often been unpredictable and full of rich surprise. Paul would call it grace.

REFERENCES

Ascough, R. S. (1997), *What Are They Saying About the Formation of Pauline Churches?* (New York: Paulist).

Aune, D. E. (1987), *The New Testament in its Literary Environment* (Philadelphia: Westminster).

Beker, C. (1980), *Paul the Apostle: The Triumph of God in Life and Thought* (Philadelphia: Fortress).

Betz, H. D. (1979). *Galatians: A Commentary on Paul's Letter to the Churches in Galatia*. Hermeneia (Philadelphia: Fortress).

Bockmuehl, M. (1995), 'A Commentator's Approach to the "Effective History" of Phillipians', *JSNT* 60: 57–88.

Brown, R. E. (1997), *An Introduction to the New Testament* (New York: Doubleday).

Bruce, F. F. (1977), *Paul: Apostle of the Heart Set Free* (Grand Rapids: Eerdmans).

Childs, B. S. (1984), *The New Testament as Canon: An Introduction* (London: SCM).

Deissmann, A. (1910), *Light from the Ancient East: The New Testament Illustrated by Recently Discovered Texts of the Graeco-Roman World* (London: Hodder & Stoughton).

Donaldson, T. L. (1994), ' "The Gospel that I Proclaim among the Gentiles" (Gal 2:2): Universalistic or Israel-Centred?', in L. Ann Jervis and Peter Richardson (eds.), *Gospel in Paul: Studies on Corinthians, Galatians and Romans for Richard N. Longenecker*,

JSNTSup 108 (Sheffield: Sheffield Academic Press), 166–93.

—— (1997), *Paul and the Gentiles: Remapping the Apostle's Convictional World* (Minneapolis: Fortress).

—— (2006), ' "The Field God Has Assigned": Geography and Mission in Paul', in Leif Vaage (ed.), *Religious Rivalries in the Early Roman Empire and the Rise of Christianity*, (ESCJ 18; Waterloo, ON: Wilfrid Laurier University Press), pp. 109–37.

—— (2007), *Judaism and the Gentiles: Jewish Patterns of Universalism (to 135 CE)*, (Waco, TX: Baylor University Press).

Dunn, J. D. G. (1988), *Romans*, WBC (2 vols: Waco, Tex.: Word).

—— (1998), *The Theology of Paul the Apostle* (Grand Rapids: Eerdmans).

Elliott, J. H. (1990), 'Paul, Galatians and the Evil Eye'. *CurTM* 17:262–73.

Funk, R. W. (1967), 'The Apostolic Parousia: Form and Significance', in W. R. Farmer, C. F. D. Moule, and R. R. Niebuhr (eds.), *Christian History and Interpretation: Studies Presented to John Knox* (Cambridge: Cambridge University Press), 249–68.

Gamble, H. (1975), 'The Redaction of the Pauline Letters and the Formation of the Pauline Corpus', *JBL* 94: 403–18.

—— (1985), *The New Testament Canon: Its Making and Meaning* (Philadelphia: Fortress).

Haenchen, E. (1971), *The Acts of the Apostles: A Commentary* (Philadelphia: Westminster).

Hengel, M. (1991), *The Pre-Christian Paul* (London: SCM).

Hengel, M., and Schwemer, A. M. (1997), *Paul between Damascus and Antioch: The Unknown Years* (Louisville, KY.: Westminster/John Knox).

Hock, R. F. (1980), *The Social Context of Paul's Ministry: Tentmaking and Apostleship* (Philadelphia: Fortress).

Hurd, J. C. (1965), *The Origin of 1 Corinthians* (New York: Seabury).

Kennedy, G. A. (1984), *New Testament Interpretation through Rhetorical Criticism* (Chapel Hill, NC: University of North Carolina Press).

Knox, J. (1950), *Chapters in a Life of Paul* (New York/Nashville: Abingdon-Cokesbury).

—— (1959), *Philemon among the Letters of Paul* (Nashville, Tenn.: Abingdon).

—— (1964), 'Romans 15:14–33 and Paul's Conception of His Apostolic Mission', *JBL* 83: 1–11.

Kümmel, W. G. (1929), *Römer 7 und die Bekehrung des Paulus* (Leipzig: Hinrichs).

Longenecker, R. N. (1990), *Galatians*, WBC (Waco, Tex.: Word).

Lüdemann, G. (1984), *Paul Apostle to the Gentiles: Studies in Chronology* (London: SCM).

Mack, B. L. (1990), *Rhetoric and the New Testament* (Minneapolis: Fortress).

Meeks, W. A. (1983), *The First Urban Christians: The Social World of the Apostle Paul* (New Haven: Yale University Press).

Montefiore, C. (1914), *Judaism and St. Paul: Two Essays* (London: Max Goschen).

Muggeridge, M., and Vidler, A. (1972), *Paul: Envoy Extraordinary* (London: Collins).

Murphy-O'Connor, J. (1996), *Paul: A Critical Life* (Oxford: Clarendon).

Rambo, L. R. (1993), *Understanding Religious Conversion* (New Haven: Yale University Press).

Ramsay, W. M. (1907), *St. Paul the Traveller and the Roman Citizen*, 9th edn. (London: Hodder & Stoughton).

Riesner, R. (1998), *Paul's Early Period: Chronology, Mission, Strategy, Theology* (Grand Rapids: Eerdmans).

Roetzel, C. J. (1998), *The Letters of Paul: Conversations in Context*, 4th edn. (Louisville, Ky.: Westminster/John Knox).

Sanders, E. P. (1977), *Paul and Palestinian Judaism: A Comparison of Patterns of Religion* (Philadelphia: Fortress).

Schoeps, H.-J. (1961), *Paul: The Theology of the Apostle in the Light of Jewish Religious History* (Philadelphia: Westminster).

Scott, J. M. (1995), *Paul and the Nations*, WUNT 84 (Tübingen: Mohr [Siebeck]).

Segal, A. F. (1990), *Paul the Convert: The Apostolate and Apostasy of Saul the Pharisee* (New Haven: Yale University Press).

Stark, R. (1996), *The Rise of Christianity: A Sociologist Reconsiders History* (Princeton: Princeton University Press).

Stendahl, K. (1976), *Paul among Jews and Gentiles, and other Essays* (Philadelphia: Fortress).

Stowers, S. K. (1986), *Letter Writing in Greco-Roman Antiquity* (Philadelphia: Westminster).

Townsend, J. T. (1985), 'Missionary Journeys in Acts and European Missionary Societies', *Society of Biblical Literature Seminar Papers*, 433–7.

Watson, F. (1986), *Paul, Judaism and the Gentiles*, SNTSMS 56 (Cambridge: Cambridge University Press).

Weima, J. A. D. (1994), *Neglected Endings: The Significance of the Pauline Letter Closings*, JSNTSup 101 (Sheffield: Sheffield Academic Press).

White, J. L. (1972), *The Form and Function of the Body of the Greek Letter* (Missoula, Mont.: SBL).

4. Romans

CRAIG C. HILL

INTRODUCTION

A. Significance. Romans is one of the eminent texts of Western history. From Augustine to Luther, from Wesley to Barth, Christian thinkers of every era have been shaped profoundly by this, the longest Pauline epistle. Romans is commonly regarded as Paul's supreme work, the consummate expression of his mature theology. Among Protestants in particular, no book has been more highly esteemed or carefully scrutinized. Above all, Romans influenced the Reformation vision of true religion as the reception of God's grace through faith. In equal and opposite reaction, however, Romans has unwittingly encouraged generations of readers from Marcion onwards to regard Judaism as the exemplarily *false* religion, a creed of merit and system of works unworthy of devotion or even of toleration. The first of these conclusions lies at the heart of Protestant–Catholic debate, the second at the centre of Jewish–Christian controversy. Not surprisingly, Roman Catholics have long questioned Protestant readings of Romans (paralleling in some ways the canonical protest of Jas 2:14–26), as Jews have long challenged the epistle's characterization of their theology. Only recently, as a consequence of post-Vatican II ecumenicity and post-Holocaust interreligious awareness, have the earlier interpretative models begun to break apart. The willingness of major scholars to cross traditional boundaries and weigh old criticisms with new seriousness is undoubtedly the most important development in modern Pauline studies. Thus, now as in the past, Romans is at the forefront of Christian theological reflection and self-understanding.

B. Provenance. 1. The Pauline authorship of Romans is not in doubt. Indeed, one might say that Romans is the 'most Pauline' epistle, since it most influences scholarly construals of Paul and most frequently is referenced in arguments about the (in)authenticity of the Deutero-Pauline letters. Also, compared to other Pauline epistles (notably Philippians and 2 Corinthians), few doubts arise concerning the literary integrity of Romans. The unity of the letter is seriously questioned only at ch. 16, which some regard as the remnant of a separate Pauline letter, appended to Romans' original conclusion in 15:33. The evidence for this view is not compelling, as is noted in the commentary on ch. 16.

2. Romans was probably composed in Corinth during Paul's final visit. Gaius, 'whose hospitality I and the whole church here enjoy' (16:23, NIV), is presumably the same figure mentioned in 1 Cor 1:14. In 15:23–33, Paul anticipates an imminent journey to Jerusalem, an itinerary that corresponds broadly to Acts 20:1–21:17. Thus, widespread consensus exists for dating Romans in the mid-50s CE, making it one of Paul's final letters (at least subsequent to his Thessalonian, Galatian, and Corinthian correspondence).

3. The letter is written 'to all God's beloved in Rome' (1:7). The city of Rome was the seat of government of the Roman republic (?5th cent.–31 BCE) and empire until 330 CE, when Constantine moved the capital to Constantinople. During the second and first centuries BCE, Rome gradually came to dominate the countries of the Mediterranean basin, including Judea, which was conquered in 63 BCE by the Roman general Pompey. The city of Rome was vast, home to approximately 1 million persons. Augustus and subsequent emperors erected monumental public works, including amphitheatres, squares, temples, forums, and libraries. Although the wealthy inhabited comfortable villas, the great majority of people were poor and lived in large tenement houses, some as tall as six storeys (*HBC* 882). The Jewish community of Rome was substantial; it is estimated that between 20,000 and 50,000 Jews lived in the city by the beginning of the first century CE (*ABD* 1048). How or when Christianity came to Rome is unknown. By mid-century, when Paul wrote Romans, the church already enjoyed a substantial reputation (1:8). A dispute within the Jewish community over Christian claims appears to stand behind the Emperor Claudius's expulsion of the Jews from Rome in 49 CE (see Acts 18:2). According to Suetonius (*Claudius*, 25.4), 'the Jews constantly made disturbances at the instigation of Chrestus', probably a mistaken form of the word Christus (Christ). Local Christians were sufficient in number and reputation in 64 CE that Nero could scapegoat them for the fire of Rome. 'Nero fastened the guilt and afflicted the most exquisite tortures on a class hated for their abominations, called Christians by the populace' (Tacitus, *Annals*, 15.44.2).

C. Literary Genre. Formally, Romans is identical to most other Pauline letters, including a salutation (identifying sender and recipients), a thanksgiving (clarifying the relationship between writer and reader and previewing the contents of the letter), a body (offering the substance of Paul's communication), and a farewell (including a final blessing and, if ch. 16 is genuine, personal greetings). In numerous other ways, however, Romans is different—as one might expect, knowing that it is the only Pauline letter written to a church neither founded by the apostle or his assistants, nor visited by him (note e.g. the lengthy self-descriptions in 1:1–6 and 15:16–21, and the deferential language of 1:11–13 and 15:22–4). The hallmark of Paul's other letters is their contingency; characteristically, they deal with specific issues that arose within a particular Pauline church (e.g. 1 Cor 1:11: 'For it has been reported to me by Chloe's people that there are quarrels among you'; 1 Cor 7:1: 'Now concerning the matters about which you wrote…'). Reading these letters is not unlike overhearing one side of a conversation. Clearly, this analogy does not apply to Romans, which is more declamation than dialogue. The letter does not address in any obvious way the Roman church's own problems. It is a single, extended theological argument, not a seriatim discussion of pastoral concerns. It thus is a letter more in form than in function. For this reason, Romans is categorized as, for example, an 'epistle' (as distinct, according to Deissmann (1927: 220), from a non-literary 'letter'), a 'Greek letter-essay' (Stirewalt 1977), an 'essay-letter' (Fitzmyer 1993), or an 'ambassadorial letter' (Jewett, cited by Fitzmyer 1993: 68–9). All such labels make the point that Romans was commissioned to a somewhat different service than the other Pauline letters. To what service, exactly, is one of the perennial issues of Pauline scholarship.

D. Purpose. 1. Paul offers few clues as to his purpose in writing to the church at Rome. He states in 1:10–11 that he prays for the Roman Christians and longs to see them, 'that I may share with you some spiritual gift to strengthen you—or rather so that we may be mutually encouraged by each other's faith… [and] that I may reap some harvest among you as I have among the rest of the Gentiles.' In 15:15, he states that 'on some points I have written to you rather boldly by way of reminder, because of the grace given me by God to be a minister of Christ Jesus to the Gentiles in the priestly service of the gospel of God, so that the offering of the Gentiles may be acceptable, sanctified by the Holy Spirit.' In 15:23–9, Paul informs his readers of his travel plans: he soon will deliver the collection to 'the saints at Jerusalem' and then visit Rome on his way to Spain, where he will engage in further missionary work (v. 20). He hopes not only to see the Roman Christians but also 'to be sent on by you, once I have enjoyed your company for a little while' (v. 24). Similarly, in vv. 28–9, Paul states that 'I know that when I come to you, I will come in the fullness of the blessing of Christ.' In 15:30–1, Paul urges his readers to pray for the success of his impending trip to Jerusalem, 'so that by God's will I may come to you with joy and be refreshed in your company.' Taken together, these statements probably indicate that Paul hoped to win the support of the Roman church for his missionary venture in Spain, and that as 'minister to the Gentiles' (Gal 2:7), he assumed a measure of pastoral responsibility for the Gentile Christians in what was, after all, the greatest city of the known world. The letter thus would have both strategic and didactic functions, to introduce and recommend Paul, and to teach and exhort his readers in the Christian faith, as Paul understood it.

2. Could not Paul have met these objectives in fewer than the 7,000 words of Romans? Was there some larger task, demanding a more extensive response? The traditional explanation is to regard Romans as Paul's theological 'last will and testament', a summary of his theology composed near the end of his career. But Paul expected both an ongoing apostolic occupation and an approaching eschatological consummation (13:11–12). Moreover, Romans is *not* a good compendium of Pauline teaching; much that is contained in Paul's other letters is absent. Why did Paul write at such length about these particular issues, most notably, the law and Judaism? Scholars have looked both to Paul's own circumstances and to the circumstances of the Roman church for answers.

3.1. What do we know about Paul's situation that might be relevant to the composition of Romans? Surely the most important datum is the recent, bitter controversy at Galatia; the letter to the Galatians includes most of the primary topics and much of the key language of Romans. Many scholars date Philippians even closer to Romans (55 CE, according to Jewett 1979). Phil 3 (probably a warning based on Paul's Galatian experience; see Hill 1992: 155–8) is reminiscent of both Galatians and Romans ('flesh...circumcision...zeal...righteousness under the Law', etc.). Thus the theology of Romans does not appear *ex nihilo*. Paul had ample cause to weigh these matters and to regard them as both important and urgent.

3.2. A second key factor is Paul's awareness of the relative failure of the church's 'Jewish mission' (Gal 2:7–8). Paul speaks of his 'sorrow and unceasing anguish' for his 'kindred according to the flesh' (9:2). It is clear that Jewish unbelief is a theological and not just a personal problem for Paul. God acted in Christ to fulfil divine promises to Israel, but the concrete result is a Gentile church. Can God be *righteous*, faithful to God's own nature and commitments, and not save Israel? (Indeed, God's righteousness is the unifying theme of the entire letter. See ROM 1:16–17.) In the face of his impending trip to Jerusalem, the problem must have appeared acute. Has God failed? And is not Paul, who calls Gentiles 'children of Abraham' (4:16) and who says that 'Christ is the end of the law' (10:4), the enemy of Israel? Is Paul's a *righteous* gospel? Hays (1989: 35) has noted with insight that Romans is 'an intertextual conversation between Paul and the voice of Scripture' in which the apostle 'labors to win the blessing of Moses and the prophets'. Gentile biblical scholarship has tended to de-Judaize Paul, thereby trivializing these struggles and rendering the central place of Rom 9–11 (on the fate of Israel) nonsensical.

3.3. A number of scholars have argued that it is Paul's impending trip to Jerusalem that most influenced his writing of Romans (e.g. Manson 1948, Jervell 1971). It is evident from 15:30–2 that Paul himself anticipated trouble in Jerusalem. Accordingly, Romans is often seen as a rehearsal of the arguments that Paul would make on his own behalf in Jerusalem. The shape of this theory varies from scholar to scholar, depending mostly upon prior conclusions about the relationship between Paul and other Jewish Christians. Does 15:31 indicate that Paul would have to defend himself to the church as well as to the Jewish authorities of Jerusalem? If so, on what issues? F. C. Baur (1873–5: i. 109–51) asserted a century and a half ago that the leaders of the Jerusalem church (notably, Peter and James) actively opposed Paul for admitting uncircumcised Gentiles into the church. It is the heirs of Baur today who make the most of Paul's conflict with the Jerusalem church. By their reading, Paul's defence in Romans of the equality of Jew and Gentile is aimed squarely at the Jerusalem Christians. This presents a heroic, classically Protestant portrait of Paul as the lone champion of Christian freedom. Despite its popularity, this hypothesis is not corroborated by the New Testament. The only substantial evidence strongly supports the contrary view, that the Jerusalem church accepted Gentiles *qua* Gentiles as Christian believers (e.g. Gal. 2:1–10; Acts 15; see Hill 1992: 103–92). This does not mean that there was no disagreement between Paul and other Jewish–Christian leaders. Paul sanctioned disobedience by Jews of certain Jewish (particularly food) laws (see 1 Cor 9:20–1), an attitude that did not endear him to many in Israel, Christian or otherwise. It is instructive that it was over food laws that Paul confronted Peter at Antioch (Gal 2:11–14); it was not the circumcising of Gentiles that precipitated the crisis but the observing of dietary laws that, in Paul's mind, recreated the distinction between Jews and Gentiles. Likewise, it is the issue of law observance *on the part of Jewish Christians* that is mentioned in association with Paul's final visit to Jerusalem in Acts (21:21, 28). Also, one should bear in mind that Paul was bidding for the practical support of the Roman church. Interjecting a dispute with the mother church (whose authority Paul himself acknowledged; e.g. Gal 2:2) hardly seems politic. Moreover, any such self-defence is subtle to the point of invisibility (cf., by contrast, the defence of 2 Cor 11–13 or the record of his public confrontation in Gal 2:11–14). Therefore, while Paul's impending Jerusalem visit may have been a factor in his composition of Romans (as in ROM D.3.1), it is highly doubtful that Romans originated as an apologia directed at the Jerusalem church.

4. The other approach is to look to the circumstances of the letter's recipients for explanations. How much Paul knew about the situation in Rome is the subject of considerable debate. His most likely source of information was Priscilla and Aquila, who, according to Acts 18:2, came to Corinth from Rome as a consequence of Claudius' expulsion of the Jews (49 CE). They are mentioned by Paul himself in 1 Cor 16:19 and (if authentic) Rom 16:3. Also mentioned in ch. 16 are several other Roman Christians. Still, it is not obvious how Paul's acquaintance with such persons might have shaped this letter. Paul made a considerable effort to introduce himself and his gospel to the Roman church, a clear signal that he regarded his audience as strangers. Many scholars attempt to link the epistle's contents to a Roman context by suggesting that the Jewish believers who returned to Rome following

Claudius' death were not accorded due respect by their Gentile coreligionists, who even went so far as to deny positions of authority to returning Jewish leaders (Marxsen 1968: 95–104; Beker 1980: 69–74). Hearing of the Gentile Christians' conduct, Paul composed this letter, at least in part as an attempt to unify the Roman church. Passages such as 11:17–21 ('do not vaunt yourselves over the branches [the Jews]') were written to teach the Gentile believers proper humility. (In tension with this purpose is the tendency of these same scholars to equate the 'weak' of ch. 14 with returning Jewish believers who continued to observe food laws: see Dunn 1988: ii. 798; cf. the counter-argument in Nanos 1996: 85–165.) This reconstruction, while not impossible, is open to question at every point (see e.g. the strong challenge of Stowers 1994). The most that can be said with certainty is that Paul wanted to demonstrate that the Gentile church had not supplanted Israel, and therefore that Gentiles had no reason to boast in their present status (11:17–36). The argument could have been formulated in response to a Jewish–Gentile conflict in the Roman church, but such a conflict is not required to explain it. Perhaps Gentile Christians in the capital city faced special temptations to triumphalism, but that tendency could hardly have been unique, as subsequent history thoroughly demonstrates.

5. Knowing the context of a statement is of first importance in determining its meaning; unfortunately, such contextual data are substantially lacking with respect to Romans. Consequently, the inherently conjectural nature of one's interpretation should be acknowledged. Sufficient evidence exists to allow for the formation of fairly detailed hypotheses; sufficient gaps in that evidence ensure that even careful hypotheses will be substantially speculative. To a large degree, we do not know why this epistle was written, and any interpretation based upon the presumption of such knowledge will be inherently circular. Because the commentary below assumes no single 'reason for Romans', it will not attempt to advance one interpretation against all others. Instead, it will seek to delineate the plausible range of interpretation. This is an admittedly confined ambition, but one that corresponds to the real limitations within which any interpreter of Romans labours.

E. Issues of Interpretation. 1. A generation ago, one might have asserted that the exegesis of Romans was complete in its essentials, pointing to the common interpretative

tradition that extended from Augustine to Bultmann and Barth. Whatever consensus might have existed prior to 1977 was fractured by the publication that year of E. P. Sanders's *Paul and Palestinian Judaism* (see Räisänen 1983: 1–15; Dunn 1988: i. pp. lxiii–lxxii). Sanders offered a critique of Pauline scholarship based on two methodological assumptions: (1) a religion ought to be understood in its own terms through an analysis of its own primary sources; and (2) an author's argumentation must not be unnaturally synthesized by later expositors; contradictory statements and approaches, where they occur, should be allowed to remain (Sanders 1977: 12). Application of the first assumption leads one to question any construal of Judaism based on the often polemical references to it in Christian writings, including the NT. The popular picture of first-century Judaism as a religion of sterile legalism, supercilious piety, and haughty self-righteousness is not supported by *Jewish* documents. When allowed to speak for themselves, first-century Jews are not heard advocating a religion of merit, the photo-negative of a uniquely Christian notion of salvation by grace. Functionally, Judaism and Christianity are quite similar: one 'gets in' by means of God's gracious calling; one then is obligated (not least by gratitude) to obey the will of God, however defined. Obviously, regarding Judaism in this way necessitates a rethinking of Paul. For example, earlier interpreters could assume that Paul had formulated his ideas about the law in response to the legalism of normative Judaism. One school saw Paul's response as a correction of Jewish abuses; the law, no longer 'misused', was still valid (Cranfield 1979: 862). Others believed that Paul rejected out of hand any notion of the law's validity since he recognized that the law itself was a primary source of human alienation (Bultmann 1952–5: i. 247). Unfortunately, both approaches account for Paul's position by making reference to a Judaism that never existed. A popular counter-proposal suggests that Paul's target was not works righteousness at all but 'Jewish national [self-]righteousness' (e.g. Dunn 1988: i. pp. lxxi–lxxii, 42–3, etc.). This move appears to vindicate Paul—he is still right about what is wrong about Judaism—but it misses the point of Sanders's critique. In effect, it substitutes a new bad Judaism for the old, now discredited bad Judaism of traditional interpretation. But the problem is not in our (previously) faulty identification of Judaism's deficiency (whose depiction in Paul varies and so is infinitely interpretable); the problem is in Paul's either/or reasoning that requires that Judaism be nullified for Christ to be necessitated (see ROM E.6). Were the disorder Jewish pride, the remedy would be Jewish humility. But for Paul the only adequate curative is Christian faith, which means that the only actual complaint is Jewish unbelief, however variously it may be explained or characterized from the Christian side (see ROM 2).

2. It is at this point that the second methodological principle, that of taking apparently contradictory material at face value, has been fruitfully applied. What does it mean if Paul's arguments about the law do not entirely cohere? Among other things, it may indicate that Paul did not *think* his way to Christian faith, that his conclusions about the law are not the result of his own pre-Christian wrestling with its supposed inadequacies. As Sanders (1977: 442–7) put it, Paul 'reasoned backwards'. He did not move from consideration of the law to Christian faith; instead, having come to faith in Christ, Paul attempted to understand as a Jewish Christian the Judaism in which he had been raised. Thus Paul never was entirely able to repudiate the law. It was, after all, God's law and as such must serve a divine, albeit negative, purpose. Two fundamental convictions, that God is the God of Israel and that God provides salvation only in Christ, were thus held together in uneasy tension, and most of what is commonly considered under the rubric 'Paul and the Law' can be understood as part of an ongoing attempt to effect a reconciliation between the two.

3. If Judaism was not the false religion of works righteousness, if the law did not function within Judaism as a *means* to salvation, what are we to make of Paul's argument? It may be claimed that Paul has set up Judaism as a straw man, the foil to all that is deemed good and true in Christianity. It seems more reasonable, however, to think that Paul is describing something quite real: not Judaism as non-Christian Jews knew it but Judaism as it would be experienced by Paul's Gentile-Christian converts. Within Judaism, one was not circumcised to *earn* membership in the people of God. Instead, circumcision marked a son of Israel's participation in God's gracious, pre-existing covenant. The situation is wholly different, however, if the subject is an adult Gentile Christian. If he accepted circumcision under compulsion, he would, by implication, be saying that his faith in Christ is insufficient to save, an inadequate basis for

participation in God's covenant. For him circumcision would therefore become a work, and Judaism a religion of works righteousness. (The same dilemma occurs when an adult Christian joins a denomination that does not recognize his or her baptism. For that person, baptism becomes an entry requirement, an indispensable 'work', however it may be construed theologically by existing church members.) Paul's argument, including his tendency to oppose the law and Christian faith as antithetical religious systems, makes a good deal more sense when viewed in this way. This does require, however, that we no longer regard Paul as an objective, disinterested observer of Judaism.

4. Other distinctive aspects of Paul's thought bear significantly on our understanding of Romans. The first concerns Pauline eschatology. In general, Paul has a decidedly future or 'not yet' orientation, reminiscent of the Gospel of Mark. In the undisputed Pauline epistles, salvation is always a future category; the paradigm of present Christian life is the cross, not the resurrection (e.g. 1 Cor 1:18; 2:2; Rom 6:5; 8:18). Present experience of the Spirit is a foretaste or seal (2 Cor 1:22) of what is to come (1 Cor 13:8–12). There is one very important exception, however, one issue in relation to which Paul consistently invokes a realized eschatology: the Gentiles. For Paul, the prophetic expectation that Gentiles would be incorporated into Israel in the last days is already being fulfilled, not least in his own ministry. (Note, for example, how Paul's description in Rom 15:25–6—see also the quotations in vv. 9–12—draws on Isa 66:18–22.) In Rom 11:25–7 Paul explains this 'mystery': present Jewish unbelief has effected a reversal of the eschatological timetable; contrary to expectation, it is the Gentiles who will enter first, after which God will act to save 'all Israel'. Much of what is peculiar to Pauline theology is derived from this perspective: admission of Gentiles is not foreshadow; it is substance. That puts Pauline theology on a fundamentally different footing from that of other Jewish-Christian leaders, and it explains how both Paul and the 'pillar apostles' (James, Cephas, and John: Gal 2:9) could have agreed to the practice of Gentile admission while utterly disagreeing as to its consequences. If there is now one people in Christ, without distinction between Jew and Gentile (Gal 3:28), then the church exists in a radically new age, from which one can radically critique what went before—especially the law, whose very stipulations drew the boundaries between Jew and Gentile. (An inevitable consequence of a realized eschatology is an increased sense of theological distance between insiders and outsiders, especially between Christians and (non-Christian) Jews; note the many pejorative references to 'the Jews' and 'the world' in Johannine literature.) The categories of Paul's thought that are derivative of the 'Gentile issue' share in the same logic, e.g. Paul's idealized Christian anthropology, according to which believers are *essentially* different from other people: they 'walk in the Spirit' and so fulfil the 'just requirements of the law' (Rom 8:4). It is always worth asking what reality Paul presupposes within a given argument. When a question relates in some way to Gentile admission, Paul's thinking shifts towards realized eschatological categories, a fact that explains many of the ambiguities within Pauline theology and the tensions between Pauline theory and practice.

5. It is important to note that Paul worked with the concepts available to him. Chief among these is the idea that the law is a single entity, given by God. This presents Paul with an insuperable difficulty. He knows by God's acceptance of Gentiles (demonstrated by gifts of the Spirit; Gal 3:2–5) that obedience to laws that distinguish Jews from Gentiles (namely circumcision, food laws, sabbath and other 'days') is no longer required. However, the law being a unity, it is necessary to challenge it *in toto*. In theory, this is no problem, because Christians possess the Spirit and have no need for a 'written code' (2:27). In practice, what Paul expects of his converts is a fairly typical Jewish morality, which he can assume for himself but which comes less naturally to his Gentile associates. Consequently, Paul is put in the awkward position of legislating rules of behaviour *ad hoc*, since he no longer has the law to draw upon for authorization. Therefore, he is forced, in effect, to reinstitute Jewish laws with Christian warrants (e.g. see Rom 1:20; 1 Cor 6:15–17; and 10:20–1). Thus it is erroneous to suppose that Paul created a law-free religion. Christianity, like Judaism, has always had norms (again, mostly Jewish); for that reason, Christians, as much as Jews, can be guilty of reducing religion to rule-keeping. In short, it is quite possible that the argument of Romans would have looked very different had Paul been able to divide the law explicitly into categories (clarifying what is rejected and what is retained), as Christians ever since the second century (e.g. *Epistle of Barnabas*) have attempted to do. Certainly, subsequent Christian ambivalence—even animosity—towards the Hebrew Bible would have been lessened had Paul taken such a course.

6. Finally, it is vital to understand that Paul consistently organized the relationship between Judaism and Christianity in such a way that non-Christian Judaism *must* be negated. Gal 2:21 reveals a great deal about the working of Paul's mind: 'I do not nullify the grace of God; for if justification comes through the law, then Christ died for nothing.' In other words, it is a zero-sum game. If God intended to save through Christ, it must have been necessary; therefore, one could not be saved apart from Christ, that is to say, through the regular practice of Jewish religion. The either/or structure of Paul's argument explains an otherwise astonishing fact: were Romans our only source, we might well conclude that Jewish theology knew nothing of mercy, grace, love, forgiveness, or atonement. As the logic stands, these necessarily become Christian categories (as do 'grace and truth' in Jn 1:17). It is interesting to note that Paul cited God's acceptance of Abraham on the basis of faith in both Gal 3 and Rom 4 and then passed in silence over virtually all subsequent Jewish history (the mention of David in Rom 4:6 being a rare exception). Needless to say, the existence of any pre- or non-Christian Judaism in which one might find right relationship with God creates a severe problem for Paul. On the one hand, he wants to argue that God saves only in Christ and that Judaism, apart from Christ, is a way of 'sin' and 'death' (Rom 7:9–11); on the other hand, Paul feels compelled to cite precedents in Judaism for God's saving *modus operandi*. The question is, can one have it both ways? Paul might have argued on the basis of essential continuity: the God of the Jews, always a God of salvation, has worked this saving purpose ultimately in Christ (an argument somewhat similar to that of Hebrews). Instead, Paul's argument traces the line of essential discontinuity, which is precisely what Marcion and other despisers of Judaism have found congenial in his thinking. One must ask if it is possible to affirm what Paul affirms (the religion of grace) without necessarily denying what Paul implicitly denies (that Judaism itself is such a religion).

COMMENTARY

Salutation (1:1–17)

Although the basic shape of the salutation is the same in all Paul's letters (an indication of the sender(s) and recipient(s) followed by a short blessing), the form is flexible and was adapted by Paul to each letter's purpose. For example, Paul wrote Galatians in part as a defence of his divinely sanctioned apostolic authority; thus he identifies himself as 'an apostle neither by human commission nor from human authorities' (Gal 1:1). The salutation in Romans is distinguished by its lengthy description of 'the gospel of God' for which Paul was set apart (vv. 2–6). Such details establish Paul's credentials and identify common ground with his audience.

As in Phil 1:1, Paul refers to himself as a 'slave' or 'servant' (*doulos*) of Jesus Christ (a designation paralleled, for example, in Jas 1:1, 2 Pet 1:1, Jude 1). It was customary for Jews to regard themselves or their leaders as 'servants of God' (Ps 19:11; 27:9; Neh 1:6; 2 Kings 18:12; Isa 20:3; Jer 7:25; Deut 32:36; etc.), and Israel itself is frequently identified as God's servant (Jer 46:27; Ezek 28:25; Isa 44:1, 45:4; etc.) (Dunn 1988: i. 7). The Christological appropriation of OT language about God is a consistent and revealing feature of the NT writings (e.g. cf. Phil 2:10–11; Isa 45:23). Also noteworthy is Paul's tendency to balance a statement about Christ with a statement about God. He wished the Romans 'grace ... and peace from [both] God our Father and the Lord Jesus Christ' (v. 7); likewise, Paul mentioned that he was 'set apart for the gospel of God ... [which is] concerning his Son' (vv. 1, 3) and offered thanks to 'God through Jesus Christ for all of you' (v. 8; cf. Rom 8:9: 'Spirit of God ... Spirit of Christ').

The mention of prophets, scriptures, and David (vv. 2–3) sounds a deliberate note of continuity with Israel's past. The connection between Paul's contemporary proclamation to Gentiles and God's ancient promises to Israel is of central importance in Romans (see esp. chs. 9–11). (On the plural 'scriptures', see Hays 1989: 34).

Many scholars think that the core of vv. 3–4 came from pre-Pauline Christian tradition, possibly in the form of an early Christological formulation (Byrne 1996: 43; Dodd 1932: 4–5). A pair of descriptions of the Son are set in parallel, distinguished by the contrasting Pauline terms 'flesh' and 'spirit':

who was descended from David *according to the flesh*
and was declared to be Son of God with power *according to the spirit* of holiness
by resurrection from the dead

Jesus' human or earthly ('according to the flesh') status as a descendant of David (see 2

Sam 7:11–16; Davidic lineage is a staple of messianic texts: Isa 11; Jer 23:5–6; Ezek 34:23–4; etc.) is mentioned only here in Paul's writings but figures prominently elsewhere in the NT (e.g. Mt 1:1; 9:27; Mk 11:10; 12:35; Lk 1:27, 32; 2:4; 2 Tim 2:8; Rev 3:7; 5:5). Also lacking support elsewhere in Paul is the early Christian idea that Jesus was appointed or designated (*horisthentos*; see TDNT v. 450–1) Son of God at the resurrection (v. 4; cf. Acts 2:36; 5:30–1; 13:33). 'With power' (whether traditional or Pauline) probably modifies the title 'Son of God' and not the verb 'declared' (Fitzmyer 1993: 235; Cranfield 1979: 62; *contra* NIV 'declared with power'), emphasizing Jesus' exalted status. ('According to the spirit of holiness' is a Semitism; cf. Ps 51:11.) It also might indicate that, at least for Paul, the resurrection *enhanced* an already existing sonship (Dunn 1988: i. 14). In citing Jesus' twofold pedigree, in flesh and in spirit, Paul makes the claim that Jesus is the anticipated Jewish Messiah—and more (as in Mk 1:1). It is Paul's expectation that these common (and apparently longstanding) Christian affirmations will be shared by his readers.

The phrase 'obedience of faith' (also mentioned in 16:26) is ambiguous. It may refer either to faith that is an expression of obedience or to obedience that is an expression of faith. Possibly, Paul intended both meanings. Clearly it is the bringing of persons to faith in Christ that is the primary goal of the Pauline mission. It is no coincidence that Paul can refer synonymously to the Jews' unbelief in 11:20 and to their disobedience in 11:31 (Cranfield 1979: 66). Elsewhere in Romans, however, Paul uses 'obedience' in the more conventional sense (5:19; 6:16; 15:18; 16:19). An interesting parallel occurs in 2 Cor 9:13, where Paul says that the Corinthians' generosity is an expression of their 'obedience to the confession of the Gospel of Christ'. The fact that Paul includes in this mission the Roman Christians themselves (v. 6) indicates at the very least that he is talking about more than the evangelization of Gentiles.

'Grace to you and peace' is the typical Pauline greeting (1 Cor 1:3; 2 Cor 1:2; Gal 1:3; etc.; it is also used in 1 and 2 Pet 1:2 and Rev 1:4). It elegantly combines the Christian word 'grace', *charis* (replacing the similar Greek greeting *chairein*; cf. Acts 15:23; 23:26; Jas 1:1), and the Jewish greeting 'peace' (*šālôm*). It thus incorporates both Gentile and Semitic as well as Christian and Jewish elements.

Thanksgiving (1:8–17)

The thanksgiving is used here, as in Paul's other letters, to express goodwill towards his audience and to remind them of (or, in the case of Romans, to establish) the terms of their association, matters that fall broadly under the heading of 'relationship mainten-ance'. The thanksgiving also serves to intro-duce the reader to key ideas and terminology, deliberately signalling the letter's overarching themes (see e.g. 1 Cor 1:4–9; Phil 1:3–11; 1 Thess 1:2–3:13; Philem 4–7). It is to the thanksgiving that one should look first for an indication of Paul's own sense of purpose in writing. (The exception is Galatians, which—not sur-prisingly, given its polemical edge—contains no thanksgiving.)

(1:8–15) Relationship Maintenance Strictly spe-aking, Paul is establishing, not maintaining, his relationship with the Roman Christians; never-theless, he stresses that his interest in and con-cern for them are not new. He has long known of and prayed for the church at Rome and has been encouraged by reports of its faithfulness. Paul indicates his hope that he 'might at last succeed in coming' to Rome (v. 10). In v. 13 he states that 'I have often intended to come to you (but thus far have been prevented)'. Paul's journey to Rome is not an afterthought; his readers should not feel slighted. The reason for the delay is spelled out in 15:22–4: Paul's mis-sionary activity in Asia and Greece (that is, amongst 'the rest of the Gentiles', v. 13) had only recently been completed. Rome, the nat-ural destination of the 'apostle to the Gentiles' (Gal 2:7), is now fully in view.

The language of 1:1–15 is highly diplomatic. Paul balances assertions of his apostolic author-ity with statements concerning his regard for and reciprocity with the Roman Christians. Paul is not the founder of Roman Christianity and so cannot assume charge over it. It is worth noting, however, that even in Paul's own churches he had no real power. Paul could exercise authority only in so far as he could persuade his audience of his right to do so (the rhetoric of Galatians and 2 Corinthians providing the best examples; see Holmberg 1978: 193–204).

v. 14, instead of dividing humanity into 'Jew and Gentile' (or 'Jew and Greek', v. 16), on this one occasion Paul uses the standard Hellenistic categories 'Greeks and barbarians' (*TDNT* i. 546–53), which by this time had come to refer to 'all races and classes within the Gentile world' (Dunn 1988: i. 33). It is not clear whether 'wise and foolish' directly parallels 'Greeks and bar-barians' (cf. the opposing conclusions of Cran-field 1979: 83; Fitzmyer 1993: 251). In either case, the point is made that the gospel transcends such distinctions. Paul is a 'debtor' (i.e. 'one under obligation'), presumably by his calling, to proclaim the gospel to all Gentiles, includ-ing, of course, the Romans themselves. It is less likely that Paul also meant to express his per-sonal indebtedness to individual Gentiles (Mor-ris 1988: 63). A further point is that even the most cultured among the Gentiles is in need of the gospel and (in the light of v. 16, immedi-ately following) that the gospel is in no way threatened by human wisdom. (The contrast between earthly wisdom and divine power (v. 16) is especially prominent in 1 Corinthians, e.g. 1:18–19; 2:4–5.)

(1:16–17) Theme Paul advances now to a state-ment of his theme: God saves all (both Jew and Greek) in the same way (by faith) by the same means (the gospel), thus demonstrating God's righteousness (God's fairness and fidelity). As this statement indicates, 'righteousness' denotes something more than 'justice' (see Stuhlmacher 1994: 29–32). Dunn (1988: i. 41) terms it 'coven-ant faithfulness' and traces the idea to the Psalms (e.g. 31:1; 51:14; 98:2) and Deutero-Isaiah (e.g. 45:8, 21; 46:13; 62:1–2) (cf. Hays, below). In Rom 3:21–6, Paul returns to the idea that 'the righteousness of God [now] has been disclosed' (v. 21). How? Not by condemning sinners, as justice demands, but by justifying them, as God's character requires. In view particularly is God's covenant obligation to Israel (see 11:27, 29: 'And this is my covenant with them, when I take away their sins...for the gifts and the calling of God are *irrevocable*'). The question of God's faithfulness (one might even say 'God's consistency') is at stake. God has worked salva-tion in Christ 'first' for the Jews (v. 16); never-theless, many Jews have not believed. Does the fact of an increasingly Gentile church demon-strate either that God's plan has been thwarted or that God's people have been rejected? For Paul, neither conclusion is possible. Instead, he sets out to demonstrate that the righteousness of God is evident precisely in God's acceptance of Gentiles (chs. 1–8), and that the inclusion of Gentiles does not invalidate God's election of Israel (chs. 9–11).

The question, 'Has God abandoned Israel?', is long familiar to Judaism. At root, it is the ques-tion of theodicy, in this case, of the evident gap between God's promises and Israel's reality, felt most acutely in time of national defeat and occupation. Richard Hays (1989: 34–83) has demonstrated powerfully that Paul used as source for his reflections in Romans the prophets and lament psalms that dealt with God's apparent abandonment of Israel. It is striking that these materials are laden with references both to God's righteousness and to God's universal salvation (e.g. Ps 97:3 (LXX); Isa 51:4–5; 52:10). It should therefore come as no surprise that Paul initiates the argument of Romans with a quotation from Hab 2:4, which not only supplies key terminology for the letter (ROM 1:17) but does so in the context of a hard-won prophetic affirmation of God's paradoxical faithfulness.

The link to the remaining, paraenetic section of Romans (chs. 12–15) has been obscured by the Protestant inclination to consider justification in exclusively juridical terms. The notion that Christians are different from others primarily in their legal standing before God owes much to a traditional (Augustinian/Lutheran) (mis)reading of Rom 7–8. The Pauline meaning of 'justification' is much broader and evidences a quite different eschatological orientation (see ROM 8). The word *dikaioun* ('to justify'; first used in 2:13 and then repeatedly throughout chs. 2–10) means literally 'to righteous'; it comes from the same root as *dikaiosunē*, 'righteousness.' It means both 'to treat as righteous' and 'to make righteous' (Käsemann 1980: 25). In other words, God both forgives sin and converts sinners in 'righteousing' the unrighteous. The relational character of righteousness (e.g. seen as God's faithfulness to Israel, above) covers both being established and being equipped as a fit partner in right relationship (e.g. in 8:2–4). The same point is made by calling the gospel 'the *power* of God *for* salvation'. Thus, the entirety of Romans may be seen to be centred, in three parts, on the theme of God's righteousness:

Chs. 1–8   God's righteousness evident in the treatment of Jew and Gentile.
Chs. 9–11   God's righteousness evident in the treatment of Israel.
Chs. 12–15 God's righteousness evident in the lives of believers.

It is not required that one probe Paul's psyche to explain the statement in v. 16 that he is 'not ashamed' of the gospel. These words echo 'the very same prophecies and lament psalms from which Paul's righteousness terminology is also drawn' (Hays 1989:38), e.g. Ps 24:2; 43:10 (LXX);

Isa 28:16 (quoted in Rom 9:33); and, of particular note, 50:7–8: 'I know that I shall not be put to shame; he who vindicates me is near' (also recalled in 8:31–9).

v. 17, 'through faith for faith' (*ek pisteōs eis pistin*) is a difficult phrase to interpret. Most often, it is taken to refer to the exclusiveness of the requirement of faith (*sola fide*); hence the NIV's 'faith from first to last'. Because *pistis* can also mean 'faithfulness' (as in 3:3, its next occurrence beyond this section), it is possible that Paul had in mind God's *pistis* (faithfulness) which engenders, is manifest in, or is recognized by (*eis*, unto) human *pistis* (faith) (cf. Barth 1933: 41; Edwards 1992: 42–3). In support of this reading, one should note that the repetition of a word to play on its double meaning is a popular convention and that *ek* (from) used with the verb 'reveal' is most readily 'understood as denoting the source of the revelation' (Dunn 1988: i. 44). An even more important consideration is the content of the revelation: God's righteousness. Given the full sense of the term 'righteousness' (above), it is reasonable to imagine Paul saying that God's righteousness is revealed in (God's) faithfulness to (human) faith. 'The one who is righteous will live by faith' is a quotation from Hab 2:4. Here Paul made use of one of only two verses in the HB that link 'faith' and 'righteous(ness)'. (The other is Gen 15:6, another of Paul's crucial proof texts; see 4:3; Gal 3:6.) Although many commentators support the NRSV's rendering, in which *ek pisteōs* ('by faith') modifies the verb 'live' (Murray 1979: 33; Fitzmyer 1993: 265), an equally strong argument can be made for the translation, 'The one who is *righteous by faith* will live' (see e.g. Käsemann 1980: 32; Sanders 1977: 484; Cranfield 1979: 101–2). ('Live' here, in contrast to Habakkuk, would refer to resurrection life.) After all, Paul speaks in Phil 3:6 of a contrasting 'righteousness under (*en*) the law.' Similarly, it is possible that *pistis* here, as in the previous verse (and the LXX of Hab 2:4, 'my faithfulness'), refers to '(God's) faithfulness'. Again, the double meaning may be deliberate.

God's Righteousness Evident in the Treatment of Jew and Gentile (1:18–8:39)

Surprisingly, Christ is mentioned only once (2:16, on the future judgement) in 1:18–3:20. Indeed, almost nothing is distinctly Christian in the remainder of the first and the whole of the second chapter of Romans. The background to these materials is Hellenistic Judaism; unquestionably, Paul's description of the human condition in vv. 18–32 borrows heavily from popular Hellenistic-Jewish descriptions of Gentiles. (The highest concentration of parallels occurs in the Wisdom of Solomon, almost certainly known to Paul.) Like Paul, Jewish apologists characteristically attacked Gentile idolatry and sexual misconduct. ('For the idea of making idols was the beginning of fornication', Wis 14:12; cf. vv. 22–7.) Some also claim that behind ch. 2 lies an otherwise unknown Hellenistic synagogue sermon (see below). It is reasonable to suppose that Paul used stock materials to construct a foundation upon which the more distinctive elements of his argument would be built. This strategy is reminiscent of his citation of the Christological formulae in 1:3–4, which served to establish common ground with his readers.

Beginning in 3:21–6, Paul returns to an explicitly Christian vantage point. Interestingly, the same paragraph reintroduces the theme of righteousness (vv. 21, 22, 25, and 26; like 'Christ', 'righteousness' is mentioned only once in passing (3:5) in the previous chapter and a half). God's righteousness has been disclosed 'through faith in Jesus Christ for all who believe' (v. 22). The work of Christ is characterized as 'a sacrifice of atonement by his blood' that brings 'redemption' to those who believe (vv. 24–5). But why is such a disclosure, such an atonement, such a redemption necessary? If Christ is the solution, what precisely is the problem? Clearly, it is the job of 1:18–3:20 to inform us. Specifically, this section functions to justify Paul's own summary in 3:22b–23: 'For there is no distinction, since all have sinned and fall short of the glory of God.'

1:18–32 All are without Excuse The structure of the argument in 1:18–3:20 is not obvious. Commonly, 1:18–32 is read as an indictment of Gentile wickedness and 2:1–3:20 as the extension of that indictment to the Jews (Fitzmyer 1992: 269–71). Paul's approach is probably more subtle. In a sense, 1:18–32 sets a trap for the imaginary Jewish interlocutor introduced in 2:2. The description of human wickedness *seems* to be aimed exclusively at Gentiles; it *appears* to assume the typical contrast between Jewish probity and Gentile depravity. Nevertheless, nowhere does Paul indicate that he is describing only Gentiles; indeed, the Jewish/Gentile distinction is not made explicit until 2:9. Moreover, elements of vv. 18–31 hark back to the darker moments and practices of Israel's past. It is especially likely that the worship of

the golden calf (and perhaps the Israelites' subsequent revelry) of Ex 32 is in view. In Acts 7:41, Stephen referred to that incident and concluded, 'God...*handed them over* to worship the host of heaven'. *Paradidōmi* ('handed over') is the same verb used by Paul in vv. 24, 26, and 28 in reference to God's judgement. (The idea might go back to the OT passage quoted in the subsequent verses of Acts 7 (42–3), Am 5:25–7, which criticizes Jewish idolatry in the wilderness and speaks of God 'deporting/sending away' (*metoikizō*) the Jews to Damascus.) Also, Paul borrows language from Ps 106:20 and Jer 2:11, both of which deal with Israelite idolatry. Pious readers might accept God's judgement on conduct such as Paul describes, not realizing that they themselves stand under the same condemnation. Ch. 2 is written to make this point explicit.

v. 18, 'For the wrath of God is revealed from heaven against...those who...suppress the truth'. For Paul, the problem is not that God is unknowable; the problem is that humanity does not want to know God (cf. Wis 13:1–9). Accordingly, the idol worshipper does not seek to do the will of God; he seeks a god to do his will. Creature dethrones creator, and cosmic order is turned upside down (v. 24). Three times (vv. 23, 25, 26) human beings are said to have "exchanged" or "substituted" one reality for another' (*HBC* 1136). God's response in each case is to 'give up' or 'hand over' humanity to its own desires (vv. 24, 26, 28). For Paul, sin carries within itself its own punishment (Achtemeier 1985: 40), and the sinner's most terrible judgement is to be left alone. vv. 26–31, while it is true that Paul saw the reversal of the created order manifest in homosexual relations, it is notable that his list also included such transgressions as covetousness, envy, boastfulness, and gossip. It would be difficult not to locate oneself somewhere in this catalogue—which, of course, is just the point. The knowledge of God that humanity suppresses is a moral knowledge. They 'know God's decree, that those who practise such things deserve to die', and still they disobey and even applaud the disobedience of others (v. 27). Humanity is utterly 'without excuse' (v. 20), especially the excuse of ignorance.

Of course, Paul's fictive conversation partner (see below) would not plead ignorance. But does a Jew's knowledge of God put him or her in a superior position? Can knowledge of God's law deliver from God's judgement? It is to such questions that Paul's description of the human condition in vv. 18–32 has been leading.

(2:1–3:20) The Impartiality of God Scholars since Bultmann have made much of the similarities between Paul's rhetoric in Romans and the *diatribe*, a form of argumentation in which a Cynic or Stoic philosopher taught students by 'debating' an imaginary opponent (Bultmann 1910; Stowers, 1981). Although some scholars question whether or to what extent the diatribe was an established rhetorical form, there can be no doubt that diatribe *style* is present in Romans (Fitzmyer 1993: 91). At numerous points beginning in ch. 2 (also 3:1–9; 3:27–4:25; 9:19–21; 10:14–21; 11:17–24; 14:4–12), Paul addresses and even responds to the objections of an interlocutor (most often with an impassioned 'By no means!' (*mē genoito*); 3:4, 6, 31; 6:2, 15; 7:7, 13; 9:14; 11:1, 11). The effect is to pull the reader into the 'conversation' on Paul's side. Rhetorically, the diatribe confers argumentative dynamism without ceding authorial control. It remains in the rhetor's power to choose what questions to ask and what answers to accept.

Because Paul's dialogue partner of 2:1–16 is not identified explicitly, some commentators have isolated this section from 2:17–3:20, in which Paul plainly addresses a Jewish interlocutor (Barrett 1957: 43; Morris 1988: 107; Ziesler 1989: 80–1). It is more likely that the whole of 2:1–3:20 speaks to perceived Jewish attitudes and that any ambiguity as to the object of 2:1–16 is expressly eliminated by the direct address of v. 17. Stuhlmacher (1994: 39) made the intriguing suggestion that Paul delayed identifying the interlocutor for dramatic effect; 2:17 thus functions like Nathan's statement to David in 2 Sam 12:7: 'You are the man!' (In fact, Ps 51, understood to be David's penitential prayer, is quoted in Rom 3:4.)

The juxtaposition in vv. 28–9 of the mere outward and the true inward practice of Judaism is precedented in passages such as Deut 10:16, 30:6, and Jer 4:4, 9:26, which use the 'circumcision of the heart' metaphor to describe those whose inner commitments are consistent with their (outwardly obvious in the case of males) status as God's covenant people. The truly surprising employment of Scripture comes in v. 24, which uses Isa 52:5 to argue that Israel itself is so disobedient as to be the cause of Gentile blasphemy. This is 'a stunning misreading of the text' (Hays 1989: 45). In fact, Isa 52 celebrates Israel's rescue from the injustices of the nations. (Israel has been 'oppressed without cause'; 'my people are taken away without cause', Isa 52:4, 5.)

Numerous other difficulties are associated with the interpretation of Rom 2, some of which

bear significantly upon one's understanding and evaluation of the entire letter. The first, most glaring problem is the repeated assertion that one is justified (v. 13) or receives eternal life (v. 7) on the basis of one's deeds. (The notion that God equitably judges people according to their works is common in the HB; however, such passages do not have in view the issue of eternal destiny. In v. 5, Paul specifically quotes the LXX of Ps 61 (62):13 and Prov. 24:12.) This idea appears flatly to contradict Paul's numerous other statements that one cannot be saved by one's works (e.g. 3:20; 4:2; 9:32; 11:6). One way out of the dilemma is to say that Paul wrote only of a theoretical justification; in fact, he realized that no one actually measures up to the proposed standard. Others reason that when speaking of those who 'do good' (etc.), Paul 'is implicitly referring to Christians' (Fitzmyer 1993: 297). The first proposal seems heavy-handed; in effect, it trades coherence for consistency. The second notion, that the chapter approves only Christian good works, is certainly possible, although it does little to commend Paul as a fair-minded observer of human behaviour. Alternatively, Hays (1989: 42) has suggested that Rom 2 be read in the larger context of Ps 61 (quoted in v. 5), which 'renders an account of God fully consonant with Paul's emphasis on God's kindness and forebearance'. An entirely different approach is advocated by E. P. Sanders (1983: 123), who thinks that Paul made use of a source or sources ('homiletical material from Diaspora Judaism') that contributed the desired argument for God's impartiality (and Jewish sinfulness) but included elements strikingly at odds with Pauline theology (ibid. 123–35). In general, Rom 2 reads well as a sermon preached to Jews to encourage a higher standard of Jewish conduct. (Indeed, change 'Jew' to 'Christian' and 'circumcision' to 'baptism', and the text reads like a sermon exhorting church members to live up to their calling; cf. Mt 7:21–3.) It is noteworthy that Rom 2 deals with matters known to be at issue within first-century Judaism, such as the question of 'righteous Gentiles' and the nature of true obedience (ibid. 134).

A second problem concerns the description of Jewish sinfulness in Rom 2. In 3:9, Paul states that 'we have already charged that all, both Jews and Greeks, are under the power of sin'. Paul concludes that since Jews share the same plight as Gentiles, they require the same solution, namely, Christ (3:21–6). How does Paul make his case? Given the longstanding tendency of interpreters to read Paul as if he were an existentialist—that is, one concerned with internal states and interior conflicts (see Stendahl 1963)—the actual argument of Rom 2 is surprising. Paul does not say that while most Jews most of the time meet the external demands of the law (cf. Paul's larger claim for himself in Phil 3:6), they nevertheless continue to sin inwardly, for example, by being proud of their obedience. Such a critique would not be entirely new; something like it existed in the Jesus traditions (e.g. Mt 5:21–4, 27–30; 6:1–5; 23:25–8; Lk 11:37–44). That argument would put Jews and Gentiles on equal footing without necessitating that all Jews (or even hypothetical, representative Jews) be shown to be as badly behaved as Gentiles, which seems to be the point of 2:21–4. The lack of a clear conception or language of interiority is consistently problematic for Paul. Even Rom 7, which is usually read in this way, speaks of sin as an external power that causes one to *do* or not *do* what is right (7:15). Surely, the Jews of Paul's day were not characteristically thieves, adulterers, and temple robbers.

A third difficulty is that the obvious solution to the problems posed in 2:1–29 is that Jews simply become better Jews. If Jews commit sinful acts, repentance and atonement are available to them within Judaism. Damnation is neither the sole nor the expected alternative to perfect obedience. In this context it is worth noting that when all is said and done, Paul's one substantial and consistent accusation is that the Jews have rejected their Christ. What confuses are the numerous ways such rejection can be characterized (as disobedience, unbelief, works righteousness, etc.) and the numerous deficiencies to which it can be attributed (hardheartedness, pride, self-assertion, etc.). Apart from faith in Christ, no amount of Jewish obedience, faith, or humility is going to satisfy. However it is described, this by definition is a problem that cannot have a (non-Christian) Jewish solution.

The ground shifts in 3:9, where Paul states that 'both Jews and Greeks are under the power of sin'. This statement removes the possibility that, unaided by God, either Gentile or Jew could be righteous (*contra* 2:7, 13, etc., but consistent with 7:7–24). A compilation of OT proof-texts in 3:10–18 then describes humanity's utter depravity (Eccl 7:20; Ps 5:10; 10:7; 14:1–3/ 53:2–4; 36:2; 140:4; Isa 59:7–8/Prov 1:16). Thus the problem is not so much that humans sin as that humans are incapable of not sinning. Christ is necessary for Jew as well as Gentile because only he can break sin's power. This

claim demonstrates how Paul's thinking could at times steer him in the direction of a realized eschatology (see ROM E. 4); Christians are now 'in the Spirit' and please God while others remain 'in the flesh' and cannot please God (8:3–8). This approach equalizes Jew and Gentile and so makes Christ necessary. One might object that this line of reasoning succeeds only by overstating the differences between believers and unbelievers, in particular, between Christians and Jews. Is it really the case, either in outward behaviour or inward disposition, that Christians as a group sin less than Jews? Are the rules of the church experienced so differently from the laws of the synagogue? Certainly, it would have been possible to argue for the necessity of Christ without negating Judaism as an instrument (or at least a prior instrument) of God's grace. Despite the demurral of 3:1–2, Paul's point is that with respect to the actual state of their relationship to God, Jews enjoy no advantage over Gentiles. One must ask, 'What then was the point of Judaism?' That question, in one form or another, is the central concern of the next several chapters.

(3:21–31) The Revelation of God's Righteousness vv. 21–6 are the capstone of Paul's introductory argument; Stuhlmacher (1994: 57) refers to the paragraph as 'the heart of the letter to the Romans'. Here Paul revisits the grand theme introduced in the Thanksgiving: the righteousness of God. The divine character—faithful, gracious, forgiving, and merciful—has been disclosed in Christ, specifically in Christ's death, a sacrifice for sin 'effective through faith'. Altogether apart from human initiative, God has done what God always intended to do ('attested by the law and the prophets') and so is proved righteous. It is instructive that Ps 143, quoted (v. 2, significantly emended) in Paul's statement of judgement in Rom 3:20, maintains that one is preserved by God's righteousness (Ps 143:1, 11–12), the very subject of vv. 21–6 (see Hays 1989: 51–2). Paul is deeply conscious of the interplay of God's condemning justice and God's justifying righteousness, already evident in Scripture.

That the death of Jesus decisively altered the human situation (described in 1:18–3:20) is assumed but not explained. Almost certainly, the language Paul used concerning Christ's atonement was common to first-century Christianity and required little elucidation. (See 1 Cor 15:3, where the statement that 'Christ died for our sins according to the scriptures' is included in the tradition that Paul himself received.) v. 25, 'expiation' (*hilastērion*: 'sacrifice of atonement', NRSV) probably has in view the Jewish sacrificial system. In the LXX, the same word is used to refer to the 'mercy seat', the top of the ark of the covenant, on which the blood of the sin offering was sprinkled annually on the Day of Atonement. It might (also) have as background the notion of the efficacious sacrifice of martyrs, as one finds in 4 Macc 17:22. 'Redemption' (*apolutrōsis*) originally connoted 'freedom by ransom'. In the NT, the word is used to emphasize a change in one's position that is effected entirely at God's initiative and expense. It does not require a literal 'payment' by God (e.g. to the devil), as sometimes featured in later soteriological speculation (*EDNT* 138–40).

v. 24, which states that believers are 'justified by his [God's] grace as a gift', captures a great deal of Pauline theology in a few words. Quintessentially for Paul, justification is gift, not reward (see 4:1–4; 5:15–17). It originates in God's mind, is motivated by God's character, and is 'purchased' by God's work in Christ. It is neither human invention nor human achievement; hence, it is gracious, unmerited. Obviously, it occasions no opportunity for human boasting (v. 27; see 2:17, 23; 4:2; cf. the 'positive boasting' in 5:2–3, 11; 15:17); one may as well boast of being born as boast of being justified. (Not surprisingly, boasting is a prominent Pauline theme, especially in 1 and 2 Corinthians, e.g. 1 Cor 1:29–31; 3:21; 4:7; 5:6; 2 Cor 11:12, 16–18, 30; 12:1, 5–6; cf. the favourable boasting in 1 Cor 9:15–16; 15:31; 2 Cor 1:12; 5:12; 7:4, 14; 8:24; 9:2–3; 10:8, 13, 15–17; 11:10; 12:30.) v. 25, the statement that God, in 'divine forbearance', 'passed over the sins previously committed' raises many questions. What does it mean to 'pass over' sin (from *paresis*; lit. the 'passing by' = 'letting go unpunished'; see BAGD 626), and whose sins specifically have been passed over? Did God simply not judge former sins, or was their judgement postponed, perhaps until the cross? What evaluation of Judaism and of its sacrificial system lies behind this verse? Commentators have ventured answers to these and related questions, but no one account of the passage has proved persuasive. It is clear at least that Paul regarded the death of Christ as the one final and essential sacrifice, the basis for all human salvation. Paul does not provide us with enough information to judge how, to what extent, and on what basis he considered such salvation to have been operative in the past.

v. 26, it is essential to note that the faith of which Paul speaks in vv. 27–31 (and in Romans generally) is specifically 'faith in Christ' (see also 4:23–4). Although Paul may contrast works with faith and unbelief with faith, the unspoken and yet insistent polarity is between Jewish faith in God apart from belief in Christ and Christian (whether Jewish or Gentile) faith in God including belief in Christ. In other words, it is one's response to Jesus that ultimately is at issue, however the argument may be framed. Paul believed that God was in Christ and that to believe in God now means perforce to believe in Christ; the two 'faiths' are inseparable. Accordingly, it is only Christian faith that is legitimated *as* faith. (One can observe the same dynamic clearly at work in Johannine literature, e.g. in Jn 5:23 and 1 Jn 5:10–12.) Logically, this move eliminates the problem of present Jewish (but non-Christian) belief in God; it is not actual (one might say 'sufficient') faith. Thus Paul can speak of faith in God as if it were a uniquely Christian attribute. At the same time, this approach introduces a problem: what to do with pre-Christian Jewish faith (that is, unless one claims that those such as Abraham and David, both commended in Romans, already believed in Christ). The press of this difficulty may well account for Paul's statement in v. 25 (above) concerning God's *former* dispensation of forgiveness.

In v. 27 Paul contrasts a law 'of works' with a 'law of faith'. The shift in the use of *nomos* (law) is curious and has led many to translate the word in this instance as 'principle' (i.e. the principle of faith by which boasting is excluded). Barrett (1957: 83) has argued convincingly that, for Paul, *nomos* occasionally 'means something like "religious system", often . . . but not always, the religious system of Judaism'. Such an interpretation makes sense both here and at numerous other points in Romans. v. 31, Paul asks, 'Do we then overthrow the law by this faith?' As a Jew himself, Paul cannot answer, 'Yes'. The law is still God's law. There must be some sense in which Paul's teachings (which, let us not forget, abrogate certain specific commandments; e.g. Rom 14:14) actually 'uphold the law', perhaps the law rightly understood or the law in its deeper purpose. We do not have to wait long to discover something of what the apostle had in mind.

(4:1–25) The Example of Abraham Paul has just stated that he upholds the law (3:31) and that the righteousness of God, which he proclaims, is attested in 'the law and the prophets' (3:21). It is time to make good on these claims. Religious arguments, like legal arguments, often begin with an appeal to precedent. In most democracies, a lawyer can do no better than to appeal to the nation's constitution (and, thereby, to its founders). Constitutional interpretation is both the most basic and the most consequential matter of law. Generations of case law can be overturned by a single ruling of unconstitutionality. Paul makes his first and strongest argument by appealing to the founding figure of Judaism, Abraham. What goes for Abraham, he can assume, goes for all. God's covenant with Abraham is the core of the Jewish 'constitution', subsequent 'amendments' notwithstanding. Summoning Abraham to his defence is both an inspired and (in the light of the controversy in Galatia, which seemed to revolve around the interpretation of the Abraham story, especially the commandment of circumcision in Gen 17:10; see Gal 3) probably necessary strategy. The appeal to Abraham has the added benefit of pre-empting an opponent's appeal to Moses (see Gal 3:17). 'The promise...did not come to Abraham or his descendants through the law' (4:13). According to one possible interpretation, Paul (see ROM 10:5) effectively rules 'unconstitutional' Moses' later understanding of the relationship between the law and eternal life (e.g. that 'the person who does these things will *live* by them', Lev 18:5, my emphasis).

The basic argument of Rom 4 is comparatively simple and direct. According to Gen 15:6, Abraham 'believed the Lord; and the Lord reckoned it to him as righteousness'. (What Abraham actually believed—namely, God's promise that he would have offspring—is not in view nor, naturally, is a consideration of what 'reckoning righteousness' might have meant in its original context.) Abraham was not, of himself, righteous; instead, because of his faith, he was treated (*elogisthē*: 'was credited'; a 'bookkeeping term figuratively applied to human conduct' as in Ps 106:31; 1 Macc 2:52; and Philem 18; Fitzmyer 1993: 373) as though he were righteous. His standing before God was a gift, not an attainment (see ROM 3:24). This occurred prior to the giving of the law, prior even to the requirement of circumcision. This first instance of human righteousness thus becomes the paradigm for all subsequent instances. It is very likely that Paul wrote Rom 4 with a view to popular Jewish treatments of the Abraham story that focused on the patriarch's obedient example, which in some cases even argued for his attainment of merit (e.g. 4 Ezra 9:7; 13:23). A similar reading is present in Jas 2:18–26, which

may have been formulated to counter (possibly second-generation) abuses of Pauline theology. The two sides actually make different, not opposite, points. Essentially, Paul uses the Abraham story to answer the question, How does one get 'in' (e.g. right relationship with God)? Much more characteristically, the story is used in James to exhort believers (those already 'in') to behave in a certain way, in this case to demonstrate their faith by their actions. It is entirely possible to laud Abraham's good behaviour (e.g. in obeying God's command to leave his home, Gen 12:1) without implying that Abraham was thereby sinless or perfectly righteous, which issue was not under consideration. In fact, many contemporary Jews could have accepted Paul's basic point: like Abraham, one enters into covenant with God at God's initiative and by means of God's grace. The doctrine of justification by faith is not without Jewish antecedents; the real controversy concerns, not the necessity of faith, but the content or object of faith.

The fact that Abraham had not yet been circumcised (that comes two chapters later, in Gen 17) allows Paul to claim that Abraham is exemplar to and ancestor of all faithful persons, both Jews and Gentiles (3:9–12). As proof-text, Paul cites Gen 17:5 ('I have made you the father of many nations', vv. 17–18). Gentile Christians were for Paul (and probably for most other Jewish Christians) 'children of Abraham'. It is not difficult to imagine how such claims might have rankled with non-Christian Jews, how they could have been seen to threaten the integrity, ultimately even the existence, of Israel. It is likely that such claims underlie many of the instances of persecution recorded in the NT (see Gal 5:11 and 6:12).

v. 15, the sentiment 'the law brings wrath; but where there is no law, neither is there violation' is echoed in 5:13: 'sin was indeed in the world before the law, but sin is not reckoned when there is no law' (cf. the 'passing over' of sins prior to Christ in 3:25). It also anticipates the argument of 7:7–24 ('if it had not been for the law, I would not have known sin, v. 7). Presumably, the point is that 'law makes sin into transgression' (Byrne 1996: 158). Under the law, one not only sins, one sins with explicit knowledge that one is sinning. Paul makes no attempt to co-ordinate these statements with the earlier argument that Gentiles are fairly judged by God, having 'what the law requires written on their hearts' (2:15).

vv. 19–21, the quality of Abraham's faith is vividly described. Abraham believed God against all opposing considerations and contrary appearances. The final reality was God's fidelity: God would do what God had promised. The character of faith as trust is nowhere more clearly depicted in Paul's writings. vv. 23–4, the content of justifying faith is spelled out more fully: belief in God who 'raised Jesus our Lord from the dead, who was handed over (*paredothē*) to death for our trespasses and was raised for our justification'. This description of Jesus sounds formulaic and therefore traditional; ultimately, it is dependent upon Isa 52:13–53:12 (LXX), which tells of the Suffering Servant, on whom 'the LORD laid (*paredōken*) our sins' (53:6), who 'bore (*paredothē*) their sin' (53: 12), who will 'justify many' (v. 11) (see Cranfield 1979: 251–2).

(**5:1–11**) **God's Reconciling Love as the Foundation for Legitimate Boasting** Two verbs dominate this section: 'boast' and 'reconcile'. We were told in 4:2 that Abraham had no ground for boasting before God. Similarly, 3:27 made the point that boasting is excluded (see also 2:17, 23). In Rom 5, however, boasting is neither groundless nor excluded: Paul boasts 'in the hope of sharing the glory of God' (v. 2), in 'sufferings' (v. 3), and 'in God' (v. 11). The difference, of course, is that here Paul is not, as in 2 Cor 10:13–15, 'boasting beyond limits', claiming as his own achievement something achieved by others. It is perfectly proper to boast in what God has done, rather than in what one has done for God (see ROM 3:24). And what God has done in Christ, according to Rom 5:1–11, is to reconcile (*katallassein*) humanity with God. 'Reconciliation' is return from alienation, the restoration of relationship. Its use here puts the divine–human rift in deeply personal (as opposed to exclusively forensic) terms, an estrangement that yields only to the prevailing power of God's love (v. 8). The state of reconciliation is described in v. 1 as 'peace with God'. Because reconciliation is achieved from God's side and offered when most undeserved (v. 8), the believer possesses security in the hope of eternal life (vv. 2, 5) and confidence in the midst of earthly trials (vv. 3–4). Reconciliation *is* something about which to boast.

The claim to 'boast in…sufferings' (v. 3) is distinctly ironic and distinctively Pauline. For Paul, the paradigm of Christian existence, of Christian reality, is the cross (see ROM E. 4). One's faithfulness to the crucified messiah is measured, not in gifts of power or wisdom, but in degrees of sacrifice and suffering (1 Cor 4:8–13; 2 Cor. 6:3–10; 11:21–12:21). Against the

pretensions of the so-called 'super-apostles' at Corinth, Paul wrote, 'If I must boast, I will boast of the things that show my weakness' (2 Cor 11:30). Putting the cross at the centre of his thinking (the gospel is characterized as 'the word of the cross' in 1 Cor 1:18), set Paul outside normal religious expectation, including the expectations of many of his converts. To Paul, religion was not a means by which to manipulate heavenly powers to earthly ends. God's locus in this world is disclosed in the cross, which is foolishness and weakness in human eyes (1 Cor 1:17–19). Therefore, Paul can boast in his sufferings, in the very absence of earthly rescue, in the knowledge that he travels in the footsteps of the crucified messiah, and that he will arrive someday at the place of Christ's resurrection (where 'hope does not disappoint', v. 5). It is consistent with this perspective that reconciliation is a present reality (v. 10: 'we were reconciled' to God, aorist tense), but salvation itself remains a future hope (vv. 9–10, 'we will be saved'). (The two are related by means of an *a minori ad maius* argument: if God has reconciled, how much more will God save.)

In their unreconciled state, humans are described as 'weak', 'ungodly', 'sinners', and 'enemies' of God (vv. 6, 8, 10), a portrayal that recalls the description in 1:18–32. That Paul would, by implication, refer to himself and to all other Jews as ungodly and enemies of God is astounding. A less pointed description, however, might undermine his argument concerning the absolute necessity of the atonement. It is because reconciliation with God is so entirely necessary and yet so utterly unattainable from the human side that it is so highly prized.

(**5:12–21**) **Adam and Christ** Paul found a prototype for the doctrine of justification by faith in the story of Abraham (ch. 4). He then characterized the justification won by Christ's death as reconciliation with God (5:1–11). But how can Christ's work, however meritorious in itself, save others? Can the actions of one individual affect the standing of all other persons? Yes, indeed, if that individual happens to be the archetype for subsequent humanity. In vv. 12–21, Paul turns to Adam as precedent (that is, by way of counterexample) for the universality of Christ's atonement. If all of humanity shared in Adam's disobedience, how much more (note, again, the *a minori ad maius* structure) may all humanity share in the obedience of Jesus, the very Son of God (v. 19; see also 1 Cor 15:45–9).

Paul argues on the basis of Gen 3 only that 'sin came into the world through one man'. (There were of course two human players in the Garden drama. Eve has gone missing.) He does not propound a theory ('original sin') concerning the conveyance of sin, biological or otherwise, from one generation to the next. The proof of the ubiquity of sin is the universality of its consequence: death (v. 12; Gen 3:3). The resurrection of Christ thus overturns death introduced by Adam: 'For since death came through a human being, the resurrection of the dead has also come through a human being; for as all die in Adam, so all will be made alive in Christ' (1 Cor 15:21–2). The proper order of creation, lost in the Fall, is thus in the process of being restored (8:18–25). This two-part story is complicated by the mention of the law in vv. 13–14 and 20. Sin existed prior to the giving of the law, but it was not like Adam's transgression, that is, disobedience of an explicit commandment. The law given through Moses served to increase culpability; humans again could transgress as Adam had transgressed (vv. 13–14; see 4:15). (One might note that, among other things, Paul's argument 'passes over the so-called Noachic legislation (Gen 9:4–6)'; Fitzmyer 1993: 418.) And, whereas Adam had to obey only one commandment, those living under the law have six hundred and thirteen times the opportunity for transgression: 'law came in, with the result that the trespass multiplied' (v. 20). In the light of 7:5–12, a minority of commentators have interpreted v. 20 to mean that the law was given for the express purpose (hina) of increasing (and not merely increasing the guilt of) sin (Murray 1979: 208). This would involve God in the deliberate promotion of sin which is, needless to say, a problematic assertion (cf. the relationship between the law and sin in 7:11–12).

Moses is a not accidental omission on Paul's short-list of human archetypes. By situating the law where he does (v. 20, it 'slipped in'—pareiselthen—between Adam and Christ; see Gal 3:17), Paul indicates that Moses was not the answer to Adam. The law did not provide a way out of the human dilemma; quite to the contrary, it made an already bad situation worse. Whether or not it increased the incidence of sin (a debatable point, both exegetically and practically), it heightened sin's sinfulness by exposing the deliberateness of human disobedience. The law could not give (eternal) life; it was participant in and not victor over Adam's 'dominion of death' (vv. 20–1). In the face of this stark portrayal, one could object that the law did function for many as a positive corrective and guide. A larger problem is that belief in eternal life post-dates Torah. If one enquires, like the 'rich young ruler', 'What must I do to inherit eternal life?' (Lk 10:25), one asks a question that the law is unequipped to answer. (Note that Jesus' own answer concerned doing, not merely believing, certain things.) A typical Jewish approach would be to assume that those remaining in covenant with God will inherit eternal life. Paul's answer really is no different, but the obligatory covenant is (i.e. the new covenant of 1 Cor 11:25; 2 Cor 3:6, 14, etc.).

(6:1–23) Dead to Sin and Alive to God Paul has just introduced the notion that there are two dominions, one of death, whose head is Adam, and one of life, whose head is Christ (5:21). The obvious conclusion is that believers now dwell with Christ in the dominion of life. But this cannot be the whole truth: believers sometimes disobey, and all believers die. In what sense and to what extent Christ's dominion is a *present* reality is the underlying issue in Rom 6. Paul's argument is organized around two questions: 'Should we continue in sin in order that grace may abound?' (v. 1), and 'Should we sin because we are not under law but under grace?' (v. 15). Paul's response is by now anticipated: 'By no means!' (*mē genoito*; see ROM 2:1–3:20). The first question is answered ontologically: 'How can we who died to sin go on living in it?' (v. 2). The believer has already died and 'walks in newness of life'. How? By identification with the death of Jesus in baptism (vv. 3–4). It is important to note that this identification is substantial, not moralistic; one actually participates with Jesus in his death: 'We know that our old self was crucified with him so that the body of sin might be destroyed, and we might no longer be enslaved to sin' (v. 6). Believers are a 'new creation' (2 Cor 5:17), a new kind of person who has the power not to sin (vv. 12–14, 18, etc.). (How this portrayal meshes with the description of the 'wretched self' in 7:14–25 is a major problem; see ROM 7:14–25.)

Of all NT writings, Paul's letters most pointedly exhibit the eschatological tension between the 'already' and the 'not yet'. The obvious counterpart to 'we have been buried' with Christ 'in his death' (v. 4), would be 'and we have been raised with Christ in his resurrection'. This may be the viewpoint of Ephesians (e.g. 2:1–6), but it is not the perspective of Romans. Although the situation of the believer has changed considerably, it has not changed entirely. With respect to the individual Christian, all references to resurrection and eternal life are future tense (vv. 5, 8). Believers 'walk in newness of life' (v. 4) and are 'alive to God' (v. 11); nevertheless, their experience of the 'dominion of life' is proleptic, not fully realized. Although they have 'died to sin' (v. 2), they may yet submit themselves 'to sin as its instruments' (v. 13), may once again come under the dominion of sin (v. 12). The tension between the two realities remains unresolved: humans by nature sin; believers by (their new) nature do not sin (cf. 1 Jn 1:7–2:1 with 3:6, 8–9; 5:18). Believers are human, but believers also represent a new (or 'renewed') type of humanity. One could lower the tension by diminishing the status of believers (that is, by moving towards a more exclusively future eschatology); however, such a change would thoroughly undermine Pauline theology. Paul sets the law and Christ as opposite means: what the law could not do, Christ has done (8:3). But if believers (Christians) are not substantially different from those 'under the law' (non-Christian Jews), then (by Paul's reasoning) Christ has failed. Why frame the argument in this way? Because of Paul's one overriding concern: the present equality of Jew and Gentile (see ROM E.4).

Paul's second question also concerns the relationship between believers and sin. To paraphrase v. 15, Why not sin if sin is not judged? Are those set free from sin thereby free to sin? Paul answers that such 'freedom' is illusory. People are not transferred from slavery to sin into neutral, non-allied autonomy. Instead, they pass from one allegiance, one 'slavery' (to speak 'in human terms', v. 19), to another. Believers are slaves 'of obedience' (v. 16), 'slaves of righteousness' (vv. 18–19), 'enslaved to God' (v. 22). There can be no 'freedom' to sin, since sin itself is slavery. 'Grace and sin are to one another as "either" is to "or" ' (Barth 1933: 217).

Paul stated earlier that death came through Adam's sin (5:12). vv. 20–3 make clear that all sinners earn death as their fitting 'wages' (*opsōnion*, v. 23). The language used to describe sin ('things of which you are now ashamed', v. 21) is reminiscent of the description of human wickedness in 1:18–32 ('shameless acts', 1:27). The alternative is holiness ('sanctification', NRSV) that leads to eternal life (v. 22). Something 'holy' is pure, consisting of only one thing (e.g. 'pure gold'). That believers are to be holy (or sanctified), to be one thing, is the point of the entire chapter.

(7:1–25) The Law and Sin A connection between law and sin was posited in 3:20, 4:15, 5:13, and 5:20. This is one of the most surprising and controversial claims encountered in Paul's letter, and it demands elaboration. The discussion in ch. 6, especially the concluding section on slavery and freedom, provides an opportunity for the reintroduction of the subject of the law and sin. The previous paragraphs considered reasons why believers should not sin. In vv. 1–6, Paul offers another: the believer has died not only to sin (6:3) but also to the law (vv. 1–4), which is itself a cause of sin (vv. 5–12). (On the question, 'Of what law does Paul speak?', see Fitzmyer 1993: 455.)

The marriage metaphor Paul employs is somewhat forced. The statement that 'the law is binding on a person only during a person's lifetime' (v. 1) aligns with the conclusion 'you [therefore] have died to the law through the body of Christ' (v. 4). But the one who dies in vv. 2–3 is the husband, not the wife (the believer). Is the law the husband who dies, the 'law' that governs the wife's relationship to the husband, or both? Despite the confusion, the point of vv. 2–3 appears straightforward: one who simply disregards the law (e.g. a married person who has an affair) may be judged a sinner ('an adulterer', v. 3), but one who is no longer subject to the law (a widow[er]) may not be judged by the law (may not be called an adulterer when remarrying). Someone reading 'you have died to the law … so that you may belong to another' might well ask, 'Who was the first partner—the law?' On one level, Dunn (1988: 369) is correct to say that the question is 'over-fussy'. The analogy makes a basic point and should not be pushed beyond it. On another level, however, the question is quite valid and reveals much about Paul's view of Judaism. *Whose* were those who lived under the law? Although the language is covenantal (i.e. concerning marriage), the prior covenant partner is not God. It is as though the Sinai covenant was made with the law itself.

The mention of bearing fruit in v. 4 fills out the idea in ch. 6 that believers have become 'instruments of righteousness' (v. 13), experiencing 'sanctification' to God (v. 22). God's will is not only the absence of evil but also the presence of good. Although some commentators have argued that 'bearing fruit for God' means 'begetting spiritual children', it is more likely that Paul is referring to the generation of good character and/or works (cf. Gal 5:22; Cranfield 1979: 336–7). Correspondingly, Paul refers to 'fruit for death' as the product of 'sinful passions' 'at work in our members' (v. 5).

v. 5, two new and very important ideas are introduced. The first concerns life 'in the flesh'. Up until now, 'flesh' (*sarx*) has been used to refer to physicality: Jesus was descended from David 'according to the flesh' (1:3); Abraham is 'our ancestor according to the flesh' (4:1; Paul returns to this usage in 9:3, 5). Now the term takes on board a decidedly pejorative nuance. (Paul's use of *sarx* is the subject of numerous scholarly studies; summaries may be found in *TDNT* vii. 98–151; Spicq 1994: 3:231–41; *EDNT* 3:230–3.) Being 'in the flesh' means being in the (ordinary if not 'natural') state of human alienation from God. The one in the flesh here is roughly equivalent to the 'the old self' of 6:6. While 'fleshliness' does include carnality (i.e. improper sensuality), its meaning is broader. 'Flesh' symbolizes 'the weakness and appetites of "the mortal body" ' that were the causes of sin (Dunn 1988: 370; cf. 'sinful passions' here). The juxtaposition of flesh and Spirit (v. 6) does not evidence a true matter/spirit dualism, nor does it demonstrate that Paul was an ascetic (see Käsemann 1980: 188–9). With respect to the last point, one might note that while Paul himself was unmarried, he did not prohibit marriage, and at one point he even commanded married believers to continue sexual relations (1 Cor 7:3–5). Nevertheless, it would be fair to say that physicality was, if not denigrated, then at least held in some suspicion by Paul (cf. Rom 8:10). He might have allowed for Christian marriage, but 1 Cor 7:7–9, 28 is hardly a ringing endorsement. The second idea to be introduced in v. 5 is the notion that the law *causes* (not only exposes or increases the culpability of) sin (see ROM 5:13–14). The contention that dormant passions are 'aroused by the law' anticipates (one might say, necessitates) the discussion in 7:7–20. Much the same idea has appeared before, in 1 Cor 15:56: 'The sting of death is sin, and the power of sin is the law.' Law is the parental command not to raid the biscuit tin, an injunction that draws attention to and makes all the more desirable the very thing it prohibits. As the saying goes, stolen fruit is sweetest. Nevertheless, one might dispute whether law and sin are always thus related. Does prohibition inevitably increase desire, and does 'sinful passion' require a commandment to be stirred up? Moreover, are the commands that Paul so often includes in his letters (as in Rom 12–14) somehow excluded from this dynamic?

v. 6, the contrast between 'the old written code' and 'the new life of the Spirit' seems to be dependent particularly upon the prophecy of the future covenant in Jer 31:31–4. In contrast to the Sinai covenant ('which they broke', v. 32), in the new order the law will not be taught but rather will be written 'on the hearts' of God's people (v. 33). Paul calls the law, literally, an 'old/aged letter' (*palaiotēti grammatos*), a title conveying (in line with the treatment of the old covenant in Jer 31) both decrepitude and externality. But that's not all: the metaphor of slavery is picked up from the previous chapter and applied, not to sin, but to the law itself (see Gal 4:22–31). vv. 4–6 ratchet up by several notches Paul's already negative treatment of the law. The law is no longer just an inadequate solution to the problem of sin; the law itself is the problem. Has not Paul come to the point of equating the law, God's law, with sin? He answers, 'By no means!' (v. 7). It is not really the law's fault; sin is to blame. (That sin could be a responsible 'party' evidences a decided shift in terminology.)

The argument of v. 7 is familiar: the law makes known, discloses, sin as sin (4:15; 5:13, 20). The selection of the tenth commandment (against coveting, see 13:9) is intriguing since it is one of the few OT commandments to prohibit an attitude. It is here that Paul comes closest to locating sin in one's internal states (e.g. one sins by obeying the law for the wrong reasons or by being proud of one's obedience)—an attitude that generations of commentators have attributed to him. It may be that Paul's intuition drew him in this direction, but that he lacked the conceptual tools that would have allowed him to construct such an argument. Such speculation should be tempered by the fact that the idea, if present, is dropped in the next verse: sin now is an external power that acts on the individual. The 'wretched self' of vv. 14–25 is faulted for wrongful (in) action, not for wrongful thinking or feeling: 'I can will what is right, but I cannot *do* it . . . the evil I do not want is what I *do*' (vv. 18–19). A more likely explanation is that Paul quoted the coveting prohibition because he had in mind the temptation in the Garden (Gen 3:5–6; see the discussion of Adam below): ' "For God knows that when you eat of it your eyes will be opened, and you will be like God, knowing good and evil." So when the woman saw that the tree was good for food, and that it was a delight to the eyes, and that the tree was to be desired to make one wise, she took of its fruit and ate.' In Rom 6, sin was objectified as a power to which one could yield (v. 13) and be enslaved by (v. 16). The anthropomorphizing of sin is extended in 7:8–23. Twice sin is said to have 'seized an opportunity in the commandment' (vv. 8, 11). The ultimate expression comes in v. 17: 'It is no longer I that do it, but sin that dwells within me' (repeated in v. 20). It is as though sin were a demonic being that overpowers and possesses humans. The effect is to exonerate the law: it is not the law *itself* that provokes transgression, it is sin's fault. Sin wrests control of the law and uses it as an instrument of death. The 'I' (as in 'it is no longer I that do it'), being 'in the flesh', is helpless before such an onslaught. In 7:14–8:8, it is this weakness (and not the law, which is 'holy, just, and good') that is the problem. The solution? Believers are empowered to fulfil 'the just requirement of the law' as they walk 'not according to the flesh but according to the Spirit' (8:4; recall again Jer 31).

Regarding Paul's treatment of the law in Romans, Sanders comments (1983: 76) insightfully that there is 'an organic development with a momentum towards more and more negative statements until there is a recoil in Romans 7, a recoil which produces other problems'. Among the difficulties: 'The law could no longer be said to produce sin or to multiply transgression as part of God's overall plan [the typical view in both Romans and Galatians], since the realm of sin is now considered entirely outside that plan' (ibid. 73). Moreover, God is now credited with having provided a means for attaining life (v. 10; see 10:5) that was incapable of succeeding. In other words, if the law was given to produce transgression, the law is linked to sin (against which Paul 'recoils' in v. 7); however, if the law was given by God to produce eternal life, it was doomed to failure by human weakness (or sin's power). But how could God's plan fail?

There are good reasons for thinking that Paul himself is not the implied subject, the 'I', in 7:7–26. (Compare the universalized 'I' in e.g. 1 Cor 13). Paul never lived 'apart from the law', 'the commandment' did not 'come' in his lifetime (v. 9), nor was he 'killed' by sin (v. 11). Moreover (and of considerable importance for the interpretation of Paul), vv. 14–25 describe a self-perception nearly the antithesis of Paul's own as evidenced in his letters (see ROM 2; Stendahl 1963; Sanders 1983: 76–81). The statement of Acts 23:1, 'up to this day I have lived my life with a clear conscience before God', is echoed in passages such as 2 Cor 1:12 and 4:2.

The man who wrote, 'as to righteousness under the law, [I was] blameless' (Phil 3:6) and 'I am not aware of anything against myself' (1 Cor 4:4) did not suffer from existential *angst*. The assignment for Rom 7 must have been something other than autobiography.

The one character who qualifies on all counts to be the speaker in 7:7–26 is Adam (see Stuhlmacher 1994: 106–7), the archetypal human in whom all others sinned (5:12–21). Speaking as Adam, Paul can return to the initiation of 'law', the giving of 'the commandment' (v. 9) in the Garden: 'You shall not eat of the fruit of the tree … or you shall die' (Gen 3:3). Writes Paul, 'The very commandment that promised life proved death to me' (v. 10). Instead of saving them from death, the prohibition was used to lure them to death. The identification with Adam also explains the radical anthropomorphizing of sin in this same section: sin is like the serpent that 'deceived' Adam and Eve (v. 11; Gen 3:1, 4), enticing them to covet the forbidden fruit. (They ate, desiring to be 'as God', Gen 3:5. Note the description of Eve's response in Gen 3:6.)

vv. 14–24, if Paul is speaking in the place of unregenerate humanity, especially from the perspective of Adam, it follows that these verses do not describe the situation of believers. This is not the way the passage is read by many scholars (e.g. Schlatter 1995: 160; Barrett 1957: 151–3), but it is the only interpretation that suits the chapter's larger context (cf. Dunn's (1988: 387–99) attempt to resolve the conflict in terms of eschatological tension). The status of the individual in Rom 5:12–7:6 is either/or: either dead to sin or enslaved to sin, either in the dominion of life or in the dominion of death. The same situation prevails in Rom 8: either one is in the Spirit or one is in the flesh (v. 9). The Christian anthropology of Romans is not an essay in grey. The fault of the law in Rom 7 is that it is powerless (as 8:8: 'those in the flesh cannot please God'); it makes no sense in the context of this argument that Paul would describe believers in terms of the problem and not in terms of the solution. If 7:14–24 is a description of believers, then what is 8:1–17? There is indeed a future 'edge' to Paul's eschatological perspective, but it is located elsewhere: the expectation of 8:10–11 and 18–39 has nothing to do with freedom from sin (already available to believers); Paul awaits freedom from sin's corporeal and cosmic *effects*.

v. 25, the final sentence ('So then …') makes the best claim to be a description of believers since it comes after Paul's Christian thanksgiving (v. 24). Some have argued that the verse is simply out of order or that it was originally a marginal gloss. 'For it is scarcely conceivable that, after giving thanks to God for deliverance, Paul should describe himself as being in exactly the same position as before' (Dodd 1932: 114–15). It is striking that the individual is characterized as being a 'slave' to the law and to ('the law of') sin, both 'pre-Christian' categories in Rom 5–6. Moffatt paraphrases the verse: 'Thus, left to myself, I serve . . .', which may capture Paul's meaning. At very least, one's assessment of v. 25 must take account of 8:1–7. The person in ch. 7 is 'with [the] flesh' 'a slave to the law of sin', but the believer in ch. 8 is 'not in the flesh' (v. 9) and is 'set free from the law of sin' (v. 2)! Therefore, it is possible in v. 25 that Paul describes a state to which believers may revert; it is clear that it is not the state in which he expects believers to remain.

(8:1 17) The Law of the Spirit Having described the dominion of death from which the law offers no rescue, Paul turns his attention to the alternative existence previewed in 7:6, 'the new life of the Spirit' experienced by those 'discharged from the law'. The description in 8:1–17 is rich and densely packed, containing numerous themes that figure prominently in other Pauline texts. Freed from the law, one lives beyond the reach of law's penalty: condemnation (v. 1, as in 7:3). A new system or principle, 'the law of the Spirit of life in Christ Jesus' (in contrast to the old system, 'the law of sin and of death'), now governs the believer's existence. 'Life' has a double meaning that corresponds to the two ends of the eschatological spectrum: it is a new quality of existence already enjoyed (v. 10), and it is future, eternal existence with God (vv. 11, 13). The Spirit effectuates both forms of life: in the present, the Spirit dwells in believers (v. 9) and empowers them to fulfil 'the just requirement of the law' (v. 4) and to 'put to death the deeds of the body' (v. 14); the Spirit leads believers (v. 14), witnesses to them that they are God's children (v. 16), and 'intercedes' for them 'with sighs too deep for words' (v. 26). In the future, God will raise believers to eternal life through the same Spirit (v. 11). More than anything else, it is the Spirit that marks the dawning of the new age (the 'dominion' of grace; 5:21). According to Acts (10:44–11:18), the presence of spiritual gifts amongst Gentile Christians was the decisive consideration in their admission to the church. It is instructive

that Paul's first argument against the Galatian Judaizers concerns the presence of such *charismata* amongst the Galatian converts prior to any law observance (Gal 3:1–5). (Note that Paul refers synonymously to 'the Spirit of God' and 'the Spirit of Christ' in v. 9. See ROM 1:1 above.)

v. 3, the idea of Christ's atonement, already present in 3:24–5 and 5:6–9, is reintroduced. God 'dealt with sin', something that law, allied to weak human 'flesh' (i.e. the powerless human will, as in 7:14–25), was incapable of doing. In the death of Jesus, God 'condemned sin in the flesh', that is, the condemnation of v. 1 was executed on Jesus, the only human (one 'in . . . flesh') who was undeserving of such judgement. (He was 'in the likeness of sinful flesh', that is, he was human without sinning. Cf. 2 Cor 5:21: 'For our sake he made him to be sin who knew no sin, so that in him we might become the righteousness of God.' See also Phil 2:5–11.) As before, Paul is more interested in celebrating the atonement than in explaining its mechanics.

The difference between the two types of existence is explained from the human side as a difference of fundamental disposition or direction (vv. 5–11). One who lives 'according to the flesh' (vv. 5, 12; returning to the meaning of 7:14) has a mind set 'on the things of the flesh' (vv. 5–6). What constitutes 'the things of the flesh' is not specified, but it must mean something more than 'earthly concerns', such as the provision of food and clothing (cf. 'the deeds of the body' in v. 13). Such a mindset is 'hostile to God'; it does not—it cannot—'submit to God's law' or 'please God' (vv. 7–8). (As in v. 4, Paul assumes that believers are the only ones who 'do' the law.) The best explication of the phrase is found in Rom 1:18–32, which vividly describes human nature at war with God. The essential sin is idolatry, the devotion to something as god that is not God. Again, there is no middle ground, no accommodation, no compromise. Believers are on one side of the line and unbelievers the other.

By the logic of Paul's argument, believers should now have the power to do what the 'wretched self' of Rom 7 could not, namely, obey the law. Nevertheless, the 'just requirement of the law' (equivalent to 'the law of God' in v. 7) that they fulfil cannot be precisely equivalent to Torah since it does not include such 'optional extras' as circumcision (1 Cor 7:19). The use of the singular (*to dikaiōma*) 'brings out the fact that the law's requirements are essentially a unity' (Cranfield 1979: 384). For Paul, the will of God is present in but not circumscribed by Torah. The commonplace distinction between 'the spirit' and 'the letter' of the law is not far from what Paul had in mind (Rom 7:6).

v. 15, the mention of slavery recalls the discussion in 6:16–23 but also, more fully, Gal 4:1–9 and, especially with its connection to parentage, 21–31. 'Abba' (in Aramaic, an affectionate word for father) is associated with the prayer of Jesus (Mk 14:36); its presence in the Pauline epistles (here and Gal 4:6) is noteworthy. vv. 15–16 were key to Wesley's doctrine of 'Christian assurance', the idea that believers need not doubt their standing with God, being inwardly assured by the Spirit of their adoption (see also 9:1). Paul is careful to show that adoption does not imply an 'also-ran' or second-class birthright; on the contrary, believers are fully 'heirs of God' and even 'joint heirs with Christ' (v. 17; cf. v. 29); that is, by identifying with Christ, they participate fully in the benefits won by Christ. Paul does not mean to imply that believers are equal in every way to Christ.

v. 17, the section concludes quite unexpectedly: [we are] 'heirs ... if ... we suffer'. This sudden shift to minor key signals the presence of the antagonist, death. Although sin has been overcome, its ravages, its legacy remain. ('The present time'—*ho nun kairos*, v. 18—is the label Paul gives to this 'time between the times'.) The comments made in connection with 5:3 ('we ... boast in our sufferings'), apply here: for Paul, the shape of Christian life was cruciform ('we suffer with him'; see also ROM E.4). True spirituality is dangerous and costly (1 Thess 3:4). Paul's difficult experiences with the church at Corinth (where he now writes) may well have prompted the inclusion of this amendment (cf. 1 Cor 4:8–13). 'Glory' and its cognates are used 180 times in the NT (cf. 1:23; 2:7, 10; 3:7, 23; 4:20; 5:2; 6:4; 8:18, 21; 9:4, 23; 11:36; 15:6–9; 16:27; see *TDNT* ii. 247–54; *EDNT* 1:344–9). The linkage between suffering and glory is typically Jewish (Stuhlmacher 1994: 132) and is made in a number of other NT writings (e.g. Lk 24:26; Eph 3:13; Heb 2:9–10; 1 Pet 1:11; 4:13; 5:1, 10).

(8:18–39) The Creation's Eager Longing To the woman ... [God] said,| 'I will greatly increase your pangs in childbearing;| in pain you shall bring forth children| ...' And to the man ... [God] said, |' ... cursed is the ground because of you; | in toil you shall eat of it all the days of your life; | thorns and thistles it shall bring forth for you; | and you shall eat the plants of the field. | By the sweat of your face you shall eat bread | ... you are dust, and to dust you shall return.'

According to Gen 3:14–19, nature itself was corrupted by human sin and suffers sin's mournful consequences (see 4 Ezra 7:10–14). The 'peaceable kingdom' of Eden is no more.

The poetry and power of 8:18–39 betoken the magnitude of Paul's discovery: no less than Paradise returned. God in Christ is not saving individuals only; God is at the task of saving creation, of swallowing up Adam's entire loss in Christ's complete victory. What is the source of Paul's confidence? Christ's resurrection (of which Paul himself is a witness; Gal 1:16; 1 Cor 15:8), which is no less than the end of history placarded in the midst of history (1 Cor 15:20–6). The Garden curse, death, has been broken and remains only to be shattered.

As already noted, the reader comes upon the idea of suffering abruptly in v. 17, like fine print at the end of a contract. He or she may be left second-guessing: Is this 'inheritance' worth its price? Paul is quick to put matters into perspective: seen aright, present suffering is improportionate to future glory. To know things as they are one must recognize the scope of the drama in which one participates and the scale of the denouement for which one hopes. Present suffering is not merely local; it is cosmic. Future glory is not merely personal; it is universal. All history turns on the events of recent years, all creation awaits their completion, and Paul and his readers are at the epicentre of both. In one sense, the weight of the entire cosmos is on their shoulders; in another, the entire cosmos cheers them on. Thus Rom 8:18–39 provides both explanation and incentive. One may better accept suffering if one knows its origin and anticipates its cessation. All the more, one may accept (even 'boast of', 5:3) suffering that advances some great cause. Rhetorically, 8:18–39 is not unlike the stirring speech delivered by (Shakespeare's) King Henry V to encourage his outnumbered troops to face the French at Agincourt ('We few, we happy few, we band of brothers', *Henry V*, IV. iii).

Paul says that creation (the natural world) is 'groaning in labour pains', an image that evokes both the curse (in God's words to Eve) and the promise of its reversal (new life). v. 23 captures the resultant eschatological tension: 'we ... who have the first fruits of the Spirit [the Spirit's many benefits, mentioned above], groan inwardly'. Believers are now children of God (v. 14), possessing 'a spirit of adoption' (v. 15), yet they must 'wait for adoption, the redemption of ... [their] bodies' (v. 23). It is interesting that v. 24 contains the only past tense form of the verb 'to save' (*esōthēmen*) in any of the undisputed Pauline epistles: literally, 'we were saved *in hope*.' Hope requires both object and absence. vv. 18–25 testify to a profound hope fuelled by the certainty and desirability of its object and the profundity of its absence.

v. 20, the identity of 'the one who subjected' the creation to futility is the topic of intense debate. The likely candidate is again Adam, the consequences of whose sin surely underlie the reflections of the entire paragraph. But did Adam subject the creation to futility 'in hope'? A variety of attempts have been made to get to grips with this odd phrase. For example, Cranfield (1979: 414) wrote that 'The creation was not subjected to frustration without any hope ... Paul possibly had in mind the promise in Gen 3.15 that the woman's seed would bruise the serpent's head (cf. Rom 16.20)'. An alternative solution is to regard the entire phrase 'for the creation ... who subjected it' as a parenthesis, and attach the final two words of v. 20, 'in hope', to the next phrase, as does NRSV (the original Greek text did not contain punctuation; where phrases or even sentences begin and end is by no means certain). Thus, v. 21 may complete the thought of v. 19: 'For the creation waits ... in hope that ['or because'] the creation itself will be set free ...'

It is possible that the phenomenon described in vv. 26–7 is the gift of tongues, which Paul describes in 1 Cor 14:15 as 'praying with the spirit'. The statement that 'God ... knows what is the mind of the Spirit' could refer to the fact that tongues were unintelligible to the human speaker. (According to 1 Cor 14:3, the one speaking in tongues 'utters mysteries with his [her] spirit'.) It is also possible that 'untterable groanings' (*stenagmois alalētois*, v. 26) refers, literally, to inarticulate moans. This interpretation takes into account the fact that vv. 26–7 assume universal applicability, whereas, by Paul's own account, all did not speak in tongues (1 Cor 12:4–11). On the other hand, it should be said that the second reading has more difficulty explaining the repeated assertion that the Spirit 'intercedes' on behalf of the saints. An unrelated issue concerns the degree of separation between God and Spirit in Paul's description (e.g. 'God knows what is the mind of the Spirit'; see Dunn 1988: 479–80).

v. 28 does not promise that only good things will happen to 'those who love God'. In the larger context of vv. 18–39, and the immediate context of vv. 29–30, the sentence probably means that the woes that characterize the present age, and the suffering of persecution in particular, cannot thwart God, who uses even these to accomplish the divine purpose.

Paradoxically, Paul assumes both that God predestined humans to a certain fate and that humans are responsible for that fate. Rom 9:14–26 shows that he knows the obvious objection—how can humans be held responsible for God's actions?—and that he does not possess a *rational* answer. Instead, he responds, 'Who are you, a human being, to argue with God?' (9:20). Here as elsewhere in the NT, predestination is not mentioned abstractly; it usually functions either as assurance (as in Rom 8) or as theodicy (as in Rom 9; really another form of assurance). The essential point is that, despite all appearances to the contrary (the 'all things' of v. 28), God has everything under control.

As was mentioned in connection with ROM 1:16, 'justification' in Romans combines two ideas: that God credits to believers the status of righteousness and that God empowers believers to live righteously. Both meanings may be present in v. 29: it is God's purpose that believers 'be conformed to the image of his Son'. Certainly, this means sharing in future glory, being one 'within a large family' (cf. 1 Cor 15:20). 'Image' (*eikōn*), echoing the creation account of Gen 1 (v. 26), invites an additional and fuller interpretation, that believers already share the character of Christ.

The entirety of Rom 1–8 reaches its climax in vv. 31–9. Paul's speech is fittingly dramatic, harking back again (ROM 1:16) to Isa 50:7–8 (LXX; trans. Hays 1989: 59–60): 'I know that I shall by no means be put to shame, | Because the One who justified me draws near. | Who enters into judgment with me? | Let him confront me. | Indeed, who enters into judgment with me? | Let him draw near to me. | Behold, the Lord helps me. | Who will do me harm?' By way of encouragement to his readers, Paul wrote earlier of the disproportion between present tribulation and future glory (vv. 18–25). To the same end, he now writes of the disproportion between earthly appearance and spiritual reality. For believers, the one true indicator of their position is the love of God demonstrated in the cross of Christ. (v. 32 is especially poignant because it borrows language from the story of the binding of Isaac in Gen 22: 'you have not withheld your son, your only son' (v. 12); Cranfield 1979: 436. In Rom 8:32, God makes the sacrifice that even Abraham was 'spared'; note the verbal echoes of Gen 22:12 in Rom 8:32.) With this datum, the 'everything else' of v. 32 is assured. No condemnation is more persuasive than Christ's intercession, no deprivation, no sovereignty, no distance a greater reality. 'In all these things we are more than conquerors through him who loved us.' It is a glorious vision.

God's Righteousness Evident in the Treatment of Israel (9:1–11:36)

(9:1–5) Paul's Lament over Israel In first eight chapters of Romans the Protestant Reformers found the answer to their urgent question, 'How shall we be saved?' Ironically, their close identification with Paul worked both to popularize and to obscure Paul's distinctive theological contribution. In assuming common cause with Paul, they tended to project onto Paul their own struggles with disconsolate conscience and disapproving Catholicism. So Romans came to be viewed as a kind of personal salvation manual, a road-map for guilty, lost souls in search of a forgiving, gracious God. One consequence was the orphaning of the remainder of the epistle, especially chs. 9–11, whose interest in the fate of Israel was scarcely an ongoing or pivotal Christian concern. Recent biblical scholarship has been more successful at placing Rom 9–11 where it properly belongs, at the centre (or, rhetorically, at the climax) of Paul's argument. The concern of Romans is not so much to explain justification by faith in Christ as to explain how such a soteriological system upholds God's righteousness, especially God's righteousness towards non-Christian Israel. Thus, deprived of chs. 9–11 Romans would be gravely deficient; indeed, without reading to the section's surprising conclusion in 11:25–36, one might wonder truly if unbelieving Israel's present status does not expose 'unrighteousness on God's part' (9:14).

Moving from 8:39 to 9:1 is like walking off a precipice; having scaled the resplendent heights of ch. 8, one drops by a single step to the shadowy depths of ch. 9. 'I have great sorrow and unceasing anguish in my heart' (v. 2). Why sorrow if nothing is able 'to separate us from the love of God in Christ Jesus our Lord' (8:39)? Because it appears that Israel is not among the 'us', that Israel *is* alienated from God's love. This is an intolerable conclusion against which Paul mobilizes two basic arguments. First, he contends that now as in the past, only a portion of Israel has been elect or faithful; therefore, one ought not to regard the present case as being exceptional either from the side of God or of Israel. It is evident that this answer was not fully persuasive even to Paul. The word of God might not entirely have 'failed' (v. 6), but Jewish Christianity remained a disconcertingly small success. Paul's second answer locates the solution outside present history (and therefore beyond the thwarted historical means of the Church's Jewish mission): at the return of Christ, 'all Israel', even 'disobedient' Israel, will be saved (11:25–36). In this belief, Paul finds a solution to the problem of God's apparent unrighteousness: God, being God, must save Israel.

Paul's remarks in vv. 1–5 appear to reflect Ex 32:30–4, Moses' offer to be 'blotted out of the book' for the sake of the Israelites, who had 'sinned a great sin' in constructing the golden calf at Sinai. (The Sinai incident also might be in view in Paul's description of human idolatry and rebellion in ROM 1:18–32). Not long before, in 2 Cor 3:4–11, Paul explicitly contrasted (his) Christian ministry with that of Moses at Sinai. This same historical referent might have encouraged Paul to begin speaking of the 'Israelites' (v. 4 and more generally in these three chapters) instead of the 'Jews'. 'Israel' and 'Israelite' are in any case the terms better suited to his argument; they allow Paul to treat past and present Judaism as a whole, they signal continuity with previous 'covenant communities', and they provide the common conceptual thread that runs through a series of arguments concerning the identity of God's true people.

In 3:1, Paul asked, 'Then what advantage has the Jew? Or what is the value of circumcision?' His answer, 'Much in every way,' was ambiguous. The only specific instantiation was Israel's entrustment with 'the oracles of God' (3:2). In vv. 4–5, Paul returns to the question, this time offering a significantly longer list of privileges, the ultimate of which is to provide (by earthly descent, 'according to the flesh') the world with its Messiah. The most unexpected item in the list is 'adoption', which in just the previous chapter had a distinctly—and uniquely—Christian nuance (8:15, 23; cf. Gal 4:5). Presumably, Paul now refers to something different, most likely to God's 'adoption' of Israel in the Exodus (as in Ex 4:22; Hos 11:1). It is interesting to note how such points of continuity both strengthen and weaken Paul's argument. On the one hand, God's work of universal adoption in Christ may be seen to be consistent with (and therefore made credible by) God's previous action in adopting Israel; on the other hand, to the extent that Israel already is adopted, it ought not to require readoption. For this reason, when Paul defends the necessity of Christ, as logically he is forced to do, his argument must lean heavily to the side of discontinuity. Jews cannot have any actual advantage with respect to salvation if Jews and Gentiles are both equally in need of Christ.

The enumeration of divine blessings leads Paul into doxology: 'God, who is over all, is blessed forever. Amen' (v. 5). The original Greek text did not include punctuation, which makes it possible to translate the phrase appositionally, i.e. as an explanatory remark concerning Christ (e.g. the NRSV's '. . . the Messiah, who is over all, God blessed forever'). Despite Paul's generally high Christology (ROM 1:1–5), it is very unlikely that he would have referred to Christ as 'God over all'. Some commentators note by way of contrast 1 Cor 15:24–8, in which Paul states that Christ himself 'will also be subjected to the one who put all things in subjection under him, *so that God may be all in all*' (my emphasis; Dunn 1988: 535–6).

(9:6–29) God's Consistency Evident in the Election of True Israel Once again, the issue of God's righteousness is front and centre. 'It is not as though the word of God had failed' (v. 6). The 'word of God' refers broadly to God's promises to Abraham and through him to his descendants (see 4:13–25). Why might one argue that this 'word' had failed? Because comparatively few who now recognize and experience its fulfilment in Christ are Abraham's offspring. The Jews, who ought to be first and foremost, appear to be last and least (cf. 1:16). Has God's plan for Israel been thwarted? It cannot be so. Paul argues that the divine promises to Abraham were fulfilled by the election of only a portion of Abraham's natural descendants. God chose Isaac over Ishmael, Abraham's first born. One might object that of the two sons only Isaac had the right of succession, being the sole child of Sarah, Abraham's wife. Such a protest is impossible, however, in the case of Abraham's grandson Jacob, whose elder brother was his twin (see Gen 25:19–34). The word of God was not frustrated by the 'failure' of Ishmael and Esau to obtain their natural birthright. It was through the second born, the true 'children of promise', Isaac and Jacob, that God's plan was fulfilled. The reference in vv. 27–9 to the remnant of Israel (Isa 10:22–3) makes much the same point (see 11:1–5): God's choice of a part of Israel is well precedented; so among contemporary Jews it is the Christian believers who are the elect descendants of Abraham. It is important

to recognize that Paul does not maintain this position unvaryingly; in 11:25–32, he will argue for the salvation of unbelieving Israel based upon its *continued* election. ('For the gifts and calling of God are irrevocable', 11:29.)

Paul is not making the point that physical descent from Abraham in itself is insufficient to save. For Paul, lineage is simply irrelevant to salvation. Rom 9 harks back to the argument of Rom 4, where Paul stated that Abraham's true descendants are not the 'adherents of the law' but those who 'share in the faith of Abraham' (4:14–16). The contrast between 'children of the flesh' and 'children of the promise' in v. 8 sets up an analogous human-way v God's-way dichotomy. The major difference is that Paul's argument in vv. 6–13 only indirectly concerns Gentiles. (In v. 24, he will again include Gentiles explicitly as part of God's people, although he does not employ the idea of 'promise', as he did in Rom 4.) The issue is whether 'fleshly' Israel *in toto* is the Israel for and in whom God must be shown to have acted faithfully. For Paul, at least in the context of this argument, it is not.

v. 13, the severe statement 'I have loved Jacob, but I have hated Esau' (Mal 1:2–3; see HBC 1155, on the original, probably less extreme, sense of this verse) pointedly raises the question of God's justice (vv. 14–29). Paul's first answer (citing Ex 33:19) is that it is no injustice to be merciful, to treat some people better than they deserve. The issue is not God's just or unjust response to human goodness (v. 16); election is a gracious gift, not an achievable reward. Even the hardening of Pharaoh's heart (vv. 17–18) was done to advance the cause of God's salvation (Ex 9:16). Of course, things might look different from the perspective of Pharaoh or Ishmael or Esau. Granted that election is undeserved, why elect some and not others? The problem is intensified by positing a 'reverse election' in which God hardens the hearts of the wicked. How can God find fault for what God has caused (vv. 18–19)? This is a problem with a very long history in Judaism. The belief in the omnipotence of the one true God may lead to (or, inversely, may be guided by) the conviction that God exerts control over all human circumstances. Thus the Exodus narrative states repeatedly both that Pharaoh hardened his own heart (Ex 8:14, 32; 9:34; etc.) and that God hardened Pharaoh's heart (4:21; 7:3; 9:12; etc.). The same perspective is evidenced in passages such as Deut 2:30, Josh 11:20, 1 Sam 6:6, and—most poignantly in reference to Israel itself—Isa 63:17: 'Why, O LORD, do you make us stray from your ways and harden our heart, so that we do not fear you?'

God's omnipotence is affirmed by means of the potter metaphor (Isa 29:16; 45:9–13; Jer 18:6; Wis 15:7). The potter has sovereign right over the clay, not the reverse. It is significant that Paul links this idea to a statement about God's unexpected patience towards the wicked (vv. 22–3; see Wis 11:21–12:22). If God is both just and powerful (as powerful as a potter over a lump of clay), why do the wicked exist, much less flourish? The assertion of God's omnipotence underlies all theodicy; if God controls human action, then human evil itself must originate in God. Negating this conclusion requires a limiting of God's omnipotence (often imagined as a divine self-limitation: here, for example, judgement is forestalled temporarily by God's patience; see also 2:4; Neh 9:30; 1 Pet 3:17; and 2 Pet 3:9, 15). The problem is as old as the book of Job and remains as intractable. Paul's answer is reminiscent of that of Job's latter chapters: 'Who indeed are you, a human being, to argue with God?' Logically, this is no answer at all; instead, it is a roundabout affirmation that God can be trusted. This faithful God indeed has done what was promised, calling a people out from among Gentiles (vv. 25–6) and Jews (vv. 27–9) alike. In sum, if much of 'natural' Israel is not included in true Israel, it cannot mean that God has failed. Then whose fault is it?

(9:30–10:21) Israel's Failure Explained In a sense, 9:6–29 explained Jewish unbelief 'from above', that is, from the perspective of God's purpose and election. What follows is an explanation 'from below', an account of Israel's response and hence responsibility. Several of Paul's statements in this section are difficult to untangle, but the essential point seems clear enough: Gentiles happened effortlessly upon righteousness by believing the proclamation concerning Christ. Jews, who had worked diligently to be righteous, have rejected faith in Christ, the only thing able to make them *truly* righteous. For this error they have no excuse.

The meaning of 'righteousness' is fundamental to this passage and has been the subject of intense debate (see Ziesler 1989: 251–2). In large part, the problem arises because Paul uses the term in a distinctly new, Christian sense, even in reference to Judaism. Writes Sanders (1977: 544),

Righteousness in Judaism is a term which implies the *maintenance of status* among the group of the elect; in

Paul it is a *transfer term* ... Thus when Paul says that one cannot be made righteous by works of law, he means that one cannot, by works of law, 'transfer to the body of the saved.' When Judaism said that one is righteous who obeys the law, the meaning is that one thereby stays in the covenant.

Within Judaism, one did not obey the law in the hope of transferring from one people (unrighteous, unsaved) to another (righteous, saved). Paul's faith/law antithesis presupposes that Jews were trying (and failing) by means of the law to attain a status ('righteous' = being 'saved') that could be conferred only by faith in Christ. Thus the juxtaposition of law and Christ as rival means of salvation is problematic; normally, the two serve different functions in different systems. From the side of Judaism, it is an apples-and-oranges comparison; however, from Paul's side, with the controversy at Galatia fresh in mind, the opposition between faith in Christ and works of the law was as straightforward as the distinction between chalk and cheese (see ROM E.3). One should note how readily and frequently a difference in theological nuance or emphasis is transformed polemically into an antithesis. A modern example is the contention on the part of some conservative Christians that unlike other churchgoers, they do not practise 'religion' but rather experience a 'relationship' with God. Outsiders might regard the religion/relationship antithesis as quite odd: even the most experientially oriented Christianity is still a religion; certainly others (including other Christians) affirm relationship with God. For insiders, however, the dichotomy helps to account for the existence of (so-called) Christians who reject the group's distinctive claims. Such persons can be dismissed as 'unbelievers' who strive misguidedly through 'religion' to know God. Similarly, Jews who for varying reasons reject Christian claims can be depicted as formalistic law-keepers without faith. In either case, what is offered is an insider's account of the rejection of those outsiders who ought to know better.

Paul's first explanation of Israel's fault, in vv. 31–2, is notoriously ambiguous. One might have expected Paul to say that 'Israel had pursued but did not achieve righteousness' (Cranfield 1979: 507). Instead, Paul wrote that Israel 'pursued a law of righteousness' but 'did not arrive at' (or 'attain') 'law'. The meaning of 'law', 'righteousness', 'law of righteousness', and 'attain law' in v. 31 have been debated extensively with no resulting consensus. It is not even clear whether it was the 'pursuit' of law itself or the inability to 'attain' ('catch up with', Fitzmyer 1993: 577) law that Paul faults. If the former, Paul might be saying that Israel's pursuit of 'legal righteousness' could not lead them to the law's true goal (as possibly in 10:4). If the latter, Paul might mean that Israel attempted but failed to live righteously according to the precepts of the law. In either case, succeeding verses make clear that the actual fault of the Jews is their unbelief in Christ, whom they insensibly overlooked (10:2–3), over whom they have stumbled (9:32–3, a combination of Isa 8:14 and 28:16; the same idea is repeated in 11:9–12; 1 Cor 1:23; and 1 Pet 2:6–8). As a result, they are characterized as being unsaved (10:1), 'disobedient and contrary' (10:21), 'broken off', 'cut off', 'fallen' (11:19, 22), and 'hardened' (11:7, 25). Their only hope is to 'submit to God's righteousness' (10:3), which means specifically to believe in (10:4, 9, 11; 11:20, 23), call upon (10:13), and confess (10:9–10) Christ.

Phil 3:2–9 is a close parallel to Rom 10:1–4 and helps to clarify Paul's distinction between the Jews' 'own righteousness' and the righteousness imparted by God through Christ. In Phil 3:6, Paul says that 'as to righteousness under the law', he was 'blameless', a statement in tension with the interpretation of 9:31 that suggests that the Jews erred by failing to attain just such a status. In Phil 3, 'one's own' righteousness 'under the law' is rejected not because of its unattainability but because of its inferiority. Rom 10:1–4 may be much closer to this sentiment than is Rom 1–7. While it is not stated whether persons may succeed at 'establishing their own' righteousness, it is clear that their attempt to do so misses the point. Another, superior kind of righteousness exists, in the face of which the lesser righteousness is only a distraction. Put differently, the problem is this: Judaism is experienced as a complete, self-contained religious system that does not appear to require faith in Christ. One can be a superlative ('zealous', Phil 3:6; Gal 1:14; Rom 10:2) Jew—the pre-Christian Paul is Paul's own pre-eminent example—and still be on the wrong side of the line. Essential for Paul is the belief that Judaism without Christ is unfinished, that the law itself points to Christ as its ultimate goal and fulfilment (v. 4, *telos*, probably in the sense both of intention and termination; Barrett 1957: 197). Paul's characterization of Judaism's incompleteness varies; Paul's conviction of its incompleteness does not.

Considerable debate has arisen over the relationship between the key vv. 5 and 6, focusing on the force of *de* ('but') at the beginning of the second sentence. If *de* signals a strong contrast (again, between two forms of righteousness), then Paul is stating quite boldly that Moses was wrong to assert that one could 'live' (in Paul's usage, the word probably refers to resurrection life; see ROM 1:17) by doing the law. In favour of this interpretation one may cite Gal 3:12, which quotes Lev 18:5 to similar effect: Moses' words prove that 'the law does not rest on faith' but on 'works'. One way of diminishing the contrast between the two verses is to take the reference to 'live' in v. 5 in its original sense, referring not to eternal life but rather to 'life sustained by God...in accordance with the...law' (Dunn 1988: 612). But Rom 7:10 speaks of the commandment 'that promised' but could *not* deliver 'life'; there (as possibly in 10:5–6) it is not a question of two kinds of life but of two means, one failed and the other successful, of attaining the one true, eternal life. Other interpreters find continuity, not contrast, in Paul's statements. For example, Hays (1989: 75–7) has argued that vv. 6–13 explain v. 5 by indicating what 'things' one must do in obedience to the law to find eternal life: namely, confessing, believing, and calling upon Christ. This view may be supported by the fact that Paul's second quotation, which helps to establish the principle that 'righteousness comes from faith', is also from 'Moses' (Deut 30:12–14, followed by citations of Isa 28:16 and Joel 2:32). It is instructive that those who do and those who do not see a contrast between vv. 5 and 6 link Paul's argument to v. 4 (Christ as *telos*) in essentially opposite ways: the former emphasizes Christ as the law's termination, the latter Christ as the law's goal.

Paul's first two elaborations on Deut 30:12–14 ('that is, to bring Christ down', 'that is, to bring Christ up from the dead', 10:6–7) provide 'a scriptural exclusion of any contemplation of the kind of human effort the rival mode of righteousness would involve' (Byrne 1996: 318). One need not, indeed cannot, do what God has done in Christ. The common obligation of Jews and Greeks is only to 'believe', 'confess', and 'call on the name of the Lord'.

10:14–17, Paul returns to the matter of Israel's fault. Can it be that Israel's unbelief is occasioned by simple ignorance? Do they fail to call on Christ because they have not heard 'the word of Christ' (vv. 17–18)? The 'good news' (Isa 52:7) has been delivered to them, but the report has not been received (also precedented in Isaiah: the nearby 53:2). Paul concludes his argument by offering scriptural warrant for the situation described in 9:30–1. Gentiles 'who are not a nation', 'who did not seek' God, have found God (Deut 32:21; Isa 65:1). By contrast, Israel is a 'disobedient and contrary people' to whom God's hands have been extended in vain (Isa 65:2). Thus, Paul would lay Israel's fault, its unbelief in Christ, at Israel's own feet.

(11:1–36) God's Plan for Israel Once again, Paul advances his argument with a rhetorical question concerning God's faithfulness and constancy. 'Has God rejected his people?' vv. 1–10 reiterate the answers provided in ch. 9. That only a remnant of physical Israel is true Israel is precedented in Jewish history, in this case, in the example of Elijah and the seven thousand (1 Kings 19). God has not spurned *this* Israel, that is, the portion of Israel 'whom he foreknew' (v. 2) and elected (v. 7). Again, Paul speaks of God graciously choosing some and of God hardening others (vv. 5–7; see 9:6–18), which Paul again defends by means of scriptural citation (vv. 8–10; Deut 29:4; Isa 29:10; Ps 69:22–3; see 9:17, 25–9; cf. the similar use of Isa 6:9–11 in both the synoptic tradition, e.g. Mk 4:12, and John, e.g. Jn 12:40).

v. 11, the shift in Paul's argument here is immensely important. Imagine that chs. 9–11 had ended at 11:10: 'let their eyes be darkened so that they cannot see, and keep their backs forever bent'. In that case, Paul might with good reason be regarded as a thoroughgoing Christian supersessionist. 'Israel failed to obtain what it was seeking' (v. 7), and so Israel has been set aside in favour of the church. The fact that Paul has been read this way for centuries amply demonstrates that Rom 11:11–36 has not been given its due weight as the conclusion and climax, not only of Rom 9–11, but of the argument begun in 1:16–17 concerning the righteousness of God. Paul asks, 'Have they stumbled so as to fall?' For the first time, the possibility is raised of a future change in Israel's status. Their present 'stumbling' is not to be interpreted as a permanent 'fall'. As much as Paul wanted to justify the present reality (e.g. through talk of an elect remnant), he could not accept that reality as permanently justifiable. Here at last Paul offers a strong answer to the persistent question concerning God's faithfulness towards Israel.

In conventional Jewish eschatological expectation, Israel would first be restored, and then into that redeemed Israel would stream believing Gentiles (e.g. Isa 2:1–4; 42:1–9; 49; 55:4–5; 60:1–7; 66:18–23). Paul reveals this

'mystery' (v. 25): Jewish obduracy has led to a reversal of the eschatological timetable. Now is the period of Gentile inclusion: 'through their stumbling salvation has come to the Gentiles' (v. 11); 'their stumbling means riches for the world' (v. 12); 'their rejection is the reconciliation of the world' (v. 15); 'you (Gentiles) were once disobedient to God but have now received mercy *because of* their [the Jews'] disobedience' (v. 30, my emphasis). Precisely what Paul believed happened (or could have happened in its place) is not clear. He might have imagined that Christ would have returned already had the mission to Israel succeeded. It is worth noting that the same train of thought is evident in Acts: the Jews are given a chance to repent with the promise of Christ's return (e.g. 3:17–21); increasingly, they reject the apostles' message, resulting ultimately in the martyrdom of Stephen (ch. 7), a direct consequence of which is the spread of Christianity to the Gentiles (11:19–26). This same pattern—Jewish rejection leading to Gentile opportunity—occurs repeatedly in the accounts of Paul's missionary activity in Acts (e.g. 13:13–52; 18:1–8; 28:17–28).

v. 25, the period of Gentile evangelization is impermanent: 'a hardening has come upon part of Israel, until the full number of the Gentiles has come in'. After the mission to the Gentiles is complete, God will act to bring faith to Israel and to complete the eschatological drama: 'So all Israel will be saved; as it is written, "The Deliverer will come from Zion, he will banish ungodliness from Jacob"; "and this will be my covenant with them when I take away their sins" ' (vv. 26–7, quoting Isa 59:20–1; 27:9). 'What will their acceptance be but life from the dead!' (v. 15). Interestingly, the author of Luke–Acts also maintains the expectation of a Jewish restoration following the Gentile mission (e.g. Acts 1:6–7; cf. the periodization of history in Lk 21:24: 'Jerusalem will be trampled on by the Gentiles *until the times of the Gentiles are fulfilled*,' my emphasis). Unfortunately, NT scholarship often has overlooked the presence of these ideas in Romans as well as in Luke–Acts.

So, when all is said and done, God's election of 'all Israel' stands (cf. 'full inclusion' in v. 12), and God's righteousness is vindicated (vv. 29–32). No details are offered concerning the constitution of 'all Israel'. (All Jews at all times? All Jews present at Christ's return? Cf. Sanday and Headlam (1980: 335): ' "Israel as a whole, Israel as a nation," and not...necessarily including every individual Israelite.') At very least, it is clear that this group includes many if not all who are now, from Paul's perspective, 'disobedient' (vv. 30–1) 'ungodly' (v. 26, a stunning characterization), and even 'enemies of God' (v. 28). Unlike Gal 6:16, there is no possibility here that Paul is referring to the church as ('spiritual') Israel. Ch. 11 contains two hints as to the means of Israel's eventual salvation. In vv. 11 and 14 Paul returns to a point made by his earlier quotation of Deut 32:21 (10:19): Israel will become jealous of the Gentile believers and repent. Perhaps this is sufficient means to win some to faith in Christ (11:13–14)—but 'all Israel'? That will be accomplished by God directly (v. 23), apparently in anticipation or consequence of Christ's return (v. 26; note the eschatologically oriented vv. 12 and 15). More than that Paul does not say.

vv. 17–24, Paul's understanding of the relationship between Gentile believers and Israel is explicated by means of the olive tree metaphor. The Gentiles have no true root in themselves; they are wild branches grafted into an already existing, carefully cultivated olive tree. True, they now occupy the place of natural olive branches (Jews) pruned because of their fruitlessness (their unbelief), but they have no cause to be proud. The present situation is temporary: natural branches will be grafted back in, and some wild branches may yet be 'broken off'.

It should be said that the 'mystery' revealed in 11:11–32 does not follow *logically* from 1:1–11:10. Stopping at 11:10, one would conclude that only a small remnant of Israel is or ever will be saved. The church's mission to the Jews failed, and that is that. But present appearances belie ultimate realities (cf. 8:31–9). The resolution to Paul's 'sorrow and unceasing anguish' (9:2) is found at length in his trust in the eschatological triumph of God's righteousness. The issue finally is decided, not by reason, but by faith.

Fittingly, Paul's disclosure of the divine plan leads him to doxology (vv. 33–6), an expression of awe at the greatness of God who uses even 'disobedience' to produce 'mercy' (vv. 30–1). Of course, it is not God's inscrutability or power alone that compels Paul's adoration; above all, it is God's righteousness that is proved in God's 'ways' and 'judgments'. In coming to understand God's mysterious plan for Israel, Paul has looked behind the veil and glimpsed 'riches', 'wisdom', and 'knowledge' beyond human calculation. Paul's 'hymn of adoration' (Dunn 1988: 697) crowns chs. 9–11 in much the way that 8:31–9 concluded chs. 1–8. Both passages affirm with rhetorical beauty and force the apostle's

trust in God's trustworthiness. Disputation at an end, Paul points to God's future, believes in God's triumph, and worships.

The Righteousness of God Evident in the Lives of Believers (12:1–15:13)

(12:1–2) Introduction: The Renewal of Your Minds At 12:1, Romans turns from the conceptual and argumentative to the practical and didactic. This is a shift towards more typical Pauline content; anyone familiar with Paul's Corinthian, Philippian, or Thessalonian correspondence should feel at home in the ethical exhortations of chs. 12–15. Of course, Paul here writes to a church that he neither founded nor visited, a fact evidenced by the fairly general nature of his paraenesis (see ROM C, on the lack of contingency in Romans).

Paul has laboured to defend God's righteousness, in part through attributing to believers a righteousness unrealized by the now antiquated means of law obedience. But it is one thing to speak loftily of fulfilling 'the just requirement of the law' by 'walking according to the Spirit' (8:2–4); it is quite another to mark out the steps for such a journey. What does this new righteousness look like in everyday practice? Paul provides an illustrative, not exhaustive, answer in these few chapters.

God's extraordinary mercy was described in 11:30–2. What then is the fitting ('logical', *logikos*) human response ('service' or 'worship', *latreia*, 12:1)? It is to present oneself wholly to God, from whom and through whom and in whom are all things (11:36). Offering 'your bodies a living sacrifice' connotes giving oneself continuously and entirely. Any lesser response misprizes the greatness of God's own offering.

The eschatological context of Pauline ethics is immediately evident. v. 2 begins, literally, 'Do not be conformed to *this age*.' Paul vividly characterized the old order in Rom 1:18–32; humans had 'became futile in their thinking, and their senseless minds were darkened' (1:21). The new, eschatological righteousness overmasters humanity's ancient, fallen nature: believers experience a 'renewal of...[their] minds, so that...[they] may discern what is the will of God—what is good and acceptable and perfect' (12:2b). For Paul, it is no less than a return, a 'conforming' to the original order, the re-creation of human minds not 'subjected to futility' (8:20; cf. 'new creation' in Gal 6:15; 2 Cor 5:17). Paul does not expect his readers to obtain such an exalted capability on their own. Rather, he believes that as possessors of the

Spirit, they are already equipped to live lives 'holy and acceptable to God' (12:1; see 8:1–17). Paul asks only that they be what they truly are: righteous.

(12:3–21) Exhortations for the Christian Community It is obvious that the recent Galatian controversy influenced Paul's discussion of the law in Rom 1–8. Less noticed is the impact of Paul's difficulties with the church at Corinth upon Rom 12–15. Note that Paul's first exhortation is to humility and Christian unity—not surprising, as he writes from Corinth, the native habitat of spiritual pride and factional division (see 1 Cor 1–4). It is a sermon well rehearsed: vv. 3–8 are closely paralleled by 1 Cor 12:12–28. A major difference is the list of gifts in vv. 6–8, which is more mundane than that found in 1 Cor 12:28. (Rom 12 includes gifts of exhortation, generosity, and compassion but not deeds of power, healings, and tongues. In Romans the gifts are not linked specifically to the activity of the Spirit, and the corporation of Christians is not referred to as 'the body *of* Christ.') Paul again counters disunity by challenging individual status seeking, but, outside of Corinth, he does not locate the problem specifically in the flaunting of spiritual gifts.

The listing of maxims, as in vv. 9–21, is characteristic of ancient paraenesis and is a feature commonly found near the conclusion of Paul's letters (e.g. 1 Thess 5:12–22; Phil 4:4–9). Probably Paul draws from no one source but rather from the broad stream of Christian ethical teaching, incorporating elements of the Jesus tradition, Jewish wisdom literature, and Graeco-Roman philosophy (Byrne 1996: 375). A unifying element is supplied by v. 9*a*: 'love is genuine' (*anupokritos*; lit. unhypocritical). (Contrary to NRSV, there is no imperative verb.) The discussion of the body of Christ in 1 Cor 12 was also followed (in the justly celebrated ch. 13) by an appeal to *agapē*, love. It is love alone that curbs self-assertion and so makes unity possible (Phil 2:2; 1 Pet 3:8). Accordingly, the whole of vv. 9*b*–13 is sometimes read as a description of 'unhypocritical love in action' (Achtemeier 1985: 198). Perhaps this is too tidy a summarization of Paul's wide-ranging admonitions; nevertheless, it is certain that Paul regarded love as the pre-eminent and finally only necessary command, a point he makes explicitly in 13:8–10 (and in continuity with passages such as Mk 12:28–34; Mt 5:43–8; 19:19; Jn 13:34–5; 15:12–17; Jas 2:8; 1 Jn 3:11, 23; 4:21; and 2 Jn 5).

(13:1–7) Christians and Civil Authority Paul commended his readers to 'live in harmony' and to 'live peaceably with all'; immediately after, he adjured them not to seek revenge (12:16, 18–19). A discussion of civil authority follows naturally if not necessarily from these remarks. It may be that Paul's comments reflect concern over behaviour that had contributed to the expulsion of the Jews (including Christian Jews; see Acts 18:2) from Rome only a few years before (see ROM B. 3).

Does Christian conversion, the submission to God's rule, release one from civil authority? It is reasonable to suppose that one who lives in a new age is free of the old age. But one cannot live *only* in the new aeon; on earth the ages overlap. God's dominion is not entirely realized; believers' hearts are not wholly submitted (hence Paul's admonishment in 12:2). One might regard government as an expedient necessitated by human sin; even so, it is apparent that Christians do not yet live so distant from the Fall as to make obsolete government's corrective function. And predating the fallen, evil order is the original, beneficent order of creation (see Rom 1:18–20). Is government a temporarily sanctioned accommodation or an eternally mandated institution? Like Jesus in Mk 12:17, Paul does not deal explicitly with these questions; nevertheless, his words invalidate some answers, such as regarding government as human invention or satanic usurpation.

Few if any passages in the Pauline corpus have been more subject to abuse than vv. 1–7. Paul does *not* indicate that one is required to obey public officials under all circumstances, nor does he say that every exercise of civil authority is sanctioned by God. No particular government is authorized; no universal autarchy is legitimated. Instead, Paul reiterates the common Jewish view that human governance operates under God's superintendency (Jn 19:11; Dan 2:21; Prov 8:15–16; Isa 45:1–3; Wis 6:3), that it is part of the divine order and so is meant for human good (1 Pet 2:13–14; *Ep. Arist.* 291–2). Paul's view of and desire for order is also paralleled in 1 Corinthians. Paul responded to the chaos of Corinthian worship by arguing that 'God is a God not of disorder but of peace' (14:33) and so commended his followers to do 'all things' 'decently and in order' (14:40). Here Paul advises a new group of readers to find peace by submitting to proper order (cf. 1 Cor 16:16). It is striking that Paul treated with such optimism the very Roman authority by which he himself was eventually martyred. The presentation in Rom 13 has often been contrasted with that of Rev 13, in which Rome is portrayed as a diabolical beast whose 'authority' is exercised in making 'war on the saints' (v. 7). Rom 13 and Rev 13 are not quite opposites; Paul is not attempting to account for the reality depicted in Revelation. Nevertheless, the near demonization of the state in Revelation may be a healthy canonical counterbalance to its near idealization in Romans. But both Paul and the author of Revelation share common ground in asserting God's final authority over human affairs, humanity's ultimate allegiance to God, and God's eventual victory over every opposing 'ruler, authority, and power' (1 Cor 15:24–5). Rom 13:1–7 is not easy to live with, but neither would the opposing alternative be.

(13:8–10) 'Love is the Fulfilling of the Law' In Rom 12:9, Paul offered a theme for the ethical instruction to follow: 'love is genuine.' He neatly closes this paraenetic section by returning to the subject of love. The segue in vv. 7–8 is artful: 'Pay to all what is due (*opheilas*)...Owe (*opheilete*) no one anything, except to love'. In other words, while civic obligations can and should be fulfilled, the obligation to love can never be fully discharged. The primacy of the love commandment is a NT commonplace and almost certainly goes back to Jesus himself (see ROM 12:9*a*). In Mk 12:28–34 and parallels, Jesus cites a twofold commandment, love of God (Deut 6:4–5) and love of neighbour (Lev 19:18). Paul refers only to the latter. Perhaps he did not know the double formula, or perhaps his immediate concern led him to quote only the Leviticus passage. (The four commandments listed are all from the 'second table' of the Decalogue, which deals with social relationships; Deut 5:17–18.) To be children of God is pre-eminently to have the character of God, and the pre-eminent attribute of God's character is love (Mt 5:43–8). Such love issues from the giver irrespective of the recipient's merit: 'God proves his love for us in that while we still were sinners Christ died for us' (5:8). So no fault in the neighbour and no sufficiency in the self excuses one from love. And if one shares the character of God, then indeed God's law is fulfilled.

(13:11–14) The Eschatological Context Paul completes a second *inclusio* by returning to the eschatological theme introduced in 12:2 ('Do not be conformed to this age...'). The present is characterized as a time between the times, expressed eloquently in the metaphor of night turning to day. Now is still a time of darkness, but the believer knows it to be the darkness preceding the dawn. Recognizing that 'the night is far gone' (v. 12), one rouses oneself, lays aside the secret, shameful 'works of darkness' (detailed in v. 13), dresses in 'the armour of light' (v. 12, i.e. by behaving righteously), and stands ready before the approaching day.

In 12:2, Paul asked his readers to act as those already inhabiting a new age, to live up to their high spiritual standing in Christ. The argument is reminiscent of 6:1–5: Christians are in a fundamentally new position, already having died to sin. So, 'How can we who died to sin go on living in it?' (6:2). In vv. 11–14 we find much the same idea. One who lives 'as in the day' makes 'no provision for the flesh', gives no quarter to the 'works of darkness' (v. 12). To be holy is to be unmixed, entirely sanctified to God (12:1). The temptation is to view the eschatological ethic partly as a future demand, to split the difference between old and new orders, to contrive a half-in, half-out moral standard. For Paul, such unholiness is neither permissible nor sensible.

The phrase 'put on the Lord Jesus Christ' (v. 14) appears to have originated in Christian baptismal liturgy. Compare Gal 3:27: 'As many of you as were baptized into Christ have clothed yourselves with Christ.' 'Taking off' (or 'laying aside', v. 12) and 'putting on' is the nomenclature of repentance, intrinsic to baptism (cf. the idea of the 'wedding garment' in Mt 22:11–14). To say that one 'puts on Christ' adds to repentance the concepts of spiritual identification and empowerment (cf. Gal 2:19–20). In 6:3–4 Paul wrote that 'all of us who have been baptized into Christ Jesus were baptized into his death...we have been buried with him by baptism into death, so that, just as Christ was raised from the dead by the glory of the Father, so we too might walk in newness of life'. In baptism, one participates in the death and, proleptically, in the resurrection of Christ. The believer puts on the clothing, not merely of a new self, but of Christ's own righteousness, power, and victory. This high 'Christian anthropology' is in keeping with Paul's thought elsewhere in Romans (ROM E.2; ROM 8, etc.).

(14:1–15:13) 'Pursue What Makes for Peace and for Mutual Edification' Paul began this section of Romans with an exhortation to Christian unity (12:3–8), modelled on his recent Corinthian correspondence. By way of conclusion, he returns to the same idea and source. Controversy had arisen at Corinth over the practice by some of eating meat that had been sacrificed to idols (1 Cor 8:1–13; 10:12–33). In theory, Paul was on their side: 'We are no worse off if we do not eat, and no better off if we do' (8:8). But theory is not principle, privileges are not rights, and 'knowledge' (8:1) is not wisdom. The prerogative of the 'strong' (15:1) does not outweigh the church's need for unity and the individual's need for integrity. Simply put, it is wrong to encourage another to violate conscience. 'Therefore, if food is a cause of their falling, I will never eat meat, so that I may not cause one of them to fall' (8:13). The scope and application of Paul's 'community ethic' are nowhere more clearly articulated than in 1 Cor 8 and Rom 14.

As we have seen (e.g. in 12:4–7), Paul generalizes the argument of 1 Corinthians when adapting it to Romans. The identity of 'the weak' is no longer clear; Paul does not mention food sacrificed to idols, nor do his statements about eating meat and drinking wine (v. 21) refer self-evidently to Jewish practice (although the mention of 'one day … better than another' in v. 5 probably has in view the Jewish sabbath). Rather than respond to any one practice, Paul formulates a rule of conduct that may be applied in a variety of circumstances (which, by way of example, include controversies surrounding eating, drinking, and sabbath observance). One is to live before God with faith (14:5–9, 22–3) and before others with consideration (14:1–5, 13–21). Do not look to the example of those who offend; do not be an example to those who would be offended.

Paul's ethical thinking inhabits the ground between individualism and communitarianism. It is somewhat individualistic: each person stands or falls before God alone (14:4); each must be 'fully convinced' in his or her 'own mind' (v. 5); each is accountable to the dictates of his or her 'own conviction' (v. 22). But the community has moral priority. Recognition of individual differences is meant to foster unity (as in the body metaphor); ironically, it is those who demand absolute conformity that 'pass judgement' (v. 4) and so create division. The individual is constrained both by God's judgement (vv. 7–12) and by the needs of others (vv. 13–23). One ought to please God (v. 18) and one's neighbour (15:1–2), not oneself. This is not self-annihilation; this is mutuality, the dance of reciprocating love.

The tolerant attitude evidenced in this passage belies the oft-popular image of Paul as narrow-minded traditionalist. (14:14, 'nothing is unclean in itself', attests to the radical inclination of Paul's thought.) v. 4, 'Who are you to

pass judgement on servants of another?' is reminiscent of that most-cited biblical quotation, Mt 7:1, 'Judge not, lest you be judged.' As a matter of perspective, one should bear in mind that neither Paul nor Jesus taught that one ought simply to 'behave and let behave'. The sphere of activity within which Paul allowed disagreement was significant but still restricted in size. Essentially, it consisted of matters regarded by Paul as morally indifferent (14:1: 'opinions', see 1 Cor 9). 'The kingdom of God is not food and drink' (14:17), but it is 'walking in love' (14:15). Then as now, conflict arose because of discrepant calculations of moral gravity. Inevitably, it is easier for the 'strong' (the less observant) to be tolerant of the 'weak' (the more observant) than the reverse. At what point does moral allowance turn the corner to moral abdication? Were Jewish Christians intolerant who continued to require sabbath observance (which is, after all, the fourth commandment of the Decalogue; see Mt 24:20)? In the first as in the twenty-first century, tolerance is in the eye of the beholder.

In 15:1, Paul explicitly identified himself with 'the strong' ('in faith', 14:1), a designation that he assumes rhetorically for most if not all of his audience. (What reader would want to identify with the community of the weak-but-tolerated?) The NRSV translation, 'We who are strong ought to put up with the failings of the weak,' is unfortunate. Literally, the strong are instructed to 'carry', 'support', or (by extension) 'tolerate' (*bastazō*) 'the *weaknesses* (asthenē-mata) of the 'weak'. To judge the actions of the weak as 'failings' is to commit the very error described by Paul in ch. 14.

Paul caps his exhortation to unity and mutual concern by referring to the example of Christ, 'who did not please himself' (15:3). 'Welcome' (or 'accept', 'receive', *proslambanomai*) 'one another … just as Christ has welcomed you' (15:7). The passage is similar to Phil 2:1–11, where Paul charges his readers:

Be of the same mind, having the same love, being in full accord and of one mind. Do nothing from selfish ambition or conceit, but in humility regard others as better than yourselves. Let each of you look not to your own interests, but to the interests of others. Let the same mind be in you that was in Christ Jesus … (vv. 2–5)

What follows is the well-known 'Christ hymn', a poetic description of Jesus' self-abnegation and subsequent exaltation. Rom 15:3 is somewhat different: Paul refers only obliquely to Christ's passion, quoting the lament of the righteous sufferer in Ps 69:9, 'The insults of those who insult you [God] have fallen on me.' (Psalm 69 was widely cited in early Christianity; Cranfield (1979: 733n. 1) lists 18 other NT 'quotations and echoes'.) Christ's identification with God (15:3) and with humanity (15:8) cost him honour and status, the same currency that Paul would require his readers to expend for one another (12:3–5).

Rom 15:7–13 completes the discussion of Christian life begun in 12:1. More importantly, it brings to a close the larger argument begun in 1:16. 'Christ has become a servant in order that he might confirm the promises given to the patriarchs' (v. 8) thus proving God righteous. Christ came both for Jews (v. 8) and for Gentiles (vv. 9–12), a reiteration of Paul's 'thesis statement' in 1:16–17. As he has done repeatedly before, Paul cites scriptural evidence validating the inclusion of Gentiles in the people of God (Ps 18:49; Deut 32:43 (LXX); Ps 117:1; Isa 11:10 (LXX)). In conclusion, Paul again shifts from argumentative to sacral address (cf. Rom 8:31–9; 11:33–6), now, appropriately, in the form of a benediction. The phrases 'God of hope' and 'abound in hope' evoke the eschatological expectation that grounds the believer's everyday experience. In 14:17, Paul wrote that 'the kingdom of God is not food and drink but righteousness and peace and joy in the Holy Spirit'. So Paul concludes by wishing his readers nothing less than God's dominion, both now and future.

Conclusion (15:14–16:27)

(15:14–33) The Apostle's Plans Paul began the epistle by introducing himself and his apostolic credentials to the Roman Christians and by explaining his intention to visit them in the near future (1:1–15). His language was highly diplomatic; he praised the Romans for their faith and offered that he himself would be benefited spiritually by them. v. 14 picks up where 1:15 left off. The audience again is lauded: 'you yourselves are full of goodness, filled with all knowledge'. The apostle again is politic: he acknowledges that the recipients themselves are 'able to instruct one another'. Yes, Paul has written rather boldly, but only by way of reminder (v. 15). Besides, his boldness is commensurate with his authority in Christ, carefully detailed in vv. 16–21.

Several aspects of Paul's self-description merit attention. The use of sacerdotal imagery to describe his ministry ('priestly service…the offering of the Gentiles') is telling. Paul's language

appears to echo Isa 66:18–23, a prophetic description of the eschatological incorporation of Gentiles into Israel (see also Isa 2:1–4; 42:1–9; 49; 55:4–5; 60:1–7). The 'offering of the Gentiles' (v. 16), an idea borrowed from Isa 66:20, probably consists of the Gentiles themselves (in the person of the church leaders who would accompany Paul to Jerusalem; see Barrett 1957: 275) as well as the money gathered from their congregations (vv. 25–8; Gal 2:10; 1 Cor 16:1–4; 2 Cor 8, 9). Possibly Paul entertained the idea that the impending trip to Jerusalem might prove to be the 'pilgrimage of the nations' to 'the mountain of the Lord' (Isa 2:3; as in Isa 66) that would precipitate the coming of 'the Deliverer' to Zion (11:26 = Isa 59:20–1). This hope might account for the statement in v. 19 that Paul had 'fully proclaimed' the gospel from Jerusalem to Illyricum. The conversion of a representative group from the nations (equivalent to 'the full number of the Gentiles' in 11:25) might signal the fulfilment of Isaiah's prophecy and precipitate Christ's return (note 16:20). An obvious objection is that Paul planned to go on from Jerusalem to Rome and then to Spain (v. 28). Still, hoping for the eschaton and planning for its delay are not mutually exclusive activities. As a Christian missionary, Paul had done both for years.

The legitimacy of Paul's apostolic authority was disputed at Corinth as well as Galatia, and faint aftershocks of those controversies can be felt in vv. 17–19. As a Christian leader, Paul had a number of liabilities: for example, he had not known nor was he commissioned by the historical Jesus; he had persecuted the church; his physical appearance was 'weak', and he was comparatively 'unskilled in speaking' (2 Cor 10:10; 11:6). Paul acknowledged other leading apostles but claimed to have 'outworked them all' (1 Cor 15:10). He pointed repeatedly to his ceaseless labours and continual suffering for the sake of the gospel as primary validation for his ministry. He articulated this claim in passages that are among the most dramatic and powerful in all of his letters (e.g. 1 Cor 4:8–13; 2 Cor 6:3–10; 11:21–12:21). Here in Rom 15, he emphasized not only the extent but also the success of his evangelistic effort. By such a measure, his ministry may be peerless.

Paul's statement of purpose in vv. 20–9 serves a variety of functions. First, it explains why it has taken him so long to come to Rome. Paul's job is the founding of pioneer churches (v. 20); his assignment had been the field from Jerusalem to Illyricum (v. 19). Having now completed that task (v. 23), he is prepared to advance to

Spain. Second, it details the reason for Paul's trip to Rome and makes clear that his stay there will not be permanent. (In other words, he is not coming to 'take over' the Roman church.) Third, it lets the Romans know both that he expects to be welcomed (vv. 24, 29) and that he hopes to be supported by them in his mission to Spain (v. 24).

Paul asks for prayer 'that I may be rescued from the unbelievers in Judea'. It is a poignant request; according to Acts 21:27–36, Paul was arrested soon after his arrival in Jerusalem. The additional intercession, that 'my ministry to Jerusalem may be acceptable to the saints', has been seen by some as an indication that the Jerusalem church opposed the Gentile mission and so would reject the collection. Cranfield's (1979: 778) judgement is on target: '[It would] be more likely to recognize in these words evidence of Paul's spiritual and human sensitivity and freedom from self-centred complacency than to draw from them any confident conclusions about the tensions between the Jerusalem church and Paul.' (See also Fitzmyer 1993:726.) Contrary to the assertions of the Tübingen School, it is extremely improbable that the leaders of the Jerusalem church opposed the inclusion of uncircumcised Gentiles (see ROM D.3.3, above; cf. Gal 2:1–10; Acts 15:1–29). However, it is entirely likely that they took issue with Paul's conclusion that *Jews* no longer need obey certain parts of the law. (It is instructive that the charge raised in connection with Paul's arrival in Jerusalem concerned Jewish—not Gentile—law observance, Acts 21:21). For most Jewish Christians (e.g. the author of the Gospel of Matthew), the key issue apparently was not the Judaizing of Gentiles but the Gentilizing of Jews. It also is worth noting that Phil 4:18 uses similar priestly language in reference to the 'acceptability' of a monetary offering, but no interpreter suggests that the status of the Philippians' gift was ever in question. (See Hill 1992: 175–8, for further discussion of the interpretation of Rom 15:31).

(16:1–27) Personal Greetings and Final Remarks Was ch. 16 part of Paul's original letter to Rome? The question arises in part because of discrepancies in the textual tradition. One early manuscript (P^{46}, *c.*200) appears originally to have omitted 16:1–23. Other versions contain ch. 16 but locate the letter's benediction (16:25–7) at the end of ch. 14. Nevertheless, the manuscript evidence for the literary integrity of Rom 1–16 is quite strong

(e.g. Sinaiticus, Vaticanus, Codex Ephraemi, etc.). According to Origen, Marcion disseminated a version of Romans that ended at ch. 14. The likeliest account is that the missing passages were gradually reattached to truncated copies of Romans, the benediction being added first at the end of ch. 14 (see Stuhlmacher's valuable discussion, 1994: 244–6).

The authenticity of ch. 16 also has been questioned because of the extensive greetings (twenty-six people in all) in vv. 3–15. Could Paul have known so many Roman Christians? Some scholars have suggested that all or part of ch. 16 was a separate letter, possibly written to commend Phoebe to the church at Ephesus. It is an intriguing but unconvincing suggestion. Rom 16 by itself hardly constitutes an independent letter; moreover, we are scarcely in a position to judge whom Paul could not have known. Clearly, it would have been to his advantage to identify as many Roman confederates as possible. (Note that he first greets Prisca and Aquila, who left Rome under Claudius' edict and who may have returned following its suspension; Acts 18:2–3.) Finally, one may cite again the compelling textual evidence for the originality of ch. 16.

Rom 16 differs from other Pauline epistolary conclusions primarily in the length of its greetings (vv. 3–16) and its blessing (vv. 23–7; see below). Each of its elements is common to other Pauline closings:

Personal recommendation (vv. 1–2) 1 Cor 16:10–11, 15–18; 1 Thess 5:12–13 (cf. Phil 4:2–3); Philem 17
Personal greetings (vv. 3–16) Philem 23–4
Final admonition (vv. 17–20a) 1 Cor 16:13–14; 2 Cor 13:11–12; Gal 6:12–17; Phil 4:4–9; 1 Thess 5:14–22
Grace (v. 20b (=24)) 1 Cor 16:23; 2 Cor 13:13; Gal 6:18; Phil 4:23; 1 Thess 5:28; Philem 25
Greetings from companions (vv. 21–3) 1 Cor 16:19–20; Phil 4:21–2
Identification of writer/amanuensis (v. 22) 1 Cor 16:21; Gal 6:11
Blessing (vv. 25–7) 2 Cor 13:11b; Gal 6:16; Phil 4:19–20; 1 Thess 5:23–4.

The frequent mention of women in vv. 1–15 is impressive. Writes Beverly Gaventa (in Newson and Ringe 1992: 320) 'Nothing in Paul's comments justifies the conclusion that these women worked in ways that differed either in kind or in quality from the ways in which men worked.' Phoebe, probably the bearer of the letter, is referred to as a deacon (*not* 'deacon-ess', as in the RSV and MLB) and patron of the church. Nine other women are included in vv. 3–15, several of whom are commended for their ministry. Of particular interest is Junia (v. 7), who together with Andronicus (probably her husband) is said to be 'prominent among the apostles'. Almost certainly, the phrasing identi-fies both *as apostles*. For that reason, many trans-lators assumed that *Iounian* must be a contracted form of the masculine Junianus. In effect, they masculinized the name Junia, rendering it 'Junias' (e.g. RSV, NIV, NJB, NEB). But the pairing of names (as with Prisca and Aquila in v. 3) usually indicates a husband and wife; moreover, no cor-roborating example has been found for the sup-posed masculine form, while the feminine usage is very well attested (see the fine overview of the question in Dunn 1988: 894–5). In short, 'Junias' is a scandalous mistranslation.

Paul's letters often include final words of ad-monition (see table above). The exhortation in vv. 17–20 recalls the teaching in 12–15:13 con-cerning Christian unity, whose background was the recent controversy at Corinth (and second-arily at Galatia). The description of those who serve 'their own appetites' and deceive others by 'flattery' is reminiscent of Paul's account of fallen humanity in 1:18–32. On behalf of his readers, Paul assumes the best but cautions against the worst.

The stately prescript that began Romans (1:1–7) is echoed in the formal benediction in vv. 25–7. Paul again refers to his ministry of the 'gospel' (v. 25=1:1), mentions the testimony of the proph-etic writings (v. 26=1:2), and speaks of winning the Gentiles' 'obedience of faith' (v. 26=1:5). As he did in 11:36, Paul concludes with doxology, glori-fying God in whose mysterious plan and by whose eternal command the Gentiles have been brought into the communion of faith. It is a majestic crown to an extraordinary letter.

REFERENCES

Achtemeier, P. J. (1985) (ed.), *Harper's Bible Dictionary* (San Francisco: Harper).

Barrett, C. K. (1957), *A Commentary on the Epistle to the Romans*, BNTC (London: A. & C. Black).

Barth, K. (1933), *The Epistle to the Romans*, trans. E. C. Hoskyns (London: Oxford University Press).

Baur, F. C. (1873–5), *Paul, The Apostle of Jesus Christ*, trans. A. P. (vol. i), and A. Menzies (vol. ii) (2 vols.; London: Williams & Norgate).

Beker, C. (1980), *Paul the Apostle* (Philadelphia: Fortress).

Bultmann, R. (1910), *Der Stil der paulinischen Predigt und die kynischstoische Diatribe*, FRLANT 13 (Göttingen: Vandenhoeck & Ruprecht).

—— (1952–5) *Theology of the New Testament*, trans. K. Grobel (2 vols.; London: SCM).

Byrne, B. (1996), *Romans*, SP 6 (Collegeville, Minn.: Liturgical Press).

Cranfield, C. E. B. (1979), *Romans*, ICC (2 vols.; Edinburgh: T. & T. Clark).

Deissmann, A. (1927), *Light from the Ancient East*, 2nd edn. (London: Hodder & Stoughton).

Dodd, C. H. (1932), *The Epistle to the Romans*, MNTC (London: Hodder & Stoughton).

Donfried, K. P. (1991) (ed.), *The Romans Debate*, rev. edn. (Peabody, Mass.: Hendrickson).

Dunn, J. D. G. (1988), *Romans*, i. chs. 1–8; ii. chs. 9–16, WBC 38A–B (Dallas: Word).

Edwards, J. R. (1992), *Romans*, NIBC (Peabody, Mass.: Hendrickson).

Fitzmyer, J. A. (1993), *Romans*, AB 33 (New York: Doubleday).

Hays, R. B. (1989), *Echoes of Scripture in the Letters of Paul* (New Haven: Yale University Press).

Hill, C. C. (1992), *Hellenists and Hebrews* (Minneapolis: Fortress).

Holmberg, B. (1978), *Paul and Power: The Structure of Authority in the Primitive Church as Reflected in the Pauline Epistles* (Lund: Student-litteratur AB).

Jervell, J. (1971), 'The Letter to Jerusalem', ST 25. ET, Donfried (1991: 61–74).

Jewett, R. (1979), *A Chronology of Paul's Life* (Phila-delphia: Fortress).

—— (1982), 'Romans as an Ambassadorial Letter', *Interpretation*, 36: 5–20.

Käsemann, E. (1980), *Commentary on Romans*, trans. and ed. Geoffrey W. Bromiley (Grand Rapids: Eerdmans).

Manson, T. W. (1948), 'St Paul's Letter to the Romans—and Others', *BJRL* 21: 224–40. Repr. in Donfried (1991: 1–16).

Marxsen, W. (1968), *Introduction to the New Testament* (Oxford: Blackwell).

Morris, L. (1988), *The Epistle to the Romans* (Grand Rapids: Eerdman).

Murray, J. (1979), *The Epistle to the Romans*, NICNT (Grand Rapids: Eerdman).

Nanos, M. D. (1996), *The Mystery of Romans: The Jewish Context of Paul's Letter* (Minneapolis: Fortress).

Newson, C. A., and Ringe, S. H. (1992) (eds.), *The Women's Bible Commentary* (London: SPCK).

Räisänen, H. (1983), *Paul and the Law* (Tübingen: Mohr).

Sanday, W., and Headlam, A. C. (1980), *A Critical and Exegetical Commentary on the Epistle to the Romans*, 5th edn., ICC (Edinburgh: T. & T. Clark).

Sanders, E. P. (1977), *Paul and Palestinian Judaism* (Philadelphia: Fortress).

—— (1983), *Paul, the Law, and the Jewish People* (Philadelphia: Fortress).

Schlatter, A. (1995), *Romans: The Righteousness of God*, trans. S. Schatzmann (Peabody, Mass.: Hendrickson).

Spicq, C. (1994), *Theological Lexicon of the New Testament*, trans. and ed. J. D. Ernest (3 vols.; Peabody, Mass.: Hendrickson).

Stendahl, K. (1963), 'The Apostle Paul and the Introspective Conscience of the West', *HTR* 56: 199–215.

Stirewalt, L. M. Jr. (1977), 'The Form and Function of the Greek Letter-Essay', in Donfried (1991).

Stowers, S. K. (1981), *The Diatribe and Paul's Letter to the Romans*, SBLDS 57 (Chico, Calif.: Scholars Press).

—— (1994), *A Rereading of Romans* (New Haven: Yale University Press).

Stuhlmacher, P. (1994), *Paul's Letter to the Romans: A Commentary*, trans. S. J. Hafemann (Louisville, Ky.: Westminster/John Knox).

Wedderburn, A. J. M. (1988), *The Reasons for Romans*, SNTW (Edinburgh: T. & T. Clark).

Ziesler, J. (1989), *Paul's Letter to the Romans*, Trinity Press International New Testament Commentaries (London: SCM).

5. 1 Corinthians

JOHN BARCLAY

INTRODUCTION

A. Authorship. The letter claims to be written by Paul and Sosthenes (1:1) and there is no reason to doubt this ascription. As in other cases of supposedly joint authorship (e.g. 2 Cor 1:1), Paul probably took the sole responsibility (16:21). Clement accepted the letter as Paul's at the end of the first century CE (1 Clem 47) and all modern scholars concur, with doubts surrounding only certain sections (see on 11:2–16 and 14:34–5).

B. Integrity. Our earliest papyri preserve the letter whole (e.g. P46, from *c*.200 CE), but a number of scholars have argued that it is in fact a compound of several letters. Thus it has been suggested that 1 Cor 1–4 is a self-contained letter, closing in 4:14–21 with the typical close-of-letter formulae (see de Boer 1994). It is strange that the named party divisions which Paul repeatedly criticizes in chs. 1–4 are never mentioned in chs. 5–16. It is possible that the Corinthians' letter to Paul (7:1) and disturbing news about their behaviour (5:1) arrived after the initial drafting of chs. 1–4 but before they were sent to Corinth. However, the opening thanksgiving section (1:4–9) seems to anticipate themes which surface in later chapters (e.g. spiritual gifts in 1:7 and chs. 12–14), and the theme of unity (1:10) pervades the whole letter (see Mitchell 1992). Inconsistencies have been found within later chapters, for instance between an apparently softer stance on sacrificial food in 8:1–13 and 10:22–11:1, and a harder line in 10:1–22. Complex theories have been

propounded of two, four, or more original letters which have been stitched together into our 1 Corinthians (see details in *ABD* i. 1142–3). Such hypotheses are plausible in the case of 2 Corinthians, but Paul's varying rhetorical purposes can probably explain all the inconsistencies in this letter. Thus we may take 1 Corinthians as a single and unified whole.

C. Date. The letter is written from Ephesus in the spring (before Pentecost, 16:8–9). If we accept the chronology of Acts (see below), Paul founded the church in Corinth in 50–1 CE (Acts 18:1–7) and was in Ephesus two or three years later (Acts 19:1–10); thus the date of composition of this letter is some time in the period 52–5 CE.

D. Paul's Previous Dealings with the Corinthian Church. 1. It was of immense importance to Paul that he was the founder of the church in Corinth, the one who laid their foundation, however many supplementary builders they may have had (3:10). As his 'work in the Lord', the existence of the Corinthian church is, for Paul, proof enough of his apostleship (9:1–2), even if it is clear from chs. 1–4 and 9 that not all the Corinthians are willing to recognize his status or authority. Paul recalls bringing the gospel to Corinth at a time which was fraught with 'weakness, fear and trembling' (2:1–3). Some of the details which we may piece together from 1 Corinthians accord well with the narrative of this founding visit in Acts 18:1–17, for instance the conversion of Crispus (1 Cor 1:14; Acts 18:8), the contact with Prisca and Aquila (1 Cor 16:19;

Acts 18:2–3) and his labour in Corinth with his own hands (1 Cor 4:12; Acts 18:3). Paul's own comments do not allow us to date this founding visit, but Acts connects it (at its close, after 18 months) with a trial before the proconsul of Achaia, Gallio. By good fortune, an inscription enables us to date Gallio's period of office to 50–1 CE, thus giving helpfully precise parameters to the date of Paul's time in the city. Acts also mentions, as a prelude to Paul's visit, Claudius' expulsion of Jews from Rome (Acts 18:2). Conflicting evidence in our sources leads some scholars to think that that expulsion took place in 41 CE, and it has been proposed that Acts 18 actually combines the accounts of two separate visits by Paul to Corinth, one in 41 and one in 50/51 CE (see Lüdemann 1984: 157–77). However, Jews were probably not expelled from Rome until 49 CE (see Barclay 1996: 303–6), and there is thus no reason to doubt the integrity of the account in Acts 18 or the dating of Paul's initial visit to 50/51 CE.

2. Corinth was a cosmopolitan city, refounded as a Roman colony in 46 BCE, a seaport exposed to multiple influences from East and West (see *ABD* i. 1134–9 s. v. Corinth). According to Acts, Paul spent longer here than in most cities (at least 18 months, Acts 18:11, 18), a fact at least partly explained by the comparative lack of opposition he encountered in the city. The birth of the church also seems to have been unusually peaceful: Paul nowhere indicates any experience of harassment (see Barclay 1992). Paul established a core of believers, both Jews and Gentiles (1 Cor 1:22–4; 7:18), who were baptized in the name of Christ (1:13), received the Spirit (12:13) and started to meet for meals and worship in homes (11:17–34; Rom 16:23). Paul bequeathed to them a variety of credal traditions and practical instructions (15:3–5; 11:2, 23) but two factors combined to lessen his influence on the church once he had left the city. First, some of his own or subsequent converts were people of education and high social standing (see E.1) who developed independent views about the meaning of the Christian message (e.g. in relation to the resurrection of the body and sexual behaviour) and whose integration in Corinthian society made them reluctant to accept Paul's more sectarian social practices (e.g. in relation to sacrificial food). Secondly, situated at an international crossroads, the church in Corinth was visited by a variety of Christian leaders, some of whom won converts of their own and assisted the church to develop in ways of which Paul disapproved (e.g. Apollos and, probably, Peter/Cephas, 1:12; 9:4–5).

3. The first signs of conflict between Paul and the Corinthian church are preserved in Paul's reference to their reception of an earlier letter he had sent (5:9–11). This letter is now lost, but it seems to have urged a moral discipline on the church which was not well received. Perhaps in response to that letter, the Corinthians wrote a letter referred to in 7:1. It is possible to suggest some of the topics on which the Corinthians wrote to Paul: many may be introduced by the formula 'now concerning', which occurs not only in 7:1, but also in 7:25 (on the topic of virgins), 8:1 (on food offered to idols), 12:1 (on spiritual gifts), 16:1 (on the collection), and 16:12 (on Apollos). Moreover, with the aid of a little imagination, we may even reconstruct what the Corinthians thought about some of the issues Paul addresses: in some cases Paul seems to cite back at them their own formulae, such as 'all things are lawful for me' (6:12; 10:23), 'it is well for a man not to touch a woman' (7:1), and 'all of us possess knowledge' (8:1). (For a full reconstruction of this interchange see Hurd 1965; for an imaginative exercise see Frör 1995.) 1 Corinthians thus represents part of a dialogue between Paul and the Corinthians, a dialogue which, as 2 Corinthians indicates, caused considerable pain to both parties for years to come.

4. As well as the Corinthian letter, Paul has received oral reports about affairs in the church, for instance from Chloe's people (1:11) and from Stephanas, Fortunatus, and Achaicus who may have brought the letter from Corinth (16:17–18). Some of the oral reports have caused Paul great concern (1:11–13; 5:1). Now, in response to both written and oral information, Paul writes our 1 Corinthians hoping that it, and Timothy's visit (4:17), will induce the necessary changes in the church before he has to correct them in person (4:21). It is clear from 2 Corinthians that that hope was not fulfilled.

E. The Corinthian Church. 1. Recent scholarship has highlighted the importance of the social divisions in the church in Corinth and has posited the disproportionate influence of a small élite group within the church, whose attitude to their social inferiors and whose class-determined interpretations of the Christian faith underlie many of the issues addressed in this letter (see esp. Theissen 1982; Chow 1992; Clarke 1993; Martin 1995; more generally on Pauline Christians, Meeks 1983; see, however, the strong arguments to the contrary by Meggitt 1998). Paul's statement about the generally lowly make-up of the church in 1:26–8 none the less indicates that there were *some* members of education, power, or noble birth, and some named individuals seem to belong to such an upper stratum. For instance, Gaius (1:14) must be a man of some wealth to be able to house the whole church (Rom 16:23, written from Corinth); some think the church may have grown to fifty or more members. If Crispus and Sosthenes were rulers of the synagogue, as Acts 18 indicates, they must have been from wealthy families (the title normally designates financial patronage). Moreover, the Erastus who sends greetings from Corinth in Rom 16:23 is there listed as 'city treasurer'. The title might designate a lowly office, but it is extremely rare for Paul to mention the occupations of Christians and he would probably do so only if they were of social importance. It is tantalizing that an inscription from Corinth from around the middle of the first century CE mentions one Erastus (a very rare name in Corinth) as paying for a piece of pavement after his appointment as aedile. It is possible that this is the same Erastus as the one mentioned by Paul, at a subsequent and more exalted rung up the social ladder (aediles were among the highest civic leaders in Corinth; Theissen 1982: 75–83).

2. Thus the church in Corinth covered a broad social spectrum, with a few highly placed individuals who probably played a major role in shaping the life of the church and its relations with wider Corinthian society. The divisions at the Corinthian Lord's Supper (11:17–34) indicate the problems inherent in staging communal meals across such a spectrum, and the 'knowledgeable' who cared little for the scruples of their 'weaker brothers' in relation to sacrificial food (1 Cor 8–10) may have been those of higher status whose contacts with their social equals would have been greatly disrupted by taking a scrupulous stance on this matter. Other topics raised in this letter may also be related to wealth and status. The Corinthian Christians who took each other to court (6:1–8) might have been wealthy (court cases were often expensive) and were perhaps engaged in a power-struggle within the church. Speaking in tongues (1 Cor 12–14) was possibly an élitist activity (Martin 1991) and the whole spirituality of the Corinthian church probably reflects the confidence of those who accommodated their faith to their social aspirations (4:6–13). The party groupings mentioned in 1:12 may represent splits among the social élite who competed for patronage in the church. It is harder to discern how such social divisions related to the ethnic mix of the church (Jews and Gentiles) or to different opinions about sexual activity (contrast the ascetic Corinthian statement in 7:1 with the apparently libertine one in 6:12).

3. The leaders of the church in Corinth seem to have prided themselves on their status as 'spiritual people' (3:1–3; 14:37). That involved a particular eagerness for spiritual gifts (12:1; 14:12), but also a high evaluation of 'wisdom' and 'knowledge' (2:6; 8:1–3) which included the appreciation of mysteries (2:6–16; 13:1–2) and the conviction that others' so-called 'gods' are really shadows ('idols', 8:4–6). Their 'spiritual' status also encouraged a sense of 'authority'— particularly the permission to eat whatever they wished and to use their bodies however they liked (6:12; 10:23). Such an emphasis on spiritual knowledge seems to have reinforced and even extended the common Greek disparagement of the body as a paltry piece of material; as a result, there are partial parallels with the later phenomenon of Christian 'Gnosticism', though not to the extent some have claimed (e.g. Schmithals 1971). In any case, some Corinthian believers appear to have balked at Paul's notion of a resurrected body (15:12, 35–57) and others understood their new possession by the Spirit to require complete sexual abstinence (7:1, 25–39). Paul finds the claims being made by the Corinthians absurdly inflated, tantamount to claiming exemption from all the inevitable weaknesses and imperfections of the present (4:8–13; 13:8–13). It is not clear whether the Corinthians thought themselves already 'resurrected' in some final sense, or whether that is merely Paul's caricature of their position (4:8; cf. 1 Tim 2:18; Thiselton 1977–8). Paul attempts throughout the letter to puncture their pride and to redirect their sense of honour towards mutual service in the community.

F. Outline.
Prescript (1:1–3)
   Thanksgiving (1:4–9)
Appeal for Unity and for Re-evaluation of Paul's Ministry (1:10–4:21)
   The Absurdity of Party Groups (1:10–17)
   The Message of the Cross, its Recipients and Proper Medium (1:18–2:5)
   True Wisdom for Spiritual, not Bickering, Christians (2:6–3:4)
   Models of Leadership in the Church (3:5–4:5)
   Paul's Apostolic Style and Authority (4:6–21)
Sexual and Related Issues (5:1–7:40)
   Expulsion of an Immoral Member of the Church (5:1–13)

The Absurdity of Using Corinthian Courts (6:1–11)

Immorality and the Significance of the Body (6:12–20)

Celibacy and Marriage (7:1–40)

Sacrificial Food and the Dangers of Idolatry (8:1–11:1)

Debate with the 'Knowledgeable' concerning their 'Right' to Eat (8:1–13)

Paul's Example in Renouncing the 'Right' to Financial Support (9:1–23)

The Dangers of Complacency in relation to Idolatry (9:24–10:22)

Practical Guidelines on Eating and Avoiding Offence (10:23–11:1)

Issues Relating to Communal Meetings (11:2–14:40)

Praying and Prophesying with Proper Head-Covering (11:2–16)

Humiliation of Church Members at the Lord's Supper (11:17–34)

The Distribution of Spiritual Gifts in the Body of Christ (12:1–31)

The Superior and Critical Demands of Love (13:1–13)

The Superiority of Prophecy over Tongues (14:1–40)

The Resurrection of Christ and the Resurrection Body (15:1–58)

Letter Closing, with Travel Plans, Final Instructions, and Greetings (16:1–24)

COMMENTARY

Prescript (1:1–3)

This follows the form typical in the Pauline letters; sender, addressees, and greeting (cf. Gal 1:1–3). Paul mentions his apostolic calling since some in Corinth doubted this (9:1–2) and associates with himself Sosthenes, perhaps the synagogue leader mentioned in Acts 18:17, who must have been converted after the events narrated there. In referring to the church in Corinth Paul emphasizes their purity ('sanctified', 'saints', v. 2), a theme which he will later employ to reinforce the boundaries between the community and outsiders and to outlaw behaviour which soils the church (e.g. 5:6–8; 6:9–11). He also pointedly associates them with all other Christians elsewhere (v. 3). He will not allow the Corinthian Christians to exalt themselves over others (4:7), to neglect their needs (16:1–4), or to develop idiosyncratic patterns of church life (4:17; 11:16).

Thanksgiving (1:4–9)

Paul's letters generally begin with a thanksgiving, which places the life of the church in the context of God's activity and compliments the believers on their progress thus far. Despite the problems which this church poses, Paul appears genuinely grateful for its lively success, so long as it is attributed to 'the grace of God' (v. 4) by which they have been 'enriched' (v. 5). Later he will criticize the Corinthians for boasting in their spiritual virtuosity as if they had made themselves rich (vv. 7–8). Their God-given riches include every form of 'speech' and 'knowledge' (v. 5)—topics which will recur at several points in the letter (notably 1:18–3:5; 8:1–13; 13:1–2; 14:1–40), where Paul's appreciation is tempered with caution about the uses of such gifts in the community. In v. 6—which is probably best translated 'just as the testimony to Christ was confirmed among you'—Paul points forward to his discussion of the terms in which he first testified to Christ in Corinth (1:18–2:5), reminding his socially comfortable converts that all they have is based on the subversive message of Christ crucified. Their speech and knowledge are part of their enjoyment of every 'spritiual gift' (charisma, v. 7), a theme which comes to full (though again critical) expression in chs. 12–14. Notable at the end of this section are references to the future: for all their present abundance, the Corinthians still await 'the revealing of our Lord Jesus Christ' (v. 7) and the judgement which will take place on 'the day of our Lord Jesus Christ' (v. 8). Throughout this letter Paul will point forward to that future, to forestall premature judgements of his own or anyone else's ministry (v. 5), to warn against complacency in the race still unfinished (9:24–7; 10:12), and to moderate the exaggerated claims that were being made for knowledge and other spiritual gifts (13:8–13). Their only ground for confidence can be the faithfulness of God (v. 9; cf. 10:13), who has called them to participate in Christ (cf. 1:30–1). It is only by continuing in that 'fellowship' with Christ that they can face the end with confidence (cf. 16:22–4).

Appeal for Unity and for Re-evaluation of Paul's Ministry (1:10–4:21)

(1:10–17) The Absurdity of Party Groups v. 10 encapsulates the core of Paul's appeal which covers not only chs. 1–4, but also many other parts of the letter which appeal for mutual care within the church (e.g. 6:1–8; 8:1–3; 12:12–26). The 'divisions' spoken of here do not seem to prevent the church gathering together (Rom 16:23), but they damage its life, preventing its maturation (3:1–4) and negating its calling to love (13:1–13). Paul is responding in the first instance to oral reports from 'Chloe's people' (v. 11), probably the slaves of one of the members of the church. The quarrels they report concern the forming of party-groups in which members of the Corinthian church line up, in quasi-political fashion, behind Paul, Apollos, Cephas, or (apparently) Christ (v. 12). The last grouping receives no further mention in 1 Corinthians, except in Paul's insistence that *all* belong to Christ (3:22). Perhaps the statement here represents a claim by some Corinthians to a more direct allegiance to Christ. Apollos is repeatedly named in the following chapters, and his followers may have been converted through him, since we know he was in Corinth after Paul (3:6; Acts 18:24–19:1). It has often been suggested that Paul's critical words about eloquence in 1:18–2:5 may be directed against admiration of Apollos' rhetorical prowess (according to Acts 18:24 he was 'an eloquent man'). Therein may lie some truth, though Paul is careful never to criticize Apollos directly in this letter and says he has encouraged him to return to Corinth (16:12).

The Cephas party remains a matter of controversy. Had Cephas (Peter) visited Corinth, like Paul and Apollos, and thus played some role in shaping the Corinthian church? Some think that 9:5 suggests as much, others that Cephas' reputation was high enough for him to have attracted a following in Corinth without a personal presence (cf. 15:5 and Barrett 1982: 28–39). Either way, it is difficult to know what the Cephas party stood for. An old scholarly tradition (arising in the 19th cent. in the Tübingen school and revived by Goulder 1991) takes the Peter party to represent a conservative form of Jewish Christianity, which took the Jewish law as its continuing standard. However, evidence for this standpoint in Corinth is hard to find and the character and influence of the Cephas party remain an enigma. What is revealing, however, is that those who say they belong to Paul are only one segment of the Corinthian congregation. Without wanting to foster a Paul party in Corinth, Paul clearly needs to re-establish his authority over the whole church. 1 Cor 1–4 is thus characterized by a delicate balance between Paul's self-effacement, as he points to Christ and the cross, and his self-promotion as the 'father' of the Corinthian church and the model of Christian discipleship (cf. Dahl 1967).

Paul's first move is to ridicule the creation of such groups. Since the whole church belongs to Christ and constitutes his body (12:12–27) any such party splits threaten to dismember Christ (v. 13). Tactfully using the Paul party as his prime target, Paul insists that he is neither the origin of their salvation nor the one to whom they belong. Reference in v. 13 to baptism 'in [lit. into] the name of Paul' indicates that baptism was usually performed in Pauline churches 'into the name of Christ' (cf. 12:12–13; Gal 3:27). It appears that the person of the baptizer is being given special significance in Corinth and Paul thus deliberately plays down his role in this regard: he can think of very few whom he has baptized (vv. 14–16; on Crispus and Gaius see 1 COR E.1). The sudden remembering of Stephanas' household (v. 16) underlines the insignificance of Paul's role in this matter; the initial lapse of memory might be genuine, but it also serves an obvious rhetorical role. Stephanas seems to have played some leadership role in the Corinthian church (see 1 COR 16:15–18). Paul insists that his commission was to 'proclaim the gospel', not to baptize (v. 17). This does not mean he considered baptism insignificant: he assumes that all believers have been baptized (1 Cor 6:11; 12:13) and elsewhere spells out its theological significance (Rom 6:1–11). But he had a different and specialized role: to preach the gospel of Christ crucified. By immediately disowning an interest in 'eloquent wisdom' (v. 17) he prepares the way for the next section of the letter.

(1:18–2:5) The Message of the Cross, its Recipients and Proper Medium At first glance, this section might appear a digression from the topic of party divisions, a subject which does not recur till 3:4. But the conjunction of the themes of wisdom and party boasts in 3:18–23 indicates that the two are closely related. It is possible that wisdom (and specifically eloquence) was one of the bases on which Corinthian Christians were lining up behind different leaders (see above, on Apollos). But, more generally, Paul discerns in the claim of allegiance to vaunted leaders a fundamental misapprehension of the gospel, whose value-system is wholly opposed to the values of power and wisdom which the Corinthian competitiveness exhibits. Thus, typically, Paul attacks the disease which has brought about the worrying symptoms, and forces the Corinthians to recognize the counter-cultural impact of the gospel of Christ crucified, in its message (1:18–25), its chosen recipients (1:26–31), and its proper medium (2:1–5).

The message of the cross is portrayed as an uncompromising indictment of human values of wisdom and power, since it reverses their standards and undermines their pretensions. In 1:18 Paul introduces the twin antitheses of wisdom/foolishness and power/weakness, which undergird this whole section, and he embraces the apparent absurdity of his message of Christ crucified—absurd, however, only to those 'who are perishing'. The division of humanity into two groups—'those perishing' and 'those being saved' (he never says believers *have been* saved)— is similar to the dualistic spirit of apocalyptic literature, as also are the pejorative nuances in phrases like 'this age' (1:20) and 'the world' (1:21). For Paul, the turning-point of the ages is precisely in the death (and resurrection) of Christ (cf. 15:20–8). The cross of Christ marks the final indictment of vaunted human 'wisdom', the fulfilment of the prediction of Isa 29:14, cited in 1:19. With rhetorical questions, Paul calls for those reputed to be wise ('scribes' are those so reputed in the Jewish world) and declares that God has not just bypassed 'the wisdom of the world' but utterly subverted it (1:20). The failure of humankind to know God according to its own system of wisdom triggers a divine plan springing from a deeper 'wisdom of God' (1:21; cf. Rom 1:18–23). In Jewish fashion, Paul divides humankind into two: Jews and Greeks/Gentiles (the two latter are synonymous in 1:22–4, but the term 'Greek' is particularly well suited for association with wisdom). The distinction between their desires (Jews want 'signs'—that is, demonstrations of divine power—and Greeks want 'wisdom') is rhetorically over-schematized, since Jews were also interested in wisdom (e.g. the Jewish wisdom material) and Greeks were also interested in supernatural power (e.g. in healing). But it enables Paul to present the message of Christ crucified as the inverse of *all* human values. It is 'a stumbling-block' to Jews (cf. Gal 5:11; 6:12–14), particularly because of the scriptural association between 'hanging on a tree' and being accursed by God (Deut 21:22–3, cited in Gal 3:13); it is 'foolishness' to Gentiles, since this Roman punishment was universally feared as a hideously cruel and shameful death (the shame of prolonged, helpless, and public death being as devastating as its pain). But to those who are 'called' this ultimate symbol of weakness and absurdity represents, paradoxically, the precise locale where God displays his power and wisdom (1:24–5).

This negation of the human value-system is matched by God's call of believers (1:26–31). The social make-up of the Corinthian church proves Paul's point since few Corinthian Christians could claim status by education ('wise'), political influence ('powerful'), or ancestry ('of noble birth', 1:26). Although this observation plays a rhetorical function here, it must also be broadly true (for a social profile of the church, see 1 COR E.1–2). For Paul, the predominantly low-status composition of the church is no accident: it indicates precisely God's choice which aggressively 'shames' the wise and powerful in the world. To creat a rhetorical tricolon, Paul adds to his earlier twin motifs of wisdom and power a third category, the low (lit. ignoble) and despised (1:28) who shame those 'of noble birth' (1:26). He then expands this category to its fullest possible generalization: God chose the things that are not, to bring to nothing the things that are (1:28). The phrase 'the nobodies' depicts then, as now, those of no social significance, but it also evokes notions of God's creative role in bringing creation out of nothing (cf. Rom 4:17; Gal 6:15; 2 Cor 5:17). And if salvation is entirely the creation of God, no human being can claim credit or rest confidence in any human attributes of status or significance (1:29). Theologically this line of thought is parallel to Paul's assault on Jewish boasting in Rom 2–4, but here it is widened to embrace the whole human race. It is precisely the Corinthians' boasting and concomitant arrogance which Paul opposes throughout this letter (cf. 4:18; 5:2; 8:1; 13:4), and it is here exposed in its absurdity. All that salvation means in Christ (the list of abstract nouns in 1:30 sums up its meaning by reference to the core metaphors in Pauline theology) is possible only *from God* (so runs the Greek behind 'he is the source of your life', 1:30). And here Paul can rightly claim to be in continuity with the prophetic warning against self-confidence, citing (1:31) Jer 9:24, whose context warns against glorying in wisdom, power, and wealth.

Finally, Paul addresses the question of the medium by which this message is conveyed (2:1–5) recalling the terms in which he first communicated the gospel. Here he pointedly eschews rhetorical ability, despite the fact that this passage, 1:18–2:5, is one of the most rhetorically effective in the New Testament! In the Graeco-Roman world 'wisdom' was closely associated with rhetorical skill ('lofty' or 'plausible' words, 2:1, 4), which was a central element in 'secondary' education and was highly prized by a public which enjoyed listening to finely crafted speeches in the courtroom, assembly, or theatre (see Litfin 1994). Paul claims that his message was so completely focused on Christ crucified (2:2) that any decorative oratory would have been utterly inconsistent. His own weakness as messenger (2:3) matched the 'weakness' of the message, so that its powerful effect in evoking faith might be identified unmistakably as the power of the Spirit of God, not any human achievement (2:4–5). Paul here anticipates his later self-depiction as a figure of weakness and humiliation (4:9–13), characteristics which match the message of the cross (cf. 2 Cor 4:7–15; 11:21–12:10). Though they admired his letters (2 Cor 10:10), the élite Corinthian Christians clearly despised Paul's speaking abilities (2 Cor 11:6); but Paul regards his 'disability' here as precisely making visible the only 'ability' that counts, the power of God.

(2:6–3:4) True Wisdom for Spiritual, not Bickering, Christians At first sight 2:6–16 seems to shift into a different gear. After denigrating wisdom in 1:18–2:5, Paul suddenly claims to impart wisdom, and in doing so changes from the first person singular (I) to the first person plural (we)—a change then reversed in 3:1 ff. What is more, the claim to privilege the 'mature' (2:6; the Greek could be translated 'perfect') looks out of step with the notion that the cross subverts human hierarchies (1:26–9), while several terms in this section of the letter are unusual or even unique in Pauline literature (e.g. 'the depths of God', 2:10, and the contrast between the 'spiritual' and the 'unspiritual', 2:13–15; cf. 15:44–6 and Pearson 1973). Is Paul claiming access to a higher wisdom than the folly of Christ crucified? Does this passage reveal an esoteric or mystical side to Pauline theology not witnessed elsewhere?

The best explanation is that Paul is not outlining a new or more esoteric form of wisdom, but spelling out the implications of his gospel in terms that partially reflect the vocabulary and concepts of the leaders of the church in Corinth, but also in such a way that he can spring a rhetorical trap on his dialogue partners in 3:1–5. Although we cannot be fully confident in this matter, it is very likely that Paul picks up and reuses elements of the theological vocabulary of the Corinthian élite in this passage, for instance, their claim to be recipients of the revelation of the Spirit, to be 'spiritual' and not just in possession of ordinary, natural life (the 'unspiritual' of v. 14), to speak in Spirit-inspired terms to one another (2:13), and to be above critical scrutiny in such matters (2:15). Paul's skill in this passage is to accept and rework this pattern of vocabulary and then to turn it *against* the Corinthian élite in 3:1–5 when

he argues that their behaviour in fact *disqualifies* their claim to be 'spiritual'!

Paul first refers to a 'wisdom' communicated among the 'mature', which is hidden and decreed from eternity 'for our glory' (2:6–7). That may seem to confirm the élitist claims of the leaders of the Corinthian church who act as though they were already rich and filled (4:8). But Paul makes clear that he understands such concepts in an apocalyptic framework in which God's wisdom is precisely opposite to the wisdom claimed by 'the world', especially that espoused by the élite ('the rulers of this age'); similarly, the 'glory' to which we are destined is not a present but a future possession (2:9). It has often been thought that 'the rulers of this age' referred to in 2:6 and 2:8 are the supernatural forces of evil which Paul elsewhere calls 'powers' and 'authorities' (e.g. 1 Cor 15:24; Rom 8:38; cf. Col 2:15). But the precise term he uses here (*archontes*) is more naturally taken to refer to (human) 'political authorities' (cf. Rom 13:3) and their responsibility for the crucifixion (2:8) strongly suggests that Paul is thinking primarily of earthly political powers. The notion that these powers are 'doomed to perish' matches the thought of 1:28 (where the same Gk. verb is used): those considered 'something' are shamed through the cross, while the 'nothings' in this world are destined for 'glory'/honour (2:7). The shamed Crucified One turns out to be—by the same paradox as 1:25—the 'Lord of glory' (2:8).

The 'glory' which is destined for believers (2:7) is defined in 2:9 as indescribably beyond human imagination by means of a pastiche of scriptural phrases, drawn principally from Isa 64:4 and 65:17. The point here, developed in 2:10–16, is that the Spirit gives access to a realm of knowledge, and a language in which to communicate it, quite beyond normal human knowledge and communication. This is not to suggest that the gospel is inherently irrational, but that its content and what it reveals about God's paradoxical purposes go well beyond the frame of reference in which human language operates. As suggested above, some of the vocabulary here might reflect the terms in which the 'spiritual' people in Corinth distinguished themselves from those who had merely normal human abilities, the *psychikoi* (those with merely natural human life, *psychē*) translated in 2:14 as 'unspiritual'. However, by using the 'we' form throughout (e.g. 'we have received…the Spirit that is from God', 2:12), Paul suggests that these special attributes are applicable to *all* believers. Those who 'love God' (2:9; cf. 8:3) are gifted with 'the gifts of God's

Spirit' (2:14; cf. 12:1–11), which, like the cross, appear foolish by worldly standards (2:14). The Spirit therefore enables an understanding much deeper than mere human knowledge (2:15). Indeed, Paul can even claim in 2:16 that the rhetorical question of Isa 40:13 (originally phrased to expect the answer 'no one') can be used to describe a position filled by believers, who really have 'the mind of the Lord' (here taken to refer to Christ). Such bold claims indicate that Paul regards Christian faith as opening a dimension of understanding far more profound than anything offered by non-believing perspectives; this is of a piece with his assertion that the cosmos, and time, and life, and death 'belong to' believers, inasmuch as they belong to Christ (3:21–3).

But Paul's dialogue with the élite in Corinth cannot rest here. He now springs on them a rhetorical trap which *denies* to them the very spiritual superiority he had described in such glowing terms in 2:6–16. If what he has just described is the condition of the 'spiritual', let the Corinthians know that Paul could not initially impart such spiritual knowledge to them since they were merely 'people of the flesh, infants in Christ' (3:1). They cannot here be described as 'unspiritual' (2:14), since they had, as believers, received the Spirit (12:12–13); yet at the start of their Christian lives they were hardly spiritual in the terms they now claim, only 'of the flesh'—that is, ensnared in merely human patterns of thought and behaviour (cf. the flesh–Spirit antithesis in Gal 5 and Rom 8). At that stage, they could only take milk and were not ready to be weaned (3:2). But now comes Paul's really devastating blow: '*even now* you are *still* not ready, for you are *still* of the flesh' (3:2–3, emphasis added). In other words, all that Paul has been saying about 'the spiritual' and their understanding of the mysteries of God cannot really be applied to the Corinthians: he has built up the mystique of this category only to deny that the Corinthians can fit it! This is the first of many attempts in this letter to puncture the pride of the Corinthian Christians, but there is none more devastating. The basis of Paul's claim that they are still of the flesh is where the trap really bites: the jealousy and quarrelling evidenced in their claims of belonging to rival leaders (3:3–4) reveal precisely how immature they are! The party-groupings which set up rival claims to status in wisdom or in the excellence of the chosen leader indicate not how mature but how immature the Corinthian church is: their bids for superiority show just how inferior

they are, operating on the level of mere squabbling humans rather than as gifted and inspired people of the Spirit. Thus it appears that the party claims ('I belong to Paul' etc.) which seemed to disappear from sight after 1:18 were actually in the background all along. For Paul they represent a mindset determined by the values of 'this age' which have been fundamentally subverted by the message of the cross (1:18–2:5) and superseded by the new depths of understanding afforded by the Spirit (2:6–16).

(3:5–4:5) Models of Leadership in the Church
Now that he has returned to the topic of party groups in the Corinthian church (3:4), Paul constructs another line of argument against such factionalism, this time focused on leadership and its evaluation. To align oneself with one or another leader is, for Paul, to commit three cardinal errors: (1) to place leaders on a pedestal, where they do not belong; (2) to play them off inappropriately against one another; and (3) to reward them with human praise rather than leaving to God the assessment of their work. These three themes are the principal elements in the discussion of leadership in 3:5–4:5, which Paul develops by using metaphors drawn from agriculture (3:5–9), building (3:9–17), and household slavery (4:1–5). 3:18–23 forms an interlude which links this section back to 1:18–31 and points to the folly of the boasting which takes place in leadership competitions.

The agricultural metaphors in 3:5–9 emphasize the subordinate nature of Christian leadership as a task fulfilled only at the bidding of the Lord (3:5, 8) and in utter dependence on God's creative activity (3:6–7, 9). Paul and Apollos are no more than servants through whom (not *in* whom) the Corinthians believed (3:5). Paul, as founder of the church (a role he recalls frequently in this letter, cf. 3:10; 4:15; 9:2), may be said to have been its planter; Apollos' subsequent activity was to water the plants (3:6). But neither role is of any value without the gift of growth to the plants, a gift which only God can bestow (3:6–7). The Corinthians belong to the church by God's calling (1:2, 26–7), and it is God alone who is 'the source of your life in Christ Jesus' (1:30): thus it is absurd to use slogans which suggest that their leaders were themselves the creators, rather than simply the instruments, of the church's life. Moreover, the two tasks of planting and watering cannot be played off against one another: the two workers 'have a common purpose' (2:8; lit. 'are one'), so it is senseless to claim to belong to one and not to the other. They are 'working together' in an agricultural project planned and owned by God (3:9). And they will receive their reward not through human adulation but by God's assessment of their labour (3:8).

The end of 3:9 switches the metaphor to that of building, an image which governs the discussion of leadership in 3:10–15 and is then extended with reference to the temple (3:16–17). Paul the planter in 3:6 is now Paul the master builder, who laid the foundation of the church in Corinth (3:10). In this case reference is made not to Apollos, but to 'someone else' who is building on that foundation. Since within this metaphor God is less clearly the means of growth, the spotlight falls on human beings with responsibility for building, with a none-too-veiled threat that they may be performing their task badly (3:10, 12–13). The aggressive tone in Paul's voice has led many commentators to suspect that he is attacking some specific individual(s) in the church (e.g. Barrett 1971: 87–8). Moreover, it is tempting to take 3:11 as a rebuke of those who claim to belong to Cephas, on the basis of the famous rock prediction: 'You are Peter and on this rock I will build my church' (Mt 16:18). It is just possible that Paul is here attacking Peter and his influence in Corinth, though elsewhere in the letter he speaks of Peter in unpolemical terms (9:5; 15:5) and we do not know if the rock saying, which is found only in Matthew, was known in Corinth at this date. Paul is concerned at the direction of the current leadership of the church, and reveals those anxieties by warning of the consequences of building with worthless materials (3:12–15). Again the test of value comes not from present human assessment but from God's definitive judgement which will operate on 'the Day'. Building on traditional images of 'the Day of the Lord' as a fiery event (e.g. Mal 3:2–3; 4:1; cf. 2 Thess 1:7–8), Paul suggests that all worthless building materials will be consumed and the builder rewarded or punished ('suffer loss', 3:15) on the basis of what survives. The context suggests that he is referring specifically to those with leadership responsibilities, rather than to each individual believer. His basis for confidence that the builder will survive, even if his work is destroyed, is that God's grace has a secure grasp of those in Christ (cf. 5:5; 11:32). However, that does not negate the possibility that believers may somehow prise themselves away from Christ by continual and deliberate disloyalty (cf. 9:27; 10:6–12).

Indeed the seriousness of the building work being undertaken in Corinth is underlined in the extension of the metaphor to the church as a temple (3:16–17). Elsewhere, each Christian's body is described as a temple of the Holy Spirit (6:19), but here (as in 2 Cor 6:16) the church as a collective is so described. This is a striking transfer of terminology and allegiance from the Jerusalem temple, which was still standing at this time and was the object of reverence by Jews both in Palestine and in the Diaspora. Paul's Gentile converts were never instructed to pay any attention, or contribute any taxes, to that building; nor, of course, did they construct any 'temples' of their own. They were encouraged, rather, to think of themselves as a temple, the locus of God's holy presence. Thus, to inflict damage on a church community is to touch God's precious sanctuary, inviting his immediate judgement (3:17). Builders in Corinth should beware that they really build and do not destroy (cf. 8:10–11).

3:18–23 briefly interrupts the sequence of metaphors to underline once more the counter-cultural character of Christian commitment (3:18–19 echoes themes from 1:18–31). Expanding quotes from Job 5:12 and Ps 94:11, Paul emphasizes again God's opposition to the worldly standards of evaluation which undergird the Corinthians' rivalry as they boast in competing leaders (3:19–21). In fact, their slogans suggest a fundamental misapprehension of themselves and of the relationship between church and leader. Instead of saying 'I belong to Paul' (or whomever), they should recognize rather that Paul (or Apollos or Cephas) 'belong to' them (3:21–2). Although God's servants may play important roles in founding and encouraging the church, their purpose is not to win admirers or adherents but to serve the church to which they belong. By placing leaders on a pedestal the Corinthian church actually demeans itself: the leaders are there for the sake of the church, not the other way around. And Paul can expand this principle rhetorically with the claim that the world, life, death, and time are at the service of the church, because this community is not some mere club or social gathering but the centre of God's plan for the world and history (3:22; cf.6:2–3 and the expansion of this theme in Colossians and Ephesians). At least, the church has that role inasmuch as (and *only* inasmuch as) it belongs to Christ (that is the one slogan from 1:12 which Paul does not here reverse); and Christ himself belongs to God (cf. 11:3; 15:28). As the token of the new creation in the midst of 'this age', the church has a significance far greater than the leaders God uses to serve it. But its significance lies only in the fact that it belongs and bears witness to Christ, the agent of God's re-creative power in the universe.

The third metaphor of leadership is that of household slaves, specifically stewards (4:1–5). Again it is implied that such figures should not be the objects of praise (they are only agents of Christ, or of 'the mysteries of God'); but the emphasis here falls on the assessment of their work. Stewards are held accountable as to their trustworthiness (4:2), but by their masters, not by those they encounter in the course of their work (cf. Rom 14:4). At this point, Paul becomes directly personal, applying the metaphor specifically to himself as one who might come under the Corinthians' scrutiny (4:3) but who prefers to leave the judgement to his master (4:4; 'the Lord', *kyrios*, means also 'the master' of a slave). Here then emerges, what we might have suspected all along, that the party divisions in Corinth represent a critical evaluation of Paul's apostleship, inasmuch as some claim to belong to others *and not to Paul* (1:12). As in 9:3, Paul hints at a body of opposition to his authority, but he attempts to defuse it by insisting that it is inappropriate for the Corinthians to judge his behaviour, and premature as well: when the Lord comes (and not before), *he* will give full and final judgement (4:4–5). What will count then is commendation from God (4:5), not the measure of praise (or criticism) leaders currently receive from members of the church.

(4:6–21) Paul's Apostolic Style and Authority

The personal turn taken in Paul's final leadership metaphor (4:1–5) indicates the progression of the argument towards self-defence. It now becomes clear that Paul is under attack in Corinth, unfavourably compared with other leaders and criticized specifically for the poor figure he cuts and for his long absence from the scene. Paul's response requires him to confront and ridicule Corinthian pride (vv. 6–8), to describe, by contrast, his own highly vulnerable ministry (vv. 9–13), and finally to assert his fatherly authority in Corinth and announce his forthcoming visit (vv. 14–21).

Paul's first target is the inflated sense of importance in the Corinthian church, which he regards as the cause of their party rivalries: they are puffed up in comparing one leader with another, congratulating themselves on their chosen objects of allegiance (v. 6). Looking

back on 3:5–4:5, Paul says he has 'applied all this to Apollos and myself for your benefit' (v. 6). The Greek here is slightly obscure and might mean simply that he has put his discussion in the form of analogies (relating to Apollos and himself) rather than using literal speech, or that he has changed the analogies from one metaphor to another (gardener, builder, steward) to make his points as clear as possible. Another possible nuance is that he has disguised his meaning, making explicit reference to Apollos and himself, but really referring to other people (e.g. Cephas?). But it is unnecessary to attribute to Paul some subtle encoding of his message. He is simply drawing attention to his use of metaphor to indicate that he has set out these various leadership models in order to undercut the rivalries which afflict the Corinthian church. It is very hard to discern the source or meaning of the saying Paul cites in this context, 'Nothing beyond what is written' (v. 6; some suspect that the text is corrupt at this point). This looks like a slogan, but whose is it, and does it refer to Scripture or to something else that was 'written' (see Hooker 1963; Fee 1987: 166–9)? Few scholars claim to understand the allusion, which one imagines made more sense to the Corinthians than it does to us.

Paul regards Corinthian pride as manifest in a sense of special achievement and perfection. Their giftedness, which he recognized in 1:4–7, led to a sense of distinction, which easily obliterated gratitude for gifts received (v. 7). They have been *enriched* (by God, 1:5), but imagine themselves simply *rich* (v. 8); their notions of fullness and royal authority might be related to the Stoic notion of the self-sufficiency of the perfectly wise man. The sarcasm of v. 8 is an attempt to puncture that pride, and the following verses deflate it by depicting the life of the apostles (supposedly the models of the church) as the very opposite of the honour and victory which the Corinthians expect for themselves. Like those under a sentence of death, who are brought on at the end of a public spectacle to entertain the masses by their gruesome deaths, the apostles are a despicable sight, watched only to be ridiculed (v. 9). Their reputations match the folly, powerlessness, and shame of the cross (v. 10 echoes the themes of 1:18–25), and vv. 11–13 spell this out in practical terms, with some intriguing echoes of the ethos of the gospels (e.g. Mk 6:7–12; Lk 6:24–31). Included in this list of demeaning conditions of life is the fact that Paul works with his own hands (v. 12). That suggests that he is combating an ethos fostered by the social élite (who alone looked down on manual labour); in deliberate and perhaps exaggerated contrast, Paul presents himself as the scum of the earth (v. 13; cf. 1:28–9).

The polemical purpose of this self-portrait is evident when Paul declares his aim to be to 'admonish' his 'children' (v. 14); he denies that he wants to shame them (cf. however 6:5), but that cannot be ruled out as a proper result. It now becomes clear that Paul's role as founder of the church is crucial to his present bid to correct them. However many teachers and leaders may have operated in Corinth, they can have no status higher than 'guardian' (lit. childminder—the slave employed by parents to guard the safety of their children), whereas Paul is unique as their 'father' (v. 15). Paul wants to claim this role even in relation to those who were converted through other evangelists (e.g. after his departure from Corinth) and he uses it, as fathers often did in the ancient world, to require that his 'children' imitate his pattern of life and thought (v. 16). He is dispatching Timothy (perhaps with this letter) to reinforce his point, but also now promises to come in person (vv. 17–21). It appears that his long absence from Corinth has been criticized, or at least exploited, by those who think Paul's opinion about their affairs is insignificant (v. 18). With a final rhetorical flourish (still utilized by parents!) Paul offers them a choice: it is up to them whether he comes with gentleness or punishment (v. 21). This threat proved to be a fatal mistake, since Paul, when he finally did visit Corinth, found himself facing stiffer opposition than he had anticipated, and his stay proved extremely painful (2 Cor 2:1–2). The assertion of authority was to backfire in outright repudiation of Paul and still harsher criticisms of his ministry: in 2 Corinthians we can watch him trying to patch up a now deeply uneasy relationship.

Sexual and Related Issues (5:1–7:40)

(5:1–13) Expulsion of an Immoral Member of the Church The abruptness with which this chapter begins has led some to wonder whether it starts a new letter or is occasioned by some fresh news. But there are good reasons why Paul should have delayed treating such matters until now. The first four chapters of the letter, which undercut the Corinthians' pride and reassert Paul's authority, form the necessary platform for Paul to launch his specific assaults on behaviour in the Corinthian church. None of

what follows in chs. 5–16 would cut any ice in Corinth unless the members of the church were prepared to reconsider their canons of 'wisdom' and to listen to their 'father' in Christ.

The oral information to which Paul responds here was apparently rather more damning than what the Corinthians had divulged in their letter (7:1). Paul is shocked that they have tolerated a form of sexual liaison which he considers scandalous even among 'pagans', whom he takes to have minimal moral standards (cf. 1 Thess 4:5). The 'immorality' (*porneia*) concerns a prolonged relationship between a man and his father's wife, probably his stepmother and probably after the death of his father. We cannot say more about the figures involved (Clarke 1993 suggests that the man may have had financial interests in such a relationship, e.g. to secure his inheritance), except that Paul's chastisement of the man alone suggests that the woman was not a Christian (cf. vv. 12–13). Sexual relations between a man and his stepmother were generally considered incestuous, both in Judaism (e.g. Lev 18:8) and in the Graeco-Roman world (Ap. *Met.* 10.2–12), and it is therefore surprising that this Corinthian believer had got away with such behaviour thus far. It is possible that he was too important socially to be subject to criticism, and that he justified his behaviour specifically on the basis of the Christian ethos of liberty. The latter may be hinted at by Paul's expostulation: 'And you are arrogant!' (v. 2). That arrogance may exist despite such sexual activity, but it might also flourish *because of* the claim to freedom from taboos which Christian faith was understood to entail: in 6:12 (and 10:23) Paul will cite a Corinthian slogan which suggests a conscious embracing of liberty, even in sexual conduct (6:13). For the rest of this chapter Paul simply assumes that this behaviour is wrong; its perpetrator must therefore, he insists, be expelled. Later, however, in 6:12–20, he gives some reasons why he thinks a Christian must be responsible in the use of his/her body.

In vv. 2–5 Paul portrays an act of expulsion (excommunication) which may owe something to synagogue practices known to him. He imagines the church gathering like a court, to pronounce judgement 'with the power of our Lord Jesus'. Such is his own strength of feeling, and his lack of confidence in the moral values of the Corinthian Christians, that he imagines himself present 'in spirit' and declares already what verdict the church court will reach: they are to 'hand this man over to Satan for the destruction of the flesh' (v. 5). Handing over to Satan (cf. 1 Tim 1:20) probably means expulsion, on the understanding that the world outside the church is in the grip of Satan ('the god of this world', 2 Cor 4:4), but it is unclear whether 'the destruction of the flesh' implies physical harm (cf. 2 Cor 12:7), even death (cf. 1 Cor 11:30), or, more benignly, the suppression of the man's fleshly nature, that is, his propensity to sin (cf. 3:3; Gal 5:19–21). In any case, Paul regards the final result of this action as in some way salvific: 'his spirit' (the Greek lacks 'his' and might conceivably mean 'the spirit of the church') will be saved in the final judgement. The connection between destruction of the 'flesh' and salvation of the 'spirit' is obscure, and depends on the meaning of each term. Does physical suffering chasten, or death make atonement for sin, or moral correction purify the individual's spirit (see Fee 1987: 208–13)? 1 Cor 11:32 might suggest some chastening process.

vv. 6–8 highlight the danger of the Corinthians' nonchalant attitude in this matter, drawing on purity metaphors associated with Passover. v. 6 contains a proverb (cf. Gal 5:9 and Mt 13:33) concerning the disproportionate influence of a tiny substance—in this case, clearly, the single individual in the corporate body of the church. But yeast leads Paul to think of Passover, and the need before Passover to clear out all traces of the substance (Ex 12:15). The church is to become unleavened (that is, without sin) because it is, in principle, a new, unleavened substance (v. 7); Paul often calls on his converts to become in practice what they already are. They are a part of the Passover feast founded on the sacrifice of Christ, the lamb (an unparalleled use of such imagery in Paul). Then, in v. 8, the church shifts within the metaphor from the unleavened dough to partakers of the festival: the Corinthians' church life may be considered a permanent Passover meal, which must be kept free from the impurities of 'malice and evil' such as the sexual sin presently tolerated in their midst.

Thus the final paragraph of this chapter (vv. 9–13) underlines the need for the church to condemn and expel the bad influence presently festering in its midst. In v. 9 Paul refers to his earlier letter as already issuing instruction to dissociate with the 'immoral'—an instruction which seems to have been objected to in Corinth as implying complete social withdrawal, but which Paul here insists meant only separation from immoral members of the church. He now makes clear that he does not require a sectarian retreat ('going out of the world', v. 10), although later chapters will indicate that

he is unhappy with the degree of social integration which the Corinthian Christians enjoy (6:1; 10:14–22). He has no principled objection to social intercourse with unbelievers, even if they be immoral or 'idolatrous': the danger lies in association with those who have been accepted into the church as 'brothers' or 'sisters'. Paul assumes that the Corinthians will know for sure who are 'insiders' and 'outsiders' (5:12–13), probably on the basis of whether or not they have received baptism (6:9–11; 12:12–13). He regards it as far more dangerous to associate with immoral insiders than immoral outsiders, presumably because the example of the insider will be more influential on the rest of the congregation. Perhaps the Corinthians did not understand themselves to be committed to a common lifestyle or to be bound as tightly to each other as Paul here assumes. They may have thought of 'religion' as quite separate from 'ethics' and their relationships with social equals more important than their fellowship with other believers. Paul's instruction here requires that they regard moral behaviour with the utmost seriousness and that they understand themselves as a community whose intensity of involvement with one another renders them vulnerable to internal corruption (v. 13 cites from a parallel theme in Deut 17; see Rosner 1994). The harsh measures advocated ('not even to eat with such a one', v. 11) would debar the offender from the communal Lord's Supper, which, like meals generally in antiquity, was an important token of association.

(6:1–11) The Absurdity of Using Corinthian Courts
The theme of judging insiders rather than outsiders (5:12–13) leads Paul into a short digression. He will return to the topic of sexual morality at the end of ch. 6, but for now uses this opportunity to register his disapproval of Corinthian Christians who are settling their disputes with one another in the civil courts of Corinth. We do not know how many such cases there had been (perhaps only one), or precisely what they concerned, though the reference to 'defrauding' in v. 7 suggests financial disputes, which indeed were the most common cause of litigation in the Graeco-Roman world. Paul is affronted that the Corinthian Christians seem incapable of resolving their internal disputes without resorting to the judgement of 'unbelievers'. His objection lies not so much in his fear lest the community wash its dirty linen in public (he shows no concern here that it will be discredited), but

in the absurdity of asking for judgement from people far less capable than believers. Those who sit in the Corinthian courts are described as 'the unrighteous' (v. 1) and 'unbelievers' (v. 6), and Paul's objection to resorting to their judgement is not simply that they are liable to be corrupt (though, arguably, justice was a rare commodity; see Winter 1991) but that they represent 'the world' (v. 2), the realm of unbelief which is by definition inferior in understanding and integrity to the circle of 'the saints'. Here the apocalyptic dualism between 'church' and 'world' which underlay Paul's whole discourse in chs. 1–4 has its social application in his insistence that the Corinthian Christians are in a wholly different category to outsiders (cf. esp. 2:6–8). The influence of this world-view is further evident in Paul's appeal to the apocalyptic notion that God's elect are destined to judge (or rule) the world in the end-time (v. 2; cf. Dan 7:22; 1 Enoch 1:9; Rev 2:26–7). As in 3:21–3, Paul cleverly portrays the Corinthian Christians as underestimating their own importance. If they remembered their destiny in judging the world, even angels, they would not consider themselves incompetent to judge the trivial matters which they now ask others to decide (vv. 2–4). In reality, the Christian parties to these disputes probably failed to see the church as a juridical entity and looked to Corinthian judges to provide publicly recognized verdicts which would restore their social honour. In Paul's view, such outside authorities 'have no standing in the church' (v. 4; lit. are despised by the church, contrast Rom 13:1–7!). As a withering rebuke, he asks whether there is really no one in this community which so values wisdom who is wise enough to deal with this matter (v. 5)! The language here is reminiscent of Deut 1:16 (Moses' creation of courts in Israel), and the whole passage may reflect the operation of internal courts in some Diaspora Jewish communities.

In vv. 7–8 Paul steps onto a higher moral plane and asks how these lawsuits have arisen in the first place: to have them is already to lose them ('a defeat for you', v. 7). He hints at an ethic of non-retaliation reminiscent of the Sermon on the Mount, without invalidating the lesser solution of internal adjudication. It is best to accept injustice, and permissible to seek its rectification through an internal court, but it is inappropriate to ask 'the unrighteous' to judge such matters and utterly scandalous that Christians are themselves responsible for injustice in the first place—even against their fellow Christians (v. 8).

vv. 9–11 follow straight on: the wrongdoing which has given rise to the litigation threatens to place those responsible in the category of 'the wrongdoers' who will be excluded from the kingdom of God (v. 9). The theme of the kingdom of God features very rarely in Paul's theology, and is chiefly found in association with traditional formulae, as here where it is linked to a list of excluded persons (vv. 9–10; cf. Gal 5:19–21). The list here expands that offered in 5:10 and its opening with sexual sins and idolatry is parallel to Jews' denunciations of the sins they considered typical of the Gentile world (cf. Rom 1:18–31). The two terms translated (NRSV) as 'male prostitutes' and 'sodomites' (v. 9) have been the subject of some debate. The first (lit. soft people) could refer to 'womanizers' (i.e. those involved in heterosexual profligacy) but could also mean the passive partner in male homosexual acts; the second is a rare term (lit. sleeper with males) which probably designates the penetrating partner in male-with-male sex. Paul, like other Jews, considered either role in homosexual acts disgraceful (cf. Rom 1:26–7). The list also includes two terms for financial fraudulence ('thieves', 'robbers'), perhaps reflecting the character of the disputes just discussed. Such behaviour, Paul insists, cannot now characterize their Christian lives (v. 11). They have been washed, sanctified, and justified—a transformation whose description here probably alludes to the event of baptism. At that point they came under the authority of a new master ('in the name of the Lord Jesus Christ', cf. 1:13–15) and received a new identity 'in the Spirit of our God' (cf. 12:13).

(6:12–20) Immorality and the Significance of the Body The Corinthians would have agreed with Paul that their receipt of the Spirit gave them a new identity as 'spiritual people' (cf. 2:6–16). But Paul thinks that they have failed to grasp the implications of that change of identity, in particular the limits it sets on the use of their bodies. In v. 12 he twice cites a formula, 'all things are lawful for me' (cf. 10:23), which appears to be current in the Corinthian church and suggests a confident appropriation of Paul's gospel of 'freedom'. Paul does not reject it out of hand, but cautions lest its individualist emphasis ('all things are lawful for me') prove detrimental to the church as a whole: not all things are beneficial (i.e. to others). That insistence on considering the good of others will be the cornerstone of his argument concerning food in chs. 8–10 and spiritual gifts in chs. 12–14. Here Paul is also aware of how freedom can become a new slavery ('I will not be dominated by anything'); he has a lively sense of the power of sin (cf. Rom 6; Gal 5:13–24).

But Paul is most anxious lest this sense of freedom create a carelessness regarding bodily behaviour. The first part of 6:13 might again be a citation from the Corinthian church: ' "food is meant for the stomach and the stomach for food", and God will destroy both one and the other'. The reference to food anticipates the discussion of chs. 8–10, where Paul challenges the 'knowledgeable' who consider themselves immune to corruption by such a paltry phenomenon as food. In Paul's eyes this betrays a dangerously dualistic notion of the human person as possessing a spirit/soul in principle separable from the body. He fears that this might lead (or had already led) to the justification of sexual freedom on the basis that the satisfaction of sexual appetites was as insignificant as the assuaging of hunger. Thus he insists that 'the body is not for *porneia* but for the Lord and the Lord for the body' (v:13). *Porneia* was used in the Jewish tradition to refer to any sexual activity judged immoral (NRSV translates here 'fornication'). Paul will later talk about a sex with a prostitute (*pornē*, v. 15), but *porneia* could refer to anything he considered illicit (it is used also in 5:1 and 7:2). 'The body' (*sōma*) must here include the material/physical expression of our selves. In ch. 15 Paul will draw a distinction between the 'natural body' which cannot inherit the kingdom of God and the 'spiritual body' which will be the form of resurrection life (15:42–50). That complication, in the existence of two kinds of body, perhaps explains why Paul says here (v. 14) that God who raised the Lord will raise *us* up (not 'will raise *our bodies* up', as the line of argument might otherwise suggest).

None the less, Paul cannot concede that our present 'natural bodies' are irrelevant to Christian commitment. On the contrary, they are 'members'—literally, limbs—of Christ (v. 15), so that the way we handle them inevitably draws Christ into our activities. Paul exploits this notion as far as possible by a novel application of Gen 2:24 ('the two shall become one flesh') to all sexual unions, not just marriage. The physical joining in sex with a prostitute actually links Christ's body with that of a representative of sin—a union which Paul finds utterly scandalous. Hence the conclusion: 'Flee immorality' (v. 18; NRSV 'Shun fornication!'). It

is not altogether clear why this sin is here taken to be uniquely 'against the body itself', but Paul may be hinting at the way in which sexual activity affects (and therefore potentially corrupts) the whole person at the deepest point of our identity. Two final arguments underline the significance of the body for a believer. First, the body is indwelt by the Spirit of God, and thus has the sanctity of a temple (v. 19); and one does not treat a temple in a cavalier fashion (cf. 3:17). Secondly, believers come under an ownership: like slaves bought at a market (v. 20), they are answerable in totality to a master, and that includes their bodies (slaves were sometimes known simply as 'bodies'; cf. Rev 18:13).

(7:1–40) Celibacy and Marriage Paul now mentions the letter he has received from the Corinthians (v. 1), which may set the agenda for most of the rest of this letter. It is often supposed that the Corinthians meekly asked Paul's opinion on these matters, but the signs of tension in his relationship with them suggest that their approach might not have been so deferential. The subject-matter for this chapter is their statement (NRSV rightly uses inverted commas), 'It is well for a man not to touch a woman' (7:1). 'Touch' is a euphemism for sexual relations, and the statement seems to represent a principled rejection of all sexual activity. The position of those who held this view in Corinth may be deduced as: (1) Those who are single should avoid marriage (see 7:1, 8–9); (2) Those who are married should refrain from sex with their partners (see 7:3–6); (3) Those who are married should seek divorce (see 7:10–11), especially if they are married to an unbeliever (see 7:12–16); (4) Those who are engaged should not proceed to marriage (see 7:36–8). We cannot be sure why some Corinthians took this apparently ascetic stance. Early Christianity spawned many kinds of asceticism (Brown 1988), but here there may have been some denigration of the body arising from the exuberance of experience in the Spirit, combined with the assumption (widespread in antiquity) that prophecy and other activities involving special receptivity to God required withdrawal from the 'pollution' of sex. If some of the Corinthians were particularly 'eager for spiritual gifts' (14:12), 'anxious about the affairs of the Lord, that they may be holy *in body and spirit*' (v. 34), they may have regarded it as necessary to avoid sexual activity and advantageous to withdraw from, or to refuse to enter, marriage.

Paul begins his response to the Corinthians by dealing with the first three points in the summary above (vv. 1–16). He then draws back to illustrate his principle that believers should remain in the condition in which they were called, with reference to circumcision and slavery (vv. 17–24). When broaching the question of 'virgins' (unmarried persons eligible for marriage), he first expounds the advantages of detachment (vv. 25–31) and single-mindedness (vv. 32–5), before discussing the position of such virgins, together with the case of the eligible widow (vv. 36–40). Throughout he insists that marriage is not sin, and sex within marriage wholly appropriate (even necessary), but always with an unmistakable coolness. He consistently maintains that it is better, if possible, to be unmarried, provided that this does not (1) involve initiating a divorce, an action forbidden by the Lord (v. 10), or (2) subject the believer to irresistible passions, leading to sex outside marriage (vv. 2, 9). The lack of enthusiasm for marriage in its own right, for the procreation of children, or for the establishment of a Christian family (contrast Eph 5:21–6:4) is notable.

Paul starts by citing the Corinthian statement that 'it is well for a man not to touch a woman', but he cannot accept it fully, at least not within marriage. v. 2 could refer to men and women in general and their acquisition of marriage partners: 'each man should have his own wife' etc. (NRSV). But, in view of the following verses, it is perhaps more likely that it refers to married men and women who should 'have' (in the sense of 'have sexual relations with') their partners: thus, 'each husband should have sex with his own wife' etc. (Fee 1987: 277–80). The reason for Paul's advice is his concern with immoralities, perhaps with specific 'cases of immorality' (NRSV) in mind, such as those alluded to in chs. 5 and 6. Lurking throughout this chapter is Paul's fear of the power of sexual desire, which, if not fulfilled (or neutralized) within marriage, is likely to lead to sin. vv. 3–4 indicate the obligations and privileges of both marriage partners in sexual matters, with a degree of reciprocity highly unusual in antiquity; indeed almost every point in the chapter is discussed from both male and female angles. Nowhere is this more radical in effect than in the second half of v. 4. The first half, detailing the husband's authority over his wife's body, is a standard assumption in antiquity (and all other patriarchal societies). But the second, by putting the matter the other way around, undercuts assumptions of male privilege at their most sensitive point: the male body and its use in sex.

Neither party is here allowed to make unilateral decisions: any period of sexual abstinence must be by agreement and of limited duration, lest the sexual urge (Satan's tempting) prove too strong (v. 5). Such a period of abstinence may enable a Christian couple to devote themselves to prayer, a notion with some parallels in Judaism (e.g. T. Naph. 8:8).

At v. 6 is the first of many indications in this chapter that Paul is careful not to establish rules or speak more confidently than is his right (cf. vv. 25, 40). The 'this' which he here concedes may be marriage, but more probably refers to temporary abstinence from sex within marriage. Then v. 7 means: I would like everyone to be sexually continent like myself, but recognize that some have this gift and can remain unmarried, while others do not, needing to marry and to fulfil the sexual obligations of that state. The 'gift from God' (charisma) represents the ability to remain celibate without succumbing to sexual desire.

vv. 8–9 turn directly to the unmarried and widowed. Paul himself is unmarried, perhaps because his conversion disrupted his life-plans so severely. The unmarried state is his preference for all (for reasons he will detail in vv. 25–35), but he is worried again by the power of sexual passion (likened here to a fire), which some need to tame, or quench, within marriage.

What about those who are already married and are tempted to escape from marriage? Here Paul for once gives a command (cf. v. 6), though not on his own authority but on that of the Lord (v. 10). This is one of those very few places (9:14 is another) where Paul refers explicitly to the teaching of Jesus. He here cites a saying also attested (with some variations) in the Synoptics, in which Jesus declared divorce to be illegitimate (Mk 10:2–11; Mt 19:3–9; Lk 16:18). In the case of a wife he imagines a second-best option whereby she separates/divorces (vv. 13–15 suggest that these may be synonyms for Paul) but does not marry again (v. 11). Some think that his special concentration on the woman might reflect a specific case, or growing tendency, in Corinth (Wire 1990). The acceptance of this second best ('if she does separate . . . ') shows that Paul does not regard the teaching of Jesus as legislation; it sets some parameters, but allows for differences of situation. He will later acknowledge that a Christian may have to accept divorce at the hands of a non-Christian partner (v. 15), taking Jesus' principle to rule out only the initiation of divorce proceedings.

vv. 12–16 deal with the case of Christians already married to unbelievers. Paul does not recommend entering into such a partnership (7:39; cf. 2 Cor 6:14–16), but seems to envisage here the conversion of one partner in a marriage, a situation which could be fraught with difficulty if the Christian spouse disdained household idolatry (cf. 1 Pet 3:1–6). Such verses make clear that it was not always whole households which converted (cf. 1:16). In this case, Paul has no direct teaching from Jesus (v. 12), but adapts what he knows to fit the social necessities. He recommends staying in the marriage if at all possible and seems to be responding to fears that the believer is somehow defiled by this intimate contact with the 'unholy'. If the marriage is to be maintained, and if holiness or defilement are in some sense contagious, logic propels Paul to insist that the unbelieving spouse is actually made 'holy' through the believer, just as are the children of even one Christian parent (v. 14). This description of persons as being 'holy' or 'sanctified' is normally used by Paul only in relation to believers in Christ (e.g. 1:2; 6:11); it is strange to find it used here of unbelievers, whose future salvation is uncertain (v. 16). Children are mentioned here for the only time in the chapter and only as a supporting argument, and it is unclear what, if anything, is implied by their designation as 'holy' (v. 14). The verse has been used with equal force in arguments both for and against infant baptism, about which Paul never speaks explicitly. v. 15 recognizes that the non-Christian partner may not wish to continue a marriage with a spouse whose recent conversion creates tension in the marriage, and in this case Paul recommends allowing divorce for the sake of peace. Nothing here rules out remarriage, though the possibility is not mentioned. v. 16 could be translated in either an optimistic or a pessimistic sense. Optimistically ('who knows, you might save your spouse'), it undergirds the main thrust of the paragraph, urging a Christian to remain in a mixed marriage (so NRSV; REB; cf. 1 Pet 3:1–2). Translated in a pessimistic sense ('how do you know whether you will ever save your spouse?'), it discourages hopes of benefit from remaining in such a marriage and thus supports the concession of v. 15 that one may withdraw from a hopeless situation (so RSV; NIV). The former is slightly more likely.

The question of change of status leads Paul to formulate a general principle (v. 17): that you should lead whatever life is apportioned by the Lord, which is taken to be that state in which you were called. 'Called' is one of Paul's common

terms for conversion, and he seems to be talking here of the state *in which* one becomes a Christian, not a vocation *to which* one is summoned (NRSV rightly translates at vv. 20, 24, but not at v. 17). Such a policy of 'stay as you are' is indeed his general advice in this chapter (if married, don't divorce; if single, remain so), with some exceptions allowed. It is now illustrated with regard to ethnic identity and social status (cf. the three categories in Gal 3:28). Circumcision, the sign of male Jewish identity, should not be reversed (as could be done by surgery or by stretching and pinning what remains of the foreskin); similarly the foreskin should not be removed for the sake of adopting Jewish identity. Here Paul summarizes the theme of his letter to the Galatians, insisting on the relativization of such cultural markers. Accordingly v. 19 echoes statements in Galatians (5:6; 6:15), though with a different and extremely puzzling conclusion. 'Keeping the commandments of God' in any normal Jewish sense would *include* the practice of circumcision; Paul has somehow redefined the notion to filter out certain commands which he considers unnecessary in a multi-ethnic church (cf. 9:19–21).

The second illustration concerns social identity, as slave or free person (vv. 21–4). Here the same 'stay as you are' principle is applied as a general rule, with legal status similarly relativized. Christian slaves can consider themselves 'freed persons belonging to the Lord' (freed persons usually had continuing obligations to their former owners), while Christians who are free are really 'slaves of Christ' (vv. 22–3). This compensatory redescription of reality renders social location irrelevant to Christian obligation (and perhaps even inverts the assumed hierarchy of slave and free, see Martin 1990: 63–8), enabling Paul to tell those in slavery not to mind about it (v. 21). However, the second half of v. 21 contains an ambiguity which has been the focus of some debate. The Greek could be taken to urge accepting slavery, even if there is an opportunity of gaining freedom (so NRSV). However, it could equally, and perhaps better, be taken in an opposite sense, providing a partial exception to the general rule of the paragraph: 'but if you can gain your freedom, be sure to use that opportunity' (so RSV). In most cases, as Bartchy (1973) pointed out, slaves would have no choice in this matter: if an owner wished to free a slave, it would happen whether the slave wished it or not. Since the chapter does contain other exceptions to the rule of 'stay as you are', and since v. 23 suggests that Paul considered freedom a better condition than slavery, the second, more positive, reading is to be preferred. None the less, the main thrust of the paragraph illustrates the rule of status-retention, which v. 24 reiterates.

In v. 25 Paul turns to the specific case of 'virgins', that is, those not yet married. Girls were typically married off by their parents at or very soon after puberty to men who were usually several years older. Marriage and the subsequent raising of children was taken to be a civic duty (to ensure future generations), but some radical philosophers (Cynics) took it to be a distraction from their philosophical calling. In what follows, Paul will mix some such Cynic motifs with his own apocalyptic reasoning about the end of the world (see Deming 1995). In the first instance (vv. 25–31) he applies the principle of 'stay as you are' on the grounds of the 'impending crisis' (v. 26). What he has in mind is made clearer in v. 29 ('the appointed time has grown short') and v. 31 ('the present form of this world is passing away'). Paul is convinced that he lives in the last generation (cf. 1 Thess 4:15 and 1 Cor 15:52). He thus harbours the apocalyptic belief that all present social structures will be dissolved, and also that the time preceding the 'end' will be characterized by acute distress ('the impending crisis'). Under such circumstances it is clear that marriage is of little value and the raising of future generations an irrelevance. Paul cannot advocate being rid of marriage relationships already entered, since he has the Lord's word forbidding divorce (v. 10). But neither can he recommend marriage for those as yet unmarried: it would not be morally wrong (vv. 28–9) but it would only make one more vulnerable to the distress of social breakdown. In fact, even for those who are married, Paul advocates an 'eschatological detachment': let them live 'as though they had no wives', like all dealings with the world must be conducted on the basis of 'as if not' (vv. 29–31). This sentiment is paralleled in Jewish apocalyptic documents (e.g. 2 Esd 16:40 ff.). It is not entirely clear what it would mean for married men to live 'as though they had no wives' (vv. 2–5 suggest it cannot mean a withdrawal from sex), but in some general sense marriage is relativized here as an institution hardly worth investing in.

The second reason for Paul's coolness regarding marriage is spelt out in vv. 32–5. Paul wishes his converts to be 'free from anxieties', or more precisely, free from competing anxieties. Like the Cynics, Paul is impressed by the amount of attention to the marriage partner required by marriage (again he oddly fails

to mention children), regarding these as 'the affairs of the world' which constitute a distraction from 'the affairs of the Lord'. For him, marriage and family life are not part of a believer's service to the Lord but a competing interest which prevents 'unhindered devotion to the Lord' (v. 35; cf. v. 34: 'his interests are divided'). The specific reference to the woman's concern 'to be holy in body and spirit' (v. 34) may allude to the concerns of particular Corinthian women, who operated as prophets (11:2–16). Once again, Paul is cautious not to side too strongly with those who forbid marriage (v. 35), but it is clear that he considers 'good order' and 'devotion to the Lord' better served by singleness. It is possible that he considers himself in this respect a better 'worker' than other apostles who were accompanied by their wives (9:3–6; 15:10).

The next paragraph (vv. 36–8) returns to the practical matter of virgins, first signalled in v. 25. Unfortunately, the paragraph could be read in a number of different ways (see Fee 1987: 349–55). Some interpret it as concerning a young girl's father, who is responsible for marrying off his daughter: the verb used for 'he who marries his virgin' (v. 38) normally means 'he who marries her off', i.e. arranges her marriage. Then the Greek could be taken to refer to a father anxious about his treatment of his daughter, if she is getting over-age (the Greek translated in NRSV 'if his passions are strong' could be taken in this quite different sense; a girl might be considered 'overripe' in her early twenties!); then it is no sin for him to allow and arrange her marriage. The more usual interpretation of the text (adopted by the NRSV and by most commentators) takes it to speak of an unmarried man and his desire to marry, or his control over this desire. Oddly, in either case, the girl's wishes in this matter are entirely ignored. Whether Paul envisages some sort of permanent 'engagement' is unclear. As throughout the chapter, Paul allows marriage ('it is no sin') but considers it a second-best option (v. 38).

That principle is finally applied to the case of a widow (vv. 39–40; many girls were widowed quite young). By the rule of 'no divorce' (v. 10) a woman can consider remarriage only on the death of her husband (cf. Rom 7:1–4); then she may remarry 'in the Lord' (the choice cannot have been great in a small congregation). But Paul's preference for singleness is again evident (v. 40). His final sentence sums up his surprising hesitancy on this matter, unless there is irony in his claim that he *too* (as much as the 'spiritual people' in Corinth) has access to the wisdom of the Spirit (cf. 2:14–16).

Sacrificial Food and the Dangers of Idolatry (8:1–11:1)

8:1 opens a new section of the letter, on 'food sacrificed to idols', perhaps another issue raised in the Corinthian letter. At first sight, the content of ch. 9 appears out of place in this section. However, as we shall see, it actually fits perfectly as an illustration of what Paul requires of the 'people of knowledge': that they renounce their 'rights' for the sake of others. It has often been noted that Paul's softer tone on the consumption of sacrificial food in 8:1–13 and 10:23–11:1 appears inconsistent with his hard-line attitude to idolatry in 10:1–22; some have even suspected the combination of two or more letters at this point. There is indeed a certain dialectic in Paul's position regarding such food, which might mask inconsistency: he himself calls attention to this dialectic in 10:19–20. But the distinctions he draws between the different contexts in which sacrificial food is eaten, and the different intents such eating represents, make it possible for him to give such a nuanced response. Moreover, it is quite like Paul to advance an argument by a range of different strategies which may not cohere perfectly with one another (cf. his response to 'speaking in tongues' in chs. 12–14).

The issue of 'sacrificial food' arises from the fact that food consumption was frequently associated with the deities, whether by prayer, libation, or sacrifice, and that the slaughter of animals often took place in the context of temple worship. Jews, who were notoriously averse to 'alien' religious practices, abstained from food and wine which had become tainted by association with gods other than their own. The early Christian movement was generally Jewish in ethos, but in many places attracted a majority of Gentile members in churches which were prepared to abandon some distinctive Jewish practices (such as circumcision and Sabbath observance). It was thus possible for uncertainty to arise as to the proper Christian stance towards Greek and Roman deities (which Jews called 'idols'), or at least towards the meals, festivals, club-dinners, and parties which were generally accompanied by some sort of religious activity. Many kinds of food might be considered to be affected: portions could be offered on an altar in domestic or public

settings, or liquids poured out as a libation (see Willis 1985; P.D. Gooch 1993). Paul seems to be particularly concerned here with meat (8:13). Wealthy individuals or clubs often brought animals for slaughter at a temple, one portion being reserved for the deity (i.e. the priests), with the rest consumed in an ordinary meal either on the site (many temples had dining rooms) or in a private setting. Even meat sold in the meat market might have been offered to a deity, so a believer anxious to avoid any contact with idolatry might balk at the purchase of meat there and at the fare provided in taverns or in an unbeliever's house. On the other hand, dinner invitations, club meetings, family celebrations, and civic festivals were such an important part of social life that some Christians might be reluctant to adopt a rigorous stance on this issue; that would certainly affect the lives and prospects of such socially significant believers as Gaius and Erastus (see E.1).

Many ambiguities surrounded the issue of sacrificial food. Was all the meat idolatrous or only those portions specifically reserved for the deity? Was one tainted by association with idolaters at occasions when they committed idolatry, or not? What, in any case, constituted 'idolatry' and how were the images to be regarded? In Graeco-Roman culture, general reverence for the images of the deities included a range of attitudes to their relation to reality: some considered the gods to be present within the images, others that they merely represented some divine attribute. In these chapters Paul is in dialogue with a group within the Corinthian church who considered themselves knowledgeable in such matters ('we all possess knowledge', 8:1). It appears that these are an educated élite: in a spirit of confident monotheism they take idols to represent nothing at all (8:4), and reason that participation in idolatrous meals, even in idolatrous worship, was a meaningless and harmless activity. This stance was probably bolstered by social convenience, but Paul takes it seriously as a theological position which was not entirely incorrect but which could have dangerous effects both on themselves and on other, 'weaker', Christians.

(8:1–13) Debate with the 'Knowledgeable' concerning their 'Right' to Eat As in ch. 7, Paul starts by citing a phrase used in the Corinthian letter: 'all of us possess knowledge' (8:1). He will shortly deny this claim, since he is aware of vulnerable Christians in Corinth unable to take this knowing stance towards 'idols' (v. 7).

But his first reaction is against the spirit of the assertion. Although he recognizes knowledge as a gift of the Spirit (1:5; 12:8), he senses here the dangers of pride and self-interest, which subordinate care for others to the acquisition and display of one's own knowledge. Thus, once again, he warns against becoming 'puffed up' (cf. 4:6 and the same verb, translated as 'to be arrogant', in 4:19, 5:2, and 13:4) and sets the priority on the constructive capability of love (v. 2; cf. chs. 12–14). In the very claim to knowledge Paul fears the corrupting power of arrogance which needs to be humbled by recognizing the inadequacy of our present 'knowledge' and the far greater value of being 'known by' God (vv. 2–3; cf. 13:8–13).

On the basis of this caution Paul addresses the knowledge in question (vv. 4–6). Again he quotes Corinthian statements that 'no idol in the world really exists' (or, 'the idol-image represents nothing in the world') and that 'there is no God but one' (v. 4). Paul can readily agree with the second statement, a cardinal tenet of Judaism. The first contains some ambiguity (see the alternative translations just offered) and it is possible that Paul and the Corinthians understood it in different senses. Paul could accept that the image is insignificant, but, as the next verse and 10:19–20 make clear, he does not doubt the reality of the *spiritual beings* which were the object of worship in Graeco-Roman religion. If the Corinthian élite think there are no such beings (and thus participate in pagan worship as a harmless inanity), Paul will have to reprimand them severely (10:1–22). Even here he insists on the exclusivity of Christian commitment (vv. 5–6). Whatever deities others might worship—and Paul insists that they are only 'so-called gods' (cf. Gal 4:8)—'yet for us there is one God . . . and one Lord . . .' The confessional and formulaic character of v. 6 suggests the presence here of a credal statement in which we see Christology coming to birth. The Jewish Shemaʿ ('Hear, O Israel, the Lord our God is one Lord', Deut 6:4) is here split apart into a statement about *God*, the creator of the world and goal of salvation, and a matching statement about *the Lord*, now taken to mean Jesus Christ, the medium of creation and redemption. The two are clearly distinguished (cf. 3:23; 11:3; 15:27–8) but the way in which Paul reads them both out of the Jewish declaration of monotheism is suggestive of the ways in which Christian theology will struggle to define Christ's exalted status without falling into ditheism (see further Hurtado 1988 and Dunn 1991).

Before proceeding further on this theological tack, Paul reminds the élite that they are not as representative of the church as they think (v. 7) and that they have responsibilities to fellow believers which override their 'right' to eat whatever food they wish. Paul knows that, after a lifetime of worship of 'so-called gods', converts are apt to be uneasy about contact with religious practices which they consider themselves to have renounced; if they were to eat such food again, their vulnerable self-image as Christians (their 'conscience') would be 'defiled' (v. 7). In itself, food is not of decisive significance in our relationship to God (v. 8, possibly, but not certainly, another Corinthian statement). Therefore, Paul insists, nothing fundamental is lost by declining to eat certain foods; he deliberately overlooks the social loss which might result from scrupulosity regarding 'idolatrous food'. Since the 'knowledgeable' people have no grounds for insisting on such eating, Paul is entitled to warn them lest their 'liberty' (v. 9, or 'right'; the noun echoes the slogan of 6:12) cause disaster for more vulnerable Christians. The 'stumbling-block' referred to here (cf. Rom 14) signals much more than 'offence' or 'shock': it suggests causing others to fall catastrophically, resulting in their 'destruction' (v. 11). The danger Paul has in mind is that 'the weak' (those whose self-image as Christians is vulnerable) will be encouraged, or pressurized, by the example of 'the knowledgeable' to eat food which they know, or suspect, has been sacrificed to idols. While such eating may not cause the knowledgeable to falter in their Christian commitment (since they regard the idol as a 'nothing'), it could disastrously compromise the commitment of weaker Christians, who might now view themselves as having reversed their decision to renounce idolatry. Paul imagines this happening if the knowledgeable are seen 'eating in the temple of an idol' (v. 10). Later (10:14–22) he will advance other reasons for caution about such behaviour, but here he maintains his focus on the effect which this display of superior knowledge could have on the weak: in their uncertainty of self-image as Christians, they may be 'encouraged' (Paul says 'built up', with conscious irony) to follow suit, with disastrous consequences. Damage against believers for whom Christ died diminishes his work and thus constitutes sin against Christ (vv. 11–12). Rather than looking down on the weak with the disdain typical of élite classes in Graeco-Roman society, the people of knowledge are here required to take them with full seriousness, as fellow Christians (cf. 11:17–22; 12:14–26): love is more important than knowledge (vv. 1–3). Thus, to use himself as an example, Paul renounces his right to eat meat, in case it causes the collapse of another's faith-commitment (v. 13).

(9:1–23) Paul's Example in Renouncing the 'Right' to Financial Support Ch. 9 appears to veer off in a different direction from the topic of food offered to idols. Here we have Paul's impassioned plea to be regarded as an apostle in Corinth (vv. 1–2), a long series of arguments concerning his right to receive support (vv. 3–14), and then his declaration that his boast lies precisely in making no use of this right (vv. 15–18) and in offering himself, although free, as a slave of all (vv. 19–23). All this is not, however, as irrelevant as it might seem. Paul finished ch. 8 by offering himself as an example of willingness to renounce his right to eat meat, if that was necessary for the sake of others. That leads him to present himself as an example on a wider plane of this principle of renunciation of rights. He has the right as an apostle to be given his material upkeep, but for the sake of the gospel he has renounced this: although 'free' and entitled to exercise certain rights, he has chosen to make himself a slave (v. 19). But this illustration is not unproblematic, because it is precisely his refusal to accept financial support from the Corinthians which has led some to doubt whether he is an apostle at all. It is because he knows that his status is questioned by some in Corinth that Paul chooses to use this controversial matter as his illustration: thereby he can defend himself, re-assert his apostleship, and present himself as the Corinthians' model (cf. 11:1) all at the same time. This means that it is some time before Paul returns explicitly to the subject of sacrificial food, but such apparent digressions which actually advance the argument at a deeper level are typical of Paul's rhetoric (cf. ch. 13 between chs. 12 and 14).

'Freedom' may have been the watchword of the 'people of knowledge' in Corinth: it sums up their assertion of rights and that 'all things are lawful' (6:12; 8:9; 10:23). Hence Paul declares that he, too, is 'free'—in particular, endowed with the 'rights' of an apostle. His claim to apostleship was heavily contested in his generation, since he had not been a disciple of Jesus, had persecuted the church, and was often at odds with the 'mother church' in Jerusalem. Paul here rehearses the grounds for his claim: that he saw (and was commissioned by) the risen Christ (cf. 15:3–11) and that he has successfully founded

churches (vv. 1–2). He hopes that the Corinthians will recognize at least this second claim, but has to counter immediately a prejudice against his apostleship which has taken root precisely in Corinth.

While staying in Corinth, Paul had apparently supported himself entirely by his own labour (according to Acts 18:3, as a leather worker), and even when the church he founded had offered him financial support he had refused to take it (cf. 2 Cor 11:7–11). It is not entirely clear why this became a matter of principle for him in Corinth; elsewhere he acknowledges receiving support from Macedonian churches (2 Cor 11:9; Phil 4:10–20). Perhaps he feared lest wealthy Christians in Corinth might wish to use their financial patronage to influence his preaching or control his movements. In any case, the fact that he did not accept support from Corinth turned out to be a bone of contention. Other 'apostles', whom the Corinthians knew about or met, received support, probably appealing to the words of Jesus and the example of travelling missionaries in Judea and Galilee (see Theissen 1982: 27–67). To forgo this right might thus appear to place Paul at a lower level than 'real' apostles, and for Paul to support himself by *manual* labour was to demean himself in the eyes of wealthier Christians (cf. 4:12).

Thus Paul confronts directly those who 'examine' him (v. 3; the same verb is used in 2:15 and 4:3). He declares his entitlement to the same forms of material support as other apostles (vv. 4–6), making special mention of 'the brothers of the Lord' (e.g. James, 15:7), and Cephas, the hero of the Cephas group, 1:12). He then strings together an impressive collection of arguments for this entitlement (vv. 7–14). He appeals first to human parallels (soldiers, vineyard workers, and shepherds), where workers expect some return for their labour (v. 7). He then turns to the Scriptures for the same principle, offering an allegorical reading of Moses' law about the threshing ox (vv. 8–11; see Deut 25:4). It is not often that Paul appeals directly to 'the law of Moses' for moral guidance (his letters to the Galatians and Romans show what an ambiguous entity 'the law' has become for him). Nor does he usually employ allegory in his interpretation of the Scriptures (Gal 4:21–31 is the only other example), although it was a technique long-established among Hellenized Jews. In his concern to find a moral lesson in the law, Paul insists that Moses really speaks *only* about human welfare, not about oxen. Allegorists such as the Jewish philosopher Philo sometimes took both literal and allegorical meanings as valid, but sometimes, like here, considered only the allegorical worthy of God. Paul applies this verse to his situation by a double transference: in talking of oxen, God is talking about human ploughers and reapers (v.10); and this principle can be applied to those who sow spiritually, and may expect to reap in exchange (v. 11). Paul can also appeal to the benefits enjoyed by priests in a temple (v. 13) and, finally, to the direct instruction of the Lord (v. 14; cf. Mt 10:10; Lk 10:7–8; 1 Tim 5:18). It is intriguing that this should be mentioned last, and without any special emphasis or priority over the previous arguments. That may be related to the fact that Paul cites this command only to declare that it does not apply to him!

Before finishing this chain of argumentation, Paul had anticipated his conclusion (v. 12): he has the rights to which he appeals but has opted *not* to make use of them, if to do so would place an obstacle in the way of the gospel. Now it becomes clear how this whole discussion relates to Paul's instruction to 'the people of knowledge' in ch. 8. In 8:9 he had warned them that their 'right' (NRSV: 'liberty') could be a stumbling-block to the weak and should be waived if it proved to be so. Here he presents himself as a model of such voluntary renunciation of rights, for the sake of the gospel. In his case, too, Paul has the 'weak' especially in mind (v. 22 highlights his accommodation to the weak, not the strong). By refusing to accept support, Paul ensures that he is not a burden on those with little to spare: he works with his hands and thereby identifies with those who are socially and economically weak, even at the risk of offending the wealthier converts who would like Paul to accept their patronage and quit his embarrassing mode of work (Martin 1990: 117–35).

vv. 15–18 explain further this renunciation of rights and its importance for Paul. Preaching the gospel 'free of charge' was an important and distinctive feature of Paul's ministry: indeed, the sentence structure breaks down in v. 15 to reveal how emotionally significant is this 'ground for boasting'. He now plays with the theme of employment and 'pay' (the Gk. word *misthos* means both 'pay' and 'reward'). The fact that he preaches the gospel is not for Paul a matter of choice, but of necessity (v. 16; cf. Gal 1:15–16). If it were a matter of choice, he would be a free agent, and like any other free man would expect pay ('reward') for work completed.

But he is not a free agent, he is 'entrusted with a commission', that is, working for Christ as his slave-steward (v. 17; the same metaphor as in 4:1–2). Slaves do not get pay ('reward') just for doing what their owners tell them to do. Paul's 'reward' (pay) is to do what he has been instructed to do under very special conditions: to make the gospel 'free of charge'. Ironically, then, his spiritual pay is to receive no financial pay for the fulfilment of his task (v. 18).

This might look like a form of self-interest, to get some reward out of what he does, if Paul did not go on to explain his motivation in vv. 19–23. His goal is not self-gratification but the interests of the gospel, and in particular the desire to 'win' converts. Like a demagogue who enslaves himself to the populace to campaign for their rights, Paul has deliberately renounced rights and demeaned himself to advance the cause of the gospel (v. 19). His self-sacrifice is first illustrated by the chief characteristic of his mission, his cross-cultural adaptability (vv. 20–1). Among Jews he could live like a Jew: that is, among the law-observant he observes the law, although not considering himself utterly bound to it (v. 20). The purpose is to win Jews for the gospel; for, although his call was 'to the Gentiles' (Rom 1:5), Paul still associated with Jews, as his synagogue visits testify (2 Cor 11:24). Similarly, for Gentiles 'outside the law' Paul lived in a Gentile fashion, although in truth not lawless before God, but under full obligation to Christ (v. 21, 'under Christ's law'; no code of teaching is here envisaged). Again the purpose is to win Gentiles, the task in which Paul was so successful, though at the cost of his reputation among most fellow Jews, who took his adaptability to be merely opportunism (Gal 1:10). This loss of clear-cut cultural identity is paralleled by his loss of honour in 'becoming weak' (v. 22), identifying with those who possessed less knowledge and less social significance than the élite leaders of the Corinthian church. Paul is prepared to give up cultural and social rights for the sake of the gospel, and hints that only by so doing will he share its blessings (v. 23). Thus he is entitled to challenge the 'people of knowledge' in Corinth as to their willingness to do the same. If they are not willing, he suggests, they may forfeit its blessings and lose out on the salvation which they take for granted. Such is the turn his argument now takes in 9:24–10:22.

(9:24–10:22) The Dangers of Complacency in relation to Idolatry While 9:24–7 still takes the form of discourse about himself, Paul now begins to turn his own example into challenge to his Corinthian audience. He uses images from the games which would be particularly vivid in their imagination, since Corinth hosted the biennial Isthmian games, drawing participants from all over the Graeco-Roman world. Entering the race is not the same as winning it: the Corinthians still have to make sure they 'run' successfully (9:24). Sporting heroes were extremely famous in antiquity and it was well-known that they underwent very rigorous training in order to win a garland. That was a motif often used in popular philosophy to indicate the seriousness of a moral lifestyle, and Paul employs it here to urge self-discipline for the sake of a far more valuable prize, salvation (9:25). Practice, discipline, and self-control were all essential for an athlete's success, whether the sport was running or boxing (9:26). Without them, a promising career would easily be spoiled, and Paul takes seriously the possibility that he himself might be 'disqualified' by God, excluded from salvation (or at least from its 'reward', cf. 3:14–15) even after having brought others into it (9:27).

The note of warning to the Corinthians is becoming louder, but before turning the spotlight directly back on to them Paul invokes a cautionary tale from the Scriptures (10:1–13). He finds no difficulty in using scriptural narratives to illustrate God's dealings with the church, since he regards the Israelites in the desert as 'our ancestors' (10:1) even though the church he is writing to is mostly Gentile (see further Hays 1989). Paul recounts the story of Israel's disobedience in the wilderness because it illustrates precisely what he wants to warn the Corinthians about: that even those chosen by God can go badly astray; and if they do, whatever their privileges, they are liable to destruction. The fact that the story concerns idolatry and sexual immorality makes it immediately relevant to a church which worries Paul on both these scores.

Paul detects among the Corinthian Christians a sense of privileged security in which they consider themselves immune to danger. Perhaps it is on this basis that the people of knowledge have the confidence to attend idolatrous events, reckoning that nothing can harm their status as spiritual people. They may have taken particular pride in their baptism as ensuring salvation and in the Lord's Supper as replenishing their spiritual resources. Both would therefore constitute rites which, like some Graeco-Roman mysteries, confirmed their

superior status and sealed their immortality. It is probably for this reason that Paul describes the Israelites' experience in terms which match Christian rites. As they went under the cloud and through the (Red) Sea, the Israelites were 'baptized into Moses' (10:2), just as Christians were baptized into Christ (1 Cor 12:12–13; Gal 3:27); similarly, as they ate the manna and drank from the rock in the desert, they partook of 'spiritual' food and drink like that enjoyed in the Lord's Supper (10:3–4). Indeed, Paul even claims that the Israelites drew nourishment, in a sense, from Christ himself, who is identified with the rock from which the water issued (10:4). He here draws on Jewish exegesis which reflected on the fact that the Pentateuchal narratives place this rock in different locations: had it therefore 'followed' the Israelites through the desert? In some quarters this rock had also been allegorized as 'Wisdom', from which the righteous drew spiritual nourishment, and Paul may be drawing on an early Christian identification between Christ and Wisdom (cf. 1:30 and 8:6). None the less— and this is the point of the illustration—despite having access to all the same privileges as the Corinthian Christians (baptism, 'spiritual' food and drink, and even Christ himself), the Israelites were not immune from God's punishment when they went astray: in fact, most of them were destroyed (10:5).

In 10:6 and 10:11 Paul explains the principle by which he interprets the Israelites' story: these events are an example, and were written down as a warning, indicating the dangers for God's people if they entertain evil desires. Indeed, 10:11 suggests that they were written specifically for 'us', that is, the Christians who live in the final generation, the climactic junction of time Paul calls 'the ends of the ages' (cf. 7:29–31; cf. Rom 15:4). 10:7–8 runs through a list of Israel's errors, perhaps a stock résumé of the wilderness sins: idolatry, in the worship of the golden calf (10:7, citing Ex 32:6); 'sexual immorality' (porneia, see 1 COR 5:1), in forging illicit marriages with Midianite women (10:8, alluding to Num 25, where, however, the casualty figure is 24,000); putting Christ to the test (10:9, alluding to Num 21; some texts read 'the Lord', which is how the scriptural narrative puts it, but generally Paul takes 'the Lord' in the Scriptures to refer to Christ); and finally, complaining, in grumbling about God's purposes or Moses' leadership (probably alluding to Num 14 or Num 16, with the notion of the 'destroyer' transferred from Ex 12:23). In each case, the outcome is the same: the 'destruction' of the sinners. If such stories are of immediate relevance to the Corinthians as 10:11 suggests, then the warning is clear: they are in as much danger as the Israelites in the desert. Paul turns directly against the confidence of the Corinthian leaders with the warning of 10:12. No situation is uniquely difficult or inescapable, and they cannot claim to be helpless or faultless if they sin: God will enable them to endure temptation (cf. 1:8–9) and will always provide an escape route (10:13). The question is whether the Corinthians will be willing to take it and the social inconvenience it may cause.

The notion of 'escape' leads into Paul's direct instruction: 'flee from the worship of idols' (10:14). Of the wilderness sins recounted in 10:7–8, it is idolatry which is Paul's most immediate concern. He has still to confront the people of knowledge concerning their easy dismissal of the significance of 'idols' (8:4), since he fears (or knows) that this attitude will justify their convenient participation in acts of worship to idols. Addressing them, with slight condescension, as 'sensible people' (they boast of their 'knowledge', 8:1), he urges them to consider what sorts of 'partnerships' (or 'sharing', Gk. koinōnia) they are undertaking. At the Lord's Supper, the cup (known as 'the cup of blessing' because of the prayer, blessing God, which is spoken over it) is a 'partnership' in the blood of Christ. Similarly, the bread which is broken is a 'partnership' in the body of Christ (10:16). It is difficult to determine what sort of 'sacramental theology' undergirds these statements. Is the 'partnership' merely represented by the cup and bread, or actually effected by it? And what is the relationship between the cup and blood, and between the bread and body (cf. 11:24–5)? But what is clear, and what Paul is concerned to stress, is that participation in this meal signals a bond between the participant and Christ, a bond which must be exclusive of all others (10:21–2; cf. the parallel argumentation in 6:15–17).

The reference to the 'bread' and the 'body' leads Paul into a brief aside concerning the 'one body' of the church (10:17, anticipating 11:17–34 and 12:12–31), a motif which should encourage the people of knowledge to take more care of their fellow 'limbs' who have weaker consciences (cf. 10:23–4). But the main point of the paragraph is pursued again in 10:18 with reference to Jewish sacrificial practice, where partaking in sacrificial victims joins an individual to the worship offered at the altar. Paul considers that the same applies to worship and sacrifice in Graeco-Roman religion. 10:19 makes clear that he has not revoked the convictions

he set out in ch. 8: it is not that the food is significant in itself (thus the act of eating is not so much the problem), nor that the 'idol' (i.e. the image) is itself of importance (its presence or proximity at a meal is not problematic); rather, in the act of sacrifice, Gentiles devote themselves to 'demons' and thus create a 'partnership' with beings which are wholly out of bounds for a believer. Paul here uses the word daimonion, which refers in normal Greek to a supernatural being of lesser significance and more ambiguous virtue than a full god, but one not necessarily evil; in time, however, Jewish and Christian usage was literally to 'demonize' all such beings. The point here is that such a partnership is incompatible with belonging to Christ, on the Jewish principle that God is jealous of all rivals (10:22, echoing Deut 32:21). The people of knowledge may be strong compared with the weak in conscience, but they are not 'stronger than' God (10:22), that is, strong enough to withstand the sort of judgement which the wilderness stories have threatened.

Paul thus issues a ban on actions which constitute personal involvement in idolatry (worship of idols). The following paragraph (10:23–11:1) will show greater latitude regarding situations where there is no personal participation in idolatry. The hard line he takes here may appear to go further than the argument he employed in 8:4–13, where his concern was the effect of eating sacrificial food on others, rather than its threat to one's own partnership with Christ; but the difference is one of focus rather than substance. In practice, it may have been difficult to define, or to anticipate, where a believer was implicated in acts of idolatry, for instance, when attendance at a meal in a temple or in the presence of an idol might involve the banqueters in sacrifice or other acts of worship. Perhaps Paul underestimated the complexity of such situations, but it is clear at least that he cannot tolerate the forging of a link to alien entities, which, though they may not be gods, are none the less potent rivals to Christ (cf. 15:24–8).

(10:23–11:1) Practical Guidelines on Eating and Avoiding Offence The ban on participation in 'idolatry' has not yet resolved all the practical issues, since there are places and occasions where sacrificial food may be on offer without involving the believer in idolatry. In such matters, again the crucial issue is the effect of one's actions on other people, particularly other believers: we have returned full circle to the concerns of ch. 8, since Paul still maintains that love is a more valuable criterion than knowledge (8:1–3). Thus, while citing again in 10:23 the Corinthian principle of freedom (cf. 6:12), Paul insists on modifying it with reference to what 'builds up', that is, what is beneficial to others (cf. 8:1). The tendencies of the élite are to protect their own interests in such matters, advancing their social position by minimum abstentions from sacrificial food; but Paul calls them to seek, first of all, the advantage of others (10:24). In the case of food sold in the meat market (which might or might not have passed through a temple in the process of slaughter), Paul encourages complete freedom: ignorance as to the history of the food means that no one's conscience (identity as a Christian) is affected by eating this food. Most Jews were more anxious about avoiding food possibly tainted by idolatry, but Paul overrules this scruple since eating such food from a market risks no personal participation in idolatry, and since the food itself is a part of God's good creation (10:25–6, boldly citing Ps 24:1 in support). In the case of a meal at an unbeliever's house, ignorance is again encouraged for the same reasons (10:27), but here complications may arise from the involvement of other people in the meal. Paul is concerned for the 'conscience' of someone else who declares the food to have been involved in sacrifice (10:28). Because the phrase, 'This has been offered in sacrifice', does not use the Jewish/Christian term 'idolatrous', many interpreters take this informant to be a non-believer (either fellow-guest or host; e.g. Fee 1987: 483–5). But it is hard to see why Paul would be concerned with an unbeliever's conscience in this matter, and it is better to see here the same weak Christians as were in view in ch. 8 (Barrett 1971: 239–40). For *their* sake, i.e. lest they be pressurized into compromising their faith, knowledgeable Christians should refrain from such food (10:28–29a). But otherwise the basic principle remains: so long as one can give thanks with integrity, that is, eat the food as part of a relationship with God (uncompromised by partnership with demons), one should do so freely, even if others are critical (10:29b–30).

On this reading of the argument, 10:28–9a forms a digression, citing an exceptional case when liberty is to be constrained, while 10:29b–30 gives the general rule. If this is right, Paul agrees with the knowledgeable about their freedom to a large degree, but checks them at the point where their freedom causes real damage to others (cf. Rom 14:1–15:6). The last few verses of this discussion (10:31–11:1) sum up its principles. Eating and drinking are to be done 'to the glory of God', without compromise of that glory by idolatry. At the same time, no stumbling-block (the Greek echoes 8:9 and is much stronger than NRSV 'offence') is to be placed in the path of Jews or Greeks or the church (10:32). The goal should be not one's own advantage, but that of others, that they be saved and maintained in salvation (10:33, i. e. not 'destroyed' by selfish use of 'knowledge'; cf. 8:11). And, finally, Paul reminds them of the example he has described in ch. 9, not ultimately because of his own importance (he does not want a 'Paul party') but because he believes he thereby imitates Christ (11:1; cf. Rom 15:1–3).

Issues Relating to Communal Meetings (11:2–14:40)

Paul now turns to a number of topics which relate to the conduct of worship and communal meetings in the Corinthian church. The bulk of this new section concerns the exercise of spiritual gifts (chs. 12–14), but that is prefaced with discussion of two topics also related to worship, head-covering of women in prayer and prophecy (11:2–16) and the Lord's Supper (11:17–34). Paul's initial word of commendation (11:2) is probably meant to preface the whole section, since the Lord's Supper and the gifts of the Spirit were part of his legacy to the church. But on many issues, in fact, he has more criticism to offer than praise (cf. 11:22).

(11:2–16) Praying and Prophesying with Proper Head-Covering This passage, with its hierarchical ordering of male and female, has had a fateful influence through the centuries and has not enhanced Paul's reputation. It is full of awkward argumentation, so awkward that a few scholars even consider it a later addition to the letter by another hand. The issue concerns men and women who pray and prophesy in the church (vv. 4–5). Paul takes it for granted that *both* genders will participate in such important acts of church leadership (on prophecy, see ch. 14); how this tallies with the apparent ban on women's speech in church in 14:33–6 is not clear (see 1 COR 14:33–6). Most commentators rightly take the topic to be the *covering* of the head (Theissen 1987: 158–75), while a few scholars construe the Greek differently to refer to tying up (or letting loose) of *hair* (Murphy-O'Connor 1980). Men and women wore the same sort of outer garment (Gk. *himation*), which could be drawn forward from behind the neck to cover the crown of the head, or even further forward over the face as well. In normal circumstances men did not draw the *himation* forward, although Romans did in offering sacrifice at an altar. The typical customs for women are more difficult to discern, and probably varied over time and in different cultural contexts within the Graeco-Roman world (on Corinth see Thompson 1988). However, a variety of evidence suggests that, in public and in the presence of men other than family members, married women frequently covered their heads and even their faces, as a sign of modesty and as a protective barrier in the force-field of lustful stares. Young unmarried girls did not usually cover or veil themselves, but for a mature/married woman (girls were normally married at puberty) to be seen uncovered might suggest that she was somewhat 'forward', thus bringing shame both on herself and on her husband. Thus head-covering functioned both to differentiate women from men and to subordinate them.

This passage suggests that there are some women in the Corinthian church who are leading worship in prayer and prophecy with their heads uncovered. We can only speculate about the reasons for this behaviour. It is possible that the causes were quite mundane, for instance, that they felt the house-church a sufficiently 'private' context not to require head-covering, or that the ecstasy of Spirit-inspiration caused head-coverings to slip. It is normally suggested, however, that there stands some theological principle behind their activity, for instance some appeal to the baptismal formula that 'there is neither male nor female' (Gal 3:28) in order to justify the abolition of gender distinctions. It is also possible that the practice was particularly sponsored by those 'virgins' Paul addresses in ch. 7, who as unmarried women may have wished to demonstrate their special relationship to God (7:34) by renouncing a common token of relatedness to a husband (see later, Tertullian, *On the Veiling of Virgins*). Whatever the cause, the practice brings to the surface deep anxieties in Paul concerning gender distinction, and he employs a battery of arguments from theology, Scripture, custom, and 'reason' to reimpose what he insists is the universal Christian custom (v. 16).

His first move is to set up a hierarchy of 'heads', involving God, Christ, man, and woman (v. 3). 'Head' (Gk. *kephalē*) probably indicates 'authority'; some have taken it to mean 'source', but in either case the chain suggests subordination (on Christ's subordination to God, cf. 3:23 and 15:28). The use of 'head' language enables Paul to draw on both literal and metaphorical senses; the male with covered head disgraces his head (physical head and/or Christ), the female with uncovered head disgraces hers (physical and/or man, vv. 4–5). The cultural assumptions concerning 'shame' in this matter are clear in the parallels Paul draws with a woman whose hair is cut short or shaven (vv. 5–6): in both cases she was considered demeaned as a woman (cf. v. 15) and her femininity denied. Paul is concerned throughout this passage that genders should not be confused or rendered ambiguous.

v. 7 suggests a natural distinction between man (as image and glory/reflection of God) and woman (as glory/reflection of man). This represents a tendentious reading of Gen 1:26–7 (where male *and female* are created 'in the image of God'). The logic of the verse is obscure, but perhaps suggests that in worship of God the man's head should not be covered (since it brings glory to God), while the woman's should (since it brings glory to man). vv. 8–9 draw from Genesis 2 (Eve's creation from and for Adam) in order to reinforce the hierarchy suggested by the opening chain (v. 3). Thus a woman is required to have, literally, 'authority on her head' (v. 10). This must refer to the head-covering, but it is unclear whether it is a symbol of her authority to pray and prophesy (Hooker 1964), or of her submission to male authority. The reference to the angels in this verse is puzzling. Some take these as the angels who protect the orders of creation and are present at Corinthian worship to ensure order (there are some parallels to this notion at Qumran). Others regard them in a more sinister light as the successors to the 'sons of God' (Gen 6:1–4) who are liable to lust after unveiled women (Gen 6 was much discussed in Jewish apocalyptic circles, cf. 1 *Enoch* 14–16). In vv. 11–12 Paul moves to moderate some of what he has asserted by pointing to the interdependence (not equality) of women and men in the cycle of life, but 'in the Lord' suggests some specifically Christian reality. Finally, he appeals to reason (vv. 13–16). The Corinthians should know what is 'proper' in the matter of hair and head-covering. The appeal to 'nature' in v. 14 with reference to the degradation of *long hair* shows how disastrously Paul has confused 'nature' and 'custom', a confusion which has led him to support cultural norms with arguments from 'creation'. He may realize that his arguments are not likely to persuade and thus resorts finally to an abrupt dismissal of 'contentiousness', refusing to allow further discussion on this matter (v. 16).

(11:17–34) Humiliation of Church Members at the Lord's Supper Paul now turns to a topic on which reports have suggested a fundamental dysfunction in the church in relation to a rite, the Lord's Supper, which should constitute the core of church life and enact the proclamation of the gospel. The seriousness with which he takes this issue is indicated by his claim that their present form of gathering is positively harmful (v. 17), by his suggestion that the behaviour of some might mark them out as false Christians (v. 19; cf. 9:27), and by his warning that their mishandling of the Supper could lead—in fact already had led—to illness and death as divine judgement (vv. 27–32). The divisions that he hears about (v. 18) appear to be primarily social, between the élite members of the church and lower-class Christians. The 'Lord's Supper' (v. 20) was a full meal, incorporating the sharing of bread and wine but not restricted to those foodstuffs. Paul is scandalized that what was meant to be a common meal has become a display of disunity in the church. It appears that wealthier members have been bringing their own supplies for the meal, starting the meal before all had arrived and keeping their own food largely, if not entirely, for themselves, so that they consume more (and perhaps better quality) food than poorer members (vv. 20–2). It was common at dinner-parties in the Graeco-Roman world for the host to give more and better food to his more distinguished guests, and perhaps Gaius, the host to the whole church (Rom 16:23), has simply followed cultural habits unthinkingly (Theissen 1982: 145–74). Thus Paul once again has to remind the wealthier members of the church of their responsibilities to their fellow Christians of lower status: by humiliating them in this fashion they are showing contempt for the church of God (v. 22; cf. 3:16–17 and 8:12).

To correct such abuse Paul first reminds them of the tradition he passed to them (vv. 23–6). These verses are actually our first witness to the form and understanding of the Lord's Supper in the early church, being earlier than the gospel accounts (Mk 14:22–4; Mt 26:26–8; Lk 22:17–20). This is the only incident in the life of Jesus that Paul ever recounts (apart from his crucifixion) and it seems to have become fixed relatively early as the founding narrative for an important Christian rite. We cannot tell precisely how Paul

understood the identification between 'the bread' and 'the body' (v. 24) or between 'the cup' (note, not 'the wine') and 'the blood' (v. 25), though the reference to the new covenant and the notion of 'remembrance' seem to place greater emphasis on the relationship forged between the participant and the Lord than on the essence of the elements themselves. v. 26 seems to be Paul's own interpretation of the significance of the meal: through it the participants 'proclaim the Lord's death'. In the light of 1:18–2:5 it is not surprising that he finds the élitism and self-centredness of the higher-status Christians in Corinth constituting a denial of the message of Christ crucified.

Returning to the Corinthians' conduct, Paul warns them against eating and drinking 'in an unworthy manner' (v. 27). The context suggests that such carelessness about partaking in bread and wine includes the scandalous behaviour of those who humiliate other Christians at the Supper (vv. 20–2). Hence, the call to 'examine yourselves' (v. 28) must signal primarily a scrutiny of one's behaviour towards others in the church, not a general moral scrutiny of one's 'worthiness' to partake in a sacred meal. Eating and drinking requires 'discerning the body' (v. 29), discerning that the bread 'is' the body of Christ, but also that the church constitutes the body of Christ as it partakes of this 'one bread' (10:17; cf. 12:12–27). To defile the Supper is to show contempt for the church, and thus to invite the sort of judgement which God metes out to those who damage his temple (v. 29; 3:16–17). Such 'unworthy' eating makes one accountable for the body and blood of Christ (v. 27), in the sense that, rather than benefiting from the death of Christ, one is actually placed among his enemies and murderers (like 'the rulers of this age', 2:6–8). That would be to invite God's judgement (v. 29). Paul reckons some have already experienced this in illness and death (v. 30; cf. 5:5), though it is better to be judged in this way as a discipline than to be condemned utterly, like 'the world' (cf. 1:18; 3:15). The final instructions (vv. 33–4) show that the humiliation of the poorer members is still his chief concern: the 'brothers and sisters' should wait for one another and not indulge in grossly unequal feasts. The advice to satisfy hunger 'at home' (v. 34) might constitute a step towards separating the meal from the ritual sharing of bread and wine.

(12:1–31) The Distribution of Spiritual Gifts in the Body of Christ At v. 1 Paul turns directly to the issue of 'spiritual gifts' (the Greek could also mean 'spiritual people'). As ch. 14 will show, he is particularly concerned with their exercise in worship (a topic already touched on in 11:2–16). That chapter also indicates that the heart of the issue is the use of 'tongues', a gift of humanly incomprehensible speech which some Corinthian Christians apparently rate far higher than does Paul. The highly charged enthusiasm of the Corinthian church has led to an energetic use of the gifts of the Spirit (cf. 1:7) and a sense of fullness which Paul considers dangerously close to self-satisfaction (4:8). Here he is concerned lest the variety of gifts lead to disunity within the church, and create a hierarchy in which certain 'gifted' Christians despise others. The gift of tongues may be specially conducive to this sense of superiority, since it represents a dramatic and complete 'possession' by the Spirit of God, the gifted individual being considered to speak 'mysteries' (14:2) in 'the tongues of angels' (13:1). There is some evidence to suggest that such esoteric speech might be cultivated particularly by higher-status individuals, so that this gift might reinforce the status differentials which we have found to be operative in other issues addressed by Paul (Martin 1991).

Paul's first warning is against naïvety (vv. 1–3). Not every form of 'possession' is God-inspired: the Corinthians should not assume that the more dramatic the 'ecstasy', the better the gift. In their religious past they experienced 'ecstasy' (v. 2; NRSV 'enticed' would be better translated 'moved'), but that was erroneous, inducing only worship of speechless 'idols'. The gift has to be tested by its result (v. 3): clearly the Spirit of God cannot inspire someone to say 'Jesus be cursed', while the basic Christian confession 'Jesus is Lord' is attributable only to the Spirit (cf. Rom 10:9; Phil 2:11). The point may seem obvious, but 'inspiration' was (and is) a problematic claim and needed to be tested by its effects (cf. 14:29; 1 Thess 5:19–21).

But there is another and larger point to be made: that no one gift should be regarded as of unique importance or played off against others (vv. 4–11). In a formulation which points towards later trinitarian doctrine, Paul insists that the varieties of gifts and services can be traced to the same Spirit/Lord/God (vv. 4–6). v. 11 will re-emphasize this point, while suggesting that the Spirit distributes gifts to every believer ('to each one individually') and according to the Spirit's choice, not his/her own (but cf. 12:31; 14:1). Thus none can boast of having a gift, which is precisely a *gift* (*charisma* means 'gift of grace'), not a possession or an achievement

(cf. 4:7). Moreover, the gifts are given not for individual satisfaction or pride, but 'for the common good' (v. 7). Thus Paul again signals the criterion of 'benefit to others' which he has appealed to throughout (6:12; 8:1–3; 10:23–4, etc.) and which will form the theme of ch. 13 as the basis for ch. 14.

To illustrate the 'varieties of gifts', Paul gives a representative list in vv. 8–10. Parallel lists in v. 28 and in Rom 12:6–8 (cf. Eph 4:11) suggest that this is not meant to be an exhaustive inventory, but a display of the diversity which the Corinthians will recognize as operative among themselves. Some appear to overlap (e.g. utterance of wisdom and utterance of knowledge) or to be closely linked to others ('faith' in this context means the special exercise of faith required for the 'working of miracles', vv. 9–10; cf. 13:2). It is no accident that the gifts of tongues and their interpretation are placed at the bottom of the list (as also in v. 28). While not wishing to endorse explicitly a gift-hierarchy, Paul does want to demote tongues from the exalted position it holds in the estimation of some Corinthian Christians.

In v. 12 Paul introduces the metaphor of the body, which will dominate the rest of this chapter. The statement in v. 27 that 'you are the body of Christ' does not mean that the church constitutes, in some literal sense, the presence of Christ in the world; rather, the church is (like) a body which belongs to Christ, identified with the risen Christ ('so it is with Christ', v.12) but not identical to him. The body was commonly used in antiquity as a metaphor for human society (or for the whole cosmos), as a variegated organism whose diverse parts are interdependent. It was an image that could easily be exploited by élite classes to justify inequality, on the basis that it was necessary for inferior groups to play their part for the good of all (the Roman historian Livy uses it in this way). One of the striking aspects of Paul's use of the metaphor is that, in his hands, it not only justifies diversity in the church, but also works specifically *against* hierarchical notions of honour and differential importance.

The combination of diversity and unity—many limbs in one body—is the first point to be established (vv. 12–20). Baptismal formulae in v. 13 remind the Corinthians of their cultural and social diversity but also of their common access to the Spirit (cf. Gal 3:28, whose 'male and female' pairing is conspicuously absent here). vv. 14–19 illustrate the fact that a body, properly understood, must be a differentiated organism: it cannot all be of one part. Paul notably presents this fact from the point of view of a member which feels itself excluded because it is not something else (vv. 15–16). He thus identifies with the position of members of the church who are being made to feel inferior or marginalized, and insists on their rightful place within the body.

In vv. 21–6 Paul then develops this perspective by confronting the superior attitudes of the 'stronger' or more prominent Corinthian Christians. No member can dismiss others as dispensable (v. 21) because those which are apparently 'weaker' or less 'honourable' are in fact of crucial significance and accorded very great 'respect' by the rest of the body. He is thinking no doubt of the attitude we adopt to the vulnerable organs of the body and the genitalia, but his point is clearly meant to apply to the less 'honourable' members of the Corinthian church. We have noted at many points how the 'weaker' members in the church are being treated with less than full respect by higher-status Corinthian Christians (1:26–8; 8:1–13; 11:20–2). Paul here uses the body metaphor to overturn such attitudes, pointing out that the less 'respectable' are in fact accorded great respect, and that God has so designed this (vv. 22–4). This attribution of greater honour to the 'lesser' individual is based on the same principle as Paul had found in the message of the cross (1:18–2:5), where human values of power and wisdom are overturned. As in that passage, Paul finds here the solution to those pride-induced 'dissensions' which are springing up in the Corinthian church (v. 25; the same word is translated 'divisions' in 1:10). The mutuality of care for one another's interests which Paul had taught in chs. 8–10 (10:24, 32) is here illustrated by the concern of all the body's parts for the health and welfare of the rest (vv. 25–6).

The chapter is completed by making explicit the relevance of the metaphor to the Christians in Corinth (v. 27) and by another list of 'gifts' or 'appointments' (v. 28). Here some value distinctions are introduced ('first apostles' etc.) since Paul does regard some gifts as more conducive to the welfare of the body than others (as ch. 14 will illustrate); again tongues is last in the list! The point about necessary diversity in the body is finally driven home with a series of rhetorical questions (vv. 29–30) designed to undercut the notion that any one gift should be possessed by all, or that anyone is deficient in not possessing it. There is a sense in which some gifts are 'greater' (v. 31), but that is only because they

facilitate the supreme virtue which Paul will now describe.

(13:1–13) The Superior and Critical Demands of Love This chapter has sometimes been considered a self-contained 'love-hymn', pre-prepared by Paul, whose present positioning creates a somewhat disappointing descent to the practicalities of ch. 14. But in fact this prioritizing of love fits its present literary context and the precise needs of the Corinthian church exceptionally well, and in its sharp criticism of the values current among the Corinthians it is hardly an anodyne 'ode to love'. It is written in prose, not verse, but it clearly has poetic qualities both in the level of language and in its structural shaping. It falls naturally into three sections (vv. 1–3, 4–7, 8–13): the first and third match one another in their comparative evaluations of love, while the central section consists of thirteen simple verbs, arranged in order positive–negative–positive.

The first section (vv. 1–3) is made up of three conditional clauses, each complemented by a devastating statement of worthlessness. The first imagines the possession of all the possible gifts of speech which were so highly prized in Corinth, 'tongues of angels' perhaps describing the imagined content of 'speaking in tongues'. Without love, which can make such communication purposeful and beneficial to others, all such gifts, although genuinely gifts of the Spirit, are mere noise ('noisy gong' refers to the bronze products for which Corinth was famous). Similarly the powers of prophecy, knowledge, and faith (cf. 12:8–10; Mk 11:20–4) are valueless without love (v. 2). In fact, most challenging of all, even apparent acts of charity and self-sacrifice gain nothing at all, unless they are motivated and controlled by love (v. 3). A tiny textual variant could alter the sense in v. 3 from delivering the body 'that I may boast' to delivering it 'to be burned'. Commentators are evenly divided on the best reading here. It was perhaps unnecessary still to criticize boasting (cf. 4:7), so the reading 'to be burned' (e.g. in martyrdom) may be preferred. Even martyrdom is valueless unless it is founded on love.

The central stanza (vv. 4–7) provides a pen-portrait of 'love' (*agapē*), a term not coined in early Christianity but given special prominence and reshaped to express its peculiar ethos of self-sacrifice. The paragraph is made up of simple verbs or short clauses which define the quality of love, mostly by the attitudes it eschews. Two positive verbs open the list, which then contrasts love with a catalogue of spiritual failures in the Corinthian church: love is not envious (cf. 3:3), it is not boastful or arrogant (cf. 4:6, 18–19; 5:2; 8:1, etc.), it does not insist on its own way (cf. 10:24), nor rejoice in wrongdoing (cf. 5:1–2). The final four positive verbs (v. 7) expand the field of love's operation as widely as possible. Their link between love, faith, endurance, and hope matches the conglomerate of Christian virtues which Paul elsewhere uses to sum up the essence of Christian commitment (cf. v. 13; 1 Thess 1:3).

In the final paragraph (vv. 8–13) Paul returns to demonstrate the supreme value of love, now stressing not so much its indispensability (vv. 1–3) as its eternal worth. Paul is ever conscious of the provisional character of Christian existence before the *parousia* (cf. 15:19), and he cannot share the Corinthian sense of fullness (4:8). For him, the only characteristic of the present which is final and complete is love: 'love never ends' (v. 8). All other Christian qualities, even genuine gifts of the Spirit, are provisional and imperfect. The Corinthians value prophecy, tongues, and knowledge (cf. chs. 8–10 and 14), but all these, Paul insists, are only temporary phenomena (v. 8). For now, knowledge (and prophecy) are inescapably partial (v. 9), not only in the sense that they are incomplete (we know only some things) but also because they are imperfect (even what we 'know', we only partly comprehend; see P. W. Gooch 1987: 142–61). Like a child whose knowledge not only grows but also matures, so our present state of knowledge will appear 'childish' from the perspective of the final revelation (v. 11). Or, to use a different image, our present perception is inevitably indirect and distorted—in a mirror and 'dim'—while in the future we will see direct and clear, as clearly as we are already seen and known by God (v. 12; cf. 8:3). The abiding qualities, which already have a firm purchase on eternal truths, are faith, hope, and love (*not* the Corinthians' vaunted 'knowledge'). But the greatest of these, as the reflection of God's own character, is love (v. 13; cf. Rom 5:8).

(14:1–40) The Superiority of Prophecy over Tongues As the first phrase makes clear, ch. 14 draws its inspiration from the preceding eulogy of love, which is not a digression from the topic of spiritual gifts but an exposition of the virtue which enables the church to evaluate and prioritize those gifts. As concerns various forms of speech, love sets the priority as that which 'builds up' the church (v. 12; cf. 8:1). 'Building up' constitutes one of the two guiding principles of Paul's instructions concerning worship, the other being that which is 'decent' and 'orderly' (vv. 33, 40). The first part of this chapter is made up of four overlapping arguments for the superiority of prophecy over tongues (vv. 1–25). 'Prophecy' is never defined, but seems to constitute speech which instructs, encourages, consoles, or challenges its hearers (vv. 3, 24–5, 31). 'Tongues' are not foreign languages intelligible to native speakers (as are portrayed in Acts 2), but speech which is humanly unintelligible, being addressed primarily to God (v. 2). The phenomenon of such 'ecstatic speech' is quite widely attested in a variety of religions, though in antiquity it may have been specially prized by the social élite.

The first argument for the greater value of prophecy is that it strengthens the whole church, whereas tongues benefit only the individual gifted with them (vv. 1–5). Once again, Paul places a premium on what benefits the whole community (cf. 10:23–4), even if it be a less spectacular or mysterious gift than tongues. Their 'mysteries in the Spirit' (v. 2) are not understood even by fellow 'spiritual people', unless someone exercises the gift of interpretation (v. 5). Paul's wish that all speak in tongues or prophesy (v. 5) must be hypothetical (in the light of 12:29–30), but he simultaneously insists that what the Corinthians value most highly is actually of inferior value. Prophecy may be transitory and imperfect (13:8–10), but at least for the present it can be well used in the service of love.

The second argument develops the first by contrasting the unintelligibility of tongues—and therefore its worthlessness for others—with the intelligibility of prophecy (vv. 6–13). Again, the question is what benefit the speech has for others (v. 6). Tongues are as indistinct and incomprehensible as a musical instrument whose notes signify nothing to the hearer (vv. 7–8) or as a foreign language whose meaning we cannot grasp (v. 11). Paul recognizes and affirms the Corinthian 'zeal' for spiritual gifts (v. 12); nothing in this passage discourages the use of gifts as such. He simply wants the most useful (upbuilding) gifts to be regarded as of higher value, a recognition which will force the Corinthians to view themselves as a *community*, not as a collection of gifted individuals. Paul is careful not to go so far as to ban the use of tongues, but he requires that their users should expect them to be turned into something beneficial through interpretation (v. 13).

The third argument (vv. 14–19) provides a different rationale for the superiority of prophecy: it involves both spirit and mind, whereas the gift of tongues engages only the spirit. Paul is probably speaking here of 'spirit' in the sense of human spirit, though it is closely linked with, and inspired by, the Spirit of God. We might expect this contrast to imply a higher evaluation of rationality, the engagement of the mind being exalted over 'irrational' speech. But it would be hard to argue that the human mind was a higher faculty than the Spirit-inspired spirit, and Paul's cherishing of the 'mind' turns out to be not on account of its rationality so much as its intelligibility to others, the goal being once again the 'upbuilding' or instruction of the hearers (vv. 17–19). This point is made by reference to prayer, singing, and the offering of thanksgiving to God, as the discussion broadens to cover wider aspects of worship (cf. v. 6). Thus Paul forces the Corinthians to consider what is appropriate 'in church', as opposed to in private. In a communal setting, intelligible words count for everything (v. 19). Again, Paul does not discredit tongues absolutely (he claims to be even more gifted than the Corinthians, 14:18!), but requires them to reconsider their appropriateness with a view to others' needs. He is challenging the same unconcern for others which had manifested itself at the Lord's Supper (11:20–2).

The final argument (vv. 20–5) is prefaced by a stinging rebuke of the Corinthians, who seem to have prided themselves on their maturity (v. 20, whose last phrase reads literally, 'in your minds be mature'; cf. 2:6–3:4). Paul turns to the only passage in 'the law' (here meaning the Scriptures as a whole) which might be relevant to the subject of 'tongues', a warning in Isa 28:11–12 about God speaking to his disobedient people through foreigners. At first sight, the lesson Paul draws from this passage in v. 22 (tongues are a sign for unbelievers, prophecy for believers) seems to be the reverse of his illustration in vv. 23–5, where he imagines the negative effects of tongues on 'outsiders' or 'unbelievers' (the two terms are probably synonyms) and the positive effects of prophecy. The clue probably lies back in the quotation itself, which Paul has slightly modified (adding 'even then') to suggest that the 'tongues' actually bring about, or confirm, unbelief. Thus the 'sign for' phrases in v. 22 should probably be taken to mean that tongues serve to strengthen unbelief, while prophecy serves to strengthen, or bring about, belief. Thus outsiders viewing the whole church speaking in tongues will not be attracted to the faith, but simply conclude that it is a form of madness (v. 23); while if they encounter prophecy in the church, they will be led to faith by a conviction of sin, a revealing of heart-secrets, and a recognition of God's presence in the church (vv. 24–5). This is a rare depiction of what Paul imagines to be the ingredients of 'conversion', indicating the importance for him of sin and judgement (cf. 4:4–5) and of the powerful presence of God (cf. Gal 3:2–5). His own experience in his call/conversion may also be reflected here in some measure.

The discussion can now broaden out to take in wider aspects of worship (vv. 26–40). This is the most complete image we get of earliest Christian worship, though we cannot tell whether Paul's prescription matches reality in the Corinthian church, or in any other. Paul certainly imagines the participation of any member of the community (there are no designated 'ministerial' roles), bringing whatever gifts they have, provided, once again, that they contribute to the task of 'building up' (v. 26). The 'lesson' here (v. 26) means teaching, not a reading from Scripture, an activity which is strikingly absent from this list of worship activities. The theme of the chapter makes the spotlight fall particularly on tongues and prophecy. The former are not banned, but restricted in number and admissible only if interpreted. The latter also is not to become a virtuoso performance: a number of prophets should be allowed to speak, their speech weighed as to its validity (cf. 2:15; 12:3), and room made for new speakers, whose prophecy is sparked by a further 'revelation' (vv. 29–31). Paul is striving to control the exuberance of the worship meetings, but also to prevent their domination by any one figure or clique: each member of the body has its part to play and none is entitled to dismiss the contribution of others as inconvenient or unnecessary (cf. 12:14–26).

The next paragraph (14:33b–36) has been the subject of intense debate. It seems to place a total ban on women's speech in church, which is strangely inconsistent with Paul's permission in 11:2–16 that (veiled) women could pray and prophesy. Also the argument depends on a vague and uncharacteristic appeal to 'the law' (v. 34) and appears to assume that all the women will have husbands to ask 'at home' (v. 35), despite Paul's acceptance that the single and celibate option is prudent for both women and men (ch. 7). Such facts prompt one of two conclusions. Either Paul is truly inconsistent here, reacting against a threat of 'unruly' women by forbidding their verbal participation, despite what he had earlier allowed. Or this passage is an interpolation into the letter by a later editor, one who took the opportunity of the surrounding context to introduce the restrictive ethos of the Pastoral letters (e.g. 1 Tim 2:8–15, part of a letter generally regarded as written by a later Paulinist, not by Paul himself). This latter option is favoured by many commentators, and it is given slight textual support by the fact that some manuscripts place vv. 34–5 at the end of the chapter, rather than in their present location; that might indicate that they were once a marginal gloss which was inserted by scribes at varying points into the original text (see Fee 1987: 699–708). There have been numerous speculations about a particular local problem in Corinth (e.g. women who rudely interrupted prophecy, or questioned their husbands in 'weighing' their prophecies, see Jervis 1995) which might or might not explain this outburst if it is genuinely from Paul. But as it stands the passage seems to presuppose that women in all Paul's churches were wholly silent, which hardly fits what we know of women leaders in Pauline congregations (e.g. Rom 16:1–2, 3–5, 7; Phil 4:2).

Paul closes the discussion with a strong assertion of his authority (derived from the Lord) and a refusal to countenance contrary opinions even from prophets or so-called 'spiritual' people (vv. 37–8). The strength of his tone suggests that the whole chapter is directed against a dominant individual or group whose use of gifts is stifling the life of the congregation. The final verses (39–40) summarize the priorities set by the chapter and highlight the need for order; disorder is easily exploited by the strong.

The Resurrection of Christ and the Resurrection Body (15:1–58)

This chapter stands somewhat alone in the flow of topics in the letter and it may appear odd that the heavy emphasis on the cross as the heart of the gospel in chs. 1–2 should be diluted by the equal insistence here on the centrality of the resurrection (2:2 is somewhat contradicted by 15:3–5). Yet the discussion of the body in 6:12–20 gave an indication that Paul considered the Corinthians' understanding of resurrection to lie at the root of other problems in their church (see esp. 6:12–14). It is difficult to be sure how the Corinthians did understand resurrection. Were they uninterested in a future

resurrection because they considered themselves already 'raised' (cf. 4:8; 1 Tim 2:18)? Or did they disbelieve any future life after death? In fact, the main focus of the chapter (at least from v. 35 onwards) is the notion of a resurrection body, and it is most likely that the Corinthians believed in the existence of some post-mortem state, but one free from the restrictions of the body. Their belief in some form of afterlife seems implied by their practice of vicarious baptism for the dead (v. 29), but it was common in Hellenized circles (both Greek and Jewish) to consider the body an encumbrance which the soul will gladly shed after death. For Paul, their doubt about the sense or value of a 'resurrection body' suggests that they are beginning to question an essential element of their faith, the resurrection of Christ; it also indicates a lack of trust in God's creative power to bring life out of death in whatever form he chooses. Thus he insists on the apocalyptic notion of a final battle against the powers of death (vv. 20–8) and defends the idea of a resurrection body, though dispelling crude notions of physical identity between the present and the future body (vv. 35–57).

Paul begins by pointedly reminding them of the terms on which they entered the faith—terms which they must continue to accept if they are to remain secure (vv. 1–2). The important point is that these terms included belief in the resurrection of Jesus, and it is this topic which Paul emphasizes in citing a foundational credal statement (vv. 3–7). This creed is introduced in v. 3 in technical terms signifying the transmission of tradition, one which Paul must have inherited (in Antioch?) before he founded the church in Corinth (50–1 CE). It thus constitutes the earliest known Christian creed. Its structure is clear: two main 'that' clauses concerning, respectively, the death and the resurrection of Christ, each backed by reference to the Scriptures, and two supplementary 'that' clauses about the burial (reinforcing the death) and the appearances (supporting the resurrection). It is not clear precisely what scriptures are alluded to in this formula nor is it obvious where the original creed ceased: some think it ran no further than v. 5, others as far as v. 7.

This creed constitutes our earliest literary evidence to belief in the resurrection of Christ, and it is often remarked that it makes no mention of the empty tomb or of the women who witnessed the scene (and the risen Christ) according to the stories in the gospels. That silence has suggested to some the late emergence of the story of the empty tomb (first attested in Mk 16, in the late 60s CE), though others consider the silence merely accidental. In any case, it is striking that Paul supports the notion of the resurrection of Jesus purely on the grounds of the resurrection appearances. Those appearances he lists are not all easily correlated with the gospel stories, which also differ among themselves, though the appearance to Cephas may correspond to Lk 24:34, and the appearance to 'the twelve' with stories in Lk 24 and Jn 20.

One reason for Paul's concentration on these appearances is that he can add his own testimony at the end of the list (v. 8). He took his commissioning to his apostleship to be the final resurrection appearance, although Luke placed it in a quite different category in the narrative of the book of Acts. This claim to a vision of Christ was crucial to Paul's self-belief as an apostle (cf. 9:1), and it leads him into a brief digression about his apostleship (vv. 9–10), which reveals much about his sense of inferiority (as a former persecutor), his radical appreciation of grace, and his hope of outdoing other apostles (cf. 9:3–18). Returning to the topic (v. 11), he insists that the same resurrection-centred message was taught by all the apostles and was the basis of the Corinthians' faith.

The next paragraph (vv. 12–19) unearths the reason for Paul's concern that the Corinthians 'hold firm' to the message he delivered: he thinks they are beginning to waver in their faith in the resurrection of Jesus since some say 'there is no resurrection of the dead' (v. 12). As noted above, the Corinthians' doubts probably concerned the notion of a bodily resurrection, as indeed the phrase 'the resurrection of the dead' (which could be taken literally as 'the raising of corpses') might suggest a crude notion of physical reconstitution after death. Paul himself does not envisage resurrection in such crude terms, but his first reaction is to insist that to doubt the notion of a resurrection of the dead is to doubt the resurrection of Christ, which was a cardinal tenet of their creed. He now runs through a logical argument twice (vv. 13–15 and 16–19) with slight variations in emphasis. First: if there is no resurrection, then Christ has not been raised, then our preaching of that fact was worthless and so is your faith, which is based on that fact (vv. 13–14); indeed, the apostles are then vulnerable to the charge of lying about God, for claiming he raised Christ from the dead (v. 15). Secondly: if the dead are not raised, then Christ has not been raised, then

your faith is futile and 'you are still in your sins' (vv. 16–17)—that is, you cannot depend on the other part of the creed, that 'Christ died for our sins' (v. 3). That means all grounds of hope are destroyed. As far as Paul is concerned, the future hope is such a necessary counterweight to the difficulties of the 'present evil age' (Gal 1:4) that, if it were proved to be groundless, Christians would turn out to be especially pitiable. The Corinthians may not have denied all future hope, but Paul insists on depicting the whole of the slippery slope which he thinks they have started to descend.

Corinthian doubts have challenged a basic element in Paul's theology and he now demonstrates the pivotal significance of the resurrection of Jesus within the scheme of salvation (vv. 20–8). This scheme is founded on an apocalyptic notion of the age of death being succeeded and overcome by an age of life, the latter being ushered in by a cosmic act of resurrection (de Boer 1988). For Paul, the resurrection of Christ constitutes the 'first fruits' of that cosmic act (vv. 20, 23), the beginning of the harvest which heralds the proximity of the rest. Pairing Christ with Adam (cf. Rom 5:12–20), Paul finds in Christ the start of a new humanity, in which the failures of the present (encapsulated in death) are replaced by the possibilities of the future (resurrection and life). The key text in vv. 27–8 is Ps 8:6, which concerns the intended dignity of humankind: that role is now fulfilled in the 'final Adam' (cf. v. 45) and made possible through him for all (v. 22). That 'all' could be taken to mean 'the whole of humanity', thus implying a kind of universalism (cf. Rom 5:18; 11:32), though the subsequent reference to 'those who belong to Christ' (v. 23) and the earlier dismissals of nonbelievers (e.g. 1:18; 6:9–10) suggest that Paul did not carry through its universalistic potential. The cosmic transformation thus takes place in successive phases: first, the resurrection of Christ, then, at his coming, those who belong to him; 'then' (meaning probably, 'at that same moment', though some see here a further phase), it will be 'the end' when God's kingdom is complete and all the enemies of his rule are defeated. In this apocalyptic scenario the risen Christ plays a crucial role: it is through his present reign that God's enemies are being defeated (v. 25), as God puts them in subjection to him (vv. 27–8). Even so, Paul insists that Christ is ultimately subordinate to God, who is not himself, of course, subject to Christ (v. 27) but is the one to whom Christ is subject in 'handing over the kingdom' (v. 24; cf. 3:23; Rom 11:36).

The next section of the chapter (vv. 29–34) contains miscellaneous arguments which indicate the significance of belief in life beyond death. The reference to baptism 'on behalf of the dead' (v. 29) has been the subject of multiple interpretations (some of which construe the Greek quite differently). It probably refers to a rite in which a few Corinthian believers underwent a vicarious baptism in the place of those (believers?) who had died either unbaptized or 'improperly' baptized. 1:12–17 suggests that some Corinthians regarded baptism by certain figures as of great significance, and they may have wished to make up for a 'lack' in the case of those who were baptized by different leaders or in a different way. Paul does not condemn such a practice, and he is willing to use it to show that the Corinthians themselves entertain hopes for an existence beyond death.

Turning to himself, he indicates how his own life is founded on the same principle of hope (vv. 30–2). It is only because his investments lie beyond his present physical existence that he is prepared to take such risks with his life—exposed daily to the threat of death. Indeed, he has recently undergone some specially dangerous experience in Ephesus (v. 32); here 'fighting with wild beasts' must be a metaphor, or he would not have lived to tell the tale, but it is not clear what sort of crisis it refers to. The Corinthians need to be warned and shamed (vv. 32–4; cf. 4:14; 6:5). If they lose their faith in the resurrection of the dead, they have lapsed into mere hedonism (v. 32, citing Isa 22:13) and will end up corrupting their morals (v. 33, citing a popular proverb originating with the poet Menander). The final comment, that some have 'no knowledge of God' (v. 34) is particularly biting considering the Corinthians' boast of 'knowledge' (8:1, 4).

In v. 35 Paul reaches what is probably the heart of his dispute with the Corinthians: the means and meaning of a resurrection body. On this topic he attempts to preserve a fine and difficult balance. He insists on keeping the term 'body' (Gk. *sōma*) in describing the future state, but also stresses the *discontinuity* between the present and the future body, leaving somewhat ambiguous the relation between the two. The first stage of his argument (vv. 36–41) is the insistence that there are many types of 'body', each with variant degrees of 'glory': in talking about the resurrection of the dead our minds should not be restricted by what we presently experience as 'body' with its rather limited glory. The analogy of the seed (vv. 36–8) illustrates the possibility of

very different 'bodies' either side of death, and the insistence that 'God gives the seed a body as he has chosen' (v. 38) places the emphasis on *God's* re-creative power. The Corinthians' doubts indicate that they have placed their confidence in the continuation of their 'spiritual' selves beyond death, rather than in God, whose future act of resurrection will demonstrate his *sole* power over the forces of sin and death (cf. 1:30–1). The analogy also indicates the variety of different 'bodies' resulting from seeds, which is further illustrated by reference to the varieties of 'flesh' and the difference between 'heavenly' and 'earthly' bodies (vv. 39–41). In antiquity the stars and planets were generally considered to be living matter with a constitution much more glorious and ethereal than that of earthbound creatures. Paul is thus suggesting that a resurrection body could be a body of a much higher order than our present physical condition, though the point hardly works for us who know that the stars are not a different order of creation, but as physical, material, and destructible as ourselves.

vv. 42–50 apply the illustrations to the topic in hand. What is 'sown' (in death) is one kind of body—perishable, inglorious, and weak—but what is raised can be a body of a wholly different kind. One is a 'physical body': the Greek *psychikon sōma* means a body animated by a soul (*psyche*), which is here taken to be mortal and temporary. The other is a 'spiritual body': the Greek *pneumatikon sōma* indicates a body inhabited by spirit (*pneuma*), here perhaps the Spirit of God. Paul thus wishes to preserve the term 'body' but only when it is shorn of its connotations of physicality and mortality. The impersonal statements, 'it is sown a physical body, it is raised a spiritual body', leave unclear whether the physical body is itself reused in the resurrection or whether the self gains a new body quite distinct from the old. This ambiguity matches Paul's silence as to what happened to the body of Jesus and whether his tomb was empty. At least v. 50 makes clear that the present physical body ('flesh and blood') is quite unfit for 'the kingdom of God', though whether entry into that kingdom involves the *transformation* of the present body or the granting of an essentially *new* body is left undefined in this chapter and is not consistently dealt with elsewhere (cf. Rom 8:11; Phil 3:21; 2 Cor 5:1–11). vv. 45–9 develop the contrast between the *psychikon sōma* and the *pneumatikon sōma* by reference to their two prototypes: Adam, the first man, made from the dust, who became a living (but mortal) *psychē* (Gen 2:7) and Christ, the final Adam, whose origin is heaven, and who is a life-giving (and immortal) *pneuma*. Our present bodies are as perishable as Adam's ('we bear the image of the man of dust'), but the future resurrection body will bear the image of Christ (v. 49).

Thus the chapter finishes with a triumphant declaration of the hope on which the whole Christian faith depends, a 'mystery' which makes sense of the present in the light of the future (vv. 51–8; cf. 2:9–10). Although not all will die first ('sleep'), it is certainly the case that all will be changed, that is, our perishable selves will become imperishable and fit for the 'kingdom of God' (v. 50). Using traditional apocalyptic imagery, Paul imagines this great change taking place 'at the last trumpet' (v. 52; cf. 1 Thess 4:16; Rev 8:6). Since he supposes here that he and his generation will be alive at this end-point in history (cf. 7:29–31; 1 Thess 4:15, 17), he distinguishes between 'the dead' who will be raised in the new imperishable state and 'we' who will be changed from a mortal life to a new immortal state (vv. 52–4). At that moment the final enemy, death, will be destroyed (cf. v. 26), and Paul celebrates with two Scripture citations, one (v. 54) from Isa 25:8, a passage full of eschatological promises, the other (v. 55) from Hos 13:14, a passage which he wilfully reads against its grain: the prophet invited death to wield its sting, but Paul employs his words to taunt death with its ultimate powerlessness. Death's sting is already at work in the power of sin, a power derived from the law (v. 56; the themes are elaborated in Rom 6–7); but we are granted victory over both by God (cf. Rom 8:37–9). That means for now persistence in faith and action, since 'the work of the Lord' is of ultimate and lasting significance (v. 58), like love, which is its chief characteristic (13:13; 16:14).

Letter Closing, with Travel Plans, Final Instructions, and Greetings (16:1–24)

This final chapter covers a range of topics which bear on Paul's relationship to the church in Corinth, issues which either had already become problematic or would soon become so. The 'collection for the saints' (vv. 1–4) is the collection Paul had agreed to gather for the church in Jerusalem (Gal 2:10). His problem was in persuading his churches to support this project, since his intentions for this money were open to question and the necessity of the collection was not obvious to all. Paul here suggests a mechanism for regular storing of money on 'the first day of the week', that is, Sunday; nothing is implied here about worship on Sundays. He is trying to avoid a

sudden and potentially embarrassing demand for money when he arrives in Corinth. He also suggests that the Corinthians participate in its delivery, to offset suspicions about its destination. It is clear from 2 Cor 8 and 9 that this advice went unheeded and the Corinthians proved extremely unwilling to contribute to the collection (cf. 2 Cor 12:14–18). However, Rom 15:25–7 suggests that Paul was eventually successful, if the reference to Achaia there includes the church at Corinth (the capital of the province).

Paul's description of his travel plans (vv. 5–9) seems designed to explain why he is unable to visit Corinth immediately: he is detained in Ephesus for the sake of the gospel and wants to wait till he can pay more than a fleeting visit to Corinth. 4:18–19 indicated that Paul was criticized for his absence from Corinth, but the promises he now makes proved to be fateful. He subsequently decided to visit them on his way both *to* and *from* Macedonia, and then had such a painful time in Corinth that he did not come back (2 Cor 1:15–2:2). As 2 Corinthians shows, this constant shifting of plans exposed Paul to acute criticism from certain figures in the church, and undermined the church's confidence in his word.

Meanwhile, Paul is sending Timothy as his delegate (vv. 10–11). It is unclear why that visit, promised in 4:17, is now somewhat indefinite, but the note of fear concerning his reception in Corinth is revealing: if Paul's assistant is likely to be 'despised' in Corinth, Paul's own standing cannot be very secure. As for Apollos (v. 12), we can only speculate why Paul wanted him in Corinth (where he was the figurehead of a 'rival' party, 1:12) and why he was unwilling to go (v. 12). As in 3:5–9, Paul seems anxious to show that he and Apollos are not at odds nor wishing to undermine each other's work.

The general instructions of vv. 13–14 (cf. 15:58 and ch. 13) lead into a specific recommendation of the household of Stephanas (vv. 15–18). Their 'service of the saints' (v. 15) probably consisted of financial support of the church in Corinth. Given what we have glimpsed of leadership contests in the church, this strong recommendation constitutes Paul's bid to ensure that leadership remains in (or reverts to) this household: their presence with Paul at the time of writing has given him the opportunity to hear about the situation in Corinth and to mould the thinking of people who he hopes will influence the rest of the church. We cannot tell what relationship Fortunatus and Achaicus had to Stephanas; they perhaps belonged to his 'household', as slaves, freedmen, or free dependants.

The final greetings (vv. 19–24) are distinguished by special reference to Aquila and Prisca, the couple who had hosted Paul in Corinth at the foundation of the church (Acts 18:2–3). The 'holy kiss' (v. 20) may have been a common sign of recognition among Christian believers (cf. 1 Thess 5:26) and is here contrasted with a curse on any who 'has no love for the Lord' (v. 22). This is perhaps a formulaic phrase defining Christian identity (cf. 12:3), while the last words of v. 22 are a Greek transliteration of an Aramaic acclamation ('Marana tha') which must derive from early Jewish Christianity. Paul's own handwriting (v. 21; cf. Gal 6:11) gives a personal tone to the close of the letter, which has been calculated throughout to restore the allegiance of the Corinthians to himself, though not for his own sake, only in order to ensure their continuance 'in Christ Jesus' (v. 24; cf. 1:9).

REFERENCES

Barclay, J. M. G. (1992), 'Thessalonica and Corinth: Social Contrasts in Pauline Christianity', *JSNT* 47: 49–74.

—— (1996), *Jews in the Mediterranean Diaspora from Alexander to Trajan (323 BCE–117 CE)* (Edinburgh: T. & T. Clark).

Barrett, C. K. (1971), *A Commentary on the First Epistle to the Corinthians*, 2nd edn. (London: A. & C. Black).

—— (1982), *Essays on Paul* (London: SPCK).

Bartchy, S. S. (1973), *MALLON CHRESAI: First-Century Slavery and 1 Corinthians 7.21* (Missoula: Scholars Press).

Brown, P. (1988), *The Body and Society: Men, Women and Sexual Renunciation in Early Christianity* (London: Faber & Faber).

Chow, J. K. (1992), *Patronage and Power: A Study of Social Networks in Corinth* (Sheffield: JSOT).

Clarke, A. D. (1993), *Secular and Christian Leadership in Corinth: A Socio-Historical and Exegetical Study of 1 Corinthians 1–6* (Leiden: Brill).

Dahl, N. A. (1967), 'Paul and the Church at Corinth according to 1 Corinthians 1–4', in W. R. Farmer *et al.* (eds.), *Christian History and Interpretation: Studies Presented to John Knox* (Cambridge: Cambridge University Press), 313–35.

de Boer, M. C. (1988), *The Defeat of Death: Apocalyptic Eschatology in 1 Corinthians 15 and Romans 5* (Sheffield: JSOT).

—— (1994), 'The Composition of 1 Corinthians', *NTS* 40: 229–45.

Deming, W. (1995), *Paul on Marriage and Celibacy: The Hellenistic Background of 1 Corinthians 7* (Cambridge: Cambridge University Press).

Dunn, J. D. G. (1991), *The Partings of the Ways between Christianity and Judaism* (London: SCM).

Fee, G. D. (1987), *The First Epistle to the Corinthians*, New International Commentary on the New Testament, (Grand Rapids, Mich.: Eerdmans).

Frör, H. (1995), *You Wretched Corinthians!* (London: SCM).

Gooch, P. D. (1993), *Dangerous Food: 1 Corinthians 8–10 in Its Context* (Waterloo, Ont.: Wilfrid Laurier University Press).

Gooch, P. W. (1987), *Partial Knowledge: Philosophical Studies in Paul* (Notre Dame: University of Notre Dame Press).

Goulder, M. D. (1991), 'SOPHIA in 1 Corinthians', *NTS* 37: 516–34.

Hays, R. B. (1989), *Echoes of Scripture in the Letters of Paul* (New Haven: Yale University Press).

Hooker, M. D. (1963) ' "Beyond the things which are written": An Examination of 1 Cor iv. 6', *NTS* 10: 127–32, repr. in *From Adam to Christ: Essays on Paul*, (Cambridge: Cambridge University Press), 106–12.

—— (1964), 'Authority on her Head: An Examination of 1 Cor. 11.10', *NTS* 10: 410–16, repr. in *From Adam to Christ: Essays on Paul* (Cambridge: Cambridge University Press), 113–20.

Hurd, J. C. (1965), *The Origin of 1 Corinthians* (London: SPCK).

Hurtado, L. W. (1988), *One God, One Lord: Early Christian Devotion and Ancient Jewish Monotheism* (London: SCM).

Jervis, L. A. (1995), '1 Corinthians 14.34–35: A Reconsideration of Paul's Limitation of the Free Speech of Some Corinthian Women', *JSNT* 58: 51–74.

Litfin, D. (1994), *St. Paul's Theology of Proclamation: 1 Corinthians 1–4 and Greco-Roman Rhetoric* (Cambridge: Cambridge University Press).

Lüdemann, G. (1984), *Paul, Apostle to the Gentiles: Studies in Chronology* (London: SCM).

Martin, D. B. (1990), *Slavery as Salvation: The Metaphor of Slavery in Pauline Christianity* (New Haven: Yale University Press).

—— (1991), 'Tongues of Angels and Other Status Indicators', *AAR* 59: 547–89.

—— (1995), *The Corinthian Body* (New Haven: Yale University Press).

Meeks, W. A. (1983), *The First Urban Christians: The Social World of the Apostle Paul* (New Haven: Yale University Press).

Meggitt, J. J. (1998), *Paul, Poverty and Survival* (Edinburgh: T. & T. Clark).

Mitchell, M. M. (1992), *Paul and the Rhetoric of Reconciliation*, (Louisville, Ky.: Westminster/John Knox).

Murphy-O'Connor, J. (1980), 'Sex and Logic in 1 Corinthians 11.2–16', *CBQ* 42: 482–500.

Pearson, B. A. (1973), *The Pneumatikos-Psychikos Terminology in 1 Corinthians* (Missoula: Scholars Press).

Rosner, B. S. (1994), *Paul, Scripture and Ethics: A Study of 1 Corinthians 5–7* (Leiden: Brill).

Schmithals, W. (1971), *Gnosticism in Corinth* (Nashville: Abingdon).

Theissen, G. (1982), *The Social Setting of Pauline Christianity* (Edinburgh: T. & T. Clark).

—— (1987), *Psychological Aspects of Pauline Christianity* (Edinburgh: T. & T. Clark).

Thiselton, A. C. (1977–8), 'Realized Eschatology at Corinth', *NTS* 24: 510–26.

Thompson, C. L. (1988), 'Hairstyles, Head-coverings and St. Paul: Portraits from Roman Corinth', *Biblical Archaeologist*, 51: 99–115.

Willis, W. L. (1985), *Idol Meat in Corinth: The Pauline Argument in 1 Corinthians 8 and 10* (Chico, Calif.: Scholars Press).

Winter, B. (1991), 'Civil Litigation in Secular Corinth and the Church: The Forensic Background to 1 Corinthians 6.1–8', *NTS* 37: 559–72.

Wire, A. C. (1990), *The Corinthian Women Prophets* (Minneapolis: Fortress).

6. 2 Corinthians

MARGARET MACDONALD

INTRODUCTION

A. Literary Structure. 1. It is a generally held view today that 2 Corinthians is made up of more than one of Paul's letters. Although there is no MS evidence to support this theory, there are several problems in the text as we have it which raise the question of its unity. Among the more serious difficulties is the sharp break between the conciliatory tone of chs. 1–9 and the harsh, sarcastic tone of chs. 10–13. Several partition theories have been developed in order to explain these difficulties, and these theories may be divided into two major schools. (1) Some scholars divide the text into five or six fragments and then reconstruct the chronology of Paul's dealings with the Corinthians on the basis of these units (e.g. 2:14–6:13; 7:2–4 + 10:1–13:10 + 1:1–2:13; 7:5–16; 13:11–13 + ch. 8 + ch. 9 + 6:14–7:1; Betz 1992: 1149–50). (2) Other scholars do not view the points of discontinuity in chs. 1–9 as being severe enough to warrant theories of partition of those chapters, but nevertheless see a significant break between chs. 1–9 and chs. 10–13. Therefore, they argue in favour of a two-letter hypothesis. This is the position adopted here (cf. Furnish 1984: 35–41). Whether chs. 1–9 came before or after chs. 10–13 is a further subject for debate, but more scholars seem to be in favour of the priority of chs. 1–9. According to the proponents of the various partition theories, the NT work called 2 Corinthians is the product of an early editor who combined two or more fragments drawn from originally independent letters. However, some scholars continue to defend the integrity of the letter (e.g. Witherington 1995: 328–39).

2. In form and style 2 Corinthians closely resembles Paul's other works, and its authenticity has not been questioned. However, the language and content of 2 Cor 6:14–7:1 have struck many as being difficult to reconcile with Paul's other writings and, therefore, this passage has often been viewed as an interpolation.

B. Date and Social Setting. 1. In addition to the correspondence which was included in the NT, the Corinthian letters themselves bear witness to additional writings which are either non-extant or have been subsumed along with other letters within the body of 2 Corinthians (see 2 COR A.1). 1 Cor 5:9 demonstrates that Paul wrote a letter prior to 1 Corinthians, probably concerning the immoral behaviour of church members. Some have identified this letter with 2 Cor 6:14–7:1. 1 Corinthians was written around 54 CE in response to a letter from the Corinthians which had raised several questions. The events which precipitated the correspondence known as 2 Corinthians are a subject of great debate and we are limited to conjecture concerning them. One possible reconstruction of events is as follows. It appears that between the time of the composition of 1 Corinthians and 2 Corinthians (or fragments thereof), Paul paid an emergency 'sorrowful visit' to Corinth (2 Cor 2:1). This probably was the apostle's second visit to the community (cf. 2 Cor 12:14; 13:1), the first being the occasion of the founding of the community in 50 or 51 CE. It seems that this second visit did not go well (2 Cor 2:1–11; 7:12) and Paul followed it up with a 'tearful letter' (2 Cor 2:4; 2:2–11; 7:5–12). Although some have identified this letter with 2 Cor 10–13, it is more likely that it has been lost. A subsequent report to Paul that his 'tearful letter' had produced the desired effect in the community led to the composition in Macedonia in 55–6 CE of 2 Cor 1–9 (2 Cor 7:5; cf. 2 Cor 2:12–13; 8:1; 9:2). Titus apparently delivered this letter to the congregation (2 Cor 7:4–16; cf. 2 Cor 8:17–18). However, the situation deteriorated again. Some months later Paul wrote 2 Cor 10–13, also probably from Macedonia. In this letter he stated his intention to come to the community a third time (2 Cor 12:14; 13:1). (This reconstruction follows Furnish 1988: 1191–2 closely and is based on the two-letter hypothesis. For an alternative reconstruction based upon the five-(or six-)letter hypothesis see Betz 1992: 1149–52.)

2. When Paul wrote 1 Corinthians, he responded to problems involving community division and behaviour, problems he felt were incompatible with membership in Christ's body. By the time of the composition of 2 Corinthians (or various letter fragments), community problems extended to include the nature of the apostle's relationship with the Corinthians. Indeed, some wonder whether the harsh, critical—even sardonic—tone of 1 Corinthians may have alienated its recipients to the extent that a second, more conciliatory letter was required. Convinced that the relationship was severely threatened, and of the need for reconciliation, Paul set out to defend his apostolic authority. By the time that 2 Cor 10–13 was composed (See 2 COR A.1) the situation had become acute, due to the influence of apostolic rivals in the community. Throughout 2 Cor 10–13 Paul's preoccupation with these rivals is evident, but there are also insinuations in earlier chapters of threats by opponents to Paul's apostleship (e.g. 2 Cor 3:1–6). The nature of Paul's authority is a theme which runs throughout 2 Corinthians, and this text has therefore been of great interest to scholars concerned with the general question of how Paul exercised authority and distributed power in the community (Schütz 1975; Holmberg 1980; Meeks 1983; MacDonald 1988). Often these scholars draw upon social-scientific insights such as the foundational theories of the sociologist Max Weber on charisma and authority. Some of the specific issues under investigation include Paul's apostolic credentials and talents, his involvement in the collection for the Jerusalem church, and his attitude towards receiving material support from the congregation. Paul's use of a 'theology of the cross' (which locates power in weakness; 2 COR 4:7–15) to anchor his apostolic authority in a

divine mandate has also been of considerable interest.

3. Corinth became a Roman colony in 44 BCE and architectural, artefactual, and inscriptional evidence points to a strong Romanizing influence in this old Hellenistic city (Witherington 1995: 6–7). The growing awareness of the need to understand NT groups in the light of the context of Graeco-Roman society has had an important effect on the study of 2 Corinthians. For example, comparison of 2 Cor 8–9 to administrative correspondence in the empire has shed light upon the form and purpose of these chapters (Betz 1985). Increasingly, scholars are examining the influence of Greek rhetorical style upon Paul. The obvious use of such rhetorical devices as parody in 2 Cor 10–13 has invited further probing on the way Paul forms and develops his arguments in 2 Corinthians. It is now possible to say that rhetorical analysis of 2 Corinthians represents an important methodological approach, one which complements more traditional exercises in historical criticism. Rhetorical analysis sheds light on questions ranging from the purpose of the letter to its literary integrity (e.g. Young and Ford 1987; Marshall 1987; Crafton 1990; Witherington 1995). The recognition of the importance of rhetoric in the ancient world and in the letters of Paul has also contributed to a further understanding of Paul's emphasis on boasting and self-praise in 2 Corinthians. Public demonstrations of self-worth (which included performances of rhetoric) were a central means of establishing one's authority in a society which had an honour/shame orientation (Witherington 1995: 6, 432–7; 2 COR 1:12–14; 2 COR 4:1–6). Investigation of the structures of the patron–client relationship in the ancient world has also shed light on Paul's interaction with the Corinthians (Marshall 1987; Chow 1992; Witherington 1995; 2 COR 5:11–19; 2 COR 8:16–24; 2 COR 10:12–18).

C. Opponents. There has been extensive discussion concerning the identity of Paul's opponents in 2 Corinthians (e.g. Barrett 1971; Thrall 1980; Georgi 1986). The consensus is that the problems concerning opponents in 2 Corinthians must be distinguished from the factions and opposition apparent in 1 Corinthians, even though there may have been some connection between the two. In contrast to 1 Corinthians, in 2 Corinthians it is clear that the opponents were intruders, that is, they came from outside the community (2 Cor 10:13–16; 11:4, 19–20). It is also clear that they were Jewish

(2 Cor 11:22). But there has been no general agreement on the nature of their Jewish teaching (Murphy-O'Connor 1990: 817). Some have viewed the opponents as Judaizers who were connected to the Jerusalem church (Barrett 1971). Others have understood their spirituality in light of diaspora Judaism and their mission as based in the demonstration of ecstatic experiences and the performance of miracles. Hellenistic Jewish missionaries may have propounded notions of Jesus as the 'divine man' (Georgi 1986: 246–83). There are several difficulties associated with extracting information concerning these opponents and their influence in the community. It is sometimes difficult to know whether Paul is responding directly to new problems created by the opponents who have penetrated the community from the outside, or to more general tendencies in Corinth which have been exacerbated by his rivals. How one interprets the evidence is determined to a significant extent by what one makes of possible thematic connections between 1 and 2 Corinthians (Matthews 1994: 199–200). In addition, although Paul sometimes quotes his rivals directly, his polemical stance makes it difficult to extract accurate information concerning their teaching. The apostle's use of various labels for his opponents, such as 'super-apostles' (2 Cor 11:5; 12:11) and 'false apostles' (2 Cor 11:13), has also led to discussion of whether one or more groups of opponents are in view (see 2 COR 11:5–15).

D. Outline.

Introduction (1:1–11)
　　Address (1:1–2)
　　Blessing (1:3–11)
Paul the Conciliator (1:12–9:15)
　　Explanations and Future Plans (1:12–2:13)
　　The Authority of the Apostle (2:14–5:19)
　　Appeals for Reconciliation with the Apostle (5:20–7:16)
　　Appeals about the Collection (8:1–9:15)
Paul on the Attack (10:1–13:10)
　　Preliminary Defence (10:1–18)
　　The Fool's Speech (11:1–12:13)
　　Concluding Defence (12:14–13:10)
Conclusion: Greetings and Benediction (13:11–13)

COMMENTARY

Introduction (1:1–11)

(**1:1–2**) **Address** The address is in keeping with the normal pattern of Paul's letters (e.g. 1 Cor 1:1–3). Timothy is listed as the co-author. Although Sosthenes and Silvanus are also given this role in other letters, Timothy is most frequently mentioned (cf. Phil 1:1–2; Col 1:1–2; 1 Thess 1:1–2; Thess 1:1–2). It is not easy to evaluate the significance of this joint enterprise in modern terms. On the one hand, it is clear that Timothy's authority in the church was not equal to that of Paul; he was dependent upon Paul. On the other hand, Paul worked very closely with associates and they were instrumental to the success of his mission. Paul exercised his leadership as part of a team and it is misleading to think of the relationship between Paul and his fellow-workers as unilaterally hierarchical. In fact, the importance of the role of Paul's associates emerges especially clearly in 2 Corinthians (2 Cor 2:13; 7:6–16; 8:6, 16–24). At the very least we may say that Timothy is mentioned because he is with Paul and his presence serves to bolster the authority of Paul's message. In particular Timothy's previous work with the Corinthians means that his influence could enhance (or likewise detract from) Paul's position. Along with Silvanus he was involved in the establishment of the church in Corinth (2 Cor 1:19; cf. 1 Cor 4:17; 16:10–11). The addressees are described in such a way as to further corroborate this image of a network of relationships. They are described as the church of God in Corinth, including the 'saints' (a general term in the NT for believers, see *OCB* s.v.) throughout Achaia (the Roman province with Corinth as its capital). The church in Corinth belongs to a wider community held together by emissaries, letters, and hospitality. 2 Cor 1–9 and possibly also 2 Cor 10–13 were written from Macedonia (2 Cor 2:12–13; 7:5; 8:1; 9:2).

(**1:3–11**) **Blessing** As is usually the case in Paul's letters, a blessing or thanksgiving follows the greeting. Typically, the community is praised and their past relationship with the apostle is recalled. Themes to be developed at a later point are introduced. In this text the solidarity of the Corinthians with Paul in affliction is emphasized. Likewise, community and apostle share the hope of consolation. Implicitly, church members are being praised for their strength in the face of suffering. Particularly striking is the repetition of the term 'consolation' and its cognates (*paraklēsis*). It is a notion that is especially prominent in 2 Corinthians. For example, it is taken up again in 2 Cor 7:4–13, a passage illustrating that the affliction/consolation opposition must be understood in the light of the difficult relations and complicated exchanges between Paul and the Corinthians. Within the Pauline corpus, the term 'affliction' (*thlipsis*) occurs most frequently in 2 Corinthians. It is a term that can carry a wide variety of meanings (Garrett 1995), ranging from the apostle's own physical (?) sufferings (2 Cor 1:8), to the pain of a broken relationship with the Corinthians that inspired the 'severe letter' (2 Cor 2:4; cf. 7:7–8), to impoverishment (2 Cor 8:13). The affliction in Asia of which Paul speaks in 2 Cor 1:8 seems to have been so devastating that he narrowly escaped with his life. While other explanations cannot be ruled out entirely, some type of physical suffering is probably in view, brought about by persecution (perhaps in Ephesus, cf. 1 Cor 15:32) or disease. Recalling Christ's suffering in 2 Cor 1:5 serves the apostle's purposes well in order to convey the hope of comfort in the midst of affliction; as members of Christ's body, believers continue to share in his afflictions (cf. Col 1:24), but will also be comforted through him. The consolation/affliction opposition is one of many rhetorical strategies Paul employs to reinforce his authority in Corinth. The apostle's leadership clearly recalls the suffering Christ. Like Christ's authority, the apostle's authority is articulated in an unexpected way—through affliction. But this affliction carries the promise of consolation. It is meaningful because it leads to the consolation of believers, relating Paul's (and ultimately Christ's) life intimately to the circumstances of the Corinthians. The association of the consolation/affliction opposition with expressions of confidence (e.g. 2 Cor 1:7; 7:4) makes its function as an assertion of authority especially clear (Meeks 1983: 123).

Paul the Conciliator (1:12–9:15)

(1:12–2:13) Explanations and Future Plans

(1:12–14) The Community as Paul's Boast

Paul begins with a declaration of the significance of his relationship with the Corinthians before he offers the explanation of the events that have caused the Corinthians to doubt his sincerity and authority. Although it implies assertiveness, it is misleading to think of boasting as a type of bragging. Rather, it is a term that Paul employs to communicate his ultimate priorities as an apostle and to express his confidence in his mission. It is a notion that appears frequently in 2 Corinthians. Not surprisingly, Paul also speaks of his ground for boasting when he defines his rights as an apostle in 1 Cor 9:15–16. Particularly intriguing is the phrase,

'on the day of the Lord we are your boast even as you are our boast'. The reference to the 'day of the Lord' (cf. 1 Cor 5:5; Phil 1:6, 10; 2:16; 1 Thess 5:2) suggests that Paul is convinced that his relationship with the Corinthians is fundamental to the participation of both parties in the culmination of the Christ event. On that day all will be judged and the apostle is confident that his conduct will be shown to be above reproach. Moreover, the parallelism in the phrase implies mutual dependence between the two parties. The meaning of Paul's apostleship is fundamentally related to the fruit of his labours. A similar sentiment surfaces in Rom 15:22–33 where acceptance of the collection (and ultimately of his Gentile mission) by the Jerusalem church appears to be fundamental to Paul's confidence in the legitimacy of his apostleship. In 2 Corinthians, the body of the Corinthian community (the church which Paul founded) is his boast: this is the manifestation of his apostleship. The boast of the Corinthian community, however, is also rooted in their connection, and no doubt loyalty, to Paul (cf. 5:12). Closely related to the theme of boasting is Paul's claim of having behaved in the world with 'frankness' (*haplotēs*). Although there is strong MS evidence for the alternative reading of 'holiness', the immediate and broader context suggests that 'frankness' (cf. 2:17) is the most likely possibility (for a summary of the evidence see Furnish 1984: 127). The reference to frankness reflects the ancient Greek notion of the rights of citizens to speak freely and to be open, even generous, in mutual dealings. It is a term which Paul uses to describe the nature of his ministry along with the synonym 'sincerity'; this language resembles notions found elsewhere in 2 Corinthians (2:17; 3:12; 10:2). Frankness, boldness, confidence, and the act of boasting are expressions of the value placed on assertiveness in the ancient Mediterranean world. Assertiveness, especially among men, was a means of preserving one's honour—one's reputation—and was integral to claims of authority. Especially in Acts the assertiveness of the apostles functions as a means of reinforcing the validity of their message (e.g. Acts 4:13, 29, 31; 9:27–9; Reese 1993: 9–11).

(1:15–22) Change of Travel Plans

Here Paul is apparently responding to some charge of inconsistency based on a change of plan. It is impossible to be precise about the actual circumstances, but it seems that Paul's plans had changed at least twice. In 1 Cor 16:5–7 Paul announced his intention to visit Corinth briefly before going on to Macedonia. However, the plan he is accused of forfeiting here involved a visit both on the way to Macedonia and after leaving Macedonia; he would then have gone on from Corinth to Judea (probably bearing the collection). (See reconstructions of Paul's itinerary in Betz 1992: 1151; Furnish 1984: 143–4.) Although it is possible that Paul cancelled only the return phase of the anticipated double visit, most commentators believe the entire visit was cancelled (1:23). The reference to a double favour (v. 15) has a somewhat sarcastic ring. It may be in response to those who accused Paul of using flattery to win his audience; he had flattered the Corinthians with promises of a double visit (setting them above the Macedonians?) when he really had no intention of going twice (Furnish 1984: 144). Paul's response is unequivocal. He has not been fickle, answering yes and no in the same breath. In keeping with points he has made earlier in the chapter (1:12), he stresses that his actions as an apostle are based not on a human agenda but on divine initiative. He uses his critics' accusation of vacillation as an invitation to meditate on the absolute consistency of God and complete obedience of Jesus to God's will. In other words, since God is on Paul's side, inconsistency is ruled out. The place of Paul and the Corinthian community in God's plan is announced in vv. 21–2. As the one appointed by God to bring the gospel to the Corinthians, Paul in essence facilitates their joining with him as members of Christ's body. Their mutual relationship with Christ is so close that they have been anointed; they are now 'in Christ', incorporated into the Messiah, the anointed one. Receipt of the Spirit is also in keeping with messianic identity (cf. 1 Sam 16:13; Isa 61:1). Paul's arguments are not confined to doctrine. He also appeals to liturgical experiences, in his reference to the community's usual manner of giving assent: 'amen' (v. 20; cf. 1 Cor 14:16). He also recalls the experience of baptism by referring to the 'seal' and the Spirit as the first instalment of the divine promises (cf. Eph 1:13–14). In Colossians and Ephesians, remembrances of baptism play a central role in encouraging appropriate communal behaviour.

(1:23–2:13) The Painful Visit and the Letter of Tears Paul explains that it was to spare the Corinthians that he did not make another visit. We are probably to understand that between the time of the writing of 1 Corinthians and the

composition of 2 Corinthians (or any segment of this document), Paul paid a visit to the Corinthians (cf. 2 Cor 12:14; 13:1). This may well have been an emergency visit (perhaps from Ephesus) brought about by a report of trouble in the community. It is to be distinguished from the cancelled visit described in 1:16 (cf. 1:23). The 'painful visit' probably involved a conflict with an individual and a resulting lack of support from the community. Paul's language calls to mind broken relationships and betrayal but also great love (2:4); it seems that he felt his place among the Corinthians was jeopardized severely (2:5–11; 7:8–12). His visit was apparently followed by a 'tearful letter' which was probably brought to the community by Titus and which was interpreted by some as being unduly severe (7:8). It was Titus who brought news of the turnaround in events after the community had received the letter (7:6–8). Some have identified the 'tearful letter' with chs. 10–13. However, because the problem mentioned in 2:5–11 concerns an individual offender and not 'super-apostles' as in chs. 10–13, others believe that the 'painful letter' no longer exists. Although the incest case of 1 Cor 5 which Paul discusses in uncompromising terms might lead to the suggestion that the 'tearful letter' is in fact 1 Corinthians, few hold this point of view today. We are limited to conjecture, but these verses offer information about Paul's comings and goings, and hints about the setting of the composition of 2 Corinthians (or parts thereof). It seems that from Ephesus (1 Cor 16:5–8) Paul travelled to the seaport of Troas where he hoped to find his 'brother' Titus (for other brother-helpers, cf. Phil 2:25; Philem 16). Paul's longing for Titus offers us a poignant glimpse into the significance of Paul's relationship with his fellow-workers (2 COR 7:5–7). In Troas, Paul had considerable missionary success. The metaphor he uses calls to mind the importance of the household and workshop as an arena for conversion in the ancient world (see Hock 1980; MacMullen 1984: 25–42). Evangelical opportunity is described as a door being opened for him in the Lord (2:12). From Troas, Paul set out for Macedonia where he met up with (Titus 7:6). It is probable that it was from Macedonia that Paul wrote 2 Corinthians (or parts thereof). It is clear that by the time of the composition of these verses the problem of breakdown in relations between Paul and the Corinthians, caused by the case of the offender, had been resolved. The nature of the offence is to be distinguished from that discussed in 1 Cor 5 where Paul insists that the wicked person be driven out from the community like a malady that must be purged from the body (1 Cor 5:13; on the differences between 1 Cor 5:1–5 and 2 Cor 2:5–11 see detailed discussion in Furnish 1984: 164–6). In the case of 2 Corinthians, the offender has been punished by the community enough and now should be forgiven and consoled. Is Paul's leniency rooted in the nature of the offence, i.e. a challenge to his authority and not a case of immorality which is worse even than that found among the pagans (1 Cor 5:1)? It has been suggested that this offender was someone external to the community (see Barrett 1973: 212), but this theory has not gained wide acceptance. The pain/consolation opposition throughout the text is in keeping with the suffering/consolation opposition in 1:3–11. Paul uses language of contrast to move the discussion from a previously painful situation to a celebration of the nature of the reconciliation and love that now exists. But the frequently attested theme of the apostle who suffers unjustly surfaces here as well (2:3). Despite the presence of Christ, Paul and the community members will remain vulnerable to the intervention of evil until the day of the Lord. Satan can interfere with community matters and with the apostle's agenda (2:11; 11:3, 14–15; 12:7; cf. 1 Thess 2:18). He can cause innumerable misfortunes and suffering and one must always be watchful of his designs (Neyrey 1990: 176).

(2:14–5:19) The Authority of the Apostle

(2:14–3:6) The Legitimacy of Paul's Apostleship This section opens with a formula of thanksgiving which has perhaps been inspired by the good news brought by Titus of the community's compliance with the apostle's wishes (7:6–7; Thrall 1965: 129). Rich imagery is used to communicate what God has accomplished in Christ. Believers are described as being led in the manner of the triumphal procession of the general who returns victorious from battle. The notion of triumph in weakness which is so central to Paul's theology in 2 Corinthians may be in view here. It is important to note that it was the prisoners-of-war who were paraded through the streets during such processions and Paul may be identifying the apostles with them (Furnish 1988: 1194). 'Fragrance' refers to the odour of incense in sacrifice. Paul may be thinking of rituals associated with Roman celebrations of triumph or with Jewish temple practice. The image may also have been influenced by Sir 24:15 where fragrance is a sign of the presence of God/Wisdom (Murphy-O'Connor

1990: 819). In the accounts of martyrdom in later church literature, beautiful fragrance was a sign of God's presence and that God was on the side of the Christians (see *Mart. Pol.* 15). First the gospel and then the apostles are compared to a fragrance. The fragrance spreads throughout the world by means of the apostles and for some represents life, but for others, death. This black-and-white language offers a good example of 'language of belonging' and 'language of separation' which demarcates the boundaries of the community (Meeks 1983: 85–96). Here the negative perception of the outside society is particularly evident. But the fragrance is also said to spread 'in every place', implying a universal mission. There is a certain tension in Paul's letters between openness to the external society in the hope of winning new members and a strong desire to remain separate (MacDonald 1988: 32–42). In 2:16 the tone changes abruptly from thanksgiving to interrogation of the community concerning the specifics of their relationship with Paul. Before Paul engages in a dialogue concerning the objections raised against his apostleship, he raises a question designed to lead believers to the conclusion that apostolic claims must ultimately rest only in God. With the question 'Who is sufficient for these things?' he hopes to make them see the error of the presumption that an apostle's superior personal attributes are responsible for success in carrying out God's plan. The same idea is repeated in 3:5. Perhaps distinguishing himself from others who claim superior attributes, he makes the point emphatically that he is not a charlatan. The language is very strong and, given the suspicions about Paul's financial arrangements which are echoed later in the work, it is tempting to conclude that this label had been applied to him. Paul speaks literally of those who hawk (*kapēleuein*) the word of God. The Greek term occurs nowhere else in the NT but was employed by ancient critics of itinerant teachers to speak of the 'huckstering of wisdom' (Furnish 1984:178). To those who would rebuke him for his lack of letters of recommendation, Paul replies that nothing could compare with the proof of commendation that lies in their existence as a church: the Corinthians themselves are the letter. Letters of recommendation were an accepted means of ensuring hospitality and receipt of some favour in the ancient world (cf. Acts 9:2; 22:5). One of the benefits that a patron might extend to his client was such a letter. Rom 16:1–2 makes it clear that Paul himself could make use of such letters in order to introduce a church member to the community; but in his personal dealings with the Corinthians such tools were not necessary. Perhaps the letters in question came from the Jerusalem church or from a patron thought to be more impressive than Paul. We are left to wonder whether the tendency to peddle God's word and/or the absence of letters of recommendation were accusations made by the offender (2:5–11) against Paul which found support among others in Corinth. What is clear is that Paul thinks such problems do exist with other would-be apostles. In response to possible objections Paul does two things: (1) he reminds the Corinthians that apostleship makes sense only if it comes from God (ultimately, Paul's only patron). Paul's ministry is a ministry of a 'new covenant', a theme developed in depth in 3:7–18; (2) he appeals to his confidence, sincerity, and forthrightness which are important means of establishing his credibility as an authoritative teacher in the ancient world (2:17; 3:4–6; 4:1–4; 5:6–8; cf. 2 COR 1:12–14).

(3:7–18) A Minister of the New Covenant By playing with various contrasting notions such as 'letter of law/Spirit,' 'death/life', 'old covenant/new covenant', Paul compares the old relationship between God and his people with the new relationship established by God through Christ (on covenant, see ABD i. 1197–202). The issue of the letters of recommendation in 3:1–6 allows him to introduce the issue of the letter of the Jewish law. Beginning in 3:6, and continuing to v. 11, the law—the centre of the old covenant—is depicted in categorically negative terms. The letter kills and ministry based on letters chiselled on stone tablets (Ex 24:12; 31:18) leads to death (on death and the law, see ABD ii. 110–11; iv. 254–65). A very strong statement of the law's inadequacy for salvation is also found in v. 11 where the law is described as 'what was set aside' (cf. v. 7). Paul admits that the old covenant was glorious, but it has been far surpassed in glory (vv. 7–11). These verses have been judged as shedding light on Paul's view of life under the law and generally as important for understanding the birth of the church in a Jewish context. Stressing that Paul's conviction that the law condemns and kills is based on his post-conversion understanding, and is not rooted in particular personal experiences of the law's limitations for Jewish life, E. P. Sanders has argued that the apostle represented the Mosaic covenant as less glorious simply because he had found in Christ something more glorious. Paul's

thought and language proceeded from his conviction about Christ as the centre of salvation and it developed in very black-and-white terms: 'I cannot see how the development could have run the other way, from an initial conviction that the Law only condemns and kills, to a search for something which gives life, to the conviction that life comes by faith in Christ, to the statement that the Law lost its glory because a new dispensation surpasses it in glory' (Sanders 1983: 138). But there remains some ambiguity in Paul's thought (ibid. 138–9). On the one hand, the law has been set aside and does not save. But on the other hand, the old covenant may still be read profitably by members of the church: when Jews who are not members of the church read it, it is veiled, but when believers read it, it is unveiled (vv. 14–16). The reference to veiling recalls the covering that Moses placed over his face during his descent from Mt. Sinai (Ex 34:33–5; cf. 34:29–35). Some have understood the comparison between Paul's ministry and Moses' ministry that runs throughout vv. 7–18 in terms of a response to Paul's adversaries (Murphy-O'Connor 1990: 819). It has even been suggested that the source of the conflict is a midrashic document on Ex 34:29–35 that was composed by Paul's opponents and which Paul modified in these verses in the hope of correcting a mistaken view of Moses and the Mosaic covenant (Georgi 1986: 264–71). There has been considerable interest in Paul's use of Scripture here, including his dependence on the LXX and extra-biblical sources (Belleville 1993: 165–85; Stockhausen 1993: 143–64). The emphasis in vv. 7–18 is on freedom from the law (cf. Gal 5:18) and the transformation of believers. The believer's image, reflected in a mirror, becomes that of Christ (cf. 4:6; 1 Cor 11:7); and salvation involves increasing conformity to him (Murphy-O'Connor 1990: 820). The identification of Spirit with Lord (in Paul's letters usually referring to Christ) has raised doctrinal questions, but many commentators believe 'Lord' in vv. 16–18 refers directly to God (Thrall 1965: 136–7; Furnish 1984: 234–6).

(4:1–6) The Honourable Apostle Paul apparently responds to those who are denigrating his ministry by setting himself apart from his rivals. Paul's ministry is characterized by the persistence and boldness that are qualities of an honourable apostle (2 COR 1:12–14). The values of honour (public acknowledgement of worth) and shame (public denial of worth) frame the text. Shame also can have a positive value in the ancient world in the sense of 'having shame': that is, having appropriate concern for one's reputation. In this text what is shameful refers to the absence or loss of honour (on honour and shame see Plevnik 1993: 95–104). The shameful things that Paul has renounced are clearly negative: literally, 'the things of shame that one hides'. Has Paul been accused of dishonourable activity which is sequestered and secretive? The setting of the churches in private homes could certainly have fostered that impression. Paul believes that to act in a shameful manner is to display cunning and to falsify God's word (cf. 2:17). Behind Paul's declaration that he refuses to adopt shameful tactics probably lies an attempt to distance himself from rival apostles who mislead and exploit the congregation (cf. 11:20). Language of honour and shame is useful in communicating what should be valued most, i.e. what is the basis of true apostleship. Because honour and shame are rooted in the importance in the ancient Mediterranean world placed on public appraisal, these concepts also are useful in conveying the scope of evangelical mission. The central message is that the Corinthians have come to know the light of the gospel only through Paul's preaching (Furnish 1988: 1194). The reference to the veil is in keeping with 3:12–18 but gains further nuance in relation to the themes of secrecy and openness introduced here. The image of the sometimes blinding veil is part of Paul's admission that his preaching is not always successful: public acknowledgement which should follow honourable display and open statement of the truth is not always quickly forthcoming. The blindness of unbelievers, however, is not the result of Paul's tactics as an apostle but has been caused by the god of this world: Satan or Beliar (2 COR 6:14–7:1). The frequent notion of Paul's apostleship having purely divine origins is found again in vv. 5–6. In response to competitors who would 'preach themselves' (seek to gain acceptance by drawing upon personal attributes), Paul argues that he proclaims only 'Christ as Lord' (a confessional formula, Rom 10:9; 1 Cor 12:3; Phil 2:10–11). The description of Paul as the Corinthians' slave for Jesus' sake is in keeping with the frequent use of slavery as a metaphor in Pauline Christianity (cf. 1 Cor 9:16–23). Paul's self-enslavement has been recognized as a practical strategy for evangelization (low-status persons may be won through the evangelist's self-lowering) and as a rhetorical strategy for conveying the nature of his leadership. But the

theological importance of the metaphor is especially visible here. Paul's self-abasement, communicated through the image of slavery, is closely associated with the theology of the cross (4:13–18): humiliation is followed by exaltation. It has been suggested that the effectiveness of the metaphorical representation of slavery as salvation is related to the fact that in Graeco-Roman society, slavery was an ambiguous and multifaceted concept, carrying connotations both of abasement and upward mobility (Martin 1990: 129–32). There is very strong language of separation here which is reinforced by an allusion to Gen 1:3 (v. 6, cf. 2 COR 2:14–3:6); church members see, but unbelievers are blind and perishing. The light of the gospel (v. 4) shines through Paul in a world that is otherwise dark and still very much influenced by evil.

(4:7–15) **Power in Weakness** Paul's theology of the cross is proclaimed throughout 4:7–18 (cf. 1 Cor 1:17–2:5). The event of the death and resurrection of Christ means that the appearance of weakness and humiliation can carry the promise of power and exaltation (v. 14). Paul's theology of the cross (and statements about suffering) in 2 Corinthians must be understood in the light of a particular polemical context where Paul seeks to undermine the position of rivals who make too much of their personal superiority in relation to Paul's weakness. Moreover, the theology of the cross is not about passivity in suffering, but about power in suffering. With sometimes biting irony, Paul protests against his rivals who find God on the side of strength and power (10:10–11). In 2 Corinthians the paradox of the crucified Messiah is proclaimed boldly. The ambiguous symbol of a suffering saviour offers Paul many possibilities to expose the folly of those who would attack him. Paul's theology of the cross has been of interest to feminist biblical commentators, who warn of the dangers of lifting Paul's message out of context and using it to advocate passivity and meekness in the face of suffering and oppression (Matthews 1994: 214–15). But there is no doubt that the symbol locates God on the side of the suffering, the weak, and the oppressed (vv. 8–10, cf. 1 Cor 1:18–31; Bassler 1992: 331–2). In these verses the focus is on power in physical weakness. This notion is communicated through the beautiful image of the fragile clay pots which contain hidden treasure. It is also conveyed through the catalogue of hardships (vv. 8–9). Similar lists are found throughout 2 Corinthians and elsewhere in Paul's letters (6:4–5; 11:23–9;

12:10; Rom 8:35; 1 Cor 4:9–13). Scholars have examined the literary relationships between the lists within 2 Corinthians and have even speculated about what these relationships might reveal about the literary integrity of the work (Witherington 1995: 398–9). The tribulations are described with vivid language which is reminiscent of the terms employed by philosophers in the ancient world who described their struggles in the overcoming of passion and search for wisdom (Fitzgerald 1988: 65–70; 148–201). Suffering is not glorified; on the contrary, it is experienced by the apostle as unjust (Neyrey 1990: 177–9); yet it is given meaning in two ways. First, suffering allows for identification with Jesus and, ultimately, resurrection with Jesus (vv. 10–14). Secondly, Paul's suffering mirrors Jesus' suffering and hence makes Jesus' life visible in the world. 'Flesh' (*sarx*) in v. 11 is a synonym for 'body' (*sōma*) in v. 10, but the term 'flesh' (see *OCB* 231) places more emphasis on physical existence, a connotation which is highlighted throughout this text (Murphy-O'Connor 1990: 821) Because his suffering bears witness to Jesus, Paul is able to argue that his suffering is for the sake of the Corinthian church which he founded and more broadly for the sake of his evangelical mission. The reference to Ps 116:10 in v. 13 allows him to link preaching (speaking) with proclamation of faith in the midst of suffering.

(4:16–5:1) The Fragility of Mortal Existence Interest in the limited nature of physical existence is maintained throughout these verses. Paul is strikingly honest about his own frailty (perhaps in response to those who would claim that physical weakness is incompatible with apostleship; cf. 10:10). He uses the contrast between his outer nature (his visible body) and inner nature (the faith and commitment to Christ which cannot be seen) to point to ultimate reality: that which is eternal and transcends physical existence. While in other places Paul gives the impression that he expects to live until Christ's return (1 Thess 4:15, 17), here Paul confronts the harsh reality of death (5:1). Several architectural images are conflated to convey the notion of heavenly existence. The literary-historical background of these images has been of considerable interest. It has been noted that the use of the image of a tent to refer to the mortal body occurs in many Hellenistic religious and ethical texts (Furnish 1984: 293). There has been extensive discussion of the meaning of the 'house not made with hands'.

Often Paul has been understood as referring to the new spiritual body which will be given to believers (1 Cor 15:51–4). Others have argued that the text should be read in the light of Jewish and early Christian apocalyptic traditions which include the notion of an eschatological temple and new Jerusalem (2 *Apoc. Bar.* 4:3; 2 Esd 10:40–57; cf. Mk 14:58). Parallels between this passage and Phil 3:12–21 have been noted. The symbol of the heavenly commonwealth in Phil 3:20 resembles the heavenly dwelling of 5:1. If this interpretation is accepted, 5:1 should be understood as speaking primarily about believers as already belonging to another age and as having a new existence, rather than as addressing specifically the issue of the new spiritual body (Furnish 1984: 294–5; Murphy-O'Connor 1990: 821). A similar conflation of body imagery with architectural imagery occurs in Eph 2:19–22, but there the focus is clearly ecclesiological. Although many commentators have understood 5:1 as introducing a new subject, it has been included in this section because it acts as the climax of 4:16–18 which emphasizes the temporality and fragility of mortal existence (Furnish 1984: 291).

(5:2–10) Present Existence and Future Fulfilment The emphasis shifts somewhat from the limits of mortality to the ultimate shape of life with God and the nature of existence in this new eschatological age. It has been said that 5:1–10 is one of the most difficult passages in all of Paul's letters to explain adequately (Thrall 1965: 142). It has often been thought that Paul's recent escape from death (1:9) led him to doubt his previous belief that he and others would be alive at the Parousia (1 Thess 4:13–18; 1 Cor 15:51–2). The reference to nakedness in v. 3 has been instrumental to the theory that Paul is responding to fear surrounding an interim period between death of the physical body and resurrection of a new spiritual body. But this theory has also been disputed (Furnish 1984: 292–3). Paul does not really seem to be deliberately responding to a problem in the way that is so evident in 1 Thess 4:13–18. The fear of being naked may indeed refer to concern about an intermediate state between life and the adoption of the spiritual body (1 Cor 15:37–8; Barrett 1973: 154–5). Paul may be expressing his preference to avoid the intermediate condition altogether: that is, to live on earth until the resurrection (Witherington 1995: 391). But the reference to nakedness may also be a reminder of the harsh reality of final judgement (cf. 2 Cor

5:10) when a person's culpability will be exposed (Isa 47:3; Ezek 23:28–9; Murphy-O'Connor 1991: 52). An awareness of the importance of the values of honour and shame in the ancient Mediterranean world may also prove useful here (2 COR 4:1–6). In the HB nakedness is strongly associated with shame and sin. To be shamed is to be involuntarily stripped naked (Neyrey 1993: 119–21). Presence before an honourable God requires that one may not be found naked, but have put on the heavenly garment/tent (ibid. 122). Although the NRSV translation 'when we have taken it off' fits best with the theory that Paul is referring to an interim period between death and adoption of a new spiritual body, there is good reason to adopt the strongly attested alternative reading 'when we have put it on' (Furnish 1984: 268). An understanding of the values of honour and shame may also help explain how this text fits within the broader discussion of apostolic suffering and authority. When the Corinthians turn against Paul might they be stripping him naked and/or rendering themselves exposed before a God who makes believers accountable for what has been done 'in the body' (v. 10)? That questions about Paul's apostleship are not far removed from the main argument here is made clear by the double assertion of confidence by which Paul reinforces his role as an honourable apostle (vv. 6–8; 2 COR 1:12–14). Some have viewed the merger of the images of 'dwelling' and 'clothing' (cf. 1 Cor 15:53–4; Gal 3:27; Rom 13:14) to be somewhat awkward on Paul's part. However, they actually work well for Paul's purposes since they tie personal affiliation (the garment which must be put on) closely with communal commitment (the household that must be joined, the dwelling that must be entered). The main purpose of the imagery is to announce the nature of the new mode of existence: real life that 'swallows up' (*katapiein*; v. 4) all that is mortal. Comparison with Rom 8:18–27 is especially useful since it also refers to 'groaning' (Rom 8:23, 26) and highlights the role of the Spirit, as creation waits to be released from futility and suffering. Continuing to be plagued by limitations, groaning under his 'burdens' (cf. 1:6; 4:8, 17), Paul is moving towards his ultimate goal. The contrast between being 'at home' in the body and 'at home' with the Lord in vv. 6–10 reflects the tension between present salvation and future fulfilment that is characteristic of Paul's thought. The term for being away from home (*ekdēmein*), has a wider significance than leaving one's house: literally it refers to the act of leaving one's country or going on a long journey (BAGD 238). Paul's present life is shaped by Christ whom one must continue to please until one enters the heavenly commonwealth (cf. Phil 3:20). The presence of the Spirit acts as a foretaste of future fulfilment.

(5:11–19) Warnings against Reliance on External Appearances This text relates Paul's ministry to a reversal of earthly standards and the dawning of a new creation. The reference to 'persuasion' has been understood as a reference to rhetoric, the art of persuasion. Paul is acting like an ancient rhetor who will be judged by the Corinthians according to their consciences. The picture of the ambassador who entreats the assembly (5:20) also fits with this context. Paul presents God as his ultimate judge, but this passage functions as an indirect acknowledgement of the fact that the Corinthians have put Paul on trial, and of how important it is to Paul that the Corinthians recognize his authority (v. 11; Witherington 1995: 392–3). Paul says that he is not going to commend himself to the Corinthians again (v. 11), but in fact this is exactly what he does. In saying that he will not commend himself he means that he will not adopt the self-aggrandizing tactics of his rivals who boast in outward appearances. Paul may be distinguishing himself from apostolic rivals whom he feels adopt the disreputable tactics of sophists. Sophists were commonly accused of paying too much attention to external forms (appearance, clothing, delivery) at the expense of content (Witherington 1995: 393–4; 348–50). In v. 13 Paul offers an interesting insight into the nature of the comparisons the Corinthians were making. 'Madness' here perhaps refers to religious ecstasy (Furnish 1984: 308). His rivals probably displayed ecstatic experiences in public, and accused Paul of failing to produce these experiences as evidence of his apostleship. Paul seems to be claiming that ecstatic experiences should be reserved for private worship (cf. 12:1–7). The text invites comparison with 1 Cor 14:18–19 where Paul claims to speak in tongues frequently, but where he also makes it clear that in the public arena of the *ekklēsia* he prefers understandable speech (which can include tongues if they are interpreted) to ecstatic speaking. In 1 Cor 14:23–5 he even expresses his fear that non-believers (potential converts) might witness uncontrolled glossolalia and assume that church members are mad! Warnings against reliance on external appearance, form, and display also underlie the statement that Paul no longer makes judgements from a human point of view. Paul admits that before his acceptance of Christ he judged Christ by worldly standards, perhaps according to the pathetic image of a crucified messianic impostor (v. 16). This passage offers an excellent illustration of how Paul's theological thought is fundamentally tied to the interpersonal struggles of human communities. It is reflection on the misguided nature of his rivals that leads him to locate his own priorities in the love of Christ and to articulate one of the strongest statements of universal salvation in his epistles (vv. 14–15; as reflecting credal affirmations cf. 1 Cor 15:3). By means of the doctrine of 'reconciliation' in vv. 18–19 Paul presents God's initiative, Christ's role, and his own mission (Paul is a minister of 'reconciliation'). Here Paul also may be drawing on a traditional formula (cf. Col 1:19–20; Eph 2:13–16) which he interprets in a new way. Given the predominance of the structures of patronage in the ancient world, however, it has been suggested that Paul may be casting God here as the great benefactor, Christ as the means of benefaction, and Paul as the human agent (or broker) of the stores of salvation: Paul is the one who serves (Danker 1989: 82–3; Witherington 1995: 396). In order to justify his mission and break with worldly standards, Paul ultimately relies on support for his conviction that God has transformed the world radically through Christ. The emphasis on newness and the proclamation in v. 17 'there is a new creation'—although some would translate this as 'he/she is a new creation' (see Witherington 1995: 395)—function as justifications of the birth of a new religious movement.

(5:20–7:16) Appeals for Reconciliation with the Apostle

(5:20–6:2) God Speaks through Paul This passage is thematically very closely related to the previous section. However, it introduces a new type of exhortation. As is frequently the case in Paul's letters, an appeal (v. 20; *parakaleō*) follows an affirmation (v. 19), the imperative follows the indicative. In fact, v. 20 sets in motion a series of appeals (appeals for reconciliation with Paul and concerning the collection) which continue until 9:15 (Furnish 1988: 1196). Here, Paul's apostolic authority is expressed in the very strongest of terms. Paul's human powers (his ability as a teacher or sage to influence an audience in antiquity) are secondary at this point; what is important is that God has conveyed legitimacy upon his mission. God has granted

Paul authority and in fact speaks through him. It is God who appeals through Paul to the Corinthians. The move from doctrinal affirmation to ethical imperative in this text makes Paul's conviction explicit: the act of reconciliation which overcomes humanity's estrangement from God is played out on the societal level in the reconciliation which must occur between Paul and the Corinthians. As in the related text of Rom 5:1–11, language of justification (righteousness, OCB s.v.; ABD v. 757–68) is combined with language of reconciliation (Meeks 1983: 186). The appeal is very strong, linking a broken relationship with God to a broken relationship with the Corinthians. Paul may even have feared that the Corinthians were in danger of committing apostasy (Witherington 1995: 397). The citation from Isa 49:8 emphasizes the present nature of salvation, but also reinforces the urgency of the situation. The reference to the one who knew no sin having been made sin (v. 21) may refer to the sinless Christ taking on sin as a burden or being treated as a sinner for the sake of humanity (Gal 3:13); sin may also refer to a sin-offering here (Rom 8:3; cf. Isa 53:4–10).

(6:3–13) Commendation through Hardships A common goal of ancient rhetoric was to establish the speaker's *ethos* or character (Witherington 1995: 44, 398). Paul begins with assurances that he has placed no 'obstacle' before the Corinthians. He seems to have believed that ministers were very influential in facilitating or preventing access to salvation (Murphy-O'Connor 1990: 822). Paul presents eloquent wisdom (rhetoric devoid of content) as being able to empty the cross of its power in 1 Cor 1:17. In contrast to the self-commendations adopted by others, Paul has commended himself as a servant of God (2 COR 4:1–6). As elsewhere in 2 Corinthians the metaphor of slavery, the theology of the cross, and the list of apostolic hardships work together to communicate the notion of a reversal of norms for judging claims of authority (2 COR 4:7–15). Paul's listing of a catalogue of sufferings is in keeping with the Stoic and Cynic theme that the hardships of the sage demonstrate virtue and character (Fitzgerald 1988: 199–201). Paul gives these traditional elements distinctive meaning in relation to the Christ event (Witherington 1995: 400). The stress on reputation and recognition in vv. 8–9 illustrates the importance of public acknowledgement of worth in the 'honour and shame' societies of the ancient world. But here Paul is willing to entertain the reversal even of these most basic cultural values. The military metaphor in v. 7 is developed further in 10:3–5 and even more extensively by the author of Ephesians (Eph 6:11–17). The inclusion of poverty in the list of hardships (v. 10) is especially intriguing given the concerns about the collection which underlie chs. 8–9, and the fact that questions about Paul's acceptance and/or refusal of support from church members was at the heart of confrontation with opponents (11:7–11; 12:14–18; cf. 1 Cor 9:1–18). In vv. 11–13 Paul repeats that he has demonstrated the open speech and boldness which are the hallmarks of an honourable apostle (2 COR 1:12–14) and he characterizes his relationship with the Corinthians as resembling the exchange between a father and his children (cf. 12:14).

(6:14–7:1) Warnings against Contact with Unbelievers This text seems to interrupt the appeals of 6:11–13 which are resumed at 7:2–3. A large number of occurrences of hapax legomena have been noted. The stringing together of a series of citations from Scripture which are not found elsewhere in Paul's letters (the allusions in 6:16–18 include Lev 26:12; Isa 52:11; Ezek 20:34; 2 Sam 7:14) has invited discussion. The vocabulary and ideas, especially the dualism, have been judged to be closer to the Qumran community than to Paul. Thus a great deal of doubt has been raised about the authenticity of these verses. There have been theories ranging from an 'anti-Pauline fragment' (Betz 1973: 88–108) to a 'Pauline interpolation of non-Pauline material' (Furnish 1984: 383), to a 'deliberative digression' which fits well within the present context of 2 Corinthians (Witherington 1995: 402). Some have understood this section to be part of the letter to the Corinthians mentioned in 1 Cor 5:9–11. In addition to the many literary problems this passage raises, the uncompromising distinction between believers and unbelievers (which seems to leave little room for the winning of new members) is surprising. It is difficult, for example, to harmonize the strong statement that one should not be mismatched with unbelievers (apistoi) with Paul's allowance for marriages between believers and non-believers to continue because of their evangelizing potential (1 Cor 7:12–16). However, there are points of contact between this text and others in Paul's letters where the church is envisioned as the temple of God made up of sanctified believers (1 Cor 3:16, 19) which must be kept pure. The corollary of this notion of holy temple is the view that members who threaten to bring impurity into the community should be treated as outsiders (1 Cor 5:1–5; Newton 1985: 110–14). On the question of maintaining community boundaries, it is also useful to compare this passage to 1 Cor 8 and 10 where the problem of food sacrificed to idols is discussed. Beliar is a name for Satan (or an evil spirit under Satan) which occurs frequently in Jewish intertestamental literature.

(7:2–16) Restoration of Good Relations The appeals of 6:11–13 are resumed in vv. 2–4. Many of the concepts related to the honour of Paul's apostleship such as 'boasting' and 'confidence' are reiterated (2 COR 1:12–14). The nature of the intimate connection between apostle and community and the theme of comfort and affliction (2 COR 1:3–11) are developed further in vv. 5–16. Many commentators have understood v. 5 as a resumption of the comments in 2:12–13, and this view figures prominently in theories about the partitioning of the letter (1:1–2:13; 7:5–16; 13:11–13 have been described as a 'letter of reconciliation'; Betz 1992: 1149–50). But these theories have also been disputed. It is also possible to understand the narrative beginning at v. 5 as an example of the comfort that occurs in affliction (v. 4); a comfort that is ultimately divine consolation (v. 6; Murphy-O'Connor 1990: 823). Without going so far as a theory of partition, it has been argued from a rhetorical perspective that vv. 5–16 constitute an amplification of some of the things mentioned in the narratio (explaining the disputed matter) of chs. 1 and 2. In other words, these verses represent a kind of retelling in a manner that would help Paul make his case as convincing as possible. The recapitulation may offer an indication that Paul was very concerned about the fact that he was being perceived as inconsistent with respect to his travel plans and about the results of the 'tearful letter' (2 COR 1:23–2:13; Witherington 1995: 407). Paul informs listeners that the setting of the events where he experienced comfort in affliction was Macedonia. The afflictions from which his body had no rest are described as coming from 'within' and from 'without'. It is possible that he is referring to bodily suffering in the form of internal anguish and external malady (cf. 4:16). But the terms might also have communal connotations, referring to suffering resulting from encounters with those outside the body of Christ (cf. 1 Tim 3:7) and from problems within the church community (or a combination of community difficulties and physical afflictions, such as suffering resulting from contacts with non-believers and those occurring as a result of disease). With related terminology, Paul refers throughout his correspondence to those on the outside as non-believers (1 Cor 5:12, 13; Col 4:5; 1 Thess 4:12). In v. 5 Paul may be continuing to speak with an uncompromising voice towards non-believers as he did in 6:14–7:1. In discussing the arrival of Titus, Paul fills in many details which are alluded to in 2 Cor 2. Paul was consoled by Titus' arrival and by the news that issues concerning the offender (2:6–8) had been resolved. The 'letter of tears' (2:3–4) had apparently produced the desired effect of instilling repentance (v. 10). Paul describes the Corinthians as having proved themselves to be guiltless (v. 11): they exonerated themselves by dealing appropriately with the offender and by showing that they did not have misplaced loyalties (vv. 11–12). 'The one who did wrong' refers to the offender (2 COR 1:23–2:13) and 'the one who was wronged' refers to Paul (v. 12). That what is at stake transcends the particular events of the dispute and involves the fundamental nature of Paul's relationship with the Corinthians is made clear by Paul's description of the consolation which has occurred as a longing, mourning, and zeal for the apostle (v. 7; cf. v. 12; 11:2). It is interesting to note that although Paul seeks concrete expressions of his authority by calling for loyalty to his position and by insisting that the offender be punished, at the same time he denies the ultimate importance of his personal authority; rather, the 'tearful letter' precipitated a rediscovery of the inseparable link between loyalty to Paul and loyalty to God (vv. 12–13). The contrast between godly grief and worldly grief in vv. 9–11 also represents a bestowing of salvific meaning upon the dispute. The painful experience (the Corinthians were grieved by Paul's letter, v. 8) was in actual fact the kind of godly grief which leads to 'repentance' (metanoia, vv. 9–10; see OCB 646–7; ABD v. 672–3). This is one of the few places where Paul employs the term (Rom 2:4; cf. 12:21; 2 Tim 2:25). Here it does not refer to repentance prior to entry into the church, but to believers repenting of some sin; it involves rediscovery of commitment to Paul, his gospel, and ultimately to God (Witherington 1995: 409). The subordination or denial of the obvious or earthly significance of the events in favour of an argument about divine purpose is an example of what sociologists of knowledge have called 'legitimation': the means by which the institutional world is explained and justified (Berger and Luckmann 1981: 79). Legitimation is involved

in the construction and maintenance of the 'symbolic universe' (MacDonald 1988: 16, 10–11). Opposition, deviance, or heresy can give impetus to theorizing about the symbolic universe. The development of theological thought is accelerated by challenges posed to the tradition by opponents, deviants, or heretics. In the process of theorizing, new implications of the tradition emerge and the symbolic universe is transformed (Berger and Luckmann 1981: 125). Paul's evocative theology of comfort in affliction is articulated by means of this process. The information about Titus in this passages offers a good example of the importance of Paul's co-workers to his mission. Titus may be counted as a member of the small group of Paul's closest co-workers who were clearly subject to Paul but also could act as his representatives (Holmberg 1980: 57–67). An important companion of Paul, Titus was taken along to Jerusalem where he was the focus of a dispute about whether Gentiles needed to be circumcised. Paul vigorously resisted the appeal that his Greek co-worker be circumcised (Gal 2:1–3). Although he had apparently not met the Corinthians previously, Titus became Paul's representative in an attempt to bring about a reconciliation (v. 14). It is indicated at 8:6, 16–24, that Titus was sent to Corinth a second time to conduct work in support of the collection for Jerusalem (cf. 2 Cor 12:18). The close relationship between Paul and Titus is made clear by the fact that Titus' very presence is a comfort to Paul (vv. 6–7). Titus' connection with the Corinthian community is also cast in personal and emotional terms (vv. 13–15). He somehow participates in Paul's apostleship. It is useful to view Titus as a broker of Paul's authority. The attitude of the Corinthians with respect to Titus is one of obedience and they welcome him with fear and trembling (v. 15). An understanding of the centrality of the values of honour and shame in first-century society can shed light upon what was at stake in Titus' visit to Corinth. Because Paul has previously 'boasted' to Titus about the model behaviour of the Corinthians, the community can strip Paul of all honour if it fails to live up to its reputation; the community has the power to revoke all public recognition of the apostle's worth. How they treat Titus has a direct bearing upon their patron (v. 14).

(8:1–9:15) Appeals about the Collection

(8:1–15) A Call to Fulfil Previous Commitment

Chs. 8–9 have figured prominently in theories about the fragmentation of 2 Corinthians. It has been argued that ch. 8 constitutes an 'administrative letter' which was delivered to Corinth by Titus and two 'brothers' (8:18–23). Comparison with literary parallels has revealed similarity to letters of appointment given to political or administrative emissaries (Betz 1985: 37–86, 131–9). Ch. 9 has also been viewed as an administrative letter. It may have had an advisory purpose: enlisting the help of the Achaians in bringing the collection in Corinth to fruition (ibid. 87–128, 139–40). Such partition theories have not seemed convincing to everyone. The mention of Macedonia and Titus, for example, in ch. 7 may prepare the way for the issues in chs. 8–9 and might be taken as a sign of literary integrity (Witherington 1995: 410, 413). While there is some disjunction suggested, for example, by the break in subject between 8:24 and 9:1 (with the usual formula: 'peri de', 'now concerning', e.g. 1 Cor 7:1; 8:1, 4; 12:1; 16:1), the evidence has sometimes been judged as insufficient to demand that ch. 9 be viewed as a separate letter (Murphy-O'Connor 1990: 823; Witherington 1995: 413). These chapters have been called an example of deliberative rhetoric (persuasion or dissuasion with a future orientation) designed to ensure that the audience fulfil a commitment previously made concerning the collection, and to illustrate that the apostle's behaviour with respect to the collection has been above reproach (Witherington 1995: 411). 1 Cor 16:1–4 provides the background illustrating that the collection for the relief of the Jerusalem church is something that had been initiated previously. It appears that Titus had made some progress in reviving the commitment to the collection and was being sent back to complete the task (7:6). Perhaps he used the atmosphere of reconciliation as an opportunity to invite the Corinthians to demonstrate the honour of their community by means of fulfilling their commitment to the collection (7:7–8, 10–11). In order to persuade the Corinthians, Paul appeals to the example of the Macedonians (including the Thessalonians and Philippians) who exceeded Paul's expectations in their generosity despite their extreme poverty (vv. 1–5). The Corinthians, in contrast, are described as having a surplus (v. 14). The implicit argument might be stated as follows: 'If the Macedonians in their extreme need are capable of such generosity, surely you are capable of as much!' Paul supports his argument with Christological thought. In a manner which recalls Phil 2:6–11, Paul speaks of Christ who was rich (perhaps a reference to pre-existence) becoming poor in order that the Corinthians might benefit from spiritual wealth

(v. 9). But when Paul develops the implications of this theology for life in the community, the results are surprising (vv. 10–15). We do not hear a call to imitate Christ in the radical manner of the gospel invitations to give up all to follow him. Rather the focus is one of equity, balance, reciprocity, and accommodation. Gifts should be according to one's means (v. 11). Relief for the Jerusalem church should not cause strife for the Corinthians (v. 13). The Jerusalem church's abundance (spiritual benefits, Rom 15:26–7, or future monetary surplus) may in turn come to address the Corinthians' need (v. 14). This call for fair balance and partnership is supported by a citation from the LXX (Ex 16:18). Paul operates upon the premiss that believers should not be in need. He calls for generosity, but it is important to note that he does not call for a radical redistribution of wealth here. Paul's attitude to wealth has sometimes been judged as one of 'love-patriarchalism': social differences are allowed to continue but relationships must nevertheless be transformed by concern and respect. This attitude may have contributed to the organizational effectiveness of the Pauline churches in integrating members from different strata in an urban environment (Theissen 1982: 107–8). A second aspect of Paul's approach in governing his churches is detectable in the statement that 'he does not say this as a command' (cf. 1 Cor 7:6). The respect for the autonomy of the congregation and their freedom in decision-making is a striking feature of some of Paul's exhortations (Meeks 1983: 138–9). This type of assertion of authority may be contrasted with the rule-like statements which emerge in household codes of the Deutero-Pauline letters (Col 3:18–4:1; Eph 5:21–6:9).

(8:16–24) Recommendation of Titus and the Brothers Here Paul explains the specific arrangements he has made in order to bring the collection to completion. In vv. 16–17 he highlights the independence of his co-worker Titus: a close relationship between Titus and the Corinthians is presupposed and the fact that he is going to Corinth of his own accord is stressed (cf. 8:6; 12:18; 2 COR 7:2–16). Paul appears to be setting in motion mechanisms to distance himself from the process of gathering the collection in Corinth even though he clearly believes that the activity has divine sanction (8:8–15). This 'distancing' can be further detected in the exhortation concerning the brother in vv. 18–20. Paul refers to the first individual who is to accompany Titus as 'the brother' (v. 18), while the second individual is described as '*our* brother' (v. 22). The possessive suggests a more personal relationship with the apostle: the person probably was a regular member of Paul's entourage (Furnish 1988: 1197). Paul presents the first brother's initiative as being tied to the mission of the delegation and appears to take comfort from the fact that this brother is famous in all the churches for proclaiming the good news (v. 18). But he also discloses that this brother has been 'appointed by the churches' and implies that serious difficulties have dictated the necessity of an 'external auditor' of Paul's initiatives (vv. 19–20). Paul clearly attaches special significance to the involvement of Titus in the delegation; he is described as Paul's partner and co-worker. In addition, the two unnamed individuals are described with the Greek term *apostolos*, a term which conveys leadership and authority, often translated as 'apostle' in Paul's letters (see OCB 41–2). But *apostolos* has a fluid meaning in the Pauline correspondence and in this case it seems to be a designation for an official messenger or envoy (vv. 18–19; cf. Phil 2:25). vv. 20–1 offer a very strong indication that Paul was suspected of wrongdoing with respect to the collection and that he understood the involvement of the delegation as an integral part of his defence (cf. 12:14–18). It has been suggested that the complicated relationship between Paul and the Corinthians can be understood in terms of a struggle to establish patronage, and the collection issue probably played an important part in that struggle. While the securing of support from a wealthy patron was a usual means that itinerant teachers used to earn a living, it was a means that Paul resisted for many reasons including fear that it would contribute to factions in Corinth. Instead the apostle continued to insist that he would earn his own living (cf. 1 Cor 9:12, 18). Some Corinthians probably wished to act as Paul's patron and subjected him to attack because of his departure from normal social conventions. The attack seems to have included, ironically, accusations of greed and back-handed dealings concerning money (cf. 2:17; 4:2; 6:3; 7:2; 12:16–17). Paul, in turn, sought to reverse the situation and place himself clearly in the position of patron (or agent of Christ, their ultimate benefactor; Witherington 1995: 417–19). Against such a background, the collection emerges as a particularly thorny issue, for it must be accepted by Paul in a way that does not diminish his status as a patron and does not put him in the position of being the Corinthians' client. vv. 23–4 illustrate that while he is interested in establishing the credibility of Titus and the brothers, they are brokers of his apostolic authority. He is their patron and the patron of the Corinthians, but their success as his agents in winning the Corinthians is crucial to protecting his honour. In order to encourage success, Paul calls the Corinthians to live up to their reputation, to demonstrate the reason Paul boasted about them to Titus (7:14). The implication is the same as in 7:14: if they fail to live up to their reputation, Paul will be disgraced—he will be shamed. The emotional pleas of v. 24 thus become more easily explained in the light of what is at stake. The Corinthians must prove their love openly for the delegation (love for them is love for Paul).

(9:1–5) An Appeal to Community Honour
Although it is by no means a unanimous opinion, ch. 9 has sometimes been judged to be a fragment of a separate letter (cf. 2 COR 8:1–15). One feature which appears to support the fragment theory is that in v. 2 Corinth is the subject of praise in relation to Macedonia, while in 8:2 the situation is reversed. However, there is no real contradiction here since Paul is referring to what the Macedonians have been told about the Corinthians' commitment to the collection, a commitment which they have as yet to fulfil. Both the argument about the Macedonian generosity and the point about the zeal of the Corinthians inspiring the Macedonians work together to galvanize the community into action. It is somewhat surprising that the focus in v. 2 is on Achaia while the focus in ch. 8 has been specifically on Corinth. But such a shift from the specific to the broader context of the province in which Corinth was located is in keeping with the opening of the letter (1:1). The reference to the brothers in v. 3 presupposes the discussion in 8:18–23. The emphasis on Paul's boasting about the Corinthians in vv. 2–4 is designed to repeat the same warning that has been articulated previously: the Corinthians must live up to their reputation. The importance of the values of honour and shame in shaping ethical injunctions and community life in general is clearly evident in v. 4. If Paul brings some of the Macedonians with him to Corinth and the community members have not as yet fulfilled their commitment, both the apostle and the Corinthian church will be humiliated; that is, shamed. As is also the case with the arrival of Titus and the brothers, the arrival of the Macedonians offers a potential occasion for the shaming of Paul and the Corinthian

community, and this dishonour must be avoided at all costs (cf. 7:14; 8:24). Suspicions surrounding Paul's handling of the collection emerge once again in v. 5 (cf. 8:20–1). Once again Paul gives the impression that he wants to distance himself from the process of gathering the collection by insisting that the delegation bring matters to a close before he arrives in Corinth (cf. 2 COR 8:16–24). Paul wishes the collection to be perceived as a voluntary gift and not as an 'extortion'. The Greek term translated as extortion (*pleonexia*) occurs in the list of vices in Rom 1:29, referring to covetousness (cf. 1 Cor 5:10, 11; 6:10). Related terminology also occurs in 2 Corinthians (2:11; 7:2; 12:17–18). No doubt is left by 12:17–18 that Paul was accused of fraudulent activity with respect to the collection (Furnish 1984: 428).

(**9:6–15**) **Appeals to Scripture** In this passage Paul justifies his exhortation in 9:1–5 on the basis of Scripture and with broad concepts of the significance of God's gracious actions in the world. A citation of the LXX (Ps 112:9) is included in v. 9, but there are many other allusions to Scripture throughout. The statement that 'one reaps what one sows' in v. 6 closely resembles Gal 6:7–9, but is based on a maxim which pervades the Wisdom tradition (e.g. Job 4:8; Prov 11:18, 24; 22:8; Sir 7:3; Furnish 1988: 1198). That the community's giving should not be under compulsion is in keeping with Paul's desire to respect the freedom of the congregation (cf. 8:8; Philem 8–14; 2 COR 8:1–8). Paul justifies his statement with a slightly modified reference to the LXX (Prov 22:8–9) in the proclamation that God loves the cheerful giver (cf. Rom 12:8). The premiss announced loudly in v. 8 and which underlies many of these verses is that God is the giver who makes all things possible (cf. v. 15). For the one who has received—the believer—giving in return becomes a natural expression of one's participation in God's bounty. To communicate the notion of the believer's state as 'having enough of everything', Paul uses the term *autarkeia* which expresses the Greek ideal of self-sufficiency, the precondition for human freedom. Paul modifies traditional notions, however, with his insistence that self-sufficiency is not a purely human accomplishment but is made possible by God's beneficence (Betz 1985: 110). The emphasis on divine initiative continues with the citation of Ps 112:9 where Paul probably means us to understand 'his righteousness' not as a reference to the righteousness of the person who helps the

poor (as in the psalm), but as a reference to God's righteousness (Furnish 1988: 1198). There are allusions to Isa 55:10 and Hos 10:12 in v. 10 which also support the notion of divine initiative. The images of harvest, growth, and plenty prepare the way for the announcement that the one who gives will be enriched even more (v. 11). vv. 11–13 make it clear, however, that generosity has more than the immediate effect of satisfying the need of the Jerusalem poor; it allows the Corinthians to contribute actively to the worship of God. The result of their giving is an abundance of thanksgivings to God. An alternative translation of *dokimē* in v. 13 as 'proof' rather than 'testing' (cf. 8:2, 8, 22) makes the connection with the sentiments expressed in 8:24 stand out more clearly. The collection allows for an open demonstration of their love and of their glorification of God. It is fundamentally an expression of their obedience to the gospel of Christ. Paul explains further that the generosity of the Corinthians will result in the Jerusalem Christians praying for them and expressing their love for them (v. 14). Rom 15:31 makes it clear that the apostle associates the acceptance of the collection for the Jerusalem church with the acceptance by the authorities there of what God has accomplished through Paul's ministry among the Gentiles (cf. Rom 15:31; Murphy-O'Connor 1990: 825). Perhaps Paul has these associations in mind when he joyously gives thanks to God for his indescribable gift (v. 15).

Paul on the Attack (10:1–13:10)

Chs. 1–9 reflect some problems in the community, but their tone is nevertheless often hopeful and conciliatory (e.g. 7:4–16). In contrast, the tone of chs. 10–13 is consistently harsh, anxious, and sarcastic. Therefore, most biblical scholars have accepted the theory that they originally constituted a separate letter. There is significant debate, however, as to where they fit in the chronology of letter fragments. They have frequently been identified with the 'tearful letter' mentioned in 2:3–4, 9, which means that the letter would have been written prior to chs. 1–9. Paul's more optimistic tone in the earlier chapters would then be understood as stemming from the resolution of most of the difficulties in the community. But several objections have been raised against this theory, based upon both the chronology of events suggested by the content of 2 Corinthians and the nature of the problem which is explicitly related to the 'tearful letter'. The suggestion of 7:4–16 is that at the time of composition of chs. 1–9, Titus had been to Corinth only once, while it appears that by the time 12:14–18 was composed he had been there twice. This implies that chs. 10–13 came later. Moreover, the case of the lapsed Corinthian brother dominates the concern in chs. 1–9 about the 'tearful letter' (2:3–11; cf. 7:8–12), but nowhere do we read about him in chs. 10–13. In fact, when Paul refers to the effect of the 'tearful letter' in 7:5–12, there is no explicit interest in the topic which so clearly dominates chs. 10–13: the threat of the rival apostles. Thus it seems best to consider chs. 10–13 as distinct from the 'letter of tears' and as having been composed at some point following chs. 1–9 (Furnish 1988: 1198–9). Paul's harsher approach in chs. 10–13 is the result of his struggle with apostolic rivals who have gained tremendous influence over the Corinthians in the interim and whom Paul considers as intruders. He may be revealing his awareness of the threat of 'false apostles' in 3:1–6, but by the time of composition of chs. 10–13 the situation has clearly become much worse.

(10:1–18) Preliminary Defence

(10:1–6) Claims of Divine Power These verses and indeed all of chs. 10–13 set the stage for Paul's impending visit (12:14; 13:1). Paul begins with an appeal to the example of the meekness and gentleness of Christ (v. 1). This may be his way of communicating that in his approach he is emulating the way Jesus conducted his earthly ministry. It seems more likely, however, that he is referring to Christ's voluntary debasement for the sake of salvation, revealed through the cross (cf. 8:9; Phil 2:6–11). In obeying Christ (v. 5), Paul participates in Christ's power in weakness. Although Paul perhaps expresses it most clearly in 13:3–4, all of chs. 10–13 is based upon one central conviction: the apostle's authority is rooted in the fact that his personal strength/weakness echoes the strength/weakness of the crucified/resurrected Christ. v. 1 contains a sarcastic reformulation of the accusation quoted in 10:10 about strong letters, but weak presence and speech. Paul is attacking those who evaluate him according to the criteria sophists use to judge rhetoric (Witherington 1995: 433; Furnish 1984: 462). In the process, he displays his own rhetorical skill in 'destroying arguments' and 'taking thoughts captive' in the hope of removing obstacles which stand in the way of spreading the gospel, here described as the knowledge of God (v. 5; cf. 2:14). A similar use of the imagery of siege warfare in conjunction with philosophical argumentation is made by Philo *Conf. Ling.* 128–31; cf. Prov 21:22; Furnish 1984: 458, 462).

Paul reveals further information about the nature of the case against him in the reference to opponents who accuse him of 'acting according to human standards' (lit. acting according to the flesh; v. 2). Paul previously stated that his actions are not according to human standards (1:17; cf. 1:12). Many commentators believe that Paul was rebuked on account of a lack of charismatic performances and ecstatic experiences (12:1–10; 5:11–13). This is quite ironic given the charismatic basis of his ministry. The work of the sociologist Max Weber on charisma has been employed by biblical scholars in order to shed light on Paul's apostleship (MacDonald 1988: 47–9). Paul can be understood as claiming 'charismatic authority' in the sense that he views his powers and qualities as stemming directly from divine origins and as not accessible to everyone. This attitude can be seen for example in Paul's descriptions of his divine commission (1 Cor 15:8–9; Gal 1:15–16) and when he expresses his confidence that when he preaches it is as if God were the speaker (5:18–20). He proclaims his gospel not only verbally, but also through various 'charismatic' acts (e.g. 12:12; Rom 15:19; 1 Cor 2:4; 1 Thess 1:5). Paul's charismatic authority can be seen very clearly in vv. 3–6, for in this text the apostle's very humanity is qualified by a claim to divine power. The military imagery serves Paul well here, because it communicates his belief that he is empowered by forces which are beyond this world to conquer this world (cf. 6:7). Throughout the text Paul sends the message that he will not be intimidated. When the Corinthians have demonstrated their loyalty to him, he will be ready to deal firmly with his opponents (v. 6).

(10:7–11) Accusations against Paul Denied The call to recognize what is plainly evident is designed to alert the community to danger. Behind the appeal is probably an accusation made by the intruders which has won support among the Corinthians. The opponents appear to have based their authority on a special connection to Christ (implied in 'belonging to Christ'; cf. 11:4, 13, 23). They may have claimed access to special visionary experiences of the resurrected Christ (12:1–10; 5:11–13). But since Paul's commission as an apostle was also based on such experiences (1 Cor 9:1; 15:8; Gal 1:12) yet the basis of his authority was being judged as inadequate, it is more likely that the claim concerned a special connection to the historical Jesus or to his followers, perhaps those connected with the Jerusalem church (cf. 11:22). The fact that Paul did not know the historical Jesus, had initially persecuted the church, and had entered the circle of apostles late in the game proclaiming that he had received a revelation of Christ, seems to have led to widespread questions and suspicions about his apostolic status (1 Cor 15:7–9). If the question of connection with the historical Jesus is involved in his battle with the Corinthian opponents, it is a matter of charismatic authority versus tradition. Given the importance of the appeal to tradition in Jewish teaching, it is not surprising that tension between charismatic authority and tradition can be detected in the attempts to organize the early church (Rowland 1985: 266–7). Paul is unequivocal, however, in v. 8. His authority is charismatic (2 COR 10:1–6); it was given to him by the Lord (i.e. the resurrected Christ; cf. 13:10). The concept of boasting which permeates (2 Corinthians 2 COR 1:12–14) is employed in an interesting way here and throughout chs. 10–13; its use is characterized by ambivalence and irony which becomes even more pronounced in the fool's speech of 11:1–12:13. The opponents may have accused him of boasting too much of his authority, but Paul admits that such extremes are necessary for the health of the Corinthians. Boasting and self-promotion were the conventional means of articulating where honour and shame were to be found in Graeco-Roman society (With-erington 1995: 432). Paul is faced with the difficulty of harmonizing his conviction that in the early church many of the usual criteria for determining honour have been abandoned (e.g. skill in rhetorical performance), with the necessity of communicating priorities in a cultural context which demanded public demonstrations of worth. It sometimes seems to Paul that in communicating his priorities he is resorting to worldly standards: he boasts a little too much! In v. 10 Paul quotes an accus-ation made against him directly (cf. 10:1). He has been accused of weak physical presence and poor oral performance of rhetoric. It seems that even his critics acknowledge his skill in writing rhetorical pieces (Witherington 1995: 433). In vv. 9–11 Paul admits that his letters are strong, but instead of declaring that he is equally strong in speech, he uses the opportun-ity to bring the focus of community back to the content of his letters. The true nature of his strength will be made clear through his actions when he comes to Corinth and does what he has said in his letters. Underlying these verses may be the suspicion that Paul is avoiding direct contact with the Corinthians,

perhaps relying too heavily on his talent as a letter-writer and on fellow-workers to act as his delegates.

(10:12–18) Opponents Accused of Interfer-ence In this section Paul moves from respond-ing to accusations made against him to launching some attacks of his own upon his opponents (Furnish 1988: 1199). In v. 12 he is clearly being sarcastic: he would not even presume to com-pare himself with those who commend them-selves! He probably has in mind here the use of letters of recommendation by his rivals (cf. 3:1–3). He rejects both the self-commendation of his opponents and the nature of their com-parisons with one another as completely misguided. They act according to worldly com-mendations, when only commendation by the Lord is relevant (vv. 17–18). To make his point forcefully, he draws upon the contentious notion of boasting (citing Jer 9:23–4) in order to call for a return to central priorities: boast-ing should be done only in the Lord (v. 17; cf. 1 Cor 1:31; Phil 3:3). The exact meaning of vv. 13–16 is not always clear and there are severe prob-lems in translating (esp. v. 13; see Barrett 1973: 263–6). However, the main point is clear: Paul's mission to the Corinthians has divine author-ization; his opponents have not respected his prerogatives as the founder of the community and have interfered in his 'sphere of action' (v. 16). These verses reveal the somewhat curi-ous preoccupation (at least from a modern perspective) of divisions of missionary labour. Paul's principle was that he would bring the good news only to communities where it had never been preached. 'Boasting of work already done in someone else's sphere of action' (v. 16) was 'building on someone else's foundation' (Rom 15:20). An understanding of the dynamics of patronage can shed light on Paul's exclusive claims and jealousy. Paul refers to himself as the Corinthians' spiritual parent in a way that con-veys the nature of his relationship with them as their benefactor (12:14; Witherington 1995: 418; cf. 1 Cor 4:14–16). He endowed them with the gift of salvation and, in turning to other apostles, they betray the loyalty that should exist between patron and client and fail to honour him as clients should. Paul's desire for an increasing sphere of action expressed in vv. 15–16 is a means of calling for a strengthened relationship with the Corinthian community as their patron which will free him to move on, and bring the good news to new territories (cf. Rom 15:23–4).

(11:1–12:13) The Fool's Speech

(11:1–4) The Threat of Corruption The whole of 11:1–12:13 is dominated by the concept that Paul is speaking like a fool. To a certain extent, Paul engages in parody in this section: he imitates the tactics (sophistic eloquence and rhetorical self-praise) of his opponents (Witherington 1995: 436). But the reference to foolishness in the context of v. 1 makes it clear that he is not altogether comfortable with the measures he has adopted. He is in fact engaging in the kind of comparison which he has just rejected as ultimately irrelevant, and he therefore risks giving the impression that he shares the preoccupations of his opponents (10:12–18). One can appreciate the difficulty of Paul's position; he lives in a society which demands public display of its itinerant teachers (cf. 2 COR 10:7–11). Yet there is a desperate and sometimes almost tragic sound to Paul's words, as he laments about an apostleship whose strength has not been recognized in weakness. In vv. 1–4 Paul makes use of a marriage metaphor to communicate the seriousness of the threat which has penetrated the community from the outside. The gravity of the situation as Paul perceived it would not have been missed by an audience of the time, for he appeals to the core values of honour and shame. Paul places himself in the role of father (cf. 12:14) of a virgin (the community) who is giving her in marriage to her one true husband (Christ). It is the father's duty to protect the honour of the virgin; and it is the virgin daughter's duty to remain chaste, symbolizing her shame (concern for reputation) and the shame of her whole household. But Paul fears that the virgin daughter will be violated by a seducer. The image of the corruption of the internal sanctity of the virgin daughter is a powerful means of communicating the nature of the threat which comes from the outside. Indisputable evidence is offered in v. 4 that the problem in the community is not only internal, but involves teachers from the outside who preach a message that Paul understands to be in contradiction to his own. The reference to proclamation of another Jesus may imply an appeal on the part of the 'false apostles' to greater continuity with the historical Jesus (cf. 10:7; 2 COR 10:7–11). vv. 2–3 are dense in allusions to Scripture and traditional notions of marriage. The role of the father in giving his virgin daughter in marriage is reflected in such texts as Gen 29:23 and Deut 22:13–21. The use of the marriage metaphor to address the relationship

of the community with the divine draws upon the traditional notion of marriage as a metaphor for YHWH's relationship to Israel (e.g. Hos 2:19–20). The image of the virgin (community) joining together with the bridegroom (Christ) is developed further in Eph 5:21–33. The reference to Eve being deceived by the serpent presupposes the temptation story (Gen 3:1–24). In Jewish tradition the serpent became identified with the devil (Sir 2:24; cf. Rev 20:2). Paul's interpretation here, with its overtones of seduction and sexual conquest, may reflect knowledge of a Jewish legend contained in the pseudepigrapha (2 Enoch, 31:6; cf. 1 Tim 2:13–14) where the serpent is identified with Satan and Eve's deception involves sexual seduction (Murphy-O'Connor 1990: 826).

(11:5–15) The Super-Apostles The transition from 11:4 to 11:5 implies that those who come into Corinth are described sarcastically by Paul as 'super-apostles', *tōn hyperlian apostolōn* (cf. 12:11). It has also been suggested, however, that these super-apostles are not the intruders that Paul labels so negatively as 'false apostles', *pseudapostoloi*, in v. 13 (e.g. Barrett 1971: 249–53). Paul's qualified admission that the status of the super-apostles equals his own (cf. 12:11) has sometimes led to the conclusion that they were leaders of the Jerusalem church (cf. Gal 2:9); the false apostles may then have been their envoys, whom Paul condemns categorically as intruders (v. 13; for a full summary of the debate concerning identity of super-apostles, see Furnish 1984: 502–5). But the emphasis on rhetorical performance in oral delivery (v. 6) seems to support the notion that these super-apostles are themselves the intruders, who not only rate themselves highly, but have probably also gained considerable prestige in the community (Georgi 1986: 39). v. 6 has been judged to be a frank admission by Paul of a liability (Witherington 1995: 435). In these earliest stages of church development, norms are being institutionalized with respect to judgement of apostolic legitimacy and talent, and Paul is not always able to meet group expectations. He calls for a realignment of community norms based on true knowledge of God (v. 6; cf. 10:5). Paul's shifting of labels from super-apostles to false apostles does not necessarily imply that two different groups are in view, but may stem from Paul's shifting perspectives. According to some standards (which he himself rejects) these apostles are powerful leaders. But according to the ultimate standard of God, they are merely disguising themselves as apostles of Christ (v. 13). In vv. 7–11 Paul offers a specific example of his behaviour in order to defend himself against accusations concerning his authority and credibility. The Corinthians may have harboured suspicions about Paul's attitudes to money and dealings with the collection, and these ideas may have left the opportunity ripe for the intruders to gain support. Paul has refused financial support from the Corinthians and refers to his principle ironically and with exaggeration by speaking of committing sin (v. 7), and robbing from other churches for the Corinthians' sake (v. 8). Paul continued to work as an artisan while he conducted his missionary work (1 Cor 4:12; 1 Thess 2:9), apparently refusing the support to which other apostles were entitled (1 Cor 9:12, 15–18). This refusal to accept living expenses may have been related to the desire to avoid being a client of Corinthian patrons, and to the fear of contributing to the already serious problem of community factions (2 COR 8:16–24). But it may also have led to frustration among the Corinthians who may have argued that Paul abrogated societal conventions with respect to itinerant teachers and degraded himself (and them) with manual labour. Paul makes it abundantly clear, however, in v. 10, that he has no intention of changing his approach. The reference to friends from Macedonia in v. 9 may be in response to the charge that he has allowed himself to become a client of the Macedonians. Paul reveals that he did accept special gifts from the Philippian church in Macedonia (Phil 4:10–20), but was apparently unwilling to accept such support in Corinth. The question also arises as to whether Macedonian generosity in the collection (8:1–5) was related to the nature of the patronage relationship he had with them. But Paul continues to have confidence in his boast, making it clear that his attitude towards support from the Corinthian church is a public demonstration of his honour (v. 10) and is motivated by his love for the community (v. 11). In vv. 12–15 the accusation made against Paul concerning his refusal to accept financial support from the Corinthians is transformed by him into an indication of the false apostles' inadequacy and dishonesty. Only by accepting the same attitude to support as does Paul, might these apostles show themselves to be Paul's equal (v. 12). The implication is clearly that these false apostles have been taking advantage of the Corinthians. The description of Satan disguising himself as an angel of light echoes 11:3 and reflects Jewish legends about the deception of Eve by the devil (*Apoc. Mos.* 17.1–2; *Adam and Eve* 9.1 [Latin]; *Adam and Eve* 38.1 [Slavonic]; Furnish 1984: 494–5). The use of the terms 'apostle' and 'minister' (*diakonos*) (terms Paul applies to himself) in the condemnation of the intruders suggests that, despite the polemic and the parody, the threat to Paul's apostolic authority cuts to the heart.

(11:16–21a) The 'Wise' Corinthians In v. 16 Paul repeats the appeal of 11:1 to bear with him as he plays the part of the fool. It is almost as if he is aware that he has been digressing from his main speech in 11:2–15. He explicitly states in vv. 17–18 that he is speaking not with the Lord's authority, but boasting (2 COR 1:12–14) according to the human standards of his opponents. In vv. 19–21a the apostle employs irony and engages in extreme sarcasm. He draws upon the community's reputation for thinking itself wise (1 Cor 2:6–16; 4:10; 6:4–5) and ironically refers to their willingness to entertain fools (the false apostles). The implication is that now that he counts himself as a fool, they will surely entertain him! Paul denigrates the false apostles in v. 20 in a manner that implies their charlatanism and recalls the differing attitudes towards community support which divide Paul from his opponents (11:7–15). He sarcastically proclaims that he was simply too weak to adopt the belittling tactics of his opponents (v. 21a). This is, of course, an ironic jibe at the Corinthians' blindness in recognizing the strength of true apostleship, a blindness which is made especially evident by the accusation that Paul's bodily presence is weak (10:10). What appears to be his shame (weakness) he hopes to prove is in fact his honour (power; cf. 1 Cor 12:9).

(11:21b–33) The Self-Designations of Paul's Opponents The passage 11:21b–12:10 includes the heart of the 'fool's speech'. Declaring that he is engaging in foolishness, Paul nevertheless boasts in the same terms as his opponents and insists that he shares all of their claims to authority. In the process he reveals the self-designations of his opponents. 'Hebrews,' 'Israelites', and 'descendants of Abraham' are three closely related labels pointing to a special claim of Jewish heritage (cf. Phil 3:5). It is impossible to attach a distinct significance to each term, but there may be differences of nuance. 'Hebrews' may refer primarily to ethnic descent, but also to geographical origin and familiarity with Hebrew or Aramaic (cf. Acts 6:1). With 'Israelites' the focus may be somewhat more upon a religious past, heritage, and tradition (Georgi 1986: 46). The conflict between Paul and the opponents in Corinth probably involves the question of whether the charismatic basis of the apostle's authority (a direct appeal to divine experience) is sufficient in the light of the greater appeal made to tradition by the false apostles (2 COR 10:1–6). 'Descendants of Abraham' may function to legitimate the authority they claim in propounding their particular understanding of the mission they undertake among the Gentiles: Abraham's promise was to be the father of many nations (cf. Rom 4:13–18; 9:6–8; Gal 3:16–18). The title 'ministers [or servants] of Christ' (*diakonoi Christou*), v. 23, is especially important because it represents a direct quotation of a designation that moves beyond claims concerning heritage and identity to give us a sense of how the opponents understood what they were doing (Georgi 1986: 32). The seriousness of the threat posed by the opponents may have been related to an approach and self-understanding which in many ways may have been quite similar to Paul's mission to be a minister of Christ Jesus (e.g. Rom 15:16). This is supported by the frequent use of the terms *diakonos* and *diakonia* throughout 2 Corinthians (on deacon, see OCB s.v.). The opponents' understanding of their connection with Christ may have differed from that of Paul, however, with respect to claims of a special relationship with the historical Jesus (2 COR 10:7–11; vv. 1–4, 5–15). Paul illustrates that he is a better minister/servant of Christ by describing a ministry of suffering and humiliation. He appeals once again to a catalogue of hardships (v. 23) which functions in 2 Corinthians in conjunction with the apostle's theology of the cross (vv. 30–1). This catalogue recalls the terms used by philosophers in the ancient world to describe their struggles in the overcoming of passion and in the search for wisdom (2 COR 4:7–15). But there is no heroism in Paul's attitude towards his troubles; v. 29 in fact records the sentiment of injustice in suffering. Yet suffering is far from meaningless; it offers demonstrative proof of Paul's weakness (v. 30), which is a sign of his identification with Christ (12:9). Because Paul appeals to the extent of his hardships to respond directly to the claims of superiority made by his opponents (v. 23), and because the theme of inappropriate boasting permeates the discussion (vv. 16–23), it is tempting to conclude that the opponents viewed their own apostolic struggles as heroic or as signs of their 'strength' of character. The sufferings mentioned in the catalogue of hardships cover many aspects

of Paul's life: work as an artisan (vv. 23, 27), travel (vv. 25–6), persecution (vv. 23–6), church life (vv. 26, 28). Particularly intriguing is the reference to 'false brethren' in v. 26. The same term is used by Paul to describe those who seek to impose the law on Gentile Christians in Gal 2:4 (Murphy-O'Connor 1990: 827). The list offers evidence of persecution at the hands of both Jews and Gentiles. The legal basis for the 'forty lashes' is found in Deut 25:1–3. Being 'beaten with a rod' was a Roman punishment. Although a law prohibited the imposition of this punishment on Roman citizens, it was frequently ignored; Paul protests this punishment in Acts 16:37 (cf. Acts 16:22; 1 Thess 2:2; Furnish 1984: 516). In fact, the reference to the beatings offers evidence of one of many points of contact between this text and accounts in Acts. However, as is illustrated by comparing the reference to the narrow escape from Damascus (vv. 32–3) with the account in Acts 9:23–5, the stories do not always present the same picture of the apostle. While in 2 Corinthians the story illustrates Paul's humiliation and weakness, in Acts it communicates the apostle's bravery and invincible mission (Furnish 1988: 1201).

(12:1–10) Visions and Revelations of the Lord
Paul continues his inappropriate boasting—his speaking like a fool (11:21)—by once again arguing that he can match any claims of status that his opponents might have. In v. 1 he gives the impression that he is ready to discuss the last contentious issue; he moves on to visions and revelations 'of the Lord' (probably to be understood as 'granted *by* the Lord': a genitive of origin; Furnish 1984: 524). That his reluctance to engage in this type of discourse is particularly great, however, is suggested by his description of his experience in the third person: 'I know a person in Christ...' (v. 2). Probably because of the importance attached to visions and revelations by his opponents, Paul wishes to convey the impression that such ecstatic experiences are relatively unimportant and even of no real significance for ministry. Paul's mission is based on what is seen concretely in the apostle and what is heard from the apostle (vv. 6–7). Paul emphasizes the nature of his dealings with church communities and his preaching of the gospel as definitive signs of his apostleship. But he nevertheless unwittingly offers here an indication of the significance of ecstatic religious experience for an early church group. The attitude towards it in this text appears to be more

negative than that revealed by 5:13, where competition concerning ecstatic experience may also be in view (2 COR 5:11–19). Moreover, while Paul clearly sees a great difference between the revelation of the Lord he describes in vv. 2–4 and the revelation of God's Son which led to his becoming an apostle (Gal 1:15–16), the distinction may be less apparent to his audience. Ultimately Paul's apostleship is based upon revelation, but given the situation in Corinth he obviously feels that it is prudent instead to stress his physical (and earthly) weakness which discloses the power accorded to him by the Lord. In Paul's dispute with the opponents we can perhaps sense a trace of the difficulty of determining which charismatic experience of an apostle is authentic. In the early church writing, the *Didache*, attitudes towards riches on the part of itinerant charismatics became an important guide to determining which teachers were truly gifted (*Did.* 11–13). Paul tells us very little about the shape of his revelatory experience or what it meant; but he does announce that it could have led to elation (v. 7). He tells us he was caught up (cf. 1 Thess 4:17) to the third heaven (here equated with Paradise, see vv. 2, 4; cf. *2 Enoch 7* and *Apoc. Mos.* 37.5; Murphy-O'Connor 1990: 828). Other-worldly journeys were commonly described in ancient apocalyptic literature (Furnish 1984: 525–6). The mysterious quality that one would expect of such an experience is disclosed by Paul in the admission that he does not know whether the experience was in the body or out of the body (v. 3). His reference to a lack of knowledge about the event, however, may also be a way of communicating its relative unimportance. Similarly, Paul's announcement that he heard things that should never be told could be in keeping with the notion of a sealed revelation (Dan 12:4; Rev 10:4), but could also be a means of pointing to irrelevance of the event for the essence of his apostleship (Murphy-O'Connor 1990: 828). Having abandoned the role of the fool (and the parody of his opponents' tactics), Paul admits that he was prevented from boasting (or being too elated) by a thorn in the flesh, a messenger from Satan (v. 7). Most commentators have seen here a reference to a physical ailment (physical suffering is understood by Paul as a sign that Satan's power continues to influence the world; cf. 4:4; see Neyrey 1990: 167–80), but others have argued that Paul has an external enemy in mind, a non-believer or an opponent in the church (cf. 2 Cor 11:14–15; Murphy-O'Connor 1990: 828).

Paul apparently prayed three times to the Lord to have the thorn removed (v. 8). The Lord responded by means of an oracle (v. 9). Grace is equated with power in v. 9 and refers to the force which sustains Paul and is disclosed in his weakness. Paul announces that it is his weakness that is the authentic source of his boasting, for it is a sign of the power of Christ dwelling within him. He offers a summary (v. 10) of the long catalogue of hardships in 11:23–8, but now explicitly states that he is content in his sufferings: these make known the paradox of his life as an apostle in imitation of Christ.

(12:11–13) The Signs of a True Apostle These verses are usually understood as the epilogue of the fool's speech (11:1–12:13). Paul takes up the voice of the fool once again. He has had to defend his own honour, since the Corinthians have not been commending him. This is the voice of a patron who feels he has not received the honour which is his due. Maintaining the ironic tone which dominates chs. 10–13, Paul admits that he is weak (he is nothing), but at the same time he is not at all inferior to the super-apostles whom the Corinthians admire so much (11:5; 2 COR 11:5–15). Paul tells the Corinthians that they have no reason to complain since 'the signs of a true apostle' were performed adequately among them (v. 12). The reference to 'signs' (*sēmeia*) offers evidence of the existence of institutionalized norms in the community for determining true apostleship (2 COR 10:7–11). A similar focus on charismatic performance in the process of evangelization occurs in Rom 15:19 and in Gal 3:5. But Paul's admission of the importance of 'signs and wonders and mighty works' is intriguing, given his previous attempt to play down the importance of visions and revelations to his mission (12:1–10). Paul is speaking like a fool in vv. 11–13, but he nevertheless may be offering an indication that charismatic phenomena were central to Paul's initial acceptance in a community, even though such wondrous deeds were subsumed by the apostle within the larger purpose of preaching the gospel of Christ (Rom 15:18–19). In v. 13 Paul returns to the complaint made by the Corinthians of unfair treatment in comparison to other churches. This complaint involved the apostle's refusal to accept material support from the Corinthians (his refusal to become their client). The Corinthians argued that he did not adopt the same attitude in other places (notably Macedonia: 11:7–11; 2 COR 11:5–15).

With biting sarcasm, Paul pleads for the Corinthians' forgiveness for not burdening them.

(12:14–13:10) Concluding Defence
(12:14–18) Suspicions of Wrongdoing concerning the Collection
Having appealed to the Corinthians for obedience in 10:1–18, and having supported that appeal with the 'fool's speech' in 11:1–12:13, Paul now states his intention to come to Corinth a third time and offers further arguments in support of his position. These verses have played a part in theories concerning the chronology of the letter fragments of 2 Corinthians. The passage 7:4–16 suggests that at the time of composition of chs. 1–9, Titus had only been to Corinth once, while it appears that by the time vv. 14–18 were composed he had made a second visit. This implies that chs. 10–13 came later. Paul's third visit (v. 14; cf. 13:1) appears to be the visit that he had planned (1:16) but had postponed after the second painful visit (2:1; cf. 9:4). During the first visit the community was founded. In vv. 14–16 Paul restates a principle that he defended vigorously in 11:7–11 and alluded to sarcastically in 12:13: he will continue to support himself while he is with the Corinthians (2 COR 11:5–15). Paul presents this as the natural consequence of his parental relationship with the Corinthians and of his great love for them (vv. 14–15; cf. 1 Cor 4:15). But the practical application of this principle in the community involves the acceptance of Paul as patron of the community and the obligation to honour him with their love. There were probably Corinthians who felt that the reverse should take place; they wished Paul to act as their client and accept their gifts of material support (2 COR 8:16–24). But Paul feels that this would be as ridiculous a scenario as children 'lay[ing] up' (saving) for their parents. In vv. 16–18 Paul repeats a charge of deceitful trickery brought against him by the Corinthians and defends himself against it (cf. 2 Cor 4:2). The discussion of the trip made by Titus and the brother recalls the description of the arrangements made by Paul for the impending visit in chs. 8–9. Because Paul seems so confident of his loyalty as a co-worker who accompanied Titus, the brother mentioned in v. 18 is most likely Paul's representative referred to in 8:22 and not the brother who was apparently appointed by the churches to oversee the handling of the collection as a kind of external auditor (8:18–19; 2 COR 8:16–24). vv. 14–18 present information which acts as an important complement to the material in chs. 8–9: it offers unmistakable evidence that Paul was suspected of wrongdoing

with respect to the collection and his delicate handling of the situation in chs. 8–9 should be read in that light. But the manner in which reference to the collection is fused with suspicions concerning Paul's refusal to accept material support in vv. 14–18 leads to further information about the precise nature of the suspicions of the Corinthians concerning Paul and money. Paul was probably suspected of keeping for himself some of the money that he is collecting for Jerusalem. In short, he was being accused of fraud (Furnish 1988: 1202). Paul brings the discussion of the matter to a close with rhetorical questions which he is sure will highlight his innocence (v. 18).

(12:19–21) The Motives of Paul's Defence
Paul now seeks to counter the impression that he has been engaging solely in a personal defence based on past events and has not been addressing important matters of community well-being. He insists that he has in fact been working for the sake of building up the community because he fears that a complete breakdown of the relationship between himself and the community will occur when he arrives (vv. 19–20). Given that Paul has been responding to specific problems having to do with the false apostles and with community loyalty from 10:1 until now, it is surprising to hear him frame the situation in terms of a general problem with improper behaviour ranging from quarrelling to sexual immorality (vv. 20–1). The list of vices in v. 20 appears to be conventional (cf. Gal 5:20; Murphy-O'Connor 1990: 828). While Corinth has a history of sexual immorality (1 Cor 5:1–5; cf. 1 Cor 6:15–16), the problem does not surface elsewhere in 2 Corinthians. However, Jews in the Roman world frequently drew attention to sexual immorality in attempts to describe the sin and alienation in the pagan world (Newton 1985: 102–3). It may be that Paul is aiming to cast the sin of the Corinthians in the most negative terms. Behind vv. 20–1 may lie an attempt on the part of the apostle to describe the consequences of the community's alienation from him as devastating. With all hope lost, there will be nothing left to do but mourn.

(13:1–4) The Serious Consequences of Disobedience
At first glance it may appear that the legal statement requiring two or three witnesses for a charge refers to requirements to substantiate charges against Paul (12:16). However, the rule—a citation of Deut

19:15—concerns the establishment of proper criteria for conviction and punishment (cf. Deut 19:15–21; Mt 18:16), and this fits equally well with vv. 3–4 where Paul warns the community of the possibility of punitive action. Moreover, in non-diaspora Judaism the rule was often used to support the requirement that those suspected of wrongdoing were to be warned carefully of the possibility of punishment (van Vliet 1958: 53–62; Furnish 1984: 575). In stressing his multiple previous warnings, Paul apparently feels that he has met the criteria of the rule. There is an element of foreboding in his warning that he will not be lenient. He promises proof of Christ speaking in him (2:17; 5:20; 12:19) in the form of punishment of the Corinthians. The explanation of the meaning of the Christ event in v. 4 is in keeping with credal statements in Paul's other letters (e.g. Rom 1:4): Christ was crucified in weakness but raised up to live by the power of God. Paul's union with Christ means that his life is shaped by the power of God in the same way. He shares Christ's weakness, but in dealing with the Corinthians, he will 'live with him' by the power of God. vv. 3–4 offer a good illustration of theology finding expression in concrete human interaction. The theology of the cross functions to support censure in community ethics and discipline (2 COR 4:7–15).

(13:5–10) The Purpose of Paul's Letter Paul's tone in this section is more conciliatory than in the exhortations in 13:1–4, but v. 10 makes it clear that the same message frames both passages: severe discipline of the Corinthian community is a distinct possibility. Paul states, however, that he hopes that drastic measures will not be necessary and locates the purpose of his letter in the prevention of such measures. Paul certainly feels that he has been endowed with divine power in his dealings with the Corinthians (13:4), but qualifies the authority given to him by Christ in a way that ties his treatment of the Corinthians to the central goal of his mission. Paul has been given authority to build up (v. 10; cf. 12:19) and not to tear it down (an almost identical phrase is found in 10:8; cf. 2 COR 10:7–11). The notion of 'upbuilding' (*oikodomē*) occurs frequently in the Corinthian correspondence and refers to the harmonious development of the church in accordance with God's designs (e.g. 1 Cor 3:9 and 14:26). We can only imagine the great sense of failure and defeat that Paul would have experienced if things did not turn out as he had hoped in Corinth and

there had been a tearing down (or destruction, *kathairesis*; cf. 10:4). There are, in fact, several indications throughout vv. 5–9 that Paul's sense of his own apostleship is bound up with the behaviour of the Corinthians. In an atmosphere of comparisons between apostles and challenges to apostolic authority, Paul invites the Corinthians to test themselves: have they displayed the faith that flows from the presence of Jesus among them? The implication seems to be that if they pass the test, Paul will also avoid failure (vv. 5–6). Nevertheless, to the end, Paul insists that what is most important is not the visibility of his apostolic credentials but the fact that he has acted in accordance with the truth of the gospel (vv. 7–8; cf. 4:2; 6:7). The apostle may be weak, and the Corinthians may even continue to view him as weak, as long as the Corinthians are strong; that is, strong in faith but not strong in self-importance. The relationship between apostle and community reflects the meaning of the cross. In weakness and suffering, strength and salvation are revealed. The announcement of the purpose of Paul's letter in v. 10 seems incompatible with chs. 1–9 and is often viewed as an indication that chs. 10–13 should be viewed as a separate letter. The third visit (12:14; 13:1) seems to be the one Paul intended to make after the Corinthians' contribution to the collection had been gathered (9:3–5). By the time of composition of chs. 10–13 the relationship between the Corinthians and the community had deteriorated to such an extent that Paul probably wondered whether the church would make a contribution at all and he felt a harsh letter was required to set matters straight. The reference to the people of both Macedonia and Achaia (Corinth was the capital of this province) making a generous contribution to the poor in Jerusalem (Rom 15:25–6) suggests that the letter did indeed achieve its purpose (Furnish 1988: 1202).

Conclusion: Greetings and Benediction (13:11–13) Assuming the generally held view that 2 Corinthians harmonizes at least two separate letters (chs. 1–9; 10–13), it is not clear which of the fragments originally included these verses. In addition, different translations reflect a slightly different numbering of verses. The NRSV has three verses, but some translations break the passage down into four verses, numbering 'All the saints greet you' as v. 13. 'Saints' is a general term for believers (cf. 2 COR 1:1–2), but here probably refers to the saints of Macedonia, the place where 2 Corinthians (or much of the letter) was composed (7:5; cf. 2:12–13; 8:1; 9:2). The call to greet one another with a holy kiss occurs several times in Paul's letters (e.g. Rom 16:16; 1 Cor 16:20; 1 Thess 5:26). It recalls the ritual kiss during church gatherings, which was an intimate expression of the fellowship experienced in early church groups (Meeks 1984: 109). The benediction in v. 13 is longer than usual and resembles Eph 6:23–4. The reference to the Lord Jesus Christ, God, and the Holy Spirit should not be understood as a presentation of the formal doctrine of the trinity (Thrall 1965: 183).

REFERENCES

Barrett, C. K. (1971), 'Paul's Opponents in II Corinthians', NTS 17: 233–54.

—— (1973), A Commentary on the Second Epistle to the Corinthians (London: A. & C. Black).

Bassler, J. M. (1992), '2 Corinthians', in C. Newsom and S. Ringe (eds.), The Women's Bible Commentary (Louisville, Ky.: Westminster/John Knox), 330–2.

Belleville, L. L. (1993), 'Tradition or Creation? Paul's Use of the Exodus 34 Tradition in 2 Corinthians 3.7–18', in C. Evans and J. Sanders (eds.), Paul and the Scriptures of Israel (Sheffield: JSOT), 165–85.

Berger, P. L., and Luckmann, T. (1981), The Social Construction of Reality (Harmondsworth: Penguin).

Betz, H. D. (1973), '2 Cor 6:14–7:1: An Anti-Pauline Fragment?' JBL 92: 88–108.

—— (1985), 2 Corinthians 8 and 9: A Commentary on Two Administrative Letters of the Apostle Paul, Hermeneia (Philadelphia: Fortress).

—— (1992), D. Freedman (ed.), 'Second Epistle to the Corinthians', ABD, i. 1148–54.

Chow, J. K. (1992), Patronage and Power: A Study of Social Networks in Corinth (Sheffield: JSOT).

Crafton, J. A. (1990), The Agency of the Apostle: A Dramatistic Analysis of Paul's Response to Conflict in 2 Corinthians (Sheffield: JSOT).

Danker, F. W. (1989), II Corinthians (Minneapolis: Augsburg).

Fitzgerald, J. T. (1988), Cracks in an Earthen Vessel: An Examination of the Catalogues of Hardships in the Corinthian Correspondence (Atlanta: Scholars Press).

Furnish, V. P. (1984), II Corinthians, AB (Garden City NY: Doubleday).

—— (1988), '2 Corinthians', J. L. Mays (ed.), HBC (San Francisco: Harper & Row), 1190–203.

Garrett, S. R. (1995), 'Paul's Thorn and Cultural Models of Affliction', in L. White and O. Yarbrough (eds.), The Social World of the First Christians: Essays in Honour of Wayne Meeks (Minneapolis: Fortress), 82–99.

Georgi, D. (1986), The Opponents of Paul in Second Corinthians (Philadelphia: Fortress).

Hock, R. F. (1980), The Social Context of Paul's Ministry: Tentmaking and Apostleship (Philadelphia: Fortress).

Holmberg, B. (1980), Paul and Power: The Structure of Authority in the Primitive Church as Reflected in the Pauline Epistles (Philadelphia: Fortress).

MacDonald, M. Y. (1988), The Pauline Churches: A Socio-Historical Study of Institutionalization in the Pauline and Deutero-Pauline Writings (Cambridge: Cambridge University Press).

MacMullen, R. (1984), Christianizing the Roman Empire: A. D. 100–400 (New Haven: Yale University Press).

Marshall, P. (1987), Enmity in Corinth: Social Conventions in Paul's Relations with the Corinthians (Tübingen: Mohr).

Martin, D. B. (1990), Slavery as Salvation: The Metaphor of Slavery in Pauline Christianity (New Haven: Yale University Press).

Matthews, S. (1994), '2 Corinthians', in E. S. Fiorenza (ed.), Searching the Scriptures, ii. A Feminist Commentary (New York: Crossroad), 196–217.

Meeks, W. (1983), The First Urban Christians (New Haven: Yale University Press).

Mitchell, M. M. (1991), Paul and the Rhetoric of Reconciliation (Tübingen: Mohr).

Murphy-O'Connor, J. (1990), 'The Second Letter to the Corinthians', NJBC 816–29.

—— (1991), The Theology of the Second Letter to the Corinthians (Cambridge: Cambridge University Press).

Newton, M. (1985), The Concept of Purity at Qumran and in the Letters of Paul (Cambridge: Cambridge University Press).

Neyrey, J. H. (1990), Paul, in Other Words: A Cultural Reading of his Letters (Louisville, Ky.: Westminster/John Knox).

—— (1993), 'Nudity', in J. Pilch and B. Malina (eds.), Biblical Social Values and Their Meaning (Peabody, Mass.: Hendrickson), 119–25.

Plevnik, J. (1993), 'Honour/Shame', in J. Pilch and B. Malina (eds.), Biblical Social Values and Their Meaning (Peabody, Mass.: Hendrickson), 95–104.

Reese, J. M. (1993), 'Assertiveness', in J. Pilch and B. Malina (eds.), Biblical Social Values and Their Meaning (Peabody, Mass.: Hendrickson), 9–11.

Sanders, E. P. (1983), Paul, the Law, and the Jewish People (Philadelphia: Fortress).

Schütz, J. H. (1975), Paul and the Anatomy of Apostolic Power (Cambridge: Cambridge University Press).

Stockhausen, C. K. (1993), '2 Corinthians 3 and the Principles of Pauline Exegesis', in C. Evans and J. Sanders (eds.), Paul and the Scriptures of Israel (Sheffield: JSOT), 143–64.

Theissen, G. (1982), The Social Setting of Pauline Christianity: Essays on Corinth (Philadelphia: Fortress).

Thrall, M. E. (1965), I and II Corinthians, CBC (Cambridge: Cambridge University Press).

—— (1980), 'Super-Apostles, Servants of Christ, and Servants of Satan', *JSNT* 6: 42–57.

van Vliet, H. (1958), *No Single Testimony: A Study on the Adoption of the Law of Deut. 19:15 Par. into the New Testament*, Studia Theologica Rheno-Traiectina, 4 (Utrecht: Kemink & Zoon).

Witherington III, B. (1995), *Conflict and Community in Corinth: A Socio-Rhetorical Commentary on 1 and 2 Corinthians* (Grand Rapids, Mich.: William B. Eerdmans).

Young, F., and Ford, D. F. (1987), *Meaning and Truth in 2 Corinthians* (Grand Rapids, Mich.: William B. Eerdmans).

7. Galatians

G. N. STANTON

INTRODUCTION

A. Paul and the Galatian Churches. 1. Galatians was sent as a circular letter to a group of churches in Galatia, where it would have been read aloud, perhaps on several occasions in the context of worship (1:2). This is the most passionate of Paul's letters; only 2 Cor 10–13 is partly comparable. There has never been any doubt about the authorship of Galatians: here we meet Paul's pugnacious defence of 'the truth of the gospel' (2:5), as well as his exposition of the significance of God's disclosure of Jesus Christ (1:12). Paul's letter is carefully crafted, though in places the modern reader wishes he had clarified some of his statements. We do not know whether Paul's attempt to fend off the threat of the agitators who had infiltrated the Galatian churches met with immediate success. In the long run, however, Paul was successful: his insistence that Gentiles need not observe the whole Mosaic law (including circumcision) as an integral part of their commitment to Christ won the day, but the debates on this issue rumbled on in some circles well into the latter part of the second century (cf. Justin Martyr, *Dialogue*, 47), and even occasionally thereafter.

2. In places Paul uses strong language which must have made some of the first listeners to this letter wince (cf. 3:1; 4:30; 5:12). Occasional scholarly attempts to 'improve' Paul's line of argument by removing some verses as later non-Pauline additions have not won support. We can be confident that the letter we have is very similar to the letter Paul dictated to an amanuensis before adding the final section in his own handwriting (cf. 6:11). In view of the extent to which some of Paul's key points are expressed more judiciously in some of his later letters, it is perhaps surprising that the early scribes who copied it did not make more strenuous efforts to harmonize it with the 'later', more moderate Paul.

3. Galatians was written to quite specific circumstances which are difficult to reconstruct in detail, though the main issues at stake are clear. Paul's dispute with the agitators elicited some of his most profound theological statements. Only Romans has made a greater impact on later Christian thinkers and believers. In modern times Galatians has surpassed even Romans in the role it has played in reconstructions of the history of earliest Christianity. Interpretation of Paul's accounts of the Jerusalem 'council' (2:1–10) and of his clash with Peter at Antioch (2:11–14) is always prominent in discussion of the tensions within early Christianity.

B. The Galatian Crisis. 1. In order to unravel Paul's main lines of argument in this letter, it is necessary to have some appreciation of the circumstances that led to its composition. Paul had preached in Galatia once (or possibly twice—see 4:13) before he wrote this letter. His initial visit was related to 'a physical infirmity' he experienced (4:13). Probably as the result of his ministry, house-churches were established. In spite of Paul's displeasure at the later turn of events, the warmth of his initial relationship with the Galatian Christians is reflected in several passages (e.g. 3:15; 4:12–20; 6:1).

2. At some point after Paul had left Galatia, agitators from elsewhere had undermined some of his central convictions by confusing the Galatians and 'pervert[ing] the gospel of Christ' (1:7). The clearest statements concerning the agitators' 'false teaching' are in 4:10, 5:7–12, and 6:12–13, though parts of those verses are difficult to interpret. The agitators are encouraging the Galatian Christians to observe the Jewish 'special days, and months, and seasons, and years' (4:10). They themselves are Jews who have become Christians; they have been urging the Galatian Gentile Christians to be circumcised, i.e. to become full proselytes to Judaism as part of their commitment to the gospel of Christ

(6:12–13). Paul believes that they have been selective in their approach, i.e. they have not insisted that the Galatians observe *all* the Mosaic commandments (4:3).

3. It is possible to glean a little more about the claims of the agitators by 'mirror-reading' some passages in Galatians. But as Barclay (1987) has rightly emphasized, mirror-reading is a hazardous operation. Not all Paul's statements are necessarily direct refutations of the claims of the agitators, though some scholars have assumed too readily that this is the case. Hence many questions have to be left open. For example, it is difficult to be confident about the relationship of the agitators to the 'false believers' who caused havoc among the Jerusalem Christians (2:3–6) and to 'the certain people from James' (2:12).

4. Since Paul and the agitators shared a number of convictions, it is inappropriate to refer to them as Paul's 'opponents'. They both seem to have used the term 'gospel' to refer to Christian proclamation (1:6–7). Like Paul, they believed that Jesus the Messiah was the fulfilment of the promises of Scripture. In all probability, in 4:21–31 Paul is responding to their interpretation of key passages in Genesis.

5. By mirror-reading 5:13–6:10 some scholars have claimed that Paul is opposing a second group in the Galatian churches, antinomians or Gnostics who have distorted Paul's proclamation of Christian freedom. However, in this section of his letter, Paul is far more concerned with general ethical principles than with false views. Paul is underlining two convictions: faith must be worked out in love (5:6); freedom is not an opportunity for self-indulgence, but for love of one another which is a bond as close as slavery (5:13).

C. The Recipients. 1. Where were the Galatian churches located? Scholarly opinion continues to be evenly divided between advocates of the 'north' and the 'south' Galatia theories. The former defend the traditional view that the recipients of this letter were ethnic Galatians (*Galatai*, Celts, see 3.1) who lived in the north of the Roman province; the Galatian churches were near modern Ankara. The latter note that in Paul's day the Roman province of Galatia stretched from Pontus on the Black Sea to Pamphylia on the Mediterranean coast, and insist that Paul wrote to churches at Antioch, Lystra, and Derbe in the south.

2. A decision is important for reconstruction of Paul's missionary journeys and career, but

not for the interpretation of this letter. See Longenecker (1990: lxiii–lxviii), for a full discussion.

D. Date. Dates proposed range from 49 to 58 CE. If Paul wrote in 49 or 50, Galatians would be the earliest of his letters. If Paul wrote towards the end of the 50s, Galatians was written not long before Romans. Dating Galatians is closely related to a decision on two major questions: the location of the Galatian churches, and the relationship of Gal 2:1–10 to Acts. If, as seems likely, Paul's account of his visit to Jerusalem in 2:1–10 is his equivalent of Luke's account of the Jerusalem council in Acts 15, then Galatians was written at some point after that event which is usually dated to between 49 and 51 CE. (See further GAL 2:1–10 and IPC B1.4.) The extent of the development in Paul's thinking between Galatians and Romans is only one of several issues that depend on the date one assigns to this letter. However, a decision cannot be made with any degree of confidence.

E. Genre. Of rather more importance for the exegesis of this letter is its literary genre, a question that has been prominent in recent discussion. Betz's theory that Galatians is an apologetic letter that presupposes the real or fictitious situation of the court of law has provoked lively debate. Betz (1979: 15) claims that the epistolary framework can be separated so easily 'that it appears almost as a kind of external bracket for the body of the letter'. Paul is defending himself against the accusations of his accusers before the jury that is to decide the case, i.e. the Galatians. Betz's critics acknowledge that this forensic rhetorical pattern of persuasion can be discerned in parts of chs. 1 and 2, but hardly in the letter as a whole. Some claim that Galatians is an example of deliberative rhetoric, i.e. that Paul is persuading the Galatians not to accept the claims of the agitators. While this is clearly the case in 1:6–9 and 6:12–16, this reading does not do justice to many other parts of the letter. The debate has been assessed critically by Kern (1998) who calls in question the various attempts to interpret Galatians in the light of Graeco-Roman rhetorical handbooks. Paul uses several Graeco-Roman and Jewish patterns of persuasion in what is, after all, an impassioned *letter* rather than a rhetorical discourse.

F. Structure. The introduction (1:1–9) and the conclusion (6:11–18) are clearly marked. There are three main sections in the letter. From 1:10 to 2:21 Paul relates the parts of his own story that are relevant to his overall purposes. The central arguments of the letter start at 3:1, but it is not easy to decide whether they end at 4:11, 4:30, or 5:1. The ethical exhortations in the third main section end at 6:10.

COMMENTARY

Introduction (1:1–9)

(1:1–5) Opening Greetings The literary form of the opening words is found in nearly all NT and early Christian letters: 'writer to addressees, greetings': 'Paul...to the churches of Galatia, grace to you and peace...' As in his other letters, Paul elaborates this opening formula, but only in Romans 1:1–6 is this done at greater length than in Galatians.

Paul's comments on his apostleship are striking. In numerous passages in his letters Paul refers to himself in positive terms as an apostle ('one who has been sent'). In v. 1, however, Paul stresses that his apostleship is *not* based on a 'human commission', nor has he been sent 'from human authorities'. Is this a direct response to his opponents in Galatia right at the outset of the letter? Have they been undermining Paul's authority by referring to its purely human origin, perhaps stressing that Paul had been sent as an apostle (merely) by the church at Antioch (Acts 13:1–3)? This may be the case, but as we noted above, Paul's forceful statements are not all to be read as direct responses to the jibes of his opponents. Paul emphasizes that he has been sent to the Galatian churches as an apostle by Jesus Christ and God the Father. God has shown that he is the Father of Jesus Christ by raising him to life; in vv. 3–4 God is the Father of Christians ('our Father').

In the opening phrases of several of his letters Paul refers to individual co-workers; see, for example 1 Cor 1:1, Sosthenes; 2 Cor 1:1, Timothy. In v. 2 Paul refers to an unnamed group of co-workers. The phrase, 'God's family', correctly alludes to the presence of men and women in the group, for in a context such as this, the Greek word *adelphoi*, literally 'brothers', includes 'sisters'.

Paul states that he is writing to the churches of Galatia. As noted above, it is not easy to be certain about their precise geographical location. Paul's other letters were written to individual churches, though they may soon have circulated more widely. Like 1 Peter (cf. 1:1), Galatians

was intended to be a circular letter to a group of churches probably scattered over a wide area.

In v. 4 Paul makes three comments about the significance of the death of Christ. (1) In Paul's day many Jews believed that the death of a righteous man as a martyr would expiate the sins of others (see especially 4 Macc). Here the death of Christ is linked to this conviction in what several scholars have claimed is a pre-Pauline formula. The strongest indication that this may have been the case is the use of 'sins', whereas Paul himself prefers the singular, 'sin'. (2) In what may be Paul's own filling out of an early credal statement, the death of Christ is seen as a release 'from the present evil age'. Paul implies that there is a 'coming age' which he refers to in 6:15 as 'the new creation'. This contrast between two 'ages' is characteristic of apocalyptic thought. (3) Christ's giving up of his life for our release is in accordance with the will of God. 'The death of the Son is therefore a sacrifice enacted both by him and by God; and as such it breaks the mold of the old sacrificial system. The cross, that is to say, is not a sacrifice human beings make to God; it is fundamentally God's act, and as such the inversion of the sacrificial system.' (Martyn 1997: 91)

Paul concludes his extended opening greetings with a traditional doxology (v. 5). He does not do this in his other letters. Perhaps he does so here in the knowledge that his circular letter will be read in the churches in Galatia in the context of worship.

(1:6–9) Rebuke Immediately after the opening greetings in all Paul's other letters a thanksgiving to God for the readers is included. Thanksgiving is mentioned by Paul more often, line for line, than by any other Hellenistic author, pagan or Christian (O'Brien 1977). In stark contrast to Paul's other letters, however, there is not even a hint of a note of thanksgiving in Galatians. But there is one important point of similarity here with the other letters: here too the main theme of Galatians is introduced in the sentences that follow the opening greetings.

Paul's first word after the initial greetings, *thaumazō*, 'I am astonished' must have sent a shudder through the Galatian congregations when they heard it read, for they would have expected a thanksgiving. v. 6 includes Paul's only use of the verb *metatithēmi*, 'desert'; the closest parallels in Hellenistic writers refer to the desertion of one philosophical school for another. Here, however, the context is different:

Paul is amazed that the Galatians are deserting 'the one who called you', clearly not Paul himself, but God whose call is 'in grace'. Although NRSV reads 'in the grace of Christ', 'of Christ' is not found in some early MSS; it is more likely to have been a later scribal explanatory addition than an omission. The Galatians' desertion has happened 'quickly', perhaps soon after the arrival of the agitators. The verbs in vv. 6–7 are in the present tense, confirming that the Galatians' apostasy is still happening as Paul writes.

Paul claims that the Galatians are 'turning to a different gospel', but he immediately denies that there is another gospel. The term 'gospel' has deep roots both in the Graeco-Roman world and in Isaiah. It may have been associated by the Galatians with the 'glad tidings' brought by a military victory or the birth of an emperor. In several key passages in Isaiah 40:9, 52:7, 61:1) the verb 'to proclaim good news' is used. Jesus seems to have applied the same phraseology to his own proclamation of God's coming kingly rule (e.g. Mt 11:5 11 Lk 7:22; Lk 4:16–21). Soon after Easter the noun is used as a Christian technical term for 'God's good news about Jesus Christ'. For Paul, there can be only one gospel (though see GAL 2:7); if his opponents use that term, they are perverting God's good news.

In v. 7 Paul speaks openly about the agitators for the first time. Instead of naming them, he refers to them with disdain as 'some people'. 'There are some who are confusing you' is too weak, as is REB's 'there are some who unsettle your minds'. The same verb tarassō is used in Gal 5:10 (cf. also Acts 15:24) with the sense 'intimidate': the Galatians are being frightened out of their wits by the troublemakers who, from Paul's perspective, want to pervert the gospel. In the opening phrase of v. 8 (and again in v. 9) Paul uses the plural 'we'. While this could be an editorial 'we', and simply a reference to Paul himself, Paul is probably associating his coworkers with his proclamation (cf. Gal 1:2). Paul is speaking hypothetically: he is prepared to pronounce an *anathema*, God's curse, on himself (and his circle) and even on an angel-messenger from heaven if any of them should dare to proclaim a different gospel.

In v. 9 Paul throws caution to the winds and calls down an *anathema* on those who are now proclaiming a different gospel. The phrase, 'so I now repeat' may simply refer back to v. 8; more probably it is intended as a reminder that when he was last with the Galatians, Paul had solemnly warned them of the real risk that the gospel received by the Galatians might be undermined by others. The verb 'receive' is used here (and in 1 Cor 15:3) in a technical sense to refer to the careful transmission of tradition. In 1:12 Paul seems to contradict himself when he insists that he received the gospel through a revelation of Christ and not as transmitted tradition. But the contradiction is more apparent than real: the gospel does have central themes which can be passed on from one person to another (cf. 1 Cor 15:3–5), but ultimately it is God's act of disclosure or revelation.

Paul's Story (1:10–2:21)

(1:10–12) Proclamation of the Gospel Does v. 10 belong with vv. 8–9? The word 'for' (*gar*) in the Greek suggests this; Dunn (1993: 48) (among others) takes v. 10 in this way. However, *gar* is often so weak that it need not be translated—it is ignored in the NRSV. If so, then v. 10 may be read as the beginning of a lengthy section of the letter which runs as far as 2:21.

The NRSV translation of v. 10 implies a strong contrast between the accusation against Paul that he uses rhetoric to curry favour with his audience, and Paul's own claim that in his proclamation of the gospel he seeks only God's approval. This interpretation seems to be confirmed by the strikingly similar line of argument in 1 Thess 2:4–6. However, some commentators translate the Greek verb *peithō* in its literal sense as 'persuade', and take both parts of the opening sentence of v. 10 in a negative sense: Paul is rejecting his opponents' suggestion that he seeks to persuade his audience by the force of his rhetoric, and also their claim that he is persuading God to accept Gentiles on easier terms. The final sentence of v. 10 underlines Paul's rejection of crowd-pleasing rhetoric. Paul's many references to enslavement in this letter are usually negative, but this first reference is positive: Paul insists that he is a slave of Christ.

'For I want you to know' at the beginning of v. 11 is a formula Paul uses elsewhere (e.g. 1 Cor 12:3; 15:1) to underline the importance of what follows. In spite of the strongly polemical tone of this letter, Paul refers here to the recipients as 'brothers and sisters', perhaps as a conciliatory gesture. Paul's firm threefold denial in 11c and 12 that his gospel has merely human origins is a filling out of 1:1, and probably a direct response to the jibes of his opponents. Paul's positive statement about the origin of his gospel at the end of v. 12 is one of the most important in the whole letter: it is expanded and expounded in the autobiographical sketch that follows. Paul insists that he received the gospel 'through a revelation (*apokalypsis*) of Jesus Christ'. This translation preserves the ambiguity of the Greek which can be construed either as 'Jesus Christ's disclosure of the gospel' or as 'God's disclosure of Jesus Christ as the content of the gospel'. The latter is preferable, especially in view of the filling out of v. 12 in vv. 15–16. The key noun in v. 12, *apokalypsis* is usually understood in the light of apocalyptic writings where it often refers to the unveiling of something or someone previously hidden, i.e. the 'revelation' or 'disclosure' of Jesus Christ. While not denying the validity of this traditional interpretation, Martyn (1997: 144) has argued forcefully that God's unveiling of Christ is 'basically qualified by the assertion that apocalypse is the *invasive* act that was carried out by God when he sent Christ and Christ's Spirit into the world and into human hearts' (3:23; 4:4, 6).

(1:13–17) Paul's Story, Part I When had the Galatians heard about Paul's pre-Christian way of life (v. 13)? We can only guess. Perhaps Paul had spoken about it on his initial visit to the Galatian churches. Or perhaps Paul knew that some information about his former life had circulated far and wide—well beyond the reports that had reached the churches of Judea to which he refers in 1:22–3. Or perhaps Paul had guessed or was aware that his opponents had used an account of his former way of life to undermine his authority and proclamation.

Paul's two references in vv. 13 and 14 to his way of life *in Judaism* are the only two references to Judaism in the NT. Not until the writings of Ignatius half a century later do we find 'Judaism' and 'Christianity' contrasted as two 'religions'. In earlier Jewish writings (2 and 4 Macc) 'Judaism' is used to contrast the distinctive Jewish way of life with Hellenism. In v. 14 Paul underlines twice over the 'out of the ordinary' zeal with which he observed the 'traditions of his ancestors', i.e. traditional Pharisaic interpretation of the law. Perhaps Paul is glancing sideways at the insistence of his opponents in Galatia on law observance: Paul concedes that *formerly* he himself had made the same claims concerning the law.

Paul's zeal had led him 'to persecute the church of God violently and to try to destroy it' (my tr.) The verbs are strong and in the imperfect tense: Paul's hounding of the church was not a one-off outburst, but a sustained attack which included violence. Why had

followers of Christ roused Paul's ire? Some scholars have claimed that it was lax observance of the law by Christians that provoked Paul, but Paul himself does not say this. Were there Christians in the period between the Resurrection and Paul's call who did not keep the law fully? From his letters it is difficult to discern at what point Paul changed his mind about law observance; this does not seem to have happened immediately after his call on the road to Damascus. Luke does provide some relevant evidence in Acts, but it is difficult to interpret: in Luke's perspective the claim that Stephen and the Hellenists attacked the law before Paul's call was mischievous (see Acts 6:11, 13–14). So it is not as easy as some have supposed to argue that before his call Paul was in contact with Christians who did not observe the law.

It is more likely that early Christological claims, especially concerning the Messiahship of Jesus, were the trigger for the violence Paul used against 'the church of God'. Christians were claiming that a man crucified recently as a criminal was God's Messiah, but Paul knew all too well that such a person stood under the curse of the law (Gal 3:13). Hence Paul discerned that proclamation of a crucified Messiah was implicitly a threat to the law, though even after his call as apostle to the Gentiles it seems to have taken him some time to work out the radical implications of this conclusion.

Paul does not tell his readers the location of the churches he persecuted. The phrase, 'the church (assembly) of God' is striking. This very early Christian self-designation echoes the OT references to Israel as 'the assembly of Yahweh'. Although both *synagōgē* and *ekklēsia* are used in the LXX to translate the Hebrew phrase, there is no evidence that *ekklēsia* was ever applied to the Jewish community in a given place (Meeks 1983: 80). So the early Christian use of the term *ekklēsia* was one way Christians differentiated themselves from local Jewish communities. In retaining the phrase 'of God', Paul concedes that his persecution of the church was an attack on God.

In vv. 15–17 a single, long, rather complicated Greek sentence is retained as one sentence in the NRSV; it fills out the argument of 1:11–12 considerably. Paul's two main points are clear, even though, as we shall see below, some of the details leave questions unanswered. He emphasizes that his dramatic call to proclaim God's Son among the Gentiles was on God's initiative as a revelation or disclosure of his Son (see A4 above); he did not make contact with any other

Christians in order to seek their advice or instructions, but went off on his own to Arabia.

Although it has often been customary to refer to Paul's *conversion* experience, and thereby to imply a conversion from Judaism to Christianity, Paul's carefully chosen phrases here indicate that he himself saw matters very differently. He did not decide to convert from one religion to another; in God's own time ('when it pleased God'), God *called* Paul to be an apostle to the Gentiles. Paul deliberately echoes phrases from Jer 1:4–5 and Isa 49:1, 6 to refer to his call, thereby aligning himself with the Hebrew prophets.

Paul acknowledges that there were apostles in Jerusalem before his call, but stresses that he felt no need to defer to their authority. Instead, immediately after his call he went off to 'Arabia', the kingdom of Nabataea south of Damascus. Betz (1979: 73) notes (with references) that recent excavations have brought to light a prosperous civilization with strong Hellenistic influences that was at its peak by the time of Paul's visit. Paul may have stayed in this area for up to two years, perhaps preaching in cities such as Petra to Gentiles already sympathetic to Judaism (so-called 'God-fearers') (so Hengel and Schwemer 1997: 127). This is a plausible historical reconstruction, but Paul tells us much less about his visit to Arabia than we would like to know.

At the end of v. 17 Paul reveals that he returned to Damascus following his stay in Arabia, thus implying that it was in or near Damascus that he experienced God's call. Although readers of Acts are told three times and with vivid details (9:3; 22:6; 26:12) that Paul experienced God's call near Damascus, Paul himself tells us much less in vv. 15–17, for his concerns in this letter are different. He focuses on his call to be an apostle to the Gentiles as God's initiative, and on his avoidance of those who might have been 'human sources' (cf. 1:12) for his gospel.

(1:18–24) Paul's Story, Part II: Visit to Jerusalem
When did Paul go up to Jerusalem—three years after his return to Damascus, or three years after his initial call? Most scholars prefer the latter, though the former is not impossible. The NRSV translates the key verb *historēsai* which refers to the purpose of Paul's visit to Jerusalem as 'visit', while the GNB translates 'obtain information from'. From the context 'visit' is preferable; if Paul had conceded that he obtained information from Cephas (the Aramaic form of Peter) he would have offered a hostage to fortune. No doubt during the period Paul spent as Cephas's house guest in Jerusalem he did gain some information about the life and teaching of Jesus, but from Paul's perspective that did not mean that he was dependent on Cephas for his understanding of the gospel. Some scholars have suggested that during this visit to Jerusalem Paul reached the agreement with Peter that is referred to in 2:7, but that is unlikely.

Paul is adamant about his independence from the leaders of the Jerusalem church. In v. 20 he confirms the accuracy of his autobiographical sketch with an oath. None the less it is important to bear in mind that Paul's purpose is not primarily to set out his story with chronological precision. His sketch is selective, for it is designed to rebut the claims of his opponents. Hence his repeated insistence (cf. vv. 17, 19) that with the exception of Cephas, he did not meet any of the other Jerusalem apostles. In 19b Paul adds a further exception, James the Lord's brother who is almost certainly referred to here as an apostle. However, the Greek may mean that Paul did not see any apostle (apart from Cephas)—though he did see James.

In order to underline his independence of the Jerusalem authorities Paul mentions in v. 21 that after his short visit to Cephas he then went well to the north and north-west of Jerusalem, to places in Syria (presumably including Antioch) and in neighbouring Cilicia. Defenders of the south Galatia theory believe that Paul's first visit to Galatia took place during this journey. Martyn, a defender of the north Galatia theory, believes that v. 21 tells strongly against the south Galatian theory; he notes that if Paul had visited the cities of (south) Galatia at this point, it would have suited his argument to have said so (1997: 184).

In vv. 22–3 Paul goes still further: at this time he certainly was not in contact with the Jerusalem authorities, for he was not known personally by the churches in Judea, including Jerusalem. In that area stories had circulated about his volte-face from persecutor to proclaimer, but he himself was not there, but far to the north. In v. 23 Paul quotes the report about him which had reached the Judean churches and had been received with thanksgiving to God (v. 24). No doubt only a summary is included, but some of the phrases seem to come directly from the report rather than from Paul himself. For example, Paul does not refer to the content of the Christian message as 'the faith', and he prefers the noun 'gospel/good news' to the verb 'proclaim good news'.

(2:1–10) Paul's Story, Part III: Conference in Jerusalem The meeting between Paul and Barnabas and Christians in Jerusalem was one of the most momentous events in the development of earliest Christianity. Was it intended to defuse a major crisis and to reconcile deep-seated differences? What were the main issues at stake? Although some details are unclear, the main points can be set out confidently.

The relationship of Paul's account in these verses of a conference in Jerusalem to Acts 11:29–30 and 15:1–29 has baffled scholars for many decades. A minority insists that the 'apostolic council' recorded in Acts 15 took place *after* Galatians was written. This would account for Paul's failure to refer in ch. 2 to the 'apostolic decree' (Acts 15:20, 29; 21:25) which, according to Luke, encapsulated the decisions reached at the 'apostolic council'. On this view the events recorded here are to be equated with Acts 11:29–30. However, most scholars accept that in spite of some glaring differences, there are enough similarities between the two passages to conclude that they record the same event from different perspectives. Even if Acts 15 draws on earlier sources, Luke wrote some three decades after Paul wrote Galatians—and, unlike Paul, Luke makes no claim to have been present himself. So Acts 15 should be used with great care by the interpreter of Gal 2:1–10.

'After 14 years' probably refers to Paul's call (1:15–16) rather than his visit to Cephas (1:18–19). Paul is accompanied by Barnabas who is portrayed in 2:13 as a leader in the church at Antioch, as he is in Acts 14:26–8. So Paul and Barnabas probably travelled to Jerusalem as leaders of the church in Antioch, even though, for whatever reason, Paul does not state this explicitly. Paul emphasizes that the journey was undertaken at *God's* behest, 'in response to a revelation' (v. 2), i.e. not as the result of the anxieties or the decision of the church in Antioch.

With whom in Jerusalem did Paul discuss his convictions concerning the gospel he was proclaiming to Gentiles (v. 2)? The NRSV and the REB refer to one 'private' meeting with the leaders of the Jerusalem church who play a prominent part in vv. 6–10. Some commentators (including Betz 1979 and Martyn 1997) conclude (probably correctly) that *two* meetings are referred to in the Greek of v. 2, one with the whole church in Jerusalem, followed by one with the leaders.

Paul is anxious lest his fundamental conviction that Gentiles should be accepted without the requirement of circumcision be called in question or even rejected outright (2b). In v. 3 it becomes clear that Paul and Barnabas had taken Titus with them to Jerusalem (v. 1) as a test case. At first there is no dissension: the Gentile Titus was not compelled to be circumcised (v. 3). At this point the link between Paul's story in chs. 1 and 2 and the crisis in Galatia would have become crystal clear to those who heard this letter read aloud in churches in Galatia many hundreds of miles from Jerusalem. In chs. 1 and 2 Paul is narrating selected past events in his life not because he believed that his autobiography was interesting, but because he was convinced that his story was directly relevant to the disputes in Galatia. The phrase 'compelled to be circumcised' which is used in v. 3 with reference to Titus, recurs in Gal 6:12 with reference to the Galatian Christians. In v. 5 Paul insists that the stand he took on principle in Jerusalem was 'so that the truth of the gospel might always remain with you [Galatian Christians]'.

Paul's fury at the 'false believers' who had sneaked in like spies to 'enslave us' is not disguised; it is reflected in emotive language in vv. 4–5 and in the tangled grammar, which the NRSV partly unravels. Where did this attempt to thwart 'the freedom we have in Christ Jesus' take place? Some scholars posit an earlier occasion in Antioch, partly on the basis of Acts 15:1, while others believe that the disruption took place in Jerusalem itself. Who are the 'false believers' who posed such a threat? Paul concedes that they are 'believers' ('brothers' in the Greek), but is adamant that he did not yield to their demand that Gentile Christians should be circumcised. Like the agitators in Galatia, they are perverting the gospel of Christ (1:6–7). The 'false believers' are probably not identical with 'the certain people from James' referred to in 2:12.

In v. 6 Paul insists that the Jerusalem leaders made no demands on Paul: 'they imparted nothing further to me' (REB). Here, as elsewhere in this passage, Paul is ambivalent about the Jerusalem leadership. He recognizes that they are the 'acknowledged leaders' (2:2, 6, 9) of the Jerusalem church, though he himself is unimpressed by their status, for they have no special standing in God's eyes.

In vv. 7–9 Paul spells out the agreement that was reached, one which in Paul's eyes was a victory, not a compromise. The Jerusalem leaders recognized that Paul had been entrusted *by God* with the gospel 'for the uncircumcised', just as Peter had been entrusted with the gospel 'for the circumcised'. Most scholars now accept that Paul is referring here to a division of labour along ethnic (Jew/Gentile) rather than geographical (Israel/diaspora) lines. Paul is not referring to 'two gospels', one for each ethnic group; the very idea would have appalled him, as 1:7 confirms. The recognition that God was at work in making Peter 'an apostle to the circumcised' is in stark contrast to the reference to Peter in the account of the 'incident at Antioch' which follows in 2:10–14.

At last Paul names the leaders of the Jerusalem church: James, Cephas, and John (v. 9). They are referred to as 'pillars', as in supports for a building. Agreement is sealed by giving 'the right hand of fellowship', an act that had the same meaning in antiquity as it does today. 'By implication, the agreement sets up two cooperative but independent missionary efforts' (Betz 1979: 100). The only request made by the Jerusalem leaders to Paul and Barnabas was that they should remember 'the poor', i.e. they (probably the Antioch church) should support the Jerusalem church financially. Paul had no hesitation in accepting this request. We know from 1 Cor 16:1–3 that the Galatian churches did make weekly collections for the Jerusalem church (cf. also Rom 15:25–6).

What is left unsaid in vv. 1–10 must not be forgotten. The 'false believers' fade completely from the scene at v. 5. There is not even a hint that they accepted the agreement. And if, as most scholars think, Acts 15 records a different version of the discussions in Jerusalem, Paul's failure to mention the 'apostolic decree' is significant: either Luke has anachronistically added the decree to his account of the apostolic council, or it was such an embarrassment to Paul that he could not bring himself to mention it here.

(2:11–14) Paul's Story, Part IV: Incident at Antioch The clash between Peter and Paul recorded in these verses is in sharp contrast to the amicable agreement reached at Jerusalem. In the earlier parts of Paul's story an indication of the chronology is given, but there is none here. This is one of the reasons why some scholars reverse the order of the two events narrated in ch. 2: the crisis that arose in Antioch (vv. 11–14) was resolved by the agreement reached in Jerusalem (vv. 1–10). This reconstruction avoids the difficulty that in ch. 2 Paul does not indicate the outcome of his dispute with Peter at Antioch. But in such a carefully argued letter Paul is

unlikely to have reversed the chronology, and in 2:1–10 there is no reference to food laws, the central issue at stake in Paul's clash with Peter.

Paul's failure to record the outcome of his face-to-face dispute with Peter is related to his primary concern to show that this incident has a direct bearing on the tensions in the Galatian churches. Even though the text gives no explicit indication of a change of scene from Antioch to Galatia at v. 14, most modern translations assume rather too readily that there is a major break at this point. However, the NRSV's footnote is helpful, and points the reader in the right direction: 'Some interpreters hold that the quotation extends into the following paragraph.' If so, then in 2:15–21 Paul is still addressing Peter in Antioch—but for the benefit of the troublemakers in Galatia. It is preferable to read the record of the incident at Antioch as undergoing a subtle metamorphosis in vv. 15–21 as Paul switches the focus of his attention from Antioch to Galatia.

In v. 11 Paul does not tell the reader why Peter came to Antioch (presumably from Jerusalem), nor does he give the reason for the dramatic confrontation. Only after the bald summary is given do the details emerge in vv. 12 and 13. Peter had been fully accustomed to eating with Gentiles in the church at Antioch; he was thoroughly at home in the mixed congregation there of Jews and Gentiles. But when 'certain people came from James', Peter backtracked. Presumably the visitors came at the behest of James to express the concerns of the Jerusalem church. If they were the false believers of 2:4–5, surely Paul would have said so. They were not urging abandonment of the Jerusalem accord over separate missions to Jews and to Gentiles, but raising concerns over Peter's regular practice of eating with Gentiles, a matter apparently not discussed in Jerusalem. Paul does not tell us whether the meals in question were regular meals, or the Lord's supper, or both. At this time Jews and Gentiles regularly had contact with one another, but there were differing attitudes to table fellowship. Peter and other Jewish believers seem to have been welcoming Gentiles to their tables, probably on Jewish terms. They are likely to have been 'accepting invitations to Gentile tables without asking too many questions (cf. 1 Cor 10:27), though presumably on the assumption that the Gentile believers would have been mindful of the basic food rules' (Dunn 1993: 121).

The verbs in v. 12b imply that Peter began to draw back and refrain from table fellowship over a period of time. Who was applying the pressure, and why was Peter afraid? The NRSV refers to 'fear of the circumcision faction'; this phrase is usually understood to refer to Jewish Christians who came from James and who were uneasy about what were perceived to be Antioch's lax attitudes to table fellowship with Gentiles. The REB interprets the Greek quite differently: Peter 'was afraid of the Jews'. The Jews may have been non-Christians. Longenecker (1990) and others accept R. Jewett's theory that at the time of the Antioch incident a rising tide of Jewish nationalism had provoked Jewish antagonism towards Jews who were thought to be adopting lax attitudes towards association with Gentiles. Under this political pressure, the Jerusalem Christians were 'trying to take measures to keep Gentile Christians from needlessly off ending Jewish sensibilities'. Hence the concerns of the Jersualem church were triggered by political rather than theological concerns.

These verses can be plausibly interpreted in several ways. Perhaps we have to accept that we do not know precisely why Peter acted in a way that led Paul to charge him with hypocrisy twice over in v. 13. What is clear is that Peter did not act impulsively and without support from other Jewish Christians. Even Barnabas, Paul's closest colleague (2:2, 9) 'was led astray'. It was Paul who was isolated, hence the emotive language (and perhaps even the lack of clarity) in vv. 11–14. Paul's own position becomes clear in v. 14. He believes that Peter (and Barnabas and all the other Jewish Christians) were 'not acting consistently with the truth of the gospel' when they compelled Gentiles to live like Jews, i.e. to share table fellowship with Gentiles only when meals had been prepared in accordance with Jewish dietary laws. ('Living like Jews' did not necessarily include circumcision; there is no indication that Peter was insisting that Gentile believers should be circumcised.) For Paul, a fundamental principle was at stake: Gentiles were being compelled to live like Jews in order to be accepted as members of the Antioch church. Hence Paul rounded on Peter in front of all those lined up against him. It is often pointed out that Paul's attack on Peter is at odds with his own exhortation in 6:1 to use a 'spirit of gentleness' when a fellow Christian is 'detected in transgression'.

Paul says nothing about Peter's response, and nothing about the outcome of the confrontation. Martyn (1997: 240), concludes that 'the Antioch incident ended in political defeat for Paul'. That is a possible, but not a necessary reading of the text. Perhaps Paul was more concerned to press home the theological issues at stake, as he does in the following verses, than to record the outcome of a painful episode.

(2:15–21) Works of the Law or Faith? Paul expounds vigorously the theological issues at stake in his dispute with Peter. He probably intends these verses (or at least vv. 15–18) to be part of his reply to Peter. Paul is unlikely to be recalling some seven years later the very words he used; no doubt these verses incorporate some of Paul's later reflections on the issues at stake. We do not know whether Paul formulated his convictions about 'justification by faith' in the light of his dispute with Peter, or whether he had developed them at an earlier point.

vv. 15 and 16 contain a set of programmatic statements that are expounded and underlined in the sections of Galatians that follow. In v. 15 Paul reminds Peter that both of them are Jews by birth, and hence view Gentiles as outside the law and therefore as sinners. Here Paul is echoing traditional views; perhaps he is even echoing the language used by the 'certain people from James' (v. 12). In the next verse Paul explains that v. 15 is by no means the end of the matter! In the lengthy v. 16 the phrase 'works of the law' is used three times and contrasted sharply with 'faith'. What does the former phrase refer to? Paul is refuting the claim made by the agitators in Galatia (and implicitly by Peter when he 'compel[led] the Gentiles to live like Jews', v. 14) that one's standing before God is dependent on carrying out the requirements of the Mosaic law. 'Works of the law' is taken by some scholars to refer to the Jewish 'identity markers' of sabbath, circumcision, and dietary laws, rather than to the Mosaic law *per se*, but the negative comments on the law that follow in ch. 3 make this unlikely.

Paul insists that a person is 'reckoned as righteous' by God (NRSV n.) on the basis of 'faith in Christ'. The meaning of the latter phrase is keenly discussed. It has traditionally been taken by translators and commentators to refer to the believer's faith in Christ, but a growing number of scholars insist that Paul is referring to Christ's own faithfulness to God, as in the NRSV footnote. The future tense 'will be justified' at the end of v. 16 is important; Paul is referring to the believer's ultimate standing before God.

Once again Paul includes Peter with his use of 'we' / 'our' in v. 17. Paul seems to be referring to the stand he and Peter took before Peter backtracked: they had sought to base their standing before God solely on the basis of faith—and in so doing they had been dubbed 'sinners' by some. Paul vigorously refutes this criticism, and especially the inference that Christ has become a servant of sin. In v. 18 Paul refers directly to the incident at Antioch: he would show himself to be a transgressor if he were to backtrack (as Peter did) and 'rebuild the walls of the Law that I have torn down' (Martyn 1997: 256).

In vv. 19 and 20 Paul's statements about the Christian life are positive: both the incident at Antioch and the crisis in Galatia slip into the background. Although Paul repeatedly refers to himself in the first person singular, he is speaking on behalf of all Christian believers. 'Dying to the law' (v. 19) means being separated radically from it. For Paul 'dying to the law' takes place through identification with Christ's own crucifixion and death (v. 19c). When this happens the believer's life is no longer self-centred, but Christ-centred (v. 20).

The phrase 'Christ who lives in me' is rarer in Paul than reference to the Spirit who indwells the believer. Both phrases are less common than Paul's references to Christian experience as 'in Christ' (e.g. 5:6), 'in him', 'in the Lord', or 'in the Spirit' (e.g. 5:25). In v. 20b the NRSV's 'in the flesh' is misleading, especially in view of Paul's strongly negative use of 'the flesh' in 3:3 and 5:13, 16–22. Here 'flesh' is neutral; it refers to the believer's 'present mortal life' (REB).

Paul does not often refer to Christ as 'Son' or 'Son of God'. When he does so, it is usually in a particularly rich theological context, as in Gal 1:16, 2: 20c, and 4:4–6. Both the latter passages refer to the Son's self-giving 'for us', 'for our redemption', a note first sounded in Galatians in the opening greeting at 1:4. Once again there is a division of opinion over 'faith'. Does Paul refer to the believer's faith in the Son of God, or to the Son's own faith (NRSV f.) or faithfulness?

v. 21 is a summary of the whole of vv. 15–21; in particular it underlines some of the key points of v. 16. Paul is probably responding directly to the claims of the agitators; the incident at Antioch has now faded from view. The agitators have claimed (or perhaps Paul thinks they have claimed) that Paul has wrenched asunder God's grace and the law. For Paul a person is reckoned as righteous in God's sight not through the law (synonymous in v. 20 with

the 'works of the law', v. 16) but through faith in Christ (v. 16) whose death was not in vain (v. 21c) but was an act of self-giving love for us (v. 20c).

Paul's Central Arguments (3:1–5:1)

(3:1–5) How Did You Receive the Spirit? Paul continues the argument of the preceding verses and asks pointedly whether the Galatians received the Spirit by 'works of the law' or by 'believing what you heard' (v. 2). Attention is now focused directly on the Galatians who are roundly rebuked for the second time (cf. 1:6–19). Peter and the incident at Antioch are left far behind as Paul grapples vigorously with the issues at stake in the crisis in the Galatian churches. At nearly all the key points in ch. 3 Paul's argument is grounded on Scripture, but in this opening section Paul's appeal is to the Galatians' initial reception and continuing experience of the Spirit. The Galatian Christians are upbraided twice for their foolishness (vv. 1, 3); it is not their lack of intelligence that riles Paul, but their lack of discernment. Paul draws on contemporary patterns of polemical argument in suggesting that the Galatians have been 'bewitched' by the agitators. To use a modern-day equivalent, they have had the wool pulled over their eyes. In fact Paul reminds the Galatians that he used visual imagery in his initial preaching: Jesus Christ was 'publicly exhibited as crucified'. As in 1 Cor 1:23; 2:2, Paul contrasts his preaching of the crucified Christ with the rhetorical sophistry of his opponents.

v. 3 is particularly important for Paul's argument. The Galatians have received the Spirit as the basis of their Christian experience, and they ought to continue in the Spirit (cf. 5:25). Instead, they are 'now ending with the flesh'. Paul believes that some of the Galatians have succumbed (and others may follow) to the agitators' demands that circumcision is the mark of Christian identity. Paul returns to this topic more fully at 5:2–12; 6:12–13. Paul underlines and extends his central point in this section by asking a rhetorical question in v. 5 to which he expects a resounding 'no' as an answer. The tense of the verbs is important: God continues to sustain the Galatians with the Spirit; God continues to 'work miracles' among them. We do not know what form the miracles took, but Paul's main point is clear: God's Spirit continues to be experienced powerfully in the Galatian churches. For Paul, one's standing before God (past, present, and future) is not on the basis of carrying out the requirements of the law.

(3:6–14) Abraham Believed God In v. 6 Abraham is introduced for the first time; he remains on stage until 5:1, though in some sections he lurks in the background. Given the prominence of Abraham in numerous early Jewish writings, it is not surprising that Paul also should appeal to parts of the story of Abraham. Paul takes his listeners immediately to Gen 15:6 in order to argue that 'those who believe' (including Gentiles) (vv. 7–8) are descendants of Abraham.

Paul is probably refuting the agitators' version of traditions about Abraham. They are likely to have appealed to the reference to Abraham's meritorious deeds in Gen 14 and to Abraham's acceptance of circumcision in Gen 17:4–14 as the basis of his acceptance by God. Paul, however, focuses solely on Gen 15:6 with its reference to Abraham's faith in God as the basis of his standing before God. He develops his argument from Scripture in v. 8, claiming that through Scripture (in phrases from Gen 12:3 and 18:18) God 'declared the gospel beforehand to Abraham'. God's justification of the Gentiles by faith and his bestowal of his grace, peace, and favour upon them (i.e. his blessing of them, vv. 8 and 9) is nothing new: it is anchored in Scripture, and it was always part of God's purposes.

It is difficult to be certain about Paul's line of argument in vv. 10–12. He claims that reliance on observance of the law brings a curse, not a blessing, and quotes Deut 27:26 in support. Why does the law bring a curse? Paul seems to be implying that it is impossible to carry out the requirements of the law: since those who try to do so fail to keep the law completely, they are accursed. There is a solemn warning to the Galatians here: beware of the law's siren voice, for it brings a curse, not a blessing. If this is Paul's main point in v. 10, then vv. 11 and 12 make a rather different point: they are concerned once again with the contrast between faith and keeping the law as the basis of one's standing before God. In v. 11, Hab 2:4 underpins Paul's argument concerning faith; in v. 12, Lev 18:5 is cited to confirm that the law has to do with carrying out the requirements of the law and living by them. Living by faith (v. 11) leaves no room for living by the requirements of the law (v. 12). Paul's comments on the law in vv. 10–12 are negative and harsh. The other

side of the coin is expressed positively in vv. 13–14: 'Christ redeemed us from the curse of the law . . . so that we might receive the promise of the Spirit through faith.' This section ends where it began (vv. 2–5) with a reference to the importance of God's bestowal of the Spirit. But what does 'Christ became a curse for us' mean (v. 13)? 'The thought is of Jesus acting in a representative capacity . . . the law printing its curse on Jesus, as it were, so that in his death the force of the curse was exhausted, and those held under its power were liberated' (Dunn 1993: 177, who rightly refers to 2 Cor 5:21 as an important parallel).

(3:15–29) Abraham's Offspring Paul seems to sense that the argument of the previous verses has been complex. So he pauses, and in contrast to 3:1, addresses the Galatians in endearing terms in order to secure their attention. He then provides an illustration from everyday life: one cannot annul or add to a ratified will (by means of a codicil). Paul uses a form of argument found in other Jewish writers of the time: in order to make a particular point he rejects the accepted meaning of Gen 17:8 as a reference to the promises given to Abraham and the generations of his descendants. He takes 'offspring' ('seed' in the Greek) in its literal sense in the singular to refer to one person, Christ. So God's promises were given only to Abraham and to Christ; in vv. 26–9 Paul will insist that those who belong to Christ are Abraham's offspring, not Abraham's physical, i.e. ethnic, descendants.

In v. 17 Paul returns to his illustration of v. 15, but he now uses the term *diathēkē*, which can mean either 'will' or 'covenant' to refer to God's covenant with Abraham. The law came into existence 430 years after God's covenant-promise to Abraham. There is no hint here that the law was God-given; indeed Paul's point is that as the law came *later* than the covenant ratified by God, it could neither nullify nor modify the promise to Abraham. The latter point is only implicit: in v. 15 Paul has explained that one cannot add a codicil to a will. The agitators in Galatia may well have argued along totally different lines: Gen 17 confirms that Abraham observed the law even before it was given by God to Moses at Sinai. Paul presses home his argument in v. 18. 'The law' and 'the promise' are set in antithetical opposition: 'the inheritance' given to Abraham comes via the latter, not the former. What is 'the inheritance' granted by God? It 'is the church-creating Spirit of Christ' (Martyn 1997: 343).

The obvious question now has to be faced (v. 19). If the law came into existence much later than the promise to Abraham, and is therefore secondary, why was it given at all? Answer: it was added as a supplement to the promises (this is the force of the verb used) 'because of transgressions', a phrase which has evoked much comment. Was the law added to bring about a knowledge of transgressions, or even to provide some sort of remedy for them? While the Greek can be construed in this way, in view of the negative comments on the law that follow, this interpretation is unlikely. Paul probably states that the law was given 'to cause or increase transgressions'. The next phrase 'until the offspring would come' confirms that the law's role is limited to the period between Moses and Christ. In nearly all strands of Jewish thought, and presumably in the view of the agitators, the law had been given by God permanently.

The law's secondary role is underlined by the claim that it was 'promulgated through angels' (v. 19d). The NRSV's 'ordained through angels' implies a more positive sense than the context allows. The first listeners were bound to notice the absence of explicit reference to the involvement of God in the giving of the law by God. The silence is telling, especially in view of the way God's involvement in the giving of the promise to Abraham is underlined in the Greek by the placing of 'God' at the end of v. 18. Paul concedes that a mediator was involved in the promulgation of the law (v. 19d). The statement that follows (v. 20) is one of the most puzzling in Paul's letters, but its gist is clear. A mediator, Moses, was involved. But since God is one and needs no mediator between himself and his people, God was not involved at Mt Sinai! This is indeed a radical rejection of Jewish views about the giving of the law, but it is in line with the preceding and the following comments about the role of the law.

An obvious objection is faced squarely in the verses which follow (cf. 3:19). In the light of the negative comments about the law that have been made in the preceding verses, some listeners might have concluded that the law and the promise were fundamentally opposed to one another (v. 21a). Paul adamantly resists this conclusion, and then proceeds to spell out what continuing function the law has (vv. 22–5). First of all the hypothetical possibility that the law might have brought life is considered. In

that case, Paul readily admits, God's 'rightwising' activity ('righteousness') on our behalf would be on the basis of the law. But since the law did *not* bring life, righteousness does not come as the result of keeping the law. Once again the careful listener will recall 2:16, where this theme rings out for the first time. vv. 22 and 23 are partly similar: both use the verb 'imprison', and both conclude with a reference to faith. But Paul does not simply repeat himself. In v. 22 he refers to the way Scripture has imprisoned the whole of humanity, indeed the whole of creation ('all things') under the power of sin. 'Scripture' probably refers to Deut 27:26 which Paul cited in 3:11; 'under the power of sin' is synonymous with 'under a curse' in 3:11a. This negative role played by the law had a positive outcome: so that the promise might be given to those who believe. In v. 23 Paul uses the pronoun 'we' for the first time since 3:13. The verses that follow confirm that Paul has in mind the Galatian Christians as well as himself. 'We' were imprisoned by the law; in the preceding verse sin plays this role. But the dark night did not last forever, with God's disclosure of Christ (cf. 1:12, 16) faith was revealed.

Paul clarifies his main point with an illustration in vv. 24–5. The law was our *paidagōgos* until Christ came, but with the coming of faith we are no longer under a *paidagōgos*. In many families in the Graeco-Roman world the *paidagōgos*, often a slave, played an important part in caring for children. Sometimes this person acted primarily as a teacher (hence 'pedagogue'), sometimes as a disciplinarian. What would this metaphor have meant to the listeners in Galatia when they first heard Paul's letter read aloud? The context confirms that Paul had a negative connotation in mind: the law, like the *paidagōgos*, provided unpleasant restraint for a limited period—until Christ came.

In v. 26 and in the grand finale to this section in v. 29 Paul brings discussion of who are true 'children of Abraham' back onto the agenda (cf. 3:16–19). In v. 26 those who are 'in Christ Jesus' are God's children, while in v. 29 those who 'belong to Christ' are Abraham's offspring; the expressions are synonymous. By now the listener will be well aware that one's standing before God is not grounded on law observance, but on faith. vv. 27–8 interrupt the argument of vv. 26 and 29 with a reference to baptism. Some of the phrases in these verses are found elsewhere in early Christian writings (see especially 1 Cor 12:13; Col 3:11); only the first pairing in

v. 28, 'Jew or Greek', is relevant to the immediate context. Hence several scholars conclude that Paul is here citing an early baptismal liturgy. The person who is about to be baptized removes clothing, symbolizing the old order, and in baptism is 'clothed with Christ' (v. 27). In baptism all the social distinctions that lay at the heart of the society of the day are abolished. 'Religious, social, and sexual pairs of opposites are not replaced by equality, but rather by a newly created unity' in Christ Jesus (Martyn 1997: 377). Whether this radical vision was put fully into practice by Paul himself, and in the churches he founded, is another question.

(4:1–7) The Sending of the Son As at 3:15, Paul opens this section with an illustration from daily life (vv. 1–2). In this case he modifies the illustration to suit his present purposes. The heir to an estate is in fact in a better position than a slave, for, unlike a slave, he knows that one day he will inherit his father's property. The date at which the son received his inheritance was probably fixed by law, rather than by an individual father. Nonetheless Paul's main points in vv. 3–4 are well supported by the illustration. While waiting to receive the inheritance (cf. 3:18), 'we were enslaved'. But in God's own time, freedom was made possible through the sending of his Son (vv. 3–4). Paul takes the 'enslavement' theme further in vv. 8–9: the Galatians, having been freed from slavery, now want to be enslaved all over again.

What are the 'elemental spirits of the world' (v. 3; cf. 4:8–9) which enslaved believers before their redemption, and which now attract the Galatians? The phrase probably refers to the basic materials or principles that lie at the heart of the cosmos. For a Jew, the law fulfilled that function. In any case, the context (cf. especially 4:5, 10) strongly suggests that Paul includes the law as an essential part of the 'elemental spirits'.

vv. 4–5 contain one of Paul's richest Christological statements. Several scholars have claimed that it is a pre-Pauline confessional formula, partly because some phrases are not common elsewhere in Paul's writings, and partly because of its similarity to 'sending formulae' in Rom 8:3; Jn 3:17; 1 Jn 4:9 (and cf. Mk 12:6). Here Paul develops the theme of God's sending of the prophets to Israel: Jesus as God's Son is sent to redeem those 'under the law', i.e. Jews, so that 'we', all who are 'in Christ Jesus' (cf. 3:26–9) might receive adoption. 'Born

of a woman' does not refer to the virginal conception of Jesus, but to his birth as a human being. 'Born under the law' may mean no more than 'born as a Jew', but in view of all the preceding negative statements about the law, 'under the law' probably includes a negative connotation.

The precise background to Paul's reference to believers' 'adoption as children' (v. 5) has been keenly debated. Is this phrase to be understood in the light of Graeco-Roman practices concerning the adoption of children? Or is there an OT/Jewish background? If the latter, then, as Scott (1992) has argued, Paul may have in mind an analogy with God's adoption/redemption of Israel from slavery in Egypt: believers were redeemed to adoption as sons of God from slavery under the 'elemental spirits of the world' (GAL 4:3). v. 4 refers to God's sending of his Son; in v. 6 God 'has sent the Spirit of his Son': for Paul, 'Christ/Son' and 'Spirit' are closely related and in some passages almost synonymous. In v. 6 it is the Spirit who cries out to God on behalf of the believer and calls God, 'Abba', Father. The retention of the Aramaic word 'Abba' in a letter to Greek-speaking Christians is striking; it almost certainly reflects Jesus' own preferred way of referring to God (Mk 14:36; Lk 11:2).

The argument of vv. 1–7 is brought to a climax in v. 7: the believer's adoption as a child of God means (negatively) release from enslavement to the 'elemental spirits of the world' and (positively) acceptance as an heir to God's promises to Abraham.

(4:8–11) Why Do You Want to be Enslaved Again? Paul once again speaks directly and forcefully to the Galatian Christians (cf. 3:1–5), and develops several of the themes of 4:1–7 further. Before they became Christians, Galatians were enslaved to 'beings that by nature are not gods', i.e. to idols (cf. 1 Cor 8:5; 12.2). Now as believers they have come to know, i.e. to experience, God's Spirit (cf. 3:1–5; 4:6). Paul immediately modifies this statement in v. 9b by emphasizing yet again God's initiative in redemption from enslavement to 'the weak and beggarly elemental spirits' (GAL 4:3): 'you have come ... to be known by God'.

In v. 10 the link between the elemental spirits and the law becomes explicit. What are the special 'days, and months, and seasons, and years' that the Galatians now want to observe closely, probably under the influence of the agitators? Although v. 9c, 'you want to be ensl-aved' may suggest that the Galatians have not yet succumbed to meticulous observance of the Jewish calendar, v. 10 implies that they have done so. There is general agreement that Paul is referring to observance of the Jewish sabbath and festivals. Observance of 'months' probably refers to observance of the new moon which marked the beginning of each month; precisely what is meant by 'years' is uncertain. Martyn correctly notes that Paul's argument here is not even partly anti-Jewish (1997: 417–18): God's new creation in Christ (cf. 6:15) marks the end of the distinction between 'holy times' and 'pro-fane times' that is basic to all peoples—one of the pattern of 'elemental pairs of opposites' to which the Galatians were enslaved (3:28; 4:3, 8–9).

(4:12–20) Paul's Perplexity Longenecker (1990: 184–7), has argued that v. 12 marks the opening of the final major section of the letter, the transition from the 'rebuke' section (3:1–4:11) to the 'request' section (4:12–6:10). However, the link between the emotional personal appeals of v. 11 and the entreaties in vv. 12 and 19–20 makes it preferable to align 4:12–20 closely with the preceding verses. In v. 12 Paul opens this section with a term of endearment, 'friends', which he has not used since 3:15; in v. 19 he refers to the Galatians as his 'little children'. Although vv. 12–20 have been dubbed an erratic and emotional aside, these verses make explicit Paul's passionate concern for the Galatians, a concern that begins at 1:6 with Paul's expression of astonishment at the Galatians' behaviour.

Paul's opening plea, 'become as I am', recalls the earlier autobiographical sections of the let-ter, from 1:11 to 2:14 (or even 2:18). As in several other passages in his letters (e.g. 1 Cor 4:16–17; 1 Thess 1:6; Phil 4:9), Paul refers to his own exa-mple as a model of Christian discipleship. To modern readers this smacks of bragging, but it was a conventional mode of instruction used by philosopher-teachers in Paul's day. The phrase 'I...have become as you' is an expression of Paul's friendship and solidarity with the Gal-atians. In spite of the pain the Galatians have caused Paul, he does not consider that he him-self has been wronged (v. 12c); the implication is that they have wronged God or Christ.

The Galatians know more about Paul's illness than we do (v. 13)! Presumably an illness led to Paul's initial visit to the Galatian churches—or perhaps it detained him there longer than planned. The reference to Paul's 'first' proclam-ation of the gospel may imply a second visit, but surely Paul would have referred to any second visit in this extended discussion of his relation-ship with the Galatians. Paul's illness put the Galatian Christians 'to the test' (v. 14a), probably because their pre-Christian beliefs would have tempted them to draw the inference that Paul's illness was the result of demon possession. In fact, the welcome Paul originally received could hardly have been more enthusiastic: he was wel-comed as 'an angel of God', as a representative of Christ Jesus himself. The latter phrase parallels the similar idea in Matt 10:40, where Jesus assures his disciples that whoever welcomes them, welcomes Jesus himself. vv. 15–16 express the breakdown of Paul's warm relationship with the Galatians. Although v. 15b is often taken to imply that Paul's illness was ophthalmic, it may be no more than a vivid expression of the Gal-atians' initial willingness to do almost anything in their support of Paul. v. 16 is taken as a rhet-orical question in NRSV and some other trans-lations, but the Greek can equally well be construed as an indignant expression of Paul's frustration at the Galatians' about turn. In vv. 17–18 the agitators are referred to explicitly, but as elsewhere, they are not named (cf. 1:7). The NRSV's 'they make much of you...so that you may make much of them' is too bland: the REB's double reference to 'lavishing attention' is pref-erable. Paul even claims that the agitators want to 'exclude you', i.e. to drive a wedge between Paul himself and the Galatians. The first half of v. 18 is probably an aphorism or proverb which Paul expands in order to press home his point: Paul had hoped that his absence from the Gal-atian churches would not impair his relationship with them.

The poignant expression in v. 19 of Paul's perplexity and pain has no close parallel in his other letters: Paul likens himself to a pregnant mother 'in the pain of childbirth'. His concern for the Galatians could not have been expressed more powerfully. Paul probably continues with the imagery of pregnancy in the final clause where he speaks of his hope that Christ will be 'formed', i.e. like an embryo or foetus, among the Galatians. In v. 20 Paul concludes this sec-tion with his wish to be present personally with the Galatians in the hope that their warm rela-tionship might be restored. Paul knows that his letter will have to substitute for his presence. There is no confident expectation here (or else-where) that this letter will be more effective than the agitators who are still personally present in the Galatian churches.

(4:21–5:1) The Hagar and Sarah Allegory There is no agreement on the reason for the inclusion of these verses at this point in the letter. Some scholars suggest that they are an afterthought, or have even been displaced from elsewhere. Others link them to the exhortation of the final main section of the letter. The traditional and preferable view is to take them as Paul's striking final argument in his sustained exposition that starts at 3:1.

Right up until v. 21b Paul speaks negatively about the law—32 times in all; in every case he has the law of Moses in mind. It is no exaggeration to claim that from 2:16 to v. 21a Paul's view of the law is 'consistently malignant' (Martyn 1997: 37). In v. 21b, however, Paul's tone changes dramatically: *nomos* (law) is used positively for the first time in this letter. In this verse Paul speaks with heavy irony: you Galatians who desire 'to be subject to the law', listen to what the law really says, for it does have positive things to say. This verse must have focused the minds of the Galatians sharply on Paul's central concern: heard aright, the law bears witness to the gospel, as in the allegory of Hagar and Sarah that follows.

In vv. 22 and 23 Paul summarizes parts of the Hagar–Sarah traditions from Gen 16–21. In v. 22 the reference to 'a slave woman' and 'a free woman' echo the language (but not the thought) of 3:28, and especially the opening sections of ch. 4. In v. 23 a contrast is drawn between the child 'born according to the flesh', i.e. conceived naturally, and the child born 'through the promise', i.e. following God's promise to Abraham that his aged and barren wife Sarah would bear him a son. Paul's summary is terse: neither the mothers nor the children are named. Barrett (1982: 161) has argued convincingly that Paul is responding to the agitators' interpretation of the Hagar–Sarah traditions. 'The wording implies that the story is already before the Galatians; they will know that the slave is Hagar, the free woman Sarah'. Paul explains that this is an allegory, a form of interpretation in which individuals and key details in a narrative all represent someone or something else. Allegorical interpretation was used by Philo of Alexandria, a slightly earlier contemporary of Paul's, as well as by some rabbis. Philo's allegories were more elaborate and less related to the original context than Paul's. Paul states boldly that the two women

are 'two covenants' (v. 24) even though Gen 17:21 refers to only one covenant, the one that God promises to establish with Isaac, whom Sarah will bear to Abraham. In fact Paul does not refer explicitly to the Sarah covenant, and does not even name her. Paul focuses on Hagar, who is said to come from Mount Sinai, a detail not mentioned in Genesis. Paul's further comment about Hagar in v. 25 led to several attempts by scribes to clarify his point. The NRSV provides the more difficult and therefore probably original reading; a note in the NRSV provides an equally well-attested reading, 'For Sinai is a mountain in Arabia.'

The verb *sustoixeō* 'corresponds to' in v. 25 is the key to these verses. The verb was used to refer to soldiers standing in the same line; it came to refer to the correspondence of categories in lists. Paul lines up in the same column, as it were, Hagar, Mount Sinai, children being born (even now) into slavery, the present Jerusalem who is in slavery with her children (vv. 24–5). In the other column Paul places the free woman (the unnamed Sarah), the Jerusalem above who is free, and who is our mother (v. 26). Paul does not take pains to balance the two columns precisely, for his main interest is in the contrast between two 'Jerusalems'.

Earlier in his letter Paul has been at pains to stress his independence from the Jerusalem Christian leaders (1:18–20); in 25b a further step is taken: the church of Jerusalem to whose authority the agitators appealed 'is in slavery with her children'. Paul's polemic could hardly be more acute. In stark contrast stands 'the Jerusalem above, our mother'; here Paul draws on a theme found in several OT passages (e.g. Ps 87; Isa 50:1; 66:7–11) and in Jewish writings (e.g. 4 Ezra 10:25–57). The phrase '*our* mother' is surely intended to include both Jewish and Gentile Christians. In v. 27 Paul appeals to Scripture ('it is written') to sustain his point. The preceding verses make it clear that Paul interprets Isa 54:1 as a reference to Sarah: her barrenness and desolation will be reversed, for she will bear more children than 'the one who is married', i.e. Hagar.

In v. 28 Paul's earlier frustration with the Galatians 4:19–21) gives way once again to endearment, 'my friends, you are children of the promise, like Isaac', who is now named for the first time. The contrast between Isaac and Ishmael (not named) becomes even sharper in v. 29. Paul draws attention to Ishmael's persecution of Isaac, a tradition not found in the OT itself, though several Jewish sources do mention an argument between the two. A parallel is drawn with the agitators' 'persecution' of the Galatian Christians: 'so it is now also'. v. 29 sets out a further vivid contrast: whereas Ishmael and the agitators were 'according to the flesh', Isaac and the Galatians were born 'according to the Spirit'. The Galatians' experience of the Spirit has been prominent in several earlier passages (3:1–5, 14; 4:6); the contrast between flesh and Spirit will be developed further in 5:5, 16–26.

Paul relentlessly pursues his case against the agitators with a further citation of Scripture in v. 30, where Gen 21:10 is adapted slightly to fit the present context. The argument reaches its climax in v. 31. By now the listeners in the Galatian churches should have been able to draw the conclusion themselves: they are children of the free woman, Sarah, and so are the true children of Abraham. The strong language of the citation, 'Drive out the slave and her child', should not be read as an attack on Judaism: Paul's attention is focused sharply on the agitators and their claims.

Gal 5:1 has baffled commentators in ancient as well as modern times. There are two related difficulties. Although the Greek of v. 1a is so awkward that early scribes made several attempts to tidy it up, there is now general agreement that the NRSV and similar translations are appropriate. Opinion is still keenly divided, however, on the relationship of v. 1 to its context. NRSV, REB, and many other translators and commentators appeal to the contrast between slavery and freedom as an obvious link to the preceding verses: v. 1 is taken as a ringing conclusion to the Hagar–Sarah allegory. Others, including NIV, see it as the opening of a new section in which Paul turns to exhortation, and note the link with 5:13. Still others take it as a short independent paragraph that acts as a bridge between the allegory and the new themes of chs. 5 and 6. On balance, the NRSV's punctuation is to be preferred.

Exhortations (5:2–6:10)

(5:2–12) Neither Circumcision nor Uncircumcision Paul opens this section with a solemn appeal to the Galatians: 'Mark my words' (REB). In these verses with their repeated references to circumcision, the central issue at stake in Paul's dispute with the agitators is brought out into the open. v. 2 implies that some of the Galatians are on the point of succumbing to the agitators' insistence that they should be circumcised if they wish to become true children of Abraham; v. 3 implies that some have already done so. Paul is adamant that two corollaries follow: Christ will benefit them no more, and they will be obliged to keep the whole law of Moses. Perhaps the agitators had not been frank about the latter point. There is plenty of evidence to confirm that Paul is not misrepresenting Jewish teaching in his insistence that the Galatians cannot pick and choose which parts of the law they will observe.

vv. 4 and 5 summarize many of Paul's key points: most of the phrases occur in 2:15–21, Paul's opening exposition of the chasm between being justified by the law and living by faith, through the Spirit. 'Hope' is not used elsewhere in this letter, though the general theme of waiting for future salvation is prominent. In v. 6 Paul quotes a formula that he himself has probably coined. The first half, 'neither circumcision nor uncircumcision counts for anything', is repeated almost verbatim in 6:15 and in 1 Cor 7:19, though in each case the positive statement that follows is expressed differently. In 6b faith and love are related more closely than elsewhere in Paul's letters. 'Faith working through love' rules out any suggestion that Paul's ethical teaching has no moral demands.

vv. 7–12 are linked together more loosely than vv. 2–6. Here Paul rattles off several different images, though they are all related to the overall argument. vv. 7 and 8 recall Paul's opening appeal in 1:6–9. The reference to Christian living as a running race echoes 2:2. The question, 'who prevented you?' probably also refers to running races: Who cut in on you, or who side-tracked you? Since God ('the one who calls you') is in no way responsible for this, the agitators are responsible (v. 8). They are likened in v. 9 to a little yeast which leavens the whole batch of dough, a well-known image in antiquity for the power of evil. v. 10b is taken by Martyn (1997: 475), as a reference to the leader of the agitators, 'the man who is disturbing your minds'. This is not impossible, but the NRSV's 'whoever it is that is confusing you' is preferable; as in 1:7, the reference is general. Why does Paul claim in v. 11 that he is still being persecuted? And when did Paul ever 'preach circumcision'? This verse is one of the most puzzling in this letter. Elsewhere in his letters (e.g. 1 Thess 2:16; 2 Cor 11:23–9) Paul mentions the persecution he received at the hands of his non-Christian opponents, but that is not in view here. In 4:29 Paul refers to the agitators as 'persecutors', and it is their actions which are referred to again here. They seem to have claimed mischievously or mistakenly that at some stage following his call to proclaim Christ to the Gentiles (1:15–16), Paul did 'preach circumcision'. How or why they gained that information, we do not know. Perhaps they had received a false rumour concerning the circumcision of Titus (2:3). Paul's logic is clear: the agitators still claim that he is 'preaching circumcision'. If that were the case, Paul insists, then the agitators' persecution of him would have ceased. But since it has not ceased, it must be based on misinformation. Paul is so angry with the agitators that in v. 12 he makes 'the crudest and rudest of all his extant statements' (Longenecker 1990: 234). Attempts to soften Paul's plain speaking, either by euphemisms or by interpreting these hash words figuratively as 'let them excommunicate themselves', are unconvincing.

(5:13–26) Living by the Spirit Paul now turns to general exhortations which are not directly related to the crisis in Galatia, though there are numerous linguistic links with the preceding sections. This is clearly the case in v. 13: its ringing reference to God's call to freedom is in contrast to the 'yoke of slavery' the agitators are imposing (cf. 5:1). As in 5:6b, Paul is aware that unbridled freedom can lead to antinomianism; hence Paul's insistence on loving commitment to one another which is as strong a bond as slavery.

In v. 13 Paul uses the word 'flesh' (sarx), one of the most problematic words for the translator of his letters. Earlier in Galatians 'flesh' is used in a purely neutral sense to refer to human or physical nature, but in vv. 13, 16, 17 (twice), 19, 24, and 6:8, 'flesh' is used in a negative, ethical sense to refer to a person's sinful or corrupt nature. Should the translator attempt to replicate the quite different ways in which the word is used? REB uses 'unspiritual nature' or 'old nature' for the negative references to sarx, and several different phrases for the 'neutral' uses. NRSV signals the different way in which Paul uses sarx in this section by translating it as 'self-indulgence' in v. 13, before reverting to 'flesh' in the remainder of the section.

As in 4:21b, Paul speaks about the law of Moses positively in v. 14, and cites Lev 19:18, 'love your neighbour'. Earlier in the letter the

law has consistently been referred to negatively. The NRSV's 'the whole law is summed up' is misleading, for the verb means 'fulfil'. What then is intended by 'fulfilling the whole law'? Barclay's comment is apt: it describes 'the total realization of God's will in line with the eschatological fulness of time in the coming of Christ' (1988: 40). Paul uses withering sarcasm in v. 15 to denounce in-fighting in the Galatian churches. This may perhaps have been sparked off by differing attitudes to the agitators' claims, but we cannot be sure.

'Living by the Spirit' and 'gratifying the desires of the flesh' are set in opposition to one another in v. 16 which acts as a heading to vv. 17–24. The bald statement of v. 16 is expounded in v. 17: the two ways of living are 'at war with one another' (Martyn 1997: 493). The final clause of v. 17 has long baffled exegetes. A plausible interpretation envisages that the battle between 'Spirit' and 'flesh' frustrates the wishes of the believer. In v. 18 being 'led by the Spirit' is contrasted with being 'subject to the law', themes prominent in several passages earlier in the letter (e.g. 2:16; 3:1–5; 4:6–7). In vv. 19–21 Paul sets out a list of 'the works of the flesh' (NRSV) or 'the behaviour that belongs to the unspiritual nature' (REB). In vv. 22–3 there is a list of the virtues that are the fruit of the Spirit. Lists of virtues and vices were well known in the Hellenistic world; there are partial parallels in Jewish 'two ways' traditions. While there are numerous lists of vices in the NT writings, there is no comparable juxtaposition of substantial lists of virtues and vices; perhaps the closest NT parallel is Jas 3:13–17. Although some translations list the vices of vv. 19–21 in groups, NRSV correctly treats them as a random list of 15 items. Paul rounds off the list with a solemn warning, which he says, repeats teaching he gave them earlier—presumably when he was present with them: 'those who do such things will not inherit the kingdom of God'. Here Paul may be using a common early Christian catechetical formula, for the wording is not characteristically Pauline.

The phrase 'fruit of the Spirit' (v. 22) is evocative: 'the fruit' is not the result of the believer's effort, but of the gift of the Spirit. The nine items in the list of virtues are often grouped into three groups of three, though it is doubtful whether this was Paul's intention. In the light of the opening verses of this section (vv. 13, 14) we can be more confident that Paul deliberately placed 'love' at the head of the list.

vv. 24 and 25 bring the argument of this section to a climax. Believers who identify with the crucifixion of Christ (cf. 2:19) have 'crucified the old nature' (REB). v. 25 explains how this is possible: by living by the Spirit. Although this is taken by some as the beginning of the next section of Paul's exhortations, it is better to interpret this verse (with NRSV) in conjunction with v. 24: these two verses focus on the chasm between 'flesh' and 'Spirit', the theme first set out in the 'headline' in v. 16. v. 26 is a rather bland exhortation, though v. 15 confirms that it was sorely needed in the Galatian churches.

(6:1–10) Let us Work for the Good of All
Nearly every verse in this section includes an explicit exhortation, but the links between them are loose. Even more problematic is the extent to which these exhortations are related to the specific needs of the Galatian churches. Some insist that they are very general and quite unrelated to the main arguments of the letter, while others discern close links at almost every point. A mediating position is more plausible than either extreme: Paul has adapted well-known ethical maxims to meet the needs of the Galatian Christians. Many of the maxims in this section can be read as extended expositions of several of the fruits of the Spirit listed in 5:22–3. As we shall see below, there are further important links between this section and the latter half of ch. 5.

The opening maxim in v. 1 is very general. Translated literally, the Greek reads, 'you who are spiritual'; this is taken by some to refer to a specific group within the Galatian churches. But earlier in the letter Paul has insisted that all Christians have received the Spirit (e.g. 3:1–5; 4:6), so the NRSV is appropriate: 'You who have received the Spirit'. The 'spirit of gentleness' enjoined recalls 'gentleness', one of the fruits of the Spirit (5:23). Paul's concern for the erring believer is paralleled in Mt 18:15 and Jas 5:19. What is the law of Christ which is to be fulfilled (v. 2)? Since 'fulfilling the law' in 5:14 refers to the law of Moses, the use of the similar verb here strongly suggests that 'law' here also refers to the law of Moses—as 'redefined and fulfilled by Christ in love' (Barclay 1988:134, 141). Dunn (1993:323) is even more specific: 'it means that law (Torah) as interpreted by the love command in the light of the Jesus-tradition and the Christ-event'. The maxims in vv. 3–5 come as something of an anticlimax after the rich exhortations of vv. 1–2. Perhaps they are partly related to weaknesses Paul is aware of in the Galatian churches. Or perhaps they are general maxims which have their place in nearly every community setting.

NRSV places v. 6 in a paragraph on its own, for this exhortation does not seem to be related either to those that precede or to those that follow. In 1 Cor 9:14 the right of preachers to be supported financially is asserted. This verse is rather different. It refers in general terms to the support (which surely included financial support) to be given by those under instruction in the faith to their teachers. In vv. 7–8 Paul adapts proverbial statements well known in antiquity, adding his own distinctive theological emphases. The sharp contrast between 'flesh' and 'Spirit' in v. 8 is in effect a summary of 5:16–25. The eschatological warning of 5:21c is echoed in the future tenses in v. 8, 'you will reap corruption/eternal life', and in the reference to reaping at harvest-time in v. 9.

By using the phrase 'so then', Paul indicates that v. 10 rounds off the series of exhortations which began at 5:13. The encouragement to the Galatian Christians to 'work for the good of all' encapsulates a bold vision. The churches in Galatia were tiny minorities in the societies in which they lived. As this letter emphasizes repeatedly, they had their own internal tensions and conflicts. But here they are urged to strive for the well-being of all without distinction. That special concern should be shown for those of the 'household of faith' is understandable.

Conclusion (6:11–18)
The final sentences of Paul's letters usually summarize and press home its key points. Galatians is no exception. Betz (1979: 313) correctly notes that these verses are the hermeneutical key to the whole letter. Unlike Paul's other letters, there are no personal greetings. This is as significant as the absence of the expected thanksgiving at 1:6 (GAL 1:6). In both cases a ready explanation is provided by the strained relationships between Paul and the Galatians.

Paul takes over from his amanuensis for the final sentences (cf. also 1 Cor 16:21; Col 4:18; 2 Thess 3:17; Philem 19). The reference to the 'large letters' he makes when writing himself is probably not a reference to his clumsy handwriting. When this letter was read aloud in the Galatian churches (1:2), the listeners would not have been aware of the change in handwriting. 'Large letters' probably signals the importance of the words which follow.

In vv. 12–13 Paul attacks the agitators explicitly and provides his own reasons for their insistence on circumcision. In claiming that they 'want to make a good showing in the flesh' Paul may be employing 'barbed humor, inviting the Galatians to laugh at the Teachers' (Martyn 1997: 561). It is not easy to see why an insistence on circumcision would enable them to avoid persecution. Were they currying favour with a powerful ultra-conservative group in the Jerusalem church (ibid. 562), or with a group of non-believing Jews who were incensed at the way Gentiles were being accepted into the 'people of God', i.e. as proselytes, without circumcision? We do not know. Paul claims that the agitators do not themselves obey the law (13a): they cannot pick and choose which parts of the law to observe (cf. also 5:3). Paul's final jibe is that his opponents are boasting about their success in persuading some of the Galatians to undergo circumcision (13c). There is an appropriate form of boasting, however: Christ crucified (14a; cf 3:1). For Paul the cross of Christ entails a radical break with 'the world'. Paul is not advocating a sectarian separation from the world, as 6:10 confirms; living by the Spirit entails the crucifixion of the flesh with its passions and desires (5:16, 24).

v. 15 is one of several very rich theological statements in the letter. It echoes 5:6, but caps the earlier verse with the claim that in Christ God is bringing about a new creation. The terse phrase, 'there is a new creation' is expounded in 2 Cor 5:17: the old order has passed away, everything has become new. In v. 16 Paul extends the blessing of God's peace and mercy upon those who follow this standard or rule, i.e. that there is a new creation in which the distinction between circumcised and uncircumcised is abolished.

The final phrase of v. 16 has evoked considerable discussion. Does Paul call down God's blessing upon a second group, 'the Israel of God', as well as upon those who follow the rule he has just enunciated? This interpretation is adopted by the NRSV: 'and upon the Israel of God'. Or does Paul refer boldly to Christian

believers as the Israel of God? If so, the 'and' is understood as explanatory: 'that is to say', or 'namely'. The latter interpretation is now widely accepted. If Paul does refer here to Christians as the Israel of God, what becomes of non-believing Israel? This issue does not surface in Galatians, though in due course Paul did grapple with it in Rom 9–11. In v. 17 Paul refers to the marks (*stigmata*) he bore on his body as a result of the hostility he experienced as an apostle of Christ (cf. 2 Cor 11:23–30). There may be an undercurrent of irony: it is 'the marks of Jesus' rather than the mark of circumcision which Paul bears proudly. Although the final verse is similar to the final benedictions found at the end of all Paul's letters, the reference to the grace of Christ is particularly poignant in view of the content of the letter as a whole; it echoes the opening reference in 1:6 to God's call 'in the grace of Christ'.

REFERENCES

Barclay, J. M. G. (1987), 'Mirror Reading a Polemical Letter: Galatians as a Test Case', *JSNT* 3: 73–93.

—— (1988), *Obeying the Truth: A Study of Paul's Ethics in Galatians* (Edinburgh: T. & T. Clark).

Barrett, C. K. (1982), *Essays on Paul* (London: SPCK).

Betz, H. D. (1979), *Galatians: A Commentary on Paul's Letter to the Churches in Galatia*, Hermeneia (Philadelphia: Fortress).

Dunn, J. D. G. (1993), *The Epistle to the Galatians*, BNTC (London: A. & C. Black).

Hengel, M., and Schwemer, A. M. (1997), *Paul Between Damascus and Antioch: the Unkown Years* (London: SCM).

Kern, P. H. (1998), *Rhetoric and Galatians*, SNTSMS 101 (Cambridge: Cambridge University Press).

Longenecker, R. N. (1990), *Galatians*, WBC 41 (Dallas: Word).

Martyn, J. L. (1997), *Galatians*, AB 33A (New York: Doubleday).

Meeks, W. (1983), *The First Urban Christians: the Social World of the Apostle Paul* (New Haven: Yale University Press).

O'Brien, P. T. (1977), *Introductory Thanksgivings in the Letters of Paul*, NovTSup 49 (Leiden: Brill).

Scott, J. M. (1992), *Adoption as Sons of God*, WUNT 2/48 (Tübingen: Mohr [Siebeck]).

8. Ephesians

J. D. G. DUNN

INTRODUCTION

The letter to the Ephesians is one of the most attractive documents in the NT and one to which many Christians turn when low in spirit. Its mood of elevated composure, sustained prayer, and uninhibited confidence in God (particularly chs. 1 and 3), and its vision of the church, united, growing to maturity and loved (chs. 2, 4, 5) have been uplifting and inspiring for countless individuals and communities over the centuries. This character and quality of the letter is unaffected by the disputes over its authorship and purpose.

A. Distinctive Features of Ephesians. 1. In comparison with the other Pauline letters, however, Ephesians is something of a puzzle. Unlike all the others, it is not directed to a particular church or situation or person. The words 'in Ephesus' (1:1), which most modern translations still include, are not present in the earliest and best MSS; and second-century references to the letter do not know it as sent to Ephesus (see Best 1987). The lack of specified addressees in the original text and absence of Paul's normal list of greetings are confirmed by the absence of reference to particular situations or problems known or reported to the author. This raises the question whether it was intended as a circular or catholic letter, rather like James and 1 Peter, though in these cases particular recipients are still specified.

2. The style of the letter (particularly chs. 1–3) is pleonastic, that is, marked by repetitions and redundancies. Note for example the long sentences which constitute 1:3–14 and 4:11–16 (single sentences in Greek), and the repetition and piling up of adjectives, phrases, and clauses such as we find in 1:17–19, 2:13–18, and 3:14–19. Anyone familiar with the other Pauline letters will recognize that Ephesians is exceptional on this point. If written at the same time as the other 'prison epistles' (including Philippians and Philemon), these differences become all the more striking. And if written by an unnamed amanuensis or secretary, the latter had far more scope for free composition than any of Paul's previous secretaries.

3. In some way most striking of all is the exceptionally close relationship between Ephesians and Colossians (see Mitton 1951: 279–315). Compare particularly:

Eph.	Col.	Eph.	Col.
1:15–17	1:3–4, 9–10	5:5–6	3:5–6
2:5	2:13	5:19–20	3:16
2:16	1:20–2	5:22, 25	3:18–19
4:2	3:12	6:5–9	3:22–4:1
4:16	2:19	6:21–2	4:7.
4:31–2	3:8, 12		

Such identical phraseology can be explained only if both letters were written at the same time, or, more likely (given the differences already noted), by one letter deliberately drawing upon the other. Most scholars have concluded that the character of the interdependence is best explained as Ephesians using Colossians, in part at least, as a model.

Given such features, it is hard to avoid the question: is Ephesians really a letter? Or is it better explained as a meditative and expansive summary of what Paul stood for, with his characteristic letter openings and closings added to preserve this homage to Paul appropriately in the most characteristic Pauline form?

B. Was the Letter Written by Paul? 1. The traditional view, from the second century onwards, is certainly in the affirmative. The writer names himself as Paul in both 1:1 and 3:1. But for the past 200 years the issue has been disputed, and though several prominent contemporary scholars still hold to Pauline authorship (e.g. Barth 1974 and Bruce 1984), the majority have concluded that it was most probably written by someone else. In addition to the considerations already noted, two other features have carried weight.

2. The perspective seems to be second generation: 'the apostles' are looked back to as the foundation period (2:20) and designated as especially 'holy' (3:5). The self-reference in 3:1–13 at first looks to be strong evidence of Pauline authorship, but as we read through the paragraph the measure of boasting goes well beyond what Paul had previously claimed for his own role, and sounds more and more like a eulogy penned by an ardent admirer (cf. 1 Tim 1:15–16). Even with 3:1 and 4:1, the addition of the definite article turns the humble self-designation of Philem 1 and 9 ('a prisoner of Christ Jesus') into something more like a title ('the prisoner of Christ Jesus', 'the prisoner in the Lord').

3. The theological perspective also seems to have moved beyond that of the earlier Paulines, and even that of Colossians. In particular, the cosmic Christology of Col 1:17–19 seems to have developed into the cosmic ecclesiology of Eph 1:22–3. The 'church', characteristically the local church (in house, city, or region) in the earlier Paulines, is now (for the first time) understood consistently as the universal church. The talk of grace and faith in 2:5, 8–9, certainly has a Pauline ring, but the characteristic Pauline concern regarding the law in such talk is missing: the reference in 2:9 is to 'works', not 'works of the law'; the law is mentioned only briefly in 2:15. And the eschatology is more consistently 'realized': 'salvation' is an accomplished act (2:5, 8; 6:17); they are already raised and seated with Christ 'in the heavenly places' (2:6); there is no reference to Christ's coming again (contrast 4:15).

4. All in all, the evidence is most consistent with the hypothesis that the letter was written by a disciple of Paul some time after Paul's death, presumably writing to celebrate Paul's faith and apostolic achievement and using Colossians in part as a kind of template. If, alternatively, it was Paul who composed it, we would have to envisage a Paul who had so modified his perspective and style that it comes to the same thing; that is, in effect, 'the late Paul' is little different from 'the disciple of Paul'.

C. The Issue of Pseudepigraphy. 1. Many feel uncomfortable with the view that the letter was not composed by Paul himself. Since the letter claims to be written by Paul, does the denial of Pauline authorship not amount to a questioning of the letter's integrity? And does an author who falsely claims to be someone else not forfeit our confidence in what he has written? The issue of pseudepigraphy (falsely attributed writing) seems to undermine any claim to inspiration or canonical authority for the letter.

2. The problem is serious for today's use of such a letter since it seems to attribute an immoral motive to the real author. We today take for granted the conventions of copyright and that plagiarism is unacceptable. When someone writes in another's name, therefore, we naturally assume an intention on his part to deceive, to claim falsely an authority for his writing which he himself did not possess. It needs to be remembered, however, that the conventions of copyright are a relatively recent formulation (a consequence of the invention of printing). At the time when Ephesians was written there was no clear or legal conception of authorial ownership of a piece of writing. Once written, a document was in the public domain and could be used and reused, excerpted and expanded without attribution of source and without any thought of wrongdoing. In the NT itself we may cite Matthew's use of Mark or 2 Peter's use of Jude.

3. More to the point, the history of the formation of the biblical books themselves is a clear indication that disciples and successors of the originator of highly valued tradition were able to develop that tradition in the name of its originator. Writings such as the Pentateuch and Isaiah are generally recognized to be the work of several hands over a lengthy period. The Wisdom of Solomon and the corpus known as 1 Enoch could be attributed to those named as authors long after their death, without any thought of deceit. The teaching of Jesus could be elaborated differently by the different Evangelists without any sense of impropriety.

4. Ephesians makes best sense within this tradition. A close associate or disciple of Paul, who stood within the tradition begun by Paul and was recognized to do so, was seen to represent the Pauline tradition after Paul's death and was able to re-express it in some measure in his own terms. And he did so in Paul's name, without deceit; his words were acknowledged to be appropriate sentiments to ascribe to Paul. In other words, Ephesians probably represents the Pauline heritage some little time after Paul's death as seen from within. It expresses, we may say, the transition from Paul to Pauline.

D. To Whom, From Where, When, and Why. 1. Were the letter written by Paul we could date it firmly to the early 60s, presumably from his imprisonment in Rome, and not long before his death. Would it then have been a general letter to his churches? If so, why should that purpose not be indicated? And if it was a final summation of his message we might have expected it to come more in the form of a final testament (cf. Acts 20:18–35).

2. In the light of the above conclusions, however, the more obvious answer is that Ephesians is a meditative tract on Paul's theology, teaching, and significance in the form of a Pauline letter; for unspecified use, but probably to be read in church gatherings for worship and teaching; and written some time after Paul's death, but by someone close to him, and so within ten or so years of his death (that is, some time in the 70s or 80s). The close link with Colossians, the mention of Tychicus in particular (6:21–2), and the fact that the churches of the province of Asia attracted other letters over the following decades (Rev 2–3; Ignatius) suggests that it was written in Asia, and in the event became most closely associated with Ephesus in particular.

3. More specific purposes have been suggested: for example, an early attempt to draw in Gnostic ideas, or to provide a covering letter for an early collection of Paul's letters. However, nothing in the letter itself gives any real support to such views. At best we can deduce that the churches addressed continued to be concerned about Christianity's identity as Israel's heir and about the proper integration of Jews and Gentiles within the church.

E. The Message of Ephesians in Summary. 1.

The great theme of the first three chapters is God: God whose purpose embraces all time and space and comes to focus in Christ. It is because the readers' faith and life is centred in this Christ ('in Christ' is a repeated theme) that they can have such confidence in God, based as it is both on God's resurrection of Christ from the dead and their own experience of his Holy Spirit and grace (ch. 1).

2. At the heart of God's universal purpose from eternity has been the retrieval of humanity from its state of death, the abolition of the divided state of humanity, and the bringing of all things to unity in Christ. Seen from a Jewish perspective, that deadness and dividedness had its principal manifestation in the disadvantaged state of Gentiles as contrasted with Jews. But Christ's death rendered that old division null and void and has made possible a reconciled and united community held together by Christ, which as a whole enjoys the privileges previously confined to Israel and so can function as the household of God, the place where God continues to meet with humankind (ch. 2). This reconciliation of Jew and Gentile within the gracious purpose of God was at the heart of the divine mystery which Paul in particular had been given the commission to unveil to all (ch. 3). The fact that the church is so much the medium now for the outworking of this purpose of God makes its unity and its proper working as facilitated by the ministry gifts given it all the more important. Only as it functions as the body of Christ and grows up into Christ can it fulfil the universal and cosmic role earlier ascribed to it (4:1–16).

3. Right functioning of the church also depends on believers living as the church in the world and walking in the light, with all the specific moral commitment, both positive and negative, implied. Conduct and relationships modelled on those of Christ are also part of the restoration of creation to serve its original purpose. The enabling of the Spirit in shared worship remains indispensable (4:17–5:20).

4. Particularly important, as the basic unit of society, are households and their several relationships; here too Christian households should have Christ as model and resource and thus provide a test bed for society in re-creation. At no time should they forget that they were involved in a spiritual warfare nor fail to maintain the appropriate equipment and co-operation (chs. 5:21–6:20).

F. The structure of Ephesians.

Greeting (1:1–2)
The Great Prayer and Meditation (1:3–3:21)
  The Blessing of God (1:3–14)
  Paul's Prayer (1:15–23)
  A Reminder of What God Has Already Done in Them (2:1–10)
  The New Humanity (2:11–22)
  Paul's Stewardship of the Great Mystery (3:1–13)
  The Opening Prayer Resumed (3:14–21)
The Exhortation (4:1–6:20)
  The Church in its Calling and Confession (4:1–6)
  The Character and Purpose of Ministry in the Body of Christ (4:7–16)
  How to Live as the Church in the World (4:17–32)
  Walking in the Light (5:1–20)
  Household Rules (5:21–6:9)
  Put on the Armour of God (6:10–20)
Conclusion and Benediction (6:21–4)

COMMENTARY

(1:1–2) Greeting It is typical of Paul that he adapts the normal letter address, 'X to Y, greeting' (Gk.) or 'peace' (Jewish). He emphasizes his apostleship (cf. 2 Cor 1:1; Col 1:1). He stresses the status of the recipients: they have been set apart for God ('saints') (cf. e.g. Rom 1:1; 1 Cor 1:1) and live by trust in God ('faithful') (as in Col 1:2). He transforms the Greek greeting (*chairein*) into the rich Christian term 'grace' (*charis*), and combines it with the equally rich Jewish concept of peace, wishing them the continued experience of God's generous favour ('grace') and all that makes for communal well-being ('peace'). On 'in Ephesus' see EPH. A.1.

The Great Prayer and Meditation (1:3–3:21)

(1:3–14) The Blessing of God This is one of the most beautiful passages in the Bible. It is unlike anything else in the Pauline letters (the nearest parallel is 2 Cor 1:3–11). In the Greek it can be punctuated as a single sentence. The repetition of key words, the piling up of phrases, and the circling round and steady enrichment of the central theme gives it a depth and resonance unsurpassed in Christian praise. It is a word to return to, to rest upon, to rejoice in, and not least, to enjoy. It should have been put to great music long before now.

It begins by sketching in the circle of blessing (v. 3). That circle starts with God. The word for 'blessed' (*eulogētos*) here is used only of God in the NT (e.g. Mk 14:61; Rom 1:25); it indicates that nothing more wonderful can be imagined or spoken of than God. Characteristic of this blessedness is that it reaches out to embrace God's human creatures ('with every spiritual blessing'). The circle is complete when those thus blessed affirm its source and resource in God.

This blessing is four-dimensional. It reaches from the beginning of time: chosen 'before the foundation of the world' (v. 4); predestined in love (v. 5; cf. Rom 8:29–30); the divine mystery (v. 9), that is, God's original but hidden purpose, now revealed (see 3:3–6); predestined and appointed (v. 11). And it reaches to the end of time: a plan for the fullness of time (God's appointed hour) to sum up everything in Christ (v. 10; see 1:20–3); the Spirit as the guarantee of the inheritance and the final redemption of God's own possession (v. 14). Here again the stress is on God's overarching purpose in control from the first—his good pleasure and will (vv. 5, 9), 'according to [his] purpose ... according to his counsel and will' (v. 11).

Spatial imagery is also prominent. The blessings in which believers already share are those 'in the heavenly places' (v. 3), where the symbolism of higher (heavens above earth) denotes greater bliss in a way more problematic for modern readers (see also 6:12). The final union will embrace everything in the heavens and in the earth (v. 10). Most striking of all, however, is the repeated emphasis on the location and means of this blessing as 'in him (Christ)', a phrase which occurs no less than ten times (also 'through Jesus Christ'—v. 5).

The conviction is clear: that the whole of God's purpose from the beginning focuses in and through Christ (vv. 4, 9, 11–12); that Jesus and his death were the means by which per-

sonal liberation (redemption) and the forgiveness for wrongs done had been genuinely experienced (v. 7); that Jesus himself is the 'place' in which the blessings of heaven and the Spirit are to be known in the here and now, so that the very term 'Christian' denotes a life (and death) bound up with his (vv. 3, 5, 13–14); and, not least, that Christ in a real sense constitutes the hope for the world and final reconciliation, its climax and summation point (vv. 9–10).

The blessings themselves are indicated in a series of evocative phrases: 'holy and blameless before him in love' (v. 4); adoption as God's children (cf. Gal 4:5–7), formerly estranged (v. 5); 'redemption', the image of the costly liberation of slave or captive (cf. Rom 3:24; 1 Cor 6:19–20), and the experience of forgiveness for conscience-nagging wrongs committed (v. 7; cf. Col 1:14); knowledge and sense of personal involvement in God's purpose (v. 9); an awareness of being chosen by God (v. 11); a conviction as to the truth of the gospel and of the 'salvation' (wholeness) it brings (v. 13; cf. 1 Thess 1:5); and the experience of being marked out by the Spirit as belonging to God (the function of a 'seal')—the reference will be to the impact made by the Spirit (as e.g. in Rom 5:5; 1 Cor 6:9–11), rather than to baptism—and of the assurance the Spirit brings (cf. Rom 8:14–16), as being the first instalment and guarantee of the complete redemption/liberation still to come (vv. 13–14; cf. Rom 8:23; 2 Cor 1:21–2).

But the blessing is primarily directed to God. He is the subject of the main active verbs ('blessed, chose, destined ...'). His love embraces the trustful in the sonship of the Beloved (vv. 4–6; cf. Rom 8:15–17, 29). It is his grace (the same word as in v. 2), the same outpouring of divine generosity which is the fountainhead of all human wellbeing ('his grace with which he has engraced us ... in accordance with the riches of his grace which he has lavished upon us', vv. 6–8, my tr.). He 'accomplishes all things according to his counsel and will' (v. 11). And all is 'to the praise of his glory' (vv. 6, 12, 14)—human bliss from beginning to end dependent on human recognition that God is the be-all and end-all.

It is important to note how characteristically Jewish is the language and thought. To begin a prayer to God with the evocation of his blessedness is distinctively Jewish (e.g. Ps 41:13; 72:18–19; the great Jewish prayer, the Eighteen Benedictions, 'Blessed are you, O Lord ... ', go back to Jesus' time). God's unconditional choice (v. 4) was fundamental to Israel's self-understanding (e.g. Deut 7:6–8). 'The Beloved' (v. 6) was a favourite name for Israel (e.g. Deut 33:12; Isa 5:1). The time perspective of the benediction is distinctive of Jewish apocalypses—the assurance that God's mysterious purpose is working towards its climax despite all human failure and catastrophe (vv. 9–10; cf. e.g. Dan 2:21; Mk 1:15); the Qumran community shared a similar conviction that the hidden mysteries had been revealed to them (EPH 3:1–13). And not least, there is the writer's sense that he and his readers (Gentiles included) had been embraced within the divine purpose which began with and worked through Israel: the purpose was that they should be numbered with the 'saints', the ones set apart to God (a title for Israel—e.g. Ps 16:3; 34:9), and without blemish, like Israel's sacrifices (v. 4; cf. e.g. Lev 1:3, 10; Ps 15:2); they had been appointed (lit. given a share) in Israel's 'inheritance' (vv. 11, 14), two words which would have evoked for any Jewish reader thought of the land, seed, and blessing promised to Abraham (cf. Gen 12:2–3; Deut 32:9; Jer 10:16); they were God's 'possession' (cf. Ex 19:5; Deut 14:2).

The difference is indicated, however, in the repeated 'in him'. This is the amazing feature of the benediction—the confidence and conviction that Jesus has been and is the key to unlock the mystery of God's purpose and to bring it into effect, for Gentile as well as Jew. Christianity today, long heir of elaborate creeds and dogmas regarding Christ, can scarcely appreciate what astounding claims were being made—that one who had lived only a generation or so earlier could thus unfold and embody the wonder of God's grace. So we find it equally hard to appreciate the impact which Jesus and then the message about Jesus must have made upon such hearers in the ancient Mediterranean world. It was a conviction which was not merely intellectual: the believing was matched by an experience of forgiveness, of being engraced, and of the Spirit beginning the process of reclamation of human life and community for God (vv. 7–8, 13–14). But evidently the gospel thus focused on Jesus made such sense of reality, of the whole complex of time and space, of cosmos and history, that he could be thus seen at the centre of both cosmos and history, as the one who explained the all, and always 'to the praise of God's glory'.

(1:15–23) Paul's Prayer It was conventional in ancient letters to add a thanksgiving and prayer on behalf of those to whom the letter was sent

(in Paul cf. particularly Rom 1:8–15; 1 Cor 1:4–9; Col 1:3–8). The opening words here (vv. 15–16) are typical of Paul and may indeed be modelled on Philem 4–5 and Col 1:3–4. The thanksgiving had in view particularly the two-sidedness of the readers' new relationships—faith in the Lord Jesus and love for all the saints (the 'all' might need some emphasis). Characteristic of Paul too was the habit of regular 'mention' of his converts in his prayers (Rom 1:9; Phil 1:3; 1 Thess 1:2).

But the prayer which follows surpasses anything else in Paul's letters, as rich as the preceding blessing and stretching the expectation of hope and the imagination of faith still further.

It is directed to God (not to Christ). He indeed is described as 'the God of our Lord Jesus Christ' (v. 17), with the recognition that Jesus, even in the fullness of his exalted Lordship, still acknowledges God as his God (cf. 1 Cor 15:24–8). This Christian faith, including the mind-blowing Christology of 1:22–3, is still monotheistic through and through. It is God who has done all the great work of salvation in Christ (vv. 19–23) and in whom hope is focused (vv. 17–18). He is 'the Father of glory' (v. 17; cf. Acts 7:2; Rom 6:4); the phrase should not be reduced to 'glorious Father' but should be allowed to resonate with all the overtones of God as the progenitor of all that is glorious and splendid (including v. 18). The richness of this divine resource is a repeated theme (vv. 7, 18–19; 2:4, 7; 3:8, 16).

The intercession falls into two parts. First for knowledge (vv. 17–19), knowledge being fundamental to well-being. The very diversity of the language (wisdom, revelation, knowledge, illumination) is a reminder that there are different kinds of knowledge. Here most in view is the knowledge which comes through an experience of revelation, of eyes being opened, and through the experience of personal relationship with God ('the eyes of your heart enlightened' is a wonderfully evocative phrase). When knowledge is reduced to knowledge of facts or of information which can be humanly discovered it will always be deficient for living (cf. Col. 1:9–11). Only in its richer form, dependent on inspiration from on high, does knowledge become wisdom (the echo of Isa 11:2 will be deliberate).

Here, however, the thought is directed more to the future: 'the hope to which he [God] has called you' (v. 18), a 'calling' (both invitation and summons) elaborated in the talk of the rich inheritance to be shared with the saints (see v. 14). When hope is based on such knowledge it can indeed be firm and confident. As in Col

1:4–5, so here, hope is not far from faith and love (cf. 1 Cor 13:13).

The second part (vv. 20–3) reflects further on the working of this great might of God: hope can be confident (v. 18) because the power at work in human experience (v. 19) is the same power which raised up Christ from the dead and exalted him as God's 'right-hand man'. The language was already credal (e.g. Acts 3:15; 13:30; Rom 10:9; 1 Thess 1:10) and the use of Ps 110:1 as a way of understanding what had happened to the risen Christ was well-established (e.g. Acts 2:34–5; Rom 8:34; 1 Pet 3:22). But it is here elaborated in an exceptional way.

The thought that Christ was thus set 'in the heavenly places' is peculiar to Ephesians (1:3, 20; 2:6). But the further thought that he was already dominant over all powers, both present and future, takes up Ps 110:1 combined with Ps 8:6 (1:20–2; a combination we find also in 1 Cor 15:25–7 and Heb 1:12–2:8). The combination is powerful since it links the idea of Jesus as the man/son of man who fulfils God's purpose for humanity as the climax of creation (Ps 8:4–6; cf. Heb 2:6–9) with that of Jesus as David's greater son given a share in God's sovereign rule (Ps 110:1; cf. Mk 12:35–7). The conviction obviously carried with it a psychological liberation from fear of the nameless forces which shape human existence (see 2:2 and 6:10–20). What a one was this Jesus that the note struck by his life, death, and resurrection should have had such continuing resonance and deepening reverberations in the subsequent decades.

If that was a challenging enough linkage, the final clauses (vv. 22–3) almost baffle comprehension (the major commentaries spend several pages discussing them). The climax of what God did 'in Christ' (v. 20) was to give him as 'head over all things for the church, which is his body' (vv. 22–3). The metaphor of the church as Christ's body goes back to 1 Cor 12 and Rom 12:4–8, and will later be elaborated with the idea of Christ as the head of the body (4:15–16). But here the thought is of Christ as head of all reality, given by God to or for the church (cf. Col 1:17–18). That would be a difficult enough thought, though 'head' can mean both 'ruler' and 'source' (fountainhead), and so Christ could be portrayed as embodying or epitomizing the rationale and pattern of divine creation. 'Given to/for the church' could then mean simply(!) that the church, here the universal church, had, through its faith in Christ and the God who worked through Christ, been given the key to understanding reality and

enabled to rise above all that threatened human and social life.

The chief problem is the final clause, what it means and how it relates to what has gone before—'the fullness of him who fills all in all'. Does it refer to Christ or to the church? Does it draw on ideas familiar from later Gnostic texts—Christ as a kind of cosmic being which comprises the totality of sentient reality? The answer is probably that the writer has been carried away by his language and imagery and is playing on the familiar Jewish thought of God or God's Spirit as filling the cosmos (Jer 23:24; Wis 1:7; cf. Ps 139:7). Christ now embodies that fullness (cf. Col 1:19; 2:9). And the church, his body, is (or should be!) the place where God's presence in and purpose for creation comes to its clearest expression. Would that it were so!

(2:1–10) A Reminder of What God Has Already Done in Them This is one of the most forceful statements in the Bible regarding the human condition apart from God's grace and the way in which that grace operates for salvation.

The human condition apart from grace is described in vv. 1–3 in a series of vivid clauses; note the balance between a certain givenness of human character, social conditioning, and individual responsibility. (1) They had been 'dead through trespasses and sins' (vv. 1, 5; cf. Col 2:13). 'Death' is but one metaphor among many; others include 'weak' and 'enemies' (Rom 5:6, 10; cf. EPH 2:14–16). And the experience of grace (in conversion) can itself be likened to a dying (Rom 6:5–11). But a life enmeshed in its breaches of the moral code (transgressions) and repeated failings (sins) can well be likened to a state of death, where promptings of divine grace and love evoke no real response (cf. Luke 15:24; Rom 7:7–11—'I died'). (2) Their daily conduct had been determined by the standards of society (cf. Rom 12:2), the spirit of the age (v. 2). The latter metaphor is unique in the NT ('the ruler of the power of the air'; cf. Jn 12:31 and Acts 26:18), and draws on the common understanding of the day that hostile spiritual forces influenced or determined human behaviour (hence 6:11–17). We still today speak, for example, of a criminal 'underworld' and often enough feel ourselves victims of forces, some apparently malevolent in character, that we cannot control. (3) Human responsibility becomes more evident in the talk of a life conducted 'in the passions of our flesh, following the desires of flesh and senses' (v. 3; cf. Col 3:5, 7;

Titus 3:3; 1 Pet 1:14). By 'flesh' Paul means the weakness of the physical constitution (flesh decays); life lived at that level, devoted to feeding human appetites (food, sex, power), is a life lived apart from God, subject to the law of diminishing returns and the law of increasing subserviency to self-indulgent habit (cf. Gal 5:16–21). According to Rom 1:18–32, this circle of sin-begetting-sin is also an expression of divine wrath just as is the final judgement (Rom 2:5; cf. Col 3:6). To be noted is the fact that the writer no longer speaks of 'you', as in 2:2; Christian Jews as well as Christian Gentiles are 'by nature children of wrath' (v. 3, 'all of us'; v. 5, 'we'), all equally dependent on the initiative of divine grace (cf. 2:10).

Still more, however, is said about the way in which grace had worked to change both character and context. Again, it should be noted, as throughout ch. 1, the initiative is God's from start to finish: 'But God…' (v. 4). It is his mercy, love—'rich in mercy [cf. Rom 11:30–2], out of the great love with which he loved us' (cf. Rom 5:8)—and thrice-mentioned grace (vv. 5, 7, 8) which has been decisive. And the effective medium of God's action has been Christ—'with Christ' (v. 5), 'in Christ Jesus' (vv. 6, 7, 10). The three elements in the preceding analysis are in effect taken up one by one, in each case emphasizing the role of grace and of Christ.

(1) The state of deadness in trespasses and sins has been transformed—'made alive with Christ' (v. 5). This is the language of resurrection (Jn 5:21; 8:11; 1 Cor 15:22); the final proof of God's creative power is that he overcomes death (Rom 4:17). The idea of conversion as being bound up with Christ's death, so that Christ through his death becomes as it were a passageway to new life, is prominent elsewhere in the NT (e.g. Gal 2:19–20; 1 Tim 2:11; Heb 2:9–11). In the earlier Pauline letters the thought of sharing also in Christ's resurrection is reserved for the 'not yet' future (Rom 6:5; 8:11), but here, as in Col 2:13, that too is referred to the 'already' of conversion. It is a logical development to describe the new life experienced through the Spirit (Jn 6:63; 2 Cor 3:6) as a sharing in Christ's life, that is, his risen life. Whatever the finer points of theology, however, conversion was evidently experienced in the early days of Christianity as life-giving, life-changing.

(2) Countering the captivity to 'the ruler of the power of the air', God had not only raised them with Christ to new life, but also raised them with Christ to the heavenly places (v. 6; see 1:3). The astonishing claim was necessary,

perhaps, to break the previous psychological dependency. Implicit, then, is the conviction that their lives now focused in and through Christ had in effect risen above the old captivating influences of the present world (cf. Gal 6:14; Col 2:15), or at least need have no fear of any such power (Rom 8:31–9). But more explicit here is the thought that they (writer and readers) were as it were trophies of grace to make clear to everyone the overwhelming generosity of God's purpose and its most effective implementation in and through Christ (v. 7).

(3) The answer to lives dominated by human weakness and self-indulgence is the recognition that salvation is given by grace, through faith, the very opposite of human contriving or manipulation—as a gift of God (v. 8). The language is very Pauline, but the thought has shifted somewhat from the earlier letters. (a) Salvation is here spoken of as a completed act, whereas earlier on Paul spoke of it as future (Rom 5:9–10; 13:11; 1 Cor 3:15), and of Christians as those 'being saved' (1 Cor 1:18; 2 Cor 2:15). There salvation covered the whole process of renewal and final redemption (Rom 8:23); here the thought is of the decisive character of what Christ has done and of the commitment to him and bound-up-ness with him. (b) Earlier too the talk of 'works' was always of 'the works of the law', that which was obligatory upon Jews as members of the covenant people—the key question being whether and how much of these laws were obligatory for Gentile believers. To which Paul had replied that only faith was necessary (Rom 3:19–20, 27–31; 9:30–2; Gal 2:15–16). Here the thought is broadened, or deepened. By 'works' the author here seems to mean any product of human effort: salvation is wholly and solely a 'gift' (v. 8). There is no scope for boasting in oneself, only in God (v. 9); the 'turned-in-upon-oneself-ness' of the old life (v. 3) has been given a new focus and orientation. The outcome is a complete contrast to the old way of life—God's handiwork, a new creation on the template of Christ, 'good works' such as God had made humankind for in the beginning (v. 10; cf. 4:24; 1 Cor 3:10–15). There should be a contrast, should there not, between a life lived by grace, through faith, in Christ (v. 10), and a life determined by the desires of flesh and mind (v. 3)?

(2:11–22) The New Humanity The same ground is covered again in a second review of the readers' transition from past to present (cf. 5:8). This time, however, the review is not from the more general perspective (death to life) but from the Jewish perspective on Gentile disquali-fication from grace. The assumption is that God's saving purpose for humankind had been worked out through Israel, that Gentiles had hitherto been strangers to that promise, but that now through Christ the blessing of access to God and peace with God was open to all. The resulting new reality (the 'new humanity', v. 15) is sometimes understood as a third race (Chris-tians) replacing the old division of the world into Jews and Gentiles (Lincoln 1990: 144). How-ever, it would be more in tune with the para-graph to speak of the new humanity rather as the Israel which no longer defined itself by separation from the other nations but which is redefined to embrace all who believe in (Israel's) God through Christ (cf. Rom 2:28–9; 4:11–12; Gal 3:28–9; Phil 3:3). Either way, fundamental is the thought of Christianity as continuous with Israel of old and of being given to share in Israel's blessings, and that this has only been possible in and through Christ—'he is our peace' (v. 14). That this new humanity also fulfils God's purpose in creating humankind in the first place will be indicated in 4:24.

vv. 11–12 recall the former disqualification. Characteristic of Jewish self-understanding was the conviction that circumcision was a positive identity marker 'in the flesh' which set them apart definitively from other nations as God's elect nation (Gen 17:9–14). So much so that the world could be divided from a Jewish perspec-tive into 'the uncircumcision' and 'the circum-cision'—the whole range of differences focused in this one feature (as in Gal 2:7–9). Only Jews regarded lack of circumcision as something negative; in contrast, the typical Greek regarded circumcision as a form of mutilation. The added note that circumcision was 'made . . . by human hands' is an indication that the writer saw this evaluation of 'circumcision . . . in the flesh' as a boundary separating Gentiles from God's grace to be mistaken.

v. 12 lists the blessings from which Gentiles had hitherto been disqualified in ascending order of importance. Israel was not only a na-tion-state but a religious entity (a matter of continuing confusion from that day to this). 'The covenants of promise' (as in Rom 9:4) either refer to the regularly renewed covenant with the patriarchs (starting with Gen 12:3) or include such key promises as 2 Sam 7:12–14. The worst state to be in is 'having no hope [cf. 1 Thess 4:13] and without God in the world'.

'But now in Christ Jesus' (v. 13) those disquali-fications have been removed from the nations (Gentiles). This is the subject of vv. 13–18, a nicely structured passage (chiasmus) where the repeated references to 'far off/near' and 'peace' (vv. 13–14, 17; echoing Isa 57:19; see also 6:15) bracket the central imagery of hostility recon-ciled 'in him' (vv. 14–16; see Schnackenburg 1991: 106). The key to understanding the passage is the recognition that the writer sees two hos-tilities/antagonisms as interrelated. He assumes the Jewish view (cf. 4:17–18) that Gentiles, by definition cut off from the grace given through Israel's God-given covenant(s), are distant from God (cf. Isa 49:1; 66:18–19; Acts 2:39) and in need of reconciliation with God (cf. Rom 5:10; Col 1:21). But that enmity had become entangled and confused with enmity between Jew and Gentile. Both were expressed in 'the dividing wall' (v. 14), possibly an allusion to the barrier which marked off 'the court of the Gentiles' from 'the court of Israel' in the Jerusalem tem-ple, and which Gentiles could not breach except on pain of death—symbolizing Gentile exclu-sion from the presence of God. But the main barrier was formed by the law, with particular reference to the rules (especially purity and food rules) which reinforced the separation of Jew from Gentile (v. 15; cf. Acts 10:9–16, 28, 34–5; Gal 2:11–16; Col 2:16, 21).

Consequently, for easily understandable psy-chological and social, as well as religious reasons, at the heart of Paul's gospel (himself a Jew) was the claim that God in Christ had re-solved both antagonisms, and that the one could not be reconciled in isolation from the other. The two being made one was integral to peace with God (vv. 14–15); reconciliation of either was possible only as reconciliation of both (v. 16). The theology of the cross at this point is an elaboration of the earlier 2 Cor 5:17–21 (cf. Col 1:22; 2:14). But it contains overtones of a self-sacrifice acknowledged by both sides as ending an ancient blood feud, and echoes of the sacrifice which bonded the parties to the cov-enant in Gen 15:7–21. The difference is that the one thus sacrificed continues to serve as and to maintain the bond thus created 'in him' (vv. 13, 17). The final imagery of v. 18 is of the reconciled peoples now able together to pass through the barrier which had previously divided them and together to celebrate their reconciliation in joint worship made possible by their common participation in the one Spirit (4:3–4; cf. again Phil 3:3); 3:12 says the same thing in comple-mentary terms.

The outcome is not a new national or inter-national entity, but individuals of all nations now sharing in privileges previously thought to be limited to Israel as a nation (v. 19; 3:6)— 'fellowcitizens with the saints [see 1:4; cf. Phil 3:20; Heb 12:22–3] and members of the household of God' (RSV; cf. Gal 6:10; 1 Tim 3:15; Heb 3:5–6). Those who enjoyed security both of citizenship and family/household membership would have been in a minority in many ancient cities.

The imagery of the last three verses (20–2) changes to that of a building, in particular a temple. The image was a natural one (cf. e.g. Mt 7:24–7; 1 Cor 3:9–11, 16; 1 Pet 2:5). There are three significant features here. First, the mention of 'the apostles and prophets' as the foundation (v. 20; contrast 1 Cor 3:11); given the order, the 'prophets' are probably Christian prophets (cf. 3:5; 4:11; 1 Cor 12:28). The implication seems to be that a foundation period is being looked back to (cf. Rev 21:14). Second, Christ is the cornerstone; that is, either the keystone or capstone, given that the role of foundation has already been filled (Lincoln 1990: 155–6); or the cornerstone, the first stone laid in the foundation, in relation to which all other parts of the foundation were aligned (Schnackenburg 1991: 124). The metaphor was drawn from Isa 28:16 (understood as foundation) and in early Christian apologetic was often combined with Ps 118:22 (Mt 21:42; Rom 9:33; 10:11; 1 Pet 2:4, 6–8). Third, bringing the paragraph (vv. 11–22) to a climax is the emphasis on the harmonious interrelatedness of the whole structure (see also 4:16). To be noted is the fact that it is conceived as a growing (not a static) unity, a growth dependent on harmonious working together (v. 21), an ongoing process (the tenses are all present continuous) which can only happen and be maintained 'in the Lord'.

The end result (3:22) will be a people—no longer defined in national or ethnic terms— which functions as 'a dwelling place for God'. This is the hope which always lies behind the sacramental focus of God's presence in human-built temple or earthly grown bread and wine—a people as the mode of God's presence and action in the world (cf. Ex 19:5–6; Lev 26:11–12; Ezek 37:27; 1 Pet 2:5)—but which so often falls out of focus (cf. e.g. Isa 1:10–17; Acts 7:48–9; 1 Cor 10–11). The triadic formulation—for God, in the Spirit, interlocked through Christ and growing together in Christ—reflects the theological logic which led inexorably to the subsequent Trinitarian understanding of God (cf. 1:3–14).

(3:1–13) Paul's Stewardship of the Great Mystery A personal statement in self-defence is quite a common feature in Paul's letters— earlier over his apostleship (Gal 1:1–2:10; 1 Cor 15:8–11), or missionary practice (1 Cor 9; 2 Cor 10–12), or regarding his travel plans (e.g. Rom 1:9–15). Initially ch. 3 looks like a further example and provides one of the strongest supports for the view that the letter was written by Paul himself. But as the paragraph unfolds, the claims made move well beyond anything Paul ever claimed for himself earlier—a sustained measure of boasting in spiritual insight and commission with which the earlier Paul would probably have been uncomfortable (contrast e.g. Rom 11:13, 25; 16:25–6; 1 Cor 7:40; 14:37–8; 2 Cor 10:13–18; 12:1–13). It may thus ease the problem and make for a more consistent picture of Paul to conclude that these are the words of a close, ardent disciple of Paul rather than of Paul himself.

The opening self-identification as 'the prisoner of Christ' (v. 1; also 4:1; but note the definite article) is paralleled only in Philem 1 and 9 (cf. also Phil 1:7); it thus reflects the mood of the prison epistles, Paul's imprisonment providing both opportunity to survey his previous ministry and affording fresh opportunity for witness (cf. Phil 1:13–17; Philem 10, 13). Characteristic of Paul is his conviction that his calling was 'for the sake of the Gentiles' (v. 1; Gal 1:16; Rom 11:13) and that he had been given a special engracement for the work (vv. 2, 7, 8; cf. Rom 1:5; 15:15–16; 1 Cor 9:17; 15:10; Gal 2:7–9; Col 1:29). At the end of the paragraph too (v. 13) there is an awkwardly compressed twin Pauline theme that present sufferings foreshadow future glory (Rom 5:2–5; 8:17–21; 2 Cor 4:16–17) and that Paul's sufferings work to his converts' benefit (2 Cor 1:6; 4:7–12; Gal 4:19; Col 1:24; 2 Tim 2:10).

But the main burden of the self-testimony here is the revelation made known to Paul regarding 'the mystery' and Paul's understanding of it (vv. 3–4), to which he had previously briefly alluded (1:9–10). It had also been revealed to 'his holy apostles and prophets' (v. 5; see 2:20). But the emphasis quickly reverts to the fact that it was Paul who, first and foremost, and despite being 'the very least of all the saints' (cf. 1 Cor 15:9; on 'saints' see EPH 1:2), had been given the commission (3:7–8) to unveil this mystery (3:9–11).

'Mystery' is a term which echoes the language and perspective of Jewish apocalypses (already in Dan 2:18–19, 27–30; see e.g. Caragounis 1977). Typically the thought is of the divine purpose: it had been firm from the beginning (v. 11), but had been hidden through the generations (vv. 5, 9; Rom 16:25; Col 1:26), only to be revealed now at the appointed time, at the climax of the ages (cf. 1 Cor 10:11; Gal 4:4). Jewish apocalypses and the Qumran community make similar claims regarding their own insights.

The Christian insight, particularly of Paul, however, is quite distinctive. The mystery as now unfolded was different from the mysteries perceived by their fellow Jews. It was to the effect that God's purpose from the beginning had been to give the Gentiles a share in the same inheritance, the same body, the same promise (as Israel) 'in Christ Jesus' and 'through the gospel' (v. 6). To make known this now revealed mystery to the Gentiles and to everyone (but 'everyone' might not be part of the original text) was Paul's special commission (vv. 8–9).

The thought is certainly consistent with Paul's earlier references to the divine mystery—particularly Paul's first unveiling of the mystery to resolve the excruciating problem of Israel's rejection of the gospel (Rom 11:25–32). That the mystery focuses on the Jew/Gentile issue and involves the removal of the theological significance of that distinction is less to the fore in Col 1:27, but is clearly central here in Ephesians (cf. 2:11–22). The language and imagery underline how crucial the issue was at the beginning of Christianity: the gospel as an invitation to all to share in the special relationship with God which both the Jewish and the Christian Bible assumes to have been Israel's special and distinctive prerogative, but only (Christians add) prior to the coming of Messiah Jesus (cf. Gal 3:29). If a text like this still speaks, then a sense of continuity with Israel, but transposed into a different key, remains fundamental for Christian self-understanding.

As in Col 1:27, 2:2, and 4:3, the mystery is embodied, unveiled, and implemented in Christ (vv. 4, 8–9, 11; cf. 5:32; 6:19). Inevitably and unavoidably Christ is the key to and reason for the distinctiveness of the Christian mystery (cf. 1 Cor 1:24—Christ 'the wisdom of God'). Presumably it was the impact Jesus made in his ministry (in regard to sinners discounted by 'the righteous'), and, in Paul's case particularly the impact of Christ's post-crucifixion encounter with Paul (the two cannot have been at odds otherwise Christianity would have fallen apart), which caused the first believers to see that God's grace was for all equally and without reference to national, racial, or social identity (cf. Gal

2:5–16; 3:28). As Paul saw so clearly, it followed, as day follows night, that a gospel which failed to preach that message was no gospel and a church which failed to live that message was no church. The Christ in whom such differences are not wholly discounted is not the Christ of God's mystery.

As at the end of ch. 1, the cosmic dimensions of the divine purpose are not overlooked. It is the plan of the Creator which is in view (v. 9); there is no divorce between creation and salvation here (cf. Col 1:20). The audience in view in this unfolding of divine wisdom is not just every person but every power that can be envisaged or feared (v. 10; see 1:21). And as in 1:22–3, the church is the medium through which and stage on which this richly diverse wisdom of God is enacted (v. 10; cf. 3:21). At the very least that should mean that the church is (or should be) the prototype and test bed for reconciliation between peoples and between humankind and the creation of which it is part.

The thought unwinds with a reminder of the supreme gift which Christ has brought: that 'in him' there can be a boldness and confidence of access to God (v. 12; cf. 2:18; Heb 4:16; 7:25; 1 Pet 3:18), a boldness and confidence made possible precisely because of the insight embodied in the gospel regarding God's 'unsearchable riches' and 'many-sided wisdom' (my tr.), concerning the character of creation and his purpose for all humankind. In Christ it is given to know the character of God as nowhere else so clearly, and through the trust which Christ inspires, or 'through faith in him' (cf. 3:17), humankind in its rich diversity can draw near to this God with boldness (cf. Rom 8:15–16).

(3:14–21) The Opening Prayer Resumed In effect everything from 1:3 to 3:21 is an extended prayer. The section 2:1–3:13 is as it were a meditative break within the prayer proper—on the effect of conversion (2:1–10), on the reconciliation of former hostility between Jew and Gentile (2:11–22), and on the divine mystery committed to Paul (3:1–13). The meditation has been of such a lofty character, rising repeatedly to praise for the wonder of God's purpose now enacted in Christ, that the spirit of prayer has scarcely been diminished. But now the meditation passes back to prayer proper and the prayer at the end of such a profound meditation is drawn to a fitting conclusion.

As throughout the preceding chapters, the object of the prayer and devotion is God alone. To kneel is the appropriate acknowledgement of humble submission before and dependence on such an overwhelming majesty (v. 14; cf. Rom 14:11; Phil 2:10–11). At the same time, it is God experienced and approached as Father (v. 14) which is the distinctive Christian feature (Lk 11:2; Rom 8:15–16; Gal 4:6–7). And it is no inconsistency for Christians to recognize that this same God is the source of every family and nation's identity (v. 15)—the name indicating the character of the named (cf. Ps 147:4).

The petition echoes the earlier prayer in 1:17–19. But it falls more clearly into two parts. The first (3:16–17) is a prayer for the addressees' spiritual condition. The source is again the riches of God's glory: 'glory' here is almost synonymous with 'grace' as in 1:7; God's grace is his glory. The concern is that they should be strengthened in their innermost being (cf. Rom 7:22; 2 Cor 4:16; 1 Pet 3:4); sustained firmness of conviction, commitment, and motivation will be in view (cf. Col 1:11). The means is God's Spirit, as the powerful presence of God at work within the depths of human discipleship and within the human situation.

It may seem surprising that the prayer (v. 17) is for Christ to dwell in their hearts (the tense denotes 'come to dwell' rather than 'continue to dwell'). Had Christ not already come to dwell in the hearts of believers, at their conversion (cf. Rom 8:10; Gal 2:20; Col 1:27)? But believers do often pray for something (e.g. the presence of God's Spirit in their worship) which they believe or hope to be already the case. Such a prayer is a natural expression of concerned piety. Here it reminds us that we should not transform such language (Christ indwelling the heart) into formal definitions or dogmas which can then be used to classify 'genuine' conversion or faith. Or else we should say that the prayer is for believers to be converted afresh every day. The 'faith' here refers back to the faith mentioned in 3:12. To be noted also is the overlap between the Spirit and Christ (vv. 16–17): being strengthened through the Spirit and Christ indwelling are not clearly distinct experiences (cf. Rom 8:9–11; 1 Cor 6:17; 12:4–6).

It is equally important to recognize that this spiritual strengthening and indwelling is 'rooted and founded in love' (v. 17, my tr.; note the echo of Col 2:7). The double metaphor (a living plant, a well-constructed building) was typical of Jeremiah (e.g. 1:9–10; 18:7–9; 24:6; 31:28) and is used by Paul in 1 Cor 3:10–14. The love will presumably be God's initiating love and the divinely enabled human love in response, directed both to God and to the neighbour (Mk 12:28–33).

As in the first part of the prayer proper (1:15–23), so here, the second petition pushes through the constraints of human language and imagery (3:18–19). It is a prayer once again for knowledge (as in 1:17–19)—but such knowledge! (1) To comprehend (impossible!) what we might describe as the four dimensions (a not uncommon metaphor—Lincoln 1990: 207–13; Schnackenburg 1991: 150–1) of God's love (the Gk. sentence in v. 18 is incomplete); 'with all the saints' is a reminder that only a church conscious of its own dimensions through time and space can even begin to hope for the realization of such a prayer. (2) To know (in experience) the love of Christ which goes beyond knowledge (v. 19), where words and metaphors and symbols are inadequate to the task of describing such experience (cf. Col 2:2–3). (3) With the result that they may be filled with all God's fullness! What Col 1:19 and 2:9 ascribed to Christ alone, Ephesians prays may be true also of the church (1:23; 3:19)! The goal for the church is nothing less than that it embody the presence and love of God in the way that Christ did (cf. 4:13). Here the sequence of clauses implies that such a filling is the effect of appreciating and experiencing the mystery of God's love.

The prayer is brought fittingly to an end by a benediction (vv. 20–1) whose enthusiastic language matches the hyperbole of the preceding petition (cf. Rom 11:33–6). Such a petition can be put forward since it is addressed to a God whose goodwill and enabling grace far exceed human imagining (cf. Phil 4:7). He 'is able to do beyond everything, infinitely more than we ask or think' (v. 20, my tr.); as elsewhere in Ephesians, the language tumbles over itself in the attempt to express the completeness of trust beyond vision (cf. 1:19). To be noted, however, is that the enabling power is already 'at work within us'.

The final doxology, (v. 21) ascribes glory to God both in the church and in Christ Jesus, since Christ in life, death, and resurrection is the paradigm of the one who most fully acknowledges God and the character of God, and since the church is the body of people on earth whose commitment is precisely both to live from and to live out that same acknowledgement.

The Exhortation (4:1–6:20)

(4:1–6) The Church in its Calling and Confession Paul's regular practice in his letters was to attach a sequence of appropriate exhortations to the main body of his letter. Here, even though chs. 1–3 have been more prayer than exposition, the same practice is followed. Chs. 4–6 contain mostly instruction (1) on how Christians should understand their mutual interdependence as the church (4:1–16) and (2) how they should conduct themselves in their lives within the world (4:17–5:20), (3) in their mutual responsibilities as households (5:21–6:9), and (4) in their battle against spiritual forces (6:10–20).

The exhortation begins with Paul's characteristic 'I exhort you' (v. 1; cf. Rom 12:1; 1 Thess 4:1), here with the same recall to his status as 'the prisoner' as in 3:1. The metaphor for daily conduct ('lead life') is 'to walk', a metaphor Jewish in origin (halakh means 'walk'; hence halakah, rules for conduct), which presumably reflects the fact that most moral issues arise from one's various contacts with others as one 'walks about'. The thought is not so much that a particular lifestyle or career can be regarded as a 'calling', as that the whole of life should be lived as an expression of and response to God's summons to live for him (cf. 1 Cor 1:26; 7:20; 1 Thess 2:12; 2 Thess 1:11).

No first-century Christian would need reminding that such a calling inevitably meant working and co-operating with others, with all the strains, misunderstandings, hurt feelings, and irritations which that involved. The church could never be reduced to a sequence of disparate individuals. The key to effective mutual co-operation is given in 4:2–3: a proper humbleness and meekness in self-esteem (very unmacho characteristics; cf. Phil 2:3 and Col 3:12); (2) patience and forbearance in love (cf. 1 Cor 13:4–5); and (3) an eager determination to maintain the unity of the Spirit and the peace which benefits all. To be noted is the fact that this unity is given by the Spirit, arising out of the shared experience of the one Spirit (cf. 1 Cor 12:13; Phil 2:1); it is not created by Christians, but can be destroyed by them! The peace of God (cf. 2:14–15) can function as a bond when there is genuine mutual respect (cf. Col 3:14–15).

The confession of 4:4–6 reinforces this unity by recalling its scope. It has an unconscious triadic structure—'one Spirit, one Lord, one God' (had it been more deliberate presumably 'one Spirit' would have come first in 4:4). By giving 'one God' the climactic position (4:6), and attaching to it the four 'all's, the writer reminds his readers that the ultimate foundation of Christian unity is God both in his oneness and in his allness as Creator (cf. Rom 11:36). The confession of Christ as 'one Lord' is in tune with this monotheism, or else Christian faith is misconfessed (cf. 1 Cor 8:6; 15:24–8; Phil 2:9–11). The importance of this distinctively Jewish emphasis on God as one is a reminder that the principal strains on Christian unity at this period came from the inclusion of Gentiles into Israel's privileged status (2:11–22).

That the 'one Spirit' gives the body its actual (as distinct from its confessional) oneness (v. 4), both as a shared experience (v. 3) and through the manifold workings of the Spirit's engracements, is spelled out more fully in 1 Cor 12:13–26 and Rom 12:4–8 (see also EPH 4:7–16). The 'calling' is one, because it is common to all believers (1:18; 4:1), without respect to rank or ability. In v. 5 the 'one faith' will have in mind in particular what was probably one of the earliest baptismal confessions, 'Jesus is Lord' (cf. Rom 10:9). The focus of unity is not so much a common formulation or common ritual as a common Lord; somewhat surprisingly, the Lord's Supper is not mentioned.

(4:7–16) The Character and Purpose of Ministry in the Body of Christ The paragraph is a rich elaboration of the earlier Rom 12:4–8 and 1 Cor 12:4–31. Here too it is stressed at the points of emphasis (beginning and end, vv. 7, 16): (1) that the effective functioning of the church as Christ's body depends on the recognition that each member has a function within the body and on each exercising that function; and (2) that each function is appointed and its exercise made effective by the enabling (engracement) which comes from Christ. The terms used are slightly different: the earlier Paul had spoken of 'charism' (charisma) as the function exercised in accordance with the 'grace' (charis) given (Rom 12: 6–8); here the talk is of 'grace' given in accordance with the measure of Christ's gift (v. 7). And in Rom 12 and 1 Cor 12 the head is simply another part of the body, whereas here Christ is the head of the body (v. 16; cf. 1:22). But the basic imagery is the same; that is, of the body as the model of a unity which is constituted by diversity, a unity which actually depends on the reality of mutual interdependence being expressed through the diverse engracements of its different members.

'The gift of the Messiah' (v. 7, my tr.) is elaborated in vv. 8–11. First (v. 8) by citing Ps 68:18, a passage lauding YHWH's triumph over Israel's enemies. Here it is taken as a description of Christ's exaltation, presumably in the same vein as 1 Cor 15:24–6 and Col 2:15. And the text speaks of him giving rather than receiving gifts—the character of Christ's triumph! But we know of a Jewish targum (interpretative translation) of the same passage which referred it to Moses and read it in a very similar way—Moses giving the law. So the reading here would have been quite acceptable.

The interpretation of the Psalm, which is appended (4:9–10), is probably a very early expression of the belief that Christ descended into the place of the dead ('the lower parts of the earth'; cf. Ps 63:9; Mt 12:40; 1 Pet 3:19) prior to his ascension 'far above all the heavens' (cf. 1:3, 20; 2:6; Heb 4:14; 7:26). Some think a reference to incarnation is intended by the talk of descent, but the language and imagery are focused solely on the benefits and universal effect (cf. 1:23) of Christ's resurrection and exaltation triumph; and a reference to Christ *descending* at Pentecost would be exceptional (Dunn 1989: 186–7).

'The gift of the Messiah' is elaborated, secondly, by itemizing the particular gifts given to the church (v. 11). The sequence of 'apostles…prophets…teachers' reflects the same evaluation as 1 Cor 12:28—apostles as church founders (e.g. 1 Cor 9:2), prophets and teachers as the most vital ministries in a church (Acts 13:1; Rom 12:6–7). Unexpected is the insertion of 'evangelists' as the third item (cf. Acts 21:8), and the linking of the fourth item as 'pastors and teachers'—presumably reflecting an understanding of the church as both evangelistic and pastoral in concern.

The other major elaboration of the earlier imagery of the church as Christ's body (vv. 12–16) is in terms of the purpose of these gifts and the character of the body's growth. Noteworthy is the fact that these ministries do not constitute the whole of the body's ministry, but are intended 'for the equipment or making ready of the saints: for the work of ministry, for the building up of Christ's body' (v. 12, my tr.; the punctuation is important here; otherwise Lincoln 1990: 253). The ministry of the appointed few is to facilitate the ministry of all. Only so, presumably, can *all* come to the *unity* of the faith (v. 13): the unity of the confession (4:3–6) depends on the interactive ministries of the many (vv. 7, 16), in other words, a dynamic and not a static unity. The goal (and test—1 Cor 14:3–5, 12, 17, 26) is always the upbuilding of the body. Here the voice is indeed still the voice of Paul.

This point is reinforced by the following description of the unity of the body as a process, a process of growth, a unity to be attained (v. 13) as well as maintained (4:3). Here it is characterized as a unity of faith in and knowledge of God's son: trust does not exclude knowledge

(cf. 1 Cor 13:12; Phil 3:8, 10); experience does not render trust unnecessary (cf. 2 Cor 12:1–10; Gal 4:9). The goal is maturity. The measure of that maturity is the Christ (cf. Col 1:28). What is in view, it should be noted, is a corporate maturity: such maturity is not possible for the individual; it is possible only for the church, and for the individual as part of the body of Christ.

A negative measure of such maturity (v. 14) is the church's ability to steer a straight course when the winds and waves of doctrinal speculation beat upon it—an odd change of metaphor within the sustained metaphor of the body (probably alluding to Isa 57:20; cf. Jas 1:6). The threat is all the more serious when human deceit (as in a dice game) and malice are involved, deliberate attempts to promote discordant views or counter ideologies, designed (we may infer) to boost some individual's or group's status or reputation. Here again, discernment as a gift to the congregation as a whole must normally be given precedence over the claimed insight of one or two. This fear of false teaching arising within the church smacks very much of a second-generation concern (cf. 1 Tim 4:1; Heb 13:9).

The final elaboration of the body metaphor (vv. 15–16) reverts to the imagery of growth, with Christ as both the goal and the source of its enabling (cf. 2:21; Col 2:19). The physiology implied is strange to modern ears, but the force of the metaphor is clear. The antithesis to naïve childish interest in alternative practices or views (v. 14; cf. 1 Cor 14:20–5; Heb 5:13–14) is 'speaking the truth in love' (v. 15), a balance easy to state (truth *and* love) but hard to practise (cf. Gal 4:16). It will not be accidental that the last word (v. 16) is 'love' (cf. 5:25).

(4:17–32) How to Live as the Church in the World There follows a section of more general, more or less all-purpose paraenesis, which stretches to 5:20. Unlike earlier Pauline letters, there seems to be no particular situation (in the Ephesian church or elsewhere) in view. The first part (vv. 17–24) parallels 2:1–10 in structure—a reminder (1) of the readers' Gentile past (vv. 17–19), (2) of their conversion (vv. 20–1), and (3) of God's purpose for them (vv. 22–4).

As in 2:11–12, the warning presupposes a Jewish perspective (vv. 17–19): that Gentile conduct was characterized by the futility of their vaunted reason and darkness of understanding, alienation from the life of God by their ignorance (cf. 1 Pet 1:14), and a hardness and callousness expressed in and reinforced by their self-surrender to sexual excess, impurity and greed (cf. 5:3; Col 3:5). The judgement is harsh but reflects Jewish conviction that they had been privileged with fuller insight into God's will for human conduct, and the generally higher sexual standards of Jewish communities (cf. Rom 1:21–31).

The recall to their conversion in this instance focuses on what they were then taught (vv. 20–1). Notable here is the reference to the Christ as a model for Christian conduct (cf. Rom 6:17; 15:1–3; Col 2:6); the 'truth in Jesus' is a moral truth. The 'if indeed' which begins v. 21 (my tr.; 'assuming that' RSV) is a typical Pauline cautionary note (cf. Rom 8:9, 17; 1 Cor 15:2; Col 1:23).

The exhortation which follows (vv. 22–32) takes the classic form: put off (vices) and put on (virtues) (see e.g. Schweizer 1979). The imagery is drawn from change of clothes, as indicating a change of character and lifestyle, and was familiar in the ancient world (here cf. particularly Col 3:8–12); it does not necessarily imply that a ritual change of clothes was already part of Christian baptism. Something of the moral transformation which Christian conversion entailed is here indicated (cf. 1 Cor 6:9–11), but also the Christian perception of the resulting difference in ethical values.

To be 'put off' (cf. Rom 13:12; Jas 1:21; 1 Pet 2:1) is a whole way of life characterized by 'deceitful desires' (v. 22, my tr.), the desire which constantly promises but never fully satisfies, which consumes but rarely fulfils; the 'old nature' (RSV) is marked by the twilight of desire. The antidote and alternative is a constant renewal in self-perception (v. 23; cf. Rom 12:2) and a daily assumption of and living out ('put on') the humanness which God intended and created, marked by the righteousness and holiness of God's reality (v. 24). Implicit is the conviction that Christ is the image of the new humanity, the completion of God's purpose in creating humankind, and the template for the recreation of the old humanity into the new (cf. 2:15; 4:13; Rom 13:14; Col 3:10).

The general exhortations which follow (vv. 25–32) focus particularly on personal relations and underline the importance of conversation, as a force for community building and as potentially destructive of community (cf. Jas 3:6–12). They are based on age-old proverbial wisdom, familiar among both Greek and Jewish moralists, but of no less value for that. Members of a church (of one another) should be able to speak the truth to each other (v. 25, using the

words of Zech 8:16). The proverb that anger should not be retained beyond nightfall, thereby giving scope to the devil, was a valuable elaboration of the exhortation from Ps 4:4 (vv. 26–7).

The exhortation about the thief (v. 28) breaks the sequence on speaking, but reminds of the transformation brought about in some early Christian conversions and of the need to reinforce such a conversion by a determined change of motivation and lifestyle (cf. Rom 12:8; 1 Thess 4:11; Titus 3:14). To work in order to *give* indicates a very different set of values from those which normally govern society.

The final group of exhortations (vv. 29–32) contrasts (in an a-b-a-b format) contributions to conversation which are bitter, undisciplined, angry, and malicious and thus grieve the Spirit (which should distinguish them as believers, 1:13–14), with those which are beneficial, fitting, and impart grace to the other, marked by sensitivity, thoughtfulness, and the forgiveness which they themselves had experienced from God in Christ (Col 3:13). The mature Christian community is one where the Lord's Prayer petition about forgiveness can be prayed with complete sincerity.

(5:1–20) Walking in the Light The final block of general exhortations develops the earlier antithesis between the old life and the new (cf. 2:1–10 and 4:17–24) in three sharply drawn contrasts. First, the contrast between a life modelled on the love of God and Christ (vv. 1–2) and a life mismatched with the vices which warrant the anger of God (vv. 3–7). Second, the repeated contrast between light and darkness, between a life in the light, open to and in turn reflecting light's searching rays, and a life full of hidden shamefulness (vv. 8–14). And finally, the contrasts between unwisdom and wisdom, between a life which characteristically gains its inspiration from strong drink and a life whose character and direction is given by the Spirit (vv. 15–20).

As the first sequence of general exhortations was marked by a recall to their discipleship of Christ (4:20), so the second sequence begins with a striking double call to take both God and Christ as the model for personal relationships and conduct (vv. 1–2). Paul elsewhere speaks of imitating Christ (1 Cor 11:1; 1 Thess 1:6), but not of imitating God. The thought here, however, is of the child taking the loving parent as a model, and alludes particularly to God's forgiveness (following from 4:32) and mercy (cf. Lk 6:36); see further Wild (1985). So too their conduct (walk) is to be modelled on Christ's self-giving (cf. 5:25; Gal 2:20) and sacrifice (cf. Phil 4:18 echoing Ex 29:18) as a governing principle.

Another vice list (vv. 3–5) warns against sexual sins in particular, beginning with a repetition of the characterization of their former lifestyle (4:19) and adding *porneia* (illicit sexual relations), one of the most regular members of such lists (e.g. Mk 7:21; Gal 5:19; Col 3:5). Evidently the exploitation and abuse of sex was as seductive and as destructive then as now. Gossip about such matters should be discouraged lest it promote any implication that they don't matter. Conversation between close friends can so easily degenerate into shaming and foolish talk, and become caught in the swamp between buffoonery and boorishness (where Aristotle located the uncommon third term in v. 4); this is a further reflection on the dangers of too casual speech (4:29–32). Christian conversation should be marked instead by a spirit of thankfulness (v. 4).

The vice list is rounded off by a reminder that the sexually promiscuous, the dirty-minded, and the greedy or covetous person (but the terms are masculine) will not share the inheritance of God's kingdom (v. 5). This talk about inheriting the kingdom was evidently fairly common in earliest Christianity (1 Cor 6:9–10; Gal 5:21; cf. Rev 21:8; 22:15). It linked effectively into the most prominent feature of Jesus' proclamation (about the kingdom of God, e.g. Mk 1:15), but here reflects also the developed understanding of the exalted Christ as sharing in God's kingly rule (cf. Lk 22:29–30; 1 Cor 15:24–8; Col 1:13). It also links further back into the idea of Gentiles sharing in Israel's inheritance (1:14, 18). The abhorrence of idolatry was particularly Jewish, both as a fundamental sin and as associated with the three sins just named. The idolatry and debauchery of the golden calf episode remained an unhealed sore in Israel's conscience (e.g. 1 Cor 10:6–8). But the folly of taking another as god, rather than the one Lord God of Israel, had been a lesson requiring frequent repetition.

They should beware of empty and deceptive words on this point (v. 6; cf. Rom 16:18; Col 2:4, 8). The evident fact was that human society functioned in accord with the moral order in which God had set it: as in Rom 1:18–32, the wrath or anger of God can be understood in terms of the community-destructive outworkings of such self-indulgence (v. 6; cf. 2:2–3).

The degenerative effect of promiscuous and selfishly acquisitive company (v. 7) is contrasted with the opening call to unconditional and sacrificial love (vv. 1–2).

The second set of contrasts are between light and darkness (vv. 8–14), a common metaphorical usage in religions generally to express the sharpness of the antithesis between new and old, between truth newly perceived and the old misconceptions. In the OT cf. e.g. Ps 36:9; 82:5; Prov 4:14–19; Eccl 2:13; a prominent contrast in the Dead Sea scrolls is between 'the sons of light' (the Qumran covenanters) and 'the sons of darkness' (the rest); in the NT see e.g. Mt 6:22–3; Acts 26:18; 2 Cor 4:6; Col 1:12–13; 1 Pet 2:9; 1 Jn 1:6.

The elaboration of the contrast here is a blend of the conventional and the more distinctively Christian. All would agree that goodness, righteousness, and truth are desirable virtues (v. 9), that a religious person will want to learn 'what is pleasing' to God (v. 10), and that part of the effectiveness of the imagery of light lies in the power of light to expose what would otherwise be hidden from sight (vv. 11–13). The distinctive Christian claim is that the light (the real, most effective light) is 'in the Lord' (v. 8). Equally characteristic of Paul's teaching is the claim that discernment of what pleases the Lord (v. 10) is given by renewal of the mind and through the Spirit (Rom 12:2; 1 Cor 2:14–15; Phil 1:9–10; 1 Thess 5:19–22). The power of light to expose the unsavoury and shameful recalls such passages as Jn 3:20 and 1 Cor 14:14–25 and echoes the warning notes of Mk 4:21–2 and Rom 13:11–14.

v. 14 may be a snatch of an early hymn (such as may be found under a heading such as 'The Gospel' in older hymn-books today). If sung by early congregations it would function both as a recall to their conversion, as a reminder (like Rom 13:11) that falling asleep is a constant threat to be resisted, and as a promise of final waking from sleep, resurrection from death, and enlightenment from Christ.

In the final paragraph the contrast between unwisdom and wisdom (vv. 15–17) in effect draws upon the accumulated wisdom of Proverbs, Ben Sira, the teaching of Jesus gathered in the Sermon on the Mount, and so on. But it adds the ominous note recalled from 2:2 that such wisdom is needed because the context of the life of faith is stamped by evil (v. 16). That is why conduct must be 'careful' (v. 15; still attractive is the older KJV translation, 'walk circumspectly') and the significant time (the sense of the Gk. word used here) must be 'bought up' (v. 16). The latter exhortation is just the same in Col 4:5, and the metaphor more evocative than clear, but the emphasis is presumably on discerning and acting upon all too scarce opportunities for good and the gospel in the midst of lives which are all too pressurized and constricted. v. 17 presumably says the same thing in terms closer to those already used in v. 10.

The last contrast vividly recalls Acts 2:1–4, 12–16 and reminds us that many of the earliest Christian gatherings for worship were marked by spiritual exuberance (vv. 18–20). As at Pentecost the effect of the Spirit could give an impression of drunkenness. The difference is that strong drink taken in excess resulted in debauchery and dissipation (cf. again Rom 13:13). In contrast, fullness of the Spirit came to expression most characteristically in various psalms, hymns, and spiritual songs, by which the congregation was instructed, God was praised from the heart, and life lived in a spirit of thankfulness to God. To be noted is the fact that being filled with the Spirit is not regarded as a once-for-all event; the exhortation is to be (constantly or repeatedly) filled with the Spirit (see further Fee 1994). The distinction between the various forms of song is unclear (as in Col 3:16), but presumably includes OT psalms, hymns which came to birth in Christianity (such as Lk 1:46–55 and perhaps Phil 2:6–11), and spontaneous charismatic songs (cf. 1 Cor 14:15, 26). As elsewhere in Paul prayer is made not so much *to* Christ as to God the Father *through* Christ (cf. Rom 7:25; 2 Cor 1:20; Col 3:17).

(5:21–6:9) Household Rules What follows is constructed on the framework of a table of rules for good management of the household (Balch 1981). Household management was a common concern of political theorists and ethicists in the ancient world. Naturally so, since the household was generally understood to be the basic unit of the state or society. The health of society and stability of the state therefore depended on the basic relationships within the household—husband and wife, father and children, master and slaves. The second and third generation of Christians shared this concern: no doubt partly to demonstrate the good citizenship of small house churches which might otherwise have seemed subversive of traditional social values; but no doubt partly also as a means of bearing good witness to the quality and character of the Christian household (see Schweizer 1979).

The structure is particularly close to that of Col 3:18–4:1, which probably provided the precedent for those which followed (here and 1 Pet 2:18–3:7; cf. e.g. Titus 2:1–10; *Didache* 4:9–11; 1 *Clem* 21:6–9). The core teaching is fairly conventional (good ethics are by no means exclusively Christian). But the conventional is transformed by the Christian sense that all relationships have to be lived 'in the Lord' and with the unselfish, sacrificial love of Christ as the pattern and inspiration.

In the first part of the rule (5:21–33) the transformation begins at once. That wives should be subject to their husbands (5:22; Col 3:18; 1 Pet 3:1) accorded with the moral sensibilities of the time; here we need to recall that in the law and ethos of the time households were patriarchal institutions and that the paterfamilias (father of the family) had absolute power over the other members of the family. But the rule is already softened by prefacing it with a call to be subject to one another (5:21; cf. Gal 5:13; 1 Pet 5:5): in a Christian household the power of the paterfamilias was not absolute. And the reminder that wifely submission is to be 'as to the Lord' (5:22) sets the whole relationship within the primary context of mutual disciple-ship (cf. Mk 10:42–5).

It is true that the placing of the relationship of husband and wife parallel to that of Christ and church (5:23–4) seems to set the wife in an intrinsically inferior status (cf. 1 Cor 11:3). But that again reflects the ethos of the time (the marital law which treated wives as the property of their husbands was only changed in Britain in the 19th cent.). And the main thrust of what follows is clearly intended to transfuse and transform that given relationship with the love of Christ. The paradigm for the husband is Christ as lover and saviour, not as lord and master.

The beautiful imagery of 5:25–7, so beloved at wedding ceremonies, has in view the purificatory bath which the bride took prior to and in preparation for the wedding ceremony; Christ's self-giving had an analogous cleansing in view (cf. Ezek 16:8–14). Perhaps there is a side glance at baptism, but the primary thought is of the (corporate) Christian life as equivalent to the time between betrothal and the wedding ceremony, the marriage itself only taking place at the return of Christ (cf. 2 Cor 11:2; Rev 19:7–8; 21:2, 9–10). The cleansing is evidently a spiritual cleansing, and it comes 'by the word' (5:26; cf. 1 Cor 6:11; Titus 3:5–6; Heb 10:22).

5:28–33 develops a different aspect of the imagery, drawn from Gen 2:24 (5:31; cf. Mt

19:4–6). The idea of 'the two become one flesh' invites a twofold corollary: that a healthy love of the other is inseparable from a healthy respect for oneself (5:28–9; cf. Mk 12:31; Rom 13:8–10)—an important psychological insight; and that the love of Christ sustains the mutual love of husband and wife within the corporate context of the church, of their being individually and jointly members of his body the church (5:30, 32; cf. Rom 12:5).

The final exhortation (5:33) maintains the emphasis on each and every husband's responsibility to love his own wife. The wife is not so counselled, for the love in view is not marital or family love so much as the sacrificial and non-self-serving love of the more powerful for the disadvantaged. In a situation of given inequality between husband and wife the appropriate response of the wife was to respect her husband.

The second pairing within the household code (as in Col 3:20–1) is children and parents (6:1–4). As with the submissiveness of wives, so the obligation of obedience to parents (6:1) was a widely recognized virtue in the world of the time. But again it is qualified by an 'in the Lord' (though the phrase here is missing from some important MSS). And just as noteworthy is the unusual feature in such codes, of children being directly addressed; evidently they were regarded as responsible members of the house churches where such a letter as this would be read out. As in the case of the previous exhortation to husbands (5:25–33), so here the basic exhortation of Col 3:20 is elaborated, on this occasion by drawing in the scriptural authority for it—Ex 20:12 and the slightly fuller version of Deut 5:16—with the exegetical note inserted to point out that this was the first commandment with promise. As in other similar cases, the NT writer saw no difficulty in applying a promise relating to Israel's prosperity in the promised land to Gentile believers in another part of the Mediterranean world.

In contrast, the advice to fathers is left stark (6:4). Again it is fairly conventional. Only the father is addressed: the paterfamilias had sole legal authority over his children and primary responsibility for their *paideia* (training or discipline; the classic word in this context) and instruction; at the same time it was recognized that such power unwisely handled could easily provoke or goad youths and young men to a resentment which was destructive of household order and family. Again the Christian qualification is added—'the training and instruction of the Lord' (cf. Prov 3:11).

The final pairing in the household code is slaves and masters (6:5–9). The exhortation to slaves is closely modelled on Col 3:22–5. Again it is worth noting that they too are here recognized as full members of the congregation and having responsibilities as Christians to discharge the duties which their status as slaves laid upon them (cf. 1 Tim 6:1–2; Titus 2:9–10). If any are surprised that Paul did not question the morality of slavery, they should recall that slavery only became a moral issue as a result of the slave trade (only two centuries ago), and that in the ancient world slavery was simply an economic phenomenon, slaves being essential to the smooth running of the economy (though by no means solely on the bottom rung).

The exhortation recognizes the reality of slavery: obedience had to be unquestioning and orders carried out with fear and trembling (many masters treated their slaves harshly). But the thrust of the exhortation is to provide the slaves with the right motivation, so that their service might lose its servile character and become a way of serving the Lord with sincerity of heart (6:5), doing the will of God with a will, and not (as we might say) as clock-watchers or solely to catch the master's eye or to curry favour with him (6:7). Slavery too can be a form of discipleship (cf. 1 Cor 7:20–4). At the same time, they are reminded that their earthly masters are only that (6:5), and that both slave and free will receive from their heavenly Lord the appropriate recompense according to the good they have done (6:8; cf. 2 Cor 5:10).

In 6:9 the point is driven home directly to those in the congregation who were slave-owning householders (the assumption is that the household as a whole is Christian). In the spirit of OT slave legislation (Lev 25:43), they should forbear from threatening their slaves, remembering that both they and their slaves have the same Lord in the heavenly places, and that he is an impartial master—a common OT motif (e.g. Deut 10:17; 2 Chr 19:7) echoed elsewhere in the NT (Acts 10:34; Rom 2:11; Col 3:25; Jas 2:1).

(6:10–20) Put on the Armour of God The final strand of exhortation is one of the most vivid portrayals of the Christian life as a spiritual struggle, indicating the power of the hostile forces (vv. 10–12), the means of withstanding them (vv. 13–17), and the need for co-operative effort (vv. 18–20). The metaphor, be it noted, is of warfare, not of a school debate or of a business enterprise. As a piece, it is clearly constructed from a sequence of allusions to well-established Jewish motifs, particularly that of YHWH as the Divine Warrior (Isa 59:17; Wis 5:17–20). The writer would no doubt be conscious of the fact that the armour he describes is depicted by Isaiah especially as YHWH's own armour, armour which YHWH dons to effect judgement on human sin and social injustice (Isa 59:12–18).

The spiritual opposition is described both as 'the devil' (cf. 2:2; 4:27; Jas 4:7; 1 Pet 5:8–9), and as cosmic and spiritual powers in the heavenlies (vv. 11–12; cf. Rom 8:38–9; Col 1:16; 2:15). With this information added to that of the earlier references to the heavenlies (1:3, 20; 2:6; 3:10), we are given a clearer picture of the heavenly regions—presumably as a sequence of heavens (cf. 2 Cor 12:2–3), in which the lower heavens (nearer to earth) are inhabited by hostile powers, and the upper heavens are where Christ is seated (1:20–1). Modern cosmology is very different, and the extent to which such names ('rulers, authorities, cosmic powers') were already perceived to be metaphorical is unclear. What matters is the recognition that there are forces active through human fear and greed which can captivate whole groups and even societies and wreak all forms of evil, from the most subtle ('the wiles of the devil'; cf. 4:14) to the most inhuman. Those who have lived through any three or four decades of the twentieth century should need no convincing on that score. To designate them as 'spiritual powers' helps prevent such evil from being treated lightly or superficially (they are not merely 'flesh and blood') (see e.g. Wink 1984: 84–9).

The appropriate and necessary response (given the character of this evil) is to seek a strength commensurate with and more powerful than that evil—a spiritual strength to match a spiritual crisis (cf. Rom 4:20; 1 Cor 16:13), a strength from God, the strength of God himself (v. 10; the first OT echo—Isa 40:26). Correlated with (or an elaboration of) this strength is the equipment of the Divine Warrior, 'the panoply of God' (vv. 11, 13). Only that equipment and empowering will provide the fortitude and the means to withstand in a day when evil seems to be rampant (cf. 5:16), and having done all within one's power, still to stand one's ground; the sign of God's enabling is not so much clear-cut victory over evil, as the sustained will to resist evil, come what may.

The list of equipment is inspired by earlier, briefer metaphors, and the metaphors themselves are not fixed (e.g. in 1 Thess 5:8 the breastplate is faith). Nevertheless, the appropriateness of this listing is notable.

1. *Belt* (v. 14). In a day when clothing was much looser, it was necessary for the flowing cloak to be fastened firmly by a belt, otherwise movement would be hindered and action impeded (cf. Lk 12:37; 17:8). To be caught out in deceit or falsification was like tripping over one's own clothing; the belt of truth prevents one being 'caught with one's pants down'.

2. *Breastplate* (v. 14). The metaphor draws directly on Isa 59:17 (and Wis 5:18), describing YHWH's breastplate. There it is the fact that what God does is right which makes his judgement invulnerable to criticism (of partiality). Here the thought is of God's acceptance of those who trust in him as their breastplate which keeps them equally secure in the face of hostile criticism (cf. Rom 5:1–2; 8:31–4).

3. *Shoes* (v. 15). This is a more original image, but no doubt adapted from Isa 52:7, a passage which is also echoed in Acts 10:36 and cited in Rom 10:15. Why the word 'preparation' is added is unclear, but it strengthens the impression that what is in view is the responsibility of the church and believer to speak out the gospel of peace with God. Mission is the best form of defence; the church on the move will be more surefooted in face of the encroachments of evil.

4. *Shield* (v. 16). Again the imagery is original; more typically God is a shield (e.g. Gen 15:1; Ps 18:2, 30; 28:7); in Wis 5:19 the shield is 'holiness'. But 'faith' is also appropriate (cf. 1 Pet 5:9). Faith and righteousness are two sides of the one coin in Pauline thought (Rom 1:17), just as the breastplate and shield have a similarly defensive function (hence 1 Thess 5:8). Trust itself can be exposed to quite a battering, but trust sustained keeps inviolate the one who so trusts (cf. Rom 4:16–22).

5. *Helmet* (v. 17). Here we are back with familiar imagery (Isa 59:17; 1 Thess 5:8; though in Wis 5:18 the helmet is 'impartial justice'). In 1 Thess 5:8 the helmet is 'the hope of salvation', which reflects the thought of the earlier Paulines that salvation is a still future goal (but 'hope' is confident hope). Here, however, as in 2:5 and 8, the question is raised whether the perspective has changed: that which keeps the head of the body (cf. 4:15) safe is the security of salvation realized and not just the confident hope of it.

6. *Sword* (v. 17). Notably the one offensive weapon is doubly denoted as 'of the Spirit', and as 'the word of God'. Again the imagery reflects older usage (Isa 49:2; Hos 6:5; cf. Heb 4:12). What is in mind is not just the written

word, as though the thought was simply of the believer being well versed in scripture, able to cite the appropriate passage for all occasions (cf. Mt 4:1–11). The Spirit is here seen as an inspiring force, the Spirit that inspires the word from God appropriate to the occasion (Mk 13:11; Rom 10:8–17; 1 Pet 1:25). It is no accident that the enabling of powerful speech is one of the most regular charisms and marks of the Spirit in the NT (e.g. Acts 4:8; 1 Cor 2:4–5; 12:8, 10); despite immense developments in communication, the force of the spoken word is still immeasurable.

The final stress is on prayer (vv. 18–20), not, somewhat surprisingly, as part of the continuing metaphor of spiritual armour, but emphasizing none the less (by the greater elaboration given to the request) its importance in the warfare just described. Christian soldiers must never forget that they need constant help from God. Moreover, since the previous imagery had been somewhat individualistic (despite the plural verbs), this last addition helps underline the importance of co-operation and mutual support in the warfare. Like the speaking (v. 17), the praying should look to the Spirit for inspiration (cf. Rom 8:26–7; 1 Cor 14:15; Jude 20); and the military mood is retained in the calls for alertness and application (6:18; cf. Lk 21:36).

The transition from exhortation to personal request (vv. 18–20) seems to be modelled on Col 4:2–4 (cf. Lk 21:15; Mk 14:38), with a final recapitulation of the 'mystery' motif and play on the contrast between Paul's imprisonment and his boldness as commissioned by God (3:1–12; cf. 2 Cor 3:12; 5:20; Phil 1:20; 1 Thess 2:2).

Conclusion and Benediction (6:21–4)

Most of vv. 21–2 is almost verbatim Col 4:7–8. It is of course conceivable that Paul wrote both letters at more or less the same time (thus unconsciously or deliberately giving Tychicus precisely the same commission each time). But the perspective of the letters is too different for that to be the most obvious solution. And in a letter thus far marked by its lack of specific reference to particular situations, this brief personal note rings somewhat oddly. It is more likely, then, that the author has drawn the language from Colossians to indicate the very Pauline effect he hoped his letter would have, and as an expression of what Paul would have wished to say had he himself still been able to dictate such a letter.

Since Tychicus appears only in the later Pauline letters (Col 4:7; 2 Tim 4:12; Titus 3:12;

see also Acts 20:4) he probably emerged only in the Pauline circle at a late stage; like Epaphras (Col 1:7) he is remembered as a beloved brother and faithful servant of Christ. Whatever the precise historical circumstances, the reference reminds us that there must have been regular contacts between the Pauline churches.

The final benediction (vv. 23–4) is unusual in Paul, but it strikes the regular notes of grace and peace (1:2) and links them with two of the great Pauline words—love and faith ('love with faith'). Effective also is the final balance between divine enabling ('from [both] God the Father and the Lord Jesus Christ') and human response ('all who have an undying love for our Lord Jesus Christ').

REFERENCES

Balch, D. (1981), *Let Wives be Submissive: The Domestic Code in 1 Peter* (Missoula; Scholars Press).

Barth, M. (1974), *Ephesians* (2 vols.; Garden City, NY: Doubleday).

Best, E. (1987), 'Recipients and Title of the Letter to the Ephesians: Why and When the Designation "Ephesians" ', ANRW 2. 25. 4 (Berlin: de Gruyter), 3247–79.

Bruce, F. F. (1984), *The Epistles to the Colossians to Philemon and to the Ephesians,* NICNT (Grand Rapids: Eerdmans).

Caragounis, C. C. (1977), *The Ephesian Mysterion* (Lund: Gleerup).

Dunn, J. D. G. (1989), *Christology in the Making,* 2nd edn. (London: SCM).

Fee, G. D. (1994), *God's Empowering Presence: The Holy Spirit in the Letters of Paul* (Peabody, Mass.: Hendrickson), 658–733.

Lincoln, A. T. (1990), *Ephesians,* WBC 42 (Dallas: Word).

Mitton, C. L. (1951), *The Epistle to the Ephesians* (Oxford: Clarendon).

Schnackenburg, R. (1991), *The Epistle to the Ephesians: A Commentary* (Edinburgh: T. & T. Clark).

Schweizer, E. (1979), 'Traditional Ethical Patterns in the Pauline and Post-Pauline Letters and their Development (Lists of Vices and House-Tables)', in E. Best and R. McL. Wilson (eds.), *Text and Interpretation* (Cambridge: Cambridge University Press), 195–209.

Wild, R. A. (1985), ' "Be Imitators of God": Discipleship in the Letter to the Ephesians', in F. Segovia (ed.), *Discipleship in the New Testament* (Philadelphia: Fortress), 127–43.

Wink, W. (1984), *Naming the Powers* (Philadelphia: Fortress).

9. Philippians

ROBERT MURRAY, SJ

INTRODUCTION

A. Character and Main Concerns of the Letter. 1.
Equalled only by Philemon, Philippians is the most personal of Paul's letters. Among the categories listed by ancient theorists (Malherbe 1988), it combines features of a hortatory 'letter of friendship' (Fee 1995: 214) with those of a 'patronage letter' (Bormann 1995: 161–205). Unusually for Paul, the OT is seldom cited; his argument is passionately centred on Christ, yet he often uses Stoic language (SEE PHIL E).

2. Although the letter's contents are conditioned by practical matters, the main emphasis is on strengthening the commitment and faith of the Philippian Christians, as was Paul's regular aim (Meeks 1983: 84–107). He urges them to follow the example of Christ in union with him (repeatedly expressed by 'sharing', koinōnia and its compounds), so as to grow in a Christlike mindset guiding both belief and action. This is expressed by several recurring verbs, especially phronein, 'think' or 'feel', which, together with 'rejoice', chairein, virtually structures the letter, creating a major inclusio from beginning to end.

B. The Addressees. 1.
Philippi (Bormann 1995) stood on the plain of eastern Macedonia, about 16 km inland from its port Neapolis. It was refounded as a city by Philip II of Macedon in 358–357 BCE. Prosperous from mineral deposits and its location on a main east–west route, Philippi came under Roman rule in 167 BCE. Octavian, after gaining supreme power in 31 BCE, settled veterans here and gave the city the status of a colonia with citizenship by ius italicum. The population would have been mainly Macedonians, Greeks, and Romans. Acts 16:12–40 recounts Paul's visit with Silas (about 50 CE), conversion of Lydia, and misfortunes before he revealed his citizen status. The alarm of the city magistrates and their anxiety to see the last of Paul and Silas doubtless gave Christianity a prejudiced start.

2. Apart from Acts, Philippians is our only source for the origins of this church. Lydia had been a Jewish God-fearer. All the people named in Philippians except Clement are Greek, but this does not exclude their having become Christians via Judaism. The church was doubtless mixed in ethnic and social character. It probably met in house-groups (Peterlin 1995:

135–70). By the time of the letter it had officers called episkopoi and diakonoi (1:1); presbuteroi are not mentioned. Paul refers to the Philippians' suffering for Christ (1:27–30; 2:15–17) and refers to 'opponents' (1:28), but without identifying them. Motives for hostility can be imagined on the part (respectively) of the civic authorities, the pagan public, Jews opposed to Christians, and Jewish Christians opposed to Paul.

3. The references to disunity have evoked many hypotheses (O'Brien 1991: 26–35). Theories of Gnostic opponents (Fee 1995: 19–32) are unconvincing. Tellbe (1994) plausibly suggests a crisis facing Gentile Christians unprotected by Jewish exemption from Roman cult practices. Others propose grounds for the quarrel mentioned in 4:2, especially disagreement over financial support for Paul (Peterlin 1995: 101–32, 171–216). This letter of only rarely polemical tone is subjected by some to a process which Barclay (1987) calls 'mirror-reading'; both the method and its criteria are open to criticism (Fee 1995: 7–10). Discord in the Philippian church at this time is probably best explained by the situation of Gentile converts vis-à-vis Roman civic pride and official cult and a tempting compromise offered by Jewish Christians (Tellbe 1994).

C. Paul's Situation. 1.
The common view till this century was that Paul wrote from Rome in the early 60s CE. Even if he was only under house-arrest (Acts 28:30), this could mean painful frustration. On this view 'the (praetorium) imperial guard' (1:13) and 'the emperor's [Caesar's] household' (4:22) would be in their regular bases in Rome itself.

2. Many today favour an earlier imprisonment, most preferring Ephesus in the mid-50s, about the probable time when Paul wrote 1–2 Corinthians and Romans, to which Philippians is said to be close in doctrine. Though there is no direct evidence for such an imprisonment, 1 Cor 15:32 and 2 Cor 1:8–10 might refer to it. Some epigraphic evidence is cited to argue that 'praetorium' and 'Caesar's household' could refer to a provincial governor's establishment. Communication between Philippi and Ephesus would be easier and quicker than with Rome.

3. Evaluation: in 2 Cor 11:23 Paul looks back on 'many' imprisonments, so that in theory any of them could be possible. However, the case for Ephesus is linked to the doubtful theory that Philippians is an amalgam (see PHIL D.2); the fewer letters are posited, the less need there is to suppose a shorter distance to be travelled. Similarities with Romans and 1–2 Corinthians need not tell against Philippians being dated a few years later. The epigraphic evidence is judged not relevant by Bruce (1980–1). In fine, the arguments for Ephesus have not overcome those for Rome (Fee 1995: 34–7).

D. Critical Questions. 1. Pauline authorship of Philippians is almost universally acknowledged, apart from some theories about 2:6–11.

2. The letter's unity and integrity have been challenged on grounds of apparent breaks in coherence and an order thought to be unsuited to its purpose (e.g. Collange 1979). Many hold that it has been re-edited from two or three letters by Paul, but disagree on where the cuts and rejoins are. The main reasons offered are an apparent ending and abrupt new start at 3:1, and the improbability that Paul left his thanks to the end.

3. Criticism (cf. O'Brien 1991: 10–18): no manuscript evidence suggests disturbance of the text. Any theory that an existing text has been rearranged by a redactor must show that it solves difficulties in the text better than maintaining the traditional arrangement. For Philippians it must explain credibly why and how the supposed redactor wove several letters by Paul into a new composition. In fact the problem at 3:1 is not solved but shifted from Paul to an unknown X with unknown motives. As for the postponement of thanks, Polycarp, writing to the same church at twice the length, likewise keeps business to the end (*Phil.* 13, see Lake 1912–13: i). The strongest argument, however, for the integrity of Philippians rests on appreciation of the whole as a structured masterpiece (Garland 1985; see PHIL F).

4. The theory that 2:6–11 is an already existing hymn that Paul quotes for his purpose, first proposed by Lohmeyer (1928), has come to dominate both exegesis of Philippians and study of early Christology and credal formulas, though the term 'hymn' remains imprecisely defined and the theory still takes various forms, including earlier composition by Paul. The literature is enormous; with the standard survey by Martin (1983); see now O'Brien (1991: 186–271). A rare voice questioning the theory's solidity and value for exegesis is raised by Fee (1992; 1995).

5. Evaluation: whatever the origin of this undeniably poetic passage, it actually exists only in Phil 2; the exegete must expound it in that context. If Paul quoted an existing text, by himself or another, it became part of his letter; any argument for its detachability raises similar problems to those for denying the letter's integrity (Hooker 1978). Arguments against Pauline authorship risk being circular (Fee 1995: 45). Hypotheses about the development of Christology have been allowed to determine the exegesis of the passage, again producing circular arguments. Heightened poetic style does not prove non-Pauline origin (Martin 1983: 57; Fee 1992). Recent literary analysis emphasizes that the passage is integrally embedded in its context and the whole letter. Many of its keywords recur, subtly transposed, in ch. 3 (Dalton 1979: 99–100; Garland 1985: 158–9). This does not prove it was not an already existing text, but isolating it becomes increasingly problematic.

6. These expressions of reserve, however, do not deny that the passage's theological importance reaches wider than its immediate function in Philippians, or that its pattern of Christ's descent and ascent is paralleled in other early Christological statements in solemn style.

E. 'Stoicism' in Philippians. 1. The frequency of Stoic language in Philippians is emphasized by Engberg-Pedersen (1994). The evidence is seldom noted even in larger commentaries. When compelling examples such as *autarkēs* (4:11) cannot be denied (e.g. Fee 1995: 427–35), commentators insist that Paul radically transforms Stoic themes, which are generally disparaged. Yet the use of Stoic ideas in Luke's account of Paul's sermon in Athens (Acts 17:22–31) is matched by passages in Paul's letters. In fact Stoicism had appeal for both Jewish and Christian preachers. 1 *Clement*, which should be dated not much later than 70 CE (Herron 1989), that is, only about ten years after Philippians, is full of Stoic ideas and terms, all interwoven with biblical, Jewish, and Christian themes.

2. Romans shows Paul readily adopting Stoic language for his message (e.g. 1:28, 12:2); perhaps he did this whenever he addressed converts with any degree of philosophical education. Whatever the reason, in Philippians his use of Stoic language is pervasive, serving most of his main themes: the emphasis on keeping a right mind (*phronein*), discernment to choose the better (*dokimazein ta diapheronta*), aiming (*skopein*) at the right end (*telos*); seeking contentment (*autarkeia*) in one's state, with joy (*chara*) even when suffering; community (*koinōnia*) lived out in good citizenship (*politeuesthai*) related to a state or model (*politeuma*), and still more. These expressions prove serviceable to Paul, though only up to a point; the reality of Jesus and the supreme value of knowing him in life and death, through faith and hope, are grasped only by experience (3:8–11). Yet the paradox seems true that 'it is when Paul is at his most Stoic that he is also at his most Christian' (Engberg-Pedersen 1994: 280). Paul's harnessing of Stoic ideas to the gospel in Philippians does not enter those areas where Christian Stoicism was to reveal its dangers (e.g. excessive anthropocentrism and distortions of asceticism).

F. The Structure of Philippians. The letter has a 'rondo' structure; after an 'overture' (here called 1B), comments on practical matters (sections 2, 4, and 6C) alternate with two major exhortations (sections 3 and 5) each centring on a narrative with a downward–upward movement; the first about Christ (2:5–11), the second about Paul (3:4–14). These and their contexts are linked by many corresponding words and phrases (Garland 1985: 158–9; Fee 1995: 314–15). Repetition of significant words or ideas occurs throughout the letter. *Inclusio* is used systematically, both to articulate sections of the argument and to make the letter's closing sentences echo keywords in the opening. The commentary notes these points in detail.

COMMENTARY

Introduction (1:1–11)

(**1:1–2**) **Greeting** Paul includes colleagues with himself in seven letters, and Timothy most often, but not as co-author; in 2:19–24 he occurs in the third person. Paul refers to them both as 'slaves' of Christ Jesus, as in Rom 1:1. Since this is an opening formula, it can hardly be a conscious anticipation of its application to Christ in 2:7, though this may strike a reader today. Paul uses the expression 'the saints' in six letters, thus or in the formula 'called [to be] saints'. Modern versions often paraphrase it as 'the holy people of God'; the phrase connotes the Christian claim to have been brought through faith in Christ into God's covenant people (Ex 19:6; 1 Pet 2:9–10). Though the words 'bishops and deacons' come from the Greek (see PHIL B. 2), their meanings have changed so much since their NT use that it is less misleading to render them by (e.g.) 'pastors' or 'guardians' and

'assistants'. The inclusion of these ministers, as well as the repeated 'all', five times from 1:1 to 1:8 (admittedly unusual for Paul), have been seen as a first hint of the disunity that Paul will address more clearly later (Lightfoot 1879: 67; Peterlin 1995). At this point, however, this can hardly do more than raise a suspicion. v. 2, 'Grace to you and peace' slightly varies the word order of a formula Paul uses in opening and closing greetings. The 'grace' formula is echoed in 4:23 to wrap up the whole letter. Though the Holy Spirit is expressly named only three times (1:19; 2:1; 3:3), here the formula can be called implicitly trinitarian (cf. 4:7; see Fee 1995: 48–9).

(**1:3–11**) **Thanksgiving and prayer** v. 3, Paul begins every letter to a church (except Galatians) by thanking or blessing God for the good he has heard about his addressees. Here he mingles these two reactions with his *prayer* for them (1:3–4) and with *joy* (1:5), a combination he will recommend in 4:6, as in 1 Thess 5:16–18. This paragraph is like a musical overture which anticipates themes to be heard later (PHIL F). Joy (*chara*) is the first of these; with its verb *chairein* it runs right through the letter. The focus of Paul's joy is the Philippians' sharing (*koinōnia*) with him in the gospel (1:5). *Koinōnia* is a keyword in the letter; aspects of it can be expressed by 'partnership', 'fellowship', 'union', and 'communion'. It occurs again at 2:1 and 3:10. *Koinōnos* (sharer, partner) occurs in the compound form *sunkoinōnos* at 1:7 and the related verbs at 4:14, 15. The prefix *sun-* ('together') occurs twelve times in the letter, compounded with eight nouns or verbs; it serves to enhance Paul's constant emphasis on relationship, unity and joy in community, and in sharing with him. The Philippians, of course, knew what the sharing had meant. For other readers Paul reveals it gradually: work for the gospel (1:5); prayer for him in his imprisonment and preaching, which he calls 'shar[ing] in God's grace' with him (1:7); striving side by side (1:27; 4:3) a metaphor from athletics that will recur, and finally their gifts of material support (4:15–18). v. 6, 'I am confident' (1:6): with this Paul passes from the Philippians' action to God's. (The verb recurs at 1:25, 2:24, and 3:3–4.) What Paul is confident about here is that their faith is God's 'good work', from when he began it till he brings it to completion 'by the day of Jesus Christ'. Paul returns to the interplay of human effort and God's work at 2:12–13. 'The day of Jesus Christ' is the day of his expected return; the phrase occurs again at 1:10 and 2:16. Paul refers to it as an assumed point of faith for the Philippians, a future reality though of unknown date; not a matter for overexcitement as it had been in Thessalonica. (This may perhaps lend some slight support for later dating of Philippians.)

v. 7, the key word *phronein* (see PHIL E.2) appears for the first time. Here it expresses a warm personal concern, based on mutual affection, to 'hold' others in one's 'heart'. Whose heart, holding whom? Most older versions took it as Paul's, holding that of his friends. NRSV opts for the reverse. Both are grammatically possible; the emphasis may be on the comfort Paul receives in his captivity and his service of the gospel from the thought of them, or on their thought and prayer for him in his situation. It makes little difference, because the relationship is mutual; they are *sunkoinōnoi* with Paul, they 'share in God's grace' with him. To understand the heart as Paul's perhaps makes the next sentence follow more smoothly. v. 8, Paul says his feelings are not merely his own. He lives in such union with Christ (Gal 2:20) that he experiences Christ's compassion as his own. 'Compassion' renders *splagchna*, literally 'bowels', an idiom borrowed from Hebrew, which can relate strong emotions to various internal organs.

v. 9, Paul circles back to what he began to say in v. 3. He wants them to grow in *agapē*, the kind of love he has described in 1 Cor 13, and will appeal to here in 2:1, 2. He does not say love for whom, either for himself or for each other; he simply prays that their capacity for loving may increase so that it overflows ever more and more. But he wants it to be far more than mere feeling; rather, to be directed by 'knowledge and full insight'. These words are of great importance for understanding the letter; they spell out what Paul means by *phronein*. The word rendered 'knowledge' is *epignōsis*, probably in the sense of a knowledge transcending ordinary cognition (*gnōsis*). This is best illustrated by Paul's use of the related verb in 1 Cor 13:12: 'Now I know only in part; then I will *know fully*, even as I have *been fully known*' (emphasis added); it is knowledge that at least approaches the knowledge that God has of us. 'Insight' renders *aisthēsis* which basically means perception, but the Stoics and other moral philosophers used it for moral knowledge gained by experience, and this is its probable meaning here (the only occurrence in the NT). v. 10, the verb 'determine' (*dokimazō*) primarily means the testing by which something comes to be approved. 'What is best' is literally 'the things that are different' i.e. morally better.

Such choices lived out will lead Christians to such a state that Christ at his return will find them to be 'pure and blameless'. The former word probably refers especially to motives; the latter (lit. with no stumbling) may refer both to moral steadiness and to not causing others to stumble. All this will bear the 'harvest of righteousness' through Christ's gift and to God's glory. Paul's prayer contains a whole cluster of pregnant words concerned with moral experience that develops character, and especially the capacity for loving realistically. Cf. Philem 4–7. The desired '*knowledge*' is of God; the '*insight*' is experience that builds up that knowledge; the testing of all things (1 Thess 5:21) leads to knowledge of God's will (Rom 12:2; Eph 5:10), with the purification of motives and moral firmness; all add up to the global moral term 'righteousness'. These ideas, if not the same words, reappear in Paul's central affirmation of his deepest values in 3:8–12. They are fundamental for the whole theory and practice of discernment in Christian tradition; yet it was Stoicism that provided Paul with many of the keywords: there is no need to shy away from this conclusion.

Paul's Situation and his Reactions to it (1:12–26)

(1:12–18) What has been Happening Two keywords mark off this section as another loose *inclusio*. The first is 'progress' (*prokopē*, v. 12, obscured in NRSV's 'to spread the gospel'). This is picked up again in 1:25, where the progress is on the part of Paul's addressees. The other keyword is 'confidence'; it recurs in 1:14, of Christians heartened by Paul's successful witness despite his imprisonment, and again in 1:25 of Paul trusting that he will remain some time longer for the encouragement of the Philippians. Other keywords in this section are 'gospel' (1:12, 16, 27) and 'rejoice'/'joy' (*chairō, chara*, 1:18, 25).

In the first seven verses Paul assures his readers that two aspects of his situation which might be expected to cause him pain and frustration have rather had the opposite effect. The first is his captivity. He does not describe his circumstances except by the conventional 'chains' and the implication that it would be his guards who spread favourable impressions of him around the *praetorium* (1:13 probably in the regimental sense, Lightfoot 1879: 99–104). On the alternative theories based on Rome and Ephesus, see PHIL C. The traditional view, that Paul is writing from Rome, naturally refers to Acts 28; he had come 'in chains' (28:17) with a soldier guarding him

(28:16), temporarily in a 'guesthouse' (28:23) but then for two years in lodgings where he could receive visitors (28:30). Philippians, for all its reticence, implies severer conditions than this. Perhaps after two years of waiting, on being called to have his case heard, Paul came under regulations requiring prison custody. *Apologia* (defence) in Phil 1:7 and 16 could refer to a formal hearing (cf. 2 Tim 4.6) but by reason both of its range of meaning and of its context here it can equally well refer to the 'apologetic' aspect of preaching. (Of course, such a series of events could have taken place in Ephesus, and no arguments seem decisive.) Paul does not explain how his imprisonment has encouraged Christians to witness to their faith more boldly (v. 14). Perhaps they are saying 'if Paul can do so much in chains, how much more should we dare to do in freedom?' If his guards have played a part, this could be cheering news also for his readers in a proud Roman *colonia* (Tellbe 1994: 110–11). v. 15, Paul sees two spirits at work in their activity, one of goodwill (*eudokia*) and love towards him, the other of envy (*phthonos*), rivalry (*eris*), and selfish ambition (*eritheia*, v. 17; 2:2), making some act not with pure motives (*hagiōs*, purely), but to cause Paul distress (*thlipsis*, v. 17; 4:14). The latter group is not identified, but they seem to be a part of the Christian community where Paul is. Clement of Rome, writing to Corinth not long afterwards (PHIL E.2), says that Peter and Paul were hounded to death by envy, jealousy, and rivalry (*1 Clem.* 5.2–5); see Brown and Meier (1983: 123–7; they also favour Rome as where Paul wrote Philippians, pp. 185–8). The trouble could well have begun with Jewish Christians who wanted the church to remain within Judaism and saw Paul's policy as misguided. Paul, however, regards all negative factors with a sublime equanimity, because for him they are outweighed by his supreme desire, to see Christ's gospel spreading; frustration and anger are simply overwhelmed by joy (v. 18).

(1:19–26) Paul's Hope and Confidence in Christ Paul turns from his reactions to recent events to envisage the foreseeable future. *Inclusio* markers are 'joy' (v. 26, picking up the related verb in v. 18), 'progress' (v. 25, from v. 12), and 'trusting' (v. 25, from v. 14). All three have now changed their subjects (see PHIL 1:12 and 1:18; 'joy' is now Paul's wish for the Philippians). The passage is full of the vocabulary of hope and confidence and the motives for these, and of a peaceful yet passionate equanimity, based on certainty of Christ's love. v. 19, this verse is

pivotal, grounding both Paul's joy in the situation just described and his confidence for the future: 'I know [the verb is repeated at v. 25] that…this will result in my deliverance.' Verbally this is one of the few OT allusions in Philippians; it reproduces the Greek of Job 13:16, in a passage that expresses Job's invincible trust in a transcendent justice. But in Paul's very different situation he is hardly likely to be comparing himself with Job; the coincidence of language could almost be accidental. 'Deliverance' is *sōtēria* (salvation); the NRSV's rendering seems to focus on Paul's vindication and release, but this does not exclude an implicit eschatological sense, as is clear, with reference to the Philippians in 1:28 and 2:12. Paul's first motive for confidence is his certainty that his friends pray for him as he does for them (1:4), and that their intercession is effective. Paul's second motive is revealed with the first of the three explicit references to the Holy Spirit in Philippians (see PHIL 1:2). 'Help' is *epichorēgia*, the act of supplying or providing for needs. Lightfoot (1879: 91) discusses whether the Spirit is the giver or the gift, and concludes for both. *Chorēgia* and the related verb could still retain a note of generous bounty, from their origin in sponsorship of civic celebrations by rich Athenians. v. 20, 'eager expectation' (Gk. *apokaradokia*) evokes a picture of heads strained forward in anticipation. The only other occurrence in the NT is in Rom 8:19, where Paul sees the whole of creation thus longing 'for the revealing of the children of God'. Paul hopes that he, and still more the gospel, will not be brought into public discredit, especially at his trial. In the biblical world 'shame' refers not so much to an emotion as to public worsting and discrediting; the psalmists often pray to be spared it (e.g. Ps 71:1), but to see their enemies suffering it (e.g. Ps 70:2). Positively, Paul hopes to speak 'with all boldness': the last word is *parrhēsia*, which is what Peter and John showed before the Sanhedrin (Acts 4:13). It is contrasted with being put to shame also in 1 Jn 2:28, but at the eschatological judgement, not a human trial. However, Paul's focus here, that 'Christ will be exalted now as always in my body, whether by life or by death' may have an overtone of the special sense of *parrhēsia* which developed in the NT. The word was born in political and forensic contexts, meaning freedom of speech or outspokenness. It came to connote also courage in speaking out; finally in the NT it has a special sense of confidence in God, a gift of the Holy Spirit to all who become God's children in union with

Christ, and through him have access (*prosagōgē*) to God. (See Rom 5:2; 2 Cor 3:12; Eph 3:12; Heb 4:16; 10:19; 1 Jn 3:21; 4:17; 5:14.) Paul need not have this sense fully in mind here, but he is hardly thinking merely of speaking boldly at his trial. He speaks from his awareness of constant union with Christ. If he is worsted, then Christ will be shamed in him; if he is enabled to speak well, Christ will be 'exalted' in him, and just as much if he dies as if he lives on, for neither circumstance can separate him from Christ. v. 21, thus Paul's thought flows straight into the third great expression of his spiritual equilibrium. First came prison or liberty; then being spoken of with love or with malice; now death or life, because 'to me, to live is Christ and to die is gain'. A psychological state undisturbed by fear or human attachments was the ideal for both Stoics and Epicureans; but for Paul, both his emotional balance and his whole range of values are entirely governed by his union with Christ, as he will make even clearer in 3:7–12. This serenity pervading Philippians, in contrast to Galatians and 2 Corinthians, suggests a spiritual state perhaps more appropriate to Paul's final years, and therefore to Rome. ('Gain', *kerdos*, reappears with its related verb in 3:7–8, referring to values which Paul has rejected and replaced by new ones.) He cannot make a choice even between living and dying (even though the latter would lead to his being 'with Christ' in the fullest sense) except by discerning Christ's will. This evidently leads him to decide that he must stay (v. 24); then immediately he says that he knows this with confidence (cf. 1:6, 19), for the Philippians' 'progress and joy in faith': (v. 25; cf. 2:17). Towards them, he is so far from Stoic *apatheia* as to want to come 'and share abundantly in your boasting in Christ Jesus' (v. 26). This is one of only three occurrences in Philippians of the word-group of *kauchaomai*, commonly rendered 'boast', that is so characteristic of Paul (55 of 59 instances in NT, 34 of them in 1–2 Corinthians; see *TDNT* iii. 645–54). His repeated concern with having (or not having) grounds for boasting is puzzling, especially given his teaching on 'works' in Romans 3–4; one can only conclude that the Greek words have a wider reference than self-glorification, and include joyful exultation for and with others, as seems the case here.

First Exhortation on Discipleship (1:27–2:18)

(1:27–30) Steadfastness in the Face of Opposition This paragraph is linked to what precedes,

especially by 'gospel' (1:12, 16, 27), 'salvation' (1:19, 28), and 'faith' (1:26, 29). v. 27, 'conduct yourselves' translates the verb *politeuesthai*, 'to act as a citizen' (Lightfoot 1879; Brewer 1954). NRSV misses the political sense (important also in Stoicism), though it keeps it when the related noun *politeuma* 'commonwealth' or 'citizenship' occurs in 3:20. Miller (1982) shows that Judaism had appropriated this vocabulary, and argues that Paul follows this usage, implying that the church is the New Israel; but see Engberg-Pedersen (1994: 263) and Fee (1995: 161–2). It makes a difference whether Paul is urging the Philippians to show their Christianity in good citizenship, or has transferred the verb to a purely Christian context. His wish for their steadfast unity in fidelity to the gospel (rest of 1:27) might suggest the latter, but bold resistance to their opponents (v. 28) implies the public forum. The exhortation to unanimity in Christ already anticipates 2:1–5. Is then the 'one spirit' in 1:27 simply human unanimity (as NRSV implies), or does it point to the clearer reference to the Holy Spirit in 2:1? Fee (1995: 164–6) argues plausibly for the latter. For unanimity Paul could easily have used the Stoic *homonoia* (frequent in 1 *Clement*), just as his athletic metaphors ('striving side by side', v. 27, and 'contest', v. 30, NRSV 'struggle') are Stoic clichés (Tellbe 1994: 111). What is essentially Christian is, of course, the hope of 'salvation' which 'is God's doing' (v. 28), and the sense that both faith in Christ and suffering for him are *graciously granted* (*echaristhē*) as a privilege (v. 29), which Paul sees as binding them more closely to himself in Christ, v. 30. Faith in Christ is again linked with the idea of suffering in 2:17 and 3:9–10. The 'opponents' at whose hands suffering is expected probably refers to political and social pressure to take part in the imperial cult (Tellbe 1994). If *politeuesthe* indeed refers to good citizenship, Paul would be recommending this as the best defence (cf. Polycarp, *Phil.* 10.2). But the threat is also to the Philippian church's unity, and Paul is passionately concerned that this should be in and with the suffering Christ as Paul has preached him.

(2:1–6) Unity of Minds and Hearts v. 1, the tone of appeal now rises to a more intense level of feeling through a series of 'if' clauses, regular in the rhetoric of entreaty. This more solemn tone tells against supposing a 'hymnic' style only from v. 6 onwards. In prayers, the formula typically reminds a deity of past theophanies; here the idiom implies something like 'if x means anything to you, then prove it now'. Paul appeals to what he is sure the Philippians have experienced: 'encouragement in Christ', 'consolation from love', 'sharing in the Spirit', 'compassion [see PHIL 1:8], and sympathy'. Of these, sharing, *koinōnia*, is fundamental to all the others, above all since it is in (now certainly the Holy) Spirit. At last (v. 2) comes the apodosis to the four 'ifs': '*make my joy complete*', the joy which Paul has expressed for himself in 1:4 and 18, and wished for them in 1:25. The desired response is described by four phrases which all express union of minds and hearts: two use the keyword *phronein* ('be of the same mind...of one mind'); the others are 'having the same love' (*agapē*) and 'being in full accord' (*sumpsuchoi*, united in soul). The most important words here were already established in 1:4–9, together with words compounded with *sun-*, 'together', to intensify the sense of sharing. In v. 3 Paul continues his description of the attitudes he desires by alternating dos and don'ts: not '*selfish ambition*', which he has been suffering (1:17), nor conceit (*kenodoxia*, vainglory) but rather 'humility, regard[ing] others as better than yourselves'. The last phrases are significant for the letter's unity, being echoed both in 2:7–8 and in ch. 3. v. 4, another do and don't concerns looking to 'the interests of others'. The verb is *skopeō*, 'to aim' (like *phronein*, a Stoic word); it recurs (with its noun) in 3:14–17. In Paul's present context, of course, *phronein* essentially involves a right *skopos* of mind and heart, 'as in Christ Jesus' (v. 5).

Do the attitudes (and perhaps activities) not commended in vv. 3–4 point to actual divisions within the Philippian church? Whether 1:1–4 contains hints or not, the immediately preceding exhortation in 1:27–30 now makes a reference to disunity more likely, especially on such grounds as Tellbe (1994) suggests. This will be discussed later, where clearer indications occur. Here it is not certain how far breaches of unity have actually gone. 'Selfish ambition' (2:3) could be in Paul's mind because he has suffered from its effects (1:17). Other phrases he uses may well refer to the quarrel to be mentioned in 4:2, especially if others had joined in; but surely the main thrust of this appeal, as of the passage into which it leads, is to focus the Philippians' minds on their relationship with Christ; references to human faults need to be clearer to prove an actual state of conflict.

(2:5–11) Christ, the Focus and Model for Discipleship The standpoint of the following comments is outlined in PHIL D. vv. 5–11, most commentators, accepting a hymn theory, set the passage out like verse. This displays its elegant composition in short *cola*, as found in classical artistic prose, but does not prove it to be a hymn in terms of either Semitic or Greek models. The wide and imprecise use of 'hymn' in modern discussion has not helped (O'Brien 1991: 188). The opening exhortation follows smoothly from the preceding sentences, points to Christ as model, and continues with a narrative about him in language which is certainly poetic and goes beyond Paul's usual vocabulary, but not necessarily his capacity when moved. Many keywords are echoed later, especially in ch. 3. The following exegesis takes the passage as it stands in its context. However, the possibility that Paul is adopting the structure of an existing model for credal-type statements will be considered in conclusion.

v. 5, 'Let the same mind be in you that [was] in Christ Jesus': more literally, 'be thus minded in/among yourselves as also in Christ Jesus'. The first 'in' is ambiguous in Greek; the context favours 'among', i.e. in interpersonal relations. The unexpressed verb has to be understood; more complicated ellipses have been proposed, e.g. 'which you have by virtue of your [life] in [union with]'; but '*was*' is most satisfactory. Paul points to Jesus, as known on earth, as the example for Christians in their relationships. This is rejected by some, for whom the hymn theory dictates their exegesis; they hold that the hymn was kerygmatic, proclaiming doctrinal truths about Jesus and that to make him a mere ethical model is somehow an inferior use of the hymn (cf. Martin 1983: 68–74, 84–8; Stanton 1974: 99–110; O'Brien 1991: 253–62). v. 6, 'who, though he was in the form of God': 'though' is an added interpretation; others suggest 'because' (Moule 1970). The Greek for 'was' is not the simple verb, but the participle of a stronger verb, *huparchōn*, 'existing'. Form (*morphē*) has a complex history (Behm, *TDNT* iv. 742–50). It connotes the outward aspect of something but not mere appearance; it also reflects the inward nature. Since God is incorporeal we must examine how Scripture describes theophanies. This suggests 'glory' as being what *morphē* implies, but this will not fit in v. 7, where *morphē* is that of a slave. It is desirable to keep one word in both places, and 'form' remains the least unsatisfactory. This verse already raises the question whether it refers to Christ's pre-existence or to his life on earth, but first we must read further. Paul has just used the verb 'regard' (*hēgoumai*) in exhortation (2:3), and will use it thrice of his own values in relation to Christ in 3:7–8. 'Equality with God' seems like a repetition with variation of 'being in the form of God', but not all agree on this. Indeed, the meaning of this clause is the storm-centre of modern controversy on Philippians. 'Something to be exploited' interprets one word, *harpagmon*. It is important that in the Greek the negative governs not the verb 'regard' but this noun (Carmignac 1971–2). The actual order is: 'not [as] *harpagmos* did he regard being equal to God'. The issue is not pedantic; it is between two alternative 'stories'. These depend (1) on two possible senses of *harpagmos* and (2) on what is being contrasted with what. *Harpagmos* is a verbal noun from *harpazō*, to seize or snatch. Its form raises problems (BAGD 108; Hoover 1971; O'Brien 1991: 211–16); it can refer either to the act of seizing or the thing seized, and the sentence does not indicate when in the 'story' either of these was contemplated by Christ, in his 'pre-existence' or his earthly life. This question also affects how, in the next verse, we understand 'he emptied himself' and what follows; it is relevant also to the other Pauline passage which seems to parallel this passage most closely: 'For you know the generous act [lit. grace] of our Lord Jesus Christ, that though he was rich, yet for your sakes he became poor, so that by his poverty you might become rich' (2 Cor 8:9).

The two lines of exegesis may be summarized as follows. First, most of the tradition, from the Greek fathers till recent times, assumes that vv. 6–11 are integral to their context and also that Paul believed in Christ's divinity and incarnation. Christ's being 'in the form of God' and 'equality with God' refer to his status 'before' his incarnation, which is the subject of v. 7. Christ, being by nature one with the Father, regarded this status as no *harpagmos*, i.e. not like a prize which he had won (and might fear to lose, as a freed slave would jealously treasure his new status and refuse slavish work). Instead, in trustful obedience to the Father, Christ 'emptied himself' and became not only mortal but actually like a slave, e.g. by washing feet, and above all by suffering a slave's death. The contrast implied by the placing of the negative is between Christ's status as Son of God and his acceptance of that of a slave. This summarizes the exegesis of Chrysostom (*PG* 62.217–37) and Isidore of Pelusium (*PG* 78.1071), both masters of Greek artistic prose as a living tradition.

The second line (or rather several lines, but all stemming from the same basic option) reads the negative as if it governed the verb 'regard', and *harpagmon* as a prize to be won. To mention an agent and immediately characterize him as one who did not seek to usurp divine status suggests a contrast with some figure who did that; thus some have proposed historical rulers (Seeley 1994); more have turned to the OT. Here lines diverge: one sees a contrast with rebellious deities, as in the myths (applied to human kings) in Isa 14:12–21 and Ezek 28, or (as an aetiology of evil and also against the post-exilic Jerusalem priesthood) in 1 *Enoch* (Sanders 1969). More widely canvassed is a contrast with Adam, following the tradition that he sinned by ambitious pride (*hubris*), wanting to become like God (surveyed in O'Brien 1991: 263–8); Wright (1992: 56–98) makes this integral to a comprehensive New Adam theology. But this reading of v. 6 rests on two unsafe foundations: first, that *morphē* in the NT can be a synonym for *eikōn*, the 'image' of God, as in Gen 1:26 (in favour, Martin 1983: 106–10; against, Behm in TDNT iv. 752: in Paul, *Christ* is the *eikōn* of God); and second, on an unverified assumption that the tradition ascribing such *hubris* to Adam was in existence by the time of Paul. It is not found in the OT or pre-Pauline literature; it seems to have arisen (perhaps because of the obscure similarities between Ezek 28 and Gen 2–3) by ascribing to Adam the arrogant motives of the figures in Isa 14 and Ezek 28. The earliest hint of this is probably in Josephus, *Ant.* 1.47 (Procopé 1941–). The roles of Adam in Romans and 1–2 Corinthians are clear; proponents of a contrast with him in Phil 2 have yet to prove that Adam's *hubris* was already a theme that could be referred to by mere allusion. The most likely OT reference is quite different (see below). These and other proposed backgrounds (Martin 1983: 74–93; O'Brien 1991: 193–7) which generally assume the hymn theory as proved, mostly understand Christ's position in v. 6 as referring to his lifetime on earth, and *harpagmos* as an act of usurpation which he renounced. Yet not all who interpret thus oppose pre-existence, indeed, this is increasingly (and rightly) recognized as Paul's belief, expressed both here and elsewhere.

vv. 7–8, the older exegetical line (1) takes these verses as referring first to the incarnation, then to its continuation in Jesus' life and death. Some proponents of a type (2) theory try to make them refer only to Jesus' history, but the effort is forced. The last phrase, 'even death on a cross' was declared by Lohmeyer a secondary 'Pauline addition' because it did not fit into the 'hymn' as reconstructed by him (O'Brien 1991: 230–1).

Simply on a stylistic analysis, it crowns a series of steps as a climax (not of height but of depth), the effect of which would strike ancient hearers with the force of shocking paradox (Fee 1995: 217). Its centrality for Paul is reflected in 3:10. A Christological complication was introduced by the Kenotic theory (Martin 1983: 66–8, 169–72) which interpreted the 'self-emptying' as a real abandonment of the nature of God. This misses the metaphoric character of 'he *emptied*' (*ekenōsen*; for its probable OT source see below); Chrysostom (*PG* 62.229) realized this, as part of the parable of a self-humbling king's son which he finds implicit in the the whole passage; it is explained by the following phrases in vv. 7–8. These are admittedly difficult. They are not typical of Paul's usage, and 'form', 'likeness', and *schēma* all seem rather weak ways of expressing the reality of Christ's humanity, which Paul surely wants to affirm as truly as his divinity. *Morphē* in a human context balances its previous divine context, and (as we saw) implies more than mere outward shape; but *schēma* does mean shape (though NRSV loosely renders it 'form'), while 'likeness' is also vague. And why is 'slave' mentioned before human status? The best answer lies in recognizing an allusion to the Isaian 'Servant' (Jeremias 1963; 1965). This is prima facie likely because that figure was so important for NT writers (Dodd 1952: 88–96). Though here all the words that favour an allusion are different from those usual in the NT, and imply the existence of a translation closer to the Hebrew (e.g. *doulos*, 'slave', instead of *pais*, 'boy'), the cluster of significant ideas could well form a recognizable way of hinting at the Isaian figure. Thus he 'emptied himself' could evoke 'he poured out himself' (Isa 53:12), *morphē* could allude to the Servant's lost *beauty* (Isa 52:14; 53:2), and he 'humbled himself' to Isa 53:4. This proposal has been unjustly opposed; it has more explanatory power than others. It illuminates the paradoxical choice of *morphē* to connote both Christ's divine nature and his acceptance of 'slave' status, especially if we accept that behind the Isaian Servant lies the role of the king in the pre-exilic cult (Eaton 1979: 75–84). *Doulos* is then not merely a slave as in the Graeco-Roman world but the royal Son and Servant of the divine King, living and dying in obedience (as in v. 8) as Chrysostom realized. Christ's 'self-emptying', like that of the Isaian Servant, bears an implication of *sacrificial* self-giving, lived out physically on earth, but also revealing a quality intrinsic to divine love.

Several keywords here also help to anchor the passage in the letter as a whole. 'He humbled himself' gives the model for the humility recommended in 2:3. The root occurs again, together with words formed from *morphē* and *schēma*, in 3:21. As the Son 'was found' in the human race (v. 7), so Paul hopes finally to 'be found' in him (3:9). But these recurrences are transformed in a way that depends on the second part of the 'story' of Christ. The whole passage, 2:5–11, has a downward–upward movement. The shameful death by the cross is the lowest point; vv. 9–11 are the upward-moving reversal, a second stanza in terms of poetic structure.

v. 9, 'Therefore' (*dio*) implies God's acceptance of Christ's self-offering, not necessarily a reward. The verb 'highly exalted' (*huper-hupsoō*) expresses a superlative degree of honour. Paul delights in *huper*-compounds (Fee 1995: 221). Those who take the passage primarily as a Christological statement find it strange that the resurrection is not explicitly mentioned, but it is implicit in 'exalted'. 'And gave him' (*echarisato*) is more accurately 'graciously conferred on him'; the verb used of God's giving the Philippians the grace of suffering for Christ (1:29). This echo, occurring in such close proximity, links their sufferings with Christ's glorification after his passion; the upward movement is for them too. What has been conferred is 'the name that is above every name': in biblical idiom 'name' can be personal or titular; a name has meaning and is charged with power. What name is meant here? The choice is between Jesus and *Kurios*, 'Lord'. '[S]o that at the name of Jesus every knee should bend' (v. 10) might seem to favour 'Jesus', but the confession that 'Jesus Christ is Lord' (v. 11) points decisively to the latter. 'Jesus' is his human name; *Kurios* and *Christos* are conferred titles, as in Peter's proclamation 'God has made him both Lord and Messiah, this Jesus whom you crucified' (Acts 2:36).

Christos (Heb. *māšíaḥ*) denotes the expected 'Anointed one'; *Kurios* was the regular Greek rendering of *ʾădōnāy*, the reverent equivalent of YHWH, though it had many other uses, including for the emperor. But vv. 10–11 are an adapted quotation of Isa 45:23, the context of which is that YHWH has proclaimed that he alone is God; there he says 'To me every knee shall bow, every tongue shall swear.' Paul vastly expands 'every knee', and changes 'to me' to 'at the name of Jesus'; then he changes 'swear' to 'confess' adding the object clause 'that Jesus Christ is Lord (*Kurios*).' At the beginning of the 'story' in 2:6 Jesus was 'in the form of God'; now he is 'hyper-exalted' and Paul adapts a text that denies that there is any God but YHWH, to say that God has given Jesus the supreme name, so that he may at last be adored by every being in the threefold cosmos and universally acclaimed as *Kurios*. But in this acclamation does *Kurios* function as the name YHWH, so that, God having conferred it on Jesus, a distinction is implied between God and YHWH? Or if *Kurios* functions not as a name but as an ordinary predicate, what other value for it is high enough to measure up to Paul's statements implying Jesus' divinity? (He must also have been aware of making a politically dangerous claim contrary to the imperial cult (Tellbe 1994: 111–14), but Paul's primary focus is theological.) The above dilemma seems inescapable: intolerable to Jews, and embarrassing to Christian exegetes who assume that rigorous monotheism was established long before Jesus and Paul. This is why theories of non-Jewish influences on early Christology have proliferated, encouraging theories that the 'hymn' in ch. 2 is non-Pauline. Recent research, however, is showing ever more clearly that, at least until the reconstruction of Judaism after 70 CE, Jewish theologizing took many forms and at least some were far short of the eventual monotheism (Segal 1978; Barker 1992). The total identification of YHWH with the High God *'ēl* *'elyôn*, and the redefinition of the latter's sons as angels, long remained incomplete, and the memory of how the king had been enthroned as 'Son of YHWH' haunted minds disaffected towards the second temple. The varieties of pre-rabbinic Judaism already contained the materials for the Christian interpretation of Jesus' life, death, and resurrection in relation to the divine unity. It is no longer enough to say that in v. 11 *Kurios* is 'the equivalent of Yahweh' and that 'Paul's monotheism is kept intact by the final phrase, "unto the glory of God the Father" ' as in 1 Cor 8:6, 'one God the Father...and one Lord Jesus Christ' (Fee 1995: 222, 226); this only restates the dilemma above. Paul's faith can be understood only as already essentially trinitarian.

In conclusion, vv. 5–11 are fully integrated in the letter. Paul introduces the 'story' of Jesus to encourage the Philippians to humility and mutual respect by looking at him. Within that context the upward movement, effected by God's exalting of Christ, reminds them of the divine call behind the exhortation in 2:1–5, as if to say 'as disciples and members of Christ, you do not need to think of your own interests or dignity—leave it all to God; just contemplate (*phroneite*) the whole story of Christ. Whatever

you have to suffer now, Christ is leading you to glory.' Within the letter as a whole, the passage is the climax of the first great exhortation. The second climax, in ch. 3, balances the first, both by verbal echoes and by repeating the downward–upward movement, now with reference to Paul. The movement corresponds to a pattern found (with variations) in a number of early quasi-credal statements, some more poetic in style, others less. The pattern would have taken shape in early meditation on Jesus' baptism, death, and resurrection in the light of OT texts, as in Acts 2:22–36. Its skeleton is in 2 Cor 8:9; freer variations appear in Col 1:15–20 and the Gospel of John, especially the prologue and the theme of lifting up and glorification. In early poetry we find it in the second-century *Odes of Solomon*, with typically Syrian emphasis on the descent to Sheol, in Odes 17, 22 (which brings Jesus' baptism into the pattern), 24, and 42. Since Paul was probably the earliest of all the writers involved, the variants of the pattern may well issue out from him.

(**2:12–18**) **The Response Paul Desires from the Philippians** Paul returns to direct exhortation, now illuminated by Christ's example; 'you have always obeyed' echoes 'he became obedient' (2:8), and likewise has no named object, but implies primarily God (Lightfoot 1879: 115–16), rather than Paul (as NRSV). vv. 12–13, Paul has mentioned salvation as his hope both for himself (1:19) and for the Philippians, adding 'this is God's doing' (1:28). What is added now is emphasis on human collaboration with God: 'work out your own salvation ... for it is God who is at work'. It is not, of course, autonomous labour. The force of 2:5–11 still directs the thought; the Christian's personal effort is with and in Christ. 'Fear and trembling' was proverbial from the OT; Paul usually uses it of human relations (1 Cor 2:3; 2 Cor 7:15; Eph 6:5), but here of a stance before God. At 1:15 Paul uses 'good pleasure' of attitudes favourable to himself, though usually in the NT it refers to God's benevolent will towards humankind (e.g. Lk 2:14; Eph 1:5). vv. 12–13 became a key text in all discussions of grace and free will.

v. 14, Paul echoes the Exodus story for both warning and encouragement, alluding to the people's repeated grumbling (Ex 15–17; Num 14–17) and 'arguing': with divided minds, doubting God's providence. v. 15, phrases in Deut 32:5 are turned from condemnation to encouragement: 'children of God without blemish' is what Moses said the people no longer were; Paul promises the Philippians that they can become so. A 'crooked and perverse generation' was said of the people; Paul applies it to the hostile environment in which the Philippians *shine like stars* (with perhaps a hint of Mt 5:14, 16). He uses the present tense to encourage them, but in v. 16 there is a hint of pleading; on their 'holding fast to the word of life' depends his hope of being able to 'boast [cf. 1:26] on the day of Christ [cf. 1:10] that [he] did not run in vain'—again the athletic metaphor, used as in Gal 2:2; 4:11. v. 17, he changes to a metaphor of religious intensity: 'even if I am being poured out as a libation [eight words for one in Greek, *spendomai*] over the sacrifice and the offering of your faith, I am glad and rejoice'. Here the 'priests' are the Philippians (cf. 4:18); he is ready to be part of their offering. (Paul never uses cultic or priestly terms in direct designation of his apostolic ministry, but only by way of metaphor; this is true even of the concentrated cultic language in Rom 15:16. Priestly and sacrificial language can be applied to all members of the church.) 'Offering' here renders *leitourgia*, see PHIL 1.19. It came to refer to religious worship (hence 'liturgy'), especially in the Greek Bible, but it retained its financial connotations (Peterlin 1995: 195–9). Here it combines with 'sacrifice' in a cultic metaphor, meaning the life of Christian faith. (In 2:25, 30 the financial sense is more prominent.) v. 18, Paul ends this section with a burst of joy ('I am glad') using not different words (as NRSV) but *chairō* four times, twice compounded with *sun-*, to express his own joy and to call the Philippians to the same.

Timothy and Epaphroditus, Paul's Go-Betweens (2:19–30)

This section introduces two of Paul's helpers, but tells us more about his affection for them than the reasons for their journeys. On Timothy see Acts 16:1–3; 17:14–15; 19:22; he is not named in the account of Paul's first visit to Philippi, but the Christians there know him (v. 22), doubtless from the time mentioned in Acts 20:4. Paul's praise of him as alone *iso-psuchon* (lit. equal-souled) echoes his wish that they should all be *sumpsuchoi* (2:2). Apparently speaking of his present circumstances, Paul excepts Timothy alone from a judgement more sweeping than he made in 1:15–17: 'All . . . are seeking their own interests, not those of Jesus Christ' (v. 21); he has urged the opposite attitude in 2:4. Timothy has 'served' (*edouleusen*, v. 22) 'the gospel' with Paul, like a son to him, both of them being slaves (*douloi*, 1:1) of Christ who took the form of a slave. As for

Epaphroditus, Paul calls him 'brother' and uses two *sun*-words, 'fellow-worker' and 'fellow-soldier' (v. 25). He had come with a gift (4:18) as the Philippians' envoy (*apostolos* in the sense of *šaliaḥ*, the agent of a synagogue, and *leitourgos*). Dissectors of Philippians argue that Paul would not have left his thanks to the end. Yet his appreciation is certainly implicit in vv. 25 and 30, where he uses *leitourgia* again in a 'non-liturgical' sense, for their subvention which Epaphroditus, at risk to his life, has brought. Admittedly his thanks are qualified; 'services that you could not give' (NRSV) is more literally 'your shortfall (*husterēma*) towards me'. See further PHIL 4:10–19. The Philippians had heard of Epaphroditus' illness; Paul has sent him back to relieve their anxiety about him (vv. 25–8). He wants them to receive Epaphroditus with joy and hold people like him in honour (v. 29); he hopes shortly to send Timothy for more news and then soon to come himself (vv. 19–24).

What lies behind these dealings? (See PHIL A.3.) Peterlin (1995), analysing passages in Philippians and other letters in sociological categories, sees a community of house churches, differing in social and financial status and not all equally enthusiastic about regularly supporting Paul. Epaphroditus, he suggests, was well-off and willing to discharge a *leitourgia*, but not popular with all. This is a credible picture of relationships within the community but it neglects relevant external factors. As for grounds of dissension, when Paul saw serious trouble he usually spoke out plainly. The hints of discord or the grounds for suspecting criticisms of Paul in Philippians cannot compare with the evidence in 1–2 Corinthians. Clearly he is anxious for the Philippians' unity; but he seems to see the trouble as healable by recalling them to a right mind and renewed joy in Christ (cf. PHIL 4:8).

Second Exhortation on Discipleship (3:1–4:1)

(3:1–2) Transition These verses are widely held to belong to different letters (see PHIL D.2 and most commentaries). v. 1, the first phrase, 'Finally' (*to loipon*, lit. for the rest) is often a closing formula but equally can be a mere link like 'so'. The imperative *chairete* can mean 'fare-well' but can equally remain a real imperative, 'rejoice' (as NRSV). Those who see vv. 1–2 as containing the end of a letter and the start of a fragment will take the first option in each case, but the second pair of options is perfectly possible and can support the case for the verse being a transition within one letter, as is defended here, following Reed (1996). Either way, the second sentence in v. 1 is difficult, because the three main terms in it are all obscure. (1) To what do 'the same things' refer, which Paul speaks of writing? (2) What does he mean by saying that his writing is not 'troublesome' for him? (3) What does he mean by being 'a safeguard' for his addressees? (1) On the assumption of a plurality of sources, 'the same things' are the various themes that Paul frequently addresses. On the 'integrity view', it means primarily rejoicing (just commended for the twelfth time), and probably also the warning (v. 2) that Paul is about to express, as often before (cf. 3:18). (2) Paul says that repeating this is not 'troublesome' for him, or something similar according to most interpretations. But the verb from which this adjective (oknēron) is formed primarily means 'to hesitate' or 'shrink'. Formulas using this word-group are common in Hellenistic papyrus letters in many contexts, e.g. of request or invitation: 'I say without hesitation...' or 'Don't hesitate to ask...' (Reed 1996); polite, persuasive formulas used when a writer feels tact is called for, as Paul might well here. In contrast, to say that writing the same things is 'not troublesome' seems rather pointless. (3) For his addressees, he says, his repetition is a 'safeguard' (asphales). Against what? The word negates ideas of stumbling or going wrong. Though it usually means 'safe' in a 'passive' sense (from danger, error, etc.), Paul applies it to his own action (calling for rejoicing) with reference to the effect he wants it to have on his readers, namely to stabilize and confirm them in faith and keep them from harm (what harm, we learn in v. 2). In conclusion, though the verse marks a transition, it need not be an unintelligibly harsh one: 'So go on, brothers [and sisters], rejoicing in the Lord; I don't hesitate to repeat this, while for you it is salutary.'

v. 2, the question of continuity arises again: there seems to be a sudden leap from gentleness to anger. Yet how harsh this feels depends on how one word is translated. The threefold 'look' (blepete) has often been taken as 'beware of' (as NRSV). But the latter sense normally requires a preposition not used here; without it, the probable sense is 'look hard at'. The verse is still a warning, and the strong language and its objects still have to be explained, but the tone now sounds less shrill. On a stylistic analysis (cf. Reed 1996: 84–8), the triple imperative balances the three imperatives in the three previous verses: 'receive', 'hold in honour', and 'rejoice' (2:29, 30; 3:1). The first three are addressed to friends; the second three refer to

people regarded as enemies. A parallel occurs in 3:17–19. The transition here remains arresting, but it can be seen to be bridged.

(3:2–11) Paul's 'Transvaluation of Values' through Christ Whatever personal tensions there are within the community, Paul wants to draw their minds back to Christ as he did in ch. 2, but this time by telling them his own story, how he 'emptied himself' of secure pride so as to be with Christ, and how his only aim now is to follow the 'upward call' to the end. Judaism is where he started, but non-Christian Judaism would hardly be familiar to this church formed mainly of Gentile converts. Yet they are being troubled by people urging circumcision, contrary to the Jerusalem decision (Acts 15) not to impose it on Gentile converts and Paul's efforts to uphold this. This can account for Paul's starting-point in v. 2 and (to some extent) moderate the shock of his strong language. He may be quoting expressions that he had used on previous occasions (cf. 3:18) to raise his converts' morale by mocking at opponents. The first two could be turning back terms used by the 'enemy'; the third (katatomē) is a sarcastic play on 'circumcision' (peritomē), changing the prefix to one implying destruction. It is clear that circumcision is the issue, but not an attack on Jewish Christians as such, provided they do not deny that Gentile converts are true Christians and heirs to the promises to Israel. v. 3, Paul recalls his teaching on the 'true circumcision' through faith in Christ (Rom 2:25–9); now he adds the charismatic experience of Gentile Christians 'who worship in the Spirit of God'. He wants them to remain content as they are; but he does not explain why circumcision has been urged on them. He uses his regular antithesis of 'flesh' and 'spirit', but after 3:1 there is no more anger like that in Galatians. The suggestion of Tellbe (1994: 116–20; PHIL B.3) is plausible: all circumcised Jews could enjoy the exemptions granted by Rome to Judaism as a permitted religion, even if some were now also Christians; but uncircumcised Gentile Christians, even though recognized by Jewish Christians on the basis of Acts 15, could not. If they refused to take part in the imperial cult (surely important in a proud colonia), Paul's converts would be 'disloyal citizens' and incur persecution, as they already had (1:29). The Jewish Christians offer a way out: join us and live at peace. They might insist that it would involve no infidelity to Christ; but Paul could only see it as undermining his whole work of extending membership of God's people on the sole basis of faith in Christ crucified.

vv. 4–11, this may be why Paul leaves the circumcision issue, to tell (doubtless retell) his personal story. He is a Jewish Christian, once proud of his birth, observance, and zeal (vv. 5–6; cf. Acts 26:4–11). But he has undergone a complete 'transvaluation of values', which in vv. 3–11 he expresses by a series of keywords with changed applications. He recalls his former *confidence* in Jewish practice; we have seen at 1:6, 25, and 2:24 that he now bases this only on Christ. His righteousness was once based on the law (v. 6); now, solely on his faith in Christ (v. 9). In vv. 7–8 Paul plays on an accounting metaphor of *gain* (*kerdos* and verb *kerdainō*, cf. 1:21) and *loss* (*zēmia* and verb *zēmioumai*); his assets have changed places by his new reckoning. Indeed, the metaphor of gain and loss, though quite different from that implicit in 2:6–8, corresponds in effect to Christ's regarding his divine status as 'no prize to be clung to' (*oukh harpagmon*) and, instead, 'emptying himself' (cf. Fee 1995: 314–15). The allusion continues in Paul's hope 'that I may gain Christ and be found in him' (vv. 8–9), as Christ was found in solidarity with the human race (2:7); when finally 'the books are opened', Paul hopes to be acknowledged as Christ's, because he has renounced all his assets to trust totally in him. What he now calls them (*skubala*, 'filth') recalls the invective of v. 2. v. 9 succinctly summarizes Paul's teaching on justification (Fee 1995: 319–26), which his converts would know well. v. 10 corresponds to 2:6–9 at the turning-point from descent to ascent. 'To know Christ', implies intimate, experiential knowledge, cf. 1:9; this is why Paul does not keep the order of Christ's crucifixion and exaltation, but interweaves them, just as the power of Christ's resurrection, the sharing (*koinōnia*) of his sufferings, and becoming like him in his death are experienced as interwoven in Christian prayer, liturgy, and life. As Christ was in the form of God and took the form of a slave (2:6–7), so Paul wants only to be 'con-formed' (*sum-morphizomenos*), moulded into that *morphē*. (The vocabulary recurs in 3:21.)

(3:12–16) Following the Upward Call with Paul v. 12, Paul's upward way (from v. 11) corresponds to 2:9–11, but glory is far ahead; to 'attain the resurrection' is an object of humble hope, desire, and effort. Paul knows that he has not 'obtained' (*elabon*) this or 'been made perfect' (as NRSV fn., cf. PHIL 3:15) 'but I press on' (*diōkō*, lit. pursue; last used of his former zeal in perse-

cution, 3:6), 'to grasp it (*katalabō*), as I have been grasped by Christ Jesus' (my tr.). Though the words are different, the image stands in striking counterpoint to *harpagmos* in 2:6; NRSV obscures this by using 'make [one's] own'. vv. 13–14, Paul repeats the verb, merging his accounting metaphor into that of running a race, a cliché of popular ethics that he has used before; 'straining forward' (*epekteinomenos*) renews the image in 'eager expectation' (PHIL 1:20). See further Pfitzner (1967: 134–56). 'The goal' (*skopos*; its verb *skopeō* occurs in 2:4 and 3:17) is anything aimed at, but 'prize' (*brabeion*) belongs to athletics. The aim and the prize are pursued in response to 'the upward call' (as NRSV fn.) of God in Christ Jesus.

v. 15, this completes Paul's own downward–upward 'story', which corresponds to 2:6–11; now he turns to his addressees, and first to 'those of us…who are mature' (*teleioi*, lit. perfect). At v. 12 he has just disclaimed the related verb for himself. The mystery cults used these terms to refer to grades of initiation, and Paul could on occasion draw on that vocabulary for a metaphor (e.g. 4:12); Gnostic sects used it systematically. Koester (1961–2) and others find hints of Gnostic opponents here and elsewhere, but such theories go beyond exegesis. Neither is there need to posit charismatics who have got above themselves, as in Corinth, where Paul refers, perhaps with irony, to 'the perfect' (1 Cor 2:6). Here Paul returns to his major theme of a Christlike mindset (*phronein*); he is leading up to his concluding appeals in 4:2 and 4:8. He has held up the supreme model in 2:5–11 and told his own story; he seeks to persuade, not to bludgeon. He invites any who may 'think differently' to be attentive and receptive to God's interior revelation. 'This is not the language or mode of polemics' (Fee 1995: 353).

(3:17–4:1) Citizens of earth and heaven In 3:17–19 Paul holds up examples and counter-examples. Obviously he has told his own story to invite imitation, but in calling the Philippians to be his 'fellow-imitators' (*sum-mimētai*) he puts himself beside them, as in 3:15; Christ, not Paul, is the model. Secondly, he tells them to 'observe' (*skopeite*) those who live according to the 'example (*tupos*) you have in us'; here speaks a teacher, not one demanding a personality-cult. In contrast, in vv. 18–19 Paul renews past warnings against 'many' whom (as his urgent tone shows) he regards as a serious threat. Their 'end is destruction' (*apōleia*); in 1:28 this fate awaits opponents who are probably persecutors, but

Paul's tears suggest a group within the church. They are 'enemies of the cross of Christ', yet nothing marks them as Jewish Christians. 'Their god is their belly' might refer to converts who, on the dietary issues discussed in 1 Cor 8, allow themselves too much liberty. 'Their minds are set (*phronountes*) on earthly things' and 'their glory is in their shame'—these phrases are enigmatic, but they could apply to Christians who, in face of the state cult and social pressures, chose to enjoy the sense of civic glory but with the shame of compromise, taking part in meals connected with public sacrifices and, in Paul's view, reducing Christianity to one among other acceptable philosophies.

If something like this was the case, v. 20 follows appositely: it is right to want to be good citizens, 'but our citizenship (*politeuma*) is in heaven'. *Politeuma* recalls the related verb in 1:27 and reinforces the case for taking it in civic terms, though many have understood both words more loosely in terms of way of life. The noun (often rendered 'commonwealth') refers to the state of which one is a citizen, either directly or by citizenship of an enfranchised colony, as Philippi was of Rome. Paul valued Roman citizenship and readily appealed to it at need; but just as humankind, created in God's image, has authority only by that title, so has any state. Hence for Christians (as also for Jews), God's *politeuma* is primary. Thus Paul's contemporary Philo, speaking of the patriarchs as 'sojourners on earth', says that heaven is their native land, in which they have their citizenship (*politeuontai*, Philo, *Conf. Ling.* 78–9), and a second-century apologist says exactly the same of Christians (*Letter to Diognetus*, 5). The heavenly *politeuma* is not merely an ideal; Christians' actually live in two orders, of which the earthly is under the judgement of the heavenly. They are related not only 'vertically' but also eschatologically; 'it is from there that we are expecting a Saviour (*sōtēr*), the Lord Jesus Christ'. 'Saviour' contrasts with the 'destruction' facing the 'enemies of the cross', as *sōtēria* and *apōleia* are contrasted in 1:28. But *sōtēr* was also a title used in the ruler-cult; applied to Christ it makes a higher claim for him, just as 'Christ is *Kurios*' does over against the emperor. 3:21 winds up the parallelism of chs. 2:1–18 and 3 with many significant echoes. 'He will transform [*metaschēmatisei*, *schēma*, 2:8] the body of our humiliation' (cf. 'humility', 2:3 and 'he humbled himself', 2:8, all from the same root *tapeinos* 'that it may be conformed [*sum-morphon*, cf. *morphē*, divine and then human, 2:6–7] to the body of his glory

[*doxa*, cf. 2:11 and in contrast just above, 3:19], by the power [*energeia*, cf. the twofold use of the related verb at 2:13] that also enables him to make all things subject to himself'. To savour how these echoes work, and then to see how 3:21 virtually sums up 1 Cor 15:20–8 and 2 Cor 3:18–5:10, is better than any commentary, but Fee (1995: 381–4) is good. 4:1 concludes the main exhortation: 'Therefore … stand firm in the Lord in this way'; for the rest, it overflows with words of love and joy, among which one (*epipothētoi*, beloved) echoes Epaphroditus' yearning in 2:26.

Final Exhortation, Thanks for Support, and Conclusion (4:2–23)

(4:2–3) Last Appeal for Harmony As already noted, recent exegetes find hints of disunity, and perhaps of different causes, in many passages (PHIL B.3), but 4:2 is the first place where Paul comes to naming names. Yet even here the trouble between Euodia and Syntyche is not defined more than as a failure 'to be of the same mind' (to think, *phronein*, the same). Garland (1985: 172–3) sees the whole letter as leading up to this; Peterlin (1995) constructs a total picture, defining the roles of *episkopoi*, *diakonoi*, and 'co-workers' (*sunergoi*, 2:25; 4:3); the two women are *diakonoi*, leaders of two housegroups in conflict, probably over material support of Paul. In contrast, Fee (1995: 385–400) after a survey of theories concludes that none is proven; we know neither the cause of the quarrel, nor the identity of the 'loyal companion', nor of the Clement named here, nor whether Lydia (Acts 16:14) was still there (perhaps identical with one or other of the women, or the 'companion'). The clearest indications of trouble in Philippians point to persecution and the temptation of Jewish Christianity (Tellbe 1994), but there is no hint of these as the issue in 4:2. One thing seems clear: the quarrel is serious and worries Paul; if 2:1–5 is related to it, it seems to have divided the community.

(4:4–9) Last Call to Joy, Peace, and 'Right Thinking' in Christ Yet whatever the trouble is, Paul seems confident that the cure is to recall the Philippians to the charismatic joy of their first coming to faith, exactly as he reminded their neighbours in Thessalonica how 'in spite of persecutions you received the word with joy inspired by the Holy Spirit' (1 Thess 1:6). His constant insistence on joy is not mere cheerfulness; this and following Christ with a right mind are the keys to Paul's strategy towards the Philippians. In vv. 4–7 he invites them to share the spirit of his initial greeting and prayer for them, with a few new touches. v. 5, 'Let your gentleness (*epieikēs*) be known to everyone': most versions have something similar. But the basic sense of *epieikēs* is 'seemly', decent or equitable; the phrase could be a last word on good citizenship, much as in 1 Pet 3:16. 'The Lord is near': in joy or suffering, or if the latter leads to death, all the nearer. v. 6, 'Do not worry about anything': as Paul has demonstrated regarding liberty or captivity, life or death (and is about to add, plenty or hardship). The basis is a perfect trust in God, expressed in prayer like that in 1:3–11 and here, which brings peace as in v. 7. Paul sums up his appeals for a right mind in Christ in vv. 8–9, now using a synonym as in 3:13. Few versions do justice to the heightened solemnity of tone (reminiscent of 2:1–4) and of vocabulary, which (like 2:6–11) includes several words beyond Paul's usual range. Neither there nor here need this point to a different author, despite the fact that both the rhetoric and the content of v. 8 are typical both of popular (especially Stoic) philosophy and of Hellenistic Judaism. This somewhat troubles Fee (1995: 413–19), but it need not (cf. PHIL E). Paul could harness this language to his gospel when he found it appropriate. In v. 9, as in 3:17, he reminds his pupils of what they have learned from him; he speaks with no arrogance but as a true teacher.

(4:10–23) Paul's Attitude to Gifts Received and Last Greetings The section composed of vv. 10–19 takes up from that in 2:19–30, completing the rondo pattern in the letter (PHIL F); the last appearance of several keywords marks the overall *inclusio*: rejoice, v. 10; be concerned (*phronein*), v. 10; be humbled (*tapeinousthai*, obscured in NRSV), v. 11; share (*koinōnos* words, but now in a financial idiom), vv. 14, 15; gospel, v. 15; glory, v. 20. A simple reading may find behind this and 2:19–30 no more than a simple story, to which Paul refers with modest and undemanding gratitude; but there are hints of more complicated feelings (Peterlin 1995: 209–16). The Philippian church has supported Paul generously since the beginning (vv. 15–16). Paul is, and wants to appear, duly grateful, but in the embarrassment of need (*chreia*, 2:25; v. 16) he has to speak of shortfall (*husterēma*, 2:30; *husterēsis*, v. 11; NRSV conceals this by a bland paraphrase both times). But again, he wants not to seem demanding (v. 17); hence his assurances that he has learnt to be content with whatever he has (vv. 11–13). Here Paul shows the same equanimity as in 1:18 and 22; perhaps with a touch of mock solemnity, he uses the Stoic word *autarkēs* ('self-sufficient'; NRSV 'content', v. 11) and a metaphor from the mystery cults (lit. I am initiated into everything, v. 12). But then he fears that he may seem to be indifferent to the support which he actually needs. 'Mirror-reading' runs the risk of straying into imaginative fiction; but Paul's words here, almost as much as in 2 Corinthians, do suggest that he is facing several lines of criticism. Finally he stops trying to explain, and turns to praising their gift by describing it (by a metaphor already used in 2:17) as a sacrifice pleasing to God (v. 18), and praying that God will meet all their needs. The passage ends with a doxology. We do not know how successful this letter was in restoring harmony. No evidence remains to the contrary, in contrast with what 1 *Clement* reveals about Corinth some years after Paul's letters.

The letter closes by sending usual affectionate greetings and mentioning the emperor's household (v. 22), a hint (as 1:13) of successful influence on Paul's part, perhaps through his Praetorian contacts.

REFERENCES

Barclay, J. M. G. (1987), 'Mirror-reading a Polemical Letter: Galatians as a Test Case', *JSNT* 31: 73–93.

Barker, M. (1992), *The Great Angel: A Study of Israel's Second God* (London: SPCK).

Bormann, L. (1995), *Philippi. Stadt und Christengemeinde zur Zeit des Paulus*, NovTSup 78 (Leiden: Brill).

Brewer, R. R. (1954), 'The Meaning of *Politeuesthe* in Philippians 1.27', *JBL* 73: 76–83.

Brown, R. E., and Meier, J. P. (1983), *Antioch and Rome* (New York: Paulist).

Bruce, F. F. (1980–1), 'St Paul in Macedonia: 3. The Philippian Correspondence', *BJRL* 63: 260–84.

Carmignac, J. (1971–2), 'L'importance de la place d'une négation: ΟΥΧ ΑΡΠΑΓΜΟΝ ΗΓΗΣΑΤΟ (Philippians 11.6)', *NTS* 18: 131–66.

Collange, J.-F. (1979), *The Epistle of Saint Paul to the Philippians*, tr. A. W. Heathcote (London: Epworth).

Dalton, W. (1979), 'The Integrity of Philippians', *Bib.* 60: 97–102.

Dodd, C. H. (1952), *According to the Scriptures* (Welwyn: Nisbet).

Eaton, J. (1979), *Festal Drama in Deutero-Isaiah* (London: SPCK).

Engberg-Pedersen, T. (1994), 'Stoicism in Philippians', in idem (ed.), *Paul in his Hellenistic Context* (Edinburgh: T. & T. Clark).

Fee, G. (1992), 'Philippians 2:5–11: Hymn or Exalted Pauline Prose?', *BBR* 2: 9–46.

—— (1995), *Paul's Letter to the Philippians*, NICNT (Grand Rapids: Eerdmans).

Garland, D. E. (1985), 'The Composition and Unity of Philippians', *NovT* 27: 141–73.

Herron, T. J. (1989), 'The Most Probable Date of the First Epistle of Clement to the Corinthians', *Studia Patristica*, 21, ed. E. A. Livingstone (Leuven: Peters).

Hooker, M. (1978), 'Philippians 2.6–11', in E. Ellis and E. Grasser (eds.), *Jesus und Paulus*, 2nd edn. (Göttingen: Vandenhoeck & Ruprecht).

Hoover, R. W. (1971), 'The HARPAGMOS Enigma: A Philosophical Solution', *HTR* 64: 95–119.

Jeremias, J. (1963), 'Zu Phil ii 7: ΕΑΥΤΟΝ ΕΚΕΝΩΣΕΝ', *NovT* 6: 182–9.

—— (1965), 'The Servant of God in the New Testament', in *The Servant of God*, SBT 20 (London: SCM), 97–9.

Koester, H. (1961–2), 'The Purpose of the Polemic of a Pauline Fragment (Philippians III)', *NTS* 8: 317–32.

Lake, K. (1912–13), (ed. and tr.), *The Apostolic Fathers I–II*, LCL (London: Loeb).

Lightfoot, J. B. (1879), *Saint Paul's Epistle to the Corinthians*, 4th edn. (London: Macmillan).

Lohmeyer, E. (1928), *Kyrios Jesus: Eine Untersuchung zu Phil. 2, 5–11* (Heidelberg: C. Winker).

Malherbe, A. J. (1988), *Ancient Epistolary Theorists*, SBLSBS 19 (Atlanta: Scholars Press).

Martin, R. P. (1983), *Carmen Christi: Philippians 2:5–11 in Recent Interpretation and in the Setting of Early Christian Worship*, 2nd edn. (Grand Rapids: Eerdmans).

Meeks, W. A. (1983), *The First Urban Christians: The Social World of the Apostle Paul* (New Haven: Yale University Press).

Miller, E. C. (1982), 'Πολιτεύεσθε in Philippians 1.27: Some Philological and Thematic Observations', *JSNT* 15: 86–96.

Moule, C. F. D. (1970), 'Further Reflexions on Philippians 2:5–11', in W. W. Gasque and R. P. Martin (eds.), *Apostolic History and the Gospel* (Grand Rapids: Eerdmans), 264–76.

O'Brien, P. T. (1991), *The Epistle to the Philippians: A Commentary on the Greek Text*, NIGTC (Grand Rapids: Eerdmans).

Peterlin, D. (1995), *Paul's Letter to the Philippians in the Light of Disunity in the Church*, NovTSup 79 (Leiden: Brill).

Pfitzner, V. C. (1967), *Paul and the Agon Motif*, NovTSup 16 (Leiden: Brill).

Procopé, J. (1941–), 'Hochmut', *RAC* xv. 795–858.

Reed, J. T. (1996), 'Philippians 3:1 and the Epistolary Hesitation Formulas', *JBL* 115: 63–90.

Sanders, J. A. (1969), 'Dissenting Deities and Philippians 2:1–11', *JBL* 88: 279–90.

Seeley, D. (1994), 'The Background of the Philippians Hymn', *Journal of Higher Criticism*, 1: 49–72.

Segal, A. (1978), *Two Powers in Heaven* (Leiden: Brill).

Stanton, G. V. (1974), *Jesus of Nazareth in New Testament Preaching*, SNTSMS 27 (Cambridge: Cambridge University Press).

Tellbe, M. (1994), 'The Sociological Factors behind Philippians 3:1–11 and the conflict at Philippi', *JSNT* 55: 97–121.

Wright, N. T. (1992), *The Climax of the Covenant: Christ and the Law in Pauline Theology* (Minneapolis: Fortress).

10. Colossians

JEROME MURPHY-O'CONNOR, OP

INTRODUCTION

A. Colossae. 1. The sparse unexcavated ruins of what had been a large and prosperous Hellenistic city are located in the valley of the river Lycus 12 miles east of Denzili in Turkey. Seleucid promotion of its neighbours Laodicea and Hierapolis in the third pre-Christian century ended Colossae's virtual monopoly of the wool production of the valley. None the less the cyclamen purple (*colossinus*) fleeces of Colossae (Pliny, *Nat. Hist.* 21.51) continued to rival the glossy black wool of Laodicea (Strabo, *Geog.* 12.8.6). They were the mainstay of the local economy. Access to international markets was facilitated by the location of the cities on the

great 'common highway' linking Ephesus (120 miles west) with the Euphrates (ibid. 14.2.29). The population was mainly pagan but in 213 BCE, in order to enhance commerce and trade, Antiochus III installed 2,000 Jewish families from Mesopotamia (Josephus, *Ant* 12.148–53). By 62 BCE the amount of the temple tax confiscated by the Roman governor (20 pounds of gold) reveals that there were at least 11,000 adult male Jews in the Lycus valley (Lightfoot 1904: 20).

2. The Lycus valley was evangelized by Epaphras (4:13), a native of Colossae (4:12), who had been commissioned by Paul (see COL 1:7). Paul's appreciation of the contrast between his own arrival in Philippi and Thessalonica, where he had to start from scratch each time, and his experience in Corinth (Acts 18:2–3) and Ephesus (Acts 18:19; 1 Cor 16:19), where Prisca and Aquila furnished him with a well-established base, helped him to the realization that travellers returning home would be the most effective apostles. They started with built-in advantages: they did not have to look for work, they were known and trusted, they had networks of family, friends, and acquaintances, who could be guaranteed to listen, at least initially. Most, if not all, of the converts made by Epaphras were pagans (1:21; 2:13).

3. The volcanic springs and underground rivers alerted Strabo to the unstable character of the Lycus valley, 'if any country is subject to earthquakes, Laodicea is' (*Geog.* 12.8.16). A major earthquake hit in 60 CE (Tac., *Ann.* 14.27.1). Both Laodicea and Hierapolis were rebuilt, but Colossae never recovered; note the silence of Pliny (*Nat. Hist.* 5.105). Its long slide into oblivion terminated in the ninth century CE when the site was definitively abandoned.

B. Authenticity. 1. There is no consensus regarding the authorship of Colossians. The case against authenticity has been most comprehensively argued recently by Schenk (1987) and Furnish (1992), but the reasons they assemble—style, conception of Paul's role, Christology, eschatology, and literary dependence—are not compelling.

2. Style was once thought to be the definitive argument against Pauline origin (Bujard 1973), but when analysed in a more sophisticated way it appears that Colossians is perfectly at home among the accepted letters (Neumann 1990: 213). Moreover, the stylistic variations between all the Pauline letters are far from insignificant (Kenny 1986: 80), and the influence of co-authors and secretaries can no longer be ignored (Murphy-O'Connor 1995a: 34). There is no standard of Pauline style to which doubtful letters can be compared.

3. Paul, we are told, is presented as the peerless, transcendent apostle. This is not in fact the case. The language of Colossians is certainly universalist, e.g. 'the gospel which you heard, which has been preached to every creature under heaven, and of which I, Paul, became a minister' (1:23; cf. 1:6, 28), but the lack of the article before 'minister' shows that Paul does not consider himself the unique agent, and the hyperbole is precisely paralleled by 1 Thess 1:8, both as regards tense and extension. Paul had to stress his universal, but not exclusive,

responsibility in writing to a church that he did not found directly (2:1). It is also asserted that Colossians gives Paul's sufferings a vicarious value, whereas in the authentic letters they are viewed kerygmatically. This argument has no foundation. It is due to the mistranslation of a key verse; see COL 1:24. The identification of the gospel as 'the mystery' (1:26–7; 2:2; 4:3) is a Pauline paradox, since the whole point is that it is no longer a secret. It does not, therefore, convey a different perspective on revelation.

4. The Christology of Colossians can be seen as fundamentally different from that of the authentic letters only if it is assumed that Paul was in full agreement with everything that appears in Colossians. In fact the situation is parallel to that of 1 Corinthians where Paul quotes Corinthian statements with which he is in flat disagreement. The cosmic dimension, which is most visible in 1:15–20, does not represent Paul's thought. It is quoted from a Colossian hymn, which Paul edits severely to incorporate his own vision of Christ (see COL 1:15–20). His adversaries 'had done their best to give Christ a prominent place in the realm of cosmic speculation. What they had not done, and the editor now proceeds to do, is to recognize his earthly activity' (Barrett 1994: 146). Contrast 1:19 with 2:10, and note the stress on the crucifixion (1:20; 2:14). The vision of the church as 'the body of Christ' (1:18a; 2:19) is simply a more graphic statement of the union of believers with Christ and each other (Gal 2:20; 3:27–8). The distinction between the individual Jesus Christ ('the head') and his 'body' was imposed on Paul by the circumstances at Colossae. It does not appear in 1 Cor 12:12–27 or Rom 12:4–5 because the position of Christ was not an issue in those churches.

5. It is claimed that the realized eschatology of Colossians is incompatible with the future eschatology of the authentic letters. On only two occasions, however, is the resurrection of believers presented as a past fact (2:12; 3:1), and in context this is nothing more than a vivid expression of their passage from 'death' to 'life' (2:13; cf. Rom 6:11). Standard Pauline future eschatology appears in 1:22–3, 28; 3:4, 6, 24–5.

6. The charge that Colossians is the work of a secondary imitator, because it conflates phrases from Romans, 1–2 Corinthians, Galatians, and 1 Thessalonians, exaggerates the import of verbal reminiscences, while at the same time failing to provide a justification for the proposed redactional technique in only parts of Colossians.

C. Date of Composition. 1. Of the six who send greetings to Colossae, five also salute Philemon (see COL 4:10–14). The names of Timothy (1:1; Philem 1) and Onesimus (4:9; Philem 10) appear in both letters, as does that of Archippus as one of the recipients (4:17; Philem 2). Opponents of the authenticity of Colossians claim that its author borrowed the personalia from Philemon in order to give Pauline colouring to Colossians, but cite no evidence to show that this was a normal tactic to get a forgery accepted—it was not considered necessary by the author of Ephesians—and fail to explain the changes in order and qualifications. Hence, Colossians must be dated to the same imprisonment as Philemon 4:10, 18; Philem 1, 9, 23.

2. This incarceration took place at Ephesus (1 Cor 15:32; 2 Cor 1:8) in the years 53–4, rather than at Rome in the early 60s (*contra* Dunn 1996: 41). When in Rome all Paul's attention was focused on Spain (Rom 15:24, 28), but Philem 22 and Phil 1:26; 2:24 reveal plans to visit Colossae and Philippi. The action of Onesimus is explicable only if Paul was in the vicinity of Colossae (Lampe 1985). The speed of the contacts between Paul and Philippi (Phil 2:25–30) exclude Rome as the place of imprisonment.

3. Assumptions regarding Paul's theological development cannot be given any weight in this discussion (against Bruce 1977: 411–12). Even if we could be absolutely sure of the precise chronological order of the letters, it would mean little. The letters are not homogeneous segments of an ongoing research project, each one building on its predecessor, but reactions to specific problems, in which what Paul says is conditioned by the needs of the recipients, and by his own estimate of what will be an effective response.

D. The False Teaching. 1. Hooker's (1973) view that there was no systematic false teaching at Colossae does not really account for the language of 2:8–23. Paul is reacting to a doctrinal problem, which has been described in at least forty-four different ways (Gunther 1973: 3–4)! There is a useful survey of the more notable opinions in O'Brien 1982: xxx-xxxviii. A decisive breakthrough was made by Francis's (Francis and Meeks 1973:163–207) lexicographical work on *tapeinophrosynē* and *embateuô* in 2:18, which provided a basis for an understanding of the genitive in 'worship of angels' as subjective. His outline of Jewish ascetic mysticism, which is the socio-religious framework of his hypothesis, has been developed thoroughly by Sappington (1991). The polemic material in 2:8,

16–23 contains both direct and indirect references to the content, function, and medium of revelation, as well as to the pre-requisites for its attainment. Sappington (ibid. 170) concludes, 'the Colossian error is strikingly similar to the ascetic-mystical piety of Jewish Apocalypticism. The errorists sought out heavenly ascents by means of various ascetic practices involving abstinence from eating and drinking, as well as careful observance of the Jewish festivals. These experiences of heavenly ascent climaxed in a vision of the throne [of God] and in worship offered by the heavenly hosts surrounding it. It seems that these visions also pointed to the importance of observing the Jewish festivals, probably as evidence of submission to the law of God.' There is no evidence that this attitude towards religious experience was systematically propagated at Colossae. Some of the converted Gentiles must have been God-fearers, who brought it with them from the synagogue, and proposed it as a supplement to the teaching of Epaphras.

2. This reconstruction implies that the problem with which Paul had to deal at Colossae was in no way similar to the situation he had faced in Galatia. There he had to counter a direct attack on his authority, and a vision of Christianity which in practice gave the law greater importance than Christ. Here he has to deal with a fashionable religious fad without intellectual depth, whose proponents floated in a fantasy world. His concern is to restore a sense of reality, to set the feet of the misguided on solid ground. They grasped at shadows. He had to show them that Christ was substance (2:17). The approach adopted by Paul in Galatians would have been completely inappropriate at Colossae. Understandably, therefore, the themes and terminology typical of Galatians are lacking in Colossians.

COMMENTARY

(1:1–2) Greeting Prior to his break with Antioch (Gal 2:11–14; Acts 13:1–3) Paul had been secure in his ecclesial identity (cf. 1–2 Thessalonians). Subsequently he did not represent any church (1:25), and had to identify himself as a Christ-commissioned missionary. The formula used here is a simplification of that which he adopted in Gal 1:1. The selection of Timothy from among the many with Paul (Col 4:7–14) for mention in the address suggests that he was co-author of the letter (Murphy-O'Connor 1995a: 16–34).

Rather than address the church as such (cf. 1–2 Thessalonians, Galatians, 1–2 Corinthians) Paul writes to its members as fellow-believers (cf. Rom 1:7; Phil 1:1). 'Saints' does not imply personal holiness. It reflects the usage of OT where the 'holy' is that which is 'set apart for God' (Lev 11:44). Exceptionally, 'saints' is interpreted (the *kai* is explicative; BDF §442(9)) by 'loyal', because some at Colossae, e.g. Archippus (cf. COL 4:17), had been led astray by false teaching (2:8).

The opening greeting of the Pauline letters normally mentions a double source of divine benefactions, 'from God our/ the Father and the Lord Jesus Christ'. The absence of the second element here may be due to the mention of 'in Christ' in the first part of the verse (Aletti 1993: 46).

(1:3–8) Thanksgiving In all Pauline letters, with the exception of Galatians, 1 Timothy, and Titus, the address is followed by a report on how Paul has thanked God for the recipients. When the formula 'I give thanks to the gods' appears in contemporary letters it is never a banal convention and always evokes what is upmost in the writer's mind (Schubert 1939: 173). Similarly in Paul. The thanksgiving is designed to win the favour of the readers—and so parallels the rhetorical *exordium*—but the compliments carefully reflect Paul's assessment of the state of the community, and reveal his concerns (Murphy-O'Connor 1995a: 55–64).

The length of the thanksgiving here is disputed, but even those who extend it to 1:14 (Moule 1968: 47), or even 1:23 (Aletti 1993: 49), consider 1:3–8 a subsection in which Paul notes the reasons for his gratitude (Lohse 1968: 40; O'Brien 1982: 7).

Paul's knowledge of the believers at Colossae depends on the report of Epaphras (1:4, 8), who had been deputed by Paul to evangelize the Lycus valley (1:7). The NRSV reading 'on *your* behalf' is to be rejected (cf. RSV, NJB). While the quality of its witnesses might seem worthy of confidence, the reading is excluded by the titles given to Epaphras (Abbott 1897: 200). In particular 'servant of Christ' suggests a duly authorized missionary (cf. 2 Cor 11:25; Phil 1:1). Note that Tychicus is given the same titles (4:7), and he is certainly Paul's representative. The fact that Epaphras was imprisoned (4:12–13; Philem 23), whereas Epaphroditus of Philippi was not (Phil 2:25), indicates that the authorities understood Epaphras to be Paul's agent.

Among the virtues of the Colossians Paul singles out their Christian confidence, and their love which reaches out to all (Philem 5), virtues which are inspired by their hope of a guaranteed heavenly reward (1 Thess 1:3). The Colossians had been made aware of their assured future by the preaching of Epaphras (1:6–7), which was anterior to the false teaching. The qualification of the gospel as 'the word of truth' (1:5; cf. Gal 2:5, 14) is intended to underline its reliability (Ps 119:43) by contrast with the 'empty deceit' (2:8) of the false teaching. The sterility and parochialism of the latter is indirectly stigmatized by the universal creativity of the word of God (1 Thess 2:13; 1 Cor 1:18; Rom 1:16; cf. Isa 55:10–11), a dynamic force changing the world as it is transforming the Colossians (3:16). Their experience corroborates the true understanding of the message; the 'grace of God' is not merely a favourable attitude on the part of the divinity but tangible benefaction. It is typical of Paul that he evokes love a second time (1:8); the fruit of the Spirit (Gal 5:22), it is the very being of the believer (1 Cor 13:2). This is the only mention of the Holy Spirit in Colossians.

(1:9–11) Prayer for the Future Having complimented the Colossians, Paul now reveals his attitude towards them (cf. 2:1). They have been the object of his constant concern, but his status as a prisoner (4:10) has meant that he can only pray for them. He begs God that they may know his will, that they may do good works, and that they may persevere. It is the responsibility of believers to discern what God demands of them (Phil 1:9–10). There is no longer a law to dictate their actions. The emphasis on 'wisdom,' 'understanding', and 'knowledge' as divine gifts with a purpose beyond themselves is designed to counter the false teachers' insistence on ascetical practices as prerequisites (2:16, 21–3) for visions which were an end in themselves (2:18). Paul does not exclude contemplative knowledge of God (1:10c), but it must be accompanied by fruitfulness in 'good works' (1:10b; cf. Eph 2:10; Jn 15:16). A permanent lifestyle, different from that of those who belong to the world (2:20; 2 Cor 4:7–11; Phil 2:14–16), and resistant to cowardice and a desire forvengeance, is made possible only by the power of God. His 'glory' is his visibility in history (1:27), which can only be a display of 'might' (1:11; cf. Eph 1:19).

(1:12–14) Conversion There is in fact no break in the sentence, but the importance of the contents merits a special heading. In order to motivate the thanksgiving of the Colossians Paul describes the crucial change in their existence in terms and images drawn from the liturgy of baptism (Käsemann 1964: 160). The key sentence is 1:12, which is then explained in 1:13–14 (cf. Acts 28:16). The combination of two virtual synonyms, 'the share of the portion', is common in the Essene hymns (Kuhn 1968: 117), which also attest a use of 'saints' encompassing both angels and believers (1QS 11:7–8; Benoit 1982). The Colossians have already been empowered to live in the realm of light where God's holiness is experienced. The implication is that the ascetic practices and visions advocated by the false teachers are unnecessary. 1:12–14 is the key to understanding 2:13–15 (Sappington 1991: 203).

In 1 Thess 5:5 Paul contrasted the past and present of believers in terms of 'darkness' and 'light' (cf. Rom 13:12). His use of 'power' here in conjunction with 'darkness' is meant to evoke the societal constraints which promote the inauthentic behaviour of non-believers; all are 'under the power of sin' (Rom 3:9). Deliverance is the transferral to an alternative environment identified as 'the kingdom of the son of God's love' (1:13; cf. 1 Cor 15:23–8). The genitive of quality is a Semitism ('beloved'; cf. BDF §165), but Paul chose the expression (contrast 1:7; 4:7, 9, 14) in order to give prominence to 'love', which stands at the beginning of the process of salvation (Rom 5:8). In the form displayed by Christ it is the basic characteristic of the believing community (2:2; 3:11–14; cf. Gal 3:27–8: 1 Cor 13:2). The vague 'redemption' is clarified by 'the forgiveness of sins'. The formula is found in Paul only here (cf. 2:13; 3:13), and has a liturgical ring. By incorporation into Christ ('in him') in baptism (cf. Acts 2:38) the structures of the world are replaced by new values.

(1:15–20) The Christological Hymn Note the change in the layout of the Greek text in Nestle-Aland, 27th edn. (1993). It is generally recognized that Paul here offers a corrected version of a hymn in circulation at Colossae (3:16; cf. Eph 5:19). Many efforts have been made to recreate the original form of this hymn, but none has won significant support (Schmauch 1964: 48–52; Benoit 1975). The multiplicity of hypotheses, however, underlines the reality of the problem, not the futility of the quest. No serious exegesis is possible without a decision regarding tradition and redaction. In my view the ordered repetition of formal features recommends the reconstruction of two four-line strophes:

(v. 15a)	1	Who is (the) image of the invisible God
(v. 15b)	2	Firstborn of all creation
(v. 16a)	3	For in him were created all things
(v. 16f)	4	All things through him and to him were created
(v. 18b)	1	Who is (the) beginning
(v. 18c)	2	Firstborn from the dead
(v. 19)	3	For in him was pleased all the Fullness to dwell
(v. 20a)	4	And through him to reconcile all things to him

The first lines of each strophe begin with 'who is', and the second lines with 'firstborn'. The third lines commence with 'for in him', which is followed by a verb in the passive ('were created/was pleased'), whose subject is a universal ('all things/all the Fullness'). The fourth lines contain three identical expressions, 'all things', 'through him', and 'to him'. So many correspondences must be intentional. They are the result of careful planning to achieve perfect balance between the two strophes. No one who had made such an effort would destroy the elegance of his or her creation. In consequence, the elements which break the pattern (vv. 16bcde, 17, 18ad, 20bc) must have been added by another hand. It is theoretically possible that such redactional activity had taken place before Paul incorporated the hymn into his letter. It is more probable, however, that the additions were made by Paul, because identical retouches appear in the hymn in Phil 2:6–11 (Murphy-O'Connor 1995b).

The basic theme of this hymn is the mediation of Christ, first in creation, then in reconciliation. The titles in the first two lines of each strophe evoke the figure of Wisdom—'image' (Wis 7:26), 'beginning' and 'firstborn' (Prov 8:22; Sir 1:4)—who was present with God from eternity (Wis 9:4, 9), and participant in creation (Prov 3:19; 8:30; Wis 8:5; Sir 1:9; 24:9; Ps 104:24). These titles are the reason why Paul could not simply repudiate the hymn; they were rooted in the revelation of his people. The titles are justified by the third and fourth lines of each strophe, which are introduced by 'because'. All efforts to determine in what precise sense Christ can be said to be both the instrument and the end of all creation have failed. That ambiguity, not clarity, was intended is underlined by the plethora of unsatisfying explanations of the indwelling 'Fullness' (v. 19). Only in 2:9 do we discover that 'Fullness' is a surrogate for God, who is said to 'dwell in' both people (T. Zeb. 8:2; Jub. 1:17; 1 Enoch 49:2–3; cf. 2

Cor 6:16) and places (LXX Ps 67:17). No Jew would have understood either as meaning intrinsic divinization. It is simply a way of speaking about divine favour. What the Colossians would have understood is an open question, as is the exact manner in which Christ can be both the instrument and end of reconciliation. In what possible sense can all creation, which includes inanimate beings, have offended Christ, thereby creating the need for reconcilation?

Paul saw the hymn as a perfect example of 'beguiling, persuasive speech' (2:4). Formal perfection clothes an abstract vision of a cosmic Christ. The phrases are redolent of profundity, but yield no unambiguous understanding of Christ's person and mission. The hymn could be sung or recited by all Colossian Christians in the belief that they were articulating a mystery beyond their comprehension. Initiates, on the other hand, could debate endlessly the questions that still test the ingenuity of exegetes, or develop an interpretation only remotely related to the letter of the text, e.g. the creative power of God, once thought of as Wisdom, is now thought of as Christ (see Dunn 1980: 187–94).

In addition to the truth of the titles given to Christ, Paul had a second reason to retain the hymn. It could be turned against the false teachers. By inserting v. 16b–e Paul restricts the meaning of 'all things' (v. 16a) to intelligent beings, and makes it explicit that the angelic powers are inferior to Christ who, according to the premiss of the hymn, brought them into existence and to whom they are ordered. The ineffable names of the spirit powers are drawn at random from Jewish tradition (details in Schlier 1961). There is no intention to describe grades of the celestial hierarchy (Lightfoot 1904: 150). Paul further diminishes the attractiveness to the Colossians of such powers by inserting 1:20c. Like humans (1:21; 2:13; 3:7, 13), angels also need reconciliation; 'some of the angels of heaven transgressed the word of the Lord, and behold they commit sin and transgress the law' (1 Enoch 106:13–14; cf. 2 Apoc. Bar. 56:11–13). Manifestly only good angels can be effective mediators with God, but how are mere terrestrials to know which is which? Paul allows the Colossians to draw their own conclusion regarding the futility of the exercise.

Parallel to the addition of 'death on a cross' in Phil 2:8c, Paul here insists on the brutal modality of Christ's achievement by inserting, 'making peace by the blood of his cross' (v. 20b). Whereas the traditional teaching that Paul received mentioned only the death of Christ (Rom

1:3–4; 4:25; 8:34; 10:8–9; 1 Cor 15:2–7; Gal 1:3–4; 1 Thess 1:10), he typically stresses the 'blood' of Christ (Rom 3:25; 5:9; 1 Cor 10:16; 11:25, 27). With the exception of the gospels and Heb 6:6; 12:2; Rev 11:8, he alone in the NT uses 'cross' and 'crucify' (cf. 2:14).

Paul's choice of the verb 'to make peace' probably has less to do with any supposed animosity between heavenly beings, or between celestials and terrestrials, than with the internal situation of the Colossian church, whose unity had been compromised (cf. 2:2; 3:15). The theme of unity is fundamental to the additions in vv. 17 and 18a. The former sums up the first strophe, by parodying it. 'He is before all things' echoes the ambiguity of 'firstborn' (temporal? qualitative?). The assertion that 'all things hold together' in a human being (v. 17b) gives an impression of unity whose precise meaning evaporates on inspection. Lightfoot (1904: 154) perfectly catches the spurious profundity of the expression by commenting 'He impresses upon creation that unity and solidarity which makes it a cosmos instead of a chaos'. How exactly is this achieved? 'The action of gravitation . . . is an expression of His mind'!

Paul becomes completely serious in his introduction to the second strophe. The church must be characterized by the organic unity of a living 'body' (v. 18a). The insight is but an extension and clarification of 'you are all one person in Christ Jesus' (Gal 3:28 = Col 3:11). The distinction between 'head' and 'body' does not appear in 1 Cor 12:12–27 or Rom 12:4–5 because the supremacy of Christ was not questioned at Rome or Corinth. In this instance 'head' would appear to mean both 'superior' (2:10) and 'source' (2:19). The cosmic dimension of the original hymn has been reduced to ecclesiology.

(1:21–3) The Thesis of the Letter These verses both sum up what has been said, and enunciate the major themes of the letter in inverse order. Thus they function as the rhetorical *partitio* (Aletti 1993: 120). vv. 21–2 evoke the past, present, and future of the Colossians. The passive voice 'having been alienated' must be taken seriously (v. 21; cf. 1:13; Phil 2:15); the Gentiles had inherited their polytheism and their acceptance of the false values of a corrupt society. To extricate them from this situation divine intervention was necessary, but it was not an act of glorious triumph (v. 22). 'Body of flesh' distinguishes the individual Jesus from incorporeal beings, but also hints that his death was the result of something happening to his body, the violence of the crucifixion (v. 20*b*). Reconciliation is presented as a past achievement, but this does not imply a realized eschatology, since its conditional aspect is immediately made clear ('provided that', v. 23).

The Colossians have been given the opportunity (1:12; cf. Gal 5:1) to appear guiltless at the final judgement. How precisely they must comport themselves is outlined in 3:1–4:1. More fundamentally, however, they must remain committed to the salvific vision conveyed by the gospel they initially accepted (1:5–6). The alternative against which they are warned is the theme of 2:6–23. The hyperbole of 'preached to every creature under heaven' (v. 23*b*) echoes that of 1 Thess 1:8, and the lack of the definite article before 'servant' underlines that Paul is not the sole apostle. 1:24–2:5 develops Paul's own understanding of his service of the mystery.

(1:24–2:5) Servant of the Mystery The NRSV offers a widespread mistranslation of 1:24*b*, which has given rise to a series of false problems to which a variety of answers have been proposed, some of which are used to deny Pauline authorship of Colossians (Kremer 1956). A literal translation, which respects the order of the words, simplifies the matter considerably (Aletti 1993: 135): 'I complete what is lacking in the sufferings-of-Christ-in-my-flesh' (cf. Gal 2:20; 2 Cor 4:10–11). There is no reference to the individual Jesus Christ. Paul's sufferings are those of Christ because Paul is a member of the body of Christ (cf. Phil 3:10), and because Paul's sufferings reveal the present reality of grace as those of Christ did (2 Cor 4:10–11). Paul has no choice but to struggle on until all have heard the gospel (cf. Rom 15:19; 2 Tim 4:17). He is a minister of the church (1:25), not in virtue of a human commission (1:1; cf. Gal 1:1), but in virtue of the stewardship entrusted to him by God in order to further the economy of salvation (1 Cor 4:1; 9:17). The 'word of God', which Paul preaches in word and deed, is now described as 'the mystery' (1:26; cf. Eph 3:1–9). Divinely ordained future events (for the background see Brown 1968), which for the false teachers were still a secret to be penetrated laboriously, in fact have already been made plain, not merely to a group of initiates, but to all believers. 'Glory', the brilliance of God's action in history, is the antithesis of secrecy. The content of the mystery is Christ precisely as present among the believers, no longer in Jerusalem, to which they must trek (Isa 60:1–7), but where they are (Aletti 1993: 143).

Hence all attention must be focused on him as the source of authentic, certain knowledge (2:3). The acquisition of such knowledge is not a matter of asceticism. They must be 'instructed by love' (against NRSV; cf. Spicq 1958–9: ii.202–8) in order to penetrate the riches of wisdom and knowledge hidden in Christ (2:2), who 'loved me, that is, gave himself for me' (Gal 2:20; BDF §442(9); cf. 1:22).

(2:6–23) Warning against Errors The original commitment of the Colossians was to the Christ as Jesus the Lord (2:6; Lightfoot 1904: 174). Jesus is the truth of Christ (Eph 4:21). His historicity is fundamental to salvation. The believers must not permit themselves to be returned to the domain of darkness (cf. 1:13) by accepting merely human speculation which, despite the claims made for it, in fact regresses to the basic religious perspectives common to (fallen) humanity ('elements of the world', 2:8), e.g. the need for asceticism in order to advance in religious knowledge (v. 20; GAL 4:3); see Sappington (1991: 169).

'Elementary teaching' (Heb 5:12) appears to be the best sense in this context of a term, *stoicheion* (element), which has a wide variety of meanings according to the framework in which it is used (for a survey see Bandstra 1964: 5–30). Many scholars, however, prefer to understand 'elements of the world' as the basic components of the material universe—earth, water, air, and fire. This is certainly the best-documented meaning in contemporary literature, but to make sense here it has to be understood metaphorically of (1) the basic factors in human existence, which for Paul were Law, Sin, Death, flesh, or (2) the planets which exercise control over humans and determine the calendar; such astral beings are associated with angels. Neither of these usages is attested at the time of Paul.

The function of the genitive 'of deity' (v. 9) is to explain 'Fullness', which 1:19 had left unspecified (Lohse 1968: 150; BDF §§165, 167). As in 1:19, 'indwelling' here does not mean divinization. 'Bodily' has been interpreted in at least five different ways (Moule 1968: 92–3). The two most probable are 'really' (as opposed to seemingly; cf. v. 17) and 'in physical form'. The two are not incompatible. Divine favour and salvific action are concentrated exclusively in the humanity of Christ. Necessarily, therefore, he is the sole source of fulfilment, and he has authority over all spirit forces (v. 10; Grudem 1985).

What has already been achieved for the Colossians should be a cause of thanksgiving

(v. 7). To drive this home Paul employs a series of five vivid, dramatic images (vv. 11–15), in which attempts have been made to find traditional material (Lohse 1968: 160; Wengst 1972: 186–94). The results have been inconclusive. Through Christ the whole body of flesh (and not a mere symbolic token), i.e. the entire framework of habits and desires opposed to God, has been removed (v. 11; cf. v. 18). This is true only in theory; it must be made real in practice (cf. Gal 5:13–24). The active faith of the recipient is necessary for baptism to be a dying and rising with Christ (v. 12; cf. Rom 10:9). The realized eschatology of 'you were co-raised' (cf. 3:1) must be read in the perspective of the future eschatology of 1:22, 27; 3:4, 6, 15–16. It is simply a more graphic version of 'God made alive' (v. 13). 'Life' and 'death' are used here in their existential sense of the presence and absence of virtue (cf. 2 Cor 2:16; Philo, *Fug.*, 55). With vivid imagination Paul presents humanity as having defaulted after signing an agreement to obey the will of God. The bond thus became an accusation (v. 14). God, in his generosity, forgave the fault and cancelled the debt.

The moment when this happened—'nailing it to the cross'—was the crucifixion of Christ. The image is not totally consistent, and the metaphor must not be pressed too hard. For other interpretative options see O'Brien (1982: 121–6). A new image, whose antithesis appears in 2 Cor 2:14, is introduced in v. 15. God (the emperor) awards a Roman triumph to Christ (his victorious general), who, having stripped angelic beings of their power, led them in a procession that normally ended in executions (Hafemann 1986: 18–39). Some explain the sudden appearance of 'principalities and powers' by identifying them as the angels who recorded the transgressions of humanity. In this case the 'handwriting' would be the book of life (Ps 56:8; Isa 65:6; 1 *Enoch* 81:2–4; Sappington 1991: 208–23). The mention of spirit powers, however, could have been occasioned by the situation at Colossae to which Paul now turns.

The 'therefore' introducing v. 16 implies that the direct polemic against the false teachers (vv. 16–23) stems from the doctrinal base established in vv. 9–15. The reality of Christ highlights the insubstantial nature of the proposed alternative (v. 17), which was rooted in 'a quest for higher religious experience through mystical-ascetical piety' (Carr 1973: 500). In addition to strict observance of the Jewish calendar (v. 16; cf. Isa 1:13–14; Ezek 46:4–11), the false teachers demanded fasting and/or the exclusion of

certain foods (v. 21). They believed that obedience won God's favour, and that asceticism purified the person (v. 23). Together these two constituted the 'humility' (v. 18), i.e. mortification, that was the prerequisite for revelatory experiences (Sappington 1991: 163). The NRSV translation of v. 18a should be abandoned in favour of 'Let no one condemn you, delighting in humility and the angelic worship [of God], which he has seen upon entering' (O'Brien 1982: 134). In visions the adept 'entered' the heavenly world (Francis and Meeks 1973: 163–207), and participated in the worship offered by the angels assembled around the throne of God (Isa 6; Ezek 1; 1 *Enoch* 14). It was to this other world that the false teachers had relegated Christ.

This claim to religious superiority is brutally dismissed by Paul as overweening conceit rooted in silly ideas concocted by a fleshly intelligence (v. 18b). This fundamentally egocentric attitude is the antithesis of the sharing that characterizes the Body of Christ and, in consequence, separates those who persist in it from Christ, the only source ('head'; cf. 1 Cor 11:3) of the Body's vitality (v. 19). The being of a Christian is to 'belong' to Christ (1 Cor 3:23).

What the Colossians enjoy (cf. 1:12–14; 2:11–15) is not definitive. It can be lost. Through death in Christ (v. 12) they have been freed from the religious perspectives of fallen humanity (v. 20; cf. v. 8), but they will return to a state of slavery if they again accept the values and standards of society (Gal 4:8–11). The emphasis on ascetic practices associated with Judaism (cf. LXX Isa 29:13) is due to the situation at Colossae (vv. 21–2), but the principle is of wider application (Gal 5:1, 13). Such practices might appear to exhibit spiritual strength and superiority, but in fact they indulge the egocentricity of fallen humanity because they are 'self-imposed' (v. 23).

(3:1–4:1) How the Colossians Ought to Live
Having brought out the implications of dying with Christ (2:20–3), Paul now spells out the consequences of rising with Christ (3:1–4). If believers have been raised, then their concern must be with 'above' not with 'below'. The contrast is inspired by the characterization of the practices of the false teachers in 2:23, and appears to forget that these were only means to reaching 'the things that are above' (cf. 2:18). For Paul, however, the central figure in heaven is Christ, whose authority is emphasized by his position at God's right hand (Ps 110:1; 1 Cor 15:25).

'Do not set your minds on things that are on earth' (3:2; cf. Phil 3:19), if taken literally, would negate the ethical directives which follow. Such imprecision regularly caused confusion in Paul's communities, e.g. his insistence that Christians were totally free of the Mosaic law permitted the Corinthians to conclude that they could do what they liked (cf. 1 Cor 6:12; 10:23). Paul's intention here was not to exclude involvement with society (cf. 1 Cor 5:9–10), but to prohibit acceptance of its values (cf. Rom 8:5–6). Believers no longer 'belong to the world' (2:20). By contrast with the glorious revelation at the parousia (3:4) of the intimate union between Christ and believers (cf. Gal 2:20; Phil 1:21), their new life can be considered 'hidden' (3:3), but this is relative, because the action of grace must be seen if the gospel is to spread (1:6; cf. 1 Thess 1:6–8; 4:12; 2 Cor 3:2, 18).

'Whatever in you is earthly' (3:5) is literally 'the members on the earth'. Paul identifies the parts of the body with the sins they commit (cf. Rom 6:13, 19; 2 Apoc. Bar. 49:3). The admonition does not parallel Mt 5:29–30. Lists of vices characteristic of unredeemed pagan humanity (Wis 14:22–9) have already appeared in 1 Thess 4:3–6; Gal 5:19–21. The first five mentioned here (5:5) can be related to sexuality, thought the last-mentioned has a wider extension. The connection between greed, the original sin (Rom 7:7), and idolatry is axiomatic in Judaism (cf. T. Judah, 19:1). Pagans are simply 'those who covet' (Pal. Tg. on Ex 20:17; b. Šabb. 146a). The second five vices (5:8) all involve intemperate speech that makes genuine communication impossible. The social consequences of lying (5:9a) are even more disastrous. Without trust there can be no community.

To the Galatians Paul had said 'you have put on Christ' (Gal 3:27; cf. Rom 13:14). The image of putting on a person is without parallel in antiquity, and owes its origin to the convert's assumption of a new environment by entering the church, which is the body of Christ. The insight is developed here in a contrast between 'the old man' and 'the new man' (5:9b–10). Both are primarily social concepts. The 'new man' is the sphere 'where' (3:11) the divisions which characterize society ('the old man') no longer exist (Gal 3:28). Just as society dictates the behaviour of its members, so the believing community is the source of authentic moral knowledge. The goal of the ongoing renewal of the 'new man' is a type of knowledge characterized by creativity. This can only be a knowledge born of love (Phil 1:9–10; contrast Rom 2:17–18), which empowers the other not only to see but to act. The community, which is Christ

(3:11), exemplifies the ideal of his self-sacrificing love, and enables the members to pattern their lives on his example (2 Cor 5: 14–15). Instead of the contempt that produced the divisions typical of society—Jews despised pagans, who looked down on barbarians (i.e. anyone who did not speak Greek), who spurned Scythians as the epitome of human degradation (cf. 2 Macc 4:47; 3 Macc 7:5)—the believers must make Christ present in the world by exhibiting those virtues 'which reduce or eliminate friction: ready sympathy, a generous spirit, a humble disposition, willingness to make concessions, patience, forbearance' (Moule 1968: 123). Forgiven by God they must forgive. Loved by God they must love. Unless sheathed in love no virtue can be perfect (3:14; cf. Spicq 1958–9: i. 268–75). Love alone excludes pretence. Others (details in Schmauch 1964: 80–2) translate 'the bond of perfection' and understand the genitive as purposeful ('the bond that leads to perfection') or objective ('the bond that produces perfection'). These are less satisfactory, because for Paul there is no perfection beyond love (1 Cor 13).

Fully aware of the tensions within the church at Colossae, Paul expresses a wish that peace may reign there. In society peace is often no more than an uneasy truce to be abandoned the moment an advantage presents itself. The Colossians should be grateful that they are not in that situation. Authentic peace, which is defined by reference to the self-sacrifice of Christ, is first a subjective attitude which then results in a community of love (3:15; cf. 1 Cor 7:15; 14:33). In a living body the hand cannot be at war with the foot. According to 1 Cor 6:7, members who sue one another are in fact suing themselves—a ridiculous situation.

The ideal community is not merely an absence of antagonism. There is a much more positive dimension (3:16). The expression 'word of Christ' is unique, but synthesizes a number of concepts found earlier in the letter; 'the word of the truth, the gospel' (1:5) is 'the word of God' (1:25), which is 'God's mystery, that is Christ' (2:3). Its power within each one (1:6, 10) must find socially beneficial expression. The emphasis on 'teaching and admonishing' was demanded by the presence of false teachers at Colossae, who taught some believers the hymn that Paul quotes in 1:15–20. In practice 'yourselves' means 'one another' (NRSV; cf. 3:13) but heautous (cf. 1 Cor 6:7) was chosen to underline that believers are organically unified in a single 'body', and thereby to remind them that their source of life is Christ (2:19). Theological development is part of the natural evolution of the community. In consequence, it must (a) be homogeneous with the gospel that brought the community into being (1:6), and (b) take place in a public context. 'Psalms, hymns, and spiritual songs' suggest the liturgical assembly, in which inspired insights into the mystery of Christ (1 Cor 14:26) were proffered for the consent of the community (1 Cor 14:16; cf. 1 Thess 5:21–2). Such community singing must be an expression of gratitude to God (3:16c), but so too must every other human activity (3:17). It is made possible in, through, and by Christ; thus it must mirror his comportment. But Jesus was sent because of God's fatherly concern for humanity (1:12), and so in the last analysis gratitude must be directed to God.

Generic directives are followed by three pairs of reciprocal admonitions dealing with the relations of wife–husband, child–father, and slave–master (3:18–4:1). The nature of the socio-religious matrix in which such household codes were formulated has occasioned vigorous debate (Balch 1992), whose inconclusiveness is the inevitable consequence of the wide variations within the form. Conscious of a tradition of sensible social management, Paul formulates a series of guidelines designed to persuade the Colossians to leave the mystical world of visions and angels, and to return to the real world where the fabric of daily life was woven from a multitude of interpersonal relations, of which the most basic were the three pairs listed here (Aristotle, *Politics*, 1.1253^{b}7). The only really distinctive feature is the motivation by reference to the Lord, which here means Christ (Aletti 1993: 249). The social distinctions, which are fundamental to these admonitions, can be reconciled with the abolition of such distinctions in 3:11 only on the assumption that not all members of a family were converted to Christianity.

The literal translation of 3:18 is 'women be subject to men', but the context demands limitation to marriage, as some copyists have tried to convey by various additions. The admonition that a Christian woman be submissive to her non-believing husband (3:18) is to remind her that her new freedom (cf. Gal 5:1) does not exempt her from the obligations she undertook in marriage. Such behaviour is 'fitting' for a Christian because of its missionary potential (cf. 1 Pet 3:1). The obligation to love laid on the husband (3:19) indicates that the wife is a non-believer, since Christians by definition love one

another (3:14; cf. 1 Thess 4:9). The temptation to treat her harshly might be due to her refusal to convert.

What is said to slaves stands out from the other admonitions both quantitatively and qualitatively (3:22–5). It is unlikely to have been inspired by the case of Onesimus (4:9), or by agitation among Christian slaves at Colossae (Aletti 1993: 254). Rather it reflects Paul's habitual attitude towards slaves who accepted Christianity. Within the community he took it for granted that they would show and share the love that was its most characteristic feature, but he made no effort to change the social order. Paul does not demand that Onesimus be manumitted, but that he be received 'no longer as a slave, but more than a slave, a beloved brother' (Philem 16; cf. 1 COR 7:17–24). Paul's sole concern here is that slaves should not obey orders to the letter while their hearts raged, and hate corroded their spirits. The internal tension had to be resolved in order to permit the transforming effect of grace to become visible (4:5–6). The witness value of the comportment of believers was always a major concern (cf. 1 Thess 1:6–8; 4:12; 2 Cor 4:10–11). The warning of a future judgement (3:24–5) underlines the seriousness of Paul's concern.

Christian masters also have obligations to their slaves (cf. Sir 7:20–1, 31–3). They are not required to love them or to free them, but to treat them 'justly' and 'fairly' (4:1). The terms are related as 'knowledge' and 'discernment' in Phil 1:9. In each case the first deals with the obvious and clear, whereas the second comes into play when a sure feeling for what is appropriate is required.

(4:2–6) Concluding Exhortations As Paul had given thanks (1:3) and prayed for the Colossians (1:9), so now they must do likewise (v. 2). The prayer in question is primarily petition (O'Brien 1982: 237) for the glorious return of Christ (3:4; cf. 1 Cor 16:22). Their incessant awareness of, and orientation to, this goal is the best guarantee of the vigilance required of all believers if they are to persevere (1:23). Gratitude for what they have already been given (1:12–14; 3:11–12) should enhance their attentiveness. It is typical of Paul to request prayers for himself (1 Thess 5:25; Philem 22). It is a means of participation in the mission of the church (3:3; 2 Thess 3:1; Phil 1:19). The Colossians must beseech God (a) for Paul's liberation from prison in order to continue his mission (cf. 1 Cor 16:9; 2 Cor 2:12), and (b) for his ability to 'reveal' the mystery effectively. The divine passive of 1:26 finds its human herald in 4:4' (Aletti 1993: 260). Despite Paul's emphasis on the verbal dimension of such communication, it is likely that he also has in mind the existential aspect, in which his comportment reveals Christ (2 Cor 4:10–11; cf. 1 Cor 2:1–5).

It is to this aspect that Paul now alerts the Colossians. It is not enough to pray. They must also exhibit a presence in society that will prove attractive to non-believers (v. 5; cf. 1 Thess 4:12; Phil 2:14–16). Every opportunity to induce them to believe must be availed of. The speech of Christians should be winning and witty, and tailored to the needs of each interlocutor (v. 6). They must insinuate not dominate.

(4:7–18) Final Greetings The two bearers of the letter are introduced in a chiastic pattern (vv. 7–9). Paul tactfully remains quiet regarding the personal history of Onesimus, simply noting that he has become a Christian ('brother'; cf. Philem 10), and has Paul's respect and confidence ('faithful'). The same adjectives are applied to Tychicus, who in addition is called 'minister' and 'fellow-servant in the Lord', exactly as is Epaphras (1:7; 4:12). If the latter was an official delegate of Paul to Colossae, Tychicus now enjoys the same status. He can speak for Paul with authority, not only with respect to personal news from Ephesus, but as regards the interpretation of the letter in its impact on the growth of the community (2:2).

Greetings are sent by six men with Paul, who with one exception also appear in Philemon but in a different order (Murphy-O'Connor 2007).

Col 4:10–14	Remarks	Philem 23–4
Aristarchus	<– my fellow-prisoner	Aristarchus (3)
Mark	<– cousin of Barnabas	Mark (2)
Jesus	<– called Justus	
Epaphras	<– one of you, a servant of Christ Jesus my fellow-prisoner – >	Epaphras (1)
Luke	<– beloved physician	Luke (5)
Demas		Demas (4)

It is curious that Timothy, the co-author of both letters (1:1; Philem 1), is not mentioned in either list. Aristarchus of Thessalonica is well known from several references in Acts (19:29; 20:4;

27:2). Nothing is known of Jesus who, like Paul, had taken a similar-sounding Hellenistic Roman name. It is unlikely that his name appears in Philem 23 (O'Brien 1982: 307). Mark is mentioned in Acts 12:12, 25; 15:37–9, and in 2 Tim 4:11. In a poignant note Paul remarks that these three are the only Christians of Jewish origin to have stayed with him (3:11). Had they come with him from Antioch? The implication is that the following three collaborators are Gentiles. Luke and Demas appear in 2 Tim 4:9, 11. Despite his imprisonment, Epaphras, the apostle of Colossae (1:7), remains active on behalf of his converts (3:12). He prays that they may be stable in their maturity (cf. 1:28–9), and be filled with 'everything willed by God' (Lightfoot 1904: 238), whose essence is spelt out in 2:2–3, 10. Paul's independent knowledge of how hard Epaphras had worked to establish the gospel in the Lycus valley (v. 13) must have come from Onesimus (v. 9). The testimony would have been all the more impressive coming from one who at that stage was a pagan (Philem 10). The exclusive concentration on Laodicea in what follows suggests that Epaphras had not been successful in Hierapolis.

Paul sends his personal greetings to believers in Laodicea, and in particular to the believers who assembled in the home of Nympha (v. 15). The fact that he singles out a particular individual confirms that he had never visited the Lycus valley (cf. 2:1; ROM 16). *Nymphan* could be the accusative of the feminine name Nympha (O'Brien 1982: 246) or of the masculine name Nymphas (Moule 1968: 28). There is little difficulty in deciding which of the accompanying pronouns, 'her' or 'him', is original. No copyist would change the masculine into the feminine, because of its implication regarding the status of a woman. The contrary, however, is eminently probable, given the instinctive patriarchal bias of copyists. Women were fully the equal of men in the Pauline communities (cf. 1 Cor 11:2–16), and presided over house churches (cf. Rom 16:1–2).

For the public reading of the letter at Colossae (v. 16: cf. 1 Thess 5:27) the 'whole' community (cf. Rom 16:23; 1 Cor 14:23) must have been assembled from the various house churches in the city. The exchange of letters with Laodicea implies that the differences between the two churches were significant, otherwise two letters would be pointless. None the less the two communities had enough in common to make the reading of the other's letter worthwhile. The letter sent by Paul to the Laodiceans has been the centre of a vigorous debate. The current consensus refuses to identify it with any known document (Anderson 1992). It has been constructed out of Colossians by Boismard (1999) and much more successfully out of Ephesians by Muddiman (2001).

Paul's request that Archippus should be informed of an admonition addressed to him (141:17) implies that Paul knew that he would not be present when the letter was read in public (contrast 2 Thess 3:11–12; Phil 4:2–3), even though he was part of the leadership group of a house church (Phlm 2). The most natural explanation is that Epaphras had informed Paul that Archippus had been won over by the false teachers. The desertion of a leader of his status explains the urgency of the letter. A response could not await the release of Paul or Epaphras. Had Archippus simply moved to Laodicea (Lightfoot 1904: 242) the matter would have been dealt with in that letter.

Paul regularly used secretaries (Rom 16:22), and thus had to write the last paragraph in his own hand to authenticate the letter (4:18; cf. 2 Thess 3:17; Gal 6:11; Philem 19; 1 Cor 16:21; Richards 1991: 173–7).

REFERENCES

Abbott, T. K. (1897), A Critical and Exegetical Commentary on the Epistles to the Ephesians and to the Colossians, ICC (Edinburgh: T. & T. Clark).

Aletti, J.-N. (1993), Saint Paul: Épître aux Colossiens, Ebib NS 20 (Paris: Gabalda).

Anderson, C. P. (1992), 'Laodiceans, Epistle to', ABD iv. 231–3.

Balch, D. (1992), 'Household Codes', ABD iii. 318–20.

Bandstra, A. J. (1964), Law and the Elements (Kampen: Kok).

Barrett, C. K. (1994), Paul: An Introduction to his Thought (London: Chapman).

Benoit, P. (1975), 'L'Hymne christologique de Col i, 15–20: Jugement critique sur l'état des recherches', in J. Neusner (ed.), Christianity, Judaism and Other Greco-Roman Cults: Studies for Morton Smith at Sixty. SJLA 12/1 (Leiden: Brill), i. 226–63.

—— (1982), 'Hagioi en Colossiens 1.12: Hommes ou Anges?', in M. D. Hooker and S. G. Wilson (eds.), Paul and Paulinism: Essays in Honour of C. K. Barrett (London: SPCK), 83–101.

Boismard, M.-E. (1999), La Lettre de saint Paul au Laodicéens, Cahiers de la Revue Biblique (Paris: Gabalda).

Brown, R. E. (1968), The Semitic Background of the Term 'Mystery' in the New Testament, FBBS 21 (Philadelphia: Fortress).

Bruce, F. F. (1977), Paul: Apostle of the Free Spirit (Exeter: Paternoster).

Bujard, W. (1973), Stilanalytische Untersuchungen zum Kolosserbrief als Beitrag zur Methodik von Sprachergleichen, SUNT 11 (Göttingen: Vandenhoeck & Ruprecht).

Carr, W. (1973), 'Two Notes on Colossians', JTS 24: 492–500.

Dunn, J. D. G. (1980), Christology in the Making: An Inquiry into the Origins of the Doctrine of the Incarnation (London: SCM).

—— (1996), The Epistles to the Colossians and to Philemon: A Commentary on the Greek Text. Greek New Testament Commentary (Grand Rapids: Eerdmans).

Francis, F. O., and Meeks, W. A. (1973) (eds.), Conflict at Colossae, SBLSBS 4 (Missoula: Scholar's Press).

Furnish, V. P. (1992), 'Colossians, Epistle to the', ABD i. 1090–6.

Grudem, W. (1985), 'Does kephale ("Head") Mean "Source" or "Authority" in Greek Literature? A Survey of 2,336 Examples', Trinity Journal, 6: 38–59.

Gunther, J. J. (1973), St. Paul's Opponents and Their Background: A Study of Apocalyptic and Jewish Sectarian Teachings. NovTSup 35 (Leiden: Brill).

Hafemann, S. J. (1986), Suffering and the Spirit: An Exegetical Study of II Cor. 2:14–3:3 within the Context of the Corinthian Correspondence, WUNT 2/19 (Tübingen: Mohr [Siebeck]).

Hooker, M. D. (1973), 'Were there False Teachers at Colossae?'. in B. Lindars and S. Smalley (eds.), Christ and Spirit in the New Testament: Studies in Honour of Charles Francis Digby Moule (Cambridge: Cambridge University Press).

Käsemann, E. (1964), Essays on New Testament Themes. SBT 41 (London: SCM).

Kenny, A. (1986), A Stylometric Study of the New Testament (Oxford: Clarendon).

Kremer, J. (1956), Was an den Leiden Christi noch mangelt: Eine interpretationsgeschichtliche und exegetische Untersuchung zu Kol 1, 24b, BBB 12 (Bonn: Hanstein).

Kuhn, K. G. (1968), 'The Epistle to the Ephesians in the Light of the Qumran Texts', in J. Murphy-O'Connor (ed.), Paul and Qumran (London: Chapman), 115–31.

Lampe, P. (1985), 'Keine "Sklavenflucht" des Onesimus', ZNW 76: 135–7.

Lightfoot, J. B. (1904), Saint Paul's Epistles to the Colossians and to Philemon (London: Macmillan).

Lohse, E. (1968), Die Briefe an die Kolosser und an Philemon, MeyerK (Göttingen: Vandenhoeck & Ruprecht).

Moule, C. F. D. (1968), The Epistles to the Colossians and to Philemon, CGTC (Cambridge: Cambridge University Press).

Muddiman, J. (2001), A Commentary on the Epistle to the Ephesians, Black's NT Commentaries (London/New York: Continuum).

Murphy-O'Connor, J. (1995a), 'Tradition and Redaction in Col 1:15–20', RB 102: 231–41.

—— (1995b), *Paul the Letter Writer*. GNS 41 (College-ville, Ind.: Liturgical Press).

—— (2007), 'Greeters in Col 4:10–14 and Phm 23–4', *Revue Biblique*, 114 (2007) 416–26.

Nestle-Aland (1993), *Novum Testamentum Graece, 27th edn.* (Stuttgart: Deutsche Bibelgesellschaft).

Neumann, K. J. (1990), *The Authenticity of the Pauline Epistles in the Light of Stylostatistic Analysis*, SBLDS 120 (Atlanta: Scholars Press).

O'Brien, P. T. (1982), *Colossians, Philemon*, WBC 44 (Waco: Word).

Richards, E. R. (1991), *The Secretary in the Letters of Paul*, WUNT 2/42 (Tübingen, Mohr [Siebeck]).

Sappington, T. J. (1991), *Revelation and Redemption at Colossae*, JSNTSup 53 (Sheffield: JSOT).

Schenk, W. (1987), 'Der Kolosserbrief in der neueren Forschung (1945–1985)', *ANRW* 2. 25. 4 (Berlin: de Gruyter), 3327–64.

Schlier, H. (1961), *Principalities and Powers in the New Testament*, QD 3 (Fribourg: Herder).

Schmauch, W. (1964), *Beiheft zu E. Lohmeyer: Die Briefe an die Philipper, Kolosser und an Philemon*, MeyerK (Göttingen: Vandenhoeck & Ruprecht).

Schubert, P. (1939), *Form and Function of the Pauline Thanksgivings*, BZNW 20 (Berlin: Töpelmann).

Spicq, C. (1958–9), *Agape dans le Nouveau Testament: Analyse des textes*, Ebib (2 vols.; Paris: Gabalda).

Wengst, K. (1972), *Christologische Formeln und Lieder* (Gütersloh: Mohr).

11. 1 Thessalonians

PHILIP F. ESLER

INTRODUCTION

A. Preliminary Issues. 1. Date Paul probably wrote 1 Thessalonians from Corinth within a matter of months after his initial visit to Thessalonica, in about 50–51 CE (so Best 1972: 7–13; Barclay 1993: 515). It is widely agreed that 1 Thessalonians is the earliest extant Christian text, a precious document which brilliantly illuminates one segment of the Christ-movement less than twenty years after the death of Jesus.

2. The Significance of the Epistolary Form It can hardly be without significance that the earliest document extant from the followers of Christ takes the form of a letter. Much research has been conducted recently which analyses the formal structures of Graeco-Roman epistolography (Stowers 1986), and their relation to early Christian letters, including those of Paul (Doty 1973), and 1 Thessalonians in particular (Boers 1976). But we should be careful not to miss the distinctiveness of 1 Thessalonians. While it does have many of the features seen in Graeco-Roman letters, there is no extant letter like this from the surrounding context, in that it combines personal features (such as the elaborate thanksgiving in 1:2–3:13) with instructions and end-time exhortation (Koester 1979). 1 Thessalonians, a carefully composed writing, 'is an experiment in the composition of literature which signals the momentous entry of Christianity into the literary world of antiquity' (ibid. 33).

3. An important insight of Robert Funk (1967) is that the letter substitutes for the personal presence of Paul. In this regard Funk accepts and develops the ideas of Koskenniemi (1956) that in the Greek world the letter was designed to extend the possibility of friendship between the parties after they had become separated—that is why *parousia* ('presence' or 'arrival'), *philophronēsis* ('affectionate kind treatment', 'friendship'), and *homilia* ('being together', 'communion', 'conversing') are basic to the conception of the Greek letter. 'Absent in body, but present through this letter' is a common Greek formula reflecting this phenomenon. Funk (1967: 265) suggests that Paul must have thought of his presence as the bearer of charismatic, even 'eschatological', power, even though he certainly does not equate his parousia with that of Christ and this theme is more clearly seen in 1 Cor 5:3–5 than in 1 Thessalonians.

4. It is uncertain if Paul is replying to a letter. Frame (1912: 157), Faw (1952: 220–2), and Malherbe (1990) think that he was, but most think that he was not. Paul could have learned of the situation in Thessalonica from Timothy (so Best 1972: 171 and Jewett 1986: 92).

5. Lastly, in this connection, it should be noted that most of the letters which survive from Graeco-Roman antiquity are from one individual to another and Paul is usually writing to a group or groups. We would expect this to make some difference. There is, indeed, some interest in group-oriented letters, especially those to a family (Stowers 1986: 71–6). Most of our evidence on family letters comes not from Greek epistolary theorists (preoccupied with the concerns of free adult males) but from Egyptian papyri. There is a letter from Cicero (in exile) to his family in Stowers (1986: 74–6).

6. Context Thessalonica, located at the head of the Thermaic Gulf, was founded by Cassander in *c.* 316 BCE on the site of an older city. There is some archaeological and literary evidence for the usual assemblage of Hellenistic features and buildings, such as an agora, a Serapaeum, a gymnasium, and a stadium (Vickers 1972). In due course Thessalonica passed into Roman hands, where its situation on the Via Egnatia, the great Roman road running from the Adriatic to the Black Sea, gave it great strategic and commercial significance. It is not surprising that it became the capital of the province of Macedonia. From surviving inscriptions it seems to have had a vibrant religious life, with numerous cults (Edson 1948; Donfried 1985; 1989).

7. There is little doubt that Thessalonica would have contained the same sharp division between a small wealthy, aristocratic élite and a much larger non-élite characteristic of the Graeco-Roman cities of the East. Jewett (1993) has usefully pointed out that the dominant form of housing for the non-élite would have been tenements, not the more spacious villa type houses.

B. The Nature of the Christ-Following Community in Thessalonica. 1. Jews or Gentiles or Both? In 1 Thess 1:9 Paul tells his audience they turned to God from idols to serve the one true God. This strongly suggests they were idolatrous Gentiles prior to conversion, for he would not describe Jews as turning from idolatry (de Vos 1999: 146–7). Many scholars refuse to accept this conclusion, mainly because it is contrary to what Acts 17:1–9 says, with its picture of Paul preaching in a synagogue and winning converts among Jews, God-fearers, Greeks, and rich women. But Luke is probably just following his typical pattern here (Lührmann 1990: 237–41), possibly based on his desire to depict an early movement of Christ-followers made up of Jews and Gentile God-fearers (Esler 1987: 36–45).

2. Exactly what sort of idolatry the Thessalonians had previously engaged in is uncertain. Jewett (1986: 127–32; 165–7) has mounted a significant argument that Paul's converts were impoverished manual workers who had seen Cabirus, their saviour-god, hijacked by upper-class interests. This view has, however, been

criticized as lacking evidence and also as resting on the false assumption that an end-time ideology is necessarily founded on some form of deprivation (Barclay 1993: 519–20).

3. Social Status Recent research on the social structure of Pauline communities has tended to favour socially stratified congregations with wealthy members providing a house for the meetings of the community and virtually acting as patrons to the members. But the fact that Paul does not mention the name of any person in Thessalonica raises the possibility that the whole congregation came from the poor non-élite, living in tenements (Jewett 1993). De Vos (1999: 154) sees in Thessalonica an audience of 'free-born artisans and manual-workers'. Corinth and Thessalonica thus represent very different types of the early Christ-movement (Barclay 1992). The difficult life of an urban artisan has been well described by Hock (1980: 31–47). The community may also have embraced agricultural day labourers (Schöllgen 1988: 73, 76).

4. Opposition to the Christ-Followers in Thessalonica Paul's initial proclamation in Thessalonica was attended by great conflict (*agōn*) in public (2:2). Furthermore, great affliction (*thlipsis*: 1:6) accompanied the reception of the word by the Thessalonians and, just as Paul had warned them that they would continue to be afflicted (3:4), so they are at the time he writes the letter (3:3). They have suffered at the hands of their fellow Thessalonians (2:14).

5. The best explanation for such opposition lies in the more general issue raised by Paul's aim of having the Thessalonians abandon their traditional gods in favour of the monotheistic brand of faith he was preaching, an aim achieved as far as his addressees were concerned, since they had turned to God from idols (1:9). To appreciate what this means we need to understand the everyday reality of paganism in this part of the empire (see MacMullen 1981).

6. Kinship, politics, economics, and religion were inextricably interrelated. Pagan rites were foci of economic and social interaction, playing a key role in maintaining the local political and economic system. The social dimension could be seen in crowds in theatres attached to shrines, with readings, music, and dancing (ibid. 18–24); economic aspects included coins minted and fairs attached to festivals (ibid. 25–7); and very important were meals at these festivals, generally involving meat not otherwise eaten and much wine and often partaken by *thiasoi* in small groups of diners, where the idea was found that the god might join those who were dining (cf. Plut. *Mor.* 1102A). Here gross indulgence often occurred (ibid. 36–40; cf. 1 Cor 8:10) in the *eidoleion* where the statue of the deity was located.

7. Jews and Christ-followers who abstained from these celebrations were likely to be accused of misanthropy (MacMullen 1981: 40). If people became Christ-followers in great numbers the local temples would be less frequented and the meat trade could suffer (so it was in Bithynia before Pliny's actions: *Ep.* 10.96; Mac-Mullen 1981: 41). More dangerous was the charge of atheism, since the élite believed that the *hoi polloi* needed to take part in the local worship to ensure political stability (MacMullen 1981: 2–3). Later on there is explicit reference to such behaviour as 'godlessness' (*atheotēs*), but there is no reason such a charge could not have been made in Paul's time (Barclay 1993: 515). To be respectable and decent meant taking part in the cult; old was good and new was bad. Thus, religion served to strengthen the existing social order (MacMullen 1981: 57–8). To deny the reality of the gods was absolutely unacceptable—one would be ostracized for that, even stoned in the streets (ibid. 62).

8. The particular proposal that the conflict centred on a charge that the Thessalonian followers of Jesus were contravening 'the decrees of Caesar' (explained by Judge 1971) rests on little but the historically dubious account of the Thessalonian mission in Acts 17:1–9 (also see de Vos 1999: 156–7). Nevertheless, as Donfried (1985) has argued, any abandonment of the imperial cult as part of a general rejection of idols would not have been well received in Thessalonica, where coins reveal signs of a cultic devotion to the emperor as early as 27 BCE.

C. The Character of the Letter: Theology and Identity. 1. Established Suggestions as to the Character of the Letter
There has been much interest among critics in seeking some broad description with which to characterize the nature of 1 Thessalonians. The two most popular sources for an overarching description are popular Hellenistic philosophy and rhetoric and Jewish biblical and extra-biblical traditions, since both areas, individually or jointly, have influenced what Paul has to say to his audience (Perkins 1989: 325–7). The numerous attempts to categorize 1 Thessalonians as a whole using the conceptual frameworks available to first-century Mediterranean persons can be referred

as 'emic', a useful social-scientific term (derived from 'phonemic') referring to insider, native, or indigenous points of view, as opposed to 'etic' (derived from 'phonetic'), meaning the perspective of an outsider trained in contemporary social-scientific ideas and approaches (see Headland, Pike, and Harris 1990). One of the fundamental insights of the social sciences is the fundamental importance of the distinction between these two perspectives. Yet modern persons trained in twentieth-century ideas who seek to understand—however incompletely—a pre-industrial culture removed from them in space or time will usually find it necessary to employ both emic and etic perspectives in order to translate the experience of that culture into a framework they can understand (Esler 1995: 4–8). So, we will first consider some existing solutions to the nature of the letter from an emic point of view, and then briefly propose some etic perspectives which will be employed in the Commentary.

2. The first emic perspective consists of those derived from the Hellenistic setting. Donfried (1989) and Smith (1989: 170) regard the letter as one of consolation, having as its main purpose to console (*paramuthein*) the Thessalonians at a time when they were suffering the effects of persecution. While 1 Thessalonians contains several consolatory elements (see Commentary), the existence of other dimensions, however, raises some doubt as to whether 'consolation' is appropriate as a general designation for the letter (Chapa 1994). One other dimension to the letter, most prominently advocated by Malherbe (1989c), is that of exhortation. Malherbe (1987: 68–78; 1989c) has argued that Paul's aim in the letter is closely in tune with elements of Graeco-Roman moral philosophy dealing with how, in a context of friendship between persons, one of them exhorted the others to maintain existing forms of behaviour, even though Paul modifies these traditions to accord with his own theology and interests. Malherbe (1987: 74) recognizes that hortatory themes are explicitly prominent only in 1 Thess 4–5, but argues that his self-description in chs. 1–3 serves a hortatory function by reminding them of his example.

3. The second prominent emic perspective involves Jewish traditions, expressed in biblical and extra-biblical literature, which speak of a decisive change in the cosmos which God is going to bring about. The fact that such ideas, especially expressed in the notions of the coming parousia of Christ and the salvation and

deliverance from wrath for his followers that will result (1:6–10; 4:13–18), should figure so prominently in a letter addressed largely if not exclusively to former idolaters constitutes one of the most remarkable features of 1 Thessalonians. This is especially surprising when one considers that other areas of Jewish tradition play a fairly small part in Paul's message, since although some of his statements bear marks of having originated in Israelite Scripture (as noted in the Commentary), there is, as de Vos (1999: 146–7) notes, no explicit quotation from the OT and no reference to any OT figure (such as Abraham, for example) or to cultic language. Moreover, nowhere else in Paul's letters is the theme of dramatic future redemption so pronounced (Jewett 1986: 168). At a more general level, however, it has been reasonably argued, by Perkins (1989) for example, that Paul's desire to install Jewish categories and images in the hearts and minds of his converts in Thessalonica—with its profusion of pagan cults also competing for adherents (Donfried 1985; 1989)—is a more prominent theme in the letter than moral education of the sort advocated by Malherbe and others. This proposal seems to be more in tune with the markedly non-élite status of the recipients of the letter.

4. A Social Identity Approach to 1 Thessalonians Alternative ways of characterizing 1 Thessalonians, which are capable of comprehending possibly a broader range of issues and of facilitating useful contemporary applications, can be derived from the etic perspectives developed by modern social scientists.

5. One promising approach is that offered by social identity theory, a flourishing area of social psychology developed by Henri Tajfel and others in the 1970s and 1980s (see Tajfel 1978; 1981; Tajfel and Turner 1979; 1986; Brown 1988; Robinson 1996) and utilized in a recent monograph on Galatians (Esler 1998, esp. at 40–57) and in Esler (2000) dealing with Galatians and 1 Thessalonians. This theory explores the extent to which persons acquire and maintain a valued social identity, that is, that part of their sense of self which derives from belonging to one group rather than another, a process which is likely to be the focus of stereotypification and denigration. Social identity is more significant in group-oriented cultures (such as those present in the first-century Mediterranean world) than in modern individualistic cultures (such as those of northern Europe and North America). Social identity theory always insists on the primacy of the question 'Who do we say we

are?'—which was expressed in the first-century Mediterranean world most directly in discourses of group-belonging derived from kinship or fictive kinship). Nevertheless, this theory also finds a place for ethical norms (as helping members maintain their sense of identity in new and ambiguous situations) and narratives of the past and future (as telling them who they are in relation both to where they have come from and whither they are proceeding). Even a conceptual apparatus usually (and reasonably) designated as 'theological' (and for 1 Thessalonians, see Marshall 1982) can serve a vital role in the processes of group differentiation and categorization which lie at the heart of this theory. Modern illustrations of the (often violent) dynamics of social identity lie to hand in the ethnic differentiation evident in Northern Ireland, Bosnia, Kosovo, Rwanda, and Israel/Palestine.

6. As will be noted in detail in the Commentary, 1 Thessalonians can be interpreted as an attempt by Paul to establish and maintain a desirable social identity for his Thessalonian converts in the face of the allure and threats posed by rival groups, and in relation to past, present, and future (Esler 2000). It is noteworthy, however, that in spite of Paul's seeking to nourish their group identity in a manner which includes pronounced outgroup stereotypification, he does not recommend illtreatment of outsiders (which is an all too common concomitant of such an attitude) but, on the contrary, actually advocates doing good to outsiders (3:12; 4:12). There is a strong countercultural dimension to Paul's position here.

7. It is worth noting that proposing social identity as an overall framework for interpreting the letter, with issues traditionally referred to as ethical or theological here seen as contributing to Paul's overall task of strengthening the Thessalonians' sense of who they were, in no way forecloses on any claims his ethics and theology have to a privileged ontological status. To suggest that resituating biblical data within frameworks originating in the social sciences in some way prejudices Christian truth-claims is an unfortunate misconception of the socialscientific approach to interpretation which is still entertained in some quarters where the fact that every word in the New Testament is socially embodied does not seem to be taken with sufficient seriousness.

8. While social identity theory exists at a fairly high level of abstraction, within its broad reach other areas of social-scientific research can be used in relation to particular parts of 1 Thessalonians. Chief among them are the bedrock realities of Mediterranean culture (as compellingly modelled by Malina (1993) on the basis of the work of social anthropologists in the last few decades) and millennialism, the study of how certain contemporary pre-industrial peoples in Africa, the Americas, and the South Pacific have responded to the disruption or destruction of their traditional life styles by European colonization by generating myths of future deliverance which describe the coming destruction of the Europeans and the restoration of traditional lifestyles, the return of the ancestors, the provision of cargo, and so on (Esler 1994: 96–104; Duling 1996). Jewett (1986) has applied such insights to both 1 and 2 Thessalonians.

D. Outline.

The Prescript and Thanksgiving (1:1–10)
   The Prescript (1:1)
   The Thanksgiving (1:2–10)
Paul's Ministry in Thessalonica (2:1–16)
   The Divine Basis for the Initial Visit (2:1–4)
   Their Behaviour and Example (2:5–12)
   The Response of the Thessalonians (2:13–16)
The Present Situation (2:17–3:13)
   Paul's Desire to Visit the Thessalonians (2:17–20)
   Timothy's Mission (3:1–5)
   Thankful Receipt of Timothy's Report (3:6–10)
   Prayer for the Thessalonians (3:11–13)
Living a Life Pleasing to God (4:1–12)
   Keeping the Traditions (4:1–2)
   Purity (4:3–8)
   Brotherly Love (4:9–12)
The Lord's Coming (4:13–5:11)
   The Circumstances of this Coming (4:13–18)
   The Need for Wakefulness (5:1–11)
Final Exhortations and Greetings (5:12–28)
   Honouring Leaders (5:12–13)
   Christian Identity-Indicators (5:14–22)
   Prayer for the Thessalonians (5:23–4)
   Closing Prayer and Instructions (5:25–8)

COMMENTARY

The Prescript and Thanksgiving (1:1–10)

(1:1) The Prescript Paul follows the form of opening current in Graeco-Roman letters consisting of sender(s), recipient(s), a greeting, and sometimes a prayer for health or prosperity, in that order. Here the senders are himself, Silvanus, and Timothy, with Timothy being mentioned again later (3:1–10). Paul does not describe himself in v. 1 as an apostle, although he does use that term of himself (and perhaps Silvanus and Timothy) at 2:7. The recipients are 'the congregation' (*ekklēsia*; 'church' in NRSV seems a little anachronistic here) 'of the Thessalonians (which is) in God the Father and the Lord Jesus Christ'. With this expression, in the very first verse, Paul inaugurates the issues of identity through group-belonging which will fill this letter. Social identity embraces the mere fact of belonging to a group (the 'cognitive' aspect) and its 'evaluative' and 'emotional' dimensions, that is, the positive or negative connotations members have about belonging and how they feel toward insiders and outsiders (Esler 1998: 42). Here the Thessalonians are invited to assess their membership of the congregation as extremely valuable through its close (though unexplored) relationship with their divine Father, an expression that constitutes the first of many instances of kinship language in the letter (Esler 2000), and the Lord Jesus. Although other groups are not yet mentioned, theirs is one plainly worth belonging to.

(1:2–10) The Thanksgiving This section, consisting of one long sentence, comprises the thanksgiving that Paul includes in all his letters except Galatians, after the address and greeting. For Pauline thanksgivings, see Schubert 1939. Some see this section as ending as late as 3:13, but this suggestion probably strains the notion of thanks beyond its breaking-point. v. 2, Paul notes that he constantly thanks God for the Thessalonians and mentions them in his prayers. He is obviously happy with them. v. 3, one reason for his positive regard now emerges: his memory of their work of faith (*pistis*), labour of love (*agapē*) and steadfastness of hope (*elpis*) in 'our Lord Jesus Christ' before our God and Father. The triad of faith, love, and hope, which is common in the Pauline corpus (1 Thess 5:8; Rom 5:1–5; 1 Cor 13:13; Gal 5:5–6) and later NT documents (Eph 4:2–5; Col 1:4–5; Heb 6:10–12; 10:22–4; 1 Pet 1:3–8), may well be an invention of Paul himself (Best 1972: 67). These three characteristics of becoming a follower of Christ are not just theological virtues but constitute distinctive badges of group identity. The Thessalonians, pushed to say who they were, could have given the distinctive answer, 'People characterized by faith (in Christ), love and hope'.

v. 4, Paul, describing them as 'brothers' (*adelphoi*; NRSV has 'brothers and sisters'), says he knows of their election (*eklogē*). The notion of election, with its long history antecedent to Paul of describing God's choice of Israel as his own people, is now redirected to designate the ex-idolatrous Thessalonians as a group with an extraordinary status and destiny as specially chosen by God. Here Paul both amplifies (or reiterates) their understanding of themselves and also enhances the positive connotations of belonging to such a group. The use of *adelphoi*, the first of seventeen instances in the letter, continues the kinship discourse already begun with the two references to the Father. The word may include women (so Koester 1979: 36 and NRSV), as it must do in Galatians in the light of Gal 3:28, but it is possible that here it does not, even though some women may have been converted by Paul (see Fatum 1997). v. 5, this verse, in which Paul states how his gospel came among them not only in word, but in power and in the Holy Spirit and with full conviction, outlines either the occasion and manner of their election or the grounds by which Paul inferred the fact of their election. It is essential to give Paul's reference to power and the Holy Spirit its full force and meaning. He is reminding the Thessalonians of the miracles and other charismatic phenomena (probably prophesying, glossolalia, visions, and auditions) which accompanied their reception of his preaching. Such ecstatic phenomena, although rare, if not unheard of, in domestic settings in first-century cities of the Graeco-Roman East, were characteristic of Paul's mission (Esler 1994: 40–51), as he also later reminded the Galatians (Gal 3:1–5). Charismatic phenomena created an exciting zone of Spirit-filled experience unique to his congregations. Once again, the group-differentiating element to this language should not be missed—another way of describing their identity was as a group actually filled by God. v. 6, they became his and the Lord's imitators in the way they received the word in spite of persecution (*thlipsis*) in the joy of the Holy Spirit. The difficulties experienced by the Thessalonians, already implied by the reference to their endurance in 1:3, now surface openly in relation to their initial conversion. Possible reasons for external opposition to the Thessalonians turning to Christ, especially through neglect of cults considered vital to civic well-being, were considered above (cf. 1 THESS B 4). One insight of social identity theory is that external opposition and persecution will often encourage members to act in terms of their group membership, so that such past suffering,

now brought again to mind by Paul, probably strengthened their involvement with, and commitment to, the congregation. The 'joy inspired by the Holy Spirit' probably extends to the euphoria enjoyed by those who experience powerful dissociative states caused by divine possession (Esler 1994: 42).

vv. 7–9, they 'became an example to all the believers in Macedonia and Achaia'. In other words, they provided an admirable ensemble of attributes of belonging to a Christ-believing group which was recognized as applicable to other such groups in neighbouring areas. Paul focuses on their faith (*pistis*) as the key feature (it was mentioned first in v. 3), knowledge of which has now spread so far that he has no need to say anything about them, because others tell him what success he had among the Thessalonians, how they turned from idols 'to serve a living and true God' (cf. 1 THESS B.1). Archaeological, epigraphic, numismatic, and literary evidence shows that a number of pagan cults were present in Thessalonica in Paul's time, including those of the Egyptian goddesses Serapis and Isis (who offered salvation and eternal life), Dionysus, Zeus, Asclepius, Demeter, and, most importantly, Cabirus (Edson 1948; Donfried 1985; Jewett 1986; Kloppenborg 1993). This was not unusual in the empire which exhibited a pullulation of beliefs (MacMullen 1981: 1). The pagan cults of Thessalonica represent some of the outgroups against whom the Thessalonians must now seek to distinguish themselves so as to build and maintain a positive social identity. v. 10, Paul concludes by mentioning that now they are waiting for his (i.e. God's) son from heaven, 'whom he raised from the dead—Jesus who rescues us from the wrath that is coming'. Here we see that Paul has managed to persuade his Gentile converts to accept deeply Jewish tradition relating to the Day of Anger when the wicked will be condemned and the good saved. The notion of 'the day (of judgement)' is a common feature of Israelite end-time speculation (see Joel 2:1–2; Zech 9:16; Mal 3:1–2; for the last judgement, see 1 Enoch 1:1–9; 2 Esd 7.33–44; Apoc. Abr. 29.14–29). At the same time, this brief reference to what the future holds for them, although greatly developed later in the letter, further contributes to differentiating the Thessalonians as a positively valued in-group from negatively valued outsiders (Esler 2000). Myths of the future developed by millennial movements in modern pre-industrial settings virtually always serve this function.

Paul's Ministry in Thessalonica (2:1–16)

(2:1–4) The Divine Basis for Paul's Initial Visit
vv. 1–2, addressing them again in the language of fictive kinship as 'brothers', Paul reminds the Thessalonians how fruitful has been the work which he began among them (2:1). He then offers some precise information about his inauguration of his mission in Thessalonica, mentioning that, in spite of the suffering and abuse he (and presumably Silvanus and Timothy) previously experienced (*hubristhentes*: physically assaulted and dishonoured) in Philippi, with God's aid (lit. in our God) he courageously preached God's gospel to them in the midst of great conflict (*agōn*, 'opposition' NRSV). The ill-treatment in Philippi may be the same as that recorded in Acts 16:19–24, where Paul and Silas (i.e. Silvanus of 1 Thess 1:1) were dragged to the lawcourts, experienced hostility from the crowd, and were then stripped, flogged, and thrown into prison on the order of the magistrates. Later they were delivered (Acts 16:25–40) and moved on to inaugurate the mission in Thessalonica (Acts 17:1–9). In any event, the Thessalonians must have known of the events—which involved being grossly shamed in public in a culture where honour was the primary virtue—to which Paul alludes. His point is that, in spite of this extreme type of opposition, he persevered when he came to Thessalonica, even though there too he encountered conflict (*agōn*). Paul is not 'boasting' in our modern sense in saying this. He is doing what any honourable first-century Mediterranean man would do—setting out the foundation for his claim to respect and to authority. Moreover, the references to conflict in Philippi and then in Thessalonica illustrate the extremely competitive, indeed violent, context in which Paul's efforts to establish in-groups of Christ-believers had been conducted in the face of the actions of opposing out-groups.

v. 3, Paul now begins to make more explicit the basis and nature of his activity and status. His appeal (*paraklēsis*) refers here to his initial preaching, whereas elsewhere in the letter *paraklēsis* relates to his exhortations contained within it (so 4:1). Paul denies that the source of his preaching was error, impurity, or deception, although he does not say precisely what charges against him led to this denial; presumably the Thessalonians did know (Best 1972: 93–4). It is even unclear whether he is responding to attacks from outside or inside the Christ-movement, or from Israelites or Gentiles. v. 4,

his authority comes from God. He has been approved by God to be entrusted to preach the gospel, and so he does, not to please men but the God who scrutinizes our hearts (see Jer 11:20; 1 Sam 16:7). In Mediterranean terms, Paul presents himself as the loyal client of his divine patron, who knows him fully and has entrusted him to act as a broker to others, by distributing his benefaction (the gospel) to people who will become his clients, indeed his children.

(2:5–12) Their Behaviour and Example vv. 5–6, Paul did not flatter them, that is to say, did not please the Thessalonians by attributing to them honour they did not possess, nor try to exploit them for personal gain. Nor did he seek honour (*doxa*, 'praise' NRSV) from anyone at all. Again, it is unclear precisely from which figures Paul might be distancing himself here. One possibility consists of the wandering philosophers, such as Cynics (Malherbe 1989b: 38–9) and magicians of this period, whose sincerity was questionable (see Lucian, *De morte Peregrini*, 3, 13). Alternatively or in addition, Paul may have in mind other members of the Christ-movement, such as the wandering apostles and prophets bent on living off congregations who are mentioned in the *Didache* (11.3–12), with something like the latter suggested by the next verse. v. 7, although as Christ's authorized apostle, that is, emissary or broker (*apostolos*), he held a position of considerable honour in relation to the Thessalonians, he was gentle (that is, not insisting on the benefits which rightly belonged to such an honourable position), like a wet-nurse or nursing mother comforting her children. For the word translated here as 'gentle' (*ēpioi*) there is a variant, 'infants' (*nēpioi*), which is somewhat better attested in the manuscript tradition, but the total inversion of the imagery in the rest of the verse which this reading would produce, with the Thessalonians now the children, suggests 'gentle' was the original form.

Malherbe (1989b) has drawn attention to the similarity of Paul's language in 2:1–12 to that used of ideal Cynic philosophers (as opposed to money-grubbing charlatans) by Dio Chrysostom (40–120 CE), even to the extent of Dio's using the image of the nurse to epitomize how a good philosopher will treat his audience. Malherbe's (ibid. 46, 48) conclusion, however, that Paul's use of such language suggests he need not have been replying to an attack on him, is improbable. In this conflict-ridden and group-oriented culture it was inevitable that Paul would be attacked (2:1–2) and not at all surprising that in reply he would avail himself of a convenient stock discourse, in this case, perhaps, that of genuine travelling philosophers versus false ones (Koester 1979: 42). This discourse had probably become conventional long before Dio, writing after Paul, had utilized it himself.

v. 8, the sentiment here builds on v. 7. Because Paul cared so deeply for them (*homeiromenoi*—a rare word; Koester 1979: 42) and they had become very dear (*agapētoi*) to him, he gladly decided to share with them not only the gospel but his whole being. Paul is here drawing upon the strong bonds of love and group solidarity that characterized family life in this culture. v. 9 provides a specific interpretation of how Paul shared his whole being with them. He asks the Thessalonians, (his) 'brothers', to recall that while he preached the gospel of God to them he worked night and day so as not to be a burden on them. Paul here reveals that he preached to the Thessalonians in a very low-status occupation as a craftsman of some sort (perhaps a tent-maker—Acts 18:3), not in the context of a synagogue, thus providing further evidence for the Thessalonians being a Gentile community (see 1 THESS 1:9). Hock (1980) has amply described how a craftsman's shop would have functioned as a locus for Paul's evangelism. That Paul could celebrate manual labour in this way suggests that his addressees also belonged to the non-élite in Thessalonica (Jewett 1993). This observation finds further support in the fact that there is not a single member of this congregation socially prominent enough for Paul to address by name (unlike the case in Corinth). v. 10, the Thessalonians are witnesses that he worked among them in a manner that was holy, just, and blameless. Behind this assertion may lie sentiments to the contrary that Paul was aware were being expressed about him in the city.

vv. 11–12, once again Paul returns to the pervasive family imagery of the letter, although now changing its gender, by saying that they know he treated each one of them like a father his children (v. 11), urging (*parakalein*), encouraging (*paramuthein*), and offering witness (*marturein*, 'pleading' NRSV) as to how they should 'lead a life' (lit. walk, *peripatein*) worthily of the God who called them into his kingdom and glory (v. 12). At the end of v. 12 the reference to God's kingdom and glory reinforces the elevated and honourable nature of the group to which they belong and the glorious destiny in store for them. These are central themes in the letter as a whole. They emphasize the measureless superiority of the Christ-believing ingroup to all out-groups in this environment.

The word *peripatein* in v. 12 is important (it also appears at 4:1, twice, and 4:12). It also occurs in Romans (4 times), 1 Corinthians (twice), 2 Corinthians (5 times), and Galatians (once). In the NT the verb can mean just 'to walk around' (Mk 2:9), but Paul uses it for the 'walk' of life. According to Seesemann (1967: 944–5), Paul relies on it in exhortatory contexts, particularly in the moral sense, a meaning which could only have derived from the LXX, since it is unknown in classical Greek. An LXX example of this meaning is at 2 Kings 20:3 (where Hezekiah says he has walked before God in truth and with a perfect heart) and Eccl 11:9; Sir 13:13. Yet a moral or ethical dimension alone is too narrow for v. 12 (4:1 and 4:12); it essentially means 'to live' or, within a social identity framework, 'to adopt a particular identity'.

(2:13–16) The Response of the Thessalonians Dispute rages as to whether these verses are authentic to the letter or constitute a later insertion. The case for inauthenticity was argued by Baur (1873–5), and has recently been supported by many scholars including Pearson (1971), Boers (1976: 151–2), Koester (1979: 38), and Schmidt (1983). A much more limited interpolation theory regards 2:16c as a marginal gloss inserted into the text after the sack of Jerusalem in 70 CE. Typical reasons for inauthenticity (see Koester 1979: 38) include the unnecessary resumption of the thanksgiving at 2:13, interruption of the close connection between 2:12 and 2:17, alleged non-Pauline use of Pauline terms (such as *mimētai*, 'imitators', in 2:14), the characterization of the Judeans in 2:14 as in conflict with Paul's attitude in Rom 9–11, lack of a historical point of reference for the last phrase in 2:16 ('the wrath to the end has come upon them') before 70 CE, and the absence of any allusion to these verses in 2 Thessalonians. Koester also considers a polemic against a third party would destroy the writer-recipient relationship he is trying to reshape.

It is submitted, however, that the better view is that 2:13–16 are authentic, as argued by Okeke (1980–1), Donfried (1984), Jewett (1986: 36–41), and Weatherly (1991), to name a few. There is no reason in the textual tradition to doubt their authenticity and the arguments just mentioned are unpersuasive. Thus, v. 13, beginning with a thanksgiving, marks a natural transition from Paul's message to its impact on the

Thessalonians. As to *mimētai*, Paul uses the very word and in a very similar construction at 1 Thess 1:6 (and also at 1 Cor 4:16 and 11:1), so its use at 2:14 is Pauline. Okeke (1980–1) has offered an explanation for why we should not expect Paul to follow the same argument in this letter as when addressing the Romans. This particular point can be made more emphatically, however. A social-identity approach to Galatians has revealed how far Paul will go in stereotyping Israelites even when they are a part of his congregations (Esler 1998); we would expect such attitudes to apply *a fortiori* when his audience is Gentile, as in Thessalonica. Finally, there are other possible candidates for the catastrophe referred to in 2:16, such as the riot and massacre that occurred in Jerusalem in 48 CE (Jos. *Ant.* 20.112 and *J.W.* 2.224–7; Jewett 1986: 37–9).

Even among the critics in favour of 2:13–16 being authentic, however, one sometimes encounters a wish that the verses were not Pauline (see Jewett 1986: 41), perhaps reflecting a modern aversion to the powerful in-group/out-group antipathies of the first-century Mediterranean world which are largely alien to modern North American and northern European culture and which interpreters are often slow to recognize in NT texts.

v. 13, Paul thankfully recalls their acceptance of God's word, which is active among those who believe. Here he again shows his closeness to them and also reminds them of the nature of the power present in this group, as already mentioned in 1:4. The implication is that none of the other groups in Thessalonica have anything like this to offer. v. 14, his Thessalonian 'brothers' became imitators of the Christ-following congregations (*ekklēsiai*) in Judea (who had been persecuted by other Judeans (*Ioudaioi*), because they experienced just the same treatment at the hands of their own fellow-countrymen. To translate *Ioudaioi* as 'the Jews' (with NRSV and most other trs.) misses the extent to which this people (whether living in Judea, Galilee, or further afield) were regarded by others (and saw themselves) as oriented to Judea, and to Jerusalem and the temple within it. This point becomes very clear in Book 11 of Josephus' *Jewish Antiquities*, when Cyrus sends the Judeans home to Judea; thereafter in this text Josephus almost always refers to them under this name.

For the nature of the opposition to the Thessalonians, cf. 1 THESS B.4. The opposition in Judea must have been somewhat different, as it would have drawn upon peculiarly Israelite opposition to the Christ-movement, of the sort perhaps that had previously motivated Paul himself to try to destroy it (Gal 1:13; Phil 3:6).

v. 15, Paul now attacks the Judeans just as we would expect once we shed modern notions of ethical behaviour and attempt to enter the harsh first-century Mediterranean world of violent stereotypification and vilification of out-groups. He denigrates the Judeans as those who killed the Lord Jesus (even though he had been crucified by the Romans) and the prophets and who persecuted him, acting in a way not pleasing to God and opposed to all human beings. In the last phrase Paul seems to go so far as to pick up and mouth for the benefit of his ex-idolatrous converts negative views on Judeans current in certain Graeco-Roman circles (see Stern 1974–80; Esler 1987: 76–80). The idea that the Judeans had killed the prophets was a common one among early Christ-followers (see Lk 13:34; Mt 5:12; 23:31, 35, 37; Acts 7:52; Rom 11:3). References to killing prophets are found in Scripture (1 Kings 19:10) and from extra-scriptural accounts, as in important texts such as the *Lives of the Prophets* and the *Martyrdom of Isaiah*. v. 16, thus the Judeans have hindered him from preaching to the Gentiles so that they might be saved. A possible mechanism for such hindrance emerges in the picture of how the Judeans interfered with Paul's mission in Philippi as recounted in Acts 16:11–24, if that account is historical. The result is that the Judeans have always filled their sins to the brim, perhaps referring to the repeated failure of Israel during history, and the anger has finally caught up with them. Although it is not easy to find an incident corresponding to the statement that the anger has come upon the Judeans, one possibility is the riot and massacre which occurred in Jerusalem in 48 CE (Jewett 1986: 37–8).

The Present Situation (2:17–3:13)

Paul recounts his long-standing desire to visit them, and how he sent Timothy instead. Generally, Funk (1967) argues that the traditional Greek epistolary topic of friendship (*philophronēsis*; see Koskenniemi 1956) has been transformed into a new topic of the Christian letter, 'apostolic parousia'.

(2:17–20) Paul's Desire to Visit the Thessalonians v. 17, Paul has previously described himself as a nursing mother (2:7) and as a father (2:11) to them; now he retains the familial imagery but presents himself as (for a short period) having become an orphan in relation to them—but physically, not emotionally. The notion of 'absent in body but present in mind' was a common topic in Graeco-Roman epistolography (Funk 1967: 264; Stowers 1986: 59). The expression of his eagerness to come to them, part of the friendly letter framework, is a fairly common one in Paul's letters (cf. Rom 1:11; 15:23; 2 Cor 8:16–17; Phil 1:8). v. 18, yet although he earnestly sought to be physically with them again and wanted to come to them on a number of occasions, Satan prevented him. The idea of there being a hindrance to his coming is one of the structural features Funk isolates as belonging to the apostolic parousia (also found at Rom 1:13; 15:22). Moreover, the reference to Satan suggests Paul senses a supernatural force thwarting his desired visit to the Thessalonians (Best 1972: 126–7). vv. 19–20 provide the basis for Paul's missing the Thessalonians and desiring to be with them. For it is they who are his hope, joy, and crown of his claim to honour; in the presence of his Lord Jesus at his parousia they will be his honour and his joy. Here the typical Mediterranean connection of the honour of the individual and the publicly acknowledged worth of the group to which he or she belongs comes through loud and clear. At his parousia Jesus will reward those who are his own, so that those responsible for their conversion, here Paul, will earn a massive accretion of honour and joy from so public an acknowledgement.

(3:1–5) Timothy's Mission vv. 1–2a, because he was no longer able to endure (i.e. his separation from them) he resolved to stay behind alone in Athens and send Timothy. In Acts, Paul moves from Thessalonica to Athens (17:16–34), with a brief intervening stay in Beroea (17:9–15). vv. 2–5, according to Funk's parousia schema, this is the despatch of the emissary aspect (also see 1 Cor 4:17; 16:12; 2 Cor 8:18–24; 9:3–5; 12:17–18; Phil 2:19–23), usually containing (1) a statement that someone has been or will be sent, here 1 Thess 3:2a (just noted); (2) his credentials, here 1 Thess 3.2b (Timothy is his brother and fellow-worker in God for the proclamation of the gospel of Christ); and (3) purpose, here 1 Thess 3:2c–4 (Timothy was to strengthen and encourage them in the faith, lest anyone be agitated by the current tribulations, which they knew would come, just as he had foretold when he was with them). In v. 5, Paul offers a summary of his purpose in sending Timothy: because he could no longer endure, he sent Timothy to learn about their faith, lest the tempter had been successful or his labour fruitless.

(3:6–10) Thankful Receipt of Timothy's Report v. 6, Timothy has recently returned to Paul bearing the good news of their faith (*pistis*) and love (*agapē*), that they always have a good memory of him and that they want to see him as much as he wants to see them. The first element of this good news is that the Thessalonians are preserving two parts of the (characteristic) Pauline triad mentioned at 1 Thess 1:3, namely, faith and love; these are vital attributes of the group identity Paul has wanted them to acquire. Nevertheless, Timothy's (or Paul's) omission of any mention of the third attribute—hope—may be deliberate, given what he will say to them later (4:10, 13). As the founder of a congregation who wants them to imitate him, he naturally rejoices that he is still so warmly regarded by them. According to Funk, vv. 6–9 relate to the benefits which accrue from the apostolic parousia—both to Paul and to his addressees (see also Rom 1:13; 15:32; 1 Cor 4:18–19, 21; Phil 2:19). vv. 7–8, Paul states that their faith has encouraged him in a time of every distress (*anagkē*) and persecution (*thlipsis*); if they stand firm he can go on living. Here 'faith' is a very general word denoting their whole identity as Christ-believers. Paul does not specify the affliction and tribulation and it is not possible to correlate this information with the descriptions of his activity in Acts at around this time, in either Beroea (Acts 17:10–15), Athens (Acts 17:16–34), or Corinth (Acts 18:1–17). This is another reason against putting too much reliance on Acts as a historical source for Paul's experience at this time, a problem discussed in 1 THESS B.1 in relation to the very different pictures given by Paul and Luke of the foundation of the congregation in Thessalonica. vv. 9–10, because of the Thessalonians, Paul is able to offer joyful thanksgiving to God.

v. 10, day and night he prays most earnestly to see them and—but now a darker note intrudes—to amend the shortcomings (*husterēmata*) of their faith. Shortcomings? Hitherto there has been no *explicit* mention of any deficiency in their faith (which here has the same meaning of Christ-following identity as at 3:7), even if a lack of hope was strongly implied at 3:6. Yet Paul is now opening up the theme that even among his splendid and beloved Thessalonians there are problems. Timothy's report could not, after all, have been a uniformly positive one. Accordingly, even if Funk (1967) is right to see in v. 10 an invocation for divine approval and support for the apostolic parousia (as also in Rom 1:10; 15:30–2; 1 Cor 4:19; 16:7), the fact that an absent Paul might need to be present in epistolary form to correct as well as to praise must not be forgotten.

(3:11–13) Prayer for the Thessalonians v. 11, Paul now begins the detailed text of a prayer (especially signalled by verbs in the optative mood in vv. 11, 12) which he had described in summary form in v. 10 and which continues until the end of v. 13. The first invocation (as in v. 10) is that God their Father and their Lord Jesus might guide his way to them. v. 12, the second invocation of the prayer begins to pick up the shortcomings mentioned in v. 11: Paul prays that God may make them increase and abound in love (*agapē*) for one another and for all, just as Paul does for them. Although they are characterized by love already (1 Thess 3:6), Paul prays that they will show even more love. There is room for improvement. It is significant that this love must not only be directed to the members of the congregation (a reality to be designated, quite naturally, as *philadelphia*, 'brotherly love', at 4:9) but also to everyone, that is to all outside the congregation. This represents a significant, indeed countercultural, modification of group-oriented ways of behaving which were then the norm. The theme will be taken up again later (4:12).

v. 13, thirdly, Paul prays that they (God and Jesus) may strengthen the Thessalonians' hearts in holiness so that they may be blameless before their God and Father at the parousia of their Lord Jesus with all his saints. This invocation directs the recipients of the letter to the future dimension of their existence, the return of Jesus. The omission of hope in 1 Thess 3:6 suggested certain difficulties with their understanding of what the future held in store and, before proceeding to details (4:13–18), Paul reminds them in abbreviated form of the goal of their existence. The Lord will return and they must be blameless in holiness when he does. The word 'holiness' (*hagiōsunē*) refers to the Spirit-charged zone of existence they have entered by joining the congregation; its opposites are 'impurity' (*akatharsia*, 4:7, and *porneia*, 4:3), the label for the filthy world of idolatry and immorality which they have left behind (see 1 THESS 4:3).

Living a Life Pleasing to God (4:1–12)
Lührmann (1990: 245) refers to this material, reflecting Paul's initial preaching, as 'ethics'. But 'ethics' as a differentiated province of human activity with a heavily individualistic tendency is quite a modern concept, having acquired its current status since the time of Kant (1724–1804). In the ancient world there was discussion of appropriate ways to behave, but set within wider frameworks of domestic or civic life. From the perspective of social-identity theory, on the other hand, norms for behaviour are values which define acceptable and non-acceptable attitudes and behaviours for group members. Norms bring order and predictability to the environment and thus assist in-group members to construe the world and to choose appropriate behaviour in new and ambiguous situations. Thus they maintain and enhance group identity (Brown 1988: 42–8; Esler 1998: 45). Even if critics are correct in seeing Israelite tradition, such as that found in the so-called Holiness Code of Lev 17–26 (Hodgson 1982), as lying behind some of what Paul says in 1 Thess 4:1–12, the usefulness of a social-identity approach to the material would persist. Throughout Israelite history norms, derived from the law and its interpretation, served to differentiate Israel from other groups (Esler 1998: 82–6) and Paul's reappropriation of some of those norms within a setting of the novel intergroup differentiation inaugurated with the establishment of congregations of Christ-followers is unsurprising.

(4:1–2) Keeping the Traditions v. 1, 'Finally, brothers', says Paul, thus indicating that he is moving on to a *new* series of points relating to the maintenance of their group identity which he has just signalled (in 3:6–13) is not quite as good as it should be. He wants them to 'walk' (*peripatein*: cf. 1 THESS 2:12) and to please God in accordance with the traditions they had previously received (*parelabete*) from him (no doubt when he founded the congregation), and thus to do better and better. Paul uses the word *peripateō* to create an *inclusio* in 4:1–12, by placing it (twice) at the beginning of the passage (v. 1) and once at the end (v. 12). We are justified in translating it broadly, 'be of a particular identity', an identity which certainly includes moral norms, rather than the narrower 'behave in a particular way'. The exhortation to 'please God', reminds us that a major foundation for normative behaviour among this group is the very personal one of pleasing their heavenly Father (and patron). v. 2, Paul specifically reminds them of the existence of commands, that is, the instructions relating to norms, which he had previously given 'in our Lord Jesus Christ'. The last phrase indicates that these are distinctive to Christ-followers; they are emblems of group-belonging.

(4:3–8) Purity v. 3a, God's will is their sancti-fication (*hagiasmos*). Koester (1979: 43) reason-ably moves away from too individualistic an interpretation by suggesting that *hagiasmos* should not be understood as a task of moral perfection for the individual, but as the reassess-ment of the values for dealing with each other in everyday life (i.e. it concerns relationships). Yet this really fails to bring out the full signifi-cance of this word. As suggested elsewhere (Esler 1998: 157–8), sanctification language in 1 Thessalonians (which covers *hagios* and *hagiō-sunē* at 3:13, *hagiasmos* here and at 4:4 and 7, and *hagiazō* at 5:23) provides a semantic framework for expressing the ideal identity of his Gentile converts parallel to the language of righteous-ness which Paul reactively appropriates from Israelite tradition and deploys in Galatians and Romans when the Christ-following groups he addresses also include Israelites (Esler 1998: 141–77). This is vital language in the letter relating to norms which serves to encapsulate the very distinctive identity of the Thessalonian in-group in contrast to idolatrous out-groups. vv. 3b–6 list a number of aspects to this identity, with vv. 7–8 summarizing the position. v. 3b, the first dimension to their 'sanctification' is that they refrain from *porneia*, which probably means sexual sin of all types (Best 1972: 161), which Paul presumably implies was character-istic of the idolatrous world they had left be-hind. Thus the norm (of sexual propriety) is firmly embedded in a contrast between in-group and out-group.

v. 4, is one of the most difficult verses in the letter. (God also wills that) each one of them should know 'to acquire' (or, perhaps, 'to keep'—*ktasthai*; NRSV has 'control') his *skeuos* ('vessel') in sanctification (*hagiasmos*) and hon-our. There are two main options: (1) 'to keep or control one's body', which involves giving *ktasthai* a somewhat unusual meaning, or (2) 'to acquire one's wife'. As to (1), sometimes in the post-NT Greek world (but not before) the body is called the container of the soul (Maurer 1971: 359). But Paul does refer to human bodies at 2 Cor 4:7 as 'clay vessels', bearing a treasure. Maurer (p. 365) says the reference is not to the bodies as bearing the soul but the message, but why should not this be the sense in 4:7? This interpretation of *skeuos* as body, preferred by a number of patristic writers (such as Tertullian and Chrysostom), in spite of a rather unusual sense for *ktasthai*, is the most likely meaning. Lührmann (1990: 245–7) argues strongly that *skeuos* means 'body' to include men and

women—*anthrōpoi*—as in 1 Cor 7 (which as-sumes *adelphos* and *philadelphia* as used in 1 Thes-salonians do cover both genders). This meaning also seems far better adapted to the reference to sexual misconduct in the previous verse and to what follows in v. 6 (see below).

As to (2), there is a Jewish but not a Greek background for calling a woman a vessel (Maurer 1971: 361–2: 'to use as a vessel', 'to make one's vessel', are to be regarded as estab-lished euphemisms for sexual intercourse). If so *ktasthai* (present tense) in an ingressive sense ('to gain') would mean to marry (as a defence against fornication) and in a durative sense ('to possess'—which would normally require the perfect tense) would mean to hold their own wives in esteem (as a defence against fornication—thus the phrase would correspond exactly to 1 Cor 7:2). This interpretation also fits quite well with v. 6 which would then be a warning against adultery with the wife of a member of the congregation. But this interpret-ation involves an unpleasant nuance of *skeuos* (women as containers for semen) which is un-known among Greek authors and is found only in some fairly erotic passages in Israelite works (Bassler 1995: 55).

There are other, less likely, possibilities for *skeuos*. Donfried (1985: 342) argues that it means the penis, being a reference to the strong phallic symbolism in the cults of Dionysus, Cabirus, and Samothrace prevalent in Thessalonica. With *ktasthai* it means 'to gain control over one's penis, or over the body with respect to sexual matters'. Bassler (1995) makes an inter-esting new suggestion that it refers to one's virgin partner.

v. 5, Paul contrasts this behaviour with its opposite, the lustful passion of the Gentiles who do not know God. It seems much more plausible that 'lustful passion' is a reference to how the idolatrous Gentiles treat their bodies rather than their wives. Graeco-Roman wives were meant to live respectable lives at home, bearing their children and attending to domes-tic affairs. Greek or Roman men passionately involved with their wives were regarded as odd-ities. Best's (1972: 165) attribution to Paul of the notion that 'pagan marriage is motivated by lust' is culturally indefensible. v. 6a, Paul offers another piece of advice, beginning with an in-finitive, whose connection with what has pre-ceded is difficult. It could be a new topic: '(It is God's will—understood from v. 3—that the Thessalonian converts) should not wrong (*huperbainein*) or defraud (*pleonektein*; NRSV has 'exploit') his brother in commerce (*pragmati*). This is unlikely, since it breaks up a chain of thought that is otherwise completely devoted to sexual misconduct decried in v. 3 and *pragma* in the singular is not used of commerce (Best 1972: 167). It is preferable to interpret *pragma* as 'matter' (so NRSV) or 'area', referring back to the misuse of one's body in the lustful manner of pagans. In this context *huperbainein* and *pleonektein* could have the meanings just attributed to them, in which case Paul would be warning the Thessalonians not to engage in sexual misconduct with the wives or husbands of other members of the congregation. But Paul is unlikely to have introduced such a limitation. What he is actually saying is that they should not 'outdo' (*huperbainein*) or 'gain the advantage over' (*pleonektein*) their brothers in the area of sexual conduct, that is, stop acting like the pagans around them for whom sexual conquests were a matter of pride and the more one achieved the more one had to boast about. Such competition was typical behaviour among unrelated males in this culture (Paul also attacks the same kind of attitudes and practices in Gal 5:26; Esler 1998: 230). Once again, Paul is differentiating this group from the sinful outsiders. v. 6b–c, he reminds them that God will take vengeance on this behaviour just as he had previously told them. There is a strong context for God as avenger in Israelite tradition (Deut 32:35; Ps 99:8; Mic 5:15; Nah 1:2).

v. 7, Paul begins to sum up the discussion initiated at v. 3 by reminding them of the rival brands of identity on offer: either the sanctification (*hagiasmos*), to which God has called them, or impurity (*akatharsia*), here (like the instance at 2 Cor 12:21) being related to the condition and product of *porneia* in v. 3. These words describe the stark alternatives available to in-group and out-group. v. 8, Paul next reminds them of the divine dimension to the norms that are integral to their identity: the one who 'disregards', or 'rejects' (*athetein*), does not disregard a human being but the God who puts the Holy Spirit *into* them. Paul has already reminded them of the Spirit (see 1 Thess 1:5), which above all means the powerful charismatic phenomena associated with having, in effect, God within, and he now reiterates this message in the context of group norms in the area of sexual propriety.

(4:9–12) Brotherly Love v. 9, now Paul turns to another subject, brotherly love (*philadelphia*), although still within the broad subject of the shortcomings announced at 3:10 and the need to abound even more in their *apapē* mentioned at 3:12. Brotherly love is something that Paul says he has no need to write about because they have been 'God-taught' (*theodidaktoi*) to love (*agapan*) one another.

Although there is a treatise by Plutarch on the subject, the word *philadelphia* is rare in early texts of the Christ-movement. Paul uses *philadelphia* only once elsewhere (Rom 12:10), and there are only a few instances in the rest of the NT (Heb 13:1; 1 Pet 1:22; 2 Pet 1:7 (twice)). The adjective *philadelphos* occurs at 1 Pet 3:8. There are only three instances in the Septuagint, at 4 Macc 13:23, 26; 14:1 (which Klauck (1990) sees as a source for Paul), while *philadelphos* also appears, at 2 Macc 15:14; 4 Macc 13:21; 15:10. Perhaps the connection of 'Philadelphos' with the Ptolemies has discouraged its wider use in biblical texts. Betz (1978: 232) notes that there is no obvious explanation why this term was regarded as proper in the Christian context, since it was apparently considered as just part of *agapē* and there was no further need to explain it; it may have come to Paul from Hellenized Judaism. Aasgaard (1997) has argued for striking parallels between Plutarch's understanding of *philadelphia* and Paul's thought on the subject.

Yet in a context in which Paul was intent on maintaining the appropriateness of kinship patterns from the surrounding culture to his Thessalonian congregation, the use of a word at home in Greek perceptions of the family had a lot to recommend it. More particularly, brotherly love characterizes the alternative to behaving like unrelated males always in competition, which he criticized in v. 6a. Lying close to the heart of the identity Paul is recommending to the Thessalonians is the model of harmonious relations among a respectable family in the surrounding culture (Esler 2000). While the reference to their brotherly love at v. 9 is the most obvious example, the word *adelphos* occurs four times in the passage (4:1, 6, 10 (twice)).

Theodidaktos is unattested prior to Paul; he may have coined the word. He could be alluding to Lev 19:18 (so Lührmann 1990: 248), or to Isa 54:13 or Jer 31:33–4, but this is unlikely for a Gentile congregation. Marshall (1982: 115) has a good explanation: Paul is saying that the Spirit empowers humans to love. This is in accord with Gal 5:22 (see Esler 1998: 203). Kloppenborg (1993) has suggested another source of *philadelphia*, and *theodidaktos*, namely, that Paul is utilizing the local popularity of the Dioscuri,

Castor and Pollux, whose devotion to one another was widely regarded as exemplifying *philadelphia*, and that *theodidaktoi* evokes the Dioscuri as a pattern for imitation. But such a derivation is highly unlikely from the author of 1 Thess 1:9. How is it possible, *contra* Kloppenborg, that two *pagan* gods could offer the Thessalonians 'an appropriate mimetic ideal in a situation in which disparities in moral character lead to rivalry and tension' (1993: 237)?

v. 10*a*, Paul praises them for showing *agapē* to all the brothers in the whole of Macedonia, which brings out the fundamental importance of group solidarity, a typical theme in this culture. vv. 10*b*–11, he urges them to do even better and to make it their ambition to live quietly, to mind their own affairs, and to work with their hands as he had previously warned them. The most likely explanation for this advice is that Paul wanted his audience, probably urban craftsmen and labourers of low status, to keep a low profile and therefore avoid attracting antipathy from out-groups for reasons discussed in 1 THESS B.4. Within their social level, Paul was suggesting that they live the quiet, hardworking life of honourable men (see 1 THESS 4:12). Hock (1980: 46–7) believes that this is a recommendation to keep out of politics (by paying special levies, going on embassies to Rome, entertaining the governor, undertaking public services). Such a withdrawal from public life was especially identified with the Epicureans and many more in the first century, sometimes being coupled with advocacy of philosophers of retirement and working with one's own hands. Yet Hock's proposal seems socially unrealistic in relation to a more likely audience of the urban poor who would never have been in a financial position to engage in such activities in the first place, let alone to withdraw from them. v. 12, Paul ends this section with a purpose clause: so that they may adopt a respectable identity (*peripatein euschēmonōs*; NRSV has 'behave properly towards') towards outsiders (*hoi exō*) and be dependent on no one. Thus Paul concludes with *peripatein*, the word used twice when he opened this discussion (4:1).

The Lord's Coming (4:13–5:11)

These verses deal in some detail with the future destiny of those who believe in Christ and, to a lesser extent, with those who do not. The letter has previously referred to the future in store (1:10), especially the parousia of Christ (2:19; 3:13), but now we have the events and their significance set out in some detail. Although the word 'eschatology' has been applied by NT scholars to this subject for over a century now (as an example, see Best 1972: 180), the various (and differing) theological agendas that have become attached to that word have left its meaning rather obscure, except in the vanishingly rare case of critics who indicate precisely what they mean by it. Accordingly, in what follows the data in 4:13–5:11 will be considered within two other frameworks which, although derived from social-scientific research, have the potential to throw light on this absorbing picture of the future dating to the very early stages of the Christ-movement.

First, within social-identity theory (a sub-area of social psychology—cf. 1 THESS C.5–8), a group's distinctive orientation towards the future can help foster among the members a cognitive sense of belonging to the group, and also nourish the evaluative and emotional dimensions of membership. In other words, the members tell themselves who they are—and in a very positive way—in relation to where they are going. A striking modern example of this is the Hausa, a group of Sudanese Muslims, who spend their whole life as if they are undertaking a pilgrimage, a *haj*, to Mecca, even though most of them never get there (Esler 1998: 42). Secondly, social anthropologists have investigated many groups, generally (although not always) suffering from some form of colonial oppression or disturbance of traditional ways of life, who develop or revive narratives of a coming transformation of the world which will leave them radically restored to their proper place and, often, destroy those who oppress them (Duling 1996; Esler 1993; 1994: 93–109). These phenomena are generally referred to as instances of 'millennialism' or 'millenarianism'. Examples of millenarian mythopoiesis, discussed elsewhere (Esler 1993: 187–8; 1994: 101–4), include the ghost dance among North American Indians in the late nineteenth century and the cargo cults of twentieth-century Melanesia (in the South Pacific). Jewett (1986: 161–78) has usefully applied millenarian ideas to 1 and 2 Thessalonians (the latter letter he regards as authentic). Millennialism provides a second useful etic framework for contextualizing this part of 1 Thessalonians. It is worth noting that although deprivation of some sort cannot simply be said to explain the origin of millennial movements, it is often one aspect of the experience of the membership and provides an important part of the context that needs to be taken into account in understanding its futurist myth.

(4:13–18) The Circumstances of this Coming
v. 13, Paul wants them to know that they should not grieve about those who 'are sleeping' (NRSV 'who have died'), 'as others do who have no hope'. Apparently some of the people in Thessalonica whom Paul converted have died since and worries have arisen among the Thessalonians concerning their status at the parousia of Christ. Clearly, as already noted, belief in the parousia, even though it is a vision of the future heavily indebted to Israelite tradition, is embedded in this ex-Gentile group, so that the problem is whether those who die in faith beforehand will participate in Christ's glorious return. The sharp distinction between in-group and out-groups Paul maintains throughout the letter is evident here in the reference to 'the rest who have no hope'. Hope (*elpis*) was included at 1 Thess 1:3 as one of the three primary elements of the identity of Christ-followers and the fact that Paul is worried they might be deficient in hope also surfaces in Timothy's notable failure to include it in his report to Paul of the current condition of the Thessalonians (at 1 THESS 3:6). It is beside the point to suggest that it was not correct that the rest of men had no hope whatsoever (as does Best 1972: 185); Paul is using the notion of hope to differentiate Christ-followers from other groups; the (probably inaccurate) stereotypification of the others is essential to this strategy. v. 14, Paul sets out what should be the basis for their hope: if they believe that Jesus died and rose, so also will God bring with him those who have died (lit. fallen asleep) through Jesus. In millennial movements elsewhere the return of the ancestors is a common feature of the futurist myth. Here Paul links the inclusion in the parousia of those who have already died to the belief in the death and resurrection of Jesus which was central to their faith in him.

v. 15, first emphasizing the authority of what he is about to say (it is a 'word of the Lord'; v. 15a), Paul now expands upon the precise nature of the vindication he is holding out for those who have died. Those who are living, who survive to the parousia of the Lord, will not have any advantage over those who have died (v. 15b). It is difficult to know what Paul means by a 'word of the Lord' here. Possible meanings include a saying of Jesus (not otherwise extant), a statement by a prophet among the Christ-followers, a fragment of some unknown text, or (perhaps most likely) his own view but spoken as the Lord's agent and therefore the Lord's. It is also unclear whether the 'word of

the Lord' relates only to the statement in v. 15 or whether it extends to the end of v. 17. The former is more likely, because Paul had presumably already told them the broad outline of what we have in vv. 16–17; v. 15 contains the new element that required to be supported by the appeal to authority.

vv. 16–17, the Lord himself—accompanied by a cry of command, the call of an angel, and the trumpet of God—will come down from heaven and those who have died in Christ will rise first, then those who are living, who survive, will be snatched up together with them in the clouds to a meeting with the Lord in the air, so to be with the Lord for ever. Here we have a futurist myth derived partly from Israelite tradition but given a new slant in the context of the belief in Christ's death and resurrection which saw him exalted to the right hand of God (Acts 2:33; Rom 8:34). The myth deals with Christ's descent (based on his preceding ascent to God) which presupposes a first-century cosmology in which heaven is located above the earth. The cry of command is probably to be taken as uttered by Jesus and as addressed to the dead that they should rise. A trumpet also appears in connection with resurrection and the end-time at 1 Cor 15:52 (also see Isa 27:13; Zeph 1:14–16). While most myths relate to past events, helping a particular group to gain access to its formative, primordial past (Eliade 1989), a myth of the future such as this is rather different. It serves to stress the goal rather than the basis of a social order and thus has a prescriptive rather than a proscriptive function (Doty 1986: 44–9; Esler 1993: 186). Paul's Thessalonian converts would have been reassured by the details of this narrative that another order of reality existed, and that the difficult events of their present and recent past were occurring within a context controlled by heavenly forces who would ultimately restore their fortunes beyond their wildest dreams. Yet although the creation of hope in a future vindication forms part of such mythopoiesis, it is not the end of the story. For a futurist myth such as this also creates an imaginary experience in the present of that which is to come, and thus reinforces the social identity of its addressees at a time when they are exposed to external threat (Esler 1994: 109).

(5:1–11) The Need for Wakefulness v. 1, Paul indicates that he does not need to tell them about dates and times, presumably because he has already done so. He does not want to become involved in the discussion of an end-time calendar. v. 2, what they already know is that the day of the Lord will come like a thief in the night, that is, quite unexpectedly. The 'day of the Lord' was well established in Israelite tradition. It was to be a time of joy for some and terror for others. Thus Isaiah had written that on 'that day' a great trumpet would sound and the scattered ones in Assyria and Egypt would come to worship the Lord on Jerusalem's holy mountain (Isa 27:13). Zephaniah, on the other hand, had presented a bleaker picture: a day that would be a day of wrath, of anguish and torment, of destruction and devastation, when the Lord would bring dire distress upon the people (Zeph 1:14–18). Paul must have imparted some of this material to his ex-idol-atrous converts, no doubt painting a happy future for them and an unhappy one for sinful out-groups.

v. 3, Paul illustrates his previous statement with two connected examples showing how people will not escape. First, it is just when people are saying 'peace and security' (eirēnē kai asphaleia) that suddenly disaster overtakes them just as, secondly, the pain of childbirth comes upon a pregnant woman. The latter example is a commonplace of domestic human experience (although often mentioned as a sign of the End: Mk 13:8), but the former relates to the political realities of Thessalonica. Some coins minted at Thessalonica contained slogans with the similar words 'freedom and security', probably reflecting the advantages the local élite derived from Rome and the Roman imperial cult (Jewett 1986: 124). The 'peace' to which Paul refers is presumably the Pax Romana. Paul is alluding to the fragility of the comfortable relationship between the rulers of the city and Rome (Hendrix 1984), which could at any time suffer a disastrous reverse.

vv. 4–5, Paul introduces the imagery of light and darkness to distinguish between Christ-followers, whom the day (of anger) will not 'surprise...like a thief', and others in Thessalonica. The Christ-followers are all sons of light and sons of day who do not belong to night or darkness; by implication, then, the others are sons of night and sons of darkness who do not belong to light or day. Such a powerful dualism presents very starkly the nature of the opposed identities of in-group and out-group, the first highly positive and the second very negative indeed. Here we have a good example of the stereotypical group-categorization characteristic of the way one group generates a favourable

social identity for itself. vv. 6–7, Paul persists with his continuing process of group differentiation in a related area of imagery by exhorting them not to sleep like the others (by implication, people of the night) but to keep awake and be sober—for those who sleep and those who get drunk do so at night. v. 8, since he and they belong to the day, he says, they should be sober, thus reinforcing still further the reality of group differentiation using imagery of day and night which he began way back at v. 4. Yet now he adds a new element—they should do so having put on the breastplate of faith and love and the helmet of hope of salvation. In this latter clause he summons before his readers the triad of faith, love, and hope (and in that order) which he introduced in the third verse of the letter. This is really to pile identity-descriptors on identity-descriptors!

When Paul refers to putting on (endusamenoi) the breastplate of faith and love (thōraka pisteōs kai agapēs) and the hope of salvation for a helmet (perikephalaian elpida sōtērias), he is alluding either to Isa 59.17 or Wis 5:18 (which is presumably dependent on Isaiah), or both. The Isaian passage reads: 'He put on (enedusato) righteousness as a breastplate (dikaiosunēn thōraka) and placed the helmet of salvation (perikephalaian sōtēriou) on his head', while the one from Wisdom has: 'He will put on righteousness as a breastplate (endusetai thōraka dikaiosunēn), and he will don true judgement instead of a helmet.' Paul has changed the phrase 'breastplate of righteousness' to 'breastplate of faith and love', while adding the word 'hope' to the expression 'helmet of salvation', which he otherwise retains. Paul's treatment of the possible Septuagintal source(s) means, first, that faith and love represent a way of describing the condition of being a Christ-follower analogous to that expressed by 'righteousness'. Secondly, however, the alteration indicates that in writing to Gentiles he has deliberately chosen to substitute the former for the latter, presumably because he found 'righteousness' inappropriate for such an audience (Esler 1998: 156–7). The function fulfilled by the language of holiness in relation to a Gentile audience in 1 Thessalonians is served later in relation to mixed Israelite and Gentile groups in Galatians and Romans by the discourse of righteousness.

v. 9, Paul's statement that God has destined them not for anger but for obtaining salvation through their Lord Jesus Christ makes explicit for the first time the nature of the fate, the awesome wrath of God (see Zeph 1:14–18, noted above), hanging over out-groups, who are again sharply differentiated from the believers in Christ to whom salvation will be extended. The nature of that salvation is set out in 1 Thess 4:16–17, while the ambit of the anger is not. v. 10, Jesus Christ is described as the one who died for us so that 'awake or asleep' (that is, dead, as in 1 Thess 4:13–16), we will live together with him. This the first time in Paul's correspondence that we find the important formula 'Christ died for' with a further word or words indicating the person(s) for whom he died (also see 1 Cor 15:3; 2 Cor 5:14; 5:15; Rom 5:6; 5:8; 14:15). De Jonge (1990: 233–4) has argued that this expression, which preceded Paul's use of it since he cites it in 1 Cor 15:3 as a tradition he had received, always serves as a foundation for the claim that God's salvation has become reality or at least has been inaugurated, to highlight the new state of life into which Christ-followers have been transferred. Within a social identity framework, one might add that the notion of Jesus' death for his followers is what enables the creation of their identity and also fills it with positive evaluative and emotional dimensions. v. 11, the sentiment is similar to, while going a little further than, that of 4:18.

Final Exhortations and Greetings (5:12–28)

This section contain a series of largely unrelated pieces of advice, ending with prayers.

(5:12–13) Honouring Leaders vv. 12–13, Paul asks the Thessalonians to respect those who labour amongst them, who 'care for' (or, possibly, with the NRSV, 'have charge of') 'you ... and admonish you'. He wants his addressees to esteem them very highly in love because of their work and to be at peace with one another. Best (1972: 226) reasonably suggests that we should not interpret these verses as indicating there was a ministry among the congregation in the city. The fact that the 'leaders' are described by their activities and not by titles suggests that they have none. Clearly Paul is at pains that the Thessalonians should not engage in the antagonistic conduct common among unrelated males in this culture.

(5:14–22) Christian Identity-Indicators Paul here strings together various aspects of desirable identity-indicators. Some of them are norms (that is, 'ethical' duties), but others, such as to rejoice and pray, are not. vv. 14–15, the statements here constitute what are essential norms for maintaining the identity of Christ-followers. It is noteworthy, however, that in spite of the group-differentiation that Paul has pursued throughout the letter, he specifically extends the scope of their doing good from the members of the congregation to everyone. There are limits to how far he will go with the process of group-categorization and certainly the all-too-common advocacy of violence against out-group members plays no part whatever in his perspective. vv. 16–18, rejoicing and continual prayer are essential aspects of their identity as Christ-followers. v. 19, they must not quench the Spirit, by which Paul means that they must permit the charismatic gifts associated with the coming of the Spirit—which was a major distinguishing feature of the movement and no doubt made it attractive to members, because of the euphoria Spirit-possession can produce. v. 20, prophecy is one of the gifts of the Spirit (see 1 Cor 12:10) and Paul calls on them not to despise it. vv. 21–2, Paul mentions further attitudes which should characterize the identity of the Thessalonians.

(5:23–4) Prayer for the Thessalonians vv. 23–4, Paul prays that God will sanctify (hagiazō) them, thus seeking divine renewal of the sanctification he has already made clear was central to their new identity in contrast to the world of impurity (akatharsia) around them (1 Thess 4:7). Sanctification primarily refers to their present condition, but Paul then goes on to pray that they will be blameless at the parousia. The one who calls is faithful and he will effect this.

(5:25–8) Closing Prayer and Instructions v. 25, now he asks them to pray for him (and presumably Silvanus and Timothy); this enlivens the sense of his presence to them in the letter. v. 26, the source of the holy kiss of the movement is unknown; possible sources include the historical Jesus, Judaism, or pagan religion. v. 27, suddenly Paul changes to first person singular, presumably because he has taken the stylus in his own hand to write the last few words (as at 1 Cor 16:21; Gal 6:11), and solemnly commands them to read the letter to all the brothers. It is hard to determine how all the brothers (and a textual variant adds 'holy' to brothers) relate to the Thessalonians mentioned in the first verse. Perhaps the means to ensure that those who first received the letter should read it aloud to everyone in a meeting of the congregation (Best 1972: 246–7). v. 28, Paul ends with a form of benediction which must have become conventional among Christ-followers.

REFERENCES

Aasgaard, R. (1997), 'Brotherhood in Plutarch and Paul: Its Role and Character', in H. Moxnes (ed.), *Constructing Early Christian Families: Family as Social Reality and Metaphor* (London: Routledge), 166–97.

Balch, D. L., Ferguson, E., and Meeks, W. A. (eds.) (1990), *Greeks, Romans, and Christians: Essays in Honor of Abraham J. Malherbe* (Minneapolis: Fortress).

Barclay, J. M. G. (1992), 'Thessalonica and Corinth: Social Contrasts in Pauline Christianity', *JSNT* 47: 49–74.

—— (1993), 'Conflict in Thessalonika', *CBQ* 53: 512–30.

Bassler, J. M. (1995), 'Skeuos: A Modest Proposal for Illuminating Paul's Use of Metaphor in 1 Thessalonians 4:4', in White and Yarbrough (1995: 53–66).

Baur, F. C. (1873–5) *Paul: The Apostle of Jesus Christ* (London: Williams & Norgate). German original, *Paulus, der Apostel Jesu Christi* (1845).

Best, E. (1972), *A Commentary on the First and Second Epistles to the Thessalonians*, Black's New Testament Commentaries (London: Adam & Charles Black).

Betz, H. D. (1978), 'De fraterno amore (*Moralia* 478A–492D)', in H. D. Betz (ed.) (1978), *Plutarch's Ethical Writings and Early Christian Literature* (Leiden: E. J. Brill), 231–63.

Boers, H. (1976), 'The Form Critical Study of Paul's Letters. 1 Thessalonians as a Case Study', *NTS* 22: 140–58.

Brown, R. (1988), *Group Processes: Dynamics Within and Between Groups* (Oxford: Basil Blackwell).

Chapa, J. (1994), 'Is First Thessalonians a Letter of Consolation?', *NTS* 40: 150–60.

Collins, R. F. (ed.) (1990), *The Thessalonian Correspondence* (Leuven: Leuven University Press).

De Jonge, H. J. (1990), 'The Original Setting of the *Christos Apethanen Hyper* Formula', in Collins (1990: 229–35).

Donfried, K. P. (1984), '1 Thessalonians 2:13–16 as a Test Case', *Interpretation*, 38: 242–53.

—— (1985), 'The Cults of Thessalonica and the Thessalonian Correspondence', *NTS* 31: 336–56.

—— (1989), 'Cults and the Theology of 1 Thessalonians as a Reflection of its Purpose', in M. P. Horgan and P. Kobelski (eds.), *To Touch the Text: Studies in Honor of Joseph A. Fitzmyer, S.J.* (New York: Crossroad), 243–60.

Doty, W. G. (1973), *Letters in Primitive Christianity* (Philadelphia: Fortress).

—— (1986), *Mythography: The Study of Myths and Rituals* (Alabama: University of Alabama Press).

Duling, D. C. (1996), 'Millennialism', in R. L. Rohrbaugh (ed.), *The Social Sciences and New Testament Interpretation* (Peabody, Mass.: Hendrickson), 183–205.

Edson, C. (1948), 'Cults of Thessalonica (Macedonica III)', *HTR* 41: 153–204.

Eliade, M. (1989), *The Myth of the Eternal Return* (London: Penguin).

Esler, P. F. (1987), *Community and Gospel in Luke–Acts: The Social and Political Motivations of Lucan Theology* (Cambridge: Cambridge University Press).

—— (1993), 'Political Oppression in Jewish Apocalyptic Literature: A Social-Scientific Approach', *Listening: Journal of Religion and Culture*, 28: 181–99.

—— (1994), *The First Christians in their Social Worlds: Social-Scientific Approaches to New Testament Interpretation* (London: Routledge).

—— (ed.) (1995), *Modelling Early Christianity: Social-Scientific Studies of the New Testament in Its Context* (London: Routledge).

—— (1998), *Galatians* (London: Routledge).

—— (2000), ' "Keeping it in the Family": Culture, Kinship and Identity in 1 Thessalonians and Galatians', in J. W. van Henten and A. Brenner (eds.), *Families and Family Relations as Represented in Early Judaisms and Early Christianities: Texts and Fictions*, Studies in Theology and Religion (Leiden: Deo), ii. 145–84.

Fatum, L. (1997), 'Brotherhood in Christ: A Gender Hermeneutical Reading of 1 Thessalonians', in H. Moxnes (ed.), *Constructing Early Christian Families: Family as Social Reality and Metaphor* (London: Routledge), 183–97.

Faw, C. E. (1952), 'On the Writing of First Thessalonians', *JBL* 71: 217–25.

Frame, J. E. A. (1912), *Critical and Exegetical Commentary on the Epistles of St. Paul to the Thessalonians* (New York: James Scribner's).

Funk, R. (1967), 'The Apostolic Parousia: Form and Significance', in W. R. Farmer, C. F. D. Moule, and R. R. Niebuhr (eds.), *Christian History and Interpretation: Studies Presented to John Knox* (Cambridge: Cambridge University Press), 249–68.

Headland, T. N., Pike, K. L., and Harris, M. (eds.) (1990), *Emics and Etics: The Insider/Outsider Debate*, Frontiers of Anthropology, 7 (Newbury Park, Calif.: Sage).

Hendrix, H. L. (1984), 'Thessalonicans Honor Rome', Ph.D. dissertation, Harvard University.

Hock, R. F. (1980), *The Social Context of Paul's Ministry: Tentmaking and Apostleship* (Philadelphia: Fortress).

Hodgson, R., Jr. (1982), '1 Thess. 4:1–12 and the Holiness Tradition (HT)', in K. H. Richards (ed.), *Society of Biblical Literature 1982 Seminar Papers* (Chico, Calif.: Scholars Press), 199–215.

Hooker, M. D., and Wilson, S. G. (1982) (eds.), *Paul and Paulinism: Essays in Honour of C. K. Barrett* (London: SPCK).

Jewett, R. (1986), *The Thessalonian Correspondence: Pauline Rhetoric and Millenarian Piety* (Philadelphia: Fortress).

—— (1993), 'Tenement Churches and Communal Meals in the Early Church: The Implications of a Form-Critical Analysis of 2 Thessalonians 3:10', *BR* 38: 23–42.

Judge, E. A. (1971), 'The Decrees of Caesar at Thessalonika', *RTR* 30: 1–7.

Klauck, H.-J. (1990), 'Brotherly Love in Plutarch and in 4 Maccabees', in D. L. Balch, E. Ferguson, and W. A. Meeks (eds.), *Greeks, Romans, and Christians: Essays in Honor of Abraham J. Malherbe* (Minneapolis: Fortress), 144–56.

Kloppenborg, J. S. (1993), PHILADELPHIA, THEODIDAKTOS and the Dioscuri: Rhetorical Engagement in 1 Thessalonians 4.9–12, *NTS* 39: 265–89.

Koester, H. (1979), '1 Thessalonians—Experiment in Christian Writing', in F. F. Church and T. George (eds.) (1979), *Continuity and Discontinuity in Church History: Essays Presented to George Hunston Williams on the Occasion of his 65th Birthday*, Studies in the History of Christian Thought, 19 (Leiden: E. J. Brill), 33–44.

Koskenniemi, H. (1956), *Studien zur Idee und Phraseologie des griechischen Briefes bis n. Chr* (Helsinki: Suomalainen Tiedeakatemia).

Lührmann, D. (1990), 'The Beginnings of the Church in Thessalonica', in Balch, Ferguson, and Meeks (1990: 237–49).

MacMullen, R. (1981), *Paganism in the Roman Empire* (New Haven: Yale University Press).

Malherbe, A. J. (1987), *Paul and the Thessalonians: The Philosophic Tradition of Pastoral Care* (Philadelphia: Fortress).

—— (1989a), *Paul and the Popular Philosophers* (Minneapolis: Fortress).

—— (1989b), ' "Gentle as a Nurse": The Cynic Background to 1 Thessalonians 2', in Malherbe 1989a: 35–48 (first pub. in *NovT* 12 (1970), 213–17).

—— (1989c), 'Exhortation in First Thessalonians', in Malherbe 1989a: 49–66 (first pub. in *NovT* 25 (1983), 238–56).

—— (1990), 'Did the Thessalonians Write to Paul?' in R. R. Fortna and B. R. Gaventa (eds.), *The Conversation Continues: Studies in Paul & John in Honor of J. Louis Martyn* (Nashville: Abingdon, 246–57).

Malina, B. J. (1993), *The New Testament World: Insights from Cultural Anthropology*, rev. edn. (Louisville, Ky.: Westminster/John Knox).

Marshall, I. H. (1982), 'Pauline Theology in the Thessalonian Correspondence', in Hooker and Wilson (1982: 173–83).

Maurer, C. (1971), S. V. *skeuos*, *TDNT* vii. 358–67.

Okeke, G. E. (1980–1), '1 Thess 2.13–16. The Fate of the Unbelieving Jews', *NTS* 27: 127–36.

Pearson, B. A. (1971), '1 Thessalonians 2:13–16: A Deutero-Pauline Interpolation', *HTR* 64: 79–94.

Perkins, P. (1989), '1 Thessalonians and Hellenistic Religious Practices', in M. P. Horgan and P. J. Kobelski (eds.) (1989), *To Touch the Text: Biblical and Related Studies in Honor of Joseph A. Fitzmyer* (New York: Crossroad), 325–34.

Robinson, P. (ed.) (1996), *Social Groups and Identities: Developing the Legacy of Henri Tajfel* (Oxford: Butterworth Heinnemann).

Schmidt, D. (1983), '1 Thess 2: 13–16: Lingistic Evidence for an Interpolation', *JBL* 102: 269–79.

Schöllgen, G. (1988), 'Was wissen wie über Sozialstruktur der paul-inischen Gemeinden?', *NTS* 34: 71–82.

Schubert, P. (1939), *Form and Function of the Pauline Thanksgivings*, BNZW 20 (Berlin: de Gruyter).

Seesemann, H. (1967), '*Pateō* and compounds in NT', *TDNT* v. 943–5.

Smith, A. (1989), 'The Social and Ethical Implications of the Pauline Rhetoric in 1 Thessalonians', dissertation submitted to Vanderbilt University (Ann Arbor: University Microfilms International).

Stern, M. (1974–80), *Greek and Latin Authors on Jews and Judaism* (2 vols.; Jerusalem: Israel Academy of the Arts and Sciences).

Stowers, S. K. (1986), *Letter Writing in Greco-Roman Antiquity* (Philadelphia: Westminster).

Tajfel, H. (1978), *Differentiation between Social Groups: Studies in the Social Psychology of Intergroup Relations* (London: Academic Press).

—— (1981), 'Social Stereotypes and Social Groups', in H. Tajfel, *Human Groups and Social Categories: Studies in Social Psychology* (Cambridge: Cambridge University Press).

—— and Turner, J. C. (1979), 'An Integrative Theory of Intergroup Conflict', in W. G. Austin and S. Worchel (eds.), *The Social Psychology of Intergroup Relations* (Monterey, Calif.: Brooks-Cole), 33–47.

—— (1986), 'The Social Identity Theory of Intergroup Conflict', in S. Worchel and W. G. Austin (eds.) (1986), *Psychology of Intergroup Relations* (Chicago: Nelson-Hall), 7–24.

Vickers, M. (1972), 'Hellenistic Thessaloniki', *JHS* 92: 156–70.

Vos, C. de (1999), *Church and Community Conflicts: The Relationships of the Thessalonian, Corinthian, and Philippian Churches with their Wider Civic Communities*, SBL DS 168 (Atlanta: Scholars Press).

Weatherly, J. A. (1991), 'The Authenticity of 1 Thessalonians 2.13–16: Additional Evidence', *JSNT* 42: 79–98.

White, M. L., and Yarbrough, O. L. (eds.) (1995), *The Social World of the First Christians: Essays in Honor of Wayne A. Meeks* (Philadelphia: Fortress).

12. 2 Thessalonians

PHILIP F. ESLER

INTRODUCTION

A. The problem of authenticity. 1. The dominant preliminary issue in the interpretation of 2 Thessalonians is the controversy as to whether Paul wrote this letter or not. The answer greatly affects how the letter is to be understood. It should be noted at once that there is virtually no support for reversing the traditional order of 1 and 2 Thessalonians (for reasons well explained by Jewett (1986: 24–30); *contra* Trudinger (1995), revisiting the views of J. Weiss and T. W. Manson). Doubts as to the authenticity of 2 Thessalonians are stimulated primarily by its close literary relationship to 1 Thessalonians. Many critics, but especially William Wrede (1903), have noted that the topics in the two letters are covered in the same sequence and the themes of the first letter are reflected with minor variations in the second, even if there are few examples with exactly the same wording. Thus, the renewed thanksgiving of 1 Thess 2:12 is repeated at 2 Thess 2:12, prayers in the optative mood introduced by 'the Lord (God) himself' appear at similar points (cf. 1 Thess 3:11–13 and 5:23 with 2 Thess 2:16–17 and 3:16), and there are many verbal parallels (see Menken 1994: 36–9 for the comparative data and Best 1972: 50–1). Only 2 Thess 2:1–12 has no parallel in 1 Thessalonians. On the other hand, both letters are very different in these respects from the other Pauline letters. These literary similarities occur in spite of some major differences in the contents of the two letters, especially in relation to views on the parousia (with 1 Thessalonians saying that Christ is expected to come soon and suddenly while 2 Thessalonians argues that his coming will be preceded by other events) and the lack of personal details about Paul and the Thessalonians of the type found in 1 Thess 2:1–12; 13–16; and 3:1–13. The tone of 2 Thessalonians is also generally agreed to be rather cold in comparison with that of 1 Thessalonians.

2. Many critics consider that the best explanation for such features is that 2 Thessalonians is an imitation of the other letter written later to Thessalonica or to some other community of Christ-followers which draws upon the earlier letter to enhance its authority. While those who consider 2 Thessalonians inauthentic usually seek to reconstruct a situation which would render its creation plausible, given our incomplete knowledge of the Christ-movement in the first century their failure to come up with a convincing particular audience and setting does not, as sometimes suggested (Jewett 1986: 3–18; Barclay 1993: 526), itself invalidate their arguments, although it will mean they are less than compelling. Supporters of authenticity, on the other hand, need to explain what had happened that induced Paul to write a second letter to Thessalonica using language and structure so similar to that in 1 Thessalonians; and to the present writer the difficulties with this hypothesis are greater than those raised by the view that the letter is not by Paul (see Bailey 1978–9). As Menken (1994: 27–43) argues, while no one argument is capable of sustaining a case for inauthenticity, overall this seems the preferable solution, in spite of very respectable views to the contrary. Possible explanations for 2 Thessalonians on either hypothesis will now be addressed. Particular issues relating to this debate will come up in the comments below.

B. Some Possible Explanations for 2 Thessalonians if Authentic. 1. Best (1972: 59) suggests that 2 Thessalonians was written by Paul from Corinth shortly after 1 Thessalonians 'to meet a new situation in respect of eschatology and a deteriorating situation in respect of idleness', although he notes that 'we do not know from where Paul received his information'. He proposes that Paul probably wrote with much of 1 Thessalonians in his memory rather than that he worked from a copy of 1 Thessalonians.

2. Jewett (1986: 176–8, 191–2) has a much more particular explanation. It is that 'for some reason' Paul's first letter, impacting on a community alive with millenarian excitement, actually provoked the radical members at Thessalonica, who misunderstood Paul to such an extent as to conclude that the day of the Lord had arrived and to behave in accordance with this belief (e.g. by curtailing certain everyday activities such as work). Paul responds by writing 2 Thessalonians, a refutation of this false doctrine written in a very different tone.

3. Barclay (1993) has proposed an interesting new answer to the relationship between the eschatologies in 1 and 2 Thessalonians which offers a more specific explanation for how the Thessalonians misunderstood Paul's first letter.

After noting Wrede's (1903: 526) difficulty in suggesting a convincing setting for the letter, Barclay argues that the references to fierce persecution (1:4–9), the problem of people not working (3:6–13), and the claim by some that the day of the Lord is here (2:2) suggest a specific situation. Having examined and rejected existing answers as to what 'the day of the Lord' means at 2 Thess 2:2 (see commentary), he proposes a new alternative, namely, that in 1 Thessalonians it is possible to draw a distinction which Paul did not himself draw between *parousia* (4:13–18) and the day of the Lord (5:1–11) and the latter is associated with the sudden destruction of unbelievers. So, maybe some Christians in Thessalonica reacted to a local (or perhaps widespread) disaster by claiming that it manifested the wrath of God, thereby creating turmoil and encouraging some to give up their jobs and and continue urgent, full-time evangelism. Thus Paul is compelled to write another letter perhaps only a matter of weeks after the first wherein the friendly encouragement gives way to a more frigid and authoritarian tone.

4. A major question hanging over proposals like those of Jewett and Barclay is that if Paul's first letter had been misunderstood why would he not try to persuade them with a completely new approach, rather than risking a letter which stylistically aped the earlier one, and also strongly protest about their egregious misinterpretation of the earlier letter. 2 Thess 2:2 certainly does not fulfil the latter function, in contrast with 1 Cor 5:9–13, which clearly indicates how Paul went about correcting a misimpression drawn from an earlier letter.

C. Possible Explanations for 2 Thessalonians if Inauthentic. 1. Proponents of the inauthenticity of 2 Thessalonians have come up with a variety of dates and situations for the letter. Wrede himself dated it to about 100 CE and suggested it was written not for Thessalonica (for Thessalonians would ask where it had lain all these years) but for another church which knew of the existence of other Thessalonian correspondence. Masson (1957) proposed that it was written about 100 CE to counter the belief that the day of the Lord had come. On the other hand, Marxsen (1968: 37–44; 1982) favoured an earlier date, around 70 CE, arguing that the letter was intended to counter Gnostics, especially their (false) claim that the day of the Lord had come. If Paul's letters had been collected, as generally supposed, by about 100 CE, an earlier

date for the composition of 2 Thessalonians would be preferable (see 2 THESS 3:17).

2. 2 Thessalonians has been understood as a response to millennialism in a Mediterranean context. The three substantive issues of local context recognized in the letter are the existence of some form of oppression being suffered by the addressees (1:4–6), the disturbance caused by the message that 'the day of the Lord has come' (2:1–12), and the disorderly conduct of certain Christ-followers who are refusing to work for a living. On the (preferable) assumption that these issues derive from an actual situation somewhere in the ancient Mediterranean world, and do not just comprise a notional setting aimed at allowing someone to draft a letter in Pauline style, we are faced with what modern social scientists refer to as an outbreak of millennialism. Across the world, we know of many instances of groups, generally (although not always) suffering from some form of oppression or disturbance of traditional social patterns, who generate or revive narratives of a coming transformation of the world which will radically restore them to their proper place and, often, destroy those who oppress them (Duling 1996; Esler 1993; 1994: 93–109). Examples, discussed elsewhere (Esler 1993: 187–8; 1994: 101–4), include the ghost dance among North American Indians in the late nineteenth century and the cargo cults of twentieth-century Melanesia. Jewett (1986: 161–78) has usefully applied millenarian ideas to 2 Thessalonians, although his treatment is affected by his view that the letter is authentic. The view adopted here is that millennialism provides the best framework for contextualizing the letter in a general way, even though we cannot be sure for which troubled community of first-century Christ-followers it was written. Although biblical critics generally use the now rather tired and overworked word 'eschatological', which derives from a theological agenda, to refer to end-time speculation in such texts as Dan 7–12 and 1 *Enoch*, the framework of 'millennialism' allows a fresh set of questions originating in real social experience to be posed to texts such as 2 Thessalonians. Attempts, such as that of Menken (1994), to discuss this dimension to 2 Thessalonians almost solely in relation to (the undoubtedly important) framework of end-time speculation in Israelite biblical and extra-biblical literature, have an unnecessarily limited focus.

3. It is always worth remembering that the social context of the ancient Mediterranean

world in which this example of millennialism occurred was radically different from modern, individualistic cultures of Europe and North America. The ancient Mediterranean world was one where, at an appropriate level of abstraction and without in any way denying local variations, people found meaning by belonging to groups (especially the family), honour was the principal social value, all goods (material and immaterial) were regarded as existing in finite quantities, and relationships between patrons and clients (sometimes mediated by other individuals referred to as 'brokers'; see Moxnes 1991) were common as a way of dealing with access to limited material and social goods. These are the most important of an ensemble of cultural features originally identified and applied to the NT by Bruce Malina in 1981 (now see Malina 1993).

4. The fact that Paul probably did not write 2 Thessalonians does not entail taking a condemnatory attitude to whoever—pseudonymously—claimed he had. Pseudonymity is a common feature in the Bible (Proverbs, Ecclesiastes, Isa 40–55 and 55–66), let alone in the profuse writings of the Pseudepigrapha themselves (see Bailey 1978–9: 143–5). Meade (1986) has plausibly argued that the phenomenon occurred when it was felt necessary to make traditions capable of application to new situations, so that it becomes an assertion of authoritative tradition, not literary origin. The closeness of the style of this pseudepigraphic document to 1 Thessalonians is perhaps explicable out of the high respect in which its author held Paul. It is reasonable, therefore, that some time in the first century, probably after Paul's death in Rome in the later 60s, someone faced with a situation having the three broad features mentioned above sought faithfully to reinterpret Pauline tradition in a way which would benefit those addressed. The (non-Pauline) authors of Ephesians, Titus, and 1 and 2 Timothy adopted the same strategy, although faced with very different situations.

5. In what follows I will refer to the author of this letter as 'Paul' (with inverted commas) or 'the author' because of the view taken here that the historical Paul was not its author.

D. Structure. 2 Thessalonians, like 1 Thessalonians, can be given a structure based on thematic, epistolary, or rhetorical considerations (helpfully summarized by Jewett 1986: 222–5). It is doubtful, however, whether the rigorous application of ancient rhetorical or epistolary categories to various sections of the letter does much to further our understanding of it. Accordingly, in the commentary I will adopt the following (pragmatic) structuration, essentially thematic in type, while making occasional reference to possible epistolary or rhetorical subdivisions:

Prescript (1:1–2)
Thanksgiving and Encouragement (1:3–12)
The End and the Man of Lawlessness (2:1–12)
Encouragement to Persevere (2:13–17)
Mutual Prayer (3:1–5)
Warning against Idlers (3:6–12)
Conclusion (3:13–18)

COMMENTARY

(1:1–2) Prescript This is the beginning of one long sentence (1:1–12). Rhetoricians would call this section the 'exordium'. Letters in the ancient Mediterranean began with a prescript, comprising the names of the senders and the addressees and a brief greeting, in Greek typically *chairei*, 'hail'. These verses constitute the prescript to 2 Thessalonians. The senders (Paul, Silvanus, and Timothy) and addressees ('*ekklēsia*, the community'—'church' sounds a little anachronistic—'of the Thessalonians in God our Father and the Lord Jesus Christ') are the same as in 1 Thessalonians, while the greeting has been Christianized (a practice possibly inaugurated by Paul) even further here by an additional reference to Jesus Christ as Lord and God as Father. v. 2, by invoking upon the addressees grace (*charis*) and peace (*eirēnē*; Heb. *šālôm*) from God the Father and the Lord Jesus Christ, comes close to putting them on an equal footing, unless we are meant to see God as patron and Jesus Christ as broker in accordance with common Mediterranean social patterns, that is, a mediator who gives clients access to the resources of a more powerful patron (Moxnes 1991: 248).

(1:3–12) Thanksgiving and Encouragement v. 3, after the prescript, Paul often includes a thanksgiving for the good qualities of his addressees (Rom 1:8–10; 1 Cor 1:4–8; Phil 1:3–6; but not in Galatians, where Paul is too annoyed with his audience to engage in the usual courtesies!). Yet here he says 'we *must always* give thanks to God', rather than 'we thank God', which seems to some critics a rather more formal expression, even though he does go on to mention that their faith is growing and their love for one another increasing. The first person plural may reflect the fact that three persons are named as senders of the letter, or represent an example of the 'epistolary plural', where a single writer talks of himself or herself in the plural.

v. 4, virtually all translations (including the NRSV) have 'Paul' saying something like 'we ourselves *boast*' among the communities (NRSV 'churches') of God concerning your steadfastness and faith in all persecutions (*diōgmoi*) and afflictions (*thlipseis*). But 'boast', which carries a negative connotation to modern ears, is a mistranslation. In a group-oriented culture dominated by honour as the pre-eminent virtue and always needing to be acknowledged by others, 'Paul' is saying that 'we ourselves base our claim to honourp' on the qualities mentioned. He can say this in relation to the relevant public (here 'the communities of God') either because he is intrinsically linked to the Thessalonians' endurance and faith as their progenitor, or because he is closely connected with the Thessalonian Christ-followers who now exhibit these qualities, or both. Also see 1 Thess 2:19; 2 Cor 9:2–3. The presence of persecutions and oppressions among whatever group of Christ-followers for which 2 Thessalonians was originally destined provides either the motivation for, or reinforcement of, narratives of future deliverance of the sort prominent in the text.

v. 5 begins 'This is evidence' (*endeigma*). But to what stated previously does *endeigma* refer? Possibly to their faith and steadfastness while they suffer persecution and tribulation (Best 1972: 254–5), but it is more probable, given the tight interconnection of v. 4, that it refers to the fact that Paul lays his claim to honour on these characteristics: 'our claiming honour from your endurance and faith before the other communities (who did not demur) is a sure sign that God will also count you worthy'. The judgement Paul has in mind is the judgement of God at the end-time (usually, although not very helpfully, referred to as 'eschatological') commonly described in Israelite literature (1 *Enoch* 1:1–9; 2 Esd 7.33–44; *Apoc. Abr.* 29.14–29; D. F. Russell 1964: 379–85). Without doubting their actual existence for the original audience of 2 Thessalonians, the troubles referred to in the text are capable of interpretation as the 'woes' before the end attested in other Israelite and Christian literature (Dan 12:1; 2 *Apoc. Bar.* 25.2–4; Mk 13:19, 24; Rev 7:14). Thus we see a merger of experience and religious tradition located in biblical and non-biblical Israelite literature typical of this text and other early

Christian literature. It is likely, however, that Menken (1994: 85–7) is mistaken in seeing the current sufferings of the Thessalonians (which will absolve them from future judgement) as caused by their own sinfulness, since this conflicts with the good things said about them earlier in the text.

vv. 6–7a, the sentiment here represents a rather bald example of the law of revenge (*lex talionis*). Although modern European or North American readers might find this puzzling, in ancient Mediterranean culture serious insults, which desecrated one's honour, had to be avenged. Thus God will bring vengeance on those who have dishonoured his people (see Deut 32:35–6) and therefore slighted him as well. This is a fairly common biblical theme. In particular Isa 66:6 refers to 'the voice of the LORD dealing retribution to his enemies' and Aus (1976) has suggested that this section of Isaiah may have influenced this verse and what follows. 'Rest' (*anesis*) refers to the absence of tension and trial. The persecution and oppression mentioned in vv. 6–7 may be likened to the disturbance of traditional lifestyles suffered by North American Indians or Melanesians at the hands of European conquerors or colonists. In North America and Melanesia (in the South Pacific) millennial myths developed which described a coming convulsion in the cosmos when the white people would be swept away, so that the traditional lifestyles would be restored, the ancestors return, the game revisit the plains, or cargo be dropped on the people from the sky (see Esler 1994: 101–4, and literature cited there). The punishment for the oppressors and vindication of the oppressed in 2 Thessalonians reflects a somewhat similar social experience. v. 7b, the author now specifies when (or by what means) the events just mentioned will occur, literally: 'at the revelation (*apocalypsis*) of Lord Jesus Christ from heaven with the angels of his power'. First-century Christ-followers thought Jesus had gone to heaven after his resurrection and that he would return from there (1 Thess 1:10; 4:16; 1 Cor 1:7; 1 Pet 1:7, 13). Such beliefs were fortified (if not stimulated) by Israelite traditions describing future vindicators of Israel, such as 1 *Enoch* 48:4–6 and Dan 7:13. Normally Paul uses *parousia* of the future coming of Jesus, the sole use of *apocalypsis* in this regard being at 1 Cor 1:7. The angels represent the heavenly host or court who accompany God when he comes in judgement (Zech 14:5; 1 *Enoch* 1.9), although the early Christ-movement attached them to Jesus (Mk 8:38; 13:27).

v. 8, in flaming fire, Jesus will mete out vengeance (*ekdikēsis*) on those who do not know God and those who do not obey his gospel. The notion of fire as a feature of the vengeance God would inflict on his enemies originates in the OT (Isa 66:15–16) and here the theme is linked to the activities of Jesus. There seems no basis for seeking to distinguish those mentioned into two groups comprising Gentiles and Israelites. v. 9, we now learn what the vengeance will consist of: 'the punishment of eternal destruction, separated from the presence of the Lord and from the glory of his might'. The punishment does not consist of total annihilation, but of exclusion from God and, importantly in an honour-driven society, from his exalted and powerful honour. This vision is very different from the tortured future in store for the wicked in later Christian texts. v. 10 further specifies the occasion for these events: 'when he comes to be glorified [i.e. greatly honoured] by his saints' etc., while also evoking the fate of the blessed as contrasted with that of those who will be punished. Honour is shared among groups and here his followers revel in the great things he has done. The notion of 'the day (of judgement)' is a common feature of Israelite end-time speculation (see Joel 2:1–2; Zech 9:16; Mal 3:1–2).

vv. 11–12, 'Paul' informs the Thessalonians that he regularly prays for them, by asking God to make them worthy of his calling and powerfully fulfil every good resolution and work of faith. The object of all this is specified in v. 12: 'so that the name of our Lord Jesus may be glorified [i.e. greatly honoured] in you, and you in him, according to the grace of our God and the Lord Jesus Christ'. Although this situation has been described as 'mutual glorification' (Menken 1994: 94), it is possible to improve on such a designation. For here we have the typical Mediterranean phenomenon of sharing honour among the members of a group. If we understand God as father or patron, Jesus as broker, and the believers as clients, we have a fictive kinship arrangement in which Jesus honours (and is honoured in) them and they honour (and are honoured in) him.

The final statement, 'according to the grace of our God and the Lord Jesus Christ', indicates a very close relationship between the two, if not necessarily equating Jesus with God (Best 1972: 272–3).

(2:1–12) The End and the Man of Lawlessness
v. 1, 'Paul' now moves on to what is called in epistolary nomenclature the 'body' of the letter, or in the language of rhetoric the *partitio* (covering vv. 1–2), with the *probatio* beginning at v. 3. Paul begs them in connection with 'the coming (*parousia*) of our Lord Jesus Christ and our being gathered together (*episynagōgē*) to him'. In Hellenistic Greek the word *parousia* referred to the arrival of a high official at a city or town, to the accompaniment of elaborate greetings and celebrations. But the word came to be applied to the imminent arrival of Jesus from heaven (1 Thess 2:19; 3:13; 4:15; 5:23; 1 Cor 15:23; Mt 24:27, 37, 39; Jas 5:7, 8). The notion of God gathering in his people is found in the OT, either from exile (Isa 27:13; 43:4–7; Jer 31:8) or for final salvation (2 Macc 2:7; Sir 36:10). In *Psalms of Solomon* 17.26 it is said that the Messiah will gather in the people. Modern parallels exist in the form of the individuals who focus and lead a millennial movement (Esler 1994: 99).

v. 2, the content of Paul's entreaty is that his addressees should not be quickly shaken in mind or alarmed, either by a prophetic utterance ('a spirit') or a word or letter 'as though from us', saying that 'the day of the Lord is already here'. This is one of the most important verses in the letter. 'A letter as though from us' can mean either a forgery or a letter which he did write that is now being misinterpreted. If Paul had actually written 2 Thessalonians, he would have signally failed to address either alternative. For he neither denounces the letter as a forgery nor seeks directly to correct the misinterpretation. The statement is easier to interpret on the hypothesis of pseudonymity. Paul's letters were difficult and liable to be misunderstood (see 2 Pet 3:15–16). This could have been the fate of 1 Thess 4:13–5:11. There were several statements in this passage that could have been used to support an argument that the day of the Lord had come. 2 Thess 2:2 makes good sense as an attempt by its author to counter a misinterpretation of 1 Thess 4:13–5:11.

Barclay (1993: 526), who considers 2 Thessalonians authentic, canvasses earlier suggestions as to whether the 'day of the Lord is here' means: (1) a literal event—altering the structure of the universe, which is unlikely since no such event had occurred in the experience of the audience of 2 Thessalonians; (2) an internal and personal reality, entry into a new world, which remains a popular view, especially if linked to some kind of spiritualized or Gnostic understanding of the parousia; or (3) something which has not yet occurred but is imminent, an option that is now generally regarded as grammatically impossible. Barclay himself proposes a fourth alternative. It is possible to draw from 1 Thessalonians a distinction that Paul did not himself make between *parousia* (4:13–18) and the day of the Lord (5:1–11), the latter being associated with the sudden destruction of unbelievers. Perhaps the Thessalonians interpreted certain calamitous events in the early 50s of the first century as the sudden destruction of unbelievers, thus triggering a belief that 'the day of the Lord' had arrived. If one regards the letter as inauthentic and takes what is probably the more likely view that the parousia and the day of the Lord would have been understood by the recipients of 2 Thessalonians as referring to the same event, what meaning might one attach to 'the day of the Lord is here'? One possibility is that people had appeared claiming to be Christ and that such claims were troubling the target audience of this letter (so Menken 1994: 100–1). Mk 13:6 (to be dated sometime shortly before or after 70 CE) provides a basis for this suggestion.

vv. 3–4, Paul expresses concern that someone might deceive them. Deception prior to the end is also mentioned in the Markan apocalypse (13:5) and here seems to relate to the date of the parousia. The second clause in v. 3 opens with the words 'because unless', which begin the protasis of an anacoluthon, a sentence containing two conditions, which continues until the end of v. 4 without being rounded off with an apodosis, a statement of what will happen, presumably requiring something like 'the parousia of the Lord will not occur'. The first condition required is the apostasy or rebellion (*apostasia*). The lack of specification as to who will apostasize and in what way suggests that the author could count on the original recipients of 2 Thessalonians knowing what was meant. For modern readers, however, both aspects are difficult. At a general level the word refers to the dramatic breakdown of the legal, moral, social, and even natural order which is predicted in certain Israelite and NT texts of the period before the end (*Jub.* 23:14–21; 2 Esd 5:1–13; 2 Tim 3:1–9; Jude 17–19). Yet uncertainty surrounds the issue of whom the apostasy will involve: Israelites, Christ-followers, Gentiles, or representatives from all three possible groups.

The second condition needing to be fulfilled is the revealing of 'the lawless one' (lit. the person of lawlessness: *ho anthrōpos tēs anomias*), immediately described as 'the one destined for destruction' (lit. the son of destruction). Expressions similar to these occur in the OT (Ps 89:23;

Isa 57:4) and in the Qumran literature (1QS 9:16, 22; CD 6:15; 13:14). In Jn 17:12 Judas is called 'a son of destruction'. It is then stated that he (the lawless one) 'opposes and exalts himself above every so-called god or object of worship, so that he takes his seat in the temple of God, declaring himself to be God'. While this figure plainly encapsulates the lawlessness (or the 'sin', if—as seems unlikely—the variant reading here is correct) which will characterize the apostasy preceding the End, it has not proved easy to identify him with any known character in Jewish or Christian literature. It is even unclear whether he is a human or supernatural figure, although we should be careful to avoid the modern tendency sharply to distinguish these realms. Elsewhere we find false false messiahs and prophets predicted for the time before the End (Mk 13:21–2) and presumably the person of lawlessness is somewhat similar. We must presume that in the millennial mythopoiesis (that is to say, the creation of myth, see Esler 1993: 186–7) which had already occurred in the community for which this letter was written the person of lawlessness had been allocated a central role. The details in v. 4 show how this mythopoiesis was able to draw upon existing aspects in Israelite tradition in describing how the lawless person would behave. He will be like Antiochus IV Epiphanes who tried to extirpate Israelite religion and identity (in the period 167–164 BCE), as described in 1 Macc 1:16–64 and Dan 11:36–7, Pompey (who entered the temple in Jerusalem; see *Pss Sol.* 17:11–15) and Caligula who wanted to install statues of himself in the temple (Jos. *J. W.* 2.184–5).

v. 5, 'Paul' asks if they do not remember that he used to tell them (i.e. on more than one occasion) of these things when he was still with them. This statement, loosely based on 1 Thess 3:4, serves to provide an air of reality to the pseudonymous fiction. There is no mention in 1 Thessalonians of either the apostasy or the person of lawlessness. vv. 6–7, the author affirms that 'you know what is now restraining (*katechon*) him, so that he may be revealed when his time comes. For the mystery of lawlessness (*anomia*) is already at work, but only until the one who now restrains (*katechōn*) it is removed.' These are extremely difficult verses (see Lietaert Peerbolte 1997; Powell 1997). The chief problems have to do with the movement from a restraining power or thing to a restraining person, with the person of lawlessness as the implied subject of restraint, and with the identity of the restrainer and the restraint. But even to translate the Greek using 'that or who restrains' means opting for one among several possibilities (others being 'possess' or 'hold sway'). Possibly (see below), the original readers of this letter knew what or who was meant, although the expression does not occur elsewhere in Jewish or Christian writings dealing with the End. This phenomenon may have been an element of the mythopoiesis concerning the End with which they were familiar. The answer may simply be beyond us (Best 1972: 301). Yet one option worth mentioning, suggested by Strobel (1961: 98–116) and based on the possible influence of Hab 2:3 as interpreted in Jewish and Christian tradition, is that the restraining power is God's plan of salvation and the restraining person is God himself. Less likely is the idea that the power is the Roman empire and the person is the emperor himself, especially in view of the author's lack of interest in the political realm. Lietaert Peerbolte (1997), finally, makes the interesting suggestion that these words are deliberately obscure, allowing 'Paul'—who has no answer for the delay of the parousia—to create the illusion among the readers of 2 Thessalonians that there is an answer of which the original Thessalonians were aware.

v. 8, 'then the lawless one (ho anomos) will be revealed, whom the Lord (Jesus) will destroy with the breath of his mouth, annihilating him by the manifestation of his coming.' Whatever or whoever restrains the lawless person (an equivalent of 'the person of lawlessness' at v. 3), there is no doubt that it is Jesus who will kill him once he is revealed. The author's determination to make this point leads him to it before he has actually described the lawless one's revelation (in vv. 9–10). The manner of the killing, by 'the breath of his mouth', derives from Isa 11:4 ('by the breath of his lips he will kill the impious'; LXX). vv. 9–10, in a second relative clause the author describes the coming of the lawless one as taking place through Satan's activity with 'all power, signs, lying wonders, and every kind of wicked deception for those who are perishing'. The picture of signs and wonders which will be worked by agents of evil before the End is reminiscent of Mk 13:22; Rev 13:14; 19:20. vv. 11–12, 'For this reason', presumably their failing to accept the love of the truth, God sends on them a power of delusion to make them believe in falsehood, 'so that all who have not believed the truth but took pleasure in unrighteousness (adikia) will be condemned'. Menken (1994: 117) points out that divine causality appears here to match the human causality of the preceding verse. There

is an OT context for God inspiring false prophets in 1 Kings 22:23 and Ezek 14:9, while an idea somewhat similar to what is said here occurs at Rom 1:18–32.

(2:13–17) Encouragement to Persevere vv. 13–14, quite suddenly 'Paul' changes tack, by launching into a second thanksgiving (following the precedent in 1 Thess 2:13). The reason for the thanks is that God has established the notional Thessalonian addressees (who stand for the original audience of this letter) as a differentiated and privileged group in the world, with a particular history and a glorious destiny (which links the thanks to the previous material about the End). They are 'brothers [NRSV has "brothers and sisters"] beloved by the Lord', whom God (as in OT traditions of divine election) chose 'from the beginning [though the uncertain Gk. could also mean "as the first fruits"; NRSV] for salvation through sanctification (hagiasmos) by the Spirit and through belief in the truth'. God called them to this through 'Paul's' gospel, to obtain the exalted honour (doxa) of Jesus Christ. Such descriptions serve the fundamental purpose of delineating their identity, that is, providing answers to the always vital question 'Who are we?' The word 'sanctification' in particular serves to distinguish them and their present experience from the welter of idolatry and immorality implied as characteristic of the world outside the group. On the other hand, 'salvation' expresses the future goal of their existence; it is very common for people to tell themselves who they are in terms of their sense of where they are going (Esler 1998: 42, 175). In this heavily group-oriented culture, it is natural that the members of the group will share in the honour of their most honourable and honoured leader.

v. 15, the author encourages them to stick resolutely to the traditions (paradoseis) which they have received by word of mouth (dia logou) or in a letter. It is likely that the original recipients of 2 Thessalonians would have interpreted the letter mentioned here as 1 Thessalonians. The oral proclamation referred to was presumably teaching they had already received with which 'Paul' concurred. We must imagine a situation, therefore, in which the author is saying in effect, 'Just as the Thessalonians were told by Paul to rely on his earlier letter and the teaching given them in the community, so too must you'. vv. 16–17, moving easily from thanks to intercession, 'Paul' now offers a prayer that Jesus Christ and the God 'who loved us and through grace gave us eternal comfort (*para-klēsis*) and good hope' might comfort (*parakalein*) and strengthen their hearts 'in every good work and word'. The prominence of Jesus in this prayer indicates the fairly high Christology characteristic of the letter. 'Good hope' seems to derive from mystery cults as a way of referring to life after death (Best 1972: 321); mystery cults, such as those of Eleusis, offered their adherents a relation of intense communion, often ecstatic in nature, with a god.

(3:1–5) Mutual Prayer Many critics arguing for a rhetorical structure to the letter regard v. 1 as beginning its *exhortatio*. Epistolary theorists tend to see here the beginning of a series of moral admonitions (Jewett 1986: 224–5). vv. 1–2, in a way somewhat similar to that of 1 Thess 5:25, 'Paul' asks the *adelphoi*, literally 'brothers' but presumably also meant to include female members of the congregation (so perhaps 'brethren'), to 'pray for us, so that the word of the Lord may spread rapidly and be glorified [i.e. "greatly honoured"] everywhere, just as it is among you, and that we may be rescued from wicked and evil people; for not all have faith'. If 2 Thessalonians is pseudonymous, such a sentiment conveys an aura of verisimilitude, but also serves to legitimate—that is, to explain and justify the existence and identity of—whatever community this letter was originally intended for. They would be reassured of the value of their faith and of the fact that their sharp differentiation from sinful and uncomprehending outsiders was just what Paul had indicated would be the lot of the Thessalonians. Yet a similar conclusion could be drawn if the letter is authentic, only now it would be the Thessalonians themselves for whom the point was being made. The hostile reception that Paul and his co-workers had received figures both in the clearly genuine correspondence (such as Rom 15:30–1; 2 Cor 1:8–11; and 1 Thess 2: 2) and also in the deutero-Pauline writings, such as in 2 Tim 3:10–11; 4:16–18).

v. 3, the author asserts the faithfulness of the Lord, who will strengthen and guard them from the evil one, and this quality stands in stark contrast to the lack of faith (and the evil associated with it) mentioned in the previous verse. It is noteworthy that although this statement is probably based on 1 Thess 5:24, here the faithful one is the Lord (that is, Jesus Christ) and not God, which indicates the move to a higher Christology in 2 Thessalonians. v. 4, now 'Paul' expresses his confidence in the Lord that they

are following and will continue to follow his commands. In a pseudonymous letter this is a way of encouraging the target audience to adhere to the message associated with Paul. Specifics of the instruction will be provided in 3:6–12. v. 5, 'Paul' prays that the Lord may 'direct your hearts to the love of God and to the steadfastness of Christ'. This prayer takes the audience to the source of their ability to carry out the instructions. It is probable that the author appeals to Christ's steadfastness to provide them with a role model during the current difficulties they are experiencing.

(3:6–15) Warning against Loafers v. 6, 'Paul' commands the 'Thessalonians' to avoid every member of the congregation who is living 'in a disorderly way' (*ataktōs*) and not in accordance with the tradition (*paradosis*) they received from him. The word *ataktōs* appears again at v. 11, where the author describes how certain of his addressees are behaving, and 'Paul' himself denies he behaved in such a way at v. 7. It is reasonably clear from the associations of the word in vv. 6–15 that by 'disorderly' the author means 'not in accordance with the discipline of working and supporting oneself', thus behaving like a loafer (hence 'living in idleness' in the NRSV). Scholars have long explained this idleness as rooted in 'eschatological' excitement produced by a belief in the imminence of the parousia of Christ (see R. Russell 1988: 105–7). Several examples of millennialism in modern times, moreover, have revealed that a belief in the imminent or actual transformation of the world can produce, not surprisingly, a breakdown in belief in the need for everyday activities, such as work. Rejection of work and the usual social order can be associated with exaggerated behaviour and often a belief in a return to a Golden Age which preceded the current period and its tribulations (Jewett 1986: 173–5; Esler 1994: 101). In the unknown community for whom 2 Thessalonians was written it is likely that such attitudes had made an appearance and needed to be attacked. If Menken (1994: 130–3) is correct in assuming that underlying the order which 'Paul' would like to be restored is the rule of work that originated in the sin of Adam and Eve in the garden of Eden in Gen 3:17–19, it is possible that those refusing to work were appealing to the alleged reestablishment of prelapsarian bliss to support their position.

R. Russell (1988) proposes a different view (which has been challenged recently by Romaniuk 1993), that this idleness has nothing to do with end-time excitement, but is a result of the urban poor finding support within the social networks of Christ-fearers and then giving up work. A similar view has more recently been presented by Jewett (1993), who proposes that the early Christ-movement was likely to have been located in the tenement houses of the non-élite, where the system of internal support would have been jeopardized by the refusal of some members to contribute.

vv. 7–8, 'Paul' offers himself as a model for them, inasmuch as he did not exhibit the disorder of idleness when he was amongst them, but worked day and night so as not to be a burden on them by eating at their expense. Imitation of Paul is a reasonably common theme in the genuine Pauline epistles (1 Cor 4:16, 11:1; Phil 3:17; 1 Thess 1:6). v. 8b is closely based on 1 Thess 2:9, and there are similar statements at 1 Cor 9:12; 15–18; 2 Cor 11:7–8; 12:13. In these passages, however, Paul is seeking to allay any suspicion that he preached the gospel for personal profit, while in 2 Thessalonians the point is made to encourage the target audience to imitate him in this respect. v. 9, the author notes he had a right to be supported by the congregation, even though he did not exercise it, in order to offer them a model for imitation, a theme introduced in v. 7. v. 10, by mentioning that he had previously told them in their presence that anyone unwilling to work should not be fed, 'Paul' makes explicit the precise nature of the disorder which has been implied hitherto—the fact that some members of the congregation are living off the others. There are parallels to this saying (which has been frequently cited out of its context ever since), in Prov 10:4; 12:11; 19:15; and Pseudo-Phocylides, *Sentences*, 153–4.

v. 11, here again is a reference to disorder, now with an unequivocal core meaning brought to the surface in v. 10, together with the disturbing news—expressed in a pun—that some of them are not busy at work (*ergazomenous*) but busybodies (*periergazomenous*). Presumably the author has in mind here some exaggerated type of behaviour of the sort common among millennial movements, but its precise nature remains unclear. Not only are they not working, but they are interfering with the work of others. v. 12, 'Paul' follows up the statement in v. 11 with a direct exhortation to the troublemakers here: 'to do their work quietly and to earn their own living' (lit. eat their own bread). The reference to quietness here suggests that their current state is one of loud activity or excitement, no doubt associated with the

millennial belief that 'the day of the Lord is already here' (2:2).

(3:13–18) Conclusion vv. 13–16, there is a great diversity of views among those advocating epistolary or rhetorical analyses of the letter as to where the divisions fall in these verses (Jewett 1986: 224–5). The first four verses (13–16) can either be connected with the previous section, which would mean 'Paul' wanted the 'Thessalonians' to do good to the disorderly and idle troublemakers, or, more likely, constitute a separate section at the end of the letter—beginning with a general exhortation to them to do good (v. 13). Those who do not are to be ostracized (although, as we see in the next verse, only to a limited extent) so that they may be put to shame (v. 14). Here we see the typical association in Mediterranean culture between honour and group-belonging. Nevertheless, such a person is not to be treated as an enemy, but admonished as a brother (v. 15). The person is socially separated as a form of discipline and for a limited time (subject no doubt to a change of behaviour on the malefactor's part). Exclusion from the community for various reasons and for a limited time was also practised at Qumran (see e.g. the CD 8:16–18). v. 16, 'Paul' prays that the Lord will give them peace at all times and remain with them; in 1 Cor 14:33 Paul notes that God is a God of peace not disorder.

v. 17, it was a practice in ancient letter-writing for an author to use a scribe and add a few words at the end in his own handwriting. Paul adopts this practice elsewhere in 1 Cor 16:21; Gal 6:11; Col 4:18 (leaving aside the issue of whether Colossians is authentic or not). This device would only be effective as a proof of authenticity in relation to the original of the letter, since the difference in the two hands apparent there would disappear in subsequent copies. Although the author of 2 Thessalonians seems to claim—wrongly—that this was Paul's universal practice, Jewett's (1986: 6) conclusion that this itself indicates authenticity since otherwise the author would be casting doubt on other Pauline letters not bearing the addition is unwarranted if the letter were written before the collection of Paul's letters towards the end of the first century. On the other hand, 1 Thessalonians does not bear Paul's self-attestation and this strengthens Jewett's point if 2 Thessalonians was originally directed to Christ-followers who possessed 1 Thessalonians. The self-conscious (and unique) way in which the author draws attention to the practice in 3:17 by saying that 'This is the mark' (*sēmeion*, sign) is itself suspicious. v. 18, the letter ends with a standard benediction.

REFERENCES

Aus, R. D. (1976), 'The Relevance of Isaiah 66.7 to Revelation 12 and 2 Thessalonians 1', ZNW 67: 252–68.

Bailey, J. A. (1978–9), 'Who Wrote II Thessalonians?', NTS 25:131–45.

Barclay, M. G. (1993), 'Conflict in Thessalonika', CBQ 53: 512–30.

Best, E. (1972), A Commentary on the First and Second Epistles to the Thessalonians, Black's New Testament Commentaries (London: Adam & Charles Black).

Duling, D. C. (1996), 'Millennialism', in R. L. Rohrbaugh (ed.), The Social Sciences and New Testament Interpretation (Peabody, Mass.: Hendrickson), 183–205.

Esler, P. F. (1993), 'Political Oppression in Jewish Apocalyptic Literature: A Social-Scientific Approach', in Listening: Journal of Religion and Culture, 28: 181–99.

—— (1994), The First Christians in their Social Worlds: Social-Scientific Approaches to New Testament Interpretation (London: Routledge).

—— (1998), Galatians (London: Routledge).

Jewett, R. (1986), The Thessalonian Correspondence: Pauline Rhetoric and Millenarian Piety (Philadelphia: Fortress).

—— (1993), 'Tenement Churches and Communal Meals in the Early Church: The Implications of a Form-Critical Analysis of 2 Thessalonians 3:10', Biblical Research, 38: 23–42.

Lietaert Peerbolte, L. J. (1997), 'The Katechon, Katechōn of 2 Thess. 2:6–7', NovT 39: 138–50.

Malina, B. J. (1993), The New Testament World: Insights from Cultural Anthropology, rev. edn. Orig. 1981 (Louisville, Ky.: Westminster/John Knox).

Marxsen, W. (1968), Introduction to the New Testament (Oxford: Blackwell).

—— (1982), Der zweite Thessalonicherbrief (Zurich: Theologischer Verlag).

Masson, C. (1957), Les Deux Epîtres de Saint Paul aux Thessaloniciens (Neuchatel: Delachaux and Niestlé).

Meade, D. G. (1986), Pseudonymity and Canon: An Investigation into the Relationship of Authorship and Authority in Jewish and Early Christian Tradition, WUNT 39 (Tübingen: Mohr).

Menken, M. J. J. (1994), 2 Thessalonians (London: Routledge).

Moxnes, H. (1991), 'Patron–Client Relations and the New Community in Luke–Acts', in J. H. Neyrey (ed.) (1991), The Social World of Luke–Acts: Models for Interpretation (Peabody, Mass.: Hendrickson), 241–68.

Powell, C. E. (1997), 'The Identity of the "Restrainer" in 2 Thessalonians 2:6–7', BSacr 154: 320–32.

Romaniuk, K. (1993), 'Les Thessaloniciens étaient-ils des paresseux?', ETL 69: 142–5.

Russell, D. F. (1964), The Meaning and Message of Jewish Apocalyptic (London: SCM).

Russell, R. (1988), 'The Idle in 2 Thess. 3.6–12: An Eschatological or a Social Problem?', NTS 34: 105–19.

Seesemann, H. (1967), 'Pateō and compounds in NT', TDNTv. 943–5.

Strobel, A. (1961), Untersuchungen zum eschatologischen Verzögerungs-problem: Auf Grund der Spätjüdisch-urchristlichen Geschichte von Habakuk 2, 2 ff. (Leiden: Brill).

Trudinger, P. (1995), 'The Priority of 2 Thessalonians Revisited: Some Fresh Evidence', Downside Review, 113: 31–5.

Wrede, W. (1903), Die Echtheit des zweiten Thessalonikerbrief untersucht, TU NS 9/2 (Leipzig: Hinrichs).

13.   The Pastoral Epistles

CLARE DRURY

INTRODUCTION

These three letters purporting to be from Paul to two of his close companions clearly belong together as a set. They have always been placed together in the New Testament, their concerns and language are shared. Certain key words and ideas permeate the three, connecting them and holding together what at first sight might seem a rather amorphous collection of ethical injunctions and doctrinal assertions. 1 Timothy and Titus are very similar in character and subject-matter, their teaching concentrating on church order and ethical exhortation. Sandwiched between them, 2 Timothy is more personal than the other two; Paul is in prison, while in the other two he is free. His character and behaviour in adversity are presented as models to Timothy which arouse the reader's sympathy and admiration.

A. Authorship. 1. The claim that Paul himself wrote the letters seems at first sight obvious and incontrovertible. All three begin with a greeting from the apostle and contain personal notes and asides such as 'I urge you, as I did when I was on my way to Macedonia' (1 Tim 1:3); 'I left you behind in Crete' (Titus 1:5) and 'When you come, bring the cloak that I left with Carpus at Troas, also the books and above all the parchments' (2 Tim 4:13). Combined with such emotional appeals as 2 Tim 1:3–5; 4:6–8, the impression of Pauline authorship seems clear.

2. But things are not so straightforward: signs of the late date of the letters proliferate. The organization of the church under officers such as bishops and deacons is well advanced (e.g. 1 Tim 3:1–13; 5:3–13) and mirrors the situation found in late first-century and early second-century Christian writings such as 1 *Clement* and the letters of Ignatius and Polycarp. The situation of the letters seems inauthentic too; they are addressed to two travelling companions whom 'Paul' has apparently just left (1 Tim 1:3; Titus 1:5) and expects to see again soon (1 Tim 3:14; 2 Tim 4:13; Titus 3:12). Yet they contain teaching of the most rudimentary kind which close associates might be expected to know.

3. The teaching that characterizes the Pastorals lacks the fire and passion of the original Pauline epistles; the immediacy of eschatological expectation that lay behind much of Paul's teaching (e.g. 1 Cor 7:17–31) has gone. Judgement and the future appearance of Christ are still expected, but it is the ordered life of the community that is focal. There is no mention of key Pauline ideas such as the cross, the church as the body of Christ, or covenant. Paul's struggle to identify the role of the law in his new understanding of salvation is absent; in the Pastorals, the law fulfils its normal function of identifying, restricting, and punishing evildoers (1 Tim 1:8–11). The teaching of the Pastorals focuses upon the ordered life of the community emphasizing such virtues as piety or godliness (e.g. 1 Tim 2:2; 2 Tim 3:5; Titus 1:1) and good conscience (1 Tim 1:5, 19; 3:9; 2 Tim 1:3). Individual behaviour is bound up in the well-being of the whole group, and there is a clear sense that the church has a future as a community; its organization is designed to enable sound doctrine to continue (1 Tim 4:6; 2 Tim 3:10). The ethical teaching is not solely inward-looking, but also aims to ensure that the church is acceptable to the outside world. The behaviour of its members must not draw attention to them as part of a new and suspect cult, they must conform in every way to the moral standards and expectations of the larger community.

4. By the end of the first century the figure of Paul had assumed authority for many in the church and, as his significance grew, so did narratives about his life and interpretations of his teaching. The Acts of the Apostles provides evidence of this sort of development; the figure of Paul is employed to present the author's own image of the Gentile church and its origins. In Paul's speeches in Acts there is nothing that directly contradicts the ideas we find in Paul's own letters, but the picture that emerges is one of a more conciliatory and less theologically sophisticated figure. Both Acts and the Pastoral Epistles witness to a time in the church's development when Paul had become a legendary figure and different groups were competing to be regarded as his true successors. This trend continued well into the second century: the apocryphal *Acts of Paul* provide evidence of speculation and legends which grew up around the figure of Paul. The longest and most complete of them, the *Acts of Paul and Thecla*, provides a model of the woman's role as teacher and baptizer that the Pastoral Epistles deplore (1 Tim 2:11–15). According to Marcion, the second-century heretic, Paul alone had presented the true Christian message of love and grace.

5. Thus the origin of the Pastoral Epistles begins to become clear: the author emphasizes the importance of handing on true teaching through leaders such as Timothy and Titus, authorized by Paul so that false doctrine could be refuted and its promulgators condemned, 'Timothy, guard what has been entrusted to you. Avoid the profane chatter and contradictions of what is falsely called knowledge' (1 Tim 6:20; cf. 2 Tim 2:1–2, 14–19; Titus 1:1–5; 3:8–11). While a small and declining number of scholars still argue for Pauline authorship, most prefer to see the author's modesty and his admiration for Paul behind his pseudonymity; he was passing on Pauline tradition and the credit was due to Paul rather than to him. The letters can be seen as documents written in and for a community which wanted to hold fast to what they considered true Pauline teaching in the face of persecution or opposition from different kinds of Christian teachers. On the other hand, some of Paul's teaching on practical matters—teaching about the remarriage of widows for example, and about the ideal ascetic life—is contradicted in the Pastorals (e.g. 1 Cor 7:7–8; cf. 1 Tim 2:11–15; 3:2–5). The situation the author was addressing was so different he felt he had the authority to alter Paul's original teaching.

6. This implies that the personal notes and reminiscences, which occur throughout the letters (1 Tim 1:3; 2 Tim 4:13; Titus 1:5), are conscious forgeries included to add authenticity. So some scholars (e.g. Miller 1997) have suggested that the Pastorals are a semi-pseudonymous work, containing fragments of genuine Pauline material with later teaching added to these 'notes' to form the epistles as we have them. But a growing number of scholars see the Pastorals as entirely pseudonymous. They argue for complete and intentional pseudonimity; the writer used the device of the letter form, and included the kind of personal details that would convince his readers of the letters' authenticity. If the device was successful the author's opponents would be unassailably refuted. The personal notes are trivial in nature and do not fit with details of Paul's life we know from his undoubted letters, or from the story as presented in Acts. But they were an important part of the fiction and for the author's purpose to work, the fiction must be convincing.

B. Character and Situation of the Pastorals. 1. The concerns expressed in the Pastoral Epistles focus on sound doctrine and good behaviour. The two are closely linked in the author's mind and are contrasted with the ideas and behaviour of his opponents. A group within the author's church is trying to convert members of the community to its own way of thinking and living (e.g. 1 Tim 1:3–7, 18–20; 4:1–10; 6:3–4; 2 Tim 2:24–6; 3:13–17; 4:3–5; Titus 1:10–2:2). This group of people, heterodox from our author's point of view, was having such success in persuading others of its ideas, that the Pastoral Epistles were written to contradict their theories and denounce their behaviour. They are characterized as disputatious and given to theological speculation and argument—teaching which leads to disharmony in the community (e.g. 1 Tim 6:3–10). The methods the author employs to contradict false teaching and to encourage attachment to his point of view are a combination of exhortations to virtue and condemnations of the teachings of his opponents with warnings of the dire results of following them. Because we have no independent record, we cannot be certain who the opponents were or exactly what they were teaching; we have to reconstruct what we can from the epistles themselves.

2. The author counters his opponents with his appeal to tradition. Paul, well known and revered as the apostle to the Gentiles, hands on

the tradition to two junior companions, Timothy and Titus, who, in turn, are instructed to transmit it to the communities in their care. Within these communities, officers of blameless character will be charged with preserving and handing on this sound doctrine and ethical instructions to the rest. In this way there could be no doubt of the authenticity of the teaching the author presents; it has been transmitted by a direct and faultless route. The character of the officers of the community is a major theme in 1 Timothy and Titus. They were key people in maintaining true doctrine and in keeping order and discipline within the community.

3. Alternating with instructions about church organization and ethical teaching are brief kerygmatic statements about God's plan of salvation (1 Tim 2:5–6; 3:16; 6.13–16; 2 Tim 1:9–10; 2:11–13; Titus 3:4–7). These doctrinal sections present familiar ideas about salvation history, none of them inconsistent with Pauline and other New Testament teaching. Indeed Pauline language is sometimes employed; but the ideas are not developed theologically. Their form is often rhythmical; they may be liturgical origins.

4. The organization of the church and the relationship of its members to one another is based on the Graeco-Roman household. Household codes are found elsewhere in the NT epistles (Col 3:18–4:1; Eph 5:22–6:9; 1 Pet 2:18–3:7) but their use in the Pastorals is developing so that the church can be described as the household of God (1 Tim 3:15). The development is not complete—the terminology is used sometimes in its original sense and sometimes with the sense of church office (e.g. in 1 Tim 5:1, 17, the Greek word *presbuteros* is used both for 'older man' and for 'elder') but evolution can be seen to be taking place.

5. In the passages of ethical teaching the Pastoral Epistles share some of the ideas about how a virtuous life should be lived with contemporary pagan philosophers as well as with other Christian and Jewish writers. Comparisons with the works of Plutarch, who lived in the second half of the first century, and Epictetus, a Stoic philosopher of the first half of the second century, illuminate our understanding of the Pastorals' teaching about moderation or restraint (*sōphrosunē*) and piety or godliness (*eusebeia*). These terms describe the kind of civic and private virtues that were common subjects for discussion among Greek and Roman moralists at the time. In the Pastorals the meaning of *eusebeia* is both doctrinal and ethical; it is a word used to describe the kind of lifestyle the author advocates that arises out of a belief in the doctrinal claims he makes; good behaviour is inextricably linked with belief in sound doctrine. Pagan writers also help to put in perspective social issues such as the role of women. The place of women in society was as much an issue for pagan writers as it was for Christians (see Beard, North, and Price 1998: i. 297–9).

COMMENTARY

1 Timothy

(1:1–2) The form of the opening greeting is familiar to readers of NT epistles. It follows the conventions of letter-writing of the first few centuries CE, with the sender naming himself and greeting the recipient of the letter. Here, the writer names himself as Paul, apostle of Christ Jesus, as he does with minor variations in the other two letters. The recipient here is Timothy, well known from Pauline epistles and Acts as Paul's companion and fellow-worker (e.g. Rom 16:21; 1 Cor 4:17; 16:10; Col 1:1; 1 Thess 1:1; Acts 16:1). Several points stand out in this introduction: Paul's authority is stressed and is in no doubt; not only is he an apostle of Christ Jesus, he is commanded by God. The formality of the greeting, unexpected in a letter between friends and colleagues, has contributed to the belief that the letter is inauthentic. At the heart of the greeting two unusual epithets are employed, God is called 'our Saviour' and Christ, 'our hope'. Outside the Pastorals, only in Cor 1:27 is Christ identified as 'hope' and there it is 'Christ the hope of glory'; God our Saviour is found in the Pastorals a number of times, but elsewhere in the NT only in the Magnificat (Lk 1:47) and in the doxology of the epistle of Jude (Jude 25). The writer wants to make it clear that the message he brings is the true message of salvation, so he presents himself as the apostle Paul, commissioned by God the origin of salvation. Hope and salvation are closely connected; the work of salvation started at the incarnation will be continued through the church and completed at Christ's return.

v. 2, Timothy, the recipient of the letter, is called a 'loyal child in the faith' as is Titus in Titus 1:4. The word gnēsios, translated 'loyal', implies legitimacy in the Greek. In distinction to others who will be invoked, later (e.g. Hymenaeus and Alexander, 1:20), Timothy is Paul's legitimate successor. He is a child and therefore inferior to Paul, but the tradition passed from one to the other is true and authoritative. The

threefold salutation is slightly different from those found in other Pauline letters. Grace and peace are familiar; here, mercy is added in the middle of the formula, where 'to you' is found elsewhere (e.g. Rom 1:7; 1 Cor 1:3; 2 Cor 1:2; Gal 1:3). Mercy is a particular concern in the Pastoral Epistles, where the word appears five times of the ten occurrences in the whole Pauline corpus. God the Father, or Creator, and Christ Jesus our Lord are invoked again at the end of the salutation as the origins of Christian 'virtues'.

(1:3–7) The situation envisaged at the opening of the letter is that Paul has left Timothy behind in Ephesus while he has travelled on into Macedonia. Such a situation cannot be fitted into any reconstruction of Paul's life that can be pieced together either from his own letters or from the narrative in Acts. They provide the kind of personal details that lead some readers to argue for authenticity, while others claim that it is exactly the kind of information a pseudonymous author would include to add verisimilitude to his pretence, bringing the characters to life by placing them in relationship to one another in a real setting.

Having established his credentials, the author introduces one of the main concerns of his letter; he wants to combat false teaching and to discredit the teachers. The teachers cannot be identified with any certainty, nor what they were teaching. 1:3–11 provides clues about the teaching; we are told that the opponents occupy themselves with 'myths and endless genealogies which lead to speculations' (v. 4). It may be that a Gnostic group was teaching in the author's community and perverting the faith as he understood it by mythological speculations about creation and salvation. Because his readers must have known who he was referring to, he does not need to identify his opponents specifically, but sets his view of Christian virtues such as love, a pure heart, and a good conscience against the vices of speculative theory and vain discussion.

(1:8–11) Here he adds a further dimension to the description of his opponents. They desire to be teachers of the law, presumably the Jewish law, without understanding what it is they are talking about; its true meaning is to regulate the behaviour of lawless and disobedient people. The vices listed in vv. 9–10 are an odd collection, including specific acts such as murder, matricide, and parricide alongside general characteristics such as sinfulness, unholiness, and profanity. At different levels such behaviour would incur disapproval in almost any society, not just under Jewish law. The list is obviously meant to be contrasted with the list of virtues in 1:5. The writer's central theme, that good doctrine leads to good behaviour, is contrasted with the effects of following unsound teaching. He does not explain this teaching very clearly; but simply by placing the lists alongside one another he points up the contrast.

The qualities belonging to the faith, such as love issuing from a pure heart and a good conscience, are not typical of the teaching in Paul's genuine letters. Paul would certainly not dissent from the ideas expressed, but he uses different language to describe them. The Pastor's view of the law is very different from Paul's own too. For Paul the law symbolized the old dispensation, and its relationship to salvation brought through Christ was extremely complex; it was God-given but restrictive and negative in its effects (e.g. Rom 7:4–25; Gal 3:1–14). The Pastor, on the other hand, sees it in a much more mundane way: it is a God-given guide to behaviour, which, when abused, works against sound teaching.

(1:12–17) 1:3–11 and 18–20 provide a framework for these verses. This biographical section, illustrating God's mercy to his apostle Paul, has the effect of giving Paul tremendous prominence. The section takes the form of a thanksgiving, and describes the radical volte-face of the sometime persecutor turned faithful disciple. The story is familiar not only from Acts (9:1–22; 22:3–21; 26:9–20), but also from 1 Cor 15:8–10 and Phil 3:1–5. The story of the complete conversion of the persecutor is a tale worth telling. But here more than anywhere else the fate of Paul is inextricably linked with the story of salvation. 'Christ Jesus came into the world to save sinners—of whom I am the foremost.' Paul's sinfulness is vividly described: 'I formerly a blasphemer, a persecutor, and a man of violence', but he 'received mercy' because he acted out of ignorance. The sharp contrast between the persecutor and the believer is shown to be an intentional part of God's plan so that Paul might be an example for others, to demonstrate above all the perfect patience of Jesus Christ. So the tale serves a dual purpose; Paul is a typical example of a convert, but his special case gives him a special position as an apostle as the next few verses show. Paul himself talks of his former life in 1 Cor 15:9 and Phil 3:4–8, to make a similar point, but here the language is stronger

and less forgiving. Acts is much closer to this passage when it speaks of the ignorance of unbelievers before their conversion (e.g. 3:17; 13:27; 17:23).

The central Christian belief (v. 15), that Christ Jesus came into the world to save sinners, is introduced by a formula that assumes general acceptance. The formula is found five times in the Pastoral Epistles (1 Tim 1:15; 3:1; 4:9; 2 Tim 2:11; Titus 3:8), often, as here, drawing attention to a significant doctrinal statement. It is not clear why the author uses the phrase with some doctrinal assertions and not with others. Often, as in this case, it seems that a quotation is being employed. The significance of the expression, 'Christ came into the world to save sinners', lies in the second half of the statement: the writer is not so much interested in the pre-existence of Christ, which *may* be implied, as in the soteriological effect of his coming (cf. 3:16 and 2 Tim 1:10). It introduces the idea of Paul's sinfulness which in turn shows him as a prototype believer and recipient of grace. Patience or forbearance (*makrothumia*) is a defining characteristic of God in relationship with his people in the Jewish Scriptures. The words found in Ex 34.6–7 where God is described as 'merciful and gracious, slow to anger, and abounding in steadfast love and faithfulness, keeping steadfast love for the thousandth generation' are repeated and echoed frequently in later Jewish writings to contrast the long-suffering constancy of God with the sinfulness and fickle nature of his people (Jon 4:2; 2 Macc 6:14–16; Wis 11:23; 12:16). Here the attributes have been transferred to Christ, through whom God is working out salvation. Eternal life is in the future, it is a focus for belief grounded in Christ 'our hope' (1:1) for the future and based on what has already been achieved.

(1:18–20) This section follows awkwardly from the doxology in v. 17 and it is far from clear what 'these instructions' refers to. It may look back to 1:3 where Timothy is urged to give certain instructions, or forward to the injunction to 'fight the good fight' later in the same verse. The word *paraggelia*, translated here as 'instruction', occurs with its cognates six times in 1 Timothy (cf. Tim 1:3; 4:11; 5:7; 6:13, 17) demonstrating how important was the passing on of sound doctrine through properly commissioned people. The prophecies referred to in v. 18 are not to be understood as scriptural prophecies, but recall prophetic experiences such as that described in Acts 13:1–3 and referred to in 1 Tim 4:14.

The imagery of fighting or warfare was widespread among philosophers and religious groups in the ancient world and is found elsewhere in the NT epistles (1 Cor 9:7; 2 Cor 10:3–6; Eph 6:10–17; 2 Tim 2:3–7, where the image is linked with that of athletic competition). The repetition of the virtues of faith and a good conscience from 1:5 provides a framework for the central section of this chapter. Further emphasis is given by reference to two men, Hymenaeus and Alexander, who have 'reject[ed] conscience' and 'suffered shipwreck in the faith'. They have therefore been 'turned over to Satan'. As in 1 Cor 5:5, this is a powerful image describing the radical effects of exclusion from the Christian community. Hymenaeus is mentioned again, alongside Philetus, at 2 Tim 2:17, where their talk is said to spread like gangrene. Alexander the coppersmith is mentioned in 2 Tim 4:14 where he is said to have done Paul great harm. It is impossible to say whether both refer to the same man. Their rejection of the faith is to be contrasted with the steadfastness of Paul and Timothy; by the end of the first chapter, we are left with a clear impression of the apostle and of his legitimate successor; they are the transmitters of the true teaching of the church.

Church Organization and Behaviour (2:1–3:13)

The discussion in chs. 2 and 3 changes from concern about the opposition to a description of the kind of behaviour that should characterize members of the church towards both one another and outsiders. The detailed arrangements for the leadership of this household and relationships within it suggest that the church is becoming more at home in the world. For Paul, who felt he was living at the end of the age, there was a strong tension between living in this age but belonging to the next. This not only affected his sense of purpose but his ethical teaching as well. Now the situation is different. Eschatological hope is still very much alive (e.g. 6:14–15, 18–19), but there is no sense of urgency or immediacy. There is a more long-term viewpoint; the church must be firmly established, and respectable, so as to avoid adverse publicity.

(2:1–7) Prayer is the first duty of a member of the community. Four words are used to describe the prayers, 'supplications, prayers, intercessions, and thanksgivings' but no distinction is made between them. More significant is that prayers are to be made for everyone, particularly kings and those in authority, and not just for members of the community. For God is Creator and Saviour, and desires that every human being should be saved. Prayer for the emperor caused difficulties for Jews and Christians; their refusal to acknowledge his authority sometimes led to persecutions, but there are a number of passages in the NT which follow the same line as this (Rom 13.1–7; 1 Pet 2:14, 17; Titus 3:1; Acts *passim*). The aim of such prayer was to avoid the possibility of persecution, and so lead a peaceful life 'in godliness and dignity'. There is similar teaching in other first- and second-century Jewish and Christian writers, and the reasons given often echo those given here (e.g. 1 *Clem.* 61; Tert. *Apol.* 30; Jos. *J. W.* 2.197). The nouns translated 'godliness' and 'dignity' are characteristic of the Pastorals and betray their Hellenistic setting; they translate words (*eusebeia* and *semnotēs*) found elsewhere in the NT only in Acts and 2 Peter. They illustrate the results of living in harmony with the authorities; the ability to devote oneself to the worship of God which results in a respectable and responsible life not outwardly distinct from that of their pagan neighbours. Knowledge of the truth recurs in 2 Tim 2:25; 3:7; Titus 1:1, and helps emphasize the accessibility of the Christian message to all reasonable people.

(2:5–6) presents a summary of the true teaching that is the focus of that Christian message. It appears to contain a quotation (NRSV presents it as verse), and is a succinct telling of the drama of salvation in a rhythmical and poetic form—a kind of credal statement (cf. 1 Tim 3:16; 6.13–16; 2 Tim 1:9–10; 2:11–13; Titus 3:4–7). God is one and the Saviour of all people. Christ's role is as mediator; he alone links God and humankind. His humanity is stressed to show solidarity with those he saves—the same word is used in Greek for 'human' and 'humankind'. The word 'mediator' is applied to Christ in the NT only here and in Hebrews (8:6; 9:15; 12:24, where he is mediator of the covenant as Moses was in Gal 3:19). The emphasis on a single God and a single mediator may be an attack on the kind of Gnostic 'myths and speculations' referred to in 1:4, and the stress on Christ's humanity may have been included to refute Docetism.

Christ's self-giving as a ransom, also found in Titus 2:14, uses language similar to Paul's in Romans 3:24 and 8:23 and to that used in Mk 10:45, Mt 20:28, where 'he came … to give his life as a ransom for many'. Here, by contrast, the language is totally inclusive; he gave his life as a ransom for *all*. The language of ransom implies that payment is being made to obtain the freedom of captives or slaves and has as its background both the manumission of slaves and the freeing of Israel from Egypt at the Exodus. By the time the Pastoral Epistles were written, the language of ransom had become central in Christian thought. In the context of 1:15 freedom from sin is implied. As part of God's plan for salvation, Jesus' death undoubtedly came at the right time. In the Greek the phrase 'testimony at the right time' is part of the credal statement of vv. 5–6 rather than a comment upon it.

(2:7) Paul's own role in God's plan is emphasized again. He was not only an apostle but also herald and teacher of the Gentiles. The word translated 'herald' is rare in the NT, and is found elsewhere only in 2 Tim 1:11, where it also refers to Paul, and in 2 Peter 2:5, where it refers to Noah. The cognate verb is, however, found throughout the NT. Paul's appointment as teacher of the Gentiles provides the means for God's plan for universal salvation to proceed. The picture of Paul as apostle to the Gentiles accords with that in Paul's own letters and with the narrative of his journeys in Acts. The insistence on Paul's authority is exaggerated, much more than would be necessary in a genuine letter from Paul to his friend. But in the context of this letter the insistence on authority has its place: the true message of salvation is being handed on to the next generation.

(2:8–15) Returning to the subject of prayer, Timothy is now given instructions about the necessary physical as well as emotional attitude. A distinction is drawn between the attitude suitable for men and that for women. Men are to pray with hands raised; they can pray anywhere, in private as well as in communal worship. Their emotional state 'without anger or argument' as a prerequisite to proper prayer recalls the teaching of Old Testament prophets (e.g. Hos 6:6; Am 3:14–15; 5:4–7).

The Pastor then turns to the behaviour of women. First they are to dress and behave modestly. This teaching can be paralleled in Plutarch's *Advice to a Bride and Groom*, 'It is not gold or precious stones or scarlet that makes a woman decorous, but whatever invests her with that something which betokens dignity, good behaviour and modesty' (*Mor.* 141e). Women were gaining a certain amount of freedom and independence in the Roman empire, and this

was no doubt as true among Christian women as non-Christian women. But like other conservative writers, Christian and non-Christian, the Pastor is concerned that women should remain in what he perceives as their proper, subordinate position. Other NT writers make the same sort of point, particularly about the public behaviour of women. It was necessary for the successful continuation of the faith and to avoid persecution, that women should behave in a seemly way in meetings of the community. Part of this was an insistence that women should not teach or be perceived to be in a position of authority over a man (cf. 1 Cor 14:34).

The reason given by the Pastor for women's subordination goes back to Adam and Eve (cf. 1 Cor 11:8–9). First, he claims that primacy in time implies superiority of status. Second, it was, he claims, Eve who was deceived, not Adam. He is departing from the Genesis narrative at this point. Certainly, Eve ate the fruit first, but she was quickly followed by Adam, and they were both punished. According to some Jewish traditions, Eve's sin was a sexual one, she was seduced by the serpent, so salvation could be achieved only by bearing children. An idea of this sort may lie behind 2:14–15 which places Eve's transgression in such close proximity to the solution that salvation for women rests in bearing children. In any case, a woman's most important role in the Graeco-Roman world was to be the mother of children. For the Pastor, the family and the household were the focus of the church, so bearing children and bringing them up in the faith was vital for its successful survival and growth.

The teaching about women's subordination should not be understood outside its own context. In Rom 16:1 a deacon called Phoebe is commended by Paul. His teaching in 1 Cor 11 and 14 suggests that already in the middle of the first century some women were behaving with a freedom which was unacceptable to the leaders of the church. The popular story of Thecla, told in the *Acts of Paul and Thecla*, is evidence that this trend continued into the second century.

(3:1–7) 'The saying is sure' may refer back to what has just been said, as in 4:9 or Titus 3:8, or forwards to the instructions about church offices. When the same phrase was used before in 1:15, it introduced an important Christological saying, as it does in 2 Tim 2:11. It is not quite clear here if either the preceding saying or what follows is thought by the author to have this special significance. The writer's teaching about women is important to him but so is his teaching about church officers which follows.

vv. 1b–7 concern the office of the *episkopos*, literally overseer, but translated in the NRSV as bishop. The discussion indicates that the church has reached a settled situation, where it needs capable and dignified men to run it. But the information we are given is tantalizingly incomplete, for while the qualities required of a bishop are clearly set out, his duties are not described. If, as is quite likely, one of the patterns of organization and worship in the early church was the synagogue, then the *episkopos* would, like a Jewish synagogue leader, lead the community and represent its interests in the outside world. His good character and reputation among outsiders was essential for the community's welfare and continuing stability. The parallel drawn in 3:5 between the household and the church provides another clue. Graeco-Roman households which consisted of family, slaves, and more loosely dependent groups of people were run by a paterfamilias who had complete authority. The church in the Pastoral Epistles is seen as the household of God; everyone—men, women, children, elders (*presbyteroi*), servants (*diakonoi*)—has his or her place in it and its smooth running is overseen by an *episkopos* who must be of impeccable character.

The list of virtues expected of such a community leader is conventional in both Jewish and Hellenistic societies, including that favourite 'restraint' (*sōphrosunē*, translated in the NRSV as 'temperate'). His duties include a responsibility for teaching, that is handing on the tradition as he has had it handed on to him. There are some points that may be surprising to a modern reader; the *episkopos* is expected to be married and to be the head of a household (3:2, 4–5). Furthermore he is to be 'married only once', literally, 'the husband of one wife'. Polygamy is not being forbidden here; remarriage after divorce may be in question, or it may be that the remarriage of widowers is also excluded for *episkopoi*. If so, the rules are different for different groups in the community, for young widows are encouraged to remarry (5:14). Perhaps, though, this is rather an extreme translation of the Greek; what is meant is that the *episkopos* should be a faithful husband to his wife, but that sequential monogamy is not out of the question. His conversion to Christianity must not be recent. There may have been important individuals in the community who felt that their standing or wealth qualified them to become leaders in the church. But to be an *episkopos* one must be firmly rooted in the faith; the implication must be that the church itself is firmly established too.

We do not know whether each community had one *episkopos*, or more. Ignatius, who was bishop of Antioch in Syria, argued strongly in the first decade of the second century for a monarchical episcopate, that is, having one *episkopos* as overseer of the Christian communities in each town, who presides over and is distinct from the deacons and from the elders, 'that you may be joined together in one subjection, subject to the bishop and to the presbytery, and may in all things be sanctified' (Ign. *Eph.* 2.2; cf. 20.2). But it is certain that there was no universally accepted pattern of leadership at this period, and from the Pastoral Epistles themselves no clearly defined organization can be discerned.

(**3:8–13**) Just as there is information about the character but not the duties of the *episkopos*, only the virtues necessary for a deacon are described in vv. 8–13. Indeed, the virtues of *episkopos* and deacon overlap to a great extent. This suggests that the functions were clearly understood already in the community being addressed; the issue was to find suitable people to perform the functions. The Greek word *diakonos*, translated 'deacon', originally meant 'servant', but in the apostolic fathers (e.g. *Didache* 15; Ign. *Trall.* 2, 3; Ign. *Magn.* 6, 13) and the NT Epistles it is used to describe an officer of the church (e.g. Rom 16:1; 1 Cor 3:5; Eph 6:21; Phil 1:1; 1 Thess 3:2; cf. Acts 6). The narrative in Acts 6 traces the diaconate back to the Jerusalem church when 'seven men full of the Spirit' were appointed to distribute food to the Greek-speaking widows of the church. This may be later rationalization of the origin of the office, linking the function of serving to the diaconate when its origins were already obscure. In Mk 10:45 Jesus uses the verb cognate with *diakonos* when he says 'I came not to be served but to serve'. The qualities of an *episkopos* and a deacon were similar; their roles apparently not dissimilar except for a greater emphasis on management and teaching in the case of the *episkopos*. Little information is given here about the work of a deacon, but it is clear that a test was necessary for those aspiring to become deacons to prove themselves blameless. The 'mystery of the faith', God's hidden purpose only understood by believers, refers to the true teaching of 2:5–6 and 3:16.

In the midst of the description of a deacon's character is a verse about women. The word translated 'women' also means wives in Greek, so there is a real possibility that the verse describes the qualities required in a deacon's wife rather than in a woman deacon. If that is the case, they must be as far beyond reproach as their husbands. On the other hand, Phoebe is called a deacon in Rom 16:1, so it is possible that this verse refers to the qualities such women need. If so, their role must be limited by the constraints put on women's behaviour in 2:11–12, where women were told to be submissive to men and to learn in silence, and were forbidden to teach or have authority over men. The characteristics mentioned are reminiscent of those necessary for *episkopoi* and deacons. A deacon, like an *episkopos*, must be married only once, literally 'the husband of one wife', and must be a good head of his household. Single men, slaves, and, to judge by this qualification, women, seem to be excluded from holding office. The requirements that an *episkopos* should be hospitable and a teacher are not included for deacons, but Timothy is referred to as a deacon in 4:6, and since he was expected to 'pass on all these instructions', in other words, to teach, it may be that the categories are quite fluid and ill-defined. The face that the church presents must be respectable, so all its representatives must be beyond reproach.

(3:14–16) vv. 14–15 open with a personal note designed to add verisimilitude to the fictional situation. It is common in the Pauline epistles to refer to personal travel plans, so this reference places the epistle firmly in its genre as well as supporting the picture of Paul's personal involvement. The use of the word 'household' summarizes the whole section from 2:1 to 3:13. More will be said of the household later in this letter and also in the other two. But the picture we have so far presents a picture of a solid establishment, run by responsible figures. Any assailant will have a difficult task.

The 'mystery of our religion' is described in the quoted formula which follows. For similar passages see 1 TIM 2:5–6. The word translated 'religion' is *eusebeia*; normally in the Pastorals *eusebeia* and its cognates denote piety or godliness, here it carries a sense of the system of belief that inspires piety. The earlier formula in ch. 2 dwelt on the human nature of Christ; this confessional formula consists of three pairs of contrasted statements. The main point of contrast being the last word of each line: in the first pair flesh and spirit, in the second it is angels and Gentiles, in the last pair the contrast is between the world and glory. The structure is chiastic, ABBAAB (where the earthly world is represented by A, the heavenly by B) which makes the formula memorable and helps unify the whole. In every line the verb is in the same tense and is followed by a noun in the same case preceded, with one exception, by 'in'. Heaven and earth are being contrasted and yet shown to belong together, united by the revelation of Christ and its effects. There is no direct reference to Christ's death and resurrection, nor to the end of the world, but a clear picture is created of the unifying and universal nature of the coming of Christ. Christ's triumph and glory are placed in contrast to the teachings of demons which are to be the subject of the next passage. The household of God rests on sure foundations.

(4:1–5) No attempt is made to elucidate the confessional statement, instead, the author moves on to describe dangers of his opponents' teaching, and the importance and strength of true doctrine. The contrasts between flesh and spirit, earth and heaven are emphasized by reference to revelation through the Spirit in vv. 1–2. The Spirit who inspires true prophetic utterances has foretold opposition to the faith in 'later times', or the last times. It was a commonplace idea in Jewish and Christian apocalyptic that the end would be preceded by a time of persecution and suffering (e.g. Mk 13; 1 Cor 15:24–8). The sense of urgency and immediacy are absent from the Pastoral Epistles, but there is a lingering feeling that before the end there will be difficult and dangerous times.

The opposition described in these verses comes from people whose teaching is dangerously close to that of the author and yet markedly different. It seems to be based on asceticism; marriage was rejected and so was the eating of certain foods. Paul had faced similar problems in Corinth, but his response, recommending celibacy as the ideal, was conditioned by his belief in the imminence of the end (e.g. 1 Cor 7:8–9, 25–31). The perspective of this writer is longer, he envisages a future for the church, so marriage and the procreation of children who will be brought up in the faith is important to him. Sexual asceticism would rob the church of the next generation of believers. The Pastor feels so strongly about his opponents that he claims that their teaching is inspired by demons (v. 1). His own monotheism is clear and, in contrast to such teachers as Marcion, he believes that 'everything God created is good'. Like Jesus when discussing

Jewish food laws (Mk 7:19), he believes all food may be eaten. This particular controversy may support the thesis that some, at any rate, of his opponents were Jewish.

(4:6–10) The rest of the chapter continues in the same tone; encouraging Timothy as a 'good servant' or 'deacon' to pass on to his fellow Christians the sound teaching he has received, while avoiding or rejecting the 'profane myths and old wives' tales' of the opposition. We are given little more information about the content of sound teaching or of its opposite. Presumably, both were well known to the recipients of the letter and did not need to be spelt out, but the false myths obviously play an important part in the opponents' teaching (cf. 1:4). *Eusebeia*, here translated 'godliness', appears again as the most important Christian virtue. It characterizes behaviour now and holds promise for the life to come.

In v. 9 the formula 'the saying is sure' is repeated (cf. 1:15; 3:1). Again, it is not clear whether it points back to what has gone before, or forwards, or whether it is meant to refer to the whole passage about holding fast to the faith and rejecting false teaching. v. 10 mentions hope again (cf. 1:1). As well as looking back to the historical events of Christ's life and death, attention was fixed on hope for the future (cf. 2 Cor 1:10). God's universal salvation here is more limited than in 2:6 'especially to those who believe', but there is no suggestion of an alternative fate for those who do not believe.

(4:11–16) Timothy is again addressed personally. Such personal references help to carry the fiction of Pauline authorship. He is instructed to teach, to exhort, and to read aloud: in other words, to pass on the tradition he has received from Paul, until Paul himself arrives (cf. 2:14–15). Teaching was one of the functions allocated to the *episkopos*: Timothy is not named as an *episkopos* anywhere in the Pastorals, but he is portrayed as carrying out some similar functions (in Ign. *Magn.* 3 the church is recommended to respect and obey their *episkopos* despite his youth). He is to set an example by his behaviour and deportment. He is gifted as a teacher, from the time he was commissioned by the laying on of hands by the council of elders (also referred to in 2 Tim 1:6). Laying on of hands was a means of transferring the power of the Spirit from one person to another for teaching or healing. It was a transference of authority, a commissioning or consecration to a particular office or task.

Further Matters of Church Order (5:1–6:2)

Like ch. 3, this passage concerns church organization. Here the subject is widows and elders. In Greek the word *presbuteros* is used to designate old age as well as being the title of an office in Judaism and Christianity. This can lead to ambiguity in interpretation; the natural reverence for the senior members of the group developed into hierarchical organization. For the modern reader it is not always easy to distinguish between the two uses of the term, particularly at the stage of development we see in the Pastorals when the original use is still found alongside its titular use. In vv. 1–2 the meaning is the original one, 'older men', as can be seen from the context. Later in the chapter instructions are given for *presbuteroi*, the leading 'elders' of the community.

(5:3–16) The instructions concerning widows are extremely detailed and precise compared with those relating to other groups (3:1–7, 8–13; 5:17–22). We have already seen that the position and activities of women were of particular concern to the Pastor. This group of women commands his special attention. It was regarded as a special duty among the Jews to care for widows who had no family to provide for them. This is the group referred to here as 'really widows'. Women who would otherwise be genuinely destitute deserved the community's support, whereas those who had families able to support them were not the financial responsibility of the community. The clear moral message of the author stands out in v. 8; failure to provide for widows in one's family was tantamount to a denial of the faith. Widows have a religious duty themselves: to offer prayers night and day (v. 5). But the widow 'who lives for pleasure' (v. 6) does not deserve the community's support. The reference to such women may be to highlight the plight of the 'real widow', or there may have been such a case within the community and known to the readers.

(5:9–16) It seems, however, as if 'real widow' may have a titular sense as well. The expression in v. 9, 'Let a widow be put on the list', suggests some sort of formal enrolment; perhaps, like the term 'elder', the word had acquired a technical sense. Those enrolled might consist of 'real widows' or be a separate group. In any case, qualifications for enrolment are strict and are reminiscent of those for bishops and deacons in ch. 3. The enrolled widow must be 60 years old or more, she must have been married only once, and she must have brought up children. If the widows of 5:3–5 are included in this group, they also have the religious duty to pray continuously for the community. In v. 11 the subject changes to younger widows, a group of women whose behaviour the author finds particularly unacceptable. His characterization of these young women, though it may have been based on his knowledge of one or two individuals, is a gross over-generalization, and one that has done women harm. His solution, as in 2:15, is marriage and childbearing.

(**5:17–22**) As a council, the group of elders exercised authority in the community (cf. 4:14; Titus 1:5, etc.). Here we find rules for their payment and their discipline. Some may have achieved their status as elders simply on account of their age, and a group of them, 'those who rule well', are worthy of double honour or double payment (the same word is used in Greek to denote payment and honour). Any ambiguity about the word here disappears in the light of v. 18 which contains the scriptural quotation also found in 1 Cor 9:9. There is further justification for the disciplinary procedures by an allusion to a catchphrase also quoted in Mt 10:10 and Lk 10:7.

The disciplining of elders is based on the Jewish system of public accusations supported by at least two witnesses; this has the double effect of ensuring that casual accusations are not made and that 'the rest' would be put off committing the same sin. The rest may refer to the whole community or just the other elders. Impartiality, a word used only here in the NT, is to be the basis of all judgements. Timothy is urged 'not to ordain anyone hastily'. This could imply that extra care taken about the appointment of elders would avoid the need for discipline later.

(**5:23–6:2**) Before turning to instructions for slaves, a personal instruction is given to Timothy about drinking wine. Ostensibly it is a personal note referring to Timothy's health, which helps support the impression of intimacy between the two. It may also be a roundabout way of attacking the asceticism of the writer's opponents (cf. 4:3–4). Church officials are to be neither drunkards nor ascetics. 5:24–5 contain general truths which may be meant to refer back to the elders of the previous verses, or, more generally, to members of the congregation.

(**6:1–2**) Slaves are given special instructions, though there are no corresponding instructions

for their masters as there are in other epistles (e. g. Col 3:22–4:1; Eph 6:5–9). The institution of slavery is not questioned here or elsewhere in the NT; it was seen as a necessary part of society. The only issue was how slaves should be treated by their owners, but the Pastoral Epistles are not concerned even with that issue. The slaves are divided into two groups, those who belong to non-believing masters and those whose masters are members of the community. Unquestioning obedience is demanded of the first group so that the name of the church should not fall into disrepute. Those who are slaves of Christian masters are advised not to presume on their shared beliefs, though they are all brothers and sisters, sons and daughters of one God. Nevertheless, the social constraints that exist in their everyday lives are not to be overstepped.

(**6:2b–21**) The apparently haphazard collection of teaching, unified by its hortatory character, links false teaching with bad conduct and identifies *eusebeia*, godliness or piety, with true wealth. As we have seen, piety in the Pastorals denotes the manner of life of a true believer who honours God as Creator and Redeemer of all, and who treats other human beings with respect (cf. 2:2; 4:7, 8; 5:4). It also separates sound teaching from false. False teachers believe that what they call piety is a source of mercenary gain, while 4:8 points to its real value. In vv. 3–10 piety is contrasted with all kinds of vices ranging from envy to morbid craving for controversy, from wrangling to a desire for wealth. Teaching about the vanity of riches here and in 6:17–19 frames a paragraph describing the true Christian life.

vv. 11–12 present the reverse image; the righteousness and piety of the person who shuns the attractions of wealth are contrasted with the behaviour described in vv. 3–10. The list of antisocial and untruthful behaviour in vv. 4–5 is balanced against the beliefs of one who pursues godliness, in language already familiar, Timothy is exhorted to pursue virtues which have been recommended before, and to fight the good fight. vv. 13–16 contain a doxology or liturgical formula similar to others in the Pastorals (see 1 TIM 2:5–6). It illustrates the ideas of salvation and hope with which the epistle began. God the Creator, whose glorious and transcendent nature is extolled in a series of rich images, will bring about the second manifestation of Christ at the right time. God's transcendence is thus balanced with his involvement in human history, in the two appearances of Christ, one past, one still to come. Jesus Christ is introduced, in his first manifestation, as an example of faithful testimony before Pilate. Although this does not fit neatly with any of our gospel accounts, that he supremely bore witness to the truth is undeniable for the Pastor. As with the other similar passages, the language is poetic and defies precise interpretation, but the rhetoric is clear: God is one, he desires the salvation of all believers through the mediation of his Son, Jesus Christ.

In the final injunction to Timothy the importance of handing on the tradition is repeated, for that is 'what has been entrusted' to him. 'What is falsely called knowledge' became part of the title of Irenaeus' late second-century refutation of Gnosticism.

2 Timothy

2 Timothy shares many of the concerns of 1 Timothy and Titus, and many of the same expressions, but there is a difference of tone. There are far more personal touches in this letter; people are mentioned by name, fellow-workers, friends, and relations as well as opponents. The relationship between Paul and Timothy is made to seem closer and less formal. There are more references, mostly indirect, to Paul's letters particularly to Romans.

Greeting and Warnings (1:1–18)

The opening greeting recalls that in 1 Timothy, but the call is by the will of God rather than by his command (cf. 1 Cor 1:1; 2 Cor 1:1; Col 1:1; Eph 1:1). Paul is said to be an apostle for the sake of the promise of life which is in Christ Jesus, which expands the idea of Christ Jesus, our hope, in 1 Timothy. 'In Christ' is an authentically Pauline expression, but there is no sense that the author has grasped the deep metaphysical meaning of life in Christ as understood by Paul himself. Timothy is called 'beloved' rather than 'loyal' or legitimate child here (see 1 TIM 1:1–2). Thus we already have a hint of the different tone of the letter; there is not so much concern about passing on the authentic tradition.

Paul's letters often open with a thanksgiving like this, but different Greek words are used here, perhaps because the Pauline word *euchar-isteō* which originally meant 'give thanks' had acquired special eucharistic connotations by the time this letter was written. The tension Paul himself clearly felt between his Jewish ancestry and his Christian faith is lacking here (1:3; cf. Rom 9–11). Timothy's own ancestry in the faith is exemplary: his grandmother Lois and his

mother Eunice were believers before him. Meanwhile, the closeness of the relationship between Paul and Timothy is emphasized by Paul's constant prayers for Timothy and by the emotional memory of tears and the anticipation of joy when they meet again. This, together with the naming of Timothy's mother and grandmother, provide the kind of personal details that add to the sense of authenticity. But the very fact that three generations of Christians within one family are mentioned implies a post-Pauline date; 3:15 makes it clear that Timothy had been brought up as a Christian from childhood.

From 1:6 it seems that Timothy received the laying on of hands from Paul himself rather than from the council of elders as was suggested by 1 Tim 4:14. They may refer to two separate occasions where authorization or commissioning was given for different purposes, or they may simply reflect the different tones in 1 and 2 Timothy, the latter being more personal, the former more formal and official. What is certain in both cases is that through the laying on of hands God's Spirit is passed from one to the other, whether from Paul the apostle or from the council of elders. The qualities imparted by the laying on of hands are both new and familiar in these epistles. Self-discipline translates one of the *sōphrosunē* words familiar from the other two epistles, and together with the spirit of power and love is contrasted with the spirit of cowardice. The idea of cowardice is linked with that of shame in the next paragraph, with the mention of Paul's imprisonment. The Pastor instructs Timothy not to be ashamed of bearing witness to the gospel or of Paul's imprisonment (cf. Rom 1:16). Philippians presents a clear account of his imprisonment and of its effects on Paul and his fellow Christians. Neither 1 Timothy nor Titus mentions it, but here it adds to the sense of authenticity. Paul has by now acquired the status of a hero, someone of whom his successors must not be ashamed; another indication of the late date of these letters.

The link between God's saving work in the past and the present sufferings of the apostle are continued in the kerygmatic passage that follows in 1:8–14. It is a summary of the theological doctrine of the kind the Pastor makes in 1 Timothy and Titus (cf. 1 Tim 2:5–6; 3:16; 6:13–16; 2 Tim 2:11–13; Titus 3:4–7). Like those passages, it depends on Pauline teaching, it uses some Pauline language, but is subtly and markedly different from Paul. For example, Paul rarely uses the verb 'to save' in the past tense (a notable exception being Rom 8:24, where it is in the context of future hope). The ideas expressed in v. 10 are based on the teaching in Romans 16:25-7, 'the proclamation of Jesus Christ according to the revelation of the mystery that was kept secret but is now disclosed'. The notion that God's plan of salvation was a mystery hidden from people for generations before the appearance of Christ was one that quickly took root. It created a historical schema which could link events and prophecies from Scripture not only with Christ's life and death, but into the present and up to his future reappearance. Although the idea has Pauline roots, it is expressed here in language typical of the Pastorals: Christ is described as Saviour, his appearance as *epiphaneia*, a word found in the NT only in the Pastorals (cf. 1 Tim 6:14; 2 Tim 4:1, 8; Titus 2:13) and in 2 Thess 2:8. Christ's death had the effect of abolishing death and through the gospel he brought life and immortality. The Greek word translated 'immortality' actually means 'incorruptibility', an associated but not identical idea. Immortality, translating a different Greek word, is said in 1 Tim 6:16 to belong of God alone. Paul himself talked of resurrection rather than immortality, so again we are presented with Pauline ideas presented in un-Pauline terms.

(1:11–14) We are brought into the present by the reference to Paul's appointment as apostle and teacher, both familiar terms, and herald, already used once in a similar way in 1 Tim 2:7 (elsewhere in the NT only in 2 Pet 2:5). In Greek the word is related to the verb 'to preach', and to 'proclamation'. This triple role has led to Paul's imprisonment, but Paul can remain steadfast because of his trust in God and his assurance of vindication. 'What has been entrusted to me' is a better translation of 1:12 and refers back to 1 Tim 6:20; with the help of Christ and the Holy Spirit, the sound teaching will continue uncorrupted. The line beginning with Christ, and passing to Paul, now continues through Timothy.

(1:15–18) Paul is presented in these verses as being held in a prison in Rome, where he was visited by the faithful Onesiphorus. The example of Paul's faithfulness and that of Onesiphorus (cf. also 4:19) is contrasted with the behaviour of those in Asia who have turned against Paul, including two individuals, Phygelus and Hermogenes. Nothing else is known about these two men, but the verb used for 'turn away' is found also in 4:4 and Titus 1:14

where it has a sense implying the rejection of true teaching, rather than personal rejection. (A man named Hermogenes the coppersmith is mentioned in the *Acts of Paul and Thecla*, 3:1, where he is a companion of Paul but a hypocrite and flatterer. Onesiphorus is also mentioned in the next paragraph.) Ephesus, where Timothy receives these letters, was the capital of the Roman province of Asia, the western part of modern Turkey.

Charge to Timothy (2:1–3:9)

(2:1–7) Timothy is urged to 'be strong in grace' following the example of Onesiphorus. Again he is presented as the link in the chain between Paul and the church at the time of the Pastorals. He has heard Paul's gospel directly and indirectly through the teaching of others. What has been entrusted to him, he is to pass on to those who will, in their turn, teach others. But the role of a faithful Christian is not simply belief and loyal transmitting of tradition, it entails suffering as well. This is a theme that is hardly touched upon in 1 Timothy and Titus, but is prominent in 2 Timothy. Three images are used to describe this wholehearted commitment to the gospel: a Christian must be like a soldier dedicated to serving his commanding officer, like an athlete winning a race according to the rules, or like a farmer toiling over his crops. The three images are not explained; Timothy is told to work out their meaning for himself, with the help of the Lord (v. 7), but the general sense is clear. Work is involved in all three images, they are familiar from Paul's epistles and other NT works, and are found in popular teaching of the time. The first two belong quite closely together, they involve willing obedience to a commanding officer or to the rules of competition. The farming image recalls 1 Cor 9:7–12.

(2:8–13) v. 8 recalls Rom 1:3–4 and 1 Cor 15:20. It represents a formulaic summary of the author's message. Jesus Christ, whose own suffering is not mentioned but is assumed behind this passage, was raised from the dead. The Son of David, he was human, even though of royal descent. In a few words much is implied to contradict the opponents' teaching. The preaching of this message had led to Paul being held in chains like a criminal in a Roman prison. But his enthusiasm for the spreading of the gospel was not diminished or held back by his imprisonment; this epistle is meant to provide proof of that. For the sake of the gospel, Paul is even willing to be held as a criminal, innocent though he is, so that those who believe, 'the elect', may obtain salvation and share in eternal glory along with him. Salvation and glory are familiar themes in the Pastorals, but glory is normally a property of God. The idea of sharing in his glory after death or after the end of the world is, however, a frequent image in Paul (Rom 8:21, 30, etc.)

A rhythmical passage follows (vv. 11–13), introduced by the formula 'the saying is sure' (cf. 1 Tim 1:15; 3:1; 4:9; Titus 3:8). It explains in poetic form the salvation that is in Christ Jesus, for his suffering and death are patterns for the suffering and death of his followers, and the results of his endurance will be shared with those who also suffer in his name. The parallel saying in v. 12b makes the same point but in the negative, while 2:13a emphasizes that Christ remains faithful to the purposes of God whatever human beings do. The ideas are based on Rom 6, but are developed further. It is impossible to know whether the Pastor included here, as possibly elsewhere (for refs. see 2 TIM 1:9–10), existing liturgical passages, but the emphasis on the need for faithfulness in suffering fits this context perfectly.

(2:14–26) From the encouragement to remain faithful, the passage turns to countering heterodoxy. The ultimate aim set out in 2:24–6 is to bring the heterodox back into the fold. Correction rather than expulsion is the theme here (cf. 1 Tim 1:20 where Hymenaeus and Alexander have been handed over to Satan). Repentance is in God's gift, he provides the only way that the heretics can be released from the power of the devil into whose snare they have fallen. We are reminded of 1 Tim 2:4 where God desires the salvation of all.

Before we reach this conciliatory point, however, we learn something of what the opponents were teaching. They liked above all to enter into disputes about words. The Greek word, logomachein, to dispute or wrangle about words, is found in related forms also in 1 Tim 6:4 and Titus 3:9. Clearly, acceptance of sound doctrine means not asking questions or questioning definitions. A clear exposition of accepted doctrine was the only proper method of teaching. Discussion could only lead to dispute, and so must be avoided. If the teacher is above reproach, then opponents have no grounds for raising questions. As is often the case in these epistles, good behaviour and sound doctrine go hand in hand. If, like those

in 2:4–6, Timothy works at expounding the truth clearly, literally 'cutting a straight path', then he will have nothing to feel ashamed of before God or people. Profane chatter was the subject of a warning in 1 Tim 6:20, as it is here. There it was coupled with 'what is falsely called knowledge', here it is said to lead to impiety and will spread like gangrene; a vivid medical image. Hymenaeus and Philetus are singled out. Like other named people in the letters we cannot be sure whether they were known to the community at the time of writing, if they were well-known historical figures, or if they are fictitious characters introduced to make the situation more vivid and realistic. The particular impiety of the two named heretics is the belief that the resurrection has already happened. This idea was already prevalent in Paul's lifetime and resulted from one possible interpretation of his own teaching (e.g. 1 Cor 15). It became a popular idea among some Gnostics and sometimes accounted for their dismissive attitude to the physical body. The teaching of Paul was regarded as authoritative by both Gnostics and anti-Gnostics in the second century. Both groups could interpret his teaching in ways which supported their own outlook. The Pastoral Epistles stand out firmly against 'knowledge falsely so-called' and became the basis for many later anti-Gnostic positions.

The building metaphor of vv. 20–2 is common in Christianity, and is found elsewhere in the Pastorals (1 Tim 3:15), where it is associated with the author's favourite metaphor, the household of God. Behind this passage lies Isa 28:16, quoted by Paul in Rom 9:33. From the same chapter of Romans comes the inspiration for the image of different utensils. But here it is not used in the same way as in Rom 9:21, which is about election, nor in the same way as the image of different parts of the body in 1 Cor 12. At first glance it seems to be a parable about important and less important vessels, along the same lines as the body metaphor, but some of the meaning has become lost in the retelling. The NRSV translation obscures the meaning further; the words translated 'special' and 'ordinary' mean 'honourable' and 'dishonourable' in Greek. From the context we can understand the passage to be an instruction to Timothy to cleanse himself of any teaching except that advocated already as sound doctrine, thus he and those he teaches will become useful, that is honourable, utensils. Again, orthodoxy is closely bound up with ethics. The list of qualities Timothy should cultivate, begun in v. 15

but then interrupted, continues in v. 22. His youth, mentioned in 1 Tim 4:12, is not to be an excuse for immature behaviour. The qualities mentioned in vv. 22–4, are already familiar from this letter and its companions; there is particular emphasis on avoiding quarrels and controversies which is the special interest of 2 Timothy, and it is worth noticing that the injunction to be an 'apt teacher' was used in 1 Tim 3:2 of the *episkopos*.

(3:1–9) The distress of the last days was a common theme in Judaism and early Christianity. Sinfulness and corruption of all sorts would prevail for a time, but it was believed that none of this was beyond God's control or outside his purpose. The gospels present us with a picture of cosmic terrors, such as earthquakes, famines, and eclipses (e.g. Mk 13:14–27). Like the commentary on Habakkuk by the Jews of Qumran (1QpHab), and like 1 John, 2 Timothy sees the distress in terms of human sin and apostasy. A long list of such vices is added which follows the conventions of its time, but many of the vices appear elsewhere in the Pastorals, either as characteristics to be avoided or whose opposites are recommended for Christian leaders. The list in Greek has a certain coherence, lost in translation, because of alliteration at the beginning or end of the adjectives, and because the first two and last two begin with the prefix *phil-*. That these vices belong to heterodox Christians becomes clear in v. 5. Timothy, and through him the whole congregation, are warned to keep out of such people's way.

The group of people thought to be most at risk from these apostates are women. The mocking diminutive is used, 'little women', translated by the NRSV as 'silly women'. It is not immediately obvious whether 'overwhelmed by their sins and swayed by all kinds of desires' refers to their disposition towards this sort of teaching or whether they are seen as particularly sinful women. Taken in conjunction with 1 Tim 2:11–14 (and 1 Cor 14:35), it is clear that there were women in the early church anxious to learn. In Acts there are several accounts of women being attracted to the words of an apostle's preaching. Stories told about Thecla (written down in the late second century as the *Acts of Paul and Thecla*), who renounced the prospect of marriage to follow Paul and devote her life to spreading the gospel, illustrate the kind of response from women that the Pastor deprecates. Thecla's vocation is justified in the stories by miraculous escapes from death; there

is no doubt that she is portrayed as having arrived 'at a knowledge of the truth'.

Jannes and Jambres were the names given in some Jewish traditions to the Egyptian magicians summoned by Pharaoh to oppose Moses and Aaron in Ex 7:8–13 etc. Just as Moses' opponents' success was short-lived, so those who opposed the work of God now, by insinuating themselves into households, would fail before long.

Paul as Exemplar (3:10–4:8)

Paul's own steadfast character and his heroism under persecution are set out as an example of true faith. This glowing description of his character, though framed in the first person, bespeaks hagiography not autobiography. He is the model for Christians in times of persecution. The three cities, Antioch, Iconium, and Lystra, where the persecutions took place, are mentioned in Acts 13 and 14 as places where Paul and Barnabas were persecuted by the Jews, jealous of their success. Paul has not yet encountered Timothy at this point in the Acts narrative. It is probable that 2 Timothy and Acts are using the same sources here, unless one depends on the other for information. The example of Paul's persecutions illustrates the possibility of persecution for believers. But just as Paul was saved many times, so would his followers be. The opponents are held up as contrasts to Paul's character (3:14). The situation described at the beginning of the chapter will go from bad to worse as more and more people are led astray. The same situation was foreseen in 1 Tim 4:1. A chain reaction will take place; after one person has been deceived into believing the opponents' falsehoods, he, in turn, will deceive others.

(3:14–17) As well as having the model of Paul before him, Timothy must continue to follow the teachings of the sacred writings, an expression used by Greek-speaking Jews to describe their bible. He has been taught Scripture from childhood; the reference is to his mother and grandmother (2 Tim 1:5), but he has also had teachers such as Paul. Scripture is rarely quoted in the Pastoral Epistles, and there is no description or explanation of the development of Christianity out of and away from Judaism. It is probable that opposition is coming, at any rate some of the time, from Jewish Christians, but apart from differences about myths, genealogies, and the law, we are not told much about where the differences lie. Here Scripture, presumably including the law, is given un-equivocal approval. If the NRSV translation of 3:16 is taken, the usefulness of all Scripture arises from the fact that it is divinely inspired. The alternative reading in the margin assumes that only those passages inspired by God are useful, i.e. it assumes that some parts are not so inspired. This was indeed the belief among some early Gnostic groups such as the Marcio-nites, so it makes most sense to follow the NRSV translation. It is the usefulness of Scrip-ture that is the significant point; different kinds of usefulness are immediately listed. v. 17, 'everyone who belongs to God' (cf. 1 Tim 6:11), probably refers to anyone in a position to teach or lead the congregation; such a person needs to be well versed in Scripture as well as in Christian doctrine. The result will be good works (as in 1 Tim 2:10).

Ch. 4 contains more intensely personal ma-terial than any other part of the Pastoral Epis-tles. The first section gives the impression, like 1:3–7 of being a personal 'testament'; the passing on of instructions from an important person to his followers is a literary form found elsewhere in the NT, but it also has a long scriptural tradition (e.g. Deut 31:24, Isa 8:16). Its content is kerygmatic, like other doctrinal passages in the Pastorals; this is the most solemn both in form and content. Judgement is mentioned for the first time, which adds a note of real serious-ness; in the presence of God the Saviour, Christ will judge the living and the dead. A picture of a God who had to approve one's behaviour oc-curs in 2:14–19, but without mentioning judge-ment. Here, in language reminiscent of 1 Cor 15:21–8 (cf. Acts 10:42; 1 Pet 4:5), judgement becomes explicit. But the favourite terminology of the Pastorals is not absent; Christ's appear-ing, or *epiphaneia*, referring to his second com-ing, recurs in 1 Tim 6:14; 2 Tim 4:8; and Titus 2:13 (and in 2 Tim 1:10 the same word refers to his incarnation), but 'kingdom' is mentioned only here and in 4:18. Timothy's role is to preach the gospel, in favourable and unfavour-able times, to make sure that the message is properly understood. 'The time is coming', has a sense of urgency about it, particularly as it seems to refer to events that are already begin-ning to take place (cf 3:1–9). Sound doctrine will be rejected in favour of false teaching, myths will be believed instead of the truth. The pre-diction by Paul of the events that are happening in the community addressed by the Pastorals gives the sense that present events are part of God's plan and Paul knew what was to happen.

In spite of suffering, Timothy must continue his good work, and not be put off by the apostasy of some members of the community.

Paul's death is imminent; in 2 Timothy it has been made clear that he is in prison: now, in poignant language reminiscent of Phil 2:17 (the only other use in the NT of the verb 'pour out as a libation', NRSV), Paul reveals that he is to be put to death. Looking back, Paul reviews his Christian ministry as a fight he has fought and as a race he has run, two familiar metaphors (1 Tim 6:12, cf. 1 Cor 9:25, 2 Tim 2:5; cf. Phil 2:16; 3:13–14). His life is a model to Timothy and to all believers, the reward that awaits him and others who follow him is sure; it is the garland given to victors in athletic competitions, understood by Paul to be the reward for a life of virtue, and so used also in the early church of the reward for martyrs (cf. *Mart. Pol.* 17.1; 19.2).

Personal Comments and Salutations (4:9–22)

(4:9–15) Many individuals; friends, fellow-workers, and companions of Paul are referred to, adding conviction to the pretence of Pauline authorship, and persuading some commenta-tors that at any rate fragments of the letters are genuine. Timothy must endeavour to visit Paul in prison, for, as he mentioned in 1:15, many others have left him. Only Luke remains (but cf. 4:21 where Paul seems to have several companions). Demas, whose name is found to-gether with Luke's and Mark's in Col 4:14 and Philem 24 has actually deserted him (Demas is also named in *Acts of Paul and Thecla*, as is Her-mogenes the coppersmith, cf. 2 Tim 1:15; this is possibly the same person as in 4:14. Both are said to be hypocrites). Crescens and Titus seem to have left but not deserted him. Tychicus is also mentioned in Titus 3:12 and in Acts 20:4; Col 4:7; Eph 6:21. The reference to the cloak, books, and parchment left behind at Troas adds a final touch of verisimilitude to the picture. Alexander, possibly the same person as the Alexander of 1 Tim 1:20, is mentioned as an enemy. He may be the Alexander of Acts 19:33 who was a Jewish silversmith, not a copper-smith. At any rate this Alexander was well known to the community as an opponent.

(4:16–18) It is difficult to identify Paul's 'first defence' (4:16) with anything we hear about in Acts or in the other epistles, apart possibly from that mentioned in Phil 1:7, 16. There it is the defence of the gospel that is referred to, here, it seems to be a more technical court appearance.

However, historical identification is neither possible nor necessary to understand the picture the author is presenting. Paul has survived one trial; the trial resulted in his desertion by his friends, but he was enabled to defend the gospel with God's help. 'All the Gentiles' probably refers to those at his trial, but may be a reference to his whole Gentile mission. That time he survived, the next time he will be saved for God's heavenly kingdom. He expects to die now, but his death will not be the end (cf. 4:8).

(4:19–21) The final greetings name some familiar and some unfamiliar people. Prisca and Aquila are mentioned in an almost identical way at the end of Romans (16:3, cf. 1 Cor 16:9 where they themselves send greetings). Onesiphorus is familiar from 1:16. Erastus was the name of the city treasurer of Corinth (Rom 16:23), and in Acts 19:22 Paul sends a man called Erastus with Timothy from Ephesus to Macedonia. Trophimus appeared in Acts 20:4; 21:29, as an inhabitant of Ephesus. None of Paul's current companions are mentioned elsewhere in the NT. Perhaps they were names familiar to the community. As a further personal touch Paul urges Timothy to travel before winter, because travel during that season was difficult and dangerous (cf. Titus 3:12).

The final blessing is modelled on those in Gal 6:18; Phil 4:23; and Philem 25.

Titus

Greetings and Instructions on Dealing with Deceivers (1:1–16)

(1:1–4) The opening greeting of Titus is longer and fuller than its counterparts in 1 and 2 Timothy and includes a summary of the gospel message. Paul is named again as the sender, but here he is called slave as well as apostle as in Rom 1:1. Faith and knowledge of the truth are said to accord with godliness or *eusebeia* (cf. 1 Tim 2:2, etc.). The idea of God's plan of salvation is clearly set out again, here strengthened by the assertion that God never lies. This is never explicitly said of God elsewhere in the NT but it is a thought underlying the notion of prophecy fulfilment throughout the NT. God's plan of salvation includes his promises in the past, and their fulfilment in the work of Christ, and in the work of those who proclaim the gospel, as well as the hope of eternal life. Both God and Christ are named as Saviour, because Christ carried out God's work of salvation on earth. The title 'Saviour' is used

frequently in the Pastoral Epistles; in Titus, for example, God and Christ are each described as Saviour three times. Two elements of the blessing are present in v. 4, rather than three as in 1 and 2 Timothy.

Titus, like Timothy in 1 Tim 1:2 is called 'my loyal child', in other words, legitimate successor. From Paul's own letters he is known to be a Greek whom Paul and Barnabas took to Jerusalem (Gal 2:1, 3) and who was associated with the Corinthian church (2 Cor 7:6–16; 8:6, 16–17, 23; 12:18). In 1 Tim 4:10, he is said to have been sent to Dalmatia. Like the setting of 1 and 2 Timothy, this setting is fictitious.

(1:5–9) The situation envisaged at the beginning of the epistle is that Paul has instigated a successful mission in Crete and it is now Titus' job to continue the work, 'putting it in order'. (Crete is mentioned elsewhere in the NT only in Acts 27, when Paul did not visit the island intentionally, but his ship was wrecked as it sailed past.) Putting things in order consisted first in appointing elders in every town (cf. Acts 14:23), which in turn would discourage opposition. Qualifications are given for elders here which resemble those given in 1 Tim 3 for bishops (*episkopoi*) and deacons. The use of the conjunction 'for' at the beginning of v. 7 heading the list of qualities necessary for an *episkopos* implies an overlap in their roles; perhaps, as in Jewish communities of the diaspora, the *episkopos* was drawn from the ranks of the elders. In 1 Tim (5:1, 17, 19) it is not clear that this was the case; there a council of elders with an *episkopos* at its head may have been envisaged. The *episkopos* is the steward of God's household, a favourite image of the church in the Pastorals (e.g. 1 Tim 3:4; 5:12, 15). Paul, who was fond of using metaphors of service and slavery to describe his own role, used it of himself once in 1 Cor 4:1. But there he is the steward of the mysteries of God. To the exemplary character of the *episkopos*, familiar from 1 Tim 3, is added the necessity of his having 'a firm grasp of the word', that is, a clear understanding of the Christian message. This will enable him not only to present the church's teaching clearly but also to refute those who contradict it.

(1:10–16) The character of those who contradict is then set out. That some of them are Jewish Christians now seems clear (v. 10). This fits with the impression given in 1 and 2 Timothy but not made explicit there. They are native Cretans, converted to Christianity from

Judaism and now apparently reverting in some way to their old faith and possibly advocating the circumcision of Gentile Christians. But as in 1 Tim 1:4 and 2 Tim 4:4, it is their teaching of Jewish myths that occupies the author's attention. Since we are given no further information, however, it is not possible to know whether these were Gnostic myths or more traditional scriptural myths. They also imposed Jewish commandments on their followers; perhaps food laws which the author did not accept (cf. 1 Tim 4:3–5), and which may be alluded to in 1:15. Ascetics, whether Jewish or not, who refused to eat certain foods were condemned in 1 Tim 4:4, for 'all things created by God are pure'. Here such people are condemned as having corrupt consciences; this is very strong condemnation for people whose understanding about purity is different from one's own. But it is the obverse of believing that sound faith leads to good behaviour. However, it contradicts Paul's teaching on such matters in Rom 14 and 1 Cor 8–10 where he is able to accommodate both points of view.

Membership of the Community (2:1–3:11)

The main section of Titus is reminiscent of 1 Timothy in that it describes the qualities of members of the community, interspersed with short doctrinal statements. Here the concern is not with the officers of the community, but with its ordinary members. It is introduced by the injunction to Titus to teach what is consistent with sound doctrine. This seems to entail good behaviour on the part of all members of the community. What follows resembles the lists of instructions about behaviour in other NT epistles (Col 3:18–22; Eph 5.22–33; 1 Pet 2:18–3:9), but here the grammatical form is different. Nevertheless, the list of qualities and duties required contains no surprises. Older men (not elders here; a related but not identical word is used) are encouraged to be temperate (cf. 1 Tim 6:11), serious (semnos, cf. 1 Tim 3:8, 11), and prudent (sōphrōn, cf. 1:8; 1 Tim 3:2). These are virtues that would be admired throughout the Hellenistic world but specifically Christian virtues follow; they are to be sound in faith, in love, and in endurance (cf. 1:9; 1 Tim 6:11; 2 Tim 3:10). A summary, in other words, of the qualities listed in ch. 1.

Older women have more detailed instructions: prohibitions as well as positive admonitions. This is a much more general group than the widows of 1 Tim 5. They are to be reverent, and like those in 1 Tim 3:11, they must not be slanderers or slaves to drink. They can be teachers, presumably of the younger women, certainly not of men (1 Tim 2:12), they taught the female Christian virtues and not matters of doctrine. These virtues are then listed. To the modern eye they encourage submissive attitudes; they are, however, typical of attitudes everywhere in the Graeco-Roman world (e.g. Plut. Mor. 140c, 142d). It is possible that the opponents of 'sound doctrine' taught that women could remain single and continue to lead a full Christian life, and like Thecla become an itinerant preacher (see 2 TIM 3:1–9). In any case, that kind of behaviour in no way conforms to the ideals of this author, who believes a woman's role is properly that of wife and mother, her salvation dependent on her fulfilling those roles submissively (cf. 1 Tim 2:9–15). The motivation given here, however, is to prevent the church being discredited. Nothing in the behaviour of the members of the community must attract negative comment from its neighbours.

Titus is urged to be a model for younger men in his behaviour and teaching. Here it is opponents not secular neighbours who must find no object for criticism in the behaviour of the young men. The Pastoral Epistles show no sense of their community being threatened by persecution in a serious way, but the author does not want to attract attention to the church by odd or antisocial behaviour. Paul had a similar concern about people in Corinth speaking in tongues (1 Cor 14:23–5).

Like women to their husbands, slaves are to be submissive to their masters. The teaching about slaves corresponds to contemporary thinking in every way. Just as attitudes to the position of women have changed beyond all recognition, so have attitudes towards the institution of slavery. But at the time the letter was written the institution was never really questioned, though there was discussion of the proper treatment of slaves, particularly among the Stoics (e.g. Seneca, 'On Master and Slave', Epistles, 47). In parallel household rules in other NT epistles, the behaviour of masters to slaves, husbands to wives, and fathers to children is introduced to balance the picture (Eph 6:1–9; Col 3:18–4:1; 1 Pet 2:18–3:7). The Pastoral Epistles enjoin no such commitments. The reason for the slaves' submissive and obedient attitude that the letter recommends is given in 2:10 in a way very typical of the Pastoral Epistles; they are to be 'an ornament to the doctrine of God our Saviour'. In other words, sound doctrine and ethics are inextricably linked even for slaves.

(2:11–15) contains a typical doctrinal statement, interrupted by ethical exhortations in v. 12, recalling other such passages in the other two epistles, but resembling most closely that in 2 Tim 1:9–12. The close relationship between the death of Christ and the removal of sin is here expressed more clearly than anywhere else in the three epistles and in a way that entirely conforms to Paul's own teaching. Typically for the Pastorals, the incarnation of Christ and his sacrifice are linked with the hope and expectation of his future coming. The Greek of 2:13 is ambiguous. The NRSV chooses to identify God our Saviour with Jesus Christ. Since he is nowhere else called God in the Pastoral Epistles—indeed his humanity is stressed in 1 Tim 2:5—the alternative translation, 'our great God and our Saviour Jesus Christ' is to be preferred. But, on the other hand, the immediate context of the verse with its imagery of royal epiphany might have encouraged the author to use the most exalted imagery of Christ at his parousia.

The grace of God has brought salvation to all; the soteriology of the Pastorals is almost always inclusive rather than exclusive (e.g. 1 Tim 2:4, 6). The qualities that grace enables us to learn have been mentioned before, and include words belonging to the piety (eusebeia) as well as restraint (sōphrosunē) groups. The connection between God's gracious act of salvation in Christ's coming and death with present Christian behaviour has never been expressed more clearly. The word used for redemption here is cognate with that used for ransom in 1 Tim 2:6; Christ's death is the price of redemption. The idea of purification of a people is not Pauline as ideas of ransom are, but is reminiscent of 1 Pet 2:9. The final injunction adds weight and authority to his teaching.

(3:1–2) The face the church presents is to be that of peaceful and helpful people, both in the public realm towards the government and also towards private individuals. The injunction to be subject to rulers is familiar from 1 Tim 2:2 and from Rom 13:1–7 (cf. also 1 Pet 2:13–17 where it is placed in a list of duties as it is here). 'Remind them', an expression also used in 2 Tim 2:14, seems to introduce a general instruction for the community as a whole rather than for a particular group.

(3:3–8a) The courtesy which is owed to those outside the church is explained by reference to the experience of each individual in the community before becoming Christian. Usually in the Pastorals lists like this provide a contrast between the behaviour of the opponents and that advocated for believers. Here, on the other hand, the list points up the contrast between the good moral behaviour of members of the community which arises out of sound doctrine and the same people's earlier moral turpitude. The two lists only partly correspond with one another; there are closer links with similar lists in Eph 2:2; 5:8; 1 Cor 6:11. So it is clear that lists of 'before and after' behaviour were becoming a commonplace of Christian preaching. The use of the metaphor of slavery to sin is familiar from Paul (e.g. Rom 6:6).

(3:4–8a) describes the means by which this change has come about for believers. This is the final summary of 'sound doctrine' in the epistles, signalled by 'the saying is sure' in v. 8. As always in the Pastorals, the soteriology is theocentric. God is Saviour, and salvation comes not as a reward for good deeds but from God's mercy. The incarnation, not Christ's death, is identified here as the turning-point in salvation history when God's goodness and loving kindness (philanthrōpia, lit. love for human beings) were revealed. The crucifixion is referred to only twice in the Pastorals, as the decisive soteriological moment, in 1 Tim 2:6 and Titus 2:14. The author prefers to balance the first and the future epiphanies to describe God's work of salvation; this passage can be paralleled with 2:11–14 where the future manifestation of Christ completes the process of salvation.

The decisive moment for individuals was baptism, here described as the water of rebirth and renewal; the moment when 'he saved us'. Justification by grace, a truly Pauline idea, is not explained, but like 'saved' in v. 5, the emphasis is on a past event, enabling believers to become 'heirs according to the hope of eternal life'. The process of salvation is not yet complete, but believers can feel certain of their part in it. Paul's understanding of justification is complex, but contrasts faith as the central element of salvation with works of the law. The Pastoral Epistles' emphasis, on the other hand, is on the close relationship between belief in sound doctrine and the good works which follow. The two ideas are not opposed to one another, but are distinctly different.

(3:8b–11) concerns relationships between Titus and members of the community who indulge in controversy and argument. Such behaviour is contrasted with the good works that profit the whole community. That the difficulties are caused by Jewish Christians is suggested by the fact that some of the debates concern the law. Genealogies are also mentioned as a focus of dispute as they were in 1 Tim 1:4. After two attempts at putting them straight, Titus is told to ignore such argumentative people; they are the cause of their own condemnation.

Personal Matters (3:12–16)

Personal details at the end of the book add a final touch of verisimilitude to the fictional situation. Paul hopes that Titus will come to him soon in Nicopolis, a city not mentioned elsewhere in the NT and probably to be understood as the city of Nicopolis in Epirus. Since the city does not appear in Acts and is not mentioned by Paul, any attempt to locate this letter at a particular point in Paul's life as we know it is impossible. Artemas is unknown to us. Tychi-cus was mentioned in 2 Tim 4:12 and the name appears elsewhere in the NT (Acts 20:4; Eph 6:21; Col 4:7). Zenas the lawyer is unknown but Apollos is known to us from both 1 Corinthians and Acts (1 Cor 1:12; 3:4–6, 22; 4:6; Acts 18:24; 19:1). Perhaps we are to envisage them as the bearers of the Epistle to Titus. They are to be well looked after and perhaps given financial support for their onward journey. Travel in winter was unadvisable, so Paul had decided to spend the winter in Nicopolis. A final injunction to good works precedes the final greeting.

REFERENCES

Beard, M., North, J. A., and Price, S.R.F. (1998), *Religions of Rome* (Cambridge: Cambridge University Press).

Miller, James D. (1997), *The Pastoral Letters as Composite Documents* (2 vols. Cambridge: Cambridge University Press).

14. Philemon

CRAIG S. WANSINK

INTRODUCTION

A. Paul's Imprisonment. The apostle Paul, according to 1 *Clem.* 5, 5–6, was 'in chains' seven times. In 2 Cor 11:23, Paul himself boasts of having experienced 'far more imprisonments' than his detractors. Ironically, the one who had formerly imprisoned Christians (cf. Acts 8:3; 22:4; 26:10) frequently found himself incarcerated. During one such experience, he wrote to Philemon and the church that was in his house. Only twenty-five verses long, Paul's letter is replete with rhetorical dissonance, subtlety, and wordplay. The epistle offers little insight into its provenance or dating. Whether it was written in Rome, Ephesus, Philippi, or elsewhere is not of primary concern. Whether it was written towards the end of Paul's life or towards the beginning of his mission is not revealed. Rather, the most salient aspects of the letter are Paul's rhetoric and his imprisonment (cf. vv. 10, 13, 22).

B. Onesimus. 1. Although the figure of Onesimus is not introduced until almost half-way through the letter (in v. 10), the interpretation of this figure has typically framed how the epistle has been approached. Onesimus generally is seen in one of three ways: (1) as a runaway slave (cf. Lohse 1971; R. P. Martin 1974; Caird 1976; Nordling 1991); (2) as an estranged slave, appealing to his owner's friend (*amicus domini*) (cf. Lampe 1985; Rapske 1991; Bartchy 1992); or (3) as a slave, sent by Philemon, to serve Paul in prison (cf. Knox 1959; Winter 1984; 1987; Wansink 1996).

2. The first two characterizations generally focus on vv. 11, 15, and 18, and, as discussed in the commentary below, tend to undervalue Greek wordplays, conventions of ancient slavery and, particularly, Paul's location (in prison). For a number of additional reasons, it seems unlikely that Onesimus either ran away or was estranged from his master: (1) If Onesimus had run away or faced estrangement, his owner probably would not have known where he was. Here, however, Philemon appears to have known that Onesimus was with Paul (Winter 1987). (2) It seems unreasonable to believe that Onesimus would run away from his master in order to escape *into* prison. Such a hypothesis seems to ignore Paul's imprisonment. (3) If Onesimus were estranged from Philemon and in need of reconciliation, his conversion to the

Christian faith—under such conditions—could well appear feigned and opportunistic. (4) Although Paul asks that Philemon support Onesimus, he does not request pity or forgiveness on behalf of Onesimus. Onesimus is not presented in any way as remorseful or repentant.

3. It appears that Onesimus neither ran away nor was estranged from his master. Writing from prison, Paul thanks the recipients of the epistle for their support. He sees his relationship with them as similar to that of 'partners'. And when he returns a person who had been with him in prison, he feels justified in asking that this person be received with respect and care. That is the situation in Paul's letter to the Philippians. That is also the situation in Philemon. In Philippians, Epaphroditus was messenger and minister to Paul's needs. He had been sent to Paul by the Philippians, he had served this prisoner on their behalf, and he then returned to his community. Onesimus, similarly, appears to have been sent by Philemon to serve Paul while he was in prison. During this service, however, something unique happened. Onesimus became a Christian and Paul had now found a new colleague in ministry. If the pagan slave Onesimus was sent by his owner to 'refresh' the imprisoned, if he was no runaway looking for quick redemption and forgiveness, generations of Christian interpreters have cheated Onesimus out of the integrity of his faith.

COMMENTARY

Prescript and Thanksgiving (1–7)

(1–3) Prescript The references in vv. 1 and 9 reflect Paul's first written use of the appellation 'prisoner of Christ Jesus' (cf. 2 Tim 1:8; Eph 3:1; 4:1; 3 Cor. 3.1). Some see this expression as reflecting only Paul's presence in prison. Others understand it metaphorically, in the light of triumphal marches (cf. Stuhlmacher 1981) or initiations into mystery cults (cf. Reitzenstein 1978). Most interpreters, however, see Paul's status as 'prisoner' as resulting either 'because of' or 'for the sake of' Christ Jesus (cf. PHILEM 9; PHILEM 23 offers an alternative interpretation). 'Philemon, our beloved *brother* and fellow worker' (NASB). Ironically, only one other individual in this letter is referred to as 'beloved': Onesimus (in v. 16). 'Co-worker': like the four persons mentioned in v. 24, Philemon is a fellow worker, apparently one who assists the imprisoned apostle. v. 2, 'Apphia': some commentators see her as Philemon's wife. Re-

gardless, she is a Christian (i.e. 'sister'). 'Archippus': the appellation 'fellow-soldier' (cf. Phil 2:25) does not necessarily refer to one who performs a specific task within the church. Because soldiers were well known for their loyalty, the title may represent a character attribute (for other martial imagery, see PHILEM 23). The admonitions to a certain Archippus in Col 4:17 led Knox to ask if Paul's admonitions in Philemon were directed primarily to Archippus (cf. Knox 1959). 'To the church in your house': the earliest Christians gathered and worshipped in private homes (cf. PHILEM 22). v. 3, salutation: 'Grace to you and peace'. To readers of Greek epistles, *charis* ('grace') would have sounded similar to the typical epistolary greeting *chairein* ('greetings'; cf. Jas 1:1). Paul thus uses wordplay in a way in which his greeting bears theological import. His use of the word 'peace', in the second part of this greeting, probably reflects the typical Hebrew and Aramaic salutation shalom (*šālôm*).

(4–7) Thanksgiving The thanksgiving establishes the major themes and expectations of the epistle. v. 4, although this letter is addressed to an entire house-church, the Greek makes clear that Paul's thanksgiving is now directed to one individual, presumably Philemon. v. 5, Paul acknowledges that he has heard of Philemon's 'love' and 'faith' towards Jesus and all 'the saints'. In v. 6 Paul expounds on this faith and in v. 7 the love. v. 6, 'I pray that the sharing of your faith may become effective when you perceive all the good that we [other ancient authorities read 'you'] may do for Christ'. The word for 'sharing'—*koinōnia*—is a technical term frequently associated with commerce in the Graeco-Roman world (cf. Sampley 1980). Cf. v. 17 where Paul more explicitly uses the language of commerce. Paul refers to 'the good' again in v. 14. v. 7, 'joy', a typical catchphrase of Pauline rhetoric in Philippians is frequently used during times of persecution. Paul notes his own joy and comfort in Philemon's love, 'because the hearts (*splagchna*) of the saints' had been 'refreshed' through Philemon. Here Paul sets the stage for the main concerns in the letter. Similar references reappear in v. 12, where Paul describes Onesimus as his *splagchna* and in v. 20 where Paul encourages Philemon to 'refresh my heart (*splagchna*) in Christ'. Note that around the year 110 CE, when the bishop Ignatius was being taken in chains to Rome, he wrote to the Ephesians, thanking them for 'refreshing' him through Crocus and others whom they had sent to be with him while he was a prisoner (cf. Ign. *Eph.* 2. 1–2) (cf. Wansink 1996).

Body: Paul's Request (8–20)

vv. 8–9, Paul opens his request by acknowledging that although he is 'bold enough' to command Philemon to do his duty, he would rather appeal to him 'on the basis of love' (cf. vv. 5, 7). Paul notes that he makes such an appeal as a '*presbutes*, and now also as a prisoner of Christ Jesus'. The Greek term *presbutes* has been translated both as 'old man' and as 'ambassador'. When the received text is emended (Lightfoot 1904) or when comparisons are made to 2 Cor 5:19b–20a and Eph 6:20 (cf. Stuhlmacher 1981), this word sometimes is translated as 'ambassador'. However, since Paul has just announced that he would not exploit his authority to give commands (v. 8), referring to himself now as an 'ambassador' would seem contradictory. Furthermore, recent lexical studies emphasize that 'old man' would be the most appropriate translation for this Greek term (cf. Gnilka 1982; Birdsall 1993). Paul, thus, is seeking empathy. He is old and, furthermore, he is in a situation inappropriate for a person of his age: he is a prisoner. These two epithets share at least one key characteristic: both the elderly and the imprisoned were seen as vulnerable and dependent upon others (Hock 1995). 'Prisoner of Christ Jesus': the point seems to be that prisoners were dependent on support from outsiders (cf. v. 13). At the same time, the constellation of military metaphors in this letter points to an even richer meaning for this appellation (cf. PHILEM 23). v. 10, 'Onesimus': literally 'useful' in Greek. In this first reference to Onesimus, Paul is not explicit about how these two came to be together. Apparently Philemon already knew. 'My child': in the Pauline and Deutero-Pauline literature, Onesimus, Titus (Titus 1:4), and Timothy (1 Cor 4:17; Phil 2:22; 1 Tim 1:2, 18; 2 Tim 1:2; 2:1) are the only specific individuals whom Paul refers to as his children. The language, thus, is quite intimate. As in 1 Cor 4:17 and Phil 2:22, here Paul uses the word 'child' in commending to the addressees the one whom Paul, himself, is sending. 'Whose father I have become': Onesimus was converted by the imprisoned apostle. v. 11, by postponing the word 'Onesimus' to the end of v. 10, the Greek highlights the wordplays in v. 11. Immediately we are told that Onesimus was formerly 'useless' (*achrestos*) but 'now is useful (*euchrestos*) both to you and to me'. In what respect was Onesimus 'useless' (*achrestos*)? It is difficult to

know if Paul is using this expression in a literal, figurative, or simply rhetorical sense. The reference to 'Onesimus' as having been 'useless' would have sounded ironic to the original readers of this letter. The wordplay is even more notable when we look at *achrestos* in the light of v. 10. Onesimus became a Christian while with Paul. Before Onesimus met Paul he was not a Christian. He was *achristos* (without Christ). In Koine Greek, *achristos* and *achrestos* were homophones. Thus, Paul is saying: Before Onesimus was a Christian, he was named Onesimus (or 'useful'). At that time, however, he was not truly useful, because he was *achrestos/achristos*. Now that he is a Christian, however, he is truly useful (cf. Winter 1987). As Philemon's messenger and minister to Paul, Onesimus would be useful to both persons. v. 12, 'I am sending him, that is, my own heart, back to you.' The Greek verb employed here is frequently used to refer to the return of messengers or envoys. 'My own heart' (cf. PHILEM 7, 20): the Greek word *splagchna*, translated as 'heart', is also a synonym for the Greek word *pais* (child) (cf. Artemidorus, *Oneirocritica*, 1. 44). v. 13, 'I wanted to keep him with me' (Paul wants Philemon to make his own choice; vv. 9, 14, 21), 'so that he might be of service to me in your place'. In prison, Paul would have been dependent on outsiders for food, clothing, the delivering of letters, etc. v. 14, 'I preferred to do nothing without your consent, in order that your good deed might be voluntary'. In v. 6, Paul prays that Philemon might effectively share his faith when he perceives 'all the good that we [the imprisoned?] may do for Christ'. Here Paul expects that Philemon—with free will and this knowledge—will use his goodness appropriately. v. 15, 'Perhaps this is the reason he was separated from you for a while'. Those interpreters who claim that Onesimus was a runaway slave tend to see this verse as Paul's euphemistic handling of a delicate situation (cf. Stöger 1971; Lohse 1971). The Greek word translated as 'separated', however, does not necessarily mean 'ran away'. Slaves were often separated from their owners, conducting business for them, delivering letters, helping others, or simply working where their labour was needed (cf. D. B. Martin 1990). What Paul directly acknowledges is that this separation has resulted in a change in Onesimus' status and how he is to be viewed. v. 16, 'no longer as a slave but more than a slave, a beloved brother'. Onesimus was converted in prison and just as Philemon is referred to as 'beloved' (v. 1), just as he is referred to as Paul's 'brother' (vv. 7, 20), so Onesimus here is referred to as a 'beloved brother'. vv. 17–18, 'If he has wronged you in any way, or owes you anything, charge that to my account.' The 'if' which begins this sentence makes the apodosis hypothetical (cf. C. J. Martin 1992). Onesimus did not necessarily wrong Philemon or owe him anything. At the same time, slavery in the Graeco-Roman world often resulted from personal bankruptcy or need. Under these conditions, individuals were slaves *because* they were in debt to their masters. Furthermore, even if a slave owed his master nothing, if that slave were to be freed, the owner would expect recompense: he would be reluctant to give away what he considered to be an investment. v. 19, 'I, Paul, am writing (*egrapsa*) this with my own hand'. The epistolary aorist functions like a signature on a typed letter (cf. Gal 6:11; Col 4:18; 1 Cor 16:21). Paul is serious about this request. 'I say nothing about your owing me even your own self'. Paul apparently was responsible not only for the conversion of Onesimus but also for that of Onesimus' owner. v. 20, 'Yes, brother, let me have this benefit from you in the Lord!' In v. 7, after Paul writes that the hearts of the saints had been refreshed through Philemon, he refers to him as 'brother'. Here, similarly, Paul refers to Philemon as 'brother', and asks that he benefit him by refreshing his heart in Christ. Just as Philemon refreshes 'the hearts of the saints', so he is to refresh Paul. The verse has, however, yet another implication. In v. 12, Paul refers to Onesimus as 'my heart'. Paul's reference to Onesimus in v. 20 hinges on the equation Paul makes in v. 7. Thus, when Paul writes 'let me have this benefit (*onaimēn*) from you in the Lord', the term *onaimēn* is not coincidental. In a letter inundated with wordplay, the similarities between *onaimēn* and Onesimus (*onēsimos*) would have been obvious to a Greek-speaking audience. Thus, Philemon here is called upon to refresh both Paul and Onesimus.

Final Prayer, Greetings, and Blessing (21–5)

vv. 21–2, Paul is confident about both Philemon's obedience and his own release from prison. Furthermore, he asks Philemon to prepare lodging for him. House-churches were not only for worship, Christian meetings, and moral instruction, but also for hosting travellers and guests. Just as Paul had prayed for Philemon (cf. PHILEM 4), so he asks that this community pray for him in his imprisonment. Paul employs the second person plural pronoun, clearly emphasizing his relationship with the entire community. v. 23, 'Fellow

prisoner'. The Greek *sunaichmalōtos* actually means 'fellow prisoner of war'. The term points to more than merely shared imprisonment. When Paul, by implication, refers to himself both as a 'soldier' (cf. PHILEM 2) and as a 'prisoner of war', the implication is that Paul's imprisonment followed naturally from his commitment to Christ Jesus. Like famed Roman soldiers, and like Socrates, Paul and Epaphras refused to desert their posts, regardless if it would lead to imprisonment or death (cf. Knox 1955; Wansink 1996). v. 24, Paul refers to the others with him as 'fellow workers' (cf. PHILEM 1). Of Mark, Aristarchus, Demas, and Luke, the latter figure has provoked the most interest. In 2 Tim 4:11, he is the last person to remain with the imprisoned apostle. In Col 4:14, he is called 'the beloved physician'. Because ancient sources see illness as a terrifying threat faced by the imprisoned, it is interesting to note that each of the references to Luke—the physician—appears only in epistles said to have been written from prison. v. 25, a traditional final greeting.

REFERENCES

Bartchy, S. S. (1992), 'Philemon, Epistle to', *ABD* v. 305–10.

Birdsall, J. N. (1993), ΠΡΕΣΒΥΤΗΣ 'in Philemon 9: A Study in Conjectural Emendation', *NTS* 39: 625–30.

Caird, G. B. (1976), *Paul's Letters from Prison* (Oxford: Oxford University Press).

Gnilka, J. (1982), *Der Philemonbrief* (Freiburg: Herder).

Hock, R. F. (1955), 'A Support for His Old Age: Paul's Plea on Behalf of Onesimus', in L. M. White and O. L. Yarbrough (eds.), *The Social World of the First Christians: Essays in Honor of Wayne A. Meeks* (Minneapolis: Fortress) 67–81.

Knox, J. (1955), 'Philemon', in G. A. Buttrick (ed.), *The Interpreter's Bible* (New York: Abingdon), xi. 555–73.

—— (1959), *Philemon Among the Letters of Paul: A New View of Its Place and Importance* (Nashville: Abingdon).

Lampe, P. (1985), 'Keine "Sklavenflucht" des Onesimus', *ZNW* 76: 135–7.

Lightfoot, J. B. (1904), *St Paul's Epistles to the Colossians and to Philemon* (London: Macmillan).

Lohse, E. (1971), *Colossians and Philemon*, trans. W. R. Poehlmann and R. J. Karris, Hermaneia (Philadelphia: Fortress).

Martin, C. J. (1992), 'The Rhetorical Function of Commercial Language in Paul's Letter to Philemon (Verse 18)', in D. F. Watson (ed.), *Persuasive Artistry: Studies in New Testament Rhetoric in Honor of*

George A. Kennedy, JSNTSup 50 (Sheffield: JSOT), 321–37.

Martin, D. B. (1990), *Slavery as Salvation: The Metaphor of Slavery in Pauline Christianity* (New Haven: Yale University Press).

Martin, R. P. (1974), *Colossians and Philemon*, NCB (London: Oliphants).

Nordling, J. G. (1991), 'Onesimus Fugitivus: A Defense of the Runaway Slave Hypothesis in Philemon', *JSNT* 41: 97–119.

Rapske, B. M. (1991), 'The Prisoner Paul in the Eyes of Onesimus', *NTS* 37: 187–203.

Reitzenstein, R. (1978), *Hellenistic Mystery-Religions: Their Basic Ideas and Significance*, trans. J. E. Steely (Pittsburgh: Pickwick).

Sampley, J. P. (1980), *Pauline Partnership in Christ: Christian Community and Commitment in Light of Roman Law* (Philadelphia: Fortress).

Stöger, A. (1971), *The Epistle to Philemon*, ed. J. L. McKenzie, trans. M. Dunne (New York: Herder & Herder).

Stuhlmacher, P. (1981), *Der Brief an Philemon*, EKKNT (Zürich: Benziger).

Wansink, C. S. (1996), *'Chained in Christ': The Experience and Rhetoric of Paul's Imprisonments*, JSNTSup (Sheffield: JSNT).

Winter, S. (1984), 'Methodological Observations on a New Interpretation of Paul's Letter to Philemon', *Union Seminary Quarterly Review*, 35: 3–12.

—— (1987), 'Paul's Letter to Philemon', *NTS* 33: 1–15.

Bibliographical Guide to New Testament Studies: the Pauline Epistles

3. Introduction to the Pauline Corpus

Ashton, J. (2000), *The Religion of Paul the Apostle* (New Haven: Yale University Press).

Beker, C. (1980), *Paul the Apostle: The Triumph of God in Life and Thought* (Philadelphia: Fortress).

Bruce, F. F. (1977), *Paul: Apostle of the Heart Set Free* (Grand Rapids: Eerdmans).

Donaldson, T. L. (1997), *Paul and the Gentiles: Remapping the Apostle's Convictional World* (Minneapolis: Fortress).

—— (2007), *Judaism and the Gentiles: Jewish Patterns of Universalism (to 135 CE)*, (Waco, TX: Baylor University Press).

Dunn, J. D. G. (1998), *The Theology of Paul the Apostle* (Grand Rapids: Eerdmans).

Engberg-Pedersen, T. (2000), *Paul and the Stoics* (Edinburgh: T. & T. Clark).

Hengel, M. (1991), *The pre-Christian Paul* (London: SCM).

Lüdemann, G. (1984), *Paul Apostle to the Gentiles: Studies in Chronology* (London: SCM).

Montefiore, C. (1914), *Judaism and St. Paul: Two Essays* (London: Max Goschen).

Murphy-O'Connor, J. (1996), *Paul: A Critical Life* (Oxford: Clarendon).

Riesner, R. (1998), *Paul's Early Period: Chronology, Mission, Strategy, Theology* (Grand Rapids: Eerdmans).

Sanders, E. P. (1977), *Paul and Palestinian Judaism: A Comparison of Patterns of Religion* (Philadelphia: Fortress).

Schweitzer, A. (1931), *The Mysticism of Paul the Apostle* (London: A. & C. Black).

Segal, A. F. (1990), *Paul the Convert: The Apostolate and Apostasy of Saul the Pharisee* (New Haven: Yale University Press).

4. Romans

Barrett, C. K. (1957), *A Commentary on the Epistle to the Romans*, BNTC (London: A. & C. Black).

Barth, K. (1933), *The Epistle to the Romans* (London: Oxford University Press).

Byrne, B. (1996), *Romans*, Sacra Pagina (Collegeville: Liturgical).

Cranfield, C. E. B. (1975–1979), *Romans*. ICC (2 vols.: Edinburgh: T. & T. Clark).

—— (1998), *On Romans and Other New Testament Essays* (Edinburgh: T. & T. Clark).

Donfried, K. P. (ed.) (1991), *The Romans Debate*, rev. edn. (Peabody: Hendrickson).

Dunn, J. D. G. (1988), *Romans*, WBC (2 vols.; Dallas: Word).

Fitzmyer, J. A. (1993), *Romans*, Anchor Bible (New York: Doubleday).

Hay, D. M., and Johnson, E. E., (eds.), (1995), *Pauline Theology, vol. 3 Romans* (Minneapolis: Fortress).

Moo, D. J. (1996), *The Epistle to the Romans*, NICNT (Grand Rapids: Eerdmans).

Sanday, W., and Headlam, A. C. (1902), *Romans*, ICC (Edinburgh: T. & T. Clark).

Stowers, S. K. (1994), *A Rereading of Romans* (New Haven: Yale University Press).

Wedderburn, A. J. M. (1988), *The Reason for Romans*, SNTW (Edinburgh: T. & T. Clark).

5. 1 Corinthians

Adams, E. and Horrell, D. G. (eds.) (2004), *Christianity at Corinth: The Quest for the Pauline Church*, (Louisville: Westminster John Knox Press).

Barrett, C. K. (1971), *A Commentary on the First Epistle to the Corinthians*, BNTC (London: A. & C. Black).

Chow, J. K. (1992), *Patronage and Power: A Study of Social Networks in Corinth*, JSNTSup 75 (Sheffield: JSOT).

Clark, A. D. (1993), *Secular and Christian Leadership in Corinth: A Socio-Historical and Exegetical Study of 1 Corinthians 1–6* (Leiden: Brill).

Collins, R. F. (1999), *First Corinthians*, Sacra Pagina (Collegeville: Liturgical).

Conzelmann, H. (1987), *1 Corinthians*, Hermeneia (Philadelphia: Fortress).

Fee, G. D. (1987), *The First Epistle to the Corinthians*, NICNT (Grand Rapids: Eerdmans).

Hurd, J. C. (1983), *The Origin of 1 Corinthians*, 2nd edn. (Macon, Ga.: Mercer).

Martin, D. B. (1995), *The Corinthian Body* (New Haven, Yale University Press).

Meggitt, J. J. (1998), *Paul, Poverty and Survival* (Edinburgh: T. & T. Clark).

Mitchell, M. M. (1991), *Paul and the Rhetoric of Reconciliation* (Tübingen: Mohr-Siebeck).

Murphy-O'Connor, J. (2009), *Keys to First Corinthians. Revisiting the Major Issues* (Oxford: Oxford University Press).

Theissen, G. (1982), *The Social Setting of Pauline Christianity: Essays on Corinth* (Philadelphia: Fortress).

Thiselton, A. C. (2000), *The First Epistle to the Corinthians*, NIGTC (Grand Rapids: Eerdmans).

Welborn, L. L. (2005), *Paul, the Fool of Christ. A Study of 1 Corinthians 1–4 in the Comic-Philosophic Tradition* (London: T. & T. Clark International).

Wire, A. (1990), *The Corinthian Women Prophets* (Minneapolis: Fortress).

6. 2 Corinthians

Barnett, P. (1997), *The Second Epistle to the Corinthians*, NICNT (Grand Rapids: Eerdmans).

Barrett, C. K. (1973), *A Commentary on the Second Epistle to the Corinthians*, BNTC (London: A. & C. Black).

Betz, H. D. (1985), *2 Corinthians 8 and 9: A Commentary on Two Administrative Letters of the Apostle Paul*, Hermeneia (Philadelphia: Fortress).

Crafton, J. A. (1991), *The Agency of the Apostle: A Dramatistic Analysis of Paul's Response to Conflict in 2 Corinthians*, JSNTSup 51 (Sheffield: JSOT).

Furnish V. P. (1988), *II Corinthians*, Anchor Bible (New York: Doubleday).

Georgi, D. (1986), *The Opponents of Paul in Second Corinthians* (Edinburgh: T. & T. Clark).

Lambrecht, J. (1999), *Second Corinthians*, Sacra Pagina (Collegeville: Liturgical).

McCant, V. W. (1999), *2 Corinthians* (Sheffield: Sheffield Academic Press).

Martin, R. P. (1986), *2 Corinthians*, WBC (Dallas: Word).

Murphy-O'Connor, J. (1991), *The Theology of the Second Letter to the Corinthians* (Cambridge: Cambridge University Press).

Sumney, J. L. (1991), *Identifying Paul's Opponents: The Question of Method in 2 Corinthians*, JSNTSup 40 (Sheffield: Sheffield Academic Press).

Thrall, M. E. (1994, 2000), *The Second Epistle to the Corinthians*, ICC (2 vols.; Edinburgh: T. & T. Clark).

7. Galatians

Barclay, J. M. G. (1988), *Obeying the Truth: A Study of Paul's Ethics in Galatians* (Edinburgh: T. & T. Clark).

Betz, H. D. (1979), *Galatians: A Commentary on Paul's Letter to the Churches in Galatia*, Hermeneia (Philadelphia: Fortress).

Bruce, F. F. (1982), *The Epistle to the Galatians*, NIGTC (Grand Rapids: Eerdmans).

Dunn, J. D. G. (1993), *The Epistle to the Galatians* (London: A. & C. Black).

—— (1993), *The Theology of Paul's Letter to the Galatians* (Cambridge: Cambridge University Press).

Hansen, G. (1989), *Abraham in Galations—Epistolary and Rhetorical Contexts*, JSNTSup 29 (Sheffield: Sheffield Academic Press).

Hays, R. B. (1983), *The Faith of Jesus Christ: An Investigation of the Narrative Substructure of Galatians 3: 1–4: II*, SBLDS 56 (Chico. Calif.: Scholars Press).

Kern, P. H. (1998), *Rhetoric and Galatians*, SNTSMS 101: (Cambridge: Cambridge University Press).

Longenecker, B. W. (1998), *The Triumph of Abraham's God. The Transformation of Identity in Galatians* (Edinburgh: T. & T. Clark).

Longenecker, R. N. (1990), *Galatians*, WBC (Dallas: Word).

Lührmann, D. (1992), *Galatians: A Continental Commentary* (Minneapolis: Fortress).

Martyn, J. L. (1997), *Galatians*, Anchor Bible (New York: Doubleday).

Matera, F. J. (1992), *Galatians*, Sacra Pagina (Collegeville: Liturgical).

8. Ephesians

Barth, M. (1974), *Ephesians*, Anchor Bible (2 vols; New York: Doubleday).

Best, E. (1998), *Ephesians*, ICC (Edinburgh: T. & T. Clark).

Goodspeed, E. J. (1933), *The Meaning of Ephesians* (Chicago: University of Chicago Press).

Kirby, J. C. (1968), *Ephesians, Baptism and Pentecost* (Montreal: McGill University Press).

Koester, H. (ed.) (1995), *Ephesos—Metropolis of Asia* (Valley Forge, Pa.: TPI).

Lincoln, A. T. (1990), *Ephesians*, WBC (Dallas: Word).

—— and Wedderburn, A. J. M. (1993), *The Theology of the Later Pauline Letters* (Cambridge: Cambridge University Press).

Mitton, C. L. (1951), *The Epistle to the Ephesians* (Oxford: Clarendon).

Muddiman, J. (2001), *The Epistle to the Ephesians*, CNTC (London & New York: Continuum).

O'Brien, P. T. (1999), *The Letter to the Ephesians*, PNTC (Grand Rapids: Eerdmans).

Schnackenberg, R. (1991), *The Epistle to the Ephesians* (Edinburgh: T. & T. Clark).

van Roon, A. (1974), *The Authenticity of Ephesians*, NovTSup 39 (Leiden: Brill).

9. Philippians

Beare, F. W. (1973), *The Epistle to the Philippians*, 3rd edn. (London: A. & C. Black).

Bockmuehl, M. (1998), *The Epistle to the Philippians* (London: A. & C. Black).

Boomquist, L. G. (1993), *The Function of Suffering in Philippians*, JSNTSup 78 (Sheffield: JSOT).

Fee, G. D. (1995), *The Epistle of Paul to the Philippians*, NICNT (Grand Rapids: Eerdmans).

Hawthorne, G. F. (1983), *Philippians*, WBC (Dallas: Word).

Martin, R. P. (1983), *Carmen Christi: Philippians 2:5–11 in Recent Interpretation and in the Setting of Early Christian Worship*, 2nd edn. (Grand Rapids: Eerdmans).

—— and Dodd, B. J. (eds.) (1998), *Where Christology Began: Essays on Philippians* 2 (Philadelphia: Westminster/John Knox).

O'Brien, P. T. (1991), *Philippians*, NIGTC (Grand Rapids: Eerdmans).

Peterlin, D. (1995), *Paul's Letter to the Philippians in the Light of Disunity in the Church*, NovTSup 79 (Leiden: Brill).

10. Colossians

Arnold, C. E. (1996), *The Colossian Syncretism* (Grand Rapids: Baker).

Barth, M., and Blanke, H. (1994), *Colossians*, Anchor Bible (New York: Doubleday).

DeMaris, R. E. (1994), *The Colossian Controversy*, JSNTSup 96 (Sheffield: Sheffield Academic Press).

Dunn, J. D. G. (1996), *The Epistles to the Colossians and to Philemon*, NIGTC (Grand Rapids: Eerdmans).

Francis, F. O., and Meeks, W. A. (eds.), *Conflict at Colassae*, SBLSBS 4 (Missoula: Scholar's Press).

Lohse, E. (1971), *Colossians and Philemon*, Hermeneia (Philadelphia: Fortress).

MacDonald, M. Y. (2000), *Colossians and Ephesians*, Sacra Pagina (Collegeville: Liturgical).

Martin, T. W. (1996), *By Philosophy and Empty Deceit, Colossians as Response to a Cynic Critique*, JSNTSup 118 (Sheffield: Sheffield Academic Press).

Muddiman, J. (2001), *A Commentary on the Epistle to the Ephesians*, Black's NT Commentaries (London/New York: Continuum).

Murphy-O'Connor, J. (2007), 'Greeters in Col 4:10–14 and Phm 23–4', *Revue Biblique*, 114 (2007) 416–26.

O'Brien, P. T. (1982), *Colossians and Philemon*, WBC (Dallas: Word).

Porkorný, P. (1991), *Colossians, A Commentary* (Pcabody, Mass.: Hendrickson).

11. 1 Thessalonians

Best, E. (1972), *The First and Second Epistles to the Thessalonians* (London: A. & C. Black).

Bruce, F. F. (1982), *1 and 2 Thessalonians*, WBC (Dallas: Word).

Collins, R. F. (1984), *Studies on the First Letter to the Thessalonians*. BETL 66 (Leuven: Peeters).

—— (1990), *The Thessalonian Correspondence* (Leuven: Leuven University Press).

Donfried, K. P., and Beutler, J. (2000), *The Thessalonians Debate: Methodological Discord or Methodological Synthesis?* (Grand Rapids: Eerdmans).

Jewett, R. (1986), *The Thessalonian Correspondence: Pauline Rhetoric and Millenarian Piety* (Philadelphia: Fortress).

Malherbe, A. J. (1987), *Paul and the Thessalonians: The Philosophic Tradition of Pastoral Care* (Philadelphia: Fortress).

—— (2000), *The Letters to the Thessalonians*, Anchor Bible (New York: Doubleday).

Richards, E. J. (1995), *First and Second Thessalonians*, Sacra Pagina (Collegeville: Liturgical).

Smith, A. (1995), *Comfort One Another: Reconstructing the Rhetoric and Audience of 1 Thessalonians* (Louisville: Westminster/John Knox).

Wanamaker, C. A. (1990), *The Epistles to the Thessalonians*, NIGTC (Grand Rapids: Eerdmans).

12. 2 Thessalonians

Giblin, C. H. (1967), *The Threat to the Faith. An Exegetical and Theological Re-Examination of 2 Thessalonians*. AnBib 31 (Rome: PBI).

Holland, G. S. (1988), *The Tradition that You Received from Us: 2 Thessalonians in the Pauline Tradition*, HUT (Tübingen: Mohr Siebeck).

Hughes, F. W. (1989), *Early Christian Rhetoric and 2 Thessalonians*, JSNTSup 30 (Sheffield: JSOT).

Meade, D. G. (1986), *Pseudonymity and Canon: An Investigation into the Relationship of Authorship and Authority in Jewish and Early Christian Tradition*, WUNT 39. (Tübingen: Mohr Siebeck)

13. Pastoral Epistles

Dibelius, M., and Conzelmann, H. (1972), *The Pastoral Epistles*, Hermeneia (Philadelphia: Fortress).

Donalson, L. R. (1986), *Pseudepigraphy and Ethical Argument in the Pastoral Epistles* (Tübingen: Mohr-Siebeck).

Harrison, P. N. (1921), *The Problem of the Pastoral Epistle* (Oxford: Oxford University Press).

Kelly, J. N. D. (1960), *The Pastoral Epistles* (London: A. & C. Black).

MacDonald, D. R. (1983), *The Legend of the Apostle: The Battle for Paul in Story and Canon* (Philadelphia: Fortress).

Marshall, I. H. (1998), *The Pastoral Epistles*, ICC (Edinburgh: T. & T. Clark).

Miller, J. D. (1997), *The Pastoral Letters as Composite Documents* (Cambridge: Cambridge University Press).

Mounce, W. D. (1999), *The Pastoral Epistles*, WBC (Dallas: Word).

Quinn, J. D. (1990), *Titus*, Anchor Bible (New York: Doubleday).

—— and Wacker, W. C. (2000), *The First and Second Letters to Timothy*, Eerdmans Critical Commentary (Grand Rapids: Eerdmans).

Young, F. (1994), *The Theology of the Pastoral Letters* (Cambridge: Cambridge University Press).

14. Philemon

Barth, M., and Blanke, H. (2000), *The Letter to Philemon*, Eerdmans Critical Commentary (Grand Rapids: Eerdmans).

Burthchaell, J. T. (1973), *Philemon's Problem* (Chicago: ACTA Foundation).

Fitzmyer, J. A. (2001), *The Letter to Philemon*, Anchor Bible (New York: Doubleday).

Martin, D. B. (1990), *Slavery as Salvation: The Metaphor of Slavery in Pauline Christianity* (New Haven: Yale University Press).

Petersen, N. R. (1985), *Rediscovering Paul: Philemon and the Sociology of Paul's Narrative World* (Philadelphia: Fortress).

Sampley, J. P. (1980), *Pauline Partnership in Christ: Christian Community and Commitment in Light of Roman Law* (Philadelphia: Fortress).

Wansink, C. S. (1996), *'Chained in Christ': The Experience and Rhetoric of Paul's Imprisonments*, JSNTSup 130 (Sheffield: JSOT).

Index

Aasgaard, R. 228
Abba (Father) 77/163
Abraham
    ancestor of Jews and Gentiles 70
    children chosen by God 59, 112
    faith in God 118, 161
    God's promises to 64, 161
Achaia 40–2, 44, 92, 124, 128, 139,
        140, 149, 221
Acts of the Apostles
    historical reliability 41
    life of Paul 29, 30, 245
Acts of Paul and Thecla 245, 250, 256,
        258, 259
Adam
    archetypal human, Romans
        (book) 56
    Pastoral Epistles 179
    pride in Philippians 144
    2 Thessalonians 235
adoption by God 119–20, 173
adultery
    law of God 73
    1 Thessalonians 216
afflictions
    physical suffering 95
afterlife
    see also resurrection
    1 Corinthians 91
Alexander (and Hymenaeus) 247,
        249, 257
allegory
    Hagar and Sarah 165
angels
    promulgating the law 162
anger
    of God 183–4
Antioch
    church at 152, 157, 158
    Paul 39, 121, 157–8, 258
Antiochus III (the Great) (king of Syria)
    history of Colossae 204
Antiochus IV Epiphanes (king of
        Syria) 240
    2 Thessalonians 235
apocalyptic literature
    language of 147
Apocrypha
    Protestant 6
Apollos 92, 95, 98, 99, 100, 124, 263
apostasy
    2 Thessalonians 136, 154, 240,
        258, 259
apostles
    effectiveness 205
apostolic authority 49, 63, 64, 88,
        127, 136, 140, 145, 149

Apostolic Council 157, 158
Apphia 264
Aquila (and Priscilla) 59
Arabia, Paul 156, 165
Aramaic
    early Christian Church 17
    New Testament 7, 11, 17, 21
Archippus 206, 207, 215, 264
Aretas, king of Arabia 39
Aristarchus 214, 266
armour of God 186–8
Artemas 263
asceticism
    Colossians 210, 211
    1 Corinthians 104
    Pastoral Epistles 252, 254
Athens 190, 225
atonement
    Paul's theology 32
Aune, David E. 46, 47

baptism
    on behalf of the dead 121
    Colossians 130, 170
    dying with Christ 50, 211
    idealistic origin 12
    into Moses 112
    significance of 123
Barnabas 30, 40, 158, 260
    cousin of Mark 214
    meeting with Jerusalem
        leaders 157
    Paul and 41, 157
    persecution by Jews 258
Baur, F. C. 59, 223
belief
    in God 69, 70–1
    in Jesus Christ 25, 34, 69
    resurrection of Christ 121, 230
believers
    free from the law of sin 76
    law of the Spirit 76–9
    power not to sin 72
benediction
    Romans (book) 88
Beroea 225
Betz, Hans Dieter 48
bishops 19, 191, 245, 252, 260
Black Sea 152
blessing
    Ephesians (book) 173–4
boasting 49, 69, 71, 94, 96, 98, 111,
        118, 127, 129, 137, 140, 143, 145,
        146, 147, 169, 170, 176, 178,
        194, 222
body 76–7
    Christian identity 121

as cosmos metaphor 117
    imagery 134
    physical suffering 102, 129, 147
    resurrection 121–4
    as temple of the Holy Spirit 99
Bruce, F. F. 41, 42, 170, 188, 190, 206,
        215, 237

Cabirus 217, 221, 227
Caligula 240
canon 4–5
    biblical criticism 4
    letters of Paul 6
Carpus 245
Cassander 217
Castor and Pollux 229
celibacy
    Paul 104, 252
Cephas *see* Peter
charisma, Paul 27, 94, 181
children
    household rules in
        Ephesians 185–6
    Paul 70, 73, 148, 162, 193, 199,
        265
    of promise 80
Christ *see* Jesus; Messiah
Christ hymn 87
Christianity
    see also church
    authority of the emperor 248
    contrasted with Judaism 155
    Cretan 260
    early texts 228
    eschatology 229
    exhortations by Paul 88, 184
    Gentile converts 189
    household rules 185–6
    Jewish 38, 59, 60, 79, 95, 125
    laws 62
    Lord's supper 116
    model for conduct in
        Ephesians 184
    new humanity in Ephesians
        176–8
    origins, Paul 27
    persecution 34, 38, 146, 258
    slaves 213
    unity 85, 86, 90, 181
    worship 120
Christology
    Colossians 171
    Messiahship of Jesus 155
    non-Jewish influences 198
    Philippians 190
    2 Thessalonians 117
Chrysostom 36, 196, 197, 222, 227

church
  apostolic talent 144
  belongs to God 99
  body of Christ 116–18, 205, 212,
      245
  characteristics 29
  Corinthian 29–30, 91–3, 94–5,
      108, 115, 133, 140, 145
  early developments 16
  Ephesians 170, 175, 179, 185
  Galatia 151
  groupings 16
  itinerant-settled shift 18
  Jewish origins 16
  leadership 100
  obscurity 18
  organization in Pastoral
      Epistles 245, 246, 249 ff.
  rural setting 17
  time span 17
  urban setting 17, 18
Cicero 45
circumcision
  Ephesians 177
  Galatians 177
  for Gentile proselytes 37, 41
  Jewish identity 16, 106, 159
  participation in covenant 61
  Philippians 200
civil authority, Romans (book)
      85
Clement (of Rome) 53, 189
collection for the saints
  commitment of Corinth 141
  Paul 124, 128, 148
  Paul's visit to Jerusalem 39
Colossae 204
Colossians (book) 7, 42, 46, 49, 99,
      130, 170, 171, 188, 264, 205,
      206, 207, 208, 209, 210, 211,
      212, 213, 214, 215, 216, 266,
      270
commentary
  critical 1
  reasons for using 1
  use of The Oxford Bible
      Commentary 6
community
  benefits from prophecy 119
  ethic 87
  honour 140
  instructions in Pastoral
      Epistles 261–3
confession
  triadic structure 181
consolation
  Paul 128
consolation-affliction
      antithesis 128
conversion
  attained through prophecy 120
  Colossians 207

non-believers 105
Saul (Paul) on road to
      Damascus 31
Coptic Church 4
Corinth 11
  church 11, 71, 77, 85, 90, 91, 92, 93,
      94, 97, 98, 99, 100, 101, 102,
      103, 104, 106–8, 109, 110, 111,
      114–116, 118, 119, 121, 124, 128,
      140
  Paul 48, 235
1 Corinthians 42, 91–125
  authorship 67
2 Corinthians 42, 126–150
  authenticity 126
  collection for the Saints 140, 148
covenant
  Abraham 70, 161
  Judaism 72
  Lord's Supper 102
  new 116
  Paul and the Corinthians 132
covetousness 66
creation
  being saved through Christ 77
  new 135
creeds
  Christian 174
Crescens 259
Crete 245, 260
criticism 1–3
  see also source criticism
Crocus 264
cross
  message of the 95, 97, 98, 118
  suffering and sacrifice 71
crucifixion
  attitudes towards 95
  Pastoral Epistles 1
cults
  Eleusis 242
  imperial 194
  Thessalonica 192, 202
Cynics 15, 222

Damascus
  Paul 31, 34, 38
dead
  baptism on behalf of the 121
death
  see also afterlife; dead
  Colossians 210
  God's power over 123
Deissmann, Adolf 45
deities, Greek and Roman 108
Demas 214, 259, 266
demon
  believers' relationships with 113
Denzili 204
diakonos 146, 251
diaspora 12, 32, 36, 37, 67, 99, 103,
      125, 128, 149, 158, 260

Greek language 12
Jewish communities 36
Rome 57
diatribe 67
Didache 147
Dionysus 221
Dioscuri 228
disciples
  see also apostles
  Christ as model 195–200
  Philippiaus 189–199
disobedience
  2 Corinthians 148–9
divine consolation 137
divorce
  Paul 104–107.
Dunn, James D.G. 29

ecstatic experiences 128
Eden 242
education
  Paul 37
elders
  instructions in Pastoral
      Epistles 253
election
  God's chosen children 80–1
Eleusis 242
end of the world
  see also eschatology
  2 Thessalonians 236–7
Epaphras 188, 204, 205, 206, 207,
      214
Epaphroditus 194, 202, 207, 264
Ephesians (book) 170–188
  authorship 125
  exhortation 180 ff.
  great prayer and
      meditation 173 ff.
  relationship to Colossians 170
Ephesus 170, 247, 260
  history of Colossae 204
  Pauls 189
  Timothy 247
Epictetus 246
Epicureanism
  Philippians 194
  1 Thessalonians 229
Epiphanes see Antiochus IV
Epirus 263
episkopos (bishop) 19, 251, 252, 253,
      258, 260
epistolography 216
equality, Jew and Gentile 59, 73
Erastus 93, 108, 260
eschatology
  Colossians 205, 211
  Ephesians 171
  Gentile inclusion 83
  marriage 107
  Messiah 34, 58
  realized 61

resurrection 124
Romans (book) 72, 84, 86
spiritual body 134
1 Thessalonians 229
2 Thessalonians 235
ethics
Pastoral Epistles 257
Ethiopic church
Old Testament canon 5
eucharist
see Last Supper
Euodia 202
Euphrates 204
evangelism
Ephesians 182
Paul 239, 87
Eve
deception by the serpent 144
Pastoral Epistles 250
2 Thessalonians 241
exaltation 87
exclusion
kingdom of God 177
excommunication, at Corinth 101
existence
the flesh and the spirit 101
limited nature of 134
pagan idols 109
Exodus (book)
Philippians 198
expulsion, Roman Jews 59, 92
external appearances, judging
by 135

faith
in Christianity 53
Ephesians 170, 269
Jesus as object of 22
in Judaism 34
nature of 65–66
revelation of 162
1 Thessalonians 220
2 Thessalonians 240
working through love 166
faithfulness
of the Lord 242
false believers 152, 157, 158
famine 41
fate, predestined by God 78
Father
Ephesians 180
2 Thessalonians 237
fathers
household rules in Ephesians 186
feminism
post-critical biblical study 3
final judgement
nakedness metaphor 134
finances
converts at Corinth 103
financial support, Paul 110, 124, 145,
168

flesh
contrasted with Spirit 168
weakness of the mortal body 74
food
corruption of the body 104
laws 59, 87
Lord's Supper 116
sacrificial 91, 92, 108–110, 113
Fool's Speech 144–148
forgiveness
Ephesians 183
of sins
Paul 52
form criticism 2
founding churches, Paul 42, 88
fragrance, presence of God 131
free will
omnipotence of God 80
sin 73
freedom, Christian liberty 103
Funk, R. 233
future
see also eschatology
2 Corinthians 134

Galatia
churches, relationship with
Paul 164
comparison with Colossae 206
Galatians (book) 28, 151–169
church characteristics 17
introduction and overview 151
justification by faith 51
letters from Paul 152
Paul's visits to Jerusalem 37, 40
position in chronology 41
style of content 3, 29, 205
Gallio 41
Gamaliel 37
Gaventa, Beverley 89
gender
see also women
hierarchy 115
Genesis
the fall 72
righteousness by faith 81
Gentiles
acceptance into Judaism 14, 27,
31, 35, 58, 64, 80, 260
children of Abraham 59, 70, 162,
166
circumcision 52, 59, 64, 67, 79,
105, 151, 157, 159, 166, 169, 177
compelled to live like Jews 159
equal membership 28
evangelism 44, 223, 236
God's justification of 161
idolatry 43, 66, 76, 103, 106, 113,
189, 212, 217, 226, 241
Jewish perspective in
Ephesians 172, 177
and Jews eating together 158

justification by faith 28, 31, 50, 51,
70, 71, 78, 104
new humanity in Ephesians 122,
172, 176, 183
offering of 58,
Paul 14, 20, 31, 35–38, 39, 59
Philippians 89
as sinners 159
1 Thessalonians 218, 223, 224,
227, 231, 240
Titus 138, 157, 207, 248
glory
for believers 97
earthly body 123
God 97, 115, 123, 131, 137, 192
Pastoral Epistles 121, 251, 257
suffering 71, 77, 178
1 Thessalonians 205
Gnosticism 255
Pastoral Epistles 257
Philippians 201
2 Thessalonians 236
God
see also YHWH
anger of 184
children of 254
covenants of 70, 161
the Father 179, 185
impartiality of 67
kingdom of see Kingdom of
God
knowledge of 123, 192
love of 183
mercy of 80
omnipotence 80
power of 104, 175
righteousness 59, 64–5, 68, 78,
83
salvation of 246
Saviour 247
sinners 71, 112
sovereignty of 20, 79
transcendence of 254
Trinity 178
godliness 245, 249
Goodspeed, Edgar 54
gospel
1 Corinthians 95
payment for preaching 111
proclamation of God's good
news 154
transcends human language 97
Gospel of John see John (Gospel)
Gospel of Luke see Luke (Gospel)
Gospel of Mark see Mark (Gospel)
Gospel of Matthew see Matthew
(Gospel)
gospels
see also John; Luke; Mark;
Matthew
authorship 49
inadequacies 10

gospels (*cont.*)
  Jesus' death and resurrection 24
  Jewish background 12
  purpose 11
grace
  Ephesians 171, 175, 178
  Philippians 191
  2 Thessalonians 237
Graeco-Roman greetings 47
Great Sanhedrin *see* Sanhedrin
Greek
  diaspora 12
  New Testament 7, 11
greetings, Graeco-Roman 46
guilt
  Paul's theology 50

H *see* Holiness Code
Habakkuk (book)
  righteousness by faith 65
Hagar 165
hands, laying on 253
harpagmos 196
Hausa 229
Hays. R. B. 59, 63
head coverings 115
heaven
  see also kingdom of God
  Philippians 207
Hebrew Bible (HB)
  Christian animosity 62
Hellenism
  Jewish Christians 38
  Jewish diaspora 36
  Judaism and 155
  New Testament 11, 15
heresy
  Pastoral Epistles 257
Hermogenes 256, 259
heterodoxy, Pastoral Epistles 257
Hierapolis 204, 214
hierarchy of heads 115
higher criticism *see* source criticism
historical criticism 1–3
holiness
  non-believers in a marriage 105
  Romans (book) 86
  1 Thessalonians 226
Holiness Code (H) 226
Holy Spirit
  being filled with the 185
  body as temple 99
  contrast with 'flesh' 167
  fruit 167
  Galatian churches 160
  quenching 232
  sword of the 187
  Thessalonian church 222, 228
  unity 181
honour
  community 140
  2 Thessalonians 238

hope
  Christ, Pastoral Epistles 247
  Ephesians 174
  Philippians 193
  1 Thessalonians 220–1, 225, 230
household, codes 185–6, 213, 246
hubris 196
human beings
  see men; women
humanity
  Ephesians 176–8, 183
humility
  Ephesians 181
  Paul 109
  Romans (book) 85
husbands
  Paul 251
Hymenaeus 247, 249, 257
hymns
  Christological 208
  Ephesians 185
  Essene 208
  Philippians 195

Iconium 41, 258
idleness, 2 Thessalonians 242
idolatry
  1 Corinthians 111–13
  Ephesians 184
  Paul 112
  Romans (book) 66
  sacrificial food 108–14
  sins of non-believers 66
  1 Thessalonians 217
  2 Thessalonians 241
Ignatius of Antioch 17, 19
Irenaeus 53, 255
Isaac
  birth of 165
Isaiah (prophet) 187
  Paul's misreading in Romans
    (book) 82–3
  1 Thessalonians 231
Isaian Servant 197
Isidore of Pelusium 196
Israel
  Ephesians 177
  Holiness Code 226
  ignorance of Christ 92
  Romans (book) 79–90
  wilderness wanderings 112
  YHWH and 155

Jambres 258
James (son of Zebedee) 156
James of Jerusalem 33, 158
Jannes 258
Jeremiah (prophet)
  metaphors in Ephesians 180
Jerusalem
  Apostolic Council
    deliberations 156

church in 40, 88
  Paul 30
Jesus (called Justus) 214
Jesus Christ
  see also Christ; Christology;
    disciples; Messiah
  apocalyptic discourse 13, 24
  baptism 86
  blood of 209
  body of 116, 186, 211
  church and 116, 186
  crucifixion 133, 163, 170
  death
    condemnation of sin 76
    meaning 52
  example of 195
  fulfillment of God's purpose 13,
    24, 82
  grace of 157
  Holy Spirit 157, 162
  imagery 212
  Israel 82
  Judaism 22
  leadership 22
  love 86
  new covenant 132
  New Testament and 20
  prayers 241
  reconciliation of God and
    humanity 71
  redemption by atonement 66
  rejection of 67–9
  resurrection 121–4
    I Corinthians 121–4
    Ephesians 172, 182
    Gospel accounts 22
    Paul's letters 22
  return of 226
  salvation through 231, 262
  sinners 247
  social role 22
  Son of God 11, 22, 25, 49, 63, 71,
    160, 196, 208
  sources of knowledge 20
  suffering
    on the cross 134
  Torah antithesis 33, 38, 50
  wisdom 112
Jewett, R. 220, 235
Jewish Christianity 79, 95, 125, 202
Jews
  advantage over Gentiles 79
  Antioch incident 163
  attitudes, Romans (book) 67
  authority of the Roman
    emperor 249
  church in Corinth 128
  circumcision issue 200
  Colossae 204
  and Gentiles eating
    together 158
  Gentilization 89

new humanity in
    Ephesians 176–183
Paul 128
1 Thessalonians 217
widows 253
Job (man)
    trust 193
Johannine Gospel see John
    (gospel)
John (apostle son of Zebedee)
    leader of the Jerusalem
        church 158
    Sanhedrin 193
1–3 John (Epistles) 16
John (Gospel)
    early Christian church 15
    origin of beliefs 12
joy
    Philippians 192, 202
Judaism
    see also diaspora; Jews; rabbinic
        Judaism
    before Christ 68
    Christianity contrast 155
    dietary laws 109
    early Christian church 193
    Gentiles, acceptance of 35
    God's salvation through
        Christ 51
    Hellenism 155, 203
    influence of Romans (book) 57
    law 57, 132
    monotheism 198
    New Testament 11
    Paul 31
    primary sources 60
    righteousness, Romans
        (book) 80
    sabbath 159, 164
    sacrifice 68
    sinners 67
    unbelief in Christ 58
Judea
    churches 156
    1 Thessalonians 224
judgement
    see also final judgement
    courts at Corinth 102
    worldly standards 136
justice
    divine
        mercy 83
justification by faith
    Christianity 31
    Judaism 70
    Paul 28, 50
justification by works
    Judaism 31, 50
    Moses 82
    Paul 67
    religious 'entry requirements' 61
Justus 214

kauchaomai 194
Kenotic theory 197
Kingdom of God
    excluded persons 103
    love 87
kipper see atonement
knowledge
    of God 123
    of pagan idols 192
    without love 118
Knox, John 41, 45
Kurios 197–8

language
    see also Aramaic; Greek
    biblical criticism 1
    of commerce 264
    Ephesians 173
    letters of Paul 29, 51
    New Testament 7
    Stoic 190
Laodicea 204–5, 214–15
Last Supper
    Christian rites 116
Latin culture, New Testament 11
law
    see also Torah
    Christ its fulfilment 82
    Colossians 211
    coming into existence 161
    curse of 158, 161
    Ephesians 171
    function of 162
    Pastoral Epistles 247
    performance of 49
    promulgated by angels 162
    sin and 72
    Stephen and the Hellenists 157
    works contrasted with faith 71
leadership
    1 Corinthians 98
    models of 98
    'super apostles' 144
    1 Thessalonians 232
letters
    Graeco-Roman 162
    of recommendation 131, 143
    types and styles 45
letters of Paul 27 ff.
    see also individual books
    biblical criticism 1–3
    early Christian church 16
    interpretation 28, 32, 51
    Jesus' death and resurrection
        22
    letters in Philippians 189
    literary content 27
    origin of beliefs 14
    pattern of thought 50
    rhetorical criticism 47
    style of content 48, 49
    theological content 49–53

used as chronology of his life 29,
    40
liberationism 4
liberty, Christian ethos 101
life
    means of attaining 72, 82
    models for in Ephesians 182
light
    Ephesians 184
    1 Thessalonians 221
literary criticism see source
    criticism
literature
    Bible as 1, 3
loafers 242
love
    brotherly 228
    Colossians 207, 212
    demands of 118
    divine 183
    Ephesians 182
    fulfilling the law 85
    of husband and wife 185
    Paul 118
    1 Thessalonians 220, 225
Lüdemann, Gerd 41, 42
Luke 266
    Paul 259
    Stephen and the Hellenists 155
    Stoic ideas 190
    1 Thessalonians 225
    writings of 152
Luke (Gospel)
    Septuagint 12
Luther, Martin 51
Lycus (river) 204
Lydia (person) 189, 202
Lystra 41, 152, 258

Macedonia 12, 30, 31, 32, 81, 91, 93,
    95–6, 101–10, 138, 159, 162,
    167, 179, 181, 190
    collection for the Saints 140
    Philippians 189
magic 258
Malina, B. J. 220
manual labour, Paul 110
Marcion 50, 53, 57, 62, 89, 245, 252,
    259
Mark 214
Mark (Gospel)
    inadequacies 10
marriage
    see also adultery; husbands;
        wives
    metaphor 144
    Paul 73, 104
Matthew (Gospel)
    Jewish background 12
men
    Paul 107
Menken, M. J. J. 235

mercy
  divine 83
  Pastoral Epistles 247
Messiah
  see also Christ; Jesus
  Ephesians 181
  false 240
  Jesus as 155
  Jewish expectations 34
  Jewish tradition 22
messiahship, Jesus Christ 155
metaphors
  agricultural 98
  architectural 133
  Christ and church in
    Epehesians 175
  Ephesians 10, 49, 54, 72, 130, 137,
    170–88, 206, 215, 237, 264
  Philemon (book) 42, 45–6, 53,
    189, 214, 263–7
millenium
  1 Thessalonians 3, 42, 216–34
  2 Thessalonians 49, 219, 223, 229,
    235–44
miracles
  of God 160,
missionaries
  Paul 19, 28, 110, 128
monotheism
  Ephesians 174, 181
  Judaism 108, 198
  Pastoral Epistles 252
  Paul 108, 198, 252
  1 Thessalonians 217
morality
  church at Corinth 102
  knowledge of God 62
  Romans (book) 62
Mosaic law
  Christian communities 212
  redefined 168
  requirements of 159
Moses
  comparison with Paul's
    ministry 132
  Ephesians 182
  justification by works 82
  as mediator 162
  at Sinai 79
Mount Sinat see Sinai
Murphy-O'Connor, Jerome 16, 37,
    39, 41, 42, 45, 114, 128, 131–7,
    139, 141, 144–8, 204–16
mystery, Paul and 178, 210
mystical theology, Paul 97

nakedness
  2 Corinthians 144
nativity of Jesus see Jesus Christ
Neapolis 189
New Testament
  see also gospels

background 11–15
  canon 4–5
  Christian church depicted
    in 15–20
  Greek language
  Jewish background 12, 25
  origin of writings 9
  piecemeal growth 9
  racial tension 179
  relationship with Old
    Testament 10
  role in Christian life 8, 19
  translations 2, 5, 8, 109, 149,
    158, 164, 166, 167, 170,
    238
  worship forms 19
Nicopolis 263
non-believers
  contact with 135–6
  marriage to 105
  speaking in tongues 119
Nympha 214

oaths
  New Testament 10
obedience
  of faith 63
  to parents 186
Octavian 36, 189
Odes
  of Solomon 198
offerings
  see sacrifice
Old Testament
  canon 4–5
  olive tree metaphor 84
omnipotence 80
Onesimus 46, 54, 206, 213–14,
    263–6
Onesiphorus 256, 260
oppression
  2 Thessalonians 238
oral tradition
  biblical criticism 3
  original sin 212
Orthodox canon 4
other-worldly journeys 147
oxen 112
Oxford Annotated Bible 5

paganism
  Colossians 204
  social issues 212
  1 Thessalonians 217
Palestine
  impact of Greek culture 11
parody
  2 Corinthians 144
parousia
  Pastoral Epistles 262
  1 Thessalonians 224, 229
  2 Thessalonians 235, 239

parrhēsia 193
particularistic religion 32, 35
Passover
  yeast 102
Pastoral Epistles 244–63
  authorship 244–6
  language of Paul's letters 255
  Timothy 247–60
  Titus 260–3
pastoral responsibility
  Paul 44
  Roman church 58
patience
  Ephesians 181
patriarchy 185
patronage 9, 93, 110, 111, 136, 140,
    143
Paul (apostle)
  see also letters of Paul
  Arabia 156
  authenticity of letters 214, 243
  authority
    1 Corinthians 91, 100–1, 115,
      121
    2 Corinthians 127, 131, 142
    Galatians (book) 153
    Pastoral Epistles 245
    Romans (book) 64, 88
    1 Thessalonians 222
  Barnabas 258
  boasting 129, 140, 143, 145, 194,
    222, 238
  brotherly love 228
  Colossians (book) 204
  conscience questions 109
  conversion 31–5, 130, 156
  Corinth 91, 97, 101, 124, 126, 147
  Crete 260
  cultural adaptability 111
  death of 193, 278
  as exemplar 278
  financial support 111
  Fool's Speech 143
  formative years 35–40
  Galatian churches 152, 163
  Gentiles 158, 184, 250
  hymns 208
  idolatry 112
  illness of 164
  imprisonment 177, 189, 192, 206,
    255, 263
  interdependence of men and
    women 115
  interpretation 28, 32, 51, 54
  Jesus
    commitment to 266
    slave of 154
    vision of 205
  Judaism 32, 61, 62, 155
  Judeans 224
  Laodiceans 214
  laying on of hands 255

leadership 98–100
literary legacy 27
Mosaic law 212
mystery 178
opposition 194, 252, 258
patronage 140, 143
persecution of church by 155
Peter at Antioch 158–60
Philemon 263
Philippian church 203
Praetorian contacts 203
prayers 174–5, 226
preaching 43
rhetoric 127, 263
sexual relations 101, 104
sinfulness 257–8
slavery 213
style of letters 45–9
suffering 128, 133, 137, 147, 210
tearful letter 127, 130
theology 29, 49, 50, 53, 58, 96
Thessalonica 221
tolerance 87
wealth 139
women's speech 120
Pax Romana 231
peace
  Colossians 212
  greeting in 2 Thessalonians 237
  1 Thessalonians 231
Pentateuch
  biblical criticism 2
Peter (apostle)
  as an apostle to the
    circumcised 159
  before the Sanhedrin 193
  Corinthian church 95
  death of 193
  eating with Gentiles 159
  Paul and 39, 159
Pharisees
  Paul 37
Philadelphia (brotherly love) 228
Philemon (book) 263–7
  Colossians 206
  position in chronology 42
  writing style 45
Philetus 249, 257
Philip II (king of Macedon) 189
Philippi 222
  background in Phillippians
    189
Philippians (book) 189–204
  appeal for unity 193
  authorship 190
  exhortations on
    discipleship 194–9
  knowledge of God 192
  position in chronology 42
  Stoic language 190
Philo of Alexandria 165
  Paul 202

Phoebe 89, 250, 252
Phygelus 256
Piety 13, 34, 60, 180, 206, 211, 245,
    246, 252, 254, 262
Plutarch 228, 233, 246
Polycarp
  letters of 245
  Philippians 190
polygamy 251
polytheism
  Colossians 209
Pompey 57, 240
post-critical movements 3–4
potters
  Romans (book) 81
power
  Colossians 207, 211
  Ephesians 175
  1 Thessalonians 221
  in weakness 133–4, 142, 149
prayer
  Jesus 77, 242
  for knowledge in Ephesians
    180
preaching, Paul 42
prescripts 46–7, 90, 120, 220, 230,
    237, 264
pride
  converts at Corinth 98
Priscilla (Prisca) 59, 89, 90,91, 125,
    260
promise to Abraham *see* convenant
prophecy
  see also prophets
  Paul 119
prophets
  see also prophecy
  false 240
  killing of 224
proselytism 35
Protestantism
  Romans (book) 57
proverbs
  Ephesians 183
punishment
  church at Corinth 149
purity
  1 Thessalonians 227

Qumran
  community practices 243
  early church 15

Rabban Gamaliel the Elder *see*
    Gamaliel
reconciliation
  Corinth 131, 136
  God's love 71
  Jews and Gentiles 172
redaction criticism 3
redemption
  Pastoral Epistles 262

Reformation
  Romans (book) 57
relationship maintenance 64
religion-relationship antithesis 81
religious ecstasy 135
religious persecution
  Christians 34, 38
religious phenomena, causes 38
repentance
  church at Corinth 138
  Pastoral Epistles 257
resurrection
  body 93, 120
  Ephesians 172, 176
resurrection of Jesus
  1 Corinthians 121–4
  Ephesians 182
  Romans (book) 71
Revelation (book)
  church grouping 17
  Jewish hopes 13
revelation
  Colossians 205
  of faith 162
  Jesus 1
  Paul 147
rhetoric
  deliberative 139
  Paul 47, 127, 144
rich people *see* wealth
righteousness
  believers state of 78
  by faith 6
  Ephesians 187
  of God 78, 83
  Judaism 8
  Pastoral Epistles 254
  Paul 51, 201
  Romans (book) 64
  1 Thessalonians 231
  under the law 82
rites
  Lord's supper 116
  to seal immortality 112
ritual kiss 150
rock prediction 99
Roetzel, Calvin J. 28
Roman empire
  Corinth 126
Romans (book) 57–90
  Abraham's covenant with
    God 70
  chain of influence 27
  eschatological context 86
  ethical exhortations 84
  and Galatians 75
  justification by faith 51
  law of the Spirit 76
  literary style 48, 58
  love 85
  missing passages 89
  position in chronology 42

Romans (book) (*cont.*)
  provenance 57
  sin and righteousness 71
Rome
  see also Roman empire
  Christian community 57
  civil authority 85
  expulsion of the Jews 57, 59, 92
  imperial cult 200
  Jewish community 57
  Paul 36, 88, 192, 256

sacrifice
  Jewish 113
  living 84–85
sacrificial food
  guidelines for eating 113
  idolatry 79–80, 84 91, 93,
    108–109, 113
saints
  collection for the 40, 124, 127,
    138–141, 148–149
  Colossians 206
  Philippians 191
salvation 14, 33, 60, 95, 132, 166, 171,
    194, 208, 218–219, 241, 245
  Ephesians 176, 187
  Jewish law inadequate 132
  non-believers in a marriage 105
  Pastoral Epistles 246, 255–156,
    260, 262
  Paul 60, 61
  Philippians 198
  1 Thessalonians 231
  2 Thessalonians 241
Samothrace 227
Sappington, T. J. 206
Sarah (wife of Abraham)
  as a free woman 165
Satan
  physical suffering 147
  1 Thessalonians 225
Saviour, usage 247, 260
scripture
  letters of Paul 54
  Pastoral Epistles 258
Seleucid empire
  Colossae 204
self-righteousness 61
self-sufficiency
  Graeco-Roman tradition 141
Sermon on the Mount
  Ephesians 170
servants
  of God 63
sex
  abstinence 105
  converts at Corinth 102, 104–105,
    148
  Ephesians 183
shame
  Graeco-Roman tradition 132–133

Shields 187
shoes 187
Silas (Silvanus) 128, 220, 222, 237,
sin
  see also sinners
  anthropomorphized 67, 68
  before the law was given 70
  belief in Christ 73
  Colossians 210
  Ephesians 175–176, 184
  external power 67, 74
  inevitability 68
  origins of 212
  Paul's theology 51–52
  sexual 227
Sinai, Mount 165
singers
sinners
  destruction by god 112
  Jesus 247
slavery
  Christianity 106, 212
  Graeco-Roman society 266
  household rules 186
  Pastoral Epistles 254, 261
social relationships
  Romans (book) 86
social-identity theory 219, 226, 229
Socrates
  likened to Paul 266
Solomon
  Odes of 198
Son of Man 22, 175
Sosthenes 91
source criticism
  biblical criticism 2
Spain
  Paul 44, 45, 58, 88, 89, 206
speaking in tongues 78, 93, 108, 118,
    120, 261
speech
  without love 118
Spirit *see* Holy Spirit
spirit
  architectural metaphors 133
  law of 75–76
  resurrection 63, 96
  understanding of believers 97
spirits
  elemental 50, 163
Stephanas 92, 95, 124
steward metaphor 100, 111, 260
stoicheion 210
Stoicism
  Philippians 190–194
Strabo 36, 209
subordination 115, 138, 250
suffering
  boasting of 71, 77
  catalogue of 136
  links with glory 77
  physical weakness 133

Sundays 124
'super apostles' 128, 130, 144–147
swords 187
symbolic universe 138
synagogues
  Paul 37, 43
Synoptic Gospels 2
Syntyche 202
Syria
  see Seleucid empire

Tarsus 31, 36, 37, 40
tearful letter 49, 127, 130, 137–141
temple (heavenly)
  Christian church seen as 137
Tertullian 49, 53, 115, 227
testing
  divine 141
textual criticism 2
thanksgiving
  Colossians 207
  1 Corinthians 91, 94, 120
  2 Corinthians 128, 131, 141
  Ephesians 174
  Galatian congregations 153, 156,
    168
  Philemon 264
  Philippians 191
  Romans (book) 43, 47–8, 51, 56,
    58, 64
  1 Thessalonians 158, 161–5, 216,
    220–221
  2 Thessalonians 235–24
Thecla 189–91, 245, 250, 256,
    259–262
theodidaktos 228
theology
  ditheism 109
  Paul 29, 48–50, 53, 58, 61, 73, 103,
    115, 122, 127, 131, 133, 136–138,
    146, 148, 171, 218–219
  1 Thessalonians 218–219
1 Thessalonians 2, 42, 46, 216–232
  position in chronology 40
  social identity approach 219
2 Thessalonians 49, 206, 219, 223,
    229, 235–244
  authenticity 178 235, 243
  position in chronology 42
Thessalonica 18, 52, 192, 202,
    204–205, 214–227, 230, 235
  early Christian community 217
  social context
threshing ox 110
Timothy (companion to Paul)
  Philippians 191, 199
  recipient of letters 256
  1 Thessalonians 220, 224, 225, 230
1 Timothy (book) 153, 206,
    244–250, 255, 256
2 Timothy (book) 49, 237, 244, 248,
    256–260

Titus (book) 10, 15, 16, 28, 44, 49,
    127, 130, 138–142, 148, 157,
    167, 170, 183–186, 188, 207,
    237, 244, 263, 265
Titus (fellow-worker of Paul)
    circumcision question 260
    and Corinthian church 260
    recipient of letter 260–263
tolerance, Romans (book) 87
tongues
    speaking in 78, 93, 108, 118, 119, 261
Torah
    Christ antithesis 33, 34
    eternal life 72
    interpretation of law 182
    justification by works 31
    Paul's theology 50, 53
    will of God 76–7
Townsend, John T. 44
tradition
    Jewish teaching 143
transcendence of God 254
transgressions see sin
translation
    Bible 5
Troas 130, 245, 259
Trophimus 260
twelve apostles see apostles
Tychicus 49, 171, 188, 207, 214, 240,
    263

unbelievers see non-believers
universal gospel 32
universalism 35, 122

Via Egnatia 217
vices 131, 148, 167, 183, 212, 248, 254,
    258, 181, 186, 188
virgins
    head coverings 115
    marriage metaphor 144
    marriage of 107
    Paul 105, 107, 115
    virtue 183
2 Corinthians 136

warfare
    metaphor for Christian life 186
weakness
    body metaphor, 1
        Corinthians 117–18
    Christians and sacrificial
        food 110
    Paul 143
    poor Christians 111
    theology of the cross 133
    tolerance by the strong 87
wealth
    converts in Corinth 94
    Paul 139
weddings
    Ephesians 186
wickedness
    justice of God 81
widows
    celibacy and remarriage 79, 106,
        107
    instructions in Pastoral
        Epistles 253

will of God 76
wisdom
    converts at Corinth 103, 146
    spirituality 97
    subverted by God 96, 97
    Wisdom of Solomon 5, 66,
        171
Wisdom of Solomon (book)
    canonical status 5
wives
    Paul 105
women
    see also wives
    Christianity 90, 114–15, 121
    Colossians 213
    head covering in prayer 114–16
    participation in worship 120
    Pastoral Epistles 251, 258, 261
    social position 108, 114, 115
    1 Thessalonians 227
Word of God
    failure in Israel 79
worship
    Christian 120

YHWH
    see also God
    marriage with Israel 144
    name of 197
    warrior 187

Zenas 263
Zephaniah (prophet)
    1 Thessalonians 231